JUSTICE SYSTEM

P9-CCS-885

CORRECTIONS

SENTENCING & SANCTIONS | PROBATION | PRISON | PAROLE

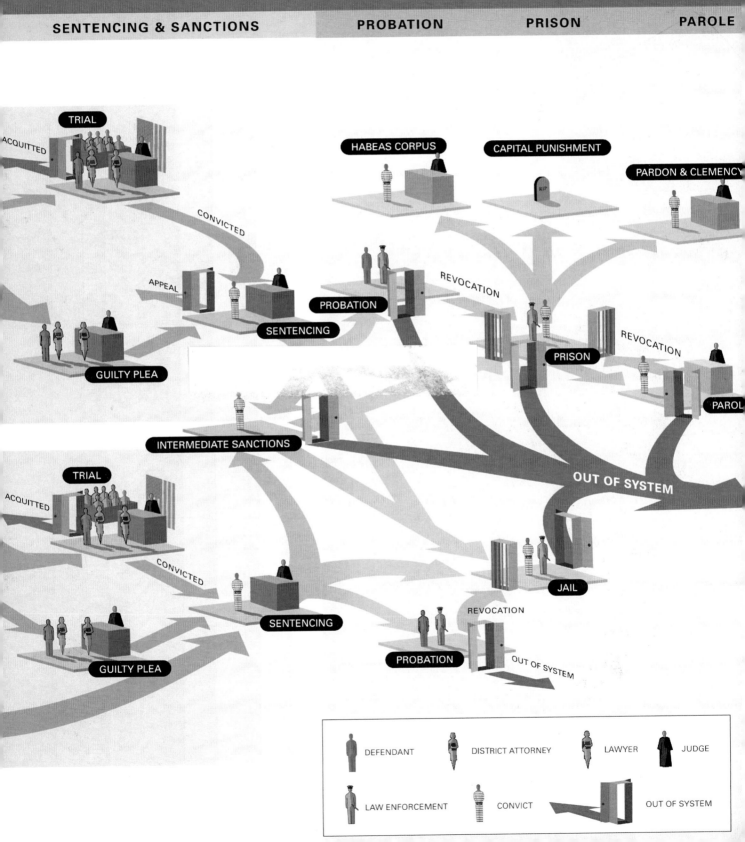

TRIAL

ACQUITTED

HABEAS CORPUS

CAPITAL PUNISHMENT

PARDON & CLEMENCY

CONVICTED

APPEAL

PROBATION

REVOCATION

SENTENCING

REVOCATION

GUILTY PLEA

PRISON

PAROL

INTERMEDIATE SANCTIONS

OUT OF SYSTEM

TRIAL

ACQUITTED

JAIL

CONVICTED

REVOCATION

SENTENCING

PROBATION

OUT OF SYSTEM

GUILTY PLEA

DEFENDANT | DISTRICT ATTORNEY | LAWYER | JUDGE

LAW ENFORCEMENT | CONVICT | OUT OF SYSTEM

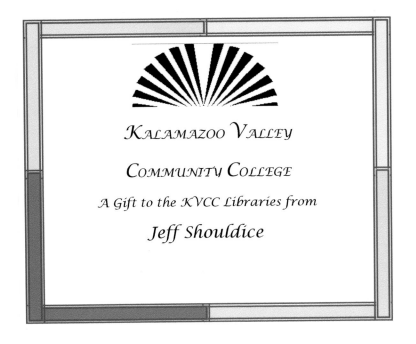

KALAMAZOO VALLEY

COMMUNITY COLLEGE

A Gift to the KVCC Libraries from

Jeff Shouldice

CRIMINAL PROCEDURE

THEORY AND PRACTICE

SECOND EDITION

Jefferson L. Ingram

University of Dayton

PEARSON

Prentice
Hall

Upper Saddle River, New Jersey
Columbus, Ohio

Library of Congress Cataloging-in-Publication Data

Ingram, Jefferson.
    Criminal procedure : theory and practice / Jefferson L. Ingram. — 2nd ed.
        p. cm.
    Includes index.
    ISBN-13: 978-0-13-135209-4
    ISBN-10:   0-13-135209-1
    1. Criminal procedure—United States.   2. Criminal procedure—United States—Cases.   3. Civil
rights—United States.   4. Civil rights—United States—Cases.   I. Title.
    KF9619.I544 2008
    345.73'05—dc22   2008013434

Vice President and Executive Publisher: Vernon Anthony
Acquisitions Editor: Tim Peyton
Development Editor: Elisa Rogers
Editorial Assistant: Alicia Kelly
Project Manager: Jessica Sykes
Production Coordination: TexTech International
Design Coordinator: Diane Y. Ernsberger
Cover Designer: Mike Fruhbeis
Cover art: Getty One
Operations Specialist: Pat Tonneman
Director of Marketing: David Gesell
Marketing Manager: Adam Kloza
Marketing Coordinator: Alicia Dysert

This book was set in Bembo by TexTech International. It was printed and bound by Hamilton Printing Co. The cover was printed by Phoenix Color Corp.

Pearson Education Ltd., London   Pearson Education Australia PtY, Ltd.
Pearson Education Singapore Pte. Ltd.   Pearson Education North Asia, Ltd., Hong Kong
Pearson Education Canada, Inc.   Pearson Educación de Mexico, S.A. de C.V.
Pearson Education—Japan   Pearson Education Malaysia Pte. Ltd.

10 9 8 7 6 5 4 3 2 1
ISBN-13: 978-0-13-135209-4
ISBN-10:   0-13-135209-1

For my Parents:
Dr. Ernagene F. Ingram and
Dr. Lewis K. Ingram

Brief Contents

Contents

2   CRIMINAL COURTS: ORGANIZATION, FUNCTION, JURISDICTION, AND THE CRIMINAL PROCESS   33

**PART TWO   ARREST, STOP AND FRISK, AND SEARCH WARRANT
PRACTICE**

5   THE CONCEPT OF STOP AND FRISK   135

6   OBTAINING AND USING SEARCH WARRANTS: PRACTICE, EXECUTION, AND RETURN   163

PART THREE   SEARCHING PERSONS AND PROPERTY

7   SEARCHES AND SEIZURES: HOUSES, PLACES, PERSONS, AND VEHICLES   193

Part Four   *MIRANDA* WARNINGS, CONFESSIONS, AND IDENTIFICATION PROCEDURES

10   *MIRANDA* PRINCIPLES: FIFTH AND SIXTH AMENDMENT INFLUENCES ON POLICE PRACTICE   309

PART FIVE   **PRETRIAL AND TRIAL CRIMINAL PROCEDURE
AND APPELLATE PRACTICE**

13   TRIAL PROCEDURE AND LEGAL RIGHTS   413

14   APPELLATE PRACTICE AND OTHER POSTTRIAL REMEDIES   445

APPENDICES

Preface

The field of criminal procedure provides part of the matrix of fairness and justice that promotes equality of treatment for persons suspected or accused of crime; therefore, it occupies an important position in the field of criminal justice. Since its genesis comes from both the Constitution of the United States and the constitutions of the several states, its substance and application will vary in some fashion from jurisdiction to jurisdiction. The decisions made by the Supreme Court of the United States, when speaking on federal constitutional issues, are binding on state criminal justice practice. Although constitutional decisions are mandatory on the states, such decisions dictate the minimal legal protections required under our federal system. Every state may go beyond the basic minimum federal guarantees by offering an accused enhanced or greater state constitutional rights. For example, a state is free to allow vicarious standing to suppress evidence following a Fourth Amendment violation, or it may require the presence of a parent or guardian before a juvenile may waive *Miranda* rights. States also may grant enhanced criminal procedure protections based on considerations of state appellate case law and state statutory law.

The constitutional and statutory rules that make up the body of law known as criminal procedure regulate how state and federal governments must treat persons accused or suspected of committing crimes. Rules dictating the way law enforcement officials interact with individuals who are mere suspects for particular crimes restrain their activities and approaches prior to the initiation of formal criminal prosecutions. When investigations have moved beyond their initial stages to the point where criminal suspects have been identified, the rules of criminal procedure provide a road map that all law enforcement officials must follow. Where officials fail to observe recognized criminal procedural rules, such deviation may jeopardize any eventual successful criminal prosecution by creating the conditions that require the suppression of otherwise admissible trial evidence or by opening any eventual conviction to appellate attack.

Similarly, when law enforcement officials have turned their work product over to the prosecutor's office, the personnel presenting the government's case must carefully follow additional rules regulating fair conduct in order to accord due process to the accused. The prosecution has no duty to win a case at all costs; it possesses the overall obligation to see that justice is the eventual outcome of the trial process. Defense attorneys have a role within the rules of criminal procedure to ensure that the government has played fairly during the investigation, pretrial, and trial phases; they also are obligated to provide a vigorous defense consistent with the Constitution and state rules and regulations.

During criminal trials, judges must carefully weigh the arguments of the contending parties, whether they are arguing over criminal procedural issues relative to the admission or exclusion of evidence or over more traditional admission of evidence under evidence codes. Whether a judge presides over pretrial issues, the trial itself, or posttrial motions or serves on an appellate panel reviewing trial-level judicial decisions, every judge possesses a duty of due process to both the prosecution and the defense. Roughly translated, due process implies fundamental fairness and fair dealing to all parties during all the important stages of the criminal justice process.

While the study of criminal procedure typically follows the case study method of instruction, where students are exposed to appellate decisions using real-world problems, this book brings together both the richness of textual description and edited appellate cases. The latest case material is available to the student at **http://www.criminalprocedurebyingram.com**, which presents edited, updated legal cases that coordinate with the book's table of contents. When a new decision by the Supreme Court of the United States alters or modifies a criminal procedure concept covered by this book, the new edited case will be placed on the book's Web site in a matrix that coordinates the new material with the respective chapter. Having the book's Web resource enables the student to both learn the traditional case precedents and integrate those principles with the latest court decisions covering a particular topic of criminal procedure.

The most significant developments, changes, and corrections in criminal procedure have generally come from landmark case decisions of the Supreme Court of the United States. Implementation of the rules contained within Supreme Court case decisions has largely been delegated to state legal systems, where state courts have developed slightly divergent interpretations and applications of these legal principles. The Federal Rules of Criminal Procedure and state rules of criminal procedure owe much of their content to the codification of legal principles announced by the Supreme Court of the United States and to common-law practice. Many states have adopted local versions of rules for criminal procedure based substantially or loosely on the Federal Rules of Criminal Procedure.

The beginning chapters of this book offer historical lessons about the Bill of Rights and the significant constitutional alterations that followed the American Civil War (1861–1865) that may not be well known to many students. The introductory chapters of the book allow the student to develop a historical context for many of the important concepts and theories in criminal procedure, as well as gain knowledge about the direction in which courts may take recent jurisprudence and build for the future. Knowledge of past legal history helps the current student or attorney appreciate the legacy that historical figures have left to this generation. Subsequent chapters detail police, attorney, and judicial practices that have developed since the adoption of the Constitution of the United States. It is the implementation of constitutional and case law principles and changes that drive most of modern criminal procedure and which the individual chapters present in an ongoing and dynamic fashion.

NEW TO THIS EDITION

The second edition of *Criminal Procedure: Theory and Practice* contains changes designed to update the work and make it easier to read and comprehend.

- The edited legal cases have been moved from the back of each chapter to within the chapter text so that the reader can study the case in the context of the relevant legal principles.
- The book presents contemporary legal cases as well as classic criminal procedure cases that illustrate and demonstrate criminal procedure concepts.
- Where appropriate, graphics and court forms have been added to support the text content.
- Learning objectives have been added to the front of each chapter to highlight the educational outcomes for the chapter. The reader who masters the learning objectives and the new terms list that follows will have attained the knowledge that the chapter contains.
- Review questions and exercises have been added to the end of each chapter to serve as a self-test to determine whether the basic learning objectives have been met.
- Also added to the end of each chapter are two edited case problems that show the practical applications of the material in each chapter. Ideally, the reader will be able to address and solve the problems suggested by the case based on the knowledge gained from mastery of the chapter. The solution to the legal problem follows the presentation of the case facts and includes a legal citation for additional study.

SUPPLEMENTS

This text is accompanied by an Instructor's Manual with Test Bank, TestGen, and PowerPoints.

ACKNOWLEDGMENTS

Although every book involves comprise concerning what material to include and what information must be left aside, every effort has been made to make those decisions properly and intelligently to benefit the reader most appropriately. Any errors or omissions belong to the author, who has received most generous assistance from everyone at Pearson Prentice Hall. The author extends thanks to Tim Peyton, Acquisitions Editor of Pearson Prentice Hall, for his guidance, support, and assistance in making this second edition possible. Very special thanks for her assistance and advice in the development and organization of this book goes to Elisa Rogers, Development Editor of Pearson Prentice Hall, whose talent, insight, and dedication greatly enhanced this book. At all times Elisa Rogers proved helpful and dedicated to this creation of this book and did it all with a sense of humor that made the author's task easier. Jessica Sykes, Project Manager at Pearson Prentice Hall, who helped keep the efforts of the author on track and on time, deserves generous thanks for her efforts. Special appreciation is extended to Douglas Korb, Associate Project Manager at TexTech, Inc. who helped keep the final editing and production of this book on schedule while maintaining its quality and integrity. The detailed work of Joy Matkowski, Editor at TexTech, Inc., helped transform the original manuscript into a text that possesses excellent readability and continuity. Her suggestions guided the author to say what he meant in a clear and concise manner that will immensely benefit the reader. The author wishes to express special thanks to Dean Lisa Kloppenberg of the University of Dayton School Of Law for significantly valuable support that enabled the research for this book to be accomplished. I wish to thank the reviewers of this edition: Rodney A. Barker, Mt. Hood Community College; Charles E. Black, Curry College; Kathleen M. Contrino, Buffalo State College; Nancy K. Dempsey, Cape Cod Community College; Carl Franklin, Southern Utah University; James P. Jernigan, Troy University and East Central Georgia Technical College; Richard G. Kuiters, Bergen Community College.

Jefferson L. Ingram
University of Dayton
February 2008

Part 1

The Criminal Procedure Matrix

The Constitution and the Bill of Rights: The Source of Protections for the Accused

Learning Objectives

1. Articulate some reasons why many citizens believed that the Articles of Confederation needed improvement or change.
2. Explain why there was a concern that the original Constitution of the United States did not contain a bill of rights.
3. Explain what the framers of the three post–Civil War amendments, the Thirteenth, Fourteenth, and Fifteenth Amendments, intended.
4. Analyze the basic theory behind the selective incorporation doctrine that gradually incorporated some of the Bill of Rights into the Due Process Clause of the Fourteenth Amendment.
5. Identify the rights in the Bill of Rights that have been incorporated into the Due Process Clause of the Fourteenth Amendment.
6. Recognize and identify the most recent right that was selectively incorporated into the Fourteenth Amendment's Due Process Clause.

Chapter Outline

1. Historical Overview: The Basis of Rights for Persons Accused of Crime
2. The Articles of Confederation
3. The Constitution: Revision in National Government
4. The Constitution: Challenges to Ratification
5. The Rationale and Need for the Bill of Rights
6. A Brief History of the Bill of Rights
7. Constitutional Developments: The Civil War Era
8. Constitutional Developments: The Thirteenth Amendment
9. Constitutional Developments: The Fourteenth Amendment
10. Constitutional Developments: The Fifteenth Amendment
11. Criminal Procedure prior to the Selective Incorporation Doctrine
12. The Selective Incorporation Doctrine: Federalization of Criminal Procedure
13. Fourth Amendment: Prohibition against Unreasonable Searches
14. Fifth Amendment: Right to a Grand Jury Indictment, Privilege against Self-Incrimination, and Prohibition against Double Jeopardy as Part of the Right to Due Process
15. Sixth Amendment: The Right to a Speedy and Public Jury Trial, the Right to Confront Witnesses, and the Right to Counsel

16. Eighth Amendment: Prohibition of
     Excessive Bail, Excessive Fines, and
     Protection against Cruel and Unusual
     Punishment

17. State Criminal Procedure: Beyond the
     Federal Constitutional Minimum
18. Summary

Key Terms

Articles of Confederation
Bill of Rights
Thirteenth Amendment
Fourteenth Amendment
Fifteenth Amendment

Selective incorporation
Grand jury indictment
Information
Privilege against self-incrimination
Speedy trial right

1. HISTORICAL OVERVIEW: THE BASIS OF RIGHTS FOR PERSONS ACCUSED OF CRIME

Over the past ten centuries, English and Western thought developed the concept that fundamental fairness should prevail in relationships between governments and their people.[1] Concepts of fairness and due process were written in the Magna Carta of 1215, a document signed by the English monarch, King John, which guaranteed individual rights that the government would respect. The Magna Carta provided, among other things, that the king would be bound by law and that the people would be free from unlawful imprisonment, would be tried by the judgment of their peers, and that justice would not be bought or sold.[2] British and colonial governments and leaders made efforts to extend some of the concepts of fundamental fairness in the Magna Carta to all persons in their relations with their governments, including those accused of criminal activities. This is not to say that there have not been miserable failures of governments to observe fundamental fairness (slavery and unfair trials, etc.) on many occasions both civil and criminal, but political thinkers of the pre– and post–Revolutionary War period, who had been influenced by concepts included in the Magna Carta and the rational theories offered during the Age of Enlightenment,[3] endeavored to enshrine fairness and due process in the written instruments of government. They believed that a static, written form of governance would assure civil and criminal justice, both in the several states and in our national government.

Despite a fairly enlightened view of justice, people in the colonies, and later in states and localities, continued to fear that a far-away government, especially a strong national one, could eventually erode their rights and institute unfair laws and practices that local people could do little to counteract. This fear resulted in compromises that created a weak central government under the Articles of Confederation and caused problems with ratification of the stronger government represented by the Constitution of the United States.

Under the Articles of Confederation, the states were free to conduct their criminal justice systems as each saw fit, with virtually no involvement with the central government. Most of the criminal justice two hundred years ago, then as now, occurred at the local level, with state and local members of the executive branch directed to take wrongdoers into custody. State and local judicial officials had the task of assuring a measure of justice, consistent with the heritage of the English common law and the common practice of the era. The overall fear of a national government interfering with local freedoms, especially ones involving crime and justice, has been a recurring American theme throughout the history of the nation, whether prior to the Articles of Confederation, during that era, or under the Constitution. The fear of a strong central government under the Constitution prompted agitation for a bill of rights to assure that the traditional rights of Englishmen[4] continued under the newest version of the national government. The fear explains the perceived need for protections from the federal government against illegal searches and seizures, the desire for grand jury indictments, the need to provide protection against double jeopardy, the desire to assure due process, and the protections against unreasonable fines, bails, and punishments. Although such fears explain many of the reasons why there is a bill of rights, other political and judicial factors and political tensions explain why these guarantees in the Bill of Rights have come to be nationalized and applied against the states in contravention of the intent of the original Framers. In some respects, the concept of selective incorporation of the Bill of Rights against the states has been to protect local individuals from overreaching or unfair treatment, not from an all-powerful national government but from increasingly powerful state governments. Civil liberties and criminal justice fairness have become federalized as a way to assure that their basic guarantees remain and continue. This chapter starts with the government under the Articles of Confederation and traces some of the later developments and constitutional trends as state and national courts interpreted the newer Constitution of the United States. These interpretations and later constitutional amendments have created a living document that, among other things, regulates much of the criminal procedure of the present day.

2. THE ARTICLES OF CONFEDERATION

At the beginning of the Revolutionary War, the colonial legislatures generally transformed themselves into governing bodies of independent states, with each state developing its own constitution. There were variations in how these independent states adapted their forms of government with new constitutions, but generally the individual states continued their forms of government in ways that were recognizable before the Declaration of Independence. Where colonial governors might once have been appointed, following independence, as a general rule, governors were elected by properly qualified voters, and the states that had two houses in their legislatures had their members elected by voters. Universal suffrage remained a future development because women were denied the right to vote and African Americans generally were not permitted to vote unless they met property owning standards.

The Continental Congress attempted to devise a constitution that would cover all of the states in a new form of government, but that proved to be a very difficult task. Concerns about how representation should be based, whether on population or by some other fair measure, consumed much of the time of members of Congress. Difficult compromises had to be made among all the states, especially those like New York and Virginia, which claimed western lands far beyond their present borders. Small states were concerned that they might end up with insufficient power and be dominated by the larger states. The resulting constitution, called the Articles of Confederation, was probably the best and strongest document that could have received enough support by a sufficient number of states to be accepted as the national charter. As is true with most negotiated documents, compromises sometimes are necessary to attain initial agreement, but necessary compromises also inject some weaknesses that may need to be corrected or renegotiated at a later time. Governmental difficulties under the Articles caused a variety of national problems.

In practice, the national government that emerged under the Articles of Confederation exhibited weaknesses that required cooperation among the states that, in many instances, was difficult to attain. Upon request from the national government under the Articles, states would furnish their allotted number of military service members, but the national government had no way to assure that the allotted number of soldiers, properly equipped, would actually show up for service. Under the Articles, the government had no central control or even influence over interstate or foreign commerce, so each individual state acted more like a sovereign nation, rather than part of a larger nation-state. A glaring weakness under the Articles of Confederation was the inability to levy and collect taxes from either the states or from individuals, while many states taxed goods coming into their respective states. From a perspective of national unity, trade, taxation, and foreign affairs, the Articles of Confederation demonstrated weaknesses that cried out for a new approach.

3. THE CONSTITUTION: REVISION IN NATIONAL GOVERNMENT

Delegates from five states responded to a Virginia call to a meeting designed to address problems affecting interstate commerce. The delegates eventually assembled in Philadelphia in 1787 to resolve interstate trade problems that the Articles of Confederation either helped create or did not solve. What developed from the meetings of the delegates during the summer of 1787, after extensive wrangling and compromise, was the United States Constitution under which we operate today. If compromises were difficult when the Articles of Confederation were drafted, they were minor compared to the issues the delegates had to deal with in writing a new document to serve as new governmental charter. The new government was to have power over interstate and foreign commerce as a way of solving one of the major problems under the Articles of Confederation. The old concerns that divided the large states and the small states with respect to representation and relative power and authority in the new government were solved by having a Senate where each state had two senators and a lower house, called the House of Representatives, where the number of representatives was to be based on a state's population. This compromise created a new problem because delegates from the slaveholding states wanted slaves counted as people and delegates from nonslaveholding states did not want to count slaves as people for the purposes of apportioning representation. Despite many conflicts concerning how to organize the government, eventually the delegates settled upon a plan that had three equal branches: legislative, executive, and judicial. The delegates eventually resolved these and many other issues and presented the document to Congress under the Articles of Confederation. Congress sent the new document to the states for consideration by state conventions called for that purpose.

4. THE CONSTITUTION: CHALLENGES TO RATIFICATION

Given the divergent opinion on political and economic matters, state ratification of the new constitution was not a foregone conclusion at the time it was submitted to the states for consideration. Article VII stated: "The ratification of the conventions of nine states, shall be sufficient for the establishment of this Constitution between the states so ratifying the same." In addition to acquiring the proper number of state votes, the merits of the new constitution created significant public discussion both for and against its adoption. One of the common arguments against adopting the new constitution concerned its lack of a bill of rights that would guarantee either individual or state rights, a concern that related back to the general fear of a strong national government. Many arguments were made that the new government created under the new constitution sacrificed state sovereignty, might levy taxes in an unfair or burdensome way, or might unfairly favor one section of the country over another. In some quarters, there was fear that the presidency might evolve into a kinglike institution or position. In many states, public meetings were raucous gatherings of partisans who argued one way or the other, and newspapers and broadsides offer their particular political wisdom both in support of ratification and in agitation against ratification.

There was strong opposition in the Commonwealth of Massachusetts, where the Anti-Federalists argued that it should be amended before it would be acceptable. The Massachusetts convention eventually voted to accept the Constitution but recommended that amendments should be considered by the first Congress under the new constitution.

> At the Massachusetts ratifying convention in early 1788, Federalists won assent for the new federal Constitution only by promising that they would support subsequent amendments that would provide a bill of rights. This concession caught on elsewhere. Without it ratification by the necessary minimum of nine states would have been impossible.[5]

Several other states that ratified the Constitution included language recommending that amendments in the form of a bill of rights be offered in the new Congress contemplated by the Constitution. Eventually a sufficient number of states through conventions indicated their respective approval for the new document, but many states expressed reservations concerning the absence of a bill of rights and urged that adoption of a bill of rights should be an early consideration of the new national government.[6] The Congress under the Articles passed a resolution that placed the Constitution of the United States as the governing document.

5. THE RATIONALE AND NEED FOR THE BILL OF RIGHTS

During the period when people in the states discussed whether the Constitution should be ratified, agitation, both for and against adoption, swirled around the nation in the form of papers, letters, and broadsides. One position argued that a bill of rights was necessary because rights would be best protected when they were enumerated or listed as rights that individuals possessed. The argument suggested that such a list of rights was necessary to prevent governmental encroachment on the rights of citizens. Others contended that if the rights were listed, the implication might be drawn that these were the only rights that existed, so that a right that was not listed did not exist. The concern remained that the federal government might become too powerful and that having a list of guaranteed rights and clear limitations on governmental prerogatives was the best way to reduce the chances of tyranny that a stronger national government might present. Guarantees that prohibited Congress from legislating about religion, the right of people to be free from unreasonable federal governmental searches, and the right not to be tried twice for the same crime were considered crucial and included within the twelve proposals the new Congress submitted to the states for consideration as amendments. Fresh remembrances of colonists transported to England for trial suggested that a right to a trial in the district where the crime was allegedly committed was an important right, and this trial right was also included within the twelve proposals. The people agitating for a bill of rights wanted to make sure that the rights traditionally enjoyed by Englishmen,[7] including a speedy public trial while represented by counsel, were guaranteed by the proposed Bill of Rights. To prevent lengthy pretrial incarceration, the Bill of Rights guaranteed the right to bail, and cruel and strange punishments were prohibited. To defuse the argument that listing rights might imply that others did not exist, the Bill of Rights noted that the inclusion of certain rights within the Constitution could not be used to deny or disparage others that were retained by the people. To ensure that the national government could not become too powerful, the proposed Bill of Rights provided that if certain powers had not been given to the national government, they belonged to the states or to the people. With the views that were expressed in the twelve proposed amendments passed by the Congress and sent to the states for ratification, the complaints of many who voted for ratification were eliminated or substantially reduced.

6. A BRIEF HISTORY OF THE BILL OF RIGHTS

With the ratification of ten of the twelve proposed changes to the Constitution, the Bill of Rights became part of the Constitution in 1791 and stands on an equal footing with all of the other original provisions of the Constitution. Some states approved all twelve of the proposed amendments while others did not approve all of them, but sufficient state approval led to the addition of the first ten amendments to the Constitution of the United States. One of the original twelve proposals for amendments, passed by the First Congress on September 25, 1789, that initially failed to be approved with the first ten amendments, finally received sufficient ratification by three-fourths of the states on May, 18, 1992.[8] The proposal became the Twenty-Seventh Amendment to the Constitution: "No law varying the compensation for the services of the Senators and Representatives, shall take effect, until an election of Representatives shall have intervened."[9]

The legislative intent of the Congress that submitted the twelve proposals to the states for consideration was that the amendments would limit or restrict the federal government in its dealings with individuals. There was no legislative intent to limit state powers when a particular state dealt with an individual because there was less fear that a state would oppress its own people. The amendments were aimed clearly and solely at placing restraints on the federal government. People did not generally believe that clear limitations on state prerogatives and powers would be necessary because individual citizens were closer to their governments in each state, and the population could control state excesses, should they occur, through the ballot box. Only after the passage of the Fourteenth Amendment, which contains a due process clause, did any argument develop that the concept of due process might include some guarantees against state activity under the Bill of Rights.[10]

In the *Slaughter-House Cases,*[11] the Louisiana Legislature had altered some of the rules for slaughtering animals in the city of New Orleans, which harmed some business owners involved in the slaughter and preparation of meat for human consumption. Among other theories, the argument offered by the affected business owners contended that the post–Civil War Thirteenth Amendment and Fourteenth Amendment to the Constitution altered the way states could legislate, based on the privileges and immunities clause in the Fourteenth Amendment. The city of New Orleans, by limiting the way meat processors could operate, the plaintiffs contended, interfered with their privileges and immunities guaranteed by the Fourteenth Amendment. The Court rejected the argument that the amendments passed following the Civil War had fundamentally changed anything, other than what the amendments were clearly designed to accomplish. The Court mentioned that the original purposes of the postwar amendments were to end slavery, make citizens of all persons born in the country, and allow the right to vote; according to the Supreme Court, the amendments were not intended to accomplish anything else.

The Bill of Rights fundamentally began to change when the Supreme Court decided *Gitlow v. New York,* 268 U.S. 652, in 1925, where the Court stated, "For present purposes we may and do assume that freedom of speech and of the press—which are protected by the First Amendment from abridgment by Congress—are among the fundamental personal rights and 'liberties' protected by the due process clause of the Fourteenth Amendment from impairment by the States."[12] The *Gitlow* case involved a prosecution for criminal anarchy in violation of New York law because Gitlow had written and orally advocated the necessity of overthrowing organized state and federal governments. The lower courts determined that the speech constituted direct incitement for others to attempt to overthrow organized government and, although the Supreme Court assumed that concepts contained within due process included freedom of speech and press, it refused to overturn the convictions. Significantly, the Court, for the first time, determined that the Due Process Clause of the Fourteenth Amendment protected the First Amendment rights of speech and of the press, a decision that was contrary to doctrine mentioned by the Court in the *Slaughterhouse Cases.* This case operated as a preview of what would later become known as the selective incorporation doctrine, where the Supreme Court incorporated many of the guarantees of the Bill of Rights into the Due Process Clause of the Fourteenth Amendment and applied them against the states.

7. CONSTITUTIONAL DEVELOPMENTS: THE CIVIL WAR ERA

In the early 1860s, eleven states of the original federal union seceded from the Union to form the Confederate States of America, causing both a civil war and a constitutional crisis. For the United States to survive as it had been envisioned by the Framers, the war had to be won and the seceded states returned to their former positions under the Constitution. Various political theories explained the former political relationship during the rebellion: Were the rebellious states considered dead states so that they would have to petition to get back into the Union, or was it impossible for a state to leave the Union and so the rebellious states were simply out of their usual position with the other states and with the federal government until the relationship was restored? No single theory ever predominated, but all of the rebellious states were eventually reintegrated into the United States. As a condition of reentry, a position that implied a particular state had left the Union, states were generally required to ratify the Thirteenth, Fourteenth, and Fifteenth Amendments to the Constitution.[13] The original Constitution contemplated voluntary ratification or rejection of constitutional amendments rather than a level of coercion to force state ratification of an amendment, but in the interests of reunification of the nation following the Civil War, Congress did not always follow settled constitutional and political theories. The ratification of these amendments eventually let to a constitutional revolution, as some of the guarantees of the Bill of Rights were determined to be fundamental rights that were essential to due process. During a course of many years, the Supreme Court engaged in a selective incorporation of some or all of the first eight amendments into the Due Process Clause of the Fourteenth Amendment, beginning with *Gitlow v. New York*[14] in 1925, when the First Amendment guarantees were considered to be inherent in the Due Process Clause of the Fourteenth Amendment. (See Section 6, this chapter.)

8. CONSTITUTIONAL DEVELOPMENTS: THE THIRTEENTH AMENDMENT

The Thirteenth Amendment, ratified in 1865, abolished slavery and involuntary servitude within the United States, except where it might be used as a punishment for a criminal conviction. This result had become one of the primary goals of the war and had followed on the heels of President Lincoln's 1863 Emancipation Proclamation, in which he ordered that all persons held as slaves in areas not controlled by the United States were to be considered free persons.

The Thirteenth Amendment clearly outlaws slavery as it was known prior to the Civil War, but some individuals have argued that different situations involving involuntary custody violated the spirit of the Thirteenth Amendment. For example, in one case, a group of Mexican nationals who had entered the United States illegally were being held against their will as material witnesses by the federal government. They contended that the Thirteenth Amendment prevented their detention while they were being paid a dollar per day as witnesses because it amounted to involuntary servitude.[15] The material witness prisoners could not afford to make bail, so they waited in jails prior to giving their testimony in a pending criminal case. Even though they were being involuntarily held by the government of the United States, they were being paid one dollar a day as compensation during the time the trial court was in session, when their presence was necessary. The Court concluded that there was no substance to the arguments made by the illegal aliens that the one dollar a day payment was so low as to impose an involuntary servitude that had been prohibited under the Thirteenth Amendment.[16]

Court cases have considered whether the federal government's act of drafting individuals for military service amounts to involuntary servitude that would violate the Thirteenth Amendment.[17] In one instance, the defendant had been indicted for failure to register under the Military Selective Service Act of 1967. In rejecting the defendant's claim, the district court noted that involuntary servitude has never been interpreted as pertaining to military service. The court believed that involuntary servitude included only forced labor such as peonage and was not intended to include lawful military service. Essentially, the Thirteenth Amendment did not infringe on the power of Congress to raise and equip an army.

Efforts of litigants to make the Thirteenth Amendment serve other purposes have traditionally been rejected by the courts, and it seems limited to its original purpose of eliminating human slavery from our nation.

9. CONSTITUTIONAL DEVELOPMENTS: THE FOURTEENTH AMENDMENT

The framers of the Fourteenth Amendment intended to make certain that persons who had formerly been held as slaves possessed citizenship, and they wanted to prohibit the individual states from infringing upon the privileges and immunities[18] that a citizen might possess. The framers of the amendment borrowed the concept of due process from the Fifth Amendment and forbade any state from denying due process to any person. At the time the Fourteenth Amendment was proposed, the concept of due process contemplated that a government must deal fairly with all of its citizens. A right that was not mentioned in the Fifth Amendment that the framers added to the Fourteenth Amendment was the concept of equal protection, which required that all states had to treat their citizens with substantial equality. The concept of due process (or a guarantee of fundamental fairness) eventually proved to be the legal vehicle that the Supreme Court used to selectively incorporate individual guarantees offered by many of the original Bill of Rights into the Due Process Clause of the Fourteenth Amendment and then apply them against state action to prevent state infringement of a federally guaranteed right. The process of incorporating some constitutional rights began with *Gitlow v. New York* when, in a criminal case, the Court assumed that the First Amendment applied to limit state action and based its decision on the Due Process Clause of the Fourteenth Amendment.[19] According to various United States Supreme Court decisions, some rights are so basic and so essential to fundamental fairness that they must be deemed to be included within the term *due process*. Among these essential rights that the Supreme Court eventually determined were necessary to due process are the right to be free from unreasonable searches and seizures, the right to a trial by jury, the right not to be tried twice for the same crime, the right to counsel, the right to a speedy and public trial, and the right not be subjected to cruel and unusual punishments. In every instance where the Court has found that these rights are essential to meeting the due process standard, it has not hesitated to hold that a particular right must be written into and considered part of the Due Process Clause of the Fourteenth Amendment.

10. CONSTITUTIONAL DEVELOPMENTS: THE FIFTEENTH AMENDMENT

The final post–Civil War amendment, the Fifteenth Amendment, effective in 1869, provided that the right of citizens of the United States to vote could not be limited by the United States or any state where that limitation was based on a person's race, color, or prior status of servitude. The intention of this amendment was not that every person, including females and newly freed slaves, would be permitted to vote; the intention was to remove disabilities relative to voting based on race and previous status as a slave. Property or gender qualifications that were otherwise necessary to be eligible to vote were not intended to be disturbed or altered by the Fifteenth Amendment. The amendment extended the franchise to anyone who could meet the existing tests or property qualifications for voting that had general application to all citizens. Consistent with the law and custom of the time, of course, the law did not allow women to vote, and the Fifteenth Amendment did not alter this fact.

11. CRIMINAL PROCEDURE PRIOR TO THE SELECTIVE INCORPORATION DOCTRINE

Prior to development of the selective incorporation doctrine, none of the individual rights or limitations on the federal government mentioned in the Bill of Rights applied in any way that limited the actions of the states. The original intent of the Bill of Rights, and especially of the first eight amendments, was to restrain only the federal government, and there was never any intention that these rights would be applied to limit state governments in their activities. In an early case, *Barron v. The Mayor and City Council of Baltimore,* 32 U.S. 243 (1833), in which a litigant contended that the takings clause of the Fifth Amendment should apply to a state so that a state would have to compensate the suing parties for injuries sustained to their wharf from actions taken by the city. The Fifth Amendment, among other rights, provided that private property would not be taken for use by the public unless the federal government compensated the owner. In making some land improvements, the diversion of streams, and other civil engineering efforts, the plaintiffs sustained damage to their property that would not have otherwise occurred but for the city's actions. The Court in *Barron* held that the Fifth Amendment provided no remedy because it "must be understood as restraining the power of the general government, not as applicable to the states."[20] The Supreme Court was simply interpreting the Constitution and the Fifth Amendment in the manner that the original Framers had intended. At this point in history, the Court was not willing to make new law by interpreting the Constitution in a way that would have given the *Barron* litigants the fair measure of justice that had been denied by the City of Baltimore. Although the *Barron* case did not involve any right of a person accused of a crime, it stands for the proposition that in the early years, the Court interpreted the Constitution based on its perceived original intent.

In later litigation, the Supreme Court of the United States decided a case involving a state criminal sanction that the defendant alleged violated the Eighth Amendment's prohibition against cruel and unusual punishment. In *Pervear v. Commonwealth,* 72 U.S. 475 (1867), the defendant possessed a federal license to keep and hold alcoholic beverages for sale, but he had been convicted of a state crime because he did not possess a state license to conduct his business. Previously, the state court had sentenced him to three months at hard labor, and he contended the punishment violated the Eighth Amendment in that it was a cruel and unusual state sentence for someone who already possessed a federal license to do exactly what he had been convicted of doing. In rejecting the defendant's argument that the Eighth Amendment prevented the Commonwealth of Massachusetts from imposing such a sentence, the *Pervear* Court noted, "We see nothing in the record, nor has anything been read to us from the statutes of the State which warrants us in saying that the laws of Massachusetts having application to this case are in conflict with the Constitution of the United States."[21] When presented with an opportunity to say that the Eighth Amendment applied in a way that limited the action of a state, the Supreme Court was simply unwilling to go against the original intent of the Framers of the Bill of Rights.[22] Such an interpretation of the post–Civil War amdendments did not last forever.

12. THE SELECTIVE INCORPORATION DOCTRINE: FEDERALIZATION OF CRIMINAL PROCEDURE

Initial efforts to get the Supreme Court to incorporate parts of the Bill of Rights into the due process clause of the Fourteenth Amendment failed in the *Slaughter-House Cases*[23] (Section 5, 6), when the Court refused to interpret the Fourteenth Amendment as doing anything more then placing the post–Civil War results in the Constitution. The Thirteenth Amendment, by its terms, clearly freed the people previously held as slaves, and the Fourteenth Amendment made every effort to protect those individuals by making them citizens and by limiting the laws than any state could enact that could restrict their newly won freedoms and citizenship.

In a 1897 case, *Chicago, Burlington & Quincy R.R. v. Chicago,*[24] where the city had taken some of the land owned by the railroad and the railroad wanted compensation, the railroad argued that the Fourteenth Amendment guarantee of due process and the Fifth Amendment prohibition against taking property without due process required compensation from the government for taking its interest in private real property. Additionally, the railroad contended that the Seventh Amendment guarantee of civil jury trials should be applied against the states. The Supreme Court affirmed the judgment of the Supreme Court of Illinois on its merits by ruling that a dollar was sufficient compensation for the interest in land actually taken. However, the Court noted.

> In our opinion, a judgment of a state court, even if it be authorized by statute, whereby private property is taken for the State or under its direction for public use, without compensation made or secured to the owner, is, upon principle and authority, wanting in the due process of law required by the Fourteenth Amendment of the Constitution of the United States, and the affirmance of such judgment by the highest court of the State is a denial by that State of a right secured to the owner by that instrument.[25]

This language opened the door for the Court to later begin incorporating some of the rights guaranteed in the Bill of Rights into the Due Process Clause of the Fourteenth Amendment. In *Gitlow v. New York,* 268 U.S. 652 (1925) (see Section 6, this chapter), the Court began the process known as selective incorporation. Although that term may not have exactly applied in 1925, hindsight permits the conclusion that the process seems to have initiated with this case. *Gitlow* involved a criminal prosecution where a defendant had been convicted and sentenced for criminal anarchy because he advocated the overthrow of all state governments and the federal government. The Court did not find the defendant's arguments persuasive that his right to free speech had been improperly curtailed, but the Court did observe:

> For present purposes we may and do assume that freedom of speech and of the press—which are protected by the First Amendment from abridgment by Congress—are among the fundamental personal rights and "liberties" protected by the due process clause of the Fourteenth Amendment from impairment by the States.[26]

Although this case did not open the floodgates to changes in the content of the Fourteenth Amendment's Due Process Clause, it appears to have initiated the process whereby other rights mentioned in the Bill of Rights would and could be applied to limit state activity by incorporating these rights into the Due Process Clause.

In the years following *Gitlow,* on a case-by-case basis, the Supreme Court of the United States determined that the Fourth Amendment guarantee against unreasonable searches and seizures, the Fifth Amendment protection against double jeopardy, the protection against self-incrimination, and other guarantees of the Bill of Rights applied to the states through the Due Process Clause of the Fourteenth Amendment. Not all of the guarantees under the Bill of Rights have been incorporated against the states as of the present time, and it remains to be seen whether those guarantees will be incorporated in future years.

13. FOURTH AMENDMENT: PROHIBITION AGAINST UNREASONABLE SEARCHES

According to the original intent, under the Fourth Amendment, "the right of the people to be secure in their persons, houses, papers, and effects, against unreasonable searches and seizures, shall not be violated" where the intruder is a federal official cloaked with federal authority. The Fourth Amendment also contains a clause that indicates no warrants shall be issued except where there is proof of probable cause that has been supported by an oath and where the warrant particularly describes the objects or people to be seized. In a landmark case, *Weeks v. United States,* 232 U.S. 383 (1914), the Court determined that where federal officials violated the Fourth Amendment by seizing private materials without the benefit of a warrant, such evidence would be suppressed from federal criminal trials. Although the new rule requiring suppression of illegally seized evidence changed federal criminal procedure, the ruling, and later ones, remained true to the concept that the Fourth Amendment limited only the federal government. The *Weeks* doctrine became known as the exclusionary rule that helped support and enforce the Fourth Amendment by removing the law enforcement incentive to violate it when securing evidence of crime. When illegally seized evidence cannot be used at trial, there is little reason to illegally seize evidence.

In a later state case, *Wolf v. Colorado,* 338 U.S. 25 (1949) (Case 1.1), the defendants had been convicted of conspiracy to commit criminal abortion by virtue of evidence illegally seized in the absence of a warrant. Had this been a federal prosecution, the Fourth Amendment would have clearly applied, and the *Weeks* exclusionary rule would have prevented the evidence from being introduced in court. In an appeal from his state court conviction to the Supreme Court, the defendant contended that the Due Process Clause of the Fourteenth Amendment required that the evidence illegally seized by state police officers should be suppressed. At that time, the Court refused to order that illegally seized evidence in state cases be suppressed from introduction into state criminal trials. In this case, the Court was not yet willing to take the next step by following the selective incorporation doctrine to incorporate the Fourth Amendment into the Due Process Clause of the Fourteenth Amendment. The *Wolf* Court noted, "[I]n a prosecution in a State court for a State crime the Fourteenth Amendment does not forbid the admission of evidence obtained by an unreasonable search and seizure."[27] The Court did express the opinion that if a state were to affirmatively sanction this type of illegal entry and seizure, the Due Process Clause of the Fourteenth Amendment would have been violated.

In 1961 in *Mapp v. Ohio,* 367 U.S. 643, the Court finally determined that the Due Process Clause of the Fourteenth Amendment included the protections involving search and seizure under the Fourth Amendment, adopted the exclusionary rule announced in *Weeks,* and applied it to state criminal trials. As a matter of due process, evidence that has been illegally seized in a state case violates the Fourth Amendment and must be excluded from proof of guilt. The Court used the doctrine of selective incorporation to determine that Fourth Amendment guarantees must be observed as part of constitutional due process. Following the *Mapp* case, evidence that has been illegally seized, whether the law enforcement person was clothed with federal or state governmental authority, must not be introduced against a person whose Fourth Amendment rights have been violated.

14. FIFTH AMENDMENT: RIGHT TO A GRAND JURY INDICTMENT, PRIVILEGE AGAINST SELF-INCRIMINATION, AND PROHIBITION AGAINST DOUBLE JEOPARDY AS PART OF THE RIGHT TO DUE PROCESS

When dealing with the Fifth Amendment and contentions that all or part of its guarantees should be included within the concept of due process of the Fourteenth Amendment, the Supreme Court of the United States has taken a case-by-case analysis, following the familiar procedure known as the selective incorporation doctrine.

In the 1880s, a defendant who had been charged, tried, and convicted of a capital offense in a state criminal trial argued that the Fifth Amendment guarantee of a grand jury indictment prior to a trial should be applied to the states through the

CASE 1.1

Leading Case Brief: Due Process Does Not Forbid the Use of Illegally Seized Evidence in State Criminal Prosecutions.

Wolf v. Colorado
Supreme Court of the United States
338 U.S. 25 (1949)

Case Facts:

Wolf and others were charged in state court by information with conspiracy to commit criminal abortion. They contended that the state illegally seized some of their records and material and used that evidence against them at trial. If the prosecution had been in a federal court, the evidence would have been excluded under the *Weeks* [*v. United States,* 232 U.S. 383 (1914)] exclusionary rule.

Legal Issue:

Does a conviction by a state court for an offense deny due process of law guaranteed by the Fourteenth Amendment solely because the same evidence would have been inadmissible in a federal trial due to a violation of the Fourth Amendment?

The Court's Ruling:

After struggling with the concept of due process, the Court determined that the case would not be reversed and that the conduct did not violate due process so that it was permissible to use the illegally seized evidence so long as the state did not make this method of seizing evidence into the state's affirmative policy.

Essence of the Court's Rationale:

* * *

Due process of law thus conveys neither formal nor fixed nor narrow requirements. It is the compendious expression for all those rights which the courts must enforce because they are basic to our free society. But basic rights do not become petrified as of any one time, even though, as a matter of human experience, some may not too rhetorically be called eternal verities.

It is of the very nature of a free society to advance in its standards of what is deemed reasonable and right. Representing as it does a living principle, due process is not confined within a permanent catalogue of what may at a given time be deemed the limits or the essentials of fundamental rights.

To rely on a tidy formula for the easy determination of what is a fundamental right for purposes of legal enforcement may satisfy a longing for certainty but ignores the movements of a free society. It belittles the scale of the conception of due process. The real clue to the problem confronting the judiciary in the application of the Due Process Clause is not to ask where the line is once and for all to be drawn but to recognize that it is for the Court to draw it by the gradual and empiric process of "inclusion and exclusion." *Davidson v. New Orleans,* 96 U.S. 97, 104. This was the Court's insight when first called upon to consider the problem; to this insight the Court has on the whole been faithful as case after case has come before it since *Davidson v. New Orleans* was decided.

The security of one's privacy against arbitrary intrusion by the police—which is at the core of the Fourth Amendment—is basic to a free society. It is therefore implicit in "the concept of ordered liberty" and as such enforceable against the States through the Due Process Clause. The knock at the door, whether by day or by night, as a prelude to a search, without authority of law but solely on the authority of the police, did not need the commentary of recent history to be condemned as inconsistent with the conception of human rights enshrined in the history and the basic constitutional documents of English-speaking peoples.

Accordingly, we have no hesitation in saying that were a State affirmatively to sanction such police incursion into privacy it would run counter to the guaranty of the Fourteenth Amendment. But the ways of enforcing such a basic right raise questions of a different order. How such arbitrary conduct should be checked, what remedies against it should be afforded, the means by which the right should be made effective, are all questions that are not to be so dogmatically answered as to preclude the varying solutions which spring from an allowable range of judgment on issues not susceptible of quantitative solution.

* * *

[The Court reviewed the various ways of enforcing the right to not be subjected to unreasonable seizures. It noted that some states excluded evidence wrongly seized and others allowed suits against the police officers. Although this case virtually indicated that the Fourth Amendment's protection against unreasonable searches was incorporated into the due process clause of the Fourteenth Amendment, the Court was not ready to dictate the same remedies for state prosecutions as it had required for cases where the federal government violated the Fourth Amendment. See *Weeks v. United States*, 232 U.S. 383 (1914).]

We hold, therefore, that in a prosecution in a State court for a State crime the Fourteenth Amendment does not forbid the admission of evidence obtained by an unreasonable search and seizure.

Affirmed. [the conviction of Wolf and others]

Case Importance:

By announcing that if a state policy affirmatively permitted the seizing of evidence in a manner that would be illegal under the Fourth Amendment that such policy would violate the due process clause, the Court was "telegraphing" that it had virtually incorporated the Fourth Amendment into the due process clause of the Fourteenth Amendment. The Court took the final step in *Mapp v. Ohio*, 367 U.S. 643 (1961).

Due Process Clause of the Fourteenth Amendment. In *Hurtado v. California*, 110 U.S. 516 (1884), the defendant had been brought to trial based upon an information[28] filed by a prosecutor that was done in accordance with due process of law as defined by California. According to the Supreme Court of the United States, the substitution of an indictment for prosecutor's information, where the defendant had assistance of counsel and where the defendant could cross-examine witnesses, did not violate the fundamental fairness required by due process of law according to the Fourteenth Amendment. This case remains good law to the present time, with the result that some states require the initiation of serious criminal prosecutions by a grand jury indictment and others offer the prosecutor a choice between filing an information against an accused and taking the case to a grand jury in the hope of procuring an indictment. Although *Hurtado* was decided long before the selective incorporation doctrine gained full force, the Court has not seen fit to overrule the decision that concepts of due process may be different in the federal arena than in state practice. So long as fundamental fairness prevails in the state process used to initiate serious criminal trials, the Supreme Court will probably not determine that the right to a grand jury indictment is required by the Fourteenth Amendment.

Although all state constitutions, in some form or other, require that the privilege against self-incrimination not be violated, some variations in the way it was applied caused criminal defendants to argue that due process under the Fourteenth Amendment required that the federal Fifth Amendment privilege against self-incrimination be recognized as a right in state criminal prosecutions. The original intent of the Framers of the Fifth Amendment was to limit the federal government. In *Malloy v. Hogan*, 378 U.S. 1 (1964) (see Case 1.2), the litigant contended that he had been held illegally in contempt of court because he asserted that the Fifth Amendment privilege

CASE 1.2

Leading Case Brief: The Fifth Amendment Privilege Against Self-Incrimination Is Incorporated into the Due Process Clause of the Fourteenth Amendment

Malloy v. Hogan, Sheriff
Supreme Court of the United States
378 U.S. 1 (1964)

Case Facts:

The petitioner, Mr. Malloy, was on probation for a gambling misdemeanor. Sixteen months later, he was ordered to testify in front of a judicial official who was investigating gambling and related activities. Mr. Malloy refused to testify, alleging that the Fifth Amendment privilege against self-incrimination allowed him to remain silent concerning gambling activity. A court found him in contempt and sent him to jail until he was willing to talk. The Superior Court and the state's top court upheld the contempt adjudication. The Connecticut Supreme Court of Errors held that the Fifth Amendment did not apply to Connecticut and extended no privilege to him. Malloy contended that the Fifth Amendment privilege against self-incrimination should limit state action when it was applied through the Due Process Clause of the Fourteenth Amendment.

Legal Issue:

Should the Fifth Amendment privilege against self-incrimination be incorporated into the Due Process Clause of the Fourteenth Amendment and assertable in a state case?

The Court's Ruling:

The Court reviewed prior cases in which some of the individual rights mentioned in the Bill of Rights had previously been incorporated into the Due Process Clause. The court found that the privilege against self-incrimination was one of the principles of a free government and therefore had to be incorporated into the Due Process Clause of the Fourteenth Amendment.

Essence of the Court's Rationale:

* * *

The extent to which the Fourteenth Amendment prevents state invasion of rights enumerated in the first eight Amendments has been considered in numerous cases in this Court since the Amendment's adoption in 1868. Although many Justices have deemed the Amendment to incorporate all eight of the Amendments, the view which has thus far prevailed dates from the decision in 1897 in *Chicago, B. & Q. R. Co. v. Chicago,* 166 U.S. 226, which held that the Due Process Clause requires the States to pay just compensation for private property taken for public use. It was on the authority of that decision that the Court said in 1908 in *Twining v. New Jersey,* supra, that "it is possible that some of the personal rights safeguarded by the first eight Amendments against National action may also be safeguarded against state action, because a denial of them would be a denial of due process of law." 211 U.S., at 99.

The Court has not hesitated to re-examine past decisions according the Fourteenth Amendment a less central role in the preservation of basic liberties than that which was contemplated by its Framers when they added the Amendment to our constitutional scheme. Thus, although the Court as late as 1922 said that "neither the Fourteenth Amendment nor any other provision of the Constitution of the United States imposes upon the States any restrictions about 'freedom of speech' . . .," *Prudential Ins. Co. v. Cheek,* 259 U.S. 530, 543, three years later *Gitlow v. New York,* 268 U.S. 652, initiated a series of decisions which today hold immune from state invasion every First Amendment protection for the cherished rights of mind and spirit—the freedoms of speech, press, religion, assembly, association, and petition for redress of grievances.

[The Court reviewed other cases that had once declared a right not applicable against the states, but were later reversed. *Palko v. Connecticut* (1937) had its decision involving the double jeopardy clause reversed. And *Mapp v. Ohio* (1961) reconsidered the earlier rejection of the Fourth Amendment and the exclusionary rule being applied to the states.]

* * *

We hold today that the Fifth Amendment's exception from compulsory self-incrimination is also protected by the Fourteenth Amendment against abridgment by the States. Decisions of the Court since *Twining* and *Adamson* have departed from the contrary view expressed in those cases. We discuss first the decisions which forbid the use of coerced confessions in state criminal prosecutions.

* * *

The marked shift to the federal standard in state cases began with *Lisenba v. California,* 314 U.S. 219, where the Court spoke of the accused's "free choice to admit, to deny, or to refuse to answer."

* * *

This conclusion is fortified by our recent decision in *Mapp v. Ohio,* 367 U.S. 643, overruling *Wolf v. Colorado,* 338 U.S. 25, which had held "that in a prosecution in a State court for a State crime the Fourteenth Amendment does not forbid the admission of evidence obtained by an unreasonable search and seizure," 338 U.S., at 33. *Mapp* held that the Fifth Amendment privilege against self-incrimination implemented the Fourth Amendment in such cases, and that the two guarantees of personal security conjoined in the Fourteenth Amendment to make the exclusionary rule obligatory upon the States.

[The Court reversed the Connecticut Supreme Court of Errors decision that the Fifth Amendment privilege against self-incrimination did not apply in a state case. On remand, the defendant will be able to assert the Fifth Amendment privilege.]

Case Importance:

By continuing to follow the selective incorporation model, the Court incorporated the Fifth Amendment privilege against self-incrimination into the Due Process Clause of the Fourteenth Amendment with the result that the Fifth Amendment privilege against self-incrimination applies in both state and federal contexts.

against self-incrimination was available to him as a witness in a state criminal proceeding in which another person was the defendant. Connecticut contended that the Fifth Amendment did not apply in this case and that Connecticut law did not give him the right not to testify against another person after he had pled guilty to a separate offense. The Supreme Court in *Malloy* reconsidered older decisions[29] that held that the Fifth Amendment privilege against self-incrimination is not protected against state action under the Due Process Clause of the Fourteenth Amendment. In taking a new look concerning whether the Fifth Amendment privilege against self-incrimination should be applied against the states, the Court noted,

> Although many Justices have deemed the Amendment to incorporate all eight of the Amendments, the view which has thus far prevailed dates from the decision in 1897 in *Chicago, B. & Q. R. Co. v. Chicago,* 166 U.S. 226, which held that the Due Process Clause requires the States to pay just compensation for private property taken for public use. It was on the authority of that decision that the Court said in 1908 in *Twining v. New Jersey, supra,* that "it is possible that some of the personal rights safeguarded by the first eight Amendments against National action may also be safeguarded against state action, because a denial of them would be a denial of due process of law." 211 U.S., at 99.[30]

The *Malloy* Court determined that the Due Process Clause of the Fourteenth Amendment incorporated the Fifth Amendment privilege against self-incrimination and that under such an interpretation the Connecticut courts had misapplied the previously nonexistent federal interpretation of the Fifth Amendment. In *Malloy,* the Supreme Court followed what has been known as the selective incorporation doctrine by determining on a case-by-case basis that various rights under the Bill of Rights exist or nest within the Due Process Clause of the Fourteenth Amendment.

In earlier litigation, the Supreme Court determined that the Fifth Amendment guarantee against being tried twice for the same crime did not apply to state criminal prosecutions. The prior case, *Palko v. Connecticut,* 302 U.S. 319 (1937), involved a defendant who had been tried for murder in the first degree but convicted of second-degree murder and given a life sentence. The defendant chose not to appeal. However, the prosecution successfully appealed the case, alleging that errors that harmed the state's case required a retrial. The reviewing court granted a new trial, after which the verdict was for first-degree murder with a death sentence. Palko appealed his second conviction to the Supreme Court of the United States and contended that what was prohibited by the Fifth Amendment's double jeopardy clause was also prohibited by the Due Process Clause of the Fourteenth Amendment. The Supreme Court rejected Palko's arguments based on prior case law and because the scheme of justice or ordered liberty would not cease to exist if a person were tried twice for the same crime. The Court said of the second trial, "Justice, however, would not perish if the accused were subject to a duty to respond to orderly inquiry."[31]

The Court reversed *Palko* in *Benton v. Maryland,* 395 U.S. 784 (1964), in a case where the defendant had been accused of burglary and larceny but the jury found him guilty of burglary and not guilty of larceny. Because of errors in the way the grand jury and the trial jury had been selected, Benton was given a new trial and convicted of both the burglary and larceny charges, even though the first jury had acquitted him of larceny. Benton's appeal argued that the double jeopardy provision of the Fifth Amendment should apply to the states and prohibit retrials of the same issue. The *Benton* Court reversed the earlier decision, *Palko v. Connecticut,* and held that the retrial of the larceny charge for which Benton had previously been acquitted violated the Fifth Amendment protection against double jeopardy, which was applicable to the states through the Due Process Clause of the Fourteenth Amendment. The *Benton* Court determined that the double jeopardy provision was "a fundamental ideal in our constitutional heritage," although the Court in *Palko* failed to acknowledge this principle.

Once again, following the doctrine of selective incorporation, the Court reconsidered one of its prior decisions and determined that another part of the Fifth Amendment involved fundamental protections that were included within the Fourteenth Amendment and were therefore enforceable against the states.

15. SIXTH AMENDMENT: THE RIGHT TO A SPEEDY AND PUBLIC JURY TRIAL, THE RIGHT TO CONFRONT WITNESSES, AND THE RIGHT TO COUNSEL

The right to a speedy trial permits the defendant an opportunity to resolve criminal charges without having them "hang over" the defendant for an indefinite time.

A defendant who waits for significant periods of time for the finality of a trial result suffers limitations on liberty, may be deprived of employment, and may be limited in his or her associations with other people. As a general rule, a delay in the initiation of a trial works to the benefit of a defendant, but sometimes delay harms the merits of a defendant's case. The Sixth Amendment contains the right to a speedy trial for federal offenses, but that guarantee originally was not intended to require a rapid resolution of criminal cases in state courts. In a landmark case, *Klopfer v. North Carolina*, 386 U.S. 213 (1967) (Case 1.3), involving criminal trespass in the context of a civil rights demonstration, the jury was unable to reach a verdict, and a mistrial had to be declared. The prosecutor requested and was granted a *nolle prosequi* with leave, which allowed the prosecutor to bring the case to trial in the future at the prosecution's discretion. In effect, there was no certainty when the matter would finally be resolved. The defendant contended that the Sixth Amendment right to a speedy trial should be applicable in a state criminal prosecution by virtue of the Due Process Clause of the Fourteenth Amendment. The Court viewed the right to a speedy trial to be as fundamental as any of the other rights guaranteed by the Sixth Amendment, and it noted that the concept has been around at least since 1215, when it appeared in the Magna Carta. Chief Justice Warren wrote, "The history of the right to a speedy trial and its reception in this country clearly establish that it is one of the most basic rights preserved by our Constitution."[32] The *Klopfer* Court, following the doctrine of selective incorporation, held that the right to speedy trial in the Sixth Amendment was incorporated into the Due Process Clause of the Fourteenth Amendment and was enforceable against the states. Klopfer was entitled to be tried within a reasonable time, or the charges had to be dismissed.

The right to a public trial prevents or reduces governmental overreaching, fraud, and other improper activities by the prosecution, the judge, or even a defense counsel. From the time of its ratification, the Sixth Amendment guaranteed that defendants would have a public trial for federal prosecutions. State constitutions and laws generally guarantee a similar right to a public trial, but in some instances, the state public trial right was not applied in the same way or manner that the federal Sixth Amendment right to a public trial had been interpreted. In the case of *In re Oliver*, 333 U.S. 257 (1948), Oliver, a state prisoner, had been called before a judge acting as a "one-person" grand jury to give testimony concerning other criminal cases. The judge found Oliver's credibility lacking and said that the story did not "jell," and while still in the context of a one-person grand jury, the judge held a secret hearing, found the defendant in criminal contempt of court, and sentenced him to sixty days of incarceration.[33] The Supreme Court reversed Oliver's conviction on the basis that a public trial had long roots in the English common law tradition and heritage and that the concept of a public trial predated the settlement of the United States. The Court determined that virtually every state, by constitution, by statute, or by judicial decision, guaranteed the right that a criminal trial would be open to the public. According to the Court, the secret procedure violated the Fourteenth Amendment guarantee that no one should be deprived of liberty without due process of law. By finding that the right to a public trial was part of due process, the Court, once again, applied the selective incorporation doctrine to the Bill of Rights by using the Fourteenth Amendment.

CASE 1.3

Leading Case Brief: Right to a Sppedy Trial Is Incorporated into the Due Process Clause of the Fourteenth Amendment

Klopfer v. North Carolina
Supreme Court of the United States
386 U.S. 213 (1967)

Case Facts:

In defendant Klopfer's misdemeanor trial, the jury failed to reach a verdict, and the court declared a mistrial. The judge ordered that the charge be continued, but eighteen months after the original indictment, the prosecutor had not brought the case up for trial. The judge permitted the prosecutor to take a *nolle prosequi,* which meant the defendant was discharged from any custody but that the prosecutor could bring the case back at any time, and the matter continued to "hang over the head" of the accused, Mr. Klopfer. When Klopfer objected and appealed, the Supreme Court of North Carolina affirmed the trial court's action, deciding that although a defendant has a right to a speedy trial where a trial is to be held, that right does not require the state to prosecute if the prosecutor, in his discretion and with the court's approval, elects to take a *nolle prosequi.* The Supreme Court of the United States granted certiorari to hear the case.

Legal Issue:

Does the Sixth Amendment guarantee of the right to a speedy trial apply to a state prosecution under the Due Process Clause of the Fourteenth Amendment, so that a state cannot delay a trial indefinitely without violating the Sixth Amendment right to a speedy trial?

The Court's Ruling:

The Justices determined that the Sixth Amendment prevented lengthy pretrial delays because the Sixth Amendment applies to the states through the Due Process Clause of the Fourteenth Amendment: the court held that the right to a speedy trial is as fundamental as any of the rights secured by the Sixth Amendment. Klopfer should have been given a speedy trial, and if

the delay in prosecuting the case was too long, the case would have to be dismissed on remand.

Essence of the Court's Rationale:

[The Court reviewed the practice followed by other states and noted that in seventeen states, where the trial has been unduly delayed, the case must be dismissed and cannot be brought again. Upon additional review, the court observed that thirty states permit a prosecutor to request a *nolle prosequi* and many allow a reinstatement at a later date. A few other states permit the use of a *nolle prosequi* with permission of the court. The Court expressed the view that the position taken by the state supreme court was erroneous.]

The petitioner is not relieved of the limitations placed upon his liberty by this prosecution merely because its suspension permits him to go "whithersoever he will." The pendency of the indictment may subject him to public scorn and deprive him of employment, and almost certainly will force curtailment of his speech, associations and participation in unpopular causes. By indefinitely prolonging this oppression, as well as the "anxiety and concern accompanying public accusation," the criminal procedure condoned in this case by the Supreme Court of North Carolina clearly denies the petitioner the right to a speedy trial which we hold is guaranteed to him by the Sixth Amendment to the Constitution of the United States.

While there has been a difference of opinion as to what provisions of this Amendment to the Constitution apply to the States through the Fourteenth Amendment, that question has been settled as to some of them in the recent cases of *Gideon v. Wainwright,* 372 U.S. 335 (1963) [due process granted assistance of counsel in felonies], and *Pointer v. Texas,* 380 U.S.

400 (1965). In the latter case, which dealt with the confrontation-of-witnesses provision, we said:

"In the light of *Gideon, Malloy* [due process guaranteed privilege against self-incrimination in state cases], and other cases cited in those opinions holding various provisions of the Bill of Rights applicable to the States by virtue of the Fourteenth Amendment, the statements made in *West* and similar cases generally declaring that the Sixth Amendment does not apply to the States can no longer be regarded as the law. We hold that petitioner was entitled to be tried in accordance with the protection of the confrontation guarantee of the Sixth Amendment, and that that guarantee, like the right against compelled self-incrimination, is 'to be enforced against the States under the Fourteenth Amendment according to the same standards that protect those personal rights against federal encroachment.' *Malloy v. Hogan,* supra, 378 U.S., at 10."

We hold here that the right to a speedy trial is as fundamental as any of the rights secured by the Sixth Amendment. That right has its roots at the very foundation of our English law heritage. Its first articulation in modern jurisprudence appears to have been made in Magna Carta (1215), wherein it was written, "We will sell to no man, we will not deny or defer to any man either justice or right"; but evidence of recognition of the right to speedy justice in even earlier times is found in the Assize of Clarendon (1166). By the late thirteenth century, justices, armed with commissions of gaol delivery and/or oyer and terminer were visiting the countryside three times a year. These justices, Sir Edward Coke wrote in Part II of his Institutes, "have not suffered the prisoner to be long detained, but at their next coming have given the prisoner full and speedy justice, . . . without detaining him long in prison." [Footnotes omitted.]

Case Importance:

The justices continued their selective incorporation of rights contained in the Bill of Rights into the Due Process Clause of the Fourteenth Amendment. From this point onward, the Sixth Amendment right to a speedy trial had to be recognized in state criminal prosecutions, and where the right is violated, the case must be dismissed and cannot be brought again.

Continuing the expansion of the Bill of Rights through selective incorporation, the Supreme Court held that the right to a jury trial under the Sixth Amendment was incorporated into the Due Process Clause of the Fourteenth Amendment in *Duncan v. Louisiana,* 391 U.S. 145 (1968). In that case, the Court found that the right to a jury trial constituted a fundamental right that was incorporated into the Due Process Clause of the Fourteenth Amendment. Duncan had been denied a trial by jury because state law considered the alleged crime to be a petty misdemeanor that carried a maximum sentence of only two years of incarceration. Justice White offered the opinion that the right to a jury trial in a state case must be granted in the same manner as the trial by jury right existed in federal criminal trials under the Sixth Amendment. In Duncan's case, a crime punishable by up to two years of incarceration was not a petty offense but had to be considered a serious offense for which the Sixth Amendment, as applied to the states, required a jury trial. In a different case involving a refinement of the right to a jury trial, *Baldwin v. New York,* 399 U.S. 145 (1970), the Court refined when the right to a jury trial existed when it held that where a potential sentence of incarceration exceeded six months, the crime could not be considered petty and that the right to a trial by jury had to be granted. The Court continued the process of selective incorporation and, in the matter of trial by jury, required the right to a jury trial in a state court whenever the right would exist in a federal criminal trial. Although due process protects the right to a jury trial, the right to a jury trial does not mean that the right is identical in state and federal trials. In highlighting the differences, the Court has determined that a jury in a state case need not have twelve jurors[34] and that juries of twelve in state cases need not always reach a unanimous verdict.[35]

Consistent with the original intent of the Framers, the Sixth Amendment guarantees the right to be able to confront and examine adverse witnesses who testify for the prosecution in a federal case. In a state prosecution in *Pointer v. Texas,* 380 U.S. 400 (1965), the chief witness against an accused in a robbery prosecution failed to show up for the trial, although the witness had testified at the preliminary hearing. The trial judge permitted the introduction of the witness's preliminary hearing transcript, a procedure that failed to permit the defendant to conduct cross-examination of the missing witness. The Supreme Court reversed the conviction on basis that the Sixth Amendment guaranteed the right of confrontation and cross-examination as applied to the states through the Due Process Clause of the Fourteenth Amendment. The Court noted, "It cannot seriously be doubted at this late date that the right of cross-examination is included in the right of an accused in a criminal case to confront the witnesses against him."[36] The Court reaffirmed *Pointer v. Texas* in a 2004 case, *Crawford v. Washington,*[37] when it reversed a case where a wife's out-of-court statement had been used against her husband without offering him the right of confrontation and cross-examination. In an earlier case involving confrontation of witnesses at criminal trials, *Washington v. Texas,* 388 U.S. 14 (1967), the Court concluded that the Sixth Amendment includes the right to have compulsory process to force witnesses to testify for an accused in a state criminal proceeding.

The right to the assistance of counsel seems so basic that there would be no doubt that it should be granted to all persons who face a state or federal prosecution. However, as originally contemplated by the Framers of the Sixth Amendment, the right to counsel applied only at federal criminal trials and was guaranteed only if a defendant could afford to pay for an attorney of the defendant's choosing. The Supreme Court recently determined that a defendant who had the ability to hire a private defense attorney was entitled to the lawyer of his or her own choosing.[38] Under the Sixth Amendment, persons who cannot afford private counsel have won the right to have appointed counsel at all critical stages of the criminal process, whether the case is to be tried in a state or federal court.

In a landmark Sixth Amendment right to counsel case, *Gideon v. Wainwright,* 372 U.S. 335 (1963), Florida prosecuted Gideon for a felony, but he had not been given the free assistance of an attorney because the state did so only in capital cases. As an indigent who was being forced to defend a felony accusation, he contended that he should be granted the Sixth Amendment assistance of counsel consistent with the guarantee of due process under the Fourteenth Amendment. The Court overruled an older precedent, *Betts v. Brady,*[39] where the *Betts* Court held that due process of law did not require an attorney to be appointed in every case. In *Gideon,* the Court determined that the Sixth Amendment's provision guaranteeing the right to counsel was a trial right that a state must grant under the Due Process Clause of the Fourteenth Amendment. The Court followed the familiar selective incorporation doctrine in granting additional rights to criminal defendants. In *Argersinger v. Hamlin,*[40] the Court refined the right to counsel in criminal prosecutions when it determined that where there was any chance of incarceration, free counsel must be given to indigent persons as a requirement of due process.

16. EIGHTH AMENDMENT: PROHIBITION OF EXCESSIVE BAIL, EXCESSIVE FINES, AND PROTECTION AGAINST CRUEL AND UNUSUAL PUNISHMENT

Although the Supreme Court has had extreme difficulty in determining exactly what constitutes cruel and unusual punishment under the Eighth Amendment,[41] the Court has decided that the cruel and unusual punishment provision applies to state criminal trials and punishments. In *Robinson v. California,* 370 U.S. 660 (1962), where a person was being prosecuted for being addicted to the use of narcotics, the Supreme Court determined that punishing somebody for being addicted to drugs violated the Due Process Clause of the Fourteenth Amendment because the Eighth Amendment prohibited the infliction of cruel and unusual punishments in state cases. The Court stated, "It is unlikely that any State at this moment in history would attempt to make it a criminal offense for a person to be mentally ill, or a leper, or to be afflicted with a venereal disease."[42] The *Robinson* Court indicated its decision when it said, "We hold that a state law which imprisons a person thus afflicted as a criminal, . . . inflicts a cruel and unusual punishment in violation of the Fourteenth Amendment."[43] The *Robinson* decision, though early in the selective incorporation of the Bill of Rights, determined that the prohibition aimed at the federal government constituted a fundamental right or bundle of rights that deserved protection from state action under the Due Process Clause of the Fourteenth Amendment.

Arguably, the excessive bail prohibition of the Eighth Amendment has not been incorporated into the Due Process Clause of the Fourteenth Amendment probably because a fair system of justice could exist where bail was not available. In fact, when an accused defendant has been denied pretrial bail or cannot afford the bail that has been set, the subsequent trial is not necessarily an unfair proceeding. The closest that the Court came to incorporating the excessive bail clause of the Eighth Amendment into the Fourteenth Amendment's Due Process Clause was in *Roper v. Simmons,* 543 U.S. 551 (2005), a case that determined that persons who were under the age of eighteen at the time of committing a capital offense could not constitutionally be given the death penalty. In *Simmons,* the Court quoted the Eighth Amendment and noted that it was applicable to the states through the Fourteenth Amendment, but the statement was not necessary to the *Simmons* decision and must not be considered as controlling, especially since bail was never an issue in *Simmons.*

As an ongoing example of selective incorporation of the Bill of Rights, the excessive fines portion of the Eighth Amendment has been incorporated into the Due Process Clause of the Fourteenth Amendment. In *Cooper Industries v. Leatherman Tool,* 532 U.S. 424 (2001),[44] the Court mentioned,

> Despite the broad discretion that States possess with respect to the imposition of criminal penalties and punitive damages, the Due Process Clause of the Fourteenth Amendment to the Federal Constitution imposes substantive limits on that discretion. That Clause makes the Eighth Amendment's prohibition against excessive fines and cruel and unusual punishments applicable to the States. *Furman v. Georgia,* 408 U.S. 238, 33 L. Ed. 2d 346, 92 S. Ct. 2726 (1972) *(per curiam).*

The *Cooper* Court cited *Furman,* a death penalty case that did not involve any excessive fines issue, so the authority for determining that the excessive fines provision has been incorporated into the due process clause may not be as secure as other incorporations of rights.

17. STATE CRIMINAL PROCEDURE: BEYOND THE FEDERAL CONSTITUTIONAL MINIMUM

Although every state must abide by Supreme Court determinations concerning selective incorporation under the Due Process Clause of the Fourteenth Amendment, each state is free to offer or to grant greater rights than the minimum threshold that is constitutionally required, according to Supreme Court decisions. If fairness or due process is viewed as a concept in which a minimum level of rights or protections is required, granting greater levels of due process and enforcing enhanced concepts of fairness would seem to be a laudable goal. For example, while most states have not extended the exclusionary rule of *Mapp v. Ohio* beyond what has been mandated by federal case law, nothing prevents a state from granting greater rights than are minimally required. In Indiana, for juveniles to properly waive *Miranda* warnings, a parent or guardian must also consent.[45] There is not any guiding case law from the Supreme Court that dictates precisely how juveniles must be given *Miranda* warnings, but Indiana takes the extra step to make sure that the warnings are understood by involving a parent or guardian in the decision.

As a general rule, a defendant does not have a federal right to counsel at any in-person lineup unless the individual has been indicted or an information has been filed against that individual. New York case law recognizes a right to counsel at an investigatory in-person lineup where an attorney-client relationship has been established.[46] In *People v. Wilson,*[47] the reversal of criminal convictions was affirmed where the defendant's attorney had made known his representation of the defendant to police officers and a corporeal lineup occurred in the absence of notice to him. This level of the right to counsel exceeds the minimum standards under case law interpreting the Constitution of the United States. In a similar fashion, Mississippi holds that the right to counsel attaches once the accused is in custody and all reasonable security measures involving evidence and persons have been completed.[48] The Supreme Court of Mississippi reversed a defendant's conviction because a witness whose identification had been tainted had identified him at trial. The witness had previously identified the defendant at a postcustody physical lineup at which the defendant had the right to counsel under Mississippi law, a right that exceeds the federal minimum right to counsel at postindictment and postinformation lineups.[49] The defendant's state right to counsel at the lineup was violated when no notice was given to the attorney. Therefore, it is clear that a state may give greater legal protections to persons in the criminal justice system than are minimally dictated by the Due Process Clause of the Fourteenth Amendment.

18. SUMMARY

English and Western philosophical and political thinkers influenced the American colonists to believe that fundamental fairness should be part of the political landscape when governments dealt with their citizens. This enlightened view of justice survived the American Revolution and found its way into state constitutions that were the part of the basis of political organization under the Articles of Confederation. When intergovernmental relations, trade, and commerce proved difficult under the Articles of Confederation, delegates responded to a Virginia call to a meeting that eventually resulted in the drafting of the Constitution of the United States. Despite challenges in obtaining ratification of the Constitution, the recommendation that a Bill of Rights be considered by the new government helped sway ratification. There were two basic positions regarding the Bill of Rights: that if human rights were enumerated, the rights not mentioned would not exist, and that if rights were not mentioned, their existence might not be honored by a powerful central government. The various proposals to guarantee rights that were suggested by several states and that were considered in the first Congress under the Constitution resulted in ratification of ten of the proposals. The ten suggested amendments to the Constitution are now known as the Bill of Rights. The intentions of the framers of the Bill of Rights were to place limits on the federal government, but they were less concerned about the possibility of state tyranny because citizens were closer to state governments and had more immediate control over them.

Following the American Civil War, the Congress proposed the Thirteenth, Fourteenth, and Fifteenth Amendments to outlaw slavery, guarantee due process and equal protection, and regulate the right to vote for citizens, respectively. Early litigation following the adoption of these amendments agitated in the direction of an expansive reading of due process, but the Supreme Court of the United States was not persuaded and limited its interpretation to the context in which they were adopted. Later litigation resulted in the gradual absorption, under the doctrine of selective incorporation, of most of the first eight amendments into the Due Process Clause of the Fourteenth Amendment. The constitutional rights originally guaranteed against infringement by the federal government in the Bill of Rights became guaranteed against infringement by state governments.

States must adhere to the minimum guarantees of constitutional rights that have been selectively incorporated into the Due Process Clause of the Fourteenth Amendment. State judicial decisions and state legislative enactments may go beyond the minimum federal constitutional requirements and recognize a greater level of protection, but they may not fall below the federal minimum threshold.

REVIEW EXERCISES AND QUESTIONS

1. What were some of the reasons that the Articles of Confederation needed some revision?

2. What reasons did some opponents offer against ratification of the present Constitution?

3. Prior to the beginning of the selective incorporation doctrine, what was the position of the Supreme Court of the United States with respect to using the Bill of Rights to place limitations on states?

4. *Wolf v. Colorado* (Section 13) came close to incorporating the exclusionary rule against the states. Why did it appear that the Court did not take the next step and incorporate the exclusionary rule from *Weeks v. United States*?

5. Assuming that the Supreme Court of the United States is in favor of extending fundamental fairness, is there a sufficiently strong reason to overrule

Hurtado v. California (Section 14) and require that states must start their serious criminal prosecutions with a grand jury indictment? Why or why not?

6. In *Palko v. Connecticut* (Section 14), the Supreme Court held that the double jeopardy clause was not part of due process under the Fourteenth Amendment. Is it possible to have a fair system of justice without prohibiting being tried twice for the same crime? Does the state have a right to a fundamentally fair trial also?

7. Why is the right to a speedy trial considered an essential part of due process applicable against the states? What is the benefit to a defendant of the right to a speedy trial?

8. Would you support the concept that states can offer greater protections based on state law or a state constitution than are minimally required by the federal Constitution? Why or why not?

HOW WOULD YOU DECIDE?

1. In the Supreme Court of the United States

Prior to and including 1962, the Kings County, California, grand jury system had excluded African Americans from participation. California does not have to use a grand jury to initiate a serious criminal prosecution. *Hurtado v. California,* 110 U.S. 516 (1884). Some California prosecutors use an information to start serious criminal cases. The Fourteenth Amendment, passed after the Civil War, guarantees everyone both due process and equal protection of the laws, and it protects these rights against state government interference. During the time that Kings County practiced racial discrimination, a grand jury returned a murder indictment against defendant-respondent Booker T. Hillery, an African American. In a pretrial motion, defendant Hillery requested that the indictment be quashed on the ground that the grand jury that indicted him had been selected in a fashion that systematically excluded black citizens from participation. Following the trial court's refusal to quash the indictment, the trial court convicted the defendant at a trial at which fundamental fairness prevailed and about which trial Mr. Hillery made no complaint.

After Hillery exhausted his California remedies, a federal district judge found in his favor and agreed that racial discrimination meant the verdict had to be reversed. The Ninth Circuit Court of Appeals agreed, and the Supreme Court granted Hillery certiorari.

How would you rule on the defendant's contention that fundamental fairness and equal protection under the Fourteenth Amendment require that his conviction based on an illegally composed grand jury be reversed?

The Court's Holding:

* * *

In 1880, this Court reversed a state conviction on the ground that the indictment charging the offense had been issued by a grand jury from which blacks had been excluded. We reasoned that deliberate exclusion of blacks "is practically a brand upon them, affixed by the law, an assertion of their inferiority, and a stimulant to that race prejudice which is an impediment to securing to individuals of the race that equal justice which the law aims to secure to all others." *Strauder v. West Virginia,* 10 Otto 303 [100 U.S. 303], 308 (1880).

* * *

When constitutional error calls into question the objectivity of those charged with bringing a defendant to judgment, a reviewing court can neither indulge a presumption of regularity nor evaluate the resulting harm. Accordingly, when the trial judge is discovered to have had some basis for rendering a biased judgment, his actual motivations are hidden from review, and we must presume that the process was impaired. See *Tumey v. Ohio,* 273 U.S. 510, 535 (1927) (reversal required when judge has financial interest in conviction, despite lack of indication that bias influenced decisions). Similarly, when a petit jury has been selected upon improper criteria or has been exposed to prejudicial publicity, we have required reversal of the conviction because the effect of the violation cannot be ascertained. See *Davis v. Georgia,* 429 U.S. 122 (1976) *(per curiam); Sheppard v. Maxwell,* 384 U.S. 333, 351–352

(1966). Like these fundamental flaws, which never have been thought harmless, discrimination in the grand jury undermines the structural integrity of the criminal tribunal itself, and is not amenable to harmless-error review.

Just as a conviction is void under the Equal Protection Clause if the prosecutor deliberately charged the defendant on account of his race, see *United States v. Batchelder,* 442 U.S. 114, 125 (1979), a conviction cannot be understood to cure the taint attributable to a charging body selected on the basis of race. Once having found discrimination in the selection of a grand jury, we simply cannot

know that the need to indict would have been assessed in the same way by a grand jury properly constituted. The overriding imperative to eliminate this systemic flaw in the charging process, as well as the difficulty of assessing its effect on any given defendant, requires our continued adherence to a rule of mandatory reversal.

* * *

The judgment of the Court of Appeals, accordingly, is affirmed. See *Vasquez, Warden v. Hillery,* 474 U.S. 254 (1986).

HOW WOULD YOU DECIDE?

2. In the Supreme Court of the United States

The federal government charged Cuauhtemoc Gonzalez-Lopez with conspiracy to distribute more than one hundred kilograms of the recreational drug marijuana in Missouri. The family of Gonzalez-Lopez hired attorney Fahle to represent him in court, and Gonzalez-Lopez also hired a California attorney, Joseph Low, to help with his representation. Since Low was not licensed in Missouri, he asked and was granted provisional authority to practice in the Missouri federal court. During one proceeding, the federal magistrate judge revoked the prior provisional acceptance to practice in the Missouri federal court on the ground that, by passing notes to Fahle during Fahle's cross-examination of a witness, Low had violated a court rule restricting the cross-examination of a witness to one counsel. With Low out of the case, the defendant eventually fired attorney Fahle and hired a third attorney, Dickhous. The new attorney wanted Low to assist him, but the trial court refused. At the conclusion of the trial, Cuauhtemoc Gonzalez-Lopez was convicted.

The Eighth Circuit Court of Appeal reversed the conviction on the ground that the Sixth Amendment had been violated because Cuauhtemoc Gonzalez-Lopez had the right to have the counsel of his choosing assist him with his defense. The appellate court also found that the district court had misinterpreted the court rule that was used to disqualify the defendant's attorney of choice, Joseph Low. The Supreme Court granted certiorari to consider the issues. Under the circumstances, does the Sixth Amendment give a defendant the right to choose his or her counsel where the lawyer is being paid by the

defendant or his family? If a person has only the right to have some attorney under the Sixth Amendment, then there has been no error.

How would you rule on the defendant's contention that where a defendant has hired legal counsel of his own choosing, a defendant has a Sixth Amendment right to have his hired counsel assist him with his defense?

The Court's Holding:

* * *

The Sixth Amendment provides that "[i]n all criminal prosecutions, the accused shall enjoy the right . . . to have the Assistance of Counsel for his defence." We have previously held that an element of this right is the right of a defendant who does not require appointed counsel to choose who will represent him. See *Wheat v. United States,* 486 U.S. 153, 159, 108 S. Ct. 1692, 100 L. Ed. 2d 140 (1988). Cf. *Powell v. Alabama,* 287 U.S. 45, 53, 53 S. Ct. 55, 77 L. Ed. 158 (1932) ("It is hardly necessary to say that, the right to counsel being conceded, a defendant should be afforded a fair opportunity to secure counsel of his own choice"). The Government here agrees, as it has previously, that "the Sixth Amendment guarantees the defendant the right to be represented by an otherwise qualified attorney whom that defendant can afford to hire, or who is willing to represent the defendant even though he is without funds." *Caplin & Drysdale, Chartered v. United States,* 491 U.S. 617, 624–625, 109 S. Ct. 2646, 109 S. Ct. 2667, 105 L. Ed. 2d 528 (1989). To be sure, the right to counsel of choice "is circumscribed in several important respects." *Wheat,* supra, at 159, 108 S. Ct. 1692, 100 L. Ed. 2d 140. But the Government does not dispute the Eighth Circuit's conclusion in this case that the District Court erroneously deprived respondent of his counsel of choice.

The Government contends, however, that the Sixth Amendment violation is not "complete" unless the defendant can show that substitute counsel was ineffective within the meaning of *Strickland v. Washington,* 466 U.S. 668, 691–696, 104 S. Ct. 2052, 80 L. Ed. 2d 674 (1984) —i.e., that substitute counsel's performance was deficient and the defendant was prejudiced by it. In the alternative, the Government contends that the defendant must at least demonstrate that his counsel of choice would have pursued a different strategy that would have created a "reasonable probability that . . . the result of the proceedings would have been different," id., at 694, 104 S. Ct. 2052, 80 L. Ed. 2d 674—in other words, that he was prejudiced [that the outcome of his trial would have been different] within the meaning of *Strickland* by the denial of his counsel of choice even if substitute counsel's performance was not constitutionally deficient.

* * *

. . . [The Sixth Amendment] commands, not that a trial be fair, but that a particular guarantee of fairness be provided—to wit, that the accused be defended by the counsel he believes to be best. "The Constitution guarantees a fair trial through the Due Process Clauses, but it defines the basic elements of a fair trial largely through the several provisions of the Sixth Amendment, including the Counsel Clause." *Strickland,* supra, at 684–685, 104 S. Ct. 2052, 80 L. Ed. 2d 674. In sum, the right at stake here is the right to counsel of choice, not the right to a fair trial; and that right was violated because the deprivation of counsel was erroneous. No additional showing of prejudice is required to make the violation "complete."

* * *

We have little trouble concluding that erroneous deprivation of the right to counsel of choice, "with consequences that are necessarily unquantifiable and indeterminate, unquestionably qualifies as 'structural error.'" [Citation omitted.] Different attorneys will pursue different strategies with regard to investigation and discovery, development of the theory of defense, selection of the jury, presentation of the witnesses, and style of witness examination and jury argument. And the choice of attorney will affect whether and on what terms the defendant cooperates with the prosecution, plea bargains, or decides instead to go to trial. In light of these myriad aspects of representation, the erroneous denial of counsel bears directly on the "framework within which the trial proceeds," *Fulminante, supra,* at 310, 111 S. Ct. 1246, 113 L. Ed. 2d 302—or indeed on whether it proceeds at all. It is impossible to know what different choices the rejected counsel would have made, and then to quantify the impact of those different choices on the outcome of the proceedings. Many counseled decisions, including those involving plea bargains and cooperation with the government, do not even concern the conduct of the trial at all. Harmless-error analysis in such a context would be a speculative inquiry into what might have occurred in an alternate universe.

* * *

The judgment of the Court of Appeals is affirmed, and the case is remanded for further proceedings consistent with this opinion. See *United States v. Gonzalez-Lopez,* 548 U.S. 140, 126 S. Ct. 2557 (2006).

ENDNOTES

1. The Charter of Liberties, proclaimed by Henry I of England on the occasion of his ascension to the throne in A.D. 1100, reduced some prerogatives of the monarch and has been considered a forerunner of the Magna Carta of 1215. The Magna Carta, signed by King John, limited some prerogatives of the British monarch while it guaranteed rights to various individuals, protecting, among other things, the freedom from unlawful imprisonment. See Section 39: "No freeman shall be taken, or imprisoned, or disseized, or outlawed, or exiled, or in any way harmed—nor will we go upon or send upon him—save by the lawful judgment of his peers or by the law of the land."

2. See Magna Carta of 1215.
3. The Age of Enlightenment refers to a period of time, mostly in the seventeenth and eighteenth centuries but with roots much earlier, when philosophers and thinkers applied reason and rationality to many areas of human thought, particularly in religious and governmental affairs. Rationality, properly applied, could create the ideal state where personal freedom flourished and the tyranny of the divine right of kings no longer existed.
4. The "rights of Englishmen" did not include universal suffrage. Men without sufficient property, women, blacks held as slaves, and free blacks could not vote unless they met property owning requirements. The Magna Carta recognized that both free and non-free persons possessed rights against unlawful imprisonments. The Supreme Court of the United States recognized in *Klopfer v. North Carolina,* 386 U.S. 213 (1967), that "the right to a speedy trial is as fundamental as any of the rights secured by the Sixth Amendment. That right has its roots at the very foundation of our English law heritage. Its first articulation in modern jurisprudence appears to have been made in Magna Carta (1215), wherein it was written, "We will sell to no man, we will not deny or defer to any man either justice or right." The "rights of Englishmen" generally applied to property-holding white men but included significant criminal procedural rights that were designed to create a system of fair trials in the colonies, generally.
5. Patrick Conley and John P. Kaminski, *The Bill of Rights and the States,* Lanham, Maryland (Rowman and Littlefield 1988), 95.
6. Ibid., p. 97. Although Massachusetts failed to ratify the Bill of Rights in the early years of the Constitution of the United States, it finally ratified it in 1939, as did Connecticut and Georgia.
7. The term Englishmen did not cover every person during most historical periods. It generally referred to males who owned a sufficient amount of property or otherwise enjoyed sufficient status to possess the "rights of Englishmen." In colonial days, the term contemplated that some colonists enjoyed all the legal rights that a similarly situated person in England would possess.
8. The Constitution of the United States of America, as Amended, p. 27, House of Representatives Document No. 102–188 (1992).
9. Ibid.
10. See *Slaughter-House Cases,* 83 U.S. 36 (1873).
11. Ibid.
12. *Gitlow v. New York,* 268 U.S. 652, 666 (1925).
13. Mississippi rejected the Thirteenth Amendment on December 4, 1865, and had not ratified it by 1992. The Constitution of the United States of America, As Amended, p. 17.
14. 268 U.S. 652.
15. See *Hurtado v. United States,* 410 U.S. 578 (1973).
16. Ibid.
17. For example, see *United States v. Chandler,* 403 U.S. 531, 1968 U.S. LEXIS 5291 (1968).
18. The concept of privileges and immunities seems to have been derived from the Constitution at Section 2 of Article 4. See *Slaughter-House Cases,* 83 U.S. 36 (1873).
19. See *Gitlow v. New York,* 268 U.S. 652 (1925).
20. *Barron v. The Mayor and City Council of Baltimore,* 32 U.S. 243, 327 (1833).
21. *Pervear v. Commonwealth,* 72 U.S. 475, 480 (1867).
22. The Fourteenth Amendment had not been ratified at the time the Court decided the *Pervear* case.
23. Ibid.
24. 166 U.S. 226 (1897).
25. *Ibid.,* 241.
26. *Gitlow v. New York,* 268 U.S. 652, 666 (1925).
27. *Wolf v. Colorado,* 338 U.S. 25, 32 (1949).
28. An information is a plain-language statement prepared by a prosecutor that accuses a particular person or persons of having committed a specifically described crime or crimes within the jurisdiction of a particular court and provides sufficient detail to give a person sufficient notice to defend the accusation. States that do not require a grand jury indictment may use this process to initiate a serious criminal proceeding.
29. See *Twining v. New Jersey,* 211 U.S. 78 (1908), and *Adamson v. California,* 332 U.S. 46 (1947).
30. *Malloy v. Hogan,* 378 U.S. 1, 2 (1964).
31. *Palko v. Connecticut,* 302 U.S. 319, 325 (1937).
32. *Klopfer v. North Carolina,* 386 U.S. 213, 226 (1967).
33. *In re Oliver,* 333 U.S. 257 (1948).
34. See *Burch v. Louisiana,* 441 U.S. 130 (1979).
35. See *Apodoca v. Oregon,* 406 U.S. 404, 1972 U.S. LEXIS 56 (1972).
36. *Pointer v. Texas,* 380 U.S. 400, 404 (1965).
37. 541 U.S. 36 (2004).
38. See *United States v. Cuauhtemoc Gonzalez-Lopez,* 126 S.Ct. 2557, 2006 LEXIS 5165 (2006).
39. 316 U.S. 455 (1942).

40. 407 U.S. 25 (1972).

41. See *McCleskey v. Kemp,* 481 U.S. 279 (1987), especially Justice Brennan's opinion, and *Furman v. Georgia,* 408 U.S. 238 (1972), and consider the several opinions.

42. *Robinson v. California,* 370 U.S. 660, 665 (1962).

43. Ibid.

44. *Cooper Industries v. Leatherman Tool,* 532 U.S. 424, 433 (2001).

45. *In the Matter of P.M.,* 861 N.E.2d 710, 714 (2007). See also Burns Ind. Code Ann. § 31-32-5-1 (2007).

46. *See People v. Wilson,* 89 N.Y.2d 754, 680 N.E.2d 598, 658 N.Y.S.2d 225, 1997 N.Y. LEXIS 738 (1997).

47. Ibid.

48. *Brooks v. State,* 903 So. 2d 691, 2005 Miss. LEXIS 191 (2005).

49. See *Kirby v. Illinois,* 406 U.S. 682, 1972 U.S. LEXIS 49 (1972).

C H A P T E R   2

Criminal Courts: Organization, Function, Jurisdiction, and the Criminal Process

Learning Objectives

1. Explain how state and federal courts are organized.
2. Be able to explain why successive prosecutions by a state and by the federal government are not considered double jeopardy.
3. Articulate why one criminal act can be a crime in two separate states.
4. Recognize and be able to articulate why some pretrial motions are considered mandatory in nature.
5. Evaluate why a prosecutor's office may not pursue every case referred by

police or by a citizen complaint, and be able to explain the rationale.
6. Assess the difference between an indictment and an information.
7. Evaluate and be able to explain the rationale behind the Supreme Court's encouragement of plea bargaining.
8. Verbally trace the trial process from jury selection to the verdict.
9. Be able to explain the essential steps of the typical appellate process.

Chapter Outline

1. An Introduction to the Criminal Justice System
2. Organization of Courts, State and Federal: A Dual System
3. Pretrial Criminal Procedure: The Initial Steps toward Prosecution
4. Initiating a Criminal Case: Complaint and Summons
5. The Charging Instruments: Indictment and Information
6. Pretrial Hearings: Probable Cause, Arraignment, and Preliminary Hearing
7. Pretrial Motion Hearings: Mandatory and Discretionary Pretrial Motions
8. Plea Negotiations
9. Jury and Nonjury Trials
10. The Trial Process
11. Selection of Jurors
12. Opening Statements
13. Prosecution's Case in Chief
14. Defense's Case in Chief
15. Prosecution Case in Rebuttal
16. Defense Case in Rejoinder
17. Motion for Judgment of Acquittal
18. Closing Arguments
19. Jury Instructions
20. Verdicts, Sentencing Process, and Posttrial Motions
21. Appellate Practice
22. State and Federal Habeas Corpus
23. Summary

Key Terms

Appellate process
Arraignment
Arrest
Bench trial
Case in chief
Case in rebuttal
Case in rejoinder
Closing argument
Complaint
Concurrent jurisdiction
Habeas corpus
Indictment

Information
Jury instructions
Jury selection
Plea negotiation
Posttrial motions
Preliminary hearing
Pretrial hearings
Pretrial motions
Prosecutor
Summons
Trial by jury
Trial court

1. AN INTRODUCTON TO THE CRIMINAL JUSTICE SYSTEM

All civilized societies recognize certain norms of human behavior and have developed methods for dealing with those individuals whose conduct seriously deviates from the expected level of normalcy. For societies that wish to deal with criminal deviancy and related behavior in a fair manner, some sort of standardized process must evolve that treats each individual in a substantially similar way, no matter what the criminal charge may involve. The states of the United States and the United States government inherited the British common law legal system[1] and have adapted it to the needs of the states and of the United States as the events of history and experience have dictated. Although the nation and the states began with a common heritage of criminal justice theory, it is not unusual to have some significant differences[2] among the state systems and between those systems and federal practice, despite great similarities.

The system of justice in the United States is a dual system that overlaps in many places, with some crimes constituting offenses under both state and federal laws. In some situations, one act may be an offense under a state law but not violate federal law. A few criminal acts may violate federal criminal law but not be recognized under state law. All jurisdictions within the territory of the United States follow a process that is roughly similar to the procedure indicated by Figure 2.1, a flow chart that has been adapted from a report of the President's Commission on Law Enforcement and Administration of Justice, 1967.[3]

This flow chart graphically represent how cases may enter the justice system, leave or be recycled, and finally be terminated out of the system with a variety of outcomes.

Where a crime has been reported and an investigation launched, the case may enter the system and exit just as quickly when sufficient evidence does not indicate that a crime has actually been committed. Alternatively, if sufficient facts and circumstances indicate that a crime has been committed, arrest may be the next step taken by police, who are members of the executive branch of government. In some situations an arrest may not be followed by a prosecution because of the exercise of discretion by the prosecutor not to pursue the case. Where criminal evidence leads toward a juvenile and indicates that the juvenile might be amenable to treatment

What is the sequence of events in the criminal justice system?

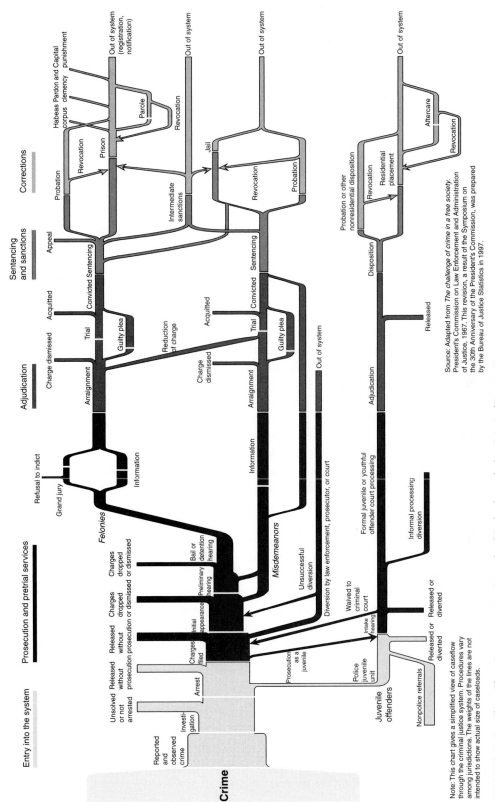

Note: This chart gives a simplified view of caseflow through the criminal justice system. Procedures vary among jurisdictions. The weights of the lines are not intended to show actual size of caseloads.

Source: Adapted from *The challenge of crime in a free society*. President's Commission on Law Enforcement and Administration of Justice, 1967. This revision, a result of the Symposium on the 30th Anniversary of the President's Commission, was prepared by the Bureau of Justice Statistics in 1997.

FIGURE 2.1   Flow Chart Demonstrating Procedural Paths through the Criminal Justice System.

within the juvenile justice system, a juvenile court typically hears and adjudicates the case. In some jurisdictions and for some accused crimes, a prosecutor may have the option to directly file a case involving a juvenile in adult court without having to persuade a juvenile court to waive juvenile jurisdiction.[4] Under such circumstances, the juvenile may be diverted from the normal procedure and receive adjudication and treatment as if the juvenile were an adult.

When facts indicate that a crime has been committed and an arrest has been made, the subject may still exit the system if the prosecutor subsequently declines to prosecute further or a judge determines that probable cause to hold the individual does not exist. In most jurisdictions, first-time offenders may be offered a diversion from the traditional prosecutorial system, and if the individual meets the requirements demanded by the diversion program, the person may be processed out of the system, typically without a criminal conviction. Where diversion is not an option or is not appropriate under the circumstances, the next major decision involves a consideration of whether the alleged offense is to be classified as a felony or as a misdemeanor.

As a general rule but not an exclusive rule in serious state prosecutions, a prosecutor empanels a grand jury to determine whether probable cause exists to believe that a particular person has committed a crime or crimes.[5] For example, an Ohio rule of criminal procedure provides that all felonies shall be prosecuted by an indictment unless the right to an indictment is waived.[6] If a grand jury returns an indictment, the accused defendant stands trial unless there is some other resolution of the criminal charge, such as a guilty plea, a guilty plea based on a plea bargain, or a dismissal. If a grand jury refuses to indict based on the facts presented to it, the accused exits the system at this point. Many states allow a prosecutor to initiate a serious criminal prosecution by the use of an information, which is a plain statement of facts accusing a particular person or persons of criminal activity, with enough additional facts to place the person on notice concerning the alleged crimes against which the accused individual must defend. Regardless of whether the case proceeds to trial based on an indictment or based on an information, the court procedures that follow do not differ.

Less serious charges involving infractions and misdemeanors may be brought on the basis of a complaint filed by police officers, by a complaint filed by a witnesses, or by the prosecutor after discussing the evidence and the situation with those individuals involved. A prosecutor may decline to prosecute a particular case for a variety of reasons; the evidence may be considered insufficient or the prosecutor's office may have a hierarchy of offenses that must be given resource priority.

Following the indictment or information, the defendant is subjected to judicial hearings, one of which may be called an arraignment. At this hearing, the charges are read to the defendant, and the court may ask for a plea to the charges. Where a grand jury has issued an indictment, a case is unlikely to be dismissed at the stage of the arraignment because a grand jury has previously determined the issue of probable cause to believe the defendant has committed a particular crime or crimes. For felony prosecutions, the issue of whether to grant bail and the conditions and amount is considered by the court at some point during the pretrial stage of a criminal prosecution, at either an arraignment, an initial appearance, or a subsequent time. If an accused offender does not have legal counsel, the hearing may be continued so that an attorney may be hired, or the judge may appoint an attorney at this hearing. In some jurisdictions, especially those that initiate serious criminal prosecutions by the use of an information, a preliminary hearing may follow the filing of an information with the court clerk, at which time the judge may require testimony that establishes probable cause to believe that the accused has done the crime or crimes, an attorney may be appointed, and bail concerns, among other issues, may be resolved.

Where the results of an arraignment or a preliminary hearing have not caused the defendant to be turned out of the criminal justice system, the accused defendant, through his or her attorney, may engage in some negotiation with the prosecutor with a view toward resolving the criminal case in a plea bargain. In most situations, both prosecution and defense must give away some of their respective strong points in order to get the opposition to agree to resolve the case. In the event that the plea negotiations do not conclude the criminal case, both prosecution and the defense must prepare for trial, at which time a guilty verdict or an acquittal is the most likely outcome.

A trial in a felony case triggers the right to a trial by jury, but in some cases a defendant takes the option of a trial by a judge rather than face a jury. Most misdemeanors generally do not carry the right to a trial by jury, but some of the more serious misdemeanors permit the defendant to demand a jury trial where the potential sentence is greater than six months.[7] According to the Supreme Court in *Lewis v. United States,* even a prosecution for multiple petty offenses does not carry the right to a trial by jury because the "Sixth Amendment reserves the jury trial right to defendants accused of serious crimes."[8] In *Blanton v. North Las Vegas,* the Court refused to interpret the Sixth Amendment as requiring a jury trial for a case where the maximum penalty was only a six-month incarceration.[9] Criminal sanctions following a verdict by a jury or a judge may range from probation to incarceration and may involve monetary fines that the defendant must pay.

Following a trial, every convicted defendant has the right to appeal and may take advantage of this right, especially where there are possibilities for a positive appellate outcome. Where a defendant wins an appeal, the higher court may order that the conviction be reversed and the defendant freed from custody, but the more likely outcome following the reversal of a conviction is to begin the criminal process virtually all over again. In cases where a defendant does not prevail during the appellate process but has been free on appellate bail, the defendant has to surrender and begin serving the sentence. In some cases where a sentencing judge has allowed probation following trial, the loss of an appeal generally has no effect on the defendant. In jurisdictions that permit parole, the possibility of parole after serving a significant part of the sentence may be available. Once the person has served all of the time, less the time that is reduced for good behavior, the defendant generally exits the criminal justice system.

Figure 2.1 graphically displays the different ways that criminal offenders are processed in, out, and through a state criminal justice system. A federal criminal case follows much the same process, except that Congress eliminated parole for federal offenses committed after November 1, 1987.[10]

2. ORGANIZATION OF COURTS, STATE AND FEDERAL: A DUAL SYSTEM

The court system in the United States is a dual system of state-based courts that have sovereign power[11] and authority and federal courts that derive their power from the federal Constitution. The power of the states to conduct criminal trials and apply punishments predates the existence of both the United States Constitution and the earlier Articles of Confederation. As Justice O'Connor, writing for the Court in *Heath v. Alabama,*[12] stated, "The States are no less sovereign with respect to each other than they are with respect to the Federal Government. Their powers to undertake criminal prosecutions derive from separate and independent sources of power and authority originally belonging to them before admission to the Union and preserved to them by the Tenth Amendment." Under our federal form of government, the states and the federal government have concurrent jurisdiction over many crimes. This means that criminal activity by one individual might violate both state and federal criminal law, and both jurisdictions could prosecute this individual for distinct federal and state crimes. For example, possession of various recreational pharmaceuticals offends both federal and state law, and an individual could be prosecuted first in a state court and later in a federal court. Armed bank robbery of a federally insured institution is an offense against the United States as well as an offense against the state in which the bank is located. For example, in an Illinois case, a defendant robbed a federally insured bank but was acquitted of federal bank robbery. The State of Illinois later successfully prosecuted the robber in a state court for state bank robbery.[13] State prosecution following an unsuccessful federal prosecution for the possession of recreational pharmaceuticals or for bank robbery would be appropriate and would not offend any federal constitutional provision.[14] In a slightly different context, criminal activity might transgress the laws of two separate states, each of which may choose to prosecute the individual for the violation of that state's law.[15]

Some criminal offenses are recognized only in a particular state and may not be considered offenses by the federal government or by other state governments. For example, speaking on a cellular telephone while driving an automobile has been prohibited by New York law, but this practice is perfectly legal under the laws of many other states and is not illegal under federal criminal law. In a different context, possession of medicinal marijuana has been approved under a state statutory scheme regulating medical marijuana in California, whereas the possession in California of the same medicinal marijuana has been prohibited by federal law.

Since the states and the federal government have dual sovereignty and concurrent jurisdiction with respect to many criminal acts, both may prosecute the same person when a criminal act violates both state and federal law. In addition, states may serially prosecute a defendant whose single act violates the law of two individual states.[16] This practice is simply the recognition of a federal system involving states that have individual sovereignty in all criminal prosecutions involving breaches of state law.

Although there may be overlapping jurisdiction shared between the states and the federal government with respect to criminal jurisdiction, the collective judicial system of the fifty states is much larger and adjudicates many times the number of cases than the judicial system of the United States. The vast majority of the criminal cases that are prosecuted are brought in state and local courts. It can be argued that the federal courts deal with many matters, both criminal and civil, that have national consequence, but state and local courts adjudicate matters of grave importance as well, whether the matters involve criminal activity, domestic relations, or business and commercial litigation. Figure 2.2, produced by the Federal Judicial Center, demonstrates the relative numbers of recent filings of state and federal courts and the relative numbers of federal court filings that involve criminal matters.[17]

State courts are generally organized on a three-tiered system, with the trial courts considered at the lowest level of the pyramid. Trial courts are known by a variety of official names, including superior courts, courts of common pleas, supreme courts, and juvenile courts. Some of the trial courts are considered courts of general jurisdiction and may try both felonies and misdemeanors; other courts, such as municipal courts or city courts, are permitted to try only misdemeanors. In the latter case, the court is said to have a limited jurisdiction, even though felony arrestees may be arraigned or face an initial court appearance in a municipal or county court. State courts of limited jurisdiction include small claims courts, juvenile courts, and domestic relations courts. These limited jurisdiction courts generally involve civil

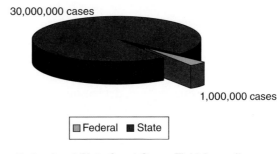

30,000,000 cases

1,000,000 cases

■ Federal ■ State

Federal and State Court Cases Field Annually

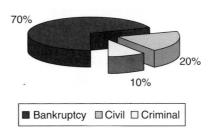

70%

20%

10%

■ Bankruptcy ▨ Civil □ Criminal

Federal Court Cases Field Annually

- Number of federal judgeships authorized: **over 1,700**
- Number of state court judgeships authorized: **almost 30,000**

FIGURE 2.2 Comparison of Federal and State Case Loads per Year.

cases, but some limited jurisdiction courts may involve criminal cases, such as a drug court. With respect to the state trial court system, these courts collectively have a broad and expansive jurisdiction that involves every type of case, from criminal, domestic relations, and tort cases to issues of state law and the state constitution. At the trial court level, witnesses introduce physical evidence, oral testimony is taken, and juries decide the results. The trial courts employ an adversarial system in which prosecution and defense emphasize the most important points of their respective positions while attempting to illuminate the flaws in the opposing side's evidence. In criminal cases, defendants are generally present in court and are represented by legal counsel, while the government is represented by a prosecutor. In the state court system, every criminal defendant is allowed to appeal to the next stage or level of the system, a court of appeal. In some jurisdictions, the court of appeal is known simply as the court of appeal or court of appeals, but the terminology may vary with the particular state. By whatever name the court of appeal may be known, it reviews the lower trial court result and decisions made by the trial judge and considers whether errors of law were made that had the effect of changing the outcome of the case. No witnesses appear at the court of appeal stage of the criminal justice process, but the defense and prosecuting attorneys representing each side prepare written briefs explaining their view of the case and either present the briefs to the court of appeals without oral argument or may request to be granted an opportunity to personally argue the merits of the case in front of the judges. The top-level court in each state court system is a state supreme court, but the official court title may be different. The function of the top-level state court with respect to criminal justice is to review the decisions of appellate courts to determine if they made the correct decision in reviewing the trial court process. The supreme court in each state has the last word in interpreting and determining the meaning of that state's law and constitution. Although not part of the state court system, criminal defendants who allege that the state judicial system violated the defendant's rights by violating federal law, the federal Constitution, or a federal treaty may be able to get the Supreme Court of the United States to hear an appeal from the top state court. When four justices of the Supreme Court of the United States vote to hear a case, a writ of certiorari is issued and the whole Court considers the defendant's allegations.

The federal courts in the United States are organized in a manner that virtually mirrors the state practice of three tiers of courts: trial courts, courts of appeal, and a supreme court. Although there are a variety of federal trial courts,[18] for criminal purposes, the typical defendant faces trial in one of the ninety-four United States district courts presided over by a federal judge. For every part of the United States, a federal district court has jurisdiction to hear legal cases involving federal law, federal treaties, or the federal Constitution. Included within this jurisdiction is the power to hear cases involving crimes against the United States. Federal district courts follow a method of operation similar to state trial courts, with prosecutors and defense attorneys appearing in court, along with a jury presided over by a judge. The prosecutors, called United States attorneys or assistant United States attorneys, present the government's case through the use of witnesses, evidence, and other exhibits. Defense attorneys are tasked with challenging the prosecution's case by calling into question the credibility of witnesses and by introducing evidence to counter matters brought to court by the prosecutor. Where a jury has been empaneled, its task is to evaluate and determine the facts and apply them to the law as explained by the federal judge. Following every criminal conviction in a federal court, the defendant has the right as a matter of law to appeal to the first level of federal appellate court, the court of appeal.

Federal appeals courts are arranged into twelve circuits that cover the entire territory of the United States.[19] Figure 2.3 below represents the geographical jurisdiction of federal courts of appeal.

For example, the Court of Appeal for the Sixth Circuit considers appeals from federal district courts from Michigan, Ohio, Kentucky, and Tennessee. Similar geographic considerations cover the remaining eleven circuits, and any person convicted of a federal offense in a particular state may appeal to the appropriate court of appeal following a conviction. Federal circuit courts of appeal do not take new evidence, as a general rule, when they consider criminal appeals. These courts review the trial rulings made by the federal district judge concerning the admission and exclusion of evidence, questions involving the application of federal law, and the overall fairness of the trial. In the courts of appeal, appellate judges generally sit in banks of three to decide criminal and other cases. When the court is faced with an issue of great importance, usually of national concern, a court of appeal may involve all the judges of the court sitting en banc to hear the appeal. When the judges sit en banc, it means that all the judges from that particular circuit sit together to hear the case. Once a case has been decided by a court of appeal, a defendant does not have a direct right to have the Supreme Court of the United States hear the case.

For a federal defendant to have the Supreme Court of the United States consider his or her case, the defendant must request that the Supreme Court granted a writ of certiorari, which means that at least four justices have voted to hear the defendant's case. The court may agree to hear a defendant's case that involves an issue of great national concern and importance, where different federal circuit courts of appeal have decided an issue differently, or where the court may wish to reconsider an old principle or a decision in light of changed circumstances. In the event that the Supreme Court decides to hear a case, the parties write and present their respective positions in a written form known as a brief. The Court considers the briefs, entertains oral

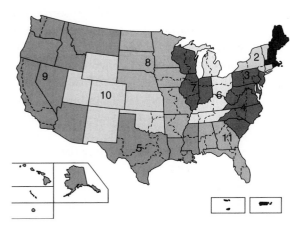

FIGURE 2.3 Geographic Jurisdiction of Federal Circuit Courts of Appeal.

arguments at the Supreme Court building, and eventually renders a written decision and opinion. There is no appeal to any higher court on any issue within its jurisdiction. There is the possibility of requesting the Court to reconsider its decision, but success with this approach is an extreme rarity.

For both the state and federal judicial systems, the three-tiered approach appears to work rather well. In both systems, the trial courts render an initial verdict that normally withstands an appeal by a defendant. Where significant errors have occurred at the trial court level, every defendant, whether state or federal, has an opportunity to have the alleged error considered by a court that has little or no connection to the original court. For extraordinary cases, the supreme court of a particular state may be willing to consider especially meritorious cases, but where a state supreme court fails to properly interpret the applicable federal constitutional provision, federal law, or federal treaty, an application to the Supreme Court of the United States is the only avenue remaining for redress of grievances.

3. PRETRIAL CRIMINAL PROCEDURE: THE INITIAL STEPS TOWARD PROSECUTION

When an investigation conducted by a police department or other law enforcement agency has gathered sufficient evidence that a criminal prosecution is either possible or likely, the focus shifts, to a degree, from the police department to the prosecutor's office. Typically, members of the prosecutor's office review the evidence presented by law enforcement officials with a view to determining whether a prosecutable case exists. Where a police investigation demonstrates that proof beyond a reasonable doubt may be possible, the prosecution needs to determine whether it is the type of case that should be pursued. Due consideration must be given to the priorities of the prosecutor's office, and the individual prosecutor must take into account the government's finite resources to determine whether the case should be brought forward to court and vigorously pursued.

While it is a given that police agencies desire the prosecution of cases they have presented to the prosecutor's office, it is possible, if not probable, that the agendas of these two law enforcement functionaries may diverge in approach and priority. Virtually every case possesses some drawback or problem that when presented in a courtroom may result in an acquittal or some other disposition. Where a case has strengths, coupled with significant weaknesses, the prosecutor may consider plea negotiations, leading to a guilty plea to a lesser included offense or, in some cases, a diversion to an alternate type of resolution.

Cases presented to the prosecutor's office may contain a variety of challenges, issues, and pretrial and trial problems that need to be resolved prior to making a decision to pursue a particular case. If a case presents Fourth Amendment search and seizure issues, the prosecutor's office must carefully analyze the legal position and the probable chances of prevailing in a defendant's pretrial motion to suppress.[20] For some cases, the outcome of a motion to suppress may drive the decision to continue the prosecution or instead drop the case. Where no search and seizure issues appear, there may still be *Miranda*[21] or Fifth Amendment confession[22] issues to be resolved prior to trial, or at least the prosecution must evaluate the probabilities of prevailing when the issues are litigated in pretrial motions to suppress. If the police allegedly have used a lineup defectively[23] or have resorted to alternative identification processes that have created legal problems,[24] definitive prosecutorial decisions may well have to await resolution of the identification issues in a case where the prosecution has been initiated. Some defendants may be in a position to raise strong arguments concerning a Sixth Amendment or statutory right to a speedy trial.[25] Constitutional Sixth Amendment speedy trial allegations must be taken seriously because the remedy is a dismissal of the case with the inability to bring it at a later time, no matter how much additional investigation may be conducted. In a small number of cases, a defendant may raise the issue of prior jeopardy, a constitutional challenge that should be resolved before trial. Collateral double jeopardy issues may exist in complicated cases[26] or where a retrial is contemplated after a reversal of the conviction upon appeal. Concerns about whether a witness or a defendant may possess some level of immunity from prosecution must be evaluated prior to coming to a conclusion regarding prosecution. Where a case cries out for prosecution but contains significant evidentiary challenges, the prosecutor's office may return to the police agency and request an additional investigatory effort. There may be questions of the defendant's competency at the time of the act and/or at the projected time of the trial. In such a case, the decision to move forward with prosecution may await a report based on a psychiatric examination. In evaluating a case, prosecution witnesses play a crucial role, which the government must consider. Because witnesses possess varying degrees of believability, credibility factors must be addressed as part of deciding whether to bring the case to trial.

4. INITIATING A CRIMINAL CASE: COMPLAINT AND SUMMONS

Accused individuals enter the criminal justice system from a variety of avenues. Many people are booked into a jail based on a police officer's determination that probable cause to arrest existed at the time the individual was taken into custody. Probable cause has been determined to exist if, at the time the arrest was made, "the facts and circumstances within their [police officers'] knowledge and of which they had reasonably trustworthy information were sufficient to warrant a prudent man in believing" a crime had been committed.[27] Other individuals enter police detention by virtue of an arrest warrant that was issued by a judicial official and executed by police. A few of the individuals in this second category enter custody by virtue of a grand jury determination that probable cause existed to believe a crime has been committed. If custody exists because of a grand jury indictment or by the issuance of an arrest warrant by a judge or magistrate, probable cause has been appropriately determined.

In misdemeanor cases, the initial information may come to the attention of law enforcement agents when a complaining witness offers evidence that starts with a formal complaint stating the operative facts of the alleged offense to which the complaining witness swears contains the truth. A witness or wronged party may file a formal complaint (Figure 2.4) that may constitute the first step in a criminal prosecution.[28]

Where sufficient evidence has been given by the witness, probable cause to arrest or to summons may exist that would cause a judicial official to act. Although this process varies widely from jurisdiction to jurisdiction, the initiation of a complaint for minor offenses often starts the criminal justice process. Alternatively, the sworn

STATE OF NEW MEXICO

COUNTY OF _____

[CITY OF _____]

IN THE _____ COURT

No. _____

Date filed: _____

STATE OF NEW MEXICO

CITY OF _____]

v.

_____, Defendant

CRIMINAL COMPLAINT

CRIME: _____ *(common name of offense or offenses)*

     The undersigned, under penalty of perjury, complains and says that on or about the _____ day of

_____, _____, in the City of _____, State of New Mexico, the above-

named defendant did: _____ *(here state the essential facts)*

contrary to Section[s] _____ *(set forth applicable section number of municipal code or*

municipal ordinance and date of adoption).

I SWEAR OR AFFIRM UNDER PENALTY OF PERJURY THAT THE FACTS SET FORTH

ABOVE ARE TRUE TO THE BEST OF MY INFORMATION AND BELIEF. I UNDERSTAND

THAT IT IS A CRIMINAL OFFENSE SUBJECT TO THE PENALTY OF IMPRISONMENT TO

MAKE A FALSE STATEMENT IN A CRIMINAL COMPLAINT.

_____

Complainant

_____

Title *(if any)*

Approved:

_____

_____

Title

FIGURE 2.4 Sample of Typical Criminal Complaint Used in State Courts.

complaint may cause law enforcement officials to conduct additional investigation that results in more serious charges or evidence that supports the initial complaint. In this situation, the police may procure an arrest warrant from a judge of the proper jurisdiction. Figure 2.5 is an example of an arrest warrant used in New Mexico.[29]

The information from the sworn complaint, as well as the results of any additional investigation, presented to a judicial official may cause that official to issue a warrant for an arrest or have a summons sent to the alleged wrongdoer. A warrant is not necessary for a lawful arrest, and in some cases, following a complaint and the development of additional information, police officers may choose to make an arrest and turn the evidence over to the prosecutor's office for a decision concerning whether to proceed further. Depending on whether the prosecutor decides to pursue the case as a misdemeanor or as a felony, the case may be heard in a municipal court, or the prosecutor may take the evidence to a grand jury for a possible criminal indictment or, if state practice permits, file an information against the suspect.

5. THE CHARGING INSTRUMENTS: INDICTMENT AND INFORMATION

Unless a defendant waives the Fifth Amendment right to a grand jury indictment, in a federal prosecution the prosecutor must initiate a serious criminal case through a grand jury indictment. Federal grand juries must have between sixteen and twenty-three grand jurors, with a foreperson appointed by the court overseeing the grand jury. At least twelve grand jurors must vote to indict, or no indictment can be issued.[30] A federal prosecutor presents witnesses in front of the grand jury and asks questions of the witnesses. Grand jurors may ask questions of each witness. The rules of evidence do not apply at grand jury proceedings, and grand jurors may consider illegally seized evidence. No defense attorney can be present, even if the potential defendant has been called as a grand jury witness. All federal offenses, other than federal criminal contempt, require a prosecutor to procure an indictment if the offense charged is punishable either by death or by imprisonment for longer than a year. The target of a federal prosecution who has not been indicted may choose to waive the requirement of an indictment in open court after having been informed of the nature of the charges that the government intends to bring.[31] A federal grand jury indictment or an information must be a plain and tightly written statement of the operative facts that the government thinks constitute the crime and must be signed by a prosecutor in the United States attorney's office. It may allege how the defendant committed the particular crime, but if that information is not known, it is not essential to the indictment or information, and it may be omitted. The official United States code that references the crime the defendant is believed to have violated must be included within the indictment. The defendant's name need not be mentioned if it is unknown; a provision within the federal rules allows a defendant to be identified by a unique DNA profile,[32] even though other identifiers are unknown at the time of indictment.

However, the Fifth Amendment requirement of a grand jury indictment does not apply to the individual states of the United States; states are free to use their version of a grand jury system or to initiate criminal prosecutions with an information. In *Hurtado v. California*[33] in 1884, the Supreme Court determined that the federal Fifth Amendment right to a grand jury indictment did not apply through the Due Process

9-210

[For use with Magistrate Court Rule 6-206
Metropolitan Court Rule 7-206, and
Municipal Court Rule 8-806]

STATE OF NEW MEXICO
[COUNTY OF_____]
[CITY OF_____]
_____ COURT   No. _____

[COUNTY OF_____]
[CITY OF_____]

v.

_____, Defendant

WARRANT FOR ARREST

THE [STATE OF NEW MEXICO] [CITY OF _____]
TO ANY OFFICER AUTHORIZED TO EXECUTE THIS WARRANT[1]:

    BASED ON A FINDING OF PROBABLE CAUSE, YOU ARE COMMANDED to arrest the above-named defendant and bring the defendant without unnecessary delay before this court[2]: to answer the charge of *(here state common name and description of offense charged)*: _____

contrary to Section(s) _____ (NMSA 1978) (OF THE MUNICIPAL ORDINANCE OF THIS MUNICIPALITY)

THIS WARRANT MAY BE EXECUTED:
    [ ]   in any jurisdiction;
    [ ]   anywhere in this state;
    [ ]   anywhere in this county;
    [ ]   anywhere in this city.

    The person obtaining this warrant shall cause it to be entered into a law enforcement information system[3]:

    [ ]   maintained by the state police.

    [ ]   _____ *(identify other law enforcement information system).*

Date: _____

_____
Judge

FIGURE 2.5   Example of a Typical Arrest Warrant.

Clause of the Fourteenth Amendment so as to require a state to use a grand jury to initiate a serious criminal case. The procedure followed in *Hurtado* substantially remains unchanged, and California prosecutors retain the option of proceeding against defendants suspected of committing serious offenses through the use of an information or by using a grand jury. In contrast, Ohio has chosen to require a grand jury for the initiation of serious criminal cases[34] and has a rule of criminal procedure that requires a grand jury indictment where the penalty may be death or life in prison.[35] When the prosecutor files an information against a state defendant, it is generally a recitation in plain English, accusing a particular person of committing a particular crime or crimes. It includes the dates, times, and operative facts about the alleged crime in order to give a defendant fair notice against which accusations he or she must defend. In the case of all lesser Ohio felonies, a prosecutor must use a grand jury indictment except where a defendant decides to waive the right to a grand jury indictment in writing and in an open court setting.[36] States generally follow the California model or the Ohio model for the initiation of a serious felony prosecution. Figure 2.6 shows a sample information form.[37]

9-203
STATE OF NEW MEXICO
COUNTY OF_____
_____ COURT   No. _____

STATE OF NEW MEXICO

v.

_____, Defendant

                                        Crime:_____
                                            (common name of offense)

CRIMINAL INFORMATION

The district attorney of _____ County, State of New Mexico, states that on or about the _____ day of _____, _____, in said County and State, the above-named defendant did: *(here state the essential facts)*
_____
_____
_____
contrary to Section[s] _____ NMSA 1978.

The names of the witnesses upon whose testimony this information is based are as follows:
_____
_____
_____.

_____
District Attorney

FIGURE 2.6 Example of an Information Used to Initiate a Criminal Case.

CASE 2.1

Leading Case Brief: The Federal Right to a Grand Jury Indictment Does Not Apply to State Practice

Hurtado v. California
Supreme Court of the United States
110 U.S. 516 (1884)

Case Facts:

In 1882, the California penal code provided that when evidence disclosed that an offense had been committed and that when probable cause existed to believe that a particular person had committed the offense, the district attorney was required to file an information charging that person with that crime. Since evidence indicated that a Hurtado had committed a capital homicide, a state prosecutor filed an information against defendant Hurtado, charging him with the murder of José Stuardo. At the trial, a jury found Hurtado guilty of capital murder, and the trial court sentenced the defendant to death.

Hurtado, through counsel, argued that the verdict and penalty were void because he had a federal constitutional right to be indicted by a grand jury rather than tried pursuant to an information in that the Fourteenth Amendment guaranteed due process of law in state cases. According to Hurtado, due process of law included the right to a grand jury indictment in his case because the Fifth Amendment right to a grand jury indictment applied to serious state criminal cases. This legal position was universally rejected from the trial court to the Supreme Court of California. The Supreme Court of the United States granted certiorari to consider Hurtado's argument that the right to a grand jury indictment was a requirement of due process under the Fourteenth Amendment.

Legal Issue:

Under the Due Process Clause of the Fourteenth Amendment, is the right to a grand jury indictment an essential element of a fair system of justice and a fair trial, so that an indictment is the only way to properly charge a capital felony in a state case?

The Court's Ruling:

A grand jury in a state case is not required by due process. The common law draws its inspiration from many sources, and there are many ways of giving fundamental fairness to a criminal accused that may not necessarily include every procedure previously offered. Were it otherwise, law would be locked in the past with no chance to adapt and adjust to new conditions while still granting fairness to defendants.

Essence of the Court's Rationale:

* * *

[I]t is maintained on behalf of the plaintiff in error [defendant Hurtado] that the phrase "due process of law" is equivalent to "law of the land" as found in the twenty-ninth chapter of Magna Charta; that by immemorial usage it has acquired a fixed, definite, and technical meaning; that it refers to and includes, not only the general principles of public liberty and private right, which lie at the foundation of all free government, but the very institutions which, venerable by time and custom, have been tried by experience and found fit and necessary for the preservation of those principles, and which, having been the birthright and inheritance of every English subject, crossed the Atlantic with the colonists and were transplanted and established in the fundamental laws of the state; that, having been originally introduced into the Constitution of the United States as a limitation upon the powers of the government, brought into being by that instrument, it has now been added as an additional security to the individual against oppression by the states themselves; that one of these institutions is that of the grand jury, an indictment or presentment by which against the accused in cases of alleged felonies is an essential part of due process of law, in order that he may not be harassed and destroyed by prosecutions founded only upon private malice or popular fury.

* * *

The Constitution of the United States was ordained, it is true, by descendants of Englishmen, who inherited the traditions of English law and history. . . . There is nothing in Magna Charta, rightly construed as a broad charter of public right and law, which ought to exclude the best ideas of all systems and of every age, and as it was the characteristic principle of the common law to draw its inspiration from every fountain of justice, we are not to assume that the sources of its supply have been exhausted. On the contrary, we should expect that the new and various experiences of our own situation and system will mould and shape it into new and not less useful forms.

* * *

In this country written constitutions were deemed essential to protect the rights and liberties of the people against the encroachments of power delegated to their governments, and the provisions of Magna Charta were incorporated into bills of rights. There were limitations upon all the powers of government, legislative as well as executive and judicial.

It necessarily happened, therefore, that as these broad and general maxims of liberty and justice held in our system a different place and performed a different function from their position and office in English constitutional history and law, they would receive and justify a corresponding and more comprehensive interpretation. Applied in England only as guards against executive usurpation and tyranny, here they have become bulwarks also against arbitrary legislation: but in that application, as it would be incongruous to measure and restrict them by the ancient customary English law, they must be held to guarantee, not particular forms of procedure, but the very substance of individual rights to life, liberty, and property.

* * *

We are to construe this phrase [due process of law] in the Fourteenth Amendment by the *usus loquendi* of the Constitution itself. The same words are contained in the Fifth Amendment. That article makes specific and express provision for perpetuating the institution of the grand jury, so far as relates to prosecutions for the more aggravated crimes under the laws of the United States. It declares that

No person shall be held to answer for capital or otherwise infamous crime, unless on a presentment or indictment of a grand jury, except in cases arising in the land or naval forces or in the militia when in actual service in time of war or public danger; nor shall any person be subject for the same offense to be twice put in jeopardy of life or limb nor shall he be compelled in any criminal cases to be a witness against himself.

It then immediately adds: "nor be deprived of life, liberty, or property without due process of law." According to a recognized canon of interpretation, especially applicable to formal and solemn instruments of constitutional law, we are forbidden to assume, without clear reason to the contrary, that any part of this most important amendment is superfluous. The natural and obvious inference is that, in the sense of the Constitution, "due process of law" was not meant or intended to include, *ex vi termini,* the institution and procedure of a grand jury in any case. The conclusion is equally irresistible, that when the same phrase was employed in the Fourteenth Amendment to restrain the action of the States, it was used in the same sense and with no greater extent; and that, if in the adoption of that amendment it had been part of its purpose to perpetuate the institution of the grand jury in all the States, it would have embodied, as did the Fifth Amendment, express declarations to that effect. Due process of law in the latter refers to that law of the land which derives its authority from the legislative power conferred upon Congress by the Constitution of the United States, exercised within the limits therein prescribed, and interpreted according to the principles of the common law. In the Fourteenth Amendment, by parity of reason, it refers to the law of the land in each state which derives its authority from the inherent and reserved powers of the state, exerted within the limits of those fundamental principles of liberty and justice which lie at the base of all our civil and political institutions, and the greatest security for which resides in the right of the people to make their own laws, and alter them at their pleasure.

The Fourteenth Amendment [as was said by Mr. Justice Bradley in *Missouri v. Lewis,* 101 U.S. 22–31] does not profess to secure to all persons in the United States the benefit of the same laws and the

(continued)

same remedies. Great diversities in these respects may exist in two states separated only by an imaginary line. On one side of this line there may be a right of trial by jury, and on the other side no such right. Each state prescribes its own modes of judicial proceeding.

* * *

Tried by these principles, we are unable to say that the substitution for a presentment or indictment by a grand jury of the proceeding by information after examination and commitment by a magistrate, certifying to the probable guilt of the defendant with the right on his part to the aid of counsel and to the cross examination of the witnesses produced for the prosecution, is not due process of law.

Case Importance:

Due process does not necessarily mean that the exact criminal processes and procedures must be identical in state and federal criminal systems of justice. Fundamental fairness can be granted in many different ways so there need not be a constitutionally required grand jury procedure in state cases.

Where a prosecutor convenes a grand jury, the practice is fairly similar, regardless of the jurisdiction. A grand jury is composed of citizens who hear evidence against an accused and come to a determination of whether probable cause exists to believe that a person has committed a crime or crimes. The grand jury meets in secret with no one present who is not necessary to the proceeding, and it deliberates with no other persons present except the grand jurors. The grand jury members may ask questions of the witnesses who appear individually before the body, and grand juries have the power to subpoena papers and documents from virtually any person, company, or legal entity. Since the power to subpoena materials is not restricted by the Fourth Amendment and its concepts of probable cause, a grand jury investigation can be rather wide-ranging. Even in investigations involving celebrated public officials or public controversies that a grand jury might be considering, because of grand jury secrecy, no one outside the grand jury knows the subject and extent of witness testimony. The testimony of any witness who publicly speaks about what he or she offered the grand jury cannot be verified, so the true facts rendered to a grand jury remain uncertain to outsiders. It is not uncommon for a grand jury witness to offer one story to the grand jury while under oath and a completely different story for public consumption.

The grand jury operates virtually independently from outside influences, save for the direction that a prosecutor might choose to give. One court noted that the independence of a grand jury and the fact that it meets in secrecy allow the grand jury to operate as

> the primary security to the innocent against "hasty, malicious and oppressive persecution; it serves the invaluable function in our society of standing between the accuser and the accused, whether the latter be an individual, minority group, or other, to determine whether a charge is founded upon reason or was dictated by an intimidating power or by malice and personal ill will."[38]

Grand jury secrecy also permits deliberation without intimidation from outside sources. Secrecy tends to prevent individuals who are targets of the grand jury but who are never indicted from experiencing reduction in social status or from being socially ostracized or shunned. As is frequently the case, the target of the grand jury's investigation may be unaware that the grand jury is considering an indictment, and the public and the press often have no idea what a grand jury is considering. In addition, grand jury secrecy has the effect of keeping witnesses from being intimidated by outside sources and allows a witness to testify fully and honestly without fear of harm from other individuals who may be targets of the grand jury. If a target is unaware that a grand jury might render an indictment, the possibility of an indicted target fleeing the jurisdiction is greatly reduced.

A sample form of an indictment in use in New Mexico has been reproduced in Figure 2.7.[39]

9-204

STATE OF NEW MEXICO
COUNTY OF _____
IN THE DISTRICT COURT

STATE OF NEW MEXICO

v.   No. _____
                                             Crime: _____
_____, Defendant   *(common name of offense)*

GRAND JURY INDICTMENT

THE GRAND JURY CHARGES:

On or about the _____ day of _____, _____, in _____ County, State of New Mexico, the above-named defendant did: *(here state the essential facts)*

_____
_____
_____.
_____
contrary to Section[s] _____ NMSA 1978.

The names of the witnesses upon whose testimony this indictment is based are as follows:

_____
_____
_____
_____

I hereby certify that the foregoing indictment is a _____ Bill.

                              _____
                              Foreperson

                              Dated:_____

APPROVED:_____
District Attorney

FIGURE 2.7 Example of a Grand Jury Indictment Form.

6. PRETRIAL HEARINGS: PROBABLE CAUSE, ARRAIGNMENT, AND PRELIMINARY HEARING

A person who has been arrested pursuant to a warrant issued by a neutral and detached judicial official does not have a right to have a judge reconsider whether to hold or release him or her. Similarly, an arrest following a grand jury indictment, at which time the grand jury determined probable cause, does not require a judicial official to immediately review the issue of probable cause. However, where a person has been taken into custody based on a complaint, on a police officer's observation, or on a multifaceted law enforcement investigation, the person has the right to have the issue of probable cause determined by a neutral and detached judicial official within a reasonable time, generally considered to be forty-eight hours.[40]

For purposes of an arraignment in a federal district court, the proceeding must be conducted publicly in open court, and the defendant must be presented with a copy of either the indictment or an information, if the defendant has consented to having the government start the case with an information. The information or indictment is read to the defendant, and the defendant is asked to enter a plea.[41] Assuming that the defendant is represented by legal counsel, the defendant may choose to plead not guilty, guilty, or nolo contendere (no contest) or may conditionally plead guilty while reserving an issue for appeal, where the defendant has been unsuccessful at suppression prior to trial. If a defendant chooses to remain mute, the court enters a plea of not guilty.[42] State arraignments are generally conducted in a similar manner. Under the Ohio procedure, the arraignment is conducted in open court. The information or indictment is read to the defendant, at who is then asked to plead. If the defendant is not represented by counsel, the court permits the defendant to hire counsel or to have counsel appointed if the defendant is indigent. In that event, the court grants continuance until representation has been secured. Under the Ohio rule and representative of general court procedure, the court informs the defendant of that the right to bail if the offense is bailable. The defendant may choose to make a statement at any time during the proceedings, but incriminating statements may be used against him or her at a later time.[43]

However, if the hearing involves a determination of issues beyond simply probable cause, it may be called a preliminary hearing in many jurisdictions. In California, preliminary hearings are for felony cases only, and the court must determine whether a crime has been committed and decide whether probable cause exists to believe that the defendant committed the crime. Since local practice varies so widely, a preliminary hearing not only may determine probable cause but also may deal with and dispose of a larger number of issues. The defendant is informed of the nature of the charges, if that has not previously occurred. If legal counsel has not been appointed previously, the judge appoints counsel for the detainee prior to proceeding. The prosecution may be required to put on a prima facie case by calling witnesses who can be cross-examined by the defendant. A failure to present a prima facie case usually results in a dismissal of the prosecution's case. At some preliminary hearings, the issue of bail may be considered, and the defendant may be required to enter a plea and to offer notice of the intent to use some affirmative defenses. Testimony given at a preliminary hearing is "frozen," or perpetuated, so that both the defense and the prosecution are aware of some of the testimony that will be given at trial. If a preliminary hearing follows a grand jury indictment, the issue of probable cause does not arise because it has been previously determined by the grand jury. According to *Coleman v. Alabama,* 399 U.S. 1 (1970), the preliminary hearing is a critical stage of the criminal justice process that requires the defendant to be represented by counsel because the presence of counsel

> is essential to protect the indigent accused against an erroneous or improper prosecution. First, the lawyer's skilled examination and cross-examination of witnesses may expose fatal weaknesses in the State's case that may lead the magistrate to refuse to bind the accused over. Second, in any event, the skilled interrogation of witnesses by an experienced lawyer can fashion a vital impeachment tool for use in cross-examination of the State's witnesses at the trial, or preserve testimony favorable to the accused of a witness who does not appear at the trial. Third, trained counsel can more effectively discover the case the State has against his client and make possible the preparation of a proper defense to meet that case at the trial. Fourth, counsel can also be influential at the preliminary hearing in making effective arguments for the accused on such matters as the necessity for an early psychiatric examination or bail.[44]

7. PRETRIAL MOTION HEARINGS: MANDATORY AND DISCRETIONARY PRETRIAL MOTIONS

Although efforts directed toward the defense of a client begin the moment the attorney is appointed by the court or is hired by the defendant, significant defense strategy begins to emerge after the preliminary hearing. The evidence presented by the prosecutor during a preliminary hearing also gives the defense attorney considerable insight into the theory that the prosecution is likely to pursue at trial. Upon request, the defense counsel must be allowed to see a considerable amount of the evidence the prosecution possesses, but the defense does not have a similar duty to disclose defense evidence and strategy, on account of the Fifth Amendment privilege against self-incrimination. In *Brady v. Maryland,* 373 U.S. 83 (1963), the Supreme Court held that "the suppression by the prosecution of evidence favorable to an accused upon request violates due process where the evidence is material either to guilt or to punishment, irrespective of the good faith or bad faith of the prosecution."[45]

Some constitutional issues must be raised prior to trial, or they are deemed to have been waived or will be difficult to raise at a later date. For example, the Fifth Amendment protection against double jeopardy, the right not to be tried twice for the same crime, generally must be raised at the pretrial stage of a criminal prosecution.[46] Since the protection is designed to prevent an improper second trial over the same crime, if it were raised after a second trial, it will have not prevented a second trial. The Sixth Amendment right to a speedy trial generally falls into the category of a mandatory pretrial motion because one of the factors used to determine whether the right has been violated involves prejudice to the defendant's case.[47] A defendant who does not claim lack of a sufficiently speedy trial creates the assumption of no complaint about the delay and implies that the delay has not harmed or otherwise prejudiced the defendant's case on the merits.

Many courts recognize that some motions must be made prior to trial because of their nature, a court rule, or a rule of criminal procedure. Failure to make a mandatory pretrial motion may result in a court's refusal to consider the motion at a later time. Generally, an allegation of some defect in the charging instrument, whether it is an indictment, an information, or a citation, constitutes a mandatory pretrial motion that in most cases will be waived if not asserted. A motion that a court lacks jurisdiction or that the charging instrument is defective in that it fails to state an offense may be considered even after the pretrial period in many jurisdictions. Motions to suppress evidence, whether based on an illegal search and seizure, an illegal confession, or other legal ground, must be made prior to trial unless some good cause is shown for the failure to raise the issue during the pretrial stage of the prosecution. Where two or more defendants are being tried together and one of the defendants wants a separate trial, a motion to sever the defendants' single trial into separate trials obviously must be offered before a joint trial starts. If a defendant has been charged with multiple offenses that the defendant believes could most justly be tried separately, a motion to sever offenses must be made prior to the initiation of the trial that charges both offenses.[48] A motion to require the prosecution to disclose any known statements made by the defendant that are within the prosecution's possession or control must be made prior to trial.[49] For a defendant's attorney to inspect and copy documents and other evidence that the prosecutor expects to use at trial, a motion to this effect must be made prior to trial.[50] A defendant's motion for a change of venue (location of the trial) obviously must be made before the trial, or it generally will be deemed to have been waived.

Discretionary pretrial motions include "any defense, objection, or request that the court can determine without a trial of the general issue."[51] A motion for a continuance may be brought during the pretrial stage or at any moment of the trial that the attorney believes that the interests of justice might demand a continuance. A defendant may wish to raise the issue of bail prior to trial, but could, where circumstances permit, make a motion for bail or ask for a reduction of bail during the trial. In a similar fashion, a prosecutor could make a motion to deny bail prior to trial, to revoke bail during trial because of changed circumstances, or to raise the bail amount during the trial based on newly discovered facts.

8. PLEA NEGOTIATIONS

A large majority of criminal cases are resolved through accommodations made by the defendant and the prosecuting attorney. The concept that a prosecutor and defense counsel would both take a close look at a pending criminal case and come to some agreement concerning its disposition without trial received judicial approval by the Supreme Court in 1971.[52] In *Santobello v. New York,* the Court approved the use of plea bargaining that resulted in pleas in criminal cases when it noted

> Disposition of charges after plea discussions is not only an essential part of the process but a highly desirable part for many reasons. It leads to prompt and largely final disposition of most criminal cases; it avoids much of the corrosive impact of enforced idleness during pretrial confinement for those who are denied release

pending trial; it protects the public from those accused persons who are prone to continue criminal conduct even while on pretrial release; and, by shortening the time between charge and disposition, it enhances whatever may be the rehabilitative prospects of the guilty when they are ultimately imprisoned.[53]

Resolution of a case may be possible when both sides in a criminal prosecution agree that there are no outstanding issues between them or that one or both are willing to compromise some issues to reach an agreement with respect to a conviction, a conviction on a lesser included offense, and/or in some cases, an agreement concerning the sentence or at least an agreement concerning the prosecutor's recommendation of a sentence. If a defendant is willing to plead guilty to a particular charge or charges, the defendant will most likely avoid the most serious of all possible charges that could have been levied, and the prosecutor gains a certain conviction. From the prosecutor's perspective, every criminal prosecution presents some challenges, and a guilty verdict from a jury or a judge is not an assured outcome for every case.

In federal prosecutions, by following the federal rules of criminal procedure[54] a defendant may plead guilty or may enter a conditional plea of guilty, by which the defendant reserves a particular right to appeal a legal issue. In the event that a defendant and a prosecutor have reached a plea agreement, the federal judge must address the defendant personally, and in open court, in an effort to assure that the defendant understands the consequences of a guilty plea. The judge must say that the defendant has the right to plead not guilty, if he or she chooses to do so, and that if the defendant pleads not guilty, the right to a jury trial is available, along with the right to counsel. The judge must indicate that a defendant who chooses to go to trial has the right to confront and cross-examine witnesses and the right, under the Fifth Amendment, not to testify. Among other matters that the judge must ensure the defendant understands is the maximum penalty that the specific charges involved might allow the judge to impose. The defendant must be made to understand how the plea agreement operates, especially if it extinguishes the right to appeal or to file a writ of habeas corpus at some future time. If the judge is satisfied that the plea has been voluntarily and freely given and that the plea agreement has been not based on threats or promises other than what has been incorporated in a written plea agreement, the judge may accept a plea bargain. Finally, the judge must determine that a factual basis for the plea exists.

A plea agreement operates like a contract. Once the defendant has agreed to the plea arrangement and pled guilty, the defendant has the right to presume that the prosecution will honor its portion of the contract. If the judge has not yet accepted the plea, it remains executory, meaning that it has yet to be put into place and no rights generally attach until the defendant has entered a plea. Once a defendant performs his or her part of the bargain, the prosecution must perform as agreed, or the defendant must be allowed to withdraw the guilty plea.

9. JURY AND NONJURY TRIALS

According to the Sixth Amendment, "In all criminal prosecutions, the accused shall enjoy the right to a speedy and public trial, by an impartial jury of the State and district wherein the crime shall have been committed." This particular legal right has been found to be binding not only on the federal government but also on all state governments,[55] but that right may not always entitle a state court defendant to a jury of twelve members or to a jury in which a unanimous decision is required. Federal criminal defendants receive a twelve-person jury, which must reach a verdict by a unanimous vote, but eleven jurors may make a decision if the parties agree that one fewer than twelve may render a decision or the judge permits eleven to continue for good cause shown.[56] Contrary to federal practice, in *Apodoca v. Oregon,* 496 U.S. 404 (1972), the Supreme Court approved a nonunanimous state jury verdict where a jury of twelve was used and where the votes of nine of twelve jurors were needed for a decision. In any event, the Sixth Amendment has been interpreted so that when the potential sentence is more than six months, a defendant is entitled to a trial by jury regardless of whether the trial occurs in a state or federal forum.[57]

The Supreme Court approved the use of a six-person jury in *Williams v. Florida,* 399 U.S. 70 (1970), for noncapital state cases, despite the defendant's objection that the Sixth Amendment right to a jury trial that was recognized in *Duncan v. Louisiana,* 391 U.S. 145 (1968), involved a twelve-person jury, the same number as in federal criminal trials. Since the *Duncan* decision, state criminal juries have ranged from twelve to five in number, but a five-person jury was rejected by the Supreme Court as not allowing sufficient numbers for proper group deliberation and as increasing the possibility of errors in the verdict if the jury became too small.[58] The Court noted in *Brown v. Louisiana,* 447 U.S. 323 (1980), that a six-person jury must reach its determinations by a unanimous verdict to meet the requirements of the Sixth Amendment as applied to the states.

To summarize, in all federal criminal prosecutions where the length of the sentence is greater than six-months, a defendant possesses the right to a trial by jury under the Sixth Amendment and the jury will have twelve persons who must reach a unanimous verdict. In state criminal prosecutions, jury numbers may range from the traditional twelve to six, with nonunanimous verdicts of 9 to 3 appropriate for twelve-person juries. No nonunanimous six-person juries have been approved as meeting the Sixth Amendment right to a jury trial, and no five-person juries are permitted in criminal cases.

When the prosecution's case is presented to a jury, the jury must perform the usual tasks, including weighing the evidence that the prosecutor presents and the opposing evidence that the defense offers, as well as considering the credibility of the witnesses who testify. The jury is not to consider evidence that the judge has ordered stricken from the record or has otherwise deemed inadmissible. Although a defendant may have a constitutional right to a trial by jury, many defendants decide to waive this right and have the case decided by a judge or, in some cases, by a three-judge panel. If a defendant takes the option of a trial by a judge, often called a bench trial, the judge's duties increase dramatically. Not only must the judge listen to the evidence and assign weight to that evidence but also the judge must exclude consideration of evidence of which the judge may have full knowledge and has ruled inadmissible. During the trial, the judge must rule on the admissibility or exclusion of evidence, deal with competency of witnesses and of evidence, and make determinations in every case where the attorneys have a conflict. The burden of proof possessed by the parties does not change, whether the trial is to a judge or to a jury. However, there are situations when a defendant would rather have a judge, who may be somewhat more "hardened" to rough or inflammatory evidence, make the factual determinations based on the evidence.

In federal criminal trials, where a defendant has the right to a trial by jury by virtue of the length of possible sentence, the trial is to a jury unless the defendant waives that right in writing, with the consent of the federal prosecutor and the judge.[59] Many states follow a similar practice by empaneling a jury unless the defendant prefers a trial to a judge and indicates that preference in writing or in open court with the approval of the judge and the prosecution.[60]

10. THE TRIAL PROCESS

From the time the prosecution makes a decision to prosecute a defendant for a particular crime or crimes, the goal is always to reach some finality, whether by plea negotiation or by resolution through a trial to a judge or jury. While the trial judge holds primary responsibility for managing a trial, both the defense and prosecution counsel have important duties. They must have prepared their witnesses for trial testimony, organized the exhibits, subpoenaed all important witnesses, considered jury selection issues, contemplated opening and closing statements, and otherwise respectively prepared for trial. Proper jury selection requires preparation for questioning prospective jurors and determining which factors exhibited by jurors would prove receptive to the attorney's position. Which witnesses to present and in which order are decisions that usually have been made prior to trial, but refinement to witness lists is often an ongoing process. Witness lists should have been served on the opposing parties by the opposing attorneys to prevent unfair surprise. Pretrial notification concerning affirmative defenses must have been made prior to trial, or a judge may refuse to allow trial testimony from a defendant's witnesses to support an alibi or other affirmative defense. In addition to the judge and attorneys, law enforcement agencies in charge of security for nonbailed defendants must arrange to have them present at the proper times. A trial is a complex matter to manage and requires that those involved perform their respective duties at the proper time in an appropriate manner so that justice is served and injustice does not occur.

11. SELECTION OF JURORS

Every defendant is entitled to an impartial jury of the state and district where the crime is alleged to have been committed. This is a Sixth Amendment right that has been made applicable to the states through the Due Process Clause of the Fourteenth Amendment. In assuring that all defendants enjoy this right, the prosecution and defense, in conjunction with the judge, must make efforts to eliminate prospective jurors who would be unfair to the defendant or to the prosecution or who might not follow the law as instructed by the judge. Every defendant has the right to have a trial jury selected from a fair cross section of the community. The jury actually selected need not mirror the fair cross section, but the jury must have been selected from a group or an array that included a fair cross section of the court's jurisdiction. Neither the defendant counsel nor the prosecutor may try to exclude jurors based on race or gender and perhaps, to a lesser extent, ethnic background or affiliation.[61] In *Batson v. Kentucky,* 476 U.S. 79 (1986), the Supreme Court reversed a conviction from a trial where the prosecutor had excluded some black prospective jurors from serving solely because of their race and offered a method to contest racially discriminatory efforts to keep African Americans from jury service. A defendant must allege that he or she is a member of a recognized group and raise some evidence that there has been discrimination. If the prosecutor cannot explain in race-neutral terms why members of a particular group appeared to have been excluded, the defendant should prevail. In *Johnson v. California,* 545 U.S. 162 (2005), the Court clarified the Batson case by explaining the three-step test to help assure that no member of a recognizable group was kept from jury service.

In federal courts and in many state courts, the trial judge conducts an examination of prospective jurors, called a voir dire, to determine the suitability of prospective jurors to hear a criminal case. In many states, the trial attorneys are responsible for conducting the examination of prospective jurors by asking questions that are designed to reveal bias, interest, or prejudice.[62] When the voir dire questioning, whether by the judge or by the attorneys, indicates that a prospective juror cannot be fair and impartial and render a jury vote based solely on the evidence presented in court, a prospective juror may be excused for cause. An unlimited number of prospective jurors may be excused for bias, interest, or apparent prejudice. In addition to excusing jurors for cause, states and federal courts permit attorneys to exercise peremptory challenges as a way of excusing prospective jurors from jury service when the attorney cannot exclude based on cause but has some other lawful reason to desire that the prospective juror not serve on that case. Peremptory challenges are limited by a court rule or by a formula that depends on the number of defendants or the type of crime that has been charged. For example, in federal criminal trials involving capital prosecutions, each side has twenty peremptory challenges, but for lesser charged offenses, each side is given only three peremptory challenges.[63] State practice, although not identical as a general rule, allows peremptory challenges based on state law or state rules of criminal procedure.[64] In virtually all jurisdictions, alternate jurors may be chosen at the court's discretion, especially if the case is expected to take months to conclude and the alternative would be to declare a mistrial in the event that one or more jurors could not continue.[65]

When the prosecution and the defense have exercised all prospective juror challenges based on cause and have exercised as many of their respective peremptory challenges as they desire or have exhausted them, the jury has been determined, and the persons selected will subsequently take their respective posts as jurors. In some jurisdictions, after the jury is sworn, the judge may offer some initial instruction to the jury concerning its duties and expected conduct. The judge may explain the order of the proceedings and offer some initial education regarding the legal principles and rules governing the trial proceeding.[66]

12. OPENING STATEMENTS

Following juror oaths, the attorneys for the respective sides are permitted, but not required, to give opening statements or, as they are often called, opening arguments.

CASE 2.2

Leading Case Brief: The Three-step Process to Prove Racial Discrimination in Jury Selection

Johnson v. California
Supreme Court of the United States
545 U.S. 162 (2005)

Case Facts:

A trial jury convicted petitioner Jay Shawn Johnson, an African American, of the assault and murder of his Caucasian girlfriend's white infant. The prosecutor used three peremptory challenges to remove all the prospective black jurors. Following a defense objection alleging that the prosecutor had used the race of the jurors improperly, the trial judge requested that the prosecutor justify the peremptory challenges on racially neutral reasons. The judge felt that the jury selections could be justified on racially neutral grounds and that the defendant failed to prove that it was more likely than not that the prosecutor had engaged in illegal discriminatory jury selection. The case was tried and decided by the jury of all white individuals.

The California Court of Appeal reversed the conviction based on the alleged improper use of peremptory challenges, but the Supreme Court of California reinstated Johnson's murder conviction on the strength of *Batson v. Kentucky,* 476 U.S. 79 (1986). According to the top California court, *Batson v. Kentucky* permitted state courts to establish fair standards with which to evaluate the sufficiency of alleged prima facie cases of purposeful jury discrimination, and the trial court had properly followed California procedure. The Supreme Court of the United States granted certiorari.

Legal Issue:

Must a defendant alleging racial discrimination in jury selection by use of peremptory challenges first demonstrate that it is more likely than not that the prosecutor's actions were based on improper group or racial bias, unless properly explained by the prosecutor?

The Court's Ruling:

In a continuing effort to remove racial discrimination from American courts, the Court held that a person making an allegation of racial discrimination did not need to prove that an event was racially motivated by a preponderance of the evidence. A lower standard served justice much better.

Essence of the Court's Rationale:

* * *

[In *Batson v. Kentucky,* 476 U.S. 79 (1986), the Court determined that a defendant may establish a prima facie case of intentional racial discrimination using a three-step process by showing that (1) he is a member of a recognizable racial group, that the prosecutor has exercised peremptory challenges to remove members of the defendant's race from the panel, and the defendant must show that these facts and circumstances raise an inference that the prosecutor used peremptory challenges to exclude jurors based on race. (2) The burden shifts to the government prosecutor to demonstrate racially neutral reasons for excluding racial minorities from the trial jury. (3) If the prosecution fails to justify its jury selections in a racially neutral manner, the defendant should prevail in his or her allegation.]

* * *

Indeed, *Batson* held that because the petitioner had timely objected to the prosecutor's decision to strike "all black persons on the venire," the trial court was in error when it "flatly rejected the objection without requiring the prosecutor to give an explanation for his action." 476 U.S. at 100. We did not hold that the petitioner had proved discrimination. Rather, we remanded the case for further proceedings

(continued)

because the trial court failed to demand an explanation from the prosecutor—i.e., to proceed to Batson's second step—despite the fact that the petitioner's evidence supported an inference of discrimination. *Ibid.*

Thus, in describing the burden-shifting framework, we assumed in Batson that the trial judge would have the benefit of all relevant circumstances, including the prosecutor's explanation, before deciding whether it was more likely than not that the challenge was improperly motivated. We did not intend the first step to be so onerous that a defendant would have to persuade the judge—on the basis of all the facts, some of which are impossible for the defendant to know with certainty—that the challenge was more likely than not the product of purposeful discrimination. Instead, a defendant satisfies the requirements of Batson's first step by producing evidence sufficient to permit the trial judge to draw an inference that discrimination has occurred.

* * *

Respondent's argument is misguided. *Batson,* of course, explicitly stated that the defendant ultimately carries the "burden of persuasion" to "'prove the existence of purposeful discrimination.'" 476 U.S. at 93 (quoting *Whitus v. Georgia,* 385 U.S. 545, 550 (1967)). This burden of persuasion "rests with, and never shifts from, the opponent of the strike." *Purkett,* 514 U.S. at 768. Thus, even if the State produces only a frivolous or utterly nonsensical justification for its strike, the case does not end—it merely proceeds to step three. *Ibid.* The first two *Batson* steps govern the production of evidence that allows the trial court to determine the persuasiveness of the defendant's constitutional claim. "It is not until the third step that the persuasiveness of the justification becomes relevant—the step in which the trial court determines whether the opponent of the strike has carried his burden of proving purposeful discrimination." *Purkett, supra,* at 768.

* * *

The *Batson* framework is designed to produce actual answers to suspicions and inferences that discrimination may have infected the jury selection process. . . . The three-step [*Batson*] process thus simultaneously serves the public purposes *Batson* is designed to vindicate and encourages "prompt rulings on objections to peremptory challenges without substantial disruption of the jury selection process." *Hernandez v. New York,* 500 U.S. 352, 358–359 (1991) (opinion of KENNEDY, J.).

* * *

In this case, the inference of discrimination was sufficient to invoke a comment by the trial judge "that 'we are very close,'" and on review, the California Supreme Court? acknowledged that "it certainly looks suspicious that all three African American prospective jurors were removed from the jury." 30 Cal.4th at 1307, 1326, 71 P.3d at 273, 286. Those inferences that discrimination may have occurred were sufficient to establish a prima facie case under *Batson.*

The facts of this case well illustrate that California's "more likely than not" standard is at odds with the prima facie inquiry mandated by *Batson.* The judgment of the California Supreme Court is therefore reversed, and the case is remanded for further proceedings not inconsistent with this opinion. It is so ordered.

Case Importance:

Persons who have been subjected to and harmed by alleged racial discrimination do not have to prove discrimination by a preponderance of the evidence but must introduce some evidence of racial discrimination that will require the opposing party to demonstrate that racial discrimination was not part of the overall procedure.

Because the prosecutor possesses the burden of proof, the prosecutor initiates the first opening statement. Of the various theories about how to make an opening statement, the most consistent approach seems to involve offering a road map of what the prosecutor believes the evidence will prove. This is the first real opportunity for the prosecutor to present his or her theory of the case and to give a preview of the evidence that the prosecutor will introduce for jury consideration. Some prosecutors explain the elements of the crime and mention that the judge will refer to these when the judge offers jury instructions at the conclusion of the trial. The prosecutor often attempts to get the jury to agree or to commit that if the government's evidence shows that all of the elements have been proven, then the jury should vote in favor of the government's position. Although the prosecutor states what he or she believes the evidence will prove, the prosecutor's statement is not evidence but a context or a matrix into which the jury may place the evidence as it evaluates the proof.

The defense attorney may offer an opening statement that immediately follows the prosecution's opening statement, offer the statement later, or decline to offer any opening statement. As a matter of trial strategy, the defense attorney may choose to wait until after the prosecution has presented its case in chief and rested its case. This strategy permits the defense attorney to make an opening statement that can take into consideration the thrust and direction of the prosecution's presentation of its case in chief. The drawback to waiting until the beginning of the defense case in chief to make an opening statement is that the prosecution gains credibility with the jury by giving an uncontested opening statement and then by launching directly into presentation of evidence adverse to the defendant. The upside to waiting is that the defense's road map will be fresh in the jurors' minds at the time of the defense presentation of evidence. In addition, the defense may benefit from being able to adjust the manner of presentation or the topics discussed in the opening statement, based on events that transpired during the prosecution's presentation of its case.

The opening statement serves as an introduction to each litigant's theory of the case and allows a little persuasive argument to be injected into the statements. The comments by the respective attorneys may help the jury understand how the case unfolds and allow it to place the events and the evidence in context. In no event may the information contained in either an opening statement or in a later closing statement be considered actual evidence in the case. The attorneys are not under oath, and they do not have firsthand information.

13. PROSECUTION'S CASE IN CHIEF

The government's case begins when the prosecutor calls the first witness to give testimony. Unless this witness is a young child or is considered a hostile witness allied with the defendant, the prosecutor is required to ask direct questions and is not permitted to ask leading questions. All evidence directed toward meeting the burden of proof, called proof beyond a reasonable doubt,[67] comes from oral testimony, exhibits and evidence introduced by witnesses, and in some jurisdictions, a view of the crime scene. Ordinary witnesses, called lay witnesses, normally present most of the evidence for the prosecution's case; these witnesses are the people who have firsthand information about what happened. Police officers who testify as witnesses for the prosecution's case generally testify as lay witnesses but may on occasion testify as expert witnesses where their education and experience qualify them with specialized knowledge that the average person does not possess. If the proof needed by the prosecution involves matters that are beyond the expertise of ordinary lay witnesses, experts that bring special expertise, knowledge, and talent in medicine, physics, science, and other areas may be brought to the witness stand and qualified as expert witnesses. These expert witnesses are permitted to give opinion evidence based on their proven expertise.

At the conclusion of the prosecutor's examination of each government witness, the defense is permitted to cross-examine that witness with a view to testing the witness's opportunity for original perception, questioning any conclusions offered by the witness, bringing out any bias or interest, and otherwise checking the credibility of the witness. The cross-examining attorney may use leading questions when interrogating a prosecution witness as a method of testing the credibility of the witness.

The prosecution may decide that the defense cross-examination of the prosecution's witness has done some damage to the prosecution's case or cast doubt on the witness's credibility. Under such circumstances, the prosecution may conduct redirect examination to rehabilitate its witness, but the subjects of the redirect are generally limited to matters discussed during the defense cross-examination. The defense counsel has the right to re-cross-examine the prosecution witness for similar reasons.

The prosecutor must use witnesses whose testimony helps to establish every element of the crime beyond a reasonable doubt. Where a prosecutor has success in going forward with the evidence and meeting the burden of proof, the prosecution will survive a defense move for a directed verdict. If a defense attorney makes a motion for a verdict of acquittal based on the argument that the prosecution failed to put on a prima facie case, the judge must consider whether the prosecution's evidence, if believed and uncontradicted, meets the burden of proof beyond a reasonable doubt. If a judge cannot say that all the elements of a crime have been proved, including jurisdiction and venue, giving every reasonable inference to the prosecution, the judge ends the case, and the defendant is discharged. This rarely happens because the prosecutor normally introduces sufficient evidence to prevent this directed verdict of acquittal, but virtually every defense counsel make this motion if there is any chance that a judge might rule in the favor of the defendant.

When the prosecution is convinced that sufficient evidence has been presented to equal proof beyond reasonable doubt and has no other witnesses or evidence to introduce, the prosecutor announces to the judge that the prosecution rests its case.

14. DEFENSE'S CASE IN CHIEF

Following the presentation of the prosecution's case in chief and the trial judge's failure to affirmatively act on the defense motion for a verdict for acquittal, the defendant's attorney must mount a defense that either demolishes the prosecutor's case or, at a bare minimum, creates reasonable doubt in the minds of the jury. Note that with the exception of affirmative defenses, a defendant has no burden of proof in any criminal case and can still prevail without introducing any evidence. The defendant may choose not to testify based on the Fifth Amendment provision against self-incrimination, and during closing arguments, the prosecutor is not permitted to call specific attention to the fact that the defendant has chosen not to testify. The defense counsel may build reasonable doubt by calling into question some of the elements of proof in the prosecution's case in chief. The defense may additionally cast doubt on the credibility of some of the prosecution's witnesses. The defense counsel also calls defense witnesses for direct examination. Just as the prosecution generally is not permitted to ask leading questions of its witnesses unless there are small children or hostile witnesses, the defense counsel must also ask direct questions. This type of interrogation contemplates receiving answers to questions of who, what, where, and when but not generally how and why. Defense testimony may include expert witnesses who have special training and qualifications and are permitted to offer opinions. Even though the experts probably do not have firsthand information about the crime, they have evidence based on tests and experiments that relate to the historical facts of the case. The prosecution is permitted to cross-examine each defense witness if it determines that it would be in the interest of justice. Just as the defense may ask leading questions of prosecution witnesses during the prosecution's case in chief, the prosecution may ask leading questions of defense witnesses during its cross-examination. The same opportunities for redirect examination and re-cross-examination exist when the parties are questioning witnesses during the defense case in chief as existed during the prosecution' case in chief. When the defense has presented all of the witnesses that it deems appropriate to a proper defense, the counsel for the defendant indicates to the judge that the defense has concluded its presentation of evidence and that the defense rests.

15. PROSECUTION CASE IN REBUTTAL

The prosecution has an opportunity to rebut the defendant's case by recalling earlier witnesses or calling new witnesses to clarify matters developed during the defense case in chief, to rebut specific defenses offered by the defendant, and to repair any damage done to the credibility of important prosecution witnesses. For example, if the defendant personally took the witness stand and surprised the prosecution by testifying to evidence that supported alibi or self-defense, the prosecution is privileged to introduce evidence that casts doubt on the alibi or demonstrates why self-defense was not appropriate under the circumstances. As a general rule, the evidence introduced by the prosecution during its case in rebuttal must relate to new material that the defense offered during its case in chief. The prosecutor must generally conduct direct examination during the presentation of the prosecution case in rebuttal and should refrain from using leading questions. For each prosecution witness called or recalled during the prosecution case in rebuttal, the defense has an opportunity to cross-examine that prosecution witness.

16. DEFENSE CASE IN REJOINDER

The defense is permitted to clarify and rebut evidence offered by the prosecution during its case in rebuttal. Continuing the process of narrowing the permitted topics, the defense may clarify matters addressed by the prosecution during its case rebuttal and is generally not permitted to introduce new topics that have not been mentioned prior to this point in the trial. The defense may introduce evidence that casts doubt on the credibility of prosecution witnesses who testified during the prosecution case in rebuttal and correct misimpressions of defense witnesses who testified during the case in chief. This is generally the defense's last opportunity to pull the defense theory together by eliminating ambiguities and uncertainties.

17. MOTION FOR JUDGMENT OF ACQUITTAL

Following the close of the defense case in rejoinder, the defense attorney may renew the motion for acquittal, which is often phrased as a motion for a directed verdict. Although this motion is rarely successful at this point in the trial, if there is a good argument that the prosecution's proof has failed or that an element of the crime was never addressed by the prosecution, this motion may succeed. According to Rule 29 of the Federal Rules of Criminal Procedure, when the defendant makes a motion to enter a judgment of acquittal because the evidence is insufficient to sustain the conviction, the court must order a judgment of acquittal if the evidence fails to prove guilt beyond a reasonable doubt.[68] This motion may be made at the close of the prosecution's case, but if the judge denies the motion, it does not prevent the defense from proceeding with its case in chief. In federal prosecutions, this motion may be renewed within seven days after the end of the trial.

18. CLOSING ARGUMENTS

Because the prosecution has the burden of proof, it has the first opportunity to present a closing argument, which is followed by the defense closing argument and finally by prosecution rebuttal.[69] The prosecution once again gets the last word, on the theory that it has the burden of proof. The attorneys for each side generally summarize their respective case presentations to reflect favorably on their respective positions while attempting to point out errors, omissions, or other problems in the opposing party's case presentation. The prosecutor is generally not permitted to offer an opinion of guilt and is prohibited under the Fifth Amendment from commenting on a defendant's failure to take the witness stand where the defendant has exercised his or her Fifth Amendment privilege not to testify. The defense counsel emphasizes the burden of proof that falls to the prosecution and calls into question, where appropriate, deficiencies in the proof of a particular element or elements, especially those that have been highly controverted during the trial. Just as a prosecutor may not personally comment on his or her view of guilt or innocence, the defense counsel also must not comment on his or her belief in the innocence of the defendant. Extreme deviations by either attorney may lead the judge to declare a mistrial, with the result that the case may have to be tried completely again.[70] If a prosecutor intentionally interjected reversible error during closing arguments in an effort to gain a mistrial, the double jeopardy provision of the Fifth Amendment may prevent a retrial.

19. JURY INSTRUCTIONS

A court's jury instructions have the purpose of educating the jury about the precise law that applies to the crimes that have been charged and the law that concerns the defenses that have been asserted. In addition to legal principles concerning the criminal charges, other general legal principles such as how to handle presumptions and inferences, the concept of judicial notice, the concept of proof beyond a reasonable doubt, and information concerning how to handle and consider affirmative defenses may be appropriate. Most states have what are called pattern jury instructions that have been approved for use in cases involving specific crimes and situations.[71] Many of these jury instructions contained within the pattern jury instructions are the result of prior litigation and clarification and are, therefore, thought to be appropriate and beyond successful appellate attack. Since the manner in which crimes may have been committed may call for jury instructions that deviate from the standard ones, jurisdictions allow prosecutors and defense counsel to propose new ones or alternative ones that are tailored specifically to fit the case being tried. For example, Rule 30 of the Ohio Rules of Criminal Procedure provides that either party may file written requests with the court that the court instruct the jury as suggested in the requests. Additionally, the parties are required to inform opposing counsel of their jury instruction requests. Prior to giving the jury instructions, the court is required under Rule 30 to inform the prosecution and defense of its proposed action with respect to the jury instructions[72] in order to give them an opportunity to object. In the event that either the prosecution or the defense disagrees with the judge's proposed instruction, the attorney for that side must inform the court of his or her objection and state the specific reasons for dissatisfaction. This allows the judge to reconsider the wording of the instruction and permits the attorney to preserve the record for appeal. An objection will the most valuable to a defendant who is subsequently convicted and believes the conviction rests on the erroneous jury instruction. Pursuant to federal Rule 30, the judge may instruct the jury either before or after closing arguments and is permitted to use both occasions to give jury instructions.

20. VERDICTS, SENTENCING PROCESS, AND POSTTRIAL MOTIONS

Once the judge finishes giving the jury its instructions, the jury assembles in a room without any outside interference or influence. Typically, the jury picks a foreman or forewoman to lend a form of order to the deliberations, but how the jury organizes itself for deliberations constitutes a matter for each jury. The only public duty of the foreman of the jury is to return the jury verdict to the court once the jury has determined the verdict. The internal workings of the jury and its deliberations are generally not subject to dispute in any forum and will not usually be the subject of any appeal, absent fraud or extreme misconduct.

The jury verdict in federal courts must be unanimous, and state courts follow this requirement in cases involving the death penalty or life in prison as a possible penalty. A unanimous vote to acquit ends the defendant's case, and that particular cause of action cannot be brought again against the defendant by the same jurisdiction. Naturally, a unanimous vote to convict means that the state has met its burden of proof and that the presumption of innocence that once existed has been extinguished. Some states, such as Florida and Georgia, operate with six-person juries, but those juries must render a unanimous verdict to constitute a verdict on the merits. In federal prosecutions where the jury vote is not unanimous and in state courts, where unanimous verdicts are required, a nonunanimous jury vote does not constitute a verdict on the merits and will generally permit a retrial of the cause of action. When the jury fails to render a unanimous vote, it is said to be a hung jury and does not produce a verdict, except in states that allow a 9 to 3 vote to render a decision for either acquittal or guilt.[73]

When the jury foreman returns the verdict to the court, a defendant has the right to have the jury polled to determine if each and every member of the jury agrees with the vote that has been reported on the jury form. This is the final chance for a juror who has been somewhat overreached by other jurors to express a dissenting vote that might indicate a lack of unanimity. Resolution where a juror dissents in open court varies, but in most instances, the jury returns to the jury room to resume deliberations.

Once the jury has rendered a verdict, that decision is turned into a judgment, whereby the trial judge sets forth the plea, including the jury's findings or the court's findings on the evidence, the adjudication, and the court's sentence. For example, under the North Dakota Rules of Criminal Procedure, Rule 32(C), "A judgment of conviction must include the plea, the verdict, and the sentence imposed." State and federal courts are under some pressure to render sentences within a reasonable time so that the convicted individual may start serving the sentence and to otherwise remove uncertainty from the direction the sentence will take.

Until recently, federal district courts were under mandatory directives to follow sentencing standards promulgated by the Federal Sentencing Guidelines.[74] One of the primary features of the sentencing guidelines that required federal judges to enhance sentences, based on specified facts that had not been determined by the jury, was determined to run contrary to earlier Supreme Court decisions. In *United States v. Booker,* 543 U.S. 220 (2005), the Supreme Court determined that enhanced sentences based on facts that had not been presented for jury determination violated the Sixth Amendment right to a jury trial. Presently, the Federal Sentencing Guidelines are considered advisory and cannot be applied in a mandatory fashion.

In federal and state courts, presentence investigations are conducted to determine whether a defendant should be sentenced at a particular level, whether the judge should consider some enhancement to the normal sentence, or whether the judge should consider a downward departure and give a lesser sentence than would typically be the case. The presentence investigation is a fairly wide-ranging study into the defendant's past criminal record, financial situation, history and characteristics, and any other relevant information.[75] As a general rule, prior to sentencing, a convicted defendant must be given an opportunity to read the presentence report. For example, under North Dakota rules,[76] prior to the sentencing, the defense counsel must be given an opportunity to speak on behalf of the defendant, and the defendant has the right to present information that might affect the sentence. Similarly, the prosecutor is given an opportunity to make a statement that might have some influence over the sentence. In an increasing number of jurisdictions, victims of a crime are permitted to have some input at the sentencing proceeding. Under federal Rule 32(i)(4),[77] the sentencing court must address any victim of the crime under consideration and permit the victim to speak or offer the court any information that the victim chooses to share with the court. After due consideration of the presentence report, along with the input of the prosecutor and the defense counsel and the defendant's statement, the judge may impose a sentence. Where probation is a possibility for the convicted offense, the judge may place a convicted defendant on probation subject to local terms and conditions.[78]

Following the imposition of sentence on a convicted defendant, courts generally must advise the defendant of his or her right of appeal. For example, under Iowa law, the sentencing court must advise the defendant of the statutory right to appeal, and a defendand who is an indigent is informed to apply to the court for the appointment of free counsel for appellant purposes. The judge also notifies the defendant that there is a requirement of filing a notice of appeal and the judge needs to advise the defendant about the consequences of failure to give notification for appeal purposes.[79] Under the federal rules of evidence, the sentencing judge must advise the convicted defendant of the right of appeal where the defendant pled not guilty and was convicted. In any event, a convicted defendant must be informed of the right to appeal the sentence that has been imposed and told that any appeal to which a convicted defendant is entitled will be without cost to the defendant if the defendant cannot afford to hire independent counsel.[80]

Postconviction proceedings can involve both defense and prosecution, although they will be seeking different remedies. The prosecution may apply for a criminal forfeiture of property owned or controlled by the convicted defendant where the property was used in the crime or had a sufficient connection to the crime.[81] Appropriate notice consistent with due process must be given to the defendant to allow the opportunity to contest the seizure. In some instances, notice of forfeiture may have been given at the time of indictment, and a jury may have rendered a judgment on forfeiture based on the evidence presented in a criminal trial.[82] In postconviction proceedings, for good cause shown, a defendant may be granted a new trial where the interests of justice require a reconsideration of the matter. Federal procedure allows a new trial based on newly discovered evidence under particular circumstances and for grounds other than newly discovered evidence.[83] For example, Iowa allows requests for new trials based on the jury receiving nonapproved evidence, an error of law by the judge, the verdict has been cast by lot, or jurors have been guilty of misconduct, among other reasons.[84]

21. APPELLATE PRACTICE

Every defendant has a statutory or state constitutional right to one appeal and has the right to receive free appellate counsel if unable to recently afford a private attorney.[85] Typically a defendant must file a notice of appeal (see Figure 2.8) within a statutorily defined time, or the right of appeal is deemed to have been waived or forfeited. Case law has provided that where a transcript is necessary for a meaningful appeal, the government must provide a transcript at its expense.[86]

An attorney who represents a convicted defendant has a duty to investigate and file a brief with the appropriate court of appeals. Appropriate representation may require the defendant to meet with the appellate attorney, and the appellate attorney must certainly read the transcript of the trial to ascertain what appealable issues exist. The appellate attorney prepares a brief that argues the law as applied to the facts, rather than attempt to reargue the facts. As a strong general rule, the facts are not arguable during the appellate process because the jury or the judge has made a determination

Local Criminal Notice of Appeal Form.

NOTICE OF APPEAL
United States District Court

_____ District of _____

_____

_____

Docket No.: _____

_____
(District Court Judge)

Notice is hereby given that _____ appeals to the United States Court of Appeals for the Second

Circuit from the judgment [_____], other [_____] _____
(specify)

entered in this action on _____.
(date)

Offense occurred after November 1, 1987   Yes   [___]   No [____]

This appeal concerns: Conviction only [___]   Sentence only [___]   Conviction and Sentence [____]

Date _____
TO

_____
(Counsel for Appellant)

Address _____

_____

_____

ADD ADDITIONAL PAGE (IF NECESSARY)   Telephone Number: _____

TO BE COMPLETED BY ATTORNEY	TRANSCRIPT INFORMATION - FORM B	
▶ **QUESTIONNAIRE**	▶ **TRANSCRIPT ORDER**	▶ DESCRIPTION OF PROCEEDINGS FOR WHICH TRANSCRIPT IS REQUIRED (INCLUDE DATE)

[_____] I am ordering a transcript
[_____] I am not ordering a transcript
Reason
    [_____] Daily copy is available
    [_____] U.S. Attorney has placed order
    [_____] Other. Attach explanation
	Prepare transcript of Dates
	[_____] Prepare proceedings _____
	[_____] Trial _____
	[_____] Sentencing _____
	[_____] Post-trial proceedings _____	

The attorney certifies that he/she will make satisfactory arrangements with the court reporter for payment of the cost of the transcript. (FRAP 10(b)).
Method of payment   [_____]   Funds [_____]   CJA Form 24 [_____]

ATTORNEY'S SIGNATURE	DATE

▶ COURT REPORTER ACKNOWLEDGMENT	To be completed by Court Reporter and forwarded to Court of Appeals.

Date order received	Estimated completion date		Estimated number of pages
	Date _____	Signature _____ (Court Reporter)	

DISTRIBUTE COPIES TO THE FOLLOWING:

1.   Original to U.S. District Court (Appeals Clerk).
2.   Copy U.S. Attorney's Office.
3.   Copy to Defendant's Attorney

4.   U.S. Court of Appeals
5.   Court Reporter (District Court)

USCA-2
FORM A REV. 8-05

FIGURE 2.8   Example of a Notice of Appeal Used in Federal District Courts.

on what facts exist and what facts were not proven. A decision concerning whether to orally argue the case before a court of appeals may rest with the appellate attorney, and most court rules of appellate practice allow a court of appeal to hear a case based only on the briefs.

On the merits of the appeal, the appellate attorney may be at a disadvantage if the trial lawyer has not properly preserved the record for appeal by making objections at appropriate times. Then the appellate attorney able to argue only the most egregious and outrageous of errors on behalf of the convicted defendant. Even where the trial attorney properly objected, errors that have not affected substantial rights of the defendant do not result in a new trial because they are not outcome determinative and are considered harmless errors. Only where the errors have seriously affected the defendant's right to a fair trial does an appellate court consider reversing a trial court judgment.

Where an appellate court rules in the defendant's favor, the court might reverse the conviction and remand the case for a new trial. In some contexts, an appellate court overturns the sentence and remands the case for a resentencing procedure. If there was some substantial defect according to which the defendant should never have been brought to trial, the reviewing court may reverse the case and remand to the trial court, with orders to dismiss the case with prejudice so that it may not be brought again. The prosecution may then appeal the case to a higher court in an attempt to have the trial verdict and sentence reinstated.

Any appeal beyond the first is based on the discretion of a state supreme court to hear the case. Most appellate cases end after the first appeal. Many criminal defendants request that the top state court in their jurisdiction consider their case on the merits, but most state courts do not entertain cases that have been decided at the intermediate appellate level. As a general rule, only where courts of appeal within one state have decided the same legal principle in two inconsistent ways do state supreme courts typically take a lower court case.

22. STATE AND FEDERAL HABEAS CORPUS

State and federal prisoners petition courts to request a grant of habeas corpus because success has the operative effect of actual freedom from incarceration, the grant of a new trial, or some other relief from the present conditions of incarceration. The petition for a writ of habeas corpus is a request that the person holding the prisoner produces his or her body for the court and explains the legality of continued custody. Although the request for a writ of habeas corpus is directed at the jailer or warden, the effect is to have the prosecutor's office defend the case against a new attack, which may involve newly discovered evidence. A request for a court to grant a writ of habeas corpus requires that all other remedies that might be available to a defendant following a conviction have been exhausted. Unless the defendant has taken every advantage of all possible avenues to have his or her conviction adjusted, the writ of habeas corpus in the state court is generally not available. In applying for a writ of habeas corpus, the defendant is alleging that he or she is being held in violation of the law or the constitution of the jurisdiction or counter to a United States law, or treaty or the federal Constitution. The opposing party in an action for a writ of habeas corpus is usually the public official who is in charge of custody of the convicted defendant. If the defendant can demonstrate that he or she is being held contrary to law after all means of appeal or redress have been exhausted, a court may issue a writ of habeas corpus directing that the individual be either retried or freed from the custody of the jailer or warden.

A denial of the writ by a trial court may be appealed to an intermediate state court of appeal and taken to the top court in the state. When the top state court refuses to hear the petition for the writ of habeas corpus after an exhaustion of state remedies, the defendant may request the Supreme Court of the United States to entertain the petition. Since the Supreme Court of the United States rarely accepts cases involving habeas corpus from state supreme courts, the typical next move for state habeas corpus litigants involves filing with a federal district court a petition for a writ of habeas corpus that makes a case for illegal detention. Essentially, the convicted defendant repeats the allegations that have been made about habeas corpus in the state court system. A federal district judge conducts a hearing to determine the merits of the allegations that the convicted defendant is being held contrary to federal law or to the Constitution of the United States. If the federal district judge does not agree with the allegations and issue a writ of habeas corpus, the convicted defendant has a difficult time appealing to proper federal circuit court of appeal. To appeal the denial of the writ of habeas corpus by a federal district court, a certificate of appealability is required from either the district court or the court of appeal. The defendant may appeal the district court's denial of the certificate of appealability to the federal court of appeal by requesting that the circuit court of appeal issue the certificate. In the event that the district court grants a certificate of appealability, the habeas corpus litigant can proceed to the court of appeals to argue the case on the merits. If a state habeas corpus litigant succeeds on the merits in a federal court of appeal, the remedies may involve a retrial, release, or any combination of relief in between.

A federal prisoner desiring a grant of habeas corpus from federal custody must first exhaust all remedies available to that individual within the federal criminal justice system. When all remedies have been attempted and failed, a federal defendant may request a district court to grant a writ of habeas corpus. Federal habeas corpus litigants face similar certificate of appealability requirements that are presented to state habeas corpus litigants. The gatekeeping feature of the certificate of appealability does not apply to habeas corpus petitions directed to the Supreme Court of the United States, which is free to accept or reject any petition.

23. SUMMARY

Federal and state court systems are organized in a similar fashion. Each system has a trial court at the lowest level, an intermediate court of appeal as the first appellate level, and a top court, frequently known as a supreme court, that serves as the court of last resort. Defendants who have been tried in state courts may appeal within the state system to have alleged errors corrected. If a defendant contends that a federal wrong has occurred within his or her trial and the defendant has exhausted all state remedies, the defendant may ask the Supreme Court of United States to hear the case. In a similar fashion, federal defendants may appeal through the federal court system and request that the Supreme Court, exercising its discretion, consider the merits of his or her appeal.

Some criminal acts may offend both state law and federal law and can be tried in either court system or both. A criminal act may violate the laws of more than one state and be subject to prosecution in each state separately without offending the concept of double jeopardy.

A person who has been accused of a crime may be required to make some pre-trial motions or be deemed to have waived the objections that were or should have been the substance of the motions. This theory allows a judge to correct an error that would otherwise remain; where the defendant makes the motion, it permits the trial judge to address the contention at the most appropriate time.

Criminal cases may be either felonies or misdemeanors and may be initiated by a complaint, an indictment, or an information, depending upon the jurisdiction and depending upon the seriousness of the offense. When a prosecutor brings a criminal case, a defendant may have an opportunity to negotiate a plea to the charge or charges. This allows criminal cases to be resolved if there is no substantial dispute concerning the facts and at the same time limits the appellate process following a guilty plea.

After a guilty verdict by a judge or a jury, a defendant may wish to appeal the verdict or sentence by alleging errors at the trial. Current interpretation of the right to counsel permits every litigant to either hire an attorney or, if the litigant is indigent, have an attorney appointed for the purposes of appeal. As a general rule, the wealth or lack of wealth of a convicted defendant should not be a bar to a meaningful appeal. When all appeals at all levels have been exhausted, and a defendant still believes that he or she is being held contrary to law, the application for a writ of habeas corpus to a state or federal court is always permitted, unless the defendant abuses the writ by frivolous or successive applications.

REVIEW EXERCISES AND QUESTIONS

1. Why are some states permitted to initiate serious criminal proceedings without using a grand jury when the Fifth Amendment appears to grant the right to a grand jury indictment?

2. Why does the concept of the prohibition against double jeopardy in the Fifth Amendment not prevent a state trial following a federal trial for the same criminal act? Explain.

3. Explain the way state courts and federal courts are organized.

4. When police have investigated an alleged criminal matter and presented it to the prosecutor's office, for what reasons might a prosecutor decline to pursue a criminal matter?

5. The case *Hurtado v. California* held that the right to a grand jury indictment did not exist in a state criminal prosecution. What was some of the Court's

reasoning for limiting the right to a grand jury indictment?

6. According to the Supreme Court in *Coleman v. Alabama,* why must defendants be offered legal counsel (free if the defendant is indigent) at a preliminary hearing?

7. Why are some pretrial motions classified as "mandatory" and generally must be made prior to a criminal trial?

8. The Supreme Court in *Santobello v. New York* approved the use of plea bargaining in criminal cases. What were some of the positive outcomes of permitting plea bargaining?

9. Does the right to a trial by jury require a jury of twelve persons in federal cases? Does the right to a jury trial mean the same thing in state criminal prosecutions?

10. What remedy does a defendant have if he or she thinks the prosecutor is using racial reasons as a basis for excluding persons from serving on the defendant's jury?
11. What purpose does the opening statement or argument have for the prosecution and for the defense?
12. Why must a convicted defendant exhaust all remedies of direct appeal before being permitted to file a writ of habeas corpus in a state or federal court?

HOW WOULD YOU DECIDE?

1. In the Supreme Court of the United States

Mr. Bartkus allegedly robbed a savings and loan association (bank) in Cook County, Illinois, that was insured by an agency of the United States government. The federal prosecutor tried the defendant for violation of 18 U.S.C § 2113, which prohibits the robbery of banks, credit unions, and savings and loan associations. Despite the efforts of the United States attorney to prosecute the defendant, the jury acquitted Bartkus. The United States attorney and the FBI delivered their evidence to a Cook County prosecutor, who procured an indictment that was substantially the same as the federal indictment but in the name of the State of Illinois. After overruling Bartkus' argument that he was being tried the second time in violation of the double jeopardy clause of the Fifth Amendment as applied to the states through the Due Process Clause of the Fourteenth Amendment, Bartkus was forced to trial and convicted of state bank robbery charges. The Fifth Amendment (provision against double jeopardy) had not been incorporated into the Fourteenth Amendment at this point in history, but the Fourteenth Amendment did require that the states grant every defendant due process.

How would you rule on the defendant's contention that fundamental fairness and due process under the Fourteenth Amendment should prevent the second trial in Illinois?

The Court's Holding:

* * *

Since the new prosecution was by Illinois, and not by the Federal Government, the claim of unconstitutionality must rest upon the Due Process Clause of the Fourteenth Amendment. Prior cases in this Court relating to successive state and federal prosecutions have been concerned with the Fifth Amendment, and the scope of its proscription of second prosecutions by the Federal Government, not with the Fourteenth Amendment's effect on state action. We are now called upon to draw on the considerations which have guided the Court in applying the limitations of the Fourteenth Amendment on state powers. We have held from the beginning and uniformly that the Due Process Clause of the Fourteenth Amendment does not apply to the States any of the provisions of the first eight amendments as such. The relevant historical materials have been canvassed by this Court and by legal scholars.

* * *

[This case was decided before the Fifth Amendment was made applicable to the states.]

In *Fox v. Ohio* argument was made to the Supreme Court that an Ohio conviction for uttering counterfeit money was invalid. This assertion of invalidity was based in large part upon the argument that since Congress had imposed federal sanctions for the counterfeiting of money, a failure to find that the Supremacy Clause precluded the States from punishing related conduct would expose an individual to double punishment. Mr. Justice Daniel, writing for the Court (with Mr. Justice McLean dissenting), recognized as true that there was a possibility of double punishment, but denied that from this flowed a finding of pre-emption, concluding instead that both the Federal and State Governments retained the power to impose criminal sanctions, the United States because of its interest in protecting the purity of its currency, the States because of their interest in protecting their citizens against fraud.

* * *

In a dozen cases decided by this Court between *Moore v. Illinois* and *United States v. Lanza* this Court had occasion to reaffirm the principle first enunciated in *Fox v. Ohio*. Since *Lanza* the Court has five times repeated the rule that successive state and federal prosecutions are not in violation of the Fifth Amendment. Indeed Mr. Justice Holmes once wrote of this rule that it "is too plain to need more than statement." One of the *post-Lanza* cases, *Jerome v. United States,* 318 U.S. 101, involved the same federal statute under which *Bartkus* was indicted and in *Jerome* this Court recognized that successive state and federal prosecutions were thereby made possible because all States had general robbery statutes. Nonetheless, a unanimous Court, as recently as 1943, accepted as unquestioned constitutional law that such successive prosecutions would not violate the proscription of double jeopardy included in the Fifth Amendment. 318 United States, at 105. 22.

[The Supreme Court affirmed the conviction of Mr. Bartkus.]

See *Bartkus v. Illinois,* 359 U.S. 121 (1959).

HOW WOULD YOU DECIDE?

2. *Supreme Court of the United States*

Mr. Santobello had been indicted on two felony counts under New York law and, after negotiating with the prosecutor, agreed to plead guilty to a lesser included offense. In return, the prosecutor's office agreed to not offer any recommendation concerning sentencing and leave that issue to the judge. Prior to sentencing, a new judge took over the duties of the original judge, and a new prosecutor took the place of the initial prosecutor. When the defendant appeared before the judge for sentencing, the prosecutor recommended that the defendant receive the maximum penalty. Santobello protested that the deal he agreed to was different than the one he actually received, that he had performed on his end of the bargain, and that the government should "hold up" its part of the bargain. The judge noted that he was not swayed by the prosecutor's recommendation and that he was always going to sentence Santobello to the maximum one year in prison once he read the presentence report.

Santobello appealed his sentence, contending that due process required that he receive the benefit of his plea agreement or that he be permitted to withdraw his plea completely and start the process from the beginning. He received no relief in the New York court system, and the Supreme Court granted certiorari.

How would you rule on the defendant's contention that due process and fundamental fairness should allow him to either specifically enforce the plea agreement or start the criminal case over again?

The Court's Holding:

* * *

This record represents another example of an unfortunate lapse in orderly prosecutorial procedures, in part, no doubt, because of the enormous increase in the workload of the often understaffed prosecutor's offices. The heavy workload may well explain these episodes, but it does not excuse them. The disposition of criminal charges by agreement between the prosecutor and the accused, sometimes loosely called "plea bargaining," is an essential component of the administration of justice. Properly administered, it is to be encouraged. If every criminal charge were subjected to a full-scale trial, the States and the Federal Government would need to multiply by many times the number of judges and court facilities.

Disposition of charges after plea discussions is not only an essential part of the process but a highly desirable part for many reasons. It leads to prompt and largely final disposition of most criminal cases; it avoids much of the corrosive impact of enforced idleness during pretrial confinement for those who are denied release pending trial; it protects the public from those accused persons who are prone to continue criminal conduct even while on pretrial release; and, by shortening the time between charge and disposition, it enhances whatever may be the rehabilitative prospects of the guilty when they are ultimately imprisoned.

* * *

We need not reach the question whether the sentencing judge would or would not have been influenced had he known all the details of the negotiations for the plea. He stated that the prosecutor's recommendation did not influence him and we have no reason to doubt that. Nevertheless, we conclude that the interests of justice and appropriate recognition of the duties of the prosecution in relation to promises made in the negotiation of pleas of guilty will be best served by remanding the case to the state courts for further consideration. The ultimate relief to which petitioner is entitled we leave to the discretion of the state court, which is in a better position to decide whether the circumstances of this case require only that there be specific performance of the agreement on the plea, in which case petitioner should be resentenced by a different judge, or whether, in the view of the state court, the circumstances require granting the relief sought by petitioner, *i.e.,* the opportunity to

withdraw his plea of guilty. We emphasize that this is in no sense to question the fairness of the sentencing judge; the fault here rests on the prosecutor, not on the sentencing judge.

[The Supreme Court vacated and remanded the case.]

See *Santobello v. New York,* 404 U.S. 257 (1971).

ENDNOTES

1. Forty-nine states follow the common law system while the state of Louisiana follows a civil law system based on the Code of Napoleon.

2. Differences include unique names for courts, different subject matter jurisdiction, and alterations in appellate process. Demonstrative of differences are the fact that many state juvenile courts have quite different procedures, and some states have eliminated an intermediate level of appeal in death penalty cases. Some states have very specialized courts, such as drug courts, where practice and procedure are not consistent with other such courts in different states.

3. The current chart is a revision of the original offered by the Symposium on the 30th Anniversary of the President's Commission and was prepared by the Bureau of Justice Studies in 1997.

4. See *People v. Chacon,* 2005 Cal. App. Unpub. LEXIS 9992 (Ca. 2005). See also *Flakes v. People,* 153 P.3d 427, 2007 Colo. LEXIS 141 (Colo. 2007), and Colorado Revised Statutes, C.R.S. 19-2-517. Direct filing.

5. "The federal Fifth Amendment right to grand jury indictment does not apply to the states; it is not a component of the due process of law guaranteed by the Fourteenth Amendment." *Ned v. State,* 119 p.3d 438, 444 (Alaska 2005), citing *Hurtado v. California,* 110 U.S. 516 (1884).

6. See Rule 7, Ohio Rules of Criminal Procedure. Ohio Crim. R. 7 (2007).

7. *Baldwin v. New York,* 399 U.S. 66 at 69, n. 6 (1970).

8. 518 U.S. 322, 327 (1996).

9. 489 U.S. 538 (1989).

10. See *History of the Federal Parole System,* United States Department of Justice, United States Parole Commission. http://www.usdoj.gov/uspc/history.pdf. September 17, 2007.

11. See *Heath v. Alabama,* 474 U.S. 82 (1985).

12. Ibid., 89.

13. See *Bartkus v. Illinois,* 359 U.S. 121 (1959). Bartkus was acquitted of federal bank robbery charges and subsequently charged and convicted of state bank robbery charges involving the same physical conduct. The Court found no constitutional difficulty, since the one act (bank robbery) had been a crime against two separate sovereigns.

14. Ibid.

15. See *Heath v. Alabama,* 474 U.S. 82 (1985). The dual sovereignty doctrine provides that, when a defendant in a single act violates the "peace and dignity" of two separate sovereigns by breaking the laws of each, he or she has committed two separate and distinct crimes. The crucial determination is whether the two governments that seek successively to prosecute a defendant for the same course of conduct can be termed separate sovereigns. This determination turns on whether the prosecuting entities' powers to undertake criminal prosecutions derive from separate and independent sources. The Court has traditionally held that state power to prosecute for crime is derived from its own inherent sovereignty and not from the federal government.

16. Ibid.

17. http://www.fjc.gov/federal/courts.nsf/autoframe? OpenForm&nav=menu2e&page=/federal/courts.nsf/ page/5DD5E0A65BA87BCA8525682400517BA5?o pendocument September 17, 2007.

18. Other federal trial courts include the United States Tax Court, the United States Court of Claims, and military courts that try offenses under the Code of Military Justice.

19. http://www.fjc.gov/federal/courts.nsf/autoframe? OpenForm&nav=menu3a&page=/federal/courts.nsf/ page/153844BD569A869285256C610059646F?o pendocument September 13, 2007.

20. See *Mapp v. Ohio,* 367 U.S. 643 (1961).
21. See *Miranda v. Arizona,* 384 U.S. 436 (1966).
22. See *United States v. Ruiz,* 536 U.S. 622 (2002), and *Schmerber v. California,* 384 U.S. 757 (1966).
23. See *Gilbert v. California,* 388 U.S. 263 (1967).
24. See *Neil v. Biggers,* 409 U.S. 188 (1972).
25. See *Barker v. Wingo,* 407 U.S. 514 (1972).
26. See *Ashe v. Swenson,* 397 U.S. 436 (1970).
27. *Beck v. Ohio,* 379 U.S. 89, 91 (1964).
28. http://www.supremecourt.nm.org/cgi-bin/download.cgi/supctforms/dc-criminal. September 18, 2007.
29. Ibid.
30. Rule 6, Federal Rules of Criminal Procedure.
31. Rule 7, Federal Rules of Criminal Procedure.
32. Ibid.
33. 110 U.S. 516 (1884).
34. O.R.C. § 2939.02. Fifteen jurors constitute the grand jury in Ohio.
35. See Ohio Constitution, § 10.
36. Rule 7, Ohio Rules of Criminal Procedure.
37. http://www.supremecourt.nm.org/supctforms/dc-criminal/VIEW/9-203.html September 18, 2007.
38. *Cochran v. State,* 256 Ga.113, 117 (1986). (Smith, J. concurring) (quoting *Wood v. Georgia,* 370 U.S. 375, 390 [1962]).
39. http://www.supremecourt.nm.org/cgi-bin/download.cgi/supctforms/dc-criminal. September 13, 2007.
40. See *County of Riverside v. McLaughlin,* 500 U.S. 44 (1991).
41. Rule 10, Federal Rules of Criminal Procedure.
42. Rule 11, Federal Rules of Criminal Procedure.
43. Rule 10, Ohio Rules of Criminal Procedure.
44. *Coleman v. Alabama,* 399 U.S. 1, 9 (1970).
45. *Brady v. Maryland,* 373 U.S. 83, 87 (1963).
46. See *Taylor v. State,* 381 Md. 602, 624 (2004), where the Court of Appeals rejected a double jeopardy claim made too late. "A reading of our cases makes clear that double jeopardy rights may be waived by failure to raise them in the trial court, and the holdings of these Supreme Court cases are not in conflict with our cases."
47. See *Barker v. Wingo,* 407 U.S. 514 (1972).
48. Rule 12, Federal Rules of Criminal Procedure.
49. Rule 16, North Dakota Rules of Criminal Procedure.
50. Ibid.
51. Rule 12(b)(1), North Dakota Rules of Criminal Procedure.
52. See *Santobello v. New York,* 404 U.S. 257 (1971).
53. Ibid., 261.
54. Rule 11, Federal Rules of Criminal Procedure.
55. See *Duncan v. Louisiana,* 391 U.S. 145, 156 (1968).
56. Rule 23, Federal Rules of Criminal Procedure.
57. See *Baldwin v. New York,* 399 U.S. 66 (1970), and *Blanton v. City of North Las Vegas,* 489 U.S. 538 (1989).
58. See *Ballew v. Georgia,* 435 U.S. 223 (1978).
59. Rule 23, Federal Rules of Criminal Procedure.
60. Rule 23, North Dakota Rules of Criminal Procedure.
61. See *Miller-El v. Cockrell,* 537 U.S. 322 (2003).
62. Rule 24(B), Ohio Rules of Criminal Procedure. See also Rule 24(a)(2), North Dakota Rules of Criminal Procedure.
63. Rule 24(b), Federal Rules of Criminal Procedure.
64. Rule 24(b), North Dakota Rules of Criminal Procedure. The rules allow four peremptory challenges when a six-person jury is empaneled and six peremptory challenges when a twelve-person jury has been selected. Multiple defendants may be granted additional peremptory challenges.
65. Rule 24, Ohio Rules of Criminal Procedure.
66. Rule 30(b)(2), North Dakota Rules of Criminal Procedure.
67. See *In re Winship,* 397 U.S. 358 (1970), in which the Court held that the standard of proof beyond a reasonable doubt was required in juvenile cases where a child had been charged with doing an act that would have been a crime if done by an adult. In dicta, routinely followed, the Court noted that the standard was required for adult criminal cases.
68. Rule 29, Federal Rules of Criminal Procedure.
69. Rule 29.1, North Dakota Rules of Criminal Procedure. See also Rule 29.1, Federal Rules of Criminal Procedure.
70. *United States v. Casas,* 425 F.3d 23, 38 (1st Cir. 2005), cert. denied, 547 U.S. 1061, 126 S. Ct. 1670, 164 L. Ed. 2d 409 (2006). In determining whether to grant declare a mistrial where prosecutorial misconduct during closing arguments has occurred, the court determines "whether prosecutorial misconduct has so poisoned the well that a new trial is required: (1) the severity of the misconduct; (2) the context in which it occurred; (3) whether the judge gave any curative instructions and the likely effect of such instructions; and (4) the strength of the evidence against the defendant."
71. See John M. Dinse, Ritchie E. Berger and Fredrick S. Lane III moaty listed on Lexis–Nexis could cite as *California Jury Instructions* (West Group, 2005).
72. Rule 30, Ohio Rules of Criminal Procedure.

73. See *Johnson v. Louisiana,* 406 U.S. 356 (1972), and Rule 31, Federal Rules of Criminal Procedure.
74. 18 U.S.C. 3553.
75. Rule 32(c), Federal Rules of Criminal Procedure.
76. Rule 32(a)(2), North Dakota Rules of Criminal Procedure.
77. Federal Rules of Criminal Procedure.
78. Rule 32 (e), North Dakota Rules of Criminal Procedure.
79. Rule 223(3)(e) Judgment, Iowa Rules of Criminal Procedure.
80. Rule 32(j), Federal Rules of Criminal Procedure.
81. See *Bennis v. Michigan,* 516 U.S. 442 (1995), where a car was forfeited to the government, and *United States v. Ursery,* 518 U.S. 267 (1996), where the forfeiture involved the defendant's house.
82. See Rule 33, Federal Rules of Criminal Procedure.
83. Ibid.
84. Rule 2.24, Iowa Rules of Criminal Procedure.
85. See *Douglas v. California,* 372 U.S. 353 (1963).
86. See *Griffin v. Illinois,* 351 U.S. 12 (1956).

The Principles of the Mapp Exclusionary Rule

Learning Objectives

1. Be able to explain what the exclusionary rule does, and give an example of how it should be applied.
2. Understand the theoretical basis for the exclusionary rule, and be able to explain the circumstances when it should not be applied.
3. Develop an understanding of why many courts hold that a government must follow its own rules, and articulate why the exclusionary rule helps to promote this goal.
4. Evaluate whether the exclusionary rule helps to enforce the requirements of the Fourth Amendment, and be able to write a paragraph advocating each position.
5. Identify how derivative evidence is excluded under the fruits of the poisonous tree doctrine, and give an example where the doctrine properly excludes evidence.
6. Comprehend and be able to explain the major exceptions to the exclusionary rule.
7. Understand why, in federal cases, a *Bivens* suit may provide an alternative remedy for some persons wronged by Fourth Amendment search and seizure violations, and articulate why the exclusionary rule does not provide a remedy in this situation.
8. Offer an example of the concept of Fourth Amendment standing, and give a concrete example of a defendant who would not possess standing.

Chapter Outline

1. Introduction to Remedies for Fourth Amendment Violations
2. Violation of the Fourth Amendment and the Exclusion of Evidence
3. The Fourth Amendment: Implementation Prior to 1914
4. The Exclusionary Rule: Enforcing the Fourth Amendment
5. Suppression of Illegally Seized Evidence
6. Basis for the Exclusionary Rule
7. Challenge to the Exclusionary Rule: The Silver Platter Doctrine
8. Application of the Exclusionary Rule to State Criminal Procedure
9. Exclusion of Derivative Evidence
10. Major Exceptions to the Exclusionary Rule
11. Exclusionary Rule Exception: The Independent Source Rule
12. Exclusionary Rule Exception: The Rule of Inevitable Discovery

Key Terms

Bivens remedy
Concept of standing
Derivative evidence
Doctrine of attenuation
Exclusionary rule
Fourth Amendment
Fruit of the poisonous tree doctrine

Good faith exception
Independent source rule
Motion to suppress
Rule of inevitable discovery
Silver platter doctrine
Vicarious standing
Writs of assistance

1. INTRODUCTION TO REMEDIES FOR FOURTH AMENDMENT VIOLATIONS

The Constitution of the United States provides for a democratic form of government, details the basic organization of the government, and guarantees a variety of personal rights to individual persons. The federal government must follow its own rules when it interacts with persons within its jurisdiction. Law-abiding citizens are to be left alone by government agents, and criminals are to be apprehended by law-abiding law enforcement agents. When the law enforcers transgress a law or constitutional provision in their effort to discover, capture, or prosecute suspected violators of criminal laws, the proper approach to confronting one lawbreaker dealing with another lawbreaker poses some interesting questions about the method of adjusting the competing equities. In his dissenting opinion in *Olmstead v. United States,*[1] Justice Brandeis offered a forceful and frequently quoted answer to the proper approach the government should take:

> In a government of laws, existence of the government will be imperilled if it fails to observe the law scrupulously. Our Government is the potent, the omnipresent teacher. For good or for ill, it teaches the whole people by its example. Crime is contagious. If the Government becomes a lawbreaker, it breeds contempt for law; it invites every man to become a law unto himself; it invites anarchy. To declare that in the administration of the criminal law the end justifies the means—to declare that the Government may commit crimes in order to secure the conviction of a private criminal—would bring terrible retribution.

In *Mapp v. Ohio,*[2] Justice Clark echoed the thoughts of Justice Brandeis: "Nothing can destroy a government more quickly than its failure to observe its own laws, or worse, its disregard of the charter of its own existence." Alternatively, should we just look the other way when law enforcement officials violate the law in an effort to promote a greater good? Or should we wonder how a society maintains its moral leadership when its own agents fail to respect and follow the basic law under which society is organized? Should we allow the wronged party to sue the wrongdoing public official?[3] The current approach excludes the evidence illegally obtained and, in effect, places the suspect and the government in the same position, legally and evidentially, that they would have occupied had the government agent not violated the law. The exclusion of illegally seized evidence has some exceptions based on logic, need, and common sense.

2. VIOLATION OF THE FOURTH AMENDMENT AND THE EXCLUSION OF EVIDENCE

Consistent with present judicial construction of the Fourth Amendment, and consistent with the case law interpreting the amendment, evidence that has been illegally seized by either a state or the federal government may be suppressed from prosecutorial introduction in a criminal trial. Suppression of evidence as a remedy for a governmental violation of the Fourth Amendment may seem to be a rather drastic measure, since the accused individual may go free as a result of a police officer's blunder. In essence, one wrongdoer goes free because another wrongdoer has violated the supreme law of the land. Arguably, to allow the use of evidence that has been illegally seized against a person who had a right of privacy concerning that property would mean that the Fourth Amendment has little force and almost no effect and has become close to a nullity. In opposition to this theory of exclusion is the thought that the evidence should be admissible against the accused wrongdoer if the wrongdoer is allowed a remedy of suit against the law enforcement official[4] who had violated the rights of the accused. In the absence of either the exclusion of evidence or the availability of a suit against the offending officer, law enforcement officials might have little incentive to respect the requirements of the Fourth Amendment. The trial exclusion of evidence illegally seized appears to be the Fourth Amendment remedy of choice for the present.

3. THE FOURTH AMENDMENT: IMPLEMENTATION PRIOR TO 1914

Prior to 1914, the Fourth Amendment had faced judicial interpretation and scrutiny in several court cases. Among these was *Boyd v. United States,* decided by the United States Supreme Court in 1886, in which the compulsory production of private papers was in question. Justice Bradley looked to the origin and intent of the Framers of the Fourth Amendment to discern the amendment's meaning and scope.[5] He recalled the lessons of history, which were more recent to him than for us, in which the British government, prior to the American Revolution, had empowered its agents to use general search warrants called writs of assistance. In many of the American colonies, British agents were issued what amounted to blank search warrants that allowed the search of private houses for personal items, personal documents and effects, and other evidence that would be used in court to convict the possessor. The colonists had protested the use of these blanket warrants in a variety of ways but to little or no avail prior to the Revolutionary War. In response to the writs of assistance and other abuses of privacy, the prohibition against unreasonable searches and seizures was grafted into the Constitution in the form of the Bill of Rights so that Americans would not have to fear that the practice of unlimited intrusion into private areas might creep back into national law enforcement practice.

Over the years since 1791, when the Bill of Rights was ratified by the required number of states, federal law enforcement practice has not always complied with what was believed to be dictated by the Fourth Amendment. Initially, there was no particular remedy against federal agents when violations of the Fourth Amendment occurred, except on a case-by-case basis. Where a defendant successfully argued that personal constitutional rights had been violated, he or she might have some modicum of success in having a conviction reversed based on illegal law enforcement activity.[6]

Justice Day, in *Weeks v. United States,* referred to the opinion of Justice Bradley[7] in explaining the original motivation and intent of the Framers of the Fourth Amendment.

> [I]t took its origin in the determination of the framers of the Amendments to the Federal Constitution to provide for that instrument a Bill of Rights, securing to the American people, among other things, those safeguards which had grown up in England to protect the people from unreasonable searches and seizures, such as were permitted under the general warrants issued under authority of the government, by which there had been invasions of the home and privacy of the citizens, and the seizure of their private papers in support of charges, real or imaginary, made against them. Such practices had also received sanction under warrants and seizures under the so-called writs of assistance, issued in the American colonies. *See* 2 Watson, Const. 1414 *et seq.* Resistance to these practices had established the principle which was enacted into the fundamental law in the Fourth Amendment, that a man's house was his castle, and not to be invaded by any general authority to search and seize his goods and papers. *Weeks v. United States,* 232 U.S. 383, 390 (1914)

The Supreme Court in *Boyd v. United States* granted a new trial where the federal government had forced the defendant to provide evidence from his private place of business in the absence of a search warrant. The *Boyd* Court did not fashion a rule of exclusion of evidence illegally seized or procured, but the use of such illegally seized evidence was deemed to create reversible error in Boyd's case. At the time *Boyd* was decided, it appeared that the Court was moving toward developing an exclusion rule that would help to enforce the Fourth Amendment, but it was not, at that time, willing to take such a step.

4. THE EXCLUSIONARY RULE: ENFORCING THE FOURTH AMENDMENT

By 1914, the Court appeared to reconsider the legality of admitting evidence in federal courts where the evidence had been illegally seized. In the case of *Weeks v. United States,* the defendant's personal residence had been entered by local police officers and a United States marshal. Both the police and the federal agent had seized evidence, which they wished to use against Weeks in a criminal gambling case. No warrant was used by any of the law enforcement agents involved in the search for evidence, and Weeks had not been present to grant any consent for the entry. Prior to trial and consistent with the practice at the time, Weeks requested the return of the documents that the federal government sought to use against him. The motion for the return of the evidence was denied, and Weeks was convicted, partly based on evidence illegally taken from his residence.

With his appeal properly before the United States Supreme Court, Weeks contended that the Fourth Amendment to the Constitution prohibited the United States marshal from making the seizure and that his conviction should be reversed. After reviewing some of the history that motivated the adoption of the Fourth Amendment and after looking at the conduct of the federal agent, Justice Day, writing for the *Weeks* Court, stated:

> We therefore reach the conclusion that the letters in question were taken from the house of the accused by an official of the United States, acting under color of his office, in direct violation of the constitutional rights of the defendant; that, having made a seasonable application for their return, which was heard and passed upon by the court, there was involved in the order refusing the application a denial of the constitutional rights of the accused, and that the court should have restored these letters to the accused. In holding them and permitting their use upon the trial, we think prejudicial error was committed. *Weeks v. United States,* 232 U.S. 383, 398 (1914)

The action of the *Weeks* Court had the effect of telling federal law enforcement agents that seizures of evidence made in the future must be in compliance with the Fourth Amendment or the evidence would not be admitted in federal courts. Consistent with the *Weeks* case, if evidence illegally seized by federal agents managed to be admitted in court against defendants whose rights were violated, upon appeal the convictions could be reversed. The ruling applied only to federal law enforcement officials and not to state officials, who were not limited in their conduct by the Fourth Amendment.[8] Interestingly enough, if federal law enforcement officials violated the Fourth Amendment in seizing evidence against a defendant, they could take the evidence to a state prosecutor, who was not limited by the Fourth Amendment, and the evidence could be used for prosecution under state law.[9]

5. SUPPRESSION OF ILLEGALLY SEIZED EVIDENCE

Although the literal language of the Fourth Amendment protects people against unreasonable searches and seizures conducted by government agents, once a violation has occurred, there is no way to reverse the wrong. Since the defendant cannot be restored to the status quo prior to the search, a process that puts the defendant nearly in the same position as he or she would have been but for the illegality would appear to be an appropriate approach. However, since the Fourth Amendment is not self-enforcing, and its text fails to provide any remedy for a governmental violation, the remedy of evidentiary exclusion is the proper procedure to pursue. Cases decided prior to 1914 rarely addressed concerns related to a remedy because the evidence illegally seized was frequently excluded on other constitutional grounds.[10]

Where the government has illegally seized evidence, current practice permits the aggrieved party to file a motion to suppress the evidence from introduction in court against that party or person. Usually the wronged party files a pretrial motion to suppress the evidence with a request to have the property returned to the defendant. A hearing is held to determine whether the defendant has a personal legal basis to complain about a violation of Fourth Amendment rights. A judge must make a determination whether, under the circumstances, the government actually violated the constitutional rights of the defendant and decide the remedy to be applied. If the judge agrees with the defendant, the evidence is ruled inadmissible for use to prove guilt;[11] where the judge believes that no violation occurred, the evidence is admissible unless excluded by the substantive rules of evidence.

6. BASIS FOR THE EXCLUSIONARY RULE

The philosophy underpinning the exclusionary rule is predicated on the belief that if the courts were to permit the use of illegally seized evidence, they would be condoning—and perhaps even become indirect participants in—Fourth Amendment transgressions. To maintain judicial propriety, courts should not sanction Fourth Amendment illegality by allowing prosecutors to introduce the fruits of illegal searches conducted by police agencies. In addition, when the incentive for law enforcement officials to violate the amendment is removed, future illegal seizures should be deterred and reduced. As Justice O'Connor explained the rationale, "The purpose of the Fourth Amendment exclusionary rule is to deter unreasonable searches, no matter how probative their fruits."[12] Although the exclusionary rule may assist an individual defendant's case, the Court has recognized that it is not a personal constitutional right, since it does not redress the injury suffered through the illegal search or seizure and does not place the injured party in the same position as if the illegality had not transpired; the damage to the constitutional right has already occurred.[13]

Although the Fourth Amendment and the exclusionary rule clearly apply to federal criminal practice, the same cannot be said for searches and seizures outside the territorial jurisdiction of the United States. When American agents conduct searches, seizures, and/or arrests in foreign countries, the Fourth Amendment and the exclusionary rule do not prevent the introduction of the evidence against the target in an American courtroom. According to the Court, there is no evidence that the drafters of the Fourth Amendment intended it to have extraterritorial effect or to be applied to foreign nationals or their property in foreign territory.[14]

7. CHALLENGE TO THE EXCLUSIONARY RULE: THE SILVER PLATTER DOCTRINE

The Court designed the exclusionary rule to limit federal law enforcement officials. State and local police, however, remained free to search and seize, and prosecutors continued to use such evidence without any federal limitation. As Justice Blackmun noted,

In *Weeks,* it was held, however, that the Fourth Amendment did not apply to state officers, and, therefore, that material seized unconstitutionally by a state officer could be admitted in a federal criminal proceeding. *United States v. Janis,* 428 U.S. 433, 444 (1976)

In actual practice, state officials conducted searches that would have been considered illegal if carried out by federal officials and then transferred the evidence to federal prosecutors, who did not hesitate to use the evidence. Such evidence was considered admissible in federal courts, since no federal official had violated the Fourth Amendment, and neither the Fourth Amendment nor the exclusionary rule applied to state officials. This practice of evidence transfer, the "silver platter doctrine," was in regular use until the Court struck it down. The Court held that evidence obtained by state law enforcement agents as the result of unreasonable searches and seizures in the absence of the involvement of federal officers must be excluded from evidentiary use against a federal defendant who makes an appropriate objection.[15]

8. APPLICATION OF THE EXCLUSIONARY RULE TO STATE CRIMINAL PROCEDURE

State criminal practice moved to conformity with the federal standard when the *Weeks* exclusionary rule was held to apply to the states in *Mapp v. Ohio* (see Case 3.1).[16] The Court determined that the constitutional guarantees of the Fourth Amendment were incorporated into the Due Process Clause of the Fourteenth Amendment, and thus required state criminal procedure to follow the federal model. With a view toward enforcing the Fourth Amendment, the *Mapp* Court thought it necessary to make the *Weeks*-based exclusionary rule applicable against the states. The net effect of *Mapp* was to make state and federal Fourth Amendment practice subject to the same limitations with respect to search and seizure.

9. EXCLUSION OF DERIVATIVE EVIDENCE

Law enforcement investigations often lead in unusual directions and produce evidence of criminal activity other than that which was originally anticipated. When police follow the path suggested by evidence that has been illegally seized or wrongfully discovered, exploiting that evidence may create admissibility problems for the prosecutor. The Supreme Court expanded the sweep of the exclusionary rule to require suppression of evidence derived from illegally obtained secondary evidence when the prosecutor's plan involved admitting it against one who had an expectation of privacy. As explained by the *Nix* Court:

> The doctrine requiring courts to suppress evidence as the tainted "fruit" of unlawful governmental conduct had its genesis in *Silverthorne Lumber Co. v. United States,* 251 U.S. 385 (1920); there, the Court held that the exclusionary rule applies not only to the illegally obtained evidence itself, but also to other incriminating evidence derived from the primary evidence. *Nix v. Williams,* 467 U.S. 431, 441 (1984)

CASE 3.1

Leading Case Brief: Illegally Seized Evidence Must Be Excluded from Court

Mapp v. Ohio
Supreme Court of the United States
367 U.S. 643 (1961)

Case Facts:

The appellant, Ms. Mapp, was convicted of knowingly having in her possession and under her control some lewd and lascivious books, pictures, and porno-type photographs. The evidence, which aided in her conviction, was taken by police officers, and as the Ohio Supreme Court admitted, was secured during the execution of an illegal search and seizure.

In the early afternoon of May 23, 1957, three policemen arrived at Mapp's home and asked to talk to her, but they would not disclose to her the topic of their inquiry while they remained on the street. In reality, the police had information that a person who had been involved in a recent bombing was present in the home.

Mapp informed the police that she would admit them only if they produced a search warrant, which the officers did not have. The officers kept the home under observation for the next three hours.

After more officers arrived several hours later, the police attempted and effectuated a break-in by smashing the glass to a rear door. When the appellant asked to see a search warrant, an officer waved a piece of paper, purporting to be a search warrant. The arrival of Mapp's attorney did nothing to aid the situation since the police would not allow him to enter the home.

The police search covered her dresser, a chest of drawers, a closet, and other areas of her bedroom. Police looked through her photo album and personal papers. The search continued through the rest of the home. A search of the basement contained the obscene materials that were used to obtain the conviction.

Over proper objection to the illegal search, at Mapp's trial, the prosecution introduced no evidence of a search warrant, and the judge permitted the introduction of the illegally seized evidence. Mapp was convicted.

The Ohio Supreme Court affirmed the conviction with the rationale that the evidence had not been taken by any outrageous process.

Legal Issue:

Should the guarantees of the Fourth Amendment be incorporated into the Due Process Clause of the Fourteenth Amendment, and the federal exclusionary rule of *Weeks v. United States* be extended to prohibit the use of illegally seized evidence in state criminal prosecutions?

The Court's Ruling:

A majority of the justices decided that due process required that the guarantees of the Fourth Amendment should be recognized as included in the Fourteenth Amendment and that evidence seized illegally should not be used in state courts against a person from whom it was taken. The ruling reversed Mapp's conviction.

Essence of the Court's Rationale:

* * *

I

* * *

[I]n *Weeks v. United States,* (1914) 232 U.S. 383, at pages 391–392, [the Court] stated that:

"The Fourth Amendment . . . put the courts of the United States and Federal officials, in the exercise of their power and authority, under limitations and restraints [and] . . . forever secure[d] the people, their persons, houses, papers, and effects, against all unreasonable searches and seizures under the guise of law . . . and the duty of giving to it force and effect is obligatory upon all entrusted under our Federal system with the enforcement of the laws."

Specifically dealing with the use of the evidence unconstitutionally seized, the Court concluded:

> "If letters and private documents can thus be seized and held and used in evidence against a citizen accused of an offense, the protection of the Fourth Amendment declaring his right to be secure against such searches and seizures is of no value, and, so far as those thus placed are concerned, might as well be stricken from the Constitution. . . ."

Finally, the Court in that case [*Weeks*] clearly stated that the use of the seized evidence involved "a denial of the constitutional rights of the accused."

* * *

This Court has ever since required of federal law officers a strict adherence to that command which this Court has held to be a clear, specific, and constitutionally required—even if judicially implied—deterrent safeguard without insistence upon which the Fourth Amendment would have been reduced to "a form of words."

* * *

While in 1949, prior to the *Wolf* case, almost two-thirds of the States were opposed to the use of the exclusionary rule, now despite the *Wolf* case, more than half of those since passing upon it . . . have . . . adopted or adhere to the *Weeks* rule. [Citations omitted.] Significantly, among those now following the rule is California, which, according to its highest court, was "compelled to reach that conclusion because other remedies have completely failed to secure compliance with the constitutional provision. . . ." *People v. Cahan,* 1955, 44 Cal.2d 434, 445, 282 P.2d 905. In connection with this California case, we note that the second basis elaborated in *Wolf* in support of its failure to enforce the exclusionary rule against the States was that "other means of protection" have been afforded the right of privacy (partially protected by the Fourth and Fourteenth Amendments). 338 U.S., at page 30.

The experience of California that other remedies have been worthless and futile is buttressed by the experience of other States. The obvious futility of relegating the Fourth Amendment to the protection of other remedies has, moreover, been recognized by this Court since *Wolf.* See *Irvine v. California,* 347 U.S. 128, 137 (1954).

* * *

[The Court incorporated the Fourth Amendment into the Due Process Clause of the Fourteenth Amendment and adopted the exclusionary rule of the *Weeks* case to enforce it.]

* * *

IV

Since the Fourth Amendment's right of privacy has been declared enforceable against the States through the Due Process Clause of the Fourteenth, it is enforceable against them by the same sanction of exclusion as is used against the Federal Government.

* * *

Having once recognized that the right of privacy embodied in the Fourth Amendment is enforceable against the States, and that the right to be secure against rude invasions by state officers, is therefore, constitutional in origin, we can no longer permit that right to remain an empty promise. . . . Our decision . . . gives to the individual no more than that which the Constitution guarantees him, to the police officer no less than that to which honest law enforcement is entitled, and, to the courts, that judicial integrity so necessary in the true administration of justice.

The judgment of the Supreme Court of Ohio is reversed and the cause remanded for further proceedings not inconsistent with this opinion.

Case Importance:

Following the *Mapp* decision, any person whose right to privacy under the Fourth Amendment has been violated by a police official may exclude from court consideration any evidence that has been seized due to the illegality of the officer's conduct if the evidence is to be used against that person. The potential incentive for police to violate the Fourth Amendment has been eliminated.

In *Wong Sun v. United States,*[17] the Court reaffirmed the principle of tainted derivative evidence exclusion when it voted to exclude evidence that law enforcement officials had obtained by exploiting an initial Fourth Amendment violation (see Case 3.2). Officers were led to a secondary evidence location by evidence that originally was illegally discovered. The Court held that the evidence in the second location would never have been discovered "but for" the agent's initial violation of the defendant's rights under the Fourth Amendment. The *Wong Sun* "fruit of the poisonous tree doctrine" permits a defendant to exclude evidence seized from locations where the defendant possessed no constitutional expectation of privacy.

In *Wong Sun,* police illegally entered a defendant's residence in the absence of probable cause and without a warrant of any kind. No incriminating physical evidence surfaced from that original search. However, the defendant gave oral evidence that implicated a second defendant and produced narcotic drugs from the home of the second defendant. The second defendant gave oral evidence and possessed drugs that implicated the first defendant in drug use and possession. Ultimately, the *Wong Sun* Court held that the first defendant could suppress evidence taken from a search of the second defendant's home, since the original illegality at the first defendant's home led to the discovery of the contraband at the second location. At first blush, this may appear to do violence to the Court's oft-repeated principle that Fourth Amendment rights are personal and cannot be asserted vicariously. Upon closer scrutiny, the evidence in *Wong Sun* was discovered by exploiting the original illegal entry to the defendant's home. But for the original illegality, no evidence against the first defendant would have been discovered.

The result of expanding the *Mapp* holding in *Wong Sun* to exclude derivative evidence from use in court to prove guilt served to enhance respect for the Fourth Amendment by removing more of the incentive to conduct illegal searches and seizures. Following *Wong Sun,* both evidence illegally seized and evidence discovered by virtue of exploiting information learned from an illegal entry are not acceptable in court if offered against one whose rights were initially violated.

10. MAJOR EXCEPTIONS TO THE EXCLUSIONARY RULE

Although supportive of defendant rights, the "fruit of the poisonous tree doctrine" derived from *Wong Sun v. United States*[18] has not seen complete favor with subsequent justices on the Supreme Court. Over the years since *Wong Sun,* the Court has recognized three legal theories that limit the exclusionary effect. The independent source rule of *Segura v. United States*[19] and of *Murray v. United States,*[20] the rule of inevitable discovery demonstrated by *Nix v. Williams,*[21] and the doctrine of attenuation described in *Wong Sun* all permit prosecutorial use of evidence illegally seized. In these exceptional situations, the justices of the Supreme Court believed strict application of the exclusionary rule would not have significantly altered the conduct or practice of law enforcement officials because the deterrent effect on police operations was viewed as marginal or nonexistent. Where there is an absence of, or a limited, deterrent effect, the rationale of the exclusionary rule is not enhanced, and courts generally refuse to suppress the evidence.

CASE 3.2

Leading Case Brief: Evidence Derivative of Illegally Obtained Evidence Must Be Excluded

Wong Sun v.
United States
Supreme Court of the United States
371 U.S. 471 (1963)

Case Facts:

James Toy and Wong Sun, a.k.a. "Sea Dog," were convicted in the Federal District Court for the Northern District of California for the knowing transportation and concealment of illegally imported heroin.

Following several weeks of surveillance of Hom Way, police arrested him and uncovered heroin in his personal possession. Hom Way told the officers that he recently purchased the drug from "Blackie Toy," who lived on Leavenworth Street in San Francisco. Police cruised the thirty-block length of the street until they discovered "Oye's Laundry" at six in the morning.

After denying entry to plainclothes officers who had appeared and requested possession of their non-existent laundry, Toy slammed the door and fled to the rear of the laundry/home. The federal narcotics agents followed Toy into his home against his will and cornered him in his bedroom. Immediately prior to Toy's flight, the officers had identified themselves as federal agents. The bedroom at the rear of the laundry was subjected to a warrantless search, and Toy was subjected to a similar search and arrest.

While the search produced no evidence of illegality, Toy promptly denied that he had any narcotics but implicated one "Johnny." Toy dutifully led the officers to the home of Johnny Yee and told the agents that they had smoked heroin the previous night.

A warrantless entry of Johnny Yee's place of residence produced less than an ounce of heroin. Just as Toy was willing to talk, so was Yee. Johnny Yee implicated Toy in heroin possession and Wong Sun as his supplier. A subsequent search of Wong Sun's residence uncovered no additional heroin.

Petitioners James Toy and Johnny Yee were arraigned almost immediately and released the same

day. Wong Sun secured his release a day later. Several days later, Toy, Yee, and Wong Sun appeared at the police station and voluntarily submitted to interrogation by agents, who prepared a statement summarizing the information obtained from each. Each man offered what amounted to a confession of guilt. Neither Toy nor Wong Sun would sign the statements, but Wong Sun admitted the accuracy of his statement.

At the trial, Johnny Yee, who was to be a government witness, did not testify. The government offered in evidence Toy's initial statements, the heroin found at Yee's home, Toy's unsigned statement, and Wong Sun's unsigned statement. Toy alleged that his initial statements and all the evidence that was derived from the illegal searches should be excluded from evidence because of the Fourth Amendment violation that occurred as his home was illegally entered. The District Court rejected his argument and allowed the admission of the evidence that led to the conviction of Toy and Wong Sun.

The Court of Appeals affirmed, and the Supreme Court granted certiorari.

Legal Issue:

Where evidence has been seized in violation of an individual's rights under the Fourth Amendment, must that evidence and any derivative evidence be excluded from the prosecutor's use for purposes of proving guilt?

The Court's Ruling:

Original evidence that has been illegally seized is excludable under the *Mapp* exclusionary rule, and derivative evidence obtained by exploiting illegally

(continued)

seized evidence may be excluded if offered against the person whose constitutional rights were originally violated by governmental agents.

Essence of the Court's Rationale:

* * *

We believe that significant differences between the cases of the two petitioners require separate discussion of each. We shall first consider the case of petitioner Toy.

I

The Court of Appeals found there was neither reasonable grounds nor probable cause for Toy's arrest. . . . It is basic that an arrest with or without a warrant must stand upon firmer ground than mere suspicion, though the arresting officer need not have in hand evidence which would suffice to convict. The quantum of information which constitutes probable cause—evidence which would "warrant a man of reasonable caution in the belief" that a felony has been committed [citation omitted]—must be measured by the facts of the particular case.

* * *

The threshold question in this case, therefore, is whether the officers could, on the information which impelled them to act, have procured a warrant for the arrest of Toy. We think that no warrant would have issued on evidence then available.

* * *

Thus we conclude that the Court of Appeals' findings that the officers' uninvited entry into Toy's living quarters was unlawful and that the bedroom arrest which followed was likewise unlawful, was fully justified on the evidence. It remains to be seen what consequences flow from this conclusion.

II

It is conceded that Toy's declarations in his bedroom are to be excluded if they are held to be "fruits" of the agents' unlawful action.

* * *

The exclusionary rule has traditionally barred from trial physical, tangible materials obtained either during or as a direct result of an unlawful invasion. It follows from our holding in *Silverman v. United States,* 365 U.S. 505, that the Fourth Amendment may protect against the overhearing of verbal statements as well as against the more traditional seizure of "papers and effects." Similarly, testimony as to matters observed during an unlawful invasion has been excluded in order to enforce the basic constitutional policies. . . .

* * *

The government argues that Toy's statements to the officers in his bedroom, although closely consequent upon the invasion which we hold unlawful, were nevertheless admissible because they resulted from "an intervening independent act of a free will." This contention, however, takes insufficient account of the circumstances. Six or seven officers had broken the door and followed on Toy's heels into the bedroom where his wife and child were sleeping. He had been almost immediately handcuffed and arrested. Under such circumstances it is unreasonable to infer that Toy's response was sufficiently an act of free will to purge the primary taint of the unlawful invasion.

The Government also contends that Toy's declarations should be admissible because they were ostensibly exculpatory, rather than incriminating. There are two answers to this argument. First, the statements soon turned out to be incriminating . . . Second, when circumstances are shown such as those which induced these declarations, it is immaterial whether the declarations be termed "exculpatory." [Footnote omitted.] Thus, we find no substantial reason to omit Toy's declarations from the protection of the exclusionary rule.

III

We now consider whether the exclusion of Toy's declarations requires also the exclusion of the narcotics taken from Yee, to which those declarations led the police. The prosecutor candidly told the trial court that "we wouldn't have found those drugs except that Mr. Toy helped us to." . . . We need not hold that all evidence is "fruit of the poisonous tree" simply because it would not have come to light but for the illegal actions of the police. Rather, the more apt question in such a case is

whether, granting establishment of the primary illegality, the evidence to which instant objection is made has been come at by exploitation of that illegality or instead by means sufficiently distinguishable to be purged of the primary taint. Maguire, *Evidence of Guilt,* 221 (1959).

We think it clear that the narcotics were "come at by the exploitation of that illegality" and hence that they may not be used against Toy.

IV

It remains only to consider Toy's unsigned statement. We need not decide whether, in light of the fact that Toy was free on his own recognizance when he made the statement, that statement was a fruit of the illegal arrest. [Citation omitted.] Since we have concluded that his declarations in the bedroom and the narcotics surrendered by Yee should not have been admitted in evidence against him, the only proofs remaining to sustain his conviction are his and Wong Sun's unsigned statements. . . .

It is a settled principle of the administration of criminal justice in the federal courts that a conviction must rest upon firmer ground than the uncorroborated admission or confession of the accused.

* * *

The import of our previous holdings is that a co-conspirator's hearsay statements may be admitted against the accused for no purpose whatever, unless made during and in furtherance of the conspiracy. Thus, as to Toy, the only possible source of corroboration is removed and his conviction must be set aside for lack of competent evidence to support it.

V

[The Court found that Wong Sun's statement could not be used to corroborate Toy's police statement. Toy's statement could not corroborate Wong Sun's statement because neither statement was made during the existence of their drug conspiracy. The only corroboration of the drug conspiracy that could be used against Wong Sun was the heroin at Toy's place and Yee's words.]

We therefore hold that petitioner Wong Sun is also entitled to a new trial. [Jimmy Toy received a new trial because there remained no admissible evidence against him.]

Case Importance:

By excluding evidence that is derivative of original Fourth Amendment illegality, the Court ensured greater respect for the Fourth Amendment and has removed most additional incentive to conduct illegal searches and seizures because once an original illegality has occurred, downstream evidence is tainted and not usable to prove guilt.

11. EXCLUSIONARY RULE EXCEPTION: THE INDEPENDENT SOURCE RULE

Where police have run afoul of the Fourth Amendment but an alternative or parallel, but legal, method of discovery of evidence exists, courts generally do not exclude the evidence.[22] The independent source rule allows trial court introduction of evidence obtained or discovered during, or as a consequence of, an illegal search and seizure, so long as the evidence was later obtained independently from proper law enforcement activity untainted by the initial illegality. In *Murray v. United States,*[23] law enforcement officials conducted an illegal search that produced evidence of criminal activities. While federal narcotics officers conducted surveillance on a warehouse that was believed to be the site of significant drug activity, they observed Murray and others driving vehicles into the warehouse and later out of it. When the vehicles and the target, Murray, later left, the agents peered into the warehouse and observed a tractor-trailer rig with a large dark container inside. Several agents illegally forced their way into the warehouse and observed, in plain view, numerous burlap-wrapped bales. Although subsequent illegal searches of the vehicles revealed quantities of marijuana, the officers left the warehouse without disturbing the contents and did not return until they possessed a search warrant

In the *Murray* case, evidence sufficient to prove probable cause to search existed before the illegal entry and illegal search and came from lawful sources. Since the illegally obtained information was not used as part of the foundation for probable cause and was not included on the affidavit for a search warrant, the Supreme Court approved the subsequent warrant-based search that resulted in various drug seizures and did not invalidate the warrant on Fourth Amendment grounds. In this case, the Court approved the execution of the search warrant because the basis for the probable cause on the warrant came from an independent and lawful source, untainted by the officer's violation of Murray's Fourth Amendment rights.

In an earlier case than *Murray, Segura v. United States,*[24] the Supreme Court approved the admissibility of evidence derived from an independent source. *Segura* involved police officers who entered a private apartment and conducted a protective sweep after an arrest of one of the occupants. No warrant or other exception allowed the entry into the premises. In the process of conducting the sweep, the officers observed, in plain view, various drug paraphernalia. Two officers remained in the apartment awaiting a warrant being procured by others, but, because of various delays, the search warrant was not issued until some nineteen hours after the initial incursion.

In executing the search warrant, the agents discovered additional drugs and records of narcotics transactions. These items were seized, together with those observed during the security check. The trial court suppressed all the evidence, and the court of appeals held that the evidence discovered in plain view on the initial entry must be suppressed, but the evidence seized during the execution of the warrant-based search should have been admitted. The court of appeals agreed with the federal trial court that the initial warrantless entry and the limited security sweep were not justified by exigent circumstances and were therefore illegal.

The Supreme Court of the United States reversed on the theory that some of the drug evidence would have eventually been seized in a lawful manner. The *Segura* Court held the opinion that the drugs and other items not observed during the initial entry but first discovered by the agents the day after the first entry, under an admittedly valid search warrant, should have been admitted because an independent source for probable cause existed. According to Chief Justice Burger:

> None of the information on which the warrant was secured was derived from or related in any way to the initial entry into petitioners' apartment; the information came from sources wholly unconnected with the entry, and was known to the agents well before the initial entry. No information obtained during the initial entry or occupation of the apartment was needed or used by the agents to secure the warrant. It is therefore beyond dispute that the information possessed by the agents before they entered the apartment constituted an independent source for the discovery and seizure of the evidence now challenged. *Segura* at 814 (1984).

So long as sufficient untainted evidence supports the existence of probable cause, warrants obtained in situations where the government has committed illegal activities will not result in the fruits of the searches being suppressed. In essence, where the evidence observed during an initial illegal search has not been used to produce probable cause to issue a warrant, and separate information proves that probable cause can be established by an independent source untainted by any illegality, courts generally uphold the validity of warrants so issued. The independent source rule may be applied where police possess two avenues or sources of obtaining evidence, one of which is illegal and the other legal. Where the two avenues are not connected, the evidence may be deemed to have an independent source and should be ruled as admissible. Therefore, there is no reason to exclude evidence that has a lawful and independent source because law enforcement officials followed a lawful method of discovery.

12. EXCLUSIONARY RULE EXCEPTION: THE RULE OF INEVITABLE DISCOVERY

Courts have recognized an additional exception to the *Mapp* exclusionary rule and the *Wong Sun* fruits of the poisonous tree doctrine, the "rule of inevitable discovery." Under this theory, where law enforcement officers find evidence through illegal means but would have discovered the same evidence through legal means, the evidence should not be excluded from use at trial. In a situation involving a clear case of inevitable discovery, the police would have lawfully obtained the evidence if no illegality had taken place, and to exclude the evidence would place the police and prosecution in a worse position than if no Fourth Amendment transgression occurred.

In the *Nix* case, information needed to find a murder victim's body was given to police by virtue of a violation of the *Miranda* principles. Probable cause to arrest Williams existed, and police took him into custody prior to transporting him back to the area where a homicide had occurred. Police were supposed to respect Williams' desire not to talk with police and had agreed with his attorney not to talk to him. While Williams was on the way back, other police officers had initiated a search for the victim's body by placing farmland in a grid pattern, searching and clearing each grid before advancing to the next parcel. The offender had placed the victim's body within one of the grids that police had yet to search. At the same time, by violating the principles of *Miranda,* the transporting officers managed to have Williams tell them the location of the body. Normally, such evidence would be excluded from court use as a *Miranda* violation. Under the circumstances of the ground search, police or other searchers would have eventually discovered the victim's body fairly soon because of the grid search plan under way. To use the theory of inevitable discovery as an exception to the rule of exclusion, the government must show that the contested evidence actually would have been discovered within a reasonable time. According to the Court in *Nix v. Williams,* 467 U.S. 431 (1984), "Exclusion of physical evidence that would inevitably have been discovered adds nothing to either the integrity or fairness of a criminal trial" and should be admitted against a defendant. Although the *Nix* decision focused on a violation of the Sixth Amendment right to counsel and the related violation of the requirements of *Miranda v. Arizona,* 384 U.S. 436 (1966), the principle of inevitable discovery is fairly applicable whenever government agents obtain evidence in violation of the defendant's constitutional rights that has a second and lawful source involving inevitable discovery.

In a clear demonstration of the rule of inevitable discovery in actual practice, police arrested a woman after observing her performing an oral sex act for money in a public place. Subsequent to the arrest, police officers retrieved the woman's purse from the vehicle of her customer and subjected it to a warrantless search, which revealed a crack cocaine pipe that contained some residue. The trial court ordered the suppression of the evidence taken from the purse, since there was no probable cause to search the person for evidence that she had performed a sexual act, and no exigent circumstances were present to justify the intrusion. The trial court rejected the rule of inevitable discovery on the theory that the cocaine evidence was not derivative but was direct evidence to which the rule of inevitable discovery should not be applied. The court of appeals reversed the trial court decision, on the grounds that the pipe inevitably would have been discovered on the woman during routine booking procedures at the local jail. While the trial court was correct that a search of the purse was not based on probable cause, the search could have been justified as being incident to a lawful arrest or under the inventory search theory, either of which would have permitted the introduction of the evidence under the rule of inevitable discovery.[25]

Another example of the rule of inevitable discovery demonstrates that evidence that would have been obtained eventually and lawfully should be admitted as an exception to the exclusionary rule. In a recent Georgia homicide case, police were called to a motel room where a woman was observed through a room window bound and motionless on a bed. Since there might have been a possibility of saving her, the manager let police into the room, where it was determined that the woman was deceased. The problem arose when an evidence technician crime scene investigator took blood sample swabs from the motel room prior to the obtaining of a search warrant. The trial court decision, affirmed upon appeal, permitted the use of the blood swab evidence because a search warrant for the motel room would have been obtained and the blood evidence inevitably obtained lawfully. As the Supreme Court of Georgia explained, "The ultimate or inevitable discovery doctrine allows admission of evidence that was discovered as a result of police error or misconduct if the State establishes by a preponderance of the evidence that the information ultimately or inevitably would have been discovered by lawful means, without reference to the police error or misconduct."[26]

13. EXCLUSIONARY RULE EXCEPTION: THE DOCTRINE OF ATTENUATION

Another aspect of *Wong Sun v. United States* involved the doctrine of attenuation, which seemed to have its genesis in *Nardone v. United States*.[27] Under this doctrine, where the evidence has been illegally seized, the prosecution may argue that although the evidence was obtained in violation of the Constitution, it has been "purged" of its taint because sufficient time and/or events have transpired since the search or discovery. As the Court explained in *United States v. Crews:*

> In the typical "fruit of the poisonous tree" case, however, the challenged evidence was acquired by the police after some initial Fourth Amendment violation, and the question before the court is whether the chain of causation proceeding from the unlawful conduct has become so attenuated or has been interrupted by some intervening circumstance so as to remove the "taint" imposed upon that evidence by the original illegality. 445 U.S. 463, 471 (1980)

In *Wong Sun,* two of the defendants returned following pretrial release to attempt to make a plea bargain with the police.[28] Several days had passed since the illegal searches and seizures; thus, the defendants had had sufficient time to independently assess the merits of confessing to the police. Wong Sun had been released on his own recognizance subsequent to his arraignment and had returned to speak with police voluntarily several days later to make the virtual confession. The *Wong Sun* Court held that the obtaining of the confession evidence was sufficiently separated (attenuated) from the illegality of the original police conduct as to not have been prompted or intimately influenced by the earlier illegal search and was, therefore, not excludable on Fourth Amendment grounds.[29]

In a more recent case,[30] following the same legal theory on attenuation, police took a man into custody on the complaint of a mother who echoed a complaint of her young son that the suspect had improperly sexually touched the small child. Police had not interviewed the child and had conducted no additional investigation before to taking the suspect to the local lockup. Although police lacked probable cause to arrest at the time they took custody of the suspect, he was not aware that his arrest was illegal and lacked probable cause. During a long period of interrogation, lasting off and on for twenty hours, the suspect made three incriminating statements that the trial court determined were admissible in court. The evidence ruling caused the defendant to plead guilty to the sexual charges, reserving his right to contest the admission of his confession-like statements. Over the government's argument that the illegal arrest was sufficiently separated or attenuated from the confession evidence, the Court of Appeals for the Sixth Circuit rejected the contention that there were intervening events that broke the connection between the illegal arrest and the defendant's statement. Despite the fact that the arrestee signed two *Miranda* waivers while he was in custody illegally, making the confessions voluntary, a *Miranda* waiver is not an event that would prove attenuation or separation from the illegal arrest. The appeals court rejected the prosecution's argument that the passage of time in custody separated the illegal arrest from the confession-like statements. In addtition, the government argued that during the time the defendant had been in custody, other officers developed new evidence that would have produced probable cause to arrest the defendant. However, neither the defendant nor the interrogating officers were aware of these facts. The reviewing court held that the "post-arrest discovery of new evidence simply cannot, under the circumstances presented here, constitute an intervening circumstance that would break the causal connection between the illegal arrest and the subsequent confessions, particularly given that neither [the defendant] nor his interrogators knew about the alleged new evidence." The Court of Appeals noted that:

> Supreme Court precedent is clear: A confession "obtained by exploitation of an illegal arrest" may not be used against a criminal defendant, *Brown v. Illinois,* 422 U.S. 590, 603, 95 S. Ct. 2254, 45 L. Ed. 2d 416 (1975), unless such confession results from "an intervening independent act of a free will" sufficient to purge the primary taint of the unlawful invasion. *Wong Sun v. United States,* 371 U.S. 471, 486, 83 S. Ct. 407, 9 L. Ed. 2d 441 (1963) (internal quotation marks and citation omitted).[31]

To permit illegally obtained evidence to be introduced under the doctrine of attenuation, a strong event or situation or a sufficient separation of time and event must have intervened that has a great force and effect to break the causation chain that originally existed between the government's illegal conduct and the defendant's act of offering of incriminating evidence.

14. EXCLUSIONARY RULE EXCEPTION: THE GOOD FAITH EXCEPTION

Where police officers act in objective good faith in following the directives of a warrant, the Court has recognized the desirability of an exception to the application of the exclusionary rule. In the companion cases of *United States v. Leon*[32] and *Massachusetts v. Sheppard,*[33] the Court adopted the "good faith" exception to the exclusionary rule. The two cases involved errors made by judges in issuing legally defective search warrants wherein the mistakes were not readily apparent to police officers. Proper procedure had been followed by the officers, who were not in a position to question the legality of the warrants issued by the judicial officials. In both cases, the officers executing the warrants acted in objective good faith. Since the purpose of the exclusionary rule was to deter illegal police conduct and not to alter judicial behavior, where police act in "good faith," the exclusionary rule cannot have its deterrent effect. In situations where the rationale of the rule is not enhanced, the reason for the remedy of exclusion disappears, and the evidence should be admitted to court. Secondarily, the Court noted that there was no evidence to suggest that the judges or magistrates ignored or attempted to subvert the Fourth Amendment. The Court could perceive no basis for believing that evidence excluded pursuant to a defective warrant would have a significant deterrent effect on judicial officials. In essence, the Court held that since the exclusionary rule was originally designed to alter police conduct, courts should not use it to punish the errors of judges and magistrates.

As a general rule, courts that follow the good faith exception to the exclusionary rule do not apply it where the magistrate or judge who issued the search warrant was misled by the police officers who made the warrant application, where the judge abandoned the judicial function and clearly failed to follow the law, where the recitation of probable cause warranted no reasonable belief in probable cause, and where the warrant appeared so facially deficient that no reasonable officer could presume it was valid.[34] A federal court of appeals upheld a trial court determination that applied the good faith exception to the exclusionary rule where the court concluded that police officers had operated in good faith. In making an investigation of a crack lab, police had conducted surveillance of a crack producer, pulled his trash from a multifamily apartment, found cocaine residue in the trash, and talked to persons who stated that the subject was "cooking up" quantities of crack. In addition, police investigated the subject's prior criminal history, which showed earlier drug convictions. The defendant contended that the officer involved in the task force should have known of the deficiencies in the affidavit, since he had been so instrumental in procuring the warrant. The trash pulls were not clearly linked to the defendant, and some of the information was stale, but the court concluded that, even though probable cause did not exist, police reliance on the warrant was objectively reasonable because the affidavit was not so lacking in indicators of probable cause that it would suggest that the officer's belief in the validity of the warrant was unreasonable. The court of appeals affirmed the trial court decision allowing the admission of the evidence; it noted that two confidential sources were used and independently corroborated, and the detective tried to obtain sufficient evidence to produce current probable cause to search. The court of appeals held that a reasonable officer would have believed that when the judge issued the particular search warrant under these facts, it was a valid warrant.[35]

In a slightly different type of case, the good faith exception has been applied to permit property forfeiture where real property had been used to grow marijuana. Under the law as it existed, police appropriately scanned the defendant's home with an infrared scanner and discovered a distinctive heat pattern consistent with cannabis cultivation. The officers used this information to procure a search warrant, the execution of which revealed a marijuana horticulture operation within the home. Subsequent to the search, the Supreme Court decided *Kyllo v. United States,* 533 U.S. 27 (2001), which held that thermal scanning of a private home by police without a warrant constituted an unreasonable search. Since the original search was reasonably believed to be legal but was later declared illegal under the Fourth Amendment in *Kyllo,* the police could not have anticipated how the Supreme Court would rule. When the federal government wanted to receive the house in a civil forfeiture action, the defendant contended that the prosecutor should not be permitted to introduce evidence of drug operations, since the government obtained the knowledge of cultivation by an illegal search. The court of appeals held that the good faith of the officers in conducting the original thermal imaging search operated to allow the introduction of the marijuana-growing operation, which supported a forfeiture of the home to the federal government.[36]

15. LIMITATIONS ON THE EXCLUSIONARY RULE: PAROLE REVOCATION HEARINGS

Evidence illegally seized under the Fourth Amendment does not have to be excluded from every legal proceeding. In parole revocation hearings, the rule of exclusion has no application because its use would be incompatible with such hearings' traditionally nonadversarial posture. Additionally, the application of the rule of exclusion would produce only incremental extra deterrence on law enforcement officials. In *Pennsylvania v. Scott,*[37] evidence of weapons possession had been seized from the parolee's home by parole officers, who conducted a warrantless raid. The search of the home followed receipt of information that indicated that Scott had been in violation of conditions of his parole. During a parole revocation hearing, Scott complained that his rights had been violated by a warrantless search of his home, and he objected to the introduction of weapon evidence on the theory that the search transgressed Fourth Amendment requirements. In rejecting Scott's complaint, Justice Thomas noted that the exclusionary rule was not mandated by the Constitution and that it should be applied only where the deterrence benefits outweighed the costs to society that the rule exacted when applied.[38] According to Justice Thomas, parole revocation hearings did not meet the test for applying the rule. As he noted in *Scott:*

> The deterrence benefits of the exclusionary rule would not outweigh these costs. As the Supreme Court of Pennsylvania recognized, application of the exclusionary rule to parole revocation proceedings would have little deterrent effect upon an officer who is unaware that the subject of his search is a parolee. In that situation, the officer will likely be searching for evidence of criminal conduct with an eye toward the introduction of the evidence at a criminal trial. The likelihood that illegally obtained evidence will be excluded from trial provides deterrence against Fourth Amendment violations, and the remote possibility that the subject is a parolee and that the evidence may be admitted at a parole revocation proceeding surely has little, if any, effect on the officer's incentives. 524 U.S. 357, 367 (1998)

Justice Thomas' opinion reflected the philosophy of refusing to apply the exclusionary rule where its deterrent effects appear almost nonexistent. Minimal deterrent effect on officer conduct should exist in any case where the searched individual was not known to be a parolee by the law enforcement agent. The officer would most likely follow the Fourth Amendment, since he or she would want to produce a prosecutable case. In the *Scott* parole revocation situation, however, the parole officers searched the residence of Scott with full knowledge that there was no warrant and probably believed that he could make no official complaint. The sole deterrent effect in *Scott* would come from compliance with the rules under which parole officers operated.

16. LIMITATIONS ON THE EXCLUSIONARY RULE: OTHER CONTEXTS

The Supreme Court has held that the exclusionary rule does not have to be applied in situations where its deterrent value would have little or no significant effect. As Justice O'Connor stated, "Where the rule's deterrent effect is likely to be marginal, or where its application offends other values central to our system of constitutional governance or the judicial process, we have declined to extend the rule to that context."[39] The application of the exclusionary rule is excused where a police officer reasonably relied on a warrant to search and the warrant was later ruled invalid for reasons unrelated to law enforcement.[40] Courts do not have to apply the rule when a defendant attempts to assert a third party's Fourth Amendment rights in an effort to exclude evidence that did not violate the defendant's constitutional rights.[41] In a case where a police officer relied on a statute that purported to give rights to search which were later deemed unconstitutional, the fruits of the search did not have to be excluded, since the officer had reasonably relied upon the constitutionality of the statute.[42] A party to a criminal case may use evidence illegally obtained to impeach a defendant without inviting application of the exclusionary rule.[43] As Justice Brennan phrased the principle, "The impeachment exception to the exclusionary rule permits the prosecution in a criminal proceeding to introduce illegally obtained evidence to impeach the defendant's own testimony."[44] In a similar vein, the Fourth Amendment's exclusionary rule does not mandate suppression of evidence seized in the absence of probable cause where the erroneous finding of probable cause resulted from clerical errors of court employees.[45] The Court rejected an invitation to apply the Fourth Amendment and its exclusionary rule in a manner that would exclude grand jury consideration of testimony based on illegally seized evidence.[46]

17. ALTERNATIVE REMEDIES TO FOURTH AMENDMENT VIOLATIONS: THE *BIVENS* CIVIL SUIT

Where an individual has been subjected to an illegal search and seizure and that person is to be tried for a criminal offense, the exclusionary rule offers a remedy that attempts to put the aggrieved individual in a similar situation as he or she would have been in, had the illegal search not occurred. However, the exclusionary rule offers no remedy to an individual who has been allegedly a victim of an illegal search and/or seizure but is not a defendant in a criminal case. Because there is no evidence to suppress and no criminal case to be tried, the aggrieved individual must look to other avenues for redress.

In *Bivens v. Six Unknown Named Agents,*[47] employees of the Federal Bureau of Narcotics entered Bivens' apartment without a warrant, in the absence of probable cause, and without the use of any recognized exception under the Fourth Amendment. The federal officers arrested Bivens for alleged narcotics violations that were without foundation. The agents manacled the petitioner in front of his wife and children, threatened to arrest the entire family, and completely searched the apartment. When no criminal case had been brought against him for a period of time, Bivens brought suit for damages in federal court, alleging that the illegal search and seizure caused him mental suffering, humiliation, and embarrassment. The legal difficulty with Mr. Bivens' suit was that federal law did not give him a clear cause of action against the agents. Ultimately, this case reached the Supreme Court of United States, which judicially created a cause of action that allowed the suit to proceed. According to Justice Brennan, part of the rationale for allowing a suit against the officers for damages for legal wrongs was not an unusual theory.

> That damages may be obtained for injuries consequent upon a violation of the Fourth Amendment by federal officials should hardly seem a surprising proposition. Historically, damages have been regarded as the ordinary remedy for an invasion of personal interests in liberty. *Bivens* at 395.

Following the *Bivens* case,[48] individuals against whom federal agents have conducted illegal searches and seizures possess a remedy in federal court to sue for damages based on violation of the Fourth Amendment. Thus, where the exclusionary rule offers no legal remedy for alleged federal government misconduct, a direct suit against the officers may be the only remedy available. In a recent case, a federal prisoner attempted to sue various employees of the federal Bureau of Prisons for personal injuries that he alleged were ultimately caused by the acts or omissions of prison officials. In a tactical move, the plaintiff dropped the allegation against the officers in their individual capacities and sued them in their official capacities. The court of appeal approved the prejudicial dismissal of the *Bivens* suit on the theory that the individual officers could be subject to a suit under the *Bivens* theory, but that they could not be sued in their official capacities because the United States had sovereign immunity with respect to the *Bivens* claims.[49] *Bivens* suits can prove to be complicated to bring and even more difficult to win on the merits.

18. LIMITS TO USE OF THE EXCLUSIONARY RULE: THE CONCEPT OF STANDING

Any person who wishes to suppress evidence alleged to have been illegally seized in violation of the Fourth Amendment must demonstrate that the government violated some personal expectation of privacy. As Justice Kennedy explained the concept, "Fourth Amendment rights are personal, and when a person objects to the search of a place and invokes the exclusionary rule, he or she must have the requisite connection to that place."[50] In another case, the Supreme Court noted, "It has long been the rule that a defendant can urge the suppression of evidence obtained in violation of the Fourth Amendment only if that defendant demonstrates that his Fourth Amendment rights were violated by the challenged search or seizure."[51] The right of privacy may be demonstrated by proof that the defendant had a possessory interest in the searched property, that the accused was legally occupying the premises, or that proof of possession of the seized evidence was crucial to proof of guilt. The government must have seized the evidence from a place where the defendant personally had a right to privacy that society generally recognizes as reasonable. Only where the government seeks to use the evidence against the one asserting the privacy right does that individual have standing to suppress the evidence. Having standing does not ensure suppression of the evidence, however; it only allows that individual the opportunity to argue that the evidence should be excluded based on a violation of the Fourth Amendment. Assuming proof of standing can successfully be made, a trial court will permit a defendant to argue that her or his personal Fourth Amendment rights were violated, but the right to argue does not ensure success in suppressing the evidence.

In a case involving standing, *Rakas v. Illinois*,[52] the Court held that a mere guest riding in a passenger car had no expectation of privacy in the automobile, since he did not assert that he was either an owner or a lessee of the vehicle (see Case 3.3). Since Rakas lacked a sufficient connection to the automobile, the trial court properly refused to entertain his motion to suppress on the theory that he lacked standing. The one individual who could have demonstrated standing would have been the owner, but the owner would have possessed standing to suppress evidence *only* if he or she were accused of criminal activities. The owner of the car could not attempt to suppress evidence sought to be used against a third person with no expectation of privacy in the motor vehicle, since Fourth Amendment rights are personal and cannot be asserted vicariously.

The *Rakas* case called into serious question the rule of automatic standing from *Jones v. United States*.[53] Under *Jones*, standing was considered automatic where the

CASE 3.3

Leading Case Brief: Defendant Must Have Standing to Suppress Illegally Seized Evidence

Rakas v. Illinois
Supreme Court of the United States
439 U.S. 128 (1978)

Case Facts:

Rakas and King were convicted of armed robbery of clothing store employees. A police description of the getaway automobile alerted other officers to the fact of the robbery and the escape of the alleged felons. After the automobile driven by a girlfriend and carrying Rakas as a passenger had been stopped, the subsequent search of the car revealed a box of shells in the glove box and a sawed-off rifle under the seat. Neither Rakas nor his codefendant, King, owned the automobile, and neither ever asserted that he owned the rifle or shells seized.

The trial court refused to consider the motion to suppress the evidence seized from the car on the ground that Rakas was merely a guest passenger in the automobile of a friend and lacked legal standing to contest the constitutionality of the search because no constitutional right of his had been possibly violated. The basis for the conclusion that Rakas had asserted no Fourth Amendment expectation of privacy in the vehicle directly related to his lack of declared ownership or possession of the car, rifle, or shells.

The trial court admitted the evidence from the car against Rakas, and both he and King were convicted. The Appellate Court of Illinois affirmed the conviction. The Illinois Supreme Court refused to hear the case, and the Supreme Court granted certiorari.

Legal Issue:

Where an automobile search has been conducted and the accused made no claim to ownership or possession of the auto or the incriminating evidence within, does such a person have standing under the Fourth Amendment to contest the legality of the search?

The Court's Ruling:

The justices determined that neither Rakas nor King had a right that had been violated. To have standing under the Fourth Amendment, a person must have experienced a legally recognized deprivation of a protected right. To have an expectation of privacy, a person must own or have a right to possess the property that was subject to or the location of the alleged illegal search and seizure. In the absence of ownership or possession, no constitutional wrong could have occurred.

Essence of the Court's Rationale:

* * *

II

Petitioners first urge us to relax or broaden the rule of standing enunciated in *Jones v. United States,* 362 U.S. 257 (1960), so that any criminal defendant at whom a search was "directed" would have standing to contest the legality of that search and object to the admission at trial of evidence obtained as a result of the search. Alternatively petitioners argue that they have standing to object to the search under *Jones* because they were "legitimately on [the] premises" at the time of the search.

The concept of standing discussed in *Jones* focuses on whether the person seeking to challenge the legality of a search as a basis for suppressing evidence was himself the "victim" of the search and seizure. *Id.,* at 261. Adoption of the so-called "target" theory advanced by petitioners would, in effect, permit a defendant to assert that a violation of the Fourth Amendment rights of a third party entitled him to have evidence suppressed at his trial.

* * *

(continued)

A

We decline to extend the rule of standing in Fourth Amendment cases in the manner suggested by petitioners. As we stated in *Alderman v. United States,* 394 U.S. 165, 174 (1969), "Fourth Amendment rights are personal rights which, like some other constitutional rights, may not be vicariously asserted." [Citations omitted.] A person who is aggrieved by an illegal search and seizure only through the introduction of damaging evidence secured by a search of a third person's premises or property has not had any of his Fourth Amendment rights infringed. And since the exclusionary rule is an attempt to effectuate the guarantee of the Fourth Amendment, *United States v. Calandra,* 414 U.S. 338, 347 (1974), it is proper to permit only defendants whose Fourth Amendment rights have been violated to benefit from the rule's protections.

* * *

C

Here, petitioners who were passengers occupying a car which they neither owned nor leased, seek to analogize their position to that of the defendant in *Jones v. United States.* In *Jones,* petitioner was present at the time of the search of an apartment which was owned by a friend. The friend had given Jones permission to use the apartment and a key to it, with which Jones had admitted himself on the day of the search. He had a suit and shirt at the apartment and had slept there "maybe the night," but his home was elsewhere. At the time of the search, Jones was the only occupant of the apartment because the lessee was away for a period of several days. Under these circumstances, this Court stated that while one wrongfully on the premises could not move to suppress evidence obtained as a result of searching them, "anyone legitimately on premises where a search occurs may challenge its legality." Petitioners argue that their occupancy of the automobile in question was comparable to that of Jones in the apartment and that they therefore have standing to contest the legality of the search—or as we have rephrased the inquiry, that they, like Jones, had their Fourth Amendment rights violated by the search.

* * *

We think that *Jones* on its facts merely stands for the unremarkable proposition that a person can have a legally sufficient interest in a place other than his own home so that the Fourth Amendment protects him from unreasonable governmental intrusion into the place.

* * *

D

Judged by the foregoing analysis, petitioners' claims must fail. They asserted neither a property nor a possessory interest in the automobile, nor an interest in the property seized. And as we have previously indicated, the fact that they were "legitimately on [the] premises" in the sense that they were in the car with the permission of its owner is not determinative of whether they had a legitimate expectation of privacy in the particular areas of the automobile searched. It is unnecessary for us to decide here whether the same expectations of privacy are warranted in a car as would be justified in a dwelling place in analogous circumstances. We have on numerous occasions pointed out that cars are not to be treated identically with houses or apartments for Fourth Amendment purposes. [Citations omitted.] But here petitioners' claim is one which would fail even in an analogous situation in a dwelling place, since they made no showing that they had any legitimate expectation of privacy in the glove compartment or area under the seat of the car in which they were merely passengers. Like the trunk of an automobile, these are areas in which a passenger *qua* passenger simply would not normally have a legitimate expectation of privacy.

* * *

III

The Illinois courts were therefore correct in concluding that it was unnecessary to decide whether the search of the car might have violated the rights secured to someone else by the Fourth and Fourteenth Amendments to the United States Constitution. Since it did not violate any rights of these petitioners, their judgment of conviction is affirmed.

Case Importance:

The rules concerning standing require that a defendant alleging a Fourth Amendment illegal search and/or seizure demonstrate that his or her constitutional rights were personally violated. A guest staying in a home has a stronger argument for standing than does a person who neither owns nor leases a motor vehicle and was only a passenger within the vehicle.

defendant had been charged with a crime involving possession or was legitimately on the premises (an apartment). In *United States v. Salvucci,*[54] the Court overruled the rule of automatic standing in *Jones* by deciding that something more than "legitimately on the premises" was required to demonstrate standing. The *Salvucci* Court noted that the reason for automatic standing had ceased to exist[55] because, in the period between *Jones* and *Salvucci,* the Court had determined that a defendant could admit possession for Fourth Amendment purposes during a suppression of evidence hearing and not have that admission of possession used against him or her at a later trial for possession of the article, in the event that the motion to suppress the evidence failed.[56] According to the *Rakas* Court, a prosecutor could claim that a defendant possessed the seized article criminally but did not have sufficient possession of the article to have been subjected to a Fourth Amendment violation.

When there is some concern that a vehicle stop was not lawful, a driver and any passenger may have standing to contend that the stop violated the Fourth Amendment rights of both persons. Rakas did not contest the stop, which was a seizure of the car in which he was riding. Most likely the reason that he did not argue the validity of the stop was because, by all accounts, it was a lawful stop. In *Brendlin v. California,* _____ U.S. _____ (2007), an officer stopped a car in which Brendlin was riding as a passenger for no objective reason, merely because the officer wanted to check its registration papers. There was no belief that the automobile was being operated illegally. Immediately after the stop, the officer recognized Brendlin as a parole violator and arrested him. A search incident to arrest revealed methamphetamine paraphernalia and other evidence that resulted in charges against Brendlin for manufacturing methamphetamine. Brendlin argued that he had been illegally seized when the car was stopped for no reason, but the trial court refused to suppress the evidence because it ruled that Brendlin had not been stopped merely because the police stopped the car and driver. The California court of appeal reversed, on the theory that Brendlin had been stopped and could argue about its legality. The Supreme Court of California reversed the lower court and held that suppression of the evidence was not required because a passenger is not seized when the driver is stopped. The Supreme Court of the United States disagreed with the top California court and reversed the case once again. The Supreme Court held that when a driver is stopped, the passenger is also seized because police are not likely to allow a passenger to walk away from the car without asking the passenger some questions, especially if the officers believed that the passenger and the driver might be involved in some common enterprise. A passenger would be seized because no reasonable person in his position would believe that he was free to terminate the encounter and walk away. As the Court observed

> Brendlin was seized from the moment Simeroth's car came to a halt on the side of the road, and it was error to deny his suppression motion on the ground that seizure occurred only at the formal arrest. It will be for the state courts to consider in the first instance whether suppression turns on any other issue.[57]

Prior cases have held that while a passenger riding in a motor vehicle may not have standing to argue about a search of the vehicle, the passenger does have standing to challenge the legality of the stop and seizure of that vehicle and his or her person.[58] Therefore, Brendlin, or someone similarly situated, has standing to argue that he was illegally stopped, seized, and searched by police but would not have standing under the Fourth Amendment as interpreted by the *Rakas v. Illinois* case to contest the search of the car's interior unless he owned it or leased it.

Standing to argue concerning an alleged illegal search and seizure requires a significant connection to the property, at least as far as residential property is concerned. In *Minnesota v. Olson,*[59] the Supreme Court recognized the defendant's Fourth Amendment expectation of privacy and standing, where Olson often stayed in part of a duplex but actually lived elsewhere. In the process of investigating a homicide, police surrounded the duplex when Olson was believed hiding within the structure. Without seeking permission to enter and with weapons drawn, officers illegally entered the duplex and discovered Olson hiding in a closet. Following his arrest, he made incriminating statements. The Supreme Court recognized that a person can have a legitimate expectation of privacy in the home of another so long as the person has a right to be on the premises and exhibits other indications that he or she expects privacy. *Olson* was different from the *Jones* case, referenced previously, because Olson did not have a key and had never been left alone in the duplex, while the guest in *Jones* had a key and was staying in the apartment while the regular renter was away. The Supreme Court held that Olson did have an expectation of privacy because the Court recognized that to hold that

> an overnight guest has a legitimate expectation of privacy in his host's home merely recognizes the everyday expectations of privacy that we all share. Staying overnight in another's home is a longstanding social custom that serves functions recognized as valuable by society. We stay in others' homes when we travel to a strange city for business or pleasure, when we visit our parents, children, or more distant relatives out of town, when we are in between jobs or homes, or when we house-sit for a friend. We will all be hosts and we will all be guests many times in our lives. From either perspective, we think that society recognizes that a houseguest has a legitimate expectation of privacy in his host's home.[60]

Thus, Olson had standing to argue that the police entered the duplex where he was hiding by violating his personal Fourth Amendment rights. Having standing does not guarantee that a defendant will win a motion to suppress evidence, only that the defendant can have his or her day in court to argue the merits of the search and seizure that occurred.

Motel and hotel guests generally have expectations of privacy in the rooms that they have rented from the hotel host. Since society and courts generally recognize this privacy, a renter of a motel room would have standing to contest a police search and seizure that occurred in his or her hotel or motel room, according settled law based on an a old case that has never been overruled.[61]

19. VICARIOUS STANDING NOT PERMITTED

Following the *Salvucci* decision, where the Supreme Court overruled the rule of automatic standing in *Jones* by deciding that something more than legitimately being on the premises of a home or apartment was required for standing, a person who wishes to suppress evidence alleged to have been illegally seized must detail precisely how his or her personal Fourth Amendment rights have been violated. Generally, a defendant must be able to demonstrate a significant proprietary or possessory interest in the property to demonstrate sufficient standing. A person has no standing to suppress evidence where a third party's premises have been illegally searched, since that person could have possessed no legitimate expectation of privacy at a third party's home.

However, even where a proprietary or significant possessory interest has not been proven, permission to use a room may prove sufficient to enable a defendant to successfully demonstrate standing, as was noted in *Minnesota v. Olson,*[62] where the legitimate occupier of an apartment did not pay rent or have a key, but the Court decided that he possessed standing to argue the merits of the case. However, when the connection to an apartment seems merely to be of a commercial nature or an arranged accommodation with the lessee, standing to argue search and seizure issues may not exist.

The Court distinguished *Olson* from a different case, *Minnesota v. Carter,*[63] where the defendants were legitimately on the premises with the consent of the lessee but had not stayed a night and did not plan an overnight visit. In the *Carter* case, the defendants were "cutting up" and bagging cocaine in a private apartment when, pursuant to an informant's tip, a police officer observed them by looking through parted curtains. While police sought a search warrant, Carter and his associates left the premises, entered an automobile, and proceeded to drive away. Police officers stopped the car, and when Carter and his associate exited, police observed a black zippered pouch and a firearm. Police arrested Carter, his business associate, and another individual and also conducted a warrantless search of the apartment. The results of the search revealed cocaine powder residue and plastic baggies used to package the cocaine.

Prior to trial, Carter and the other defendants filed a motion to suppress all evidence obtained from the later search of the apartment and the automobile, as well as to suppress several incriminating statements made by defendants to police following their arrest. The legal theory offered by the defendants' attorney contended that the initial police observation of their drug activities through the curtain was an unreasonable search in violation of the Fourth Amendment and that all evidence obtained directly or derivatively as a result of this search was inadmissible as fruit of the poisonous tree. The trial court held that the police officer had not conducted an illegal search, in connection with Carter and his accomplices, by looking in the window, and that since the two defendants were not overnight social guests, they had no standing to complain about a search and seizure within the apartment. When the case reached the Supreme Court of Minnesota, it reversed the lower court and held that Carter and the others had standing under the Fourth Amendment because they had a legitimate expectation of privacy. Therefore, since standing had been established, the Court determined that privacy existed in an apartment to do both legal and illegal activity and that the officer's observation of this illegal activity violated the two defendants' expectation of privacy under the Fourth Amendment. Pursuant to the prosecutor's request, the Supreme Court of the United States agreed to hear the Minnesota prosecutor's appeal.

In an opinion written by Chief Justice Rehnquist, the Court reversed the opinion of the Minnesota Supreme Court because it had followed a legal theory that had been obsolete for twenty years. Chief Justice Rehnquist noted that an overnight guest in a house may have a Fourth Amendment expectation of privacy but that a person legitimately on the premises for a brief time for commercial purposes does not enjoy the same expectation of privacy. According to Rehnquist, while the apartment was a dwelling place for the usual occupant, it was, for Carter and his drug-selling conspirator, simply a place to do business, which would not support a legitimate expectation of privacy under the Fourth Amendment.[64]

Thus, in *Olson,* the Court upheld the existence of a Fourth Amendment expectation of privacy because the defendant not only was legitimately on the premises but also had permission to spend the night, which gave him what society recognizes as some level of privacy as a social guest. In Carter's case, the defendant and his associates were merely using the premises of the occupant for commercial purpose for a brief time. Such activity was deemed to be quite different from being an overnight social guest in a friend's home; because of this difference, according to Chief Justice Rehnquist, Carter and his companion had no standing to even argue about a violation of privacy under the Fourth Amendment.

In addition to legitimate expectations of privacy, aggrieved parties may allege standing due to the relationship between them and the seized property. The attempt to create standing does not frequently bring success, as demonstrated by *United States v. Padilla,*[65] where members of a criminal conspiracy involved in drug trafficking attempted to allege that they had an expectation of privacy by virtue of being managers in the criminal enterprise. Law enforcement officials had seized an automobile involved in the transportation of illegal drugs at a time when the leaders of the operation were not present with the vehicle. The drug kingpins' attempt to create or allege standing where they had rented the vehicle but transferred it to other associates failed under the Fourth Amendment when they could demonstrate no personal expectation of privacy that had been violated by federal officials. In a similar and more recent case,[66] the defendant was driving a rental car and was the only person inside when it was stopped. Police arrested the defendant on an outstanding warrant and conducted a search of the motor vehicle. Since the defendant was not an authorized driver, either by the contract renter or by the rental company, he had no standing to contest the search of the car that revealed cocaine and heroin, and the drugs were properly admitted against him in court.

20. SUMMARY

Violations of the Constitution that result in illegally seized evidence may permit the person against whom the evidence is sought to have it suppressed. The individual wishing to exclude the evidence from trial must be the person whose constitutional rights have been violated. While most evidence that is the subject of suppression is alleged to have been illegally seized by virtue of a Fourth Amendment violation, similar rules of exclusion apply to other violations of the Constitution that produce evidence. The theory of the exclusionary rule contemplates that by removing the law enforcement incentive to violate the United States Constitution, and the Fourth

Amendment in particular, federal and state officials will be less likely to transgress the dictates of the law because such conduct produces no prosecution benefit. Where the exclusionary rule does not have the effect of deterring law enforcement conduct, the rule is less likely to be applied. The good faith exception, the rule of inevitable discovery, the rule of attenuation, and the independent source rule are examples of situations in which police conduct would not have been altered; for that reason, the exclusionary rule is generally not applied to exclude evidence from trial.

REVIEW EXERCISES AND QUESTIONS

1. For what reasons did the Supreme Court of the United States create the exclusionary rule under the Fourth Amendment?

2. Does the use of the Fourth Amendment's exclusionary rule put the government or police in a worse position or the same position as the prosecution would have been without the exclusionary rule?

3. How does the exclusionary rule help to enforce the Fourth Amendment? Explain.

4. What was the silver platter doctrine?

5. Evidence that has been discovered by exploiting an original Fourth Amendment violation may be excluded from use at court to prove guilt. How does this derivative evidence exclusion operate?

6. What are three major exceptions to the exclusionary rule where it is not applied to exclude evidence? Explain each one.

7. Explain why every defendant who wishes to suppress evidence generally must prove the concept of standing.

8. Consider the case where a person armed with a concealed handgun was sitting in the rear seat of a automobile when police stopped the vehicle, erroneously believing that it was stolen. The vehicle had been reported stolen earlier, but the police computer properly had been updated to show that the car was no longer in the "stolen" category. The person in the back seat was removed from the vehicle and frisked, revealing the concealed handgun. Does the person in the rear seat with the handgun have the legal ability to argue that the car, owned by another, was improperly stopped due to faulty police data? Should he be able to suppress evidence of his illegal concealed weapon? See *United States v. Anderson,* 2007 U.S. Dist. LEXIS 45137 (N.D. Ohio 2007).

9. What is a *Bivens* suit? Explain how it can be a remedy for a federal violation of the Fourth Amendment.

10. The Supreme Court generally refuses to allow what is called vicarious standing. What is vicarious standing, and why is the exclusionary rule not used in cases where someone alleges a violation of the Fourth Amendment from such a position?

HOW WOULD YOU DECIDE?

1. In the Appellate Court of Illinois

Shortly before 5:00 A.M., Marshall Mitchell went for a walk because he could not sleep and within minutes encountered two police officers who had been investigating a parked car. The officers' business with the parked car had ended, and they had no person to suspect of any crime when they observed Mitchell walking down the sidewalk. The officers stopped Mitchell and wanted to know who he was and what he was doing. Mitchell explained that he could not sleep and was out walking. He produced identification, which one officer took to the car to see if any warrants for Mitchell were outstanding. Mitchell waited until he was arrested for an outstanding "no proof of car insurance" ticket that came back on the police computer. Subsequent to a search incident to arrest on the street, he was searched again at the stationhouse, which revealed some recreational amounts of cocaine, for which he was charged. Mitchell's attorney argued that allowing police to stop and make inquiries of people walking down the street based on no articulable suspicion or other reason and run police computer checks on their names violates the Fourth Amendment's guarantee that people will be subject to only reasonable searches. The trial court ordered the suppression of the cocaine on the basis of the exclusionary rule, but the prosecution appealed the suppression of the drug, noting that the finding of the outstanding warrant removed that taint of any violation under the attenuation exception under the "fruit of the poisonous tree" doctrine.

How would you rule on the defendant's contention that the trial court properly suppressed the evidence of cocaine?

The Court's Holding:

Police have no authority to stop people who have no apparent criminal plans and who seem to be passing the time lawfully. Similarly, police may not demand identification from persons for whom police have no reasons to suspect are about to initiate criminal activity. The appellate court held that the doctrine of attenuation derived from *Wong Sun v. United States,* 371 U.S. 471 (1963) had no application to this case because there was a relatively short time from the initial illegal detention of Mitchell to the discovery of incriminating evidence. The Court also noted that the conduct of the officers of stopping an innocent-appearing person to run a warrant check was directly related to the eventual arrest. The court noted, "We also note that suppressing evidence under the present circumstances furthers the goal of the exclusionary rule. In fact, it appears to be the only way to deter the police from randomly stopping citizens for the purpose of running warrant checks. Thus, the trial court properly excluded the cocaine evidence admission in court." See *People v. Mitchell,* 2005 Ill. App. LEXIS 497 (2005).

HOW WOULD YOU DECIDE?

2. In the Supreme Court of Pennsylvania

A Pennsylvania trial court ordered suppression of a firearm seized by police from another person's car that the government wanted to introduce against the defendant, Millner. The defendant contended that the police lacked probable cause to conduct a search of the defendant's person and should not have conducted a search of the automobile in which police found the gun. Police contend that they saw Millner put the gun in the back of someone else's car. The trial court also ordered suppression of drugs taken from Millner's person because it believed while a limited frisk might have been proper, the complete search of Millner's person violated his Fourth Amendment rights. The Commonwealth did not contest the suppression of the drugs taken from Millner's person but argued that Millner had no standing to complain about the gun search in the vehicle of another. The Commonwealth's uncontradicted evidence demonstrated that the vehicle was registered to someone else and that no key, papers, or other identification was found to indicate that Millner had any interest in the car. The suppression court found that the police searched the car without a warrant and because the defendant had no obligation to inform police that it was or was not his car, the pistol should be suppressed from the trial. Therefore, the trial court ordered suppression of the gun found in the car of another, and the Commonwealth appealed.

How would you rule on the defendant's contention that the gun found in the car of another person during a warrantless police search should not be introduced against him because police searched the car illegally?

The Court's Holding:

Pennslyvania's top court believed that the Commonwealth contended correctly that no evidence in the lower court showed that Millner had any reasonable expectation of privacy in the car where police recovered the nine-millimeter pistol. Partly because Millner never claimed ownership of the car or of the pistol, the Supreme Court observed that appellee Millner

> produced no evidence that he owned the vehicle, nor did he produce evidence which remotely suggested that he had any other connection to the vehicle which could form the basis for so much as a subjective expectation of privacy. In addition, there

was nothing in the Commonwealth's evidence upon which appellee could rely to prove that he had an expectation of privacy in the Cadillac in question. The police testimony established that nothing was found in the vehicle, on appellee's person, or through a record search, to suggest any lawful connection to the car. Finally, the fact that police testified to seeing appellee put the firearm in the vehicle—a fact appellee denied—alone does not establish both a subjective and reasonable expectation of privacy in a vehicle to which he had no other legitimate connection.[67]

In addressing the standing issue under the Fourth Amendment and Pennsylvania's companion constitutional section, the Supreme Court of Pennsylvania noted,

In short, appellee failed to establish a subjective expectation of privacy in this particular vehicle, much less one that society would accept as reasonable, such that the warrantless police entry implicated his own personal privacy rights. In such a circumstance, there was no need for the Commonwealth to establish the lawfulness of the police entry into the vehicle and the seizure of the firearm, and there was no basis upon which the lower courts could properly order its suppression.[68]

Based on these findings, the Supreme Court of Pennsylvania remanded the case to the trial court to admit the pistol against the defendant-appellee Millner at his eventual trial. See *Commonwealth v. Millner,* 585 Pa. 237, 888 A.2d 680 (2005).

ENDNOTES

1. *277 U.S. 438, 485 (1928).*
2. 367 U.S. 643, 659 (1961).
3. See *Bivens v. Six Unknown Named Agents,* 403 U.S. 388 (1971), where the Court created a civil cause of action against federal employees who acted illegally in searching an apartment.
4. See Chief Justice Berger's dissent in *Bivens v. Six Unknown Named Agents,* 403 U.S. 388, 421 (1971), where he proposed a variety of remedies for Fourth Amendment violations while allowing the use of the illegally seized evidence against the person whose rights had been violated.
5. *Boyd v. United States,* 116 U.S. 616, 625 (1886).
6. See *Boyd v. United States,* 116 U.S. 616 (1886).
7. *Boyd* at 625, 626.
8. The Fourth Amendment was originally intended by its Framers and adopters to limit the federal government and was not designed to have any application to affect state law enforcement practice. The Fourth Amendment was incorporated into the Due Process Clause of the Fourteenth Amendment in *Mapp v. Ohio,* 367 U.S. 643 (1961).
9. This assumes that the evidence illegally seized by federal agents under the Fourth Amendment would tend to support a violation of state law.
10. See *Boyd v. United States,* 116 U.S. 616 (1886).
11. Illegally obtained evidence may be used for impeachment purposes where the defendant takes the witness stand and offers evidence contradictory to known but illegally seized evidence. In *Walder v. United States,* 347 U.S. 62 (1954), heroin had been illegally seized from the defendant, who denied that he ever had possession or ever sold drugs. The *Walder* Court approved the use for impeachment purposes of the evidence seized illegally in violation of the defendant's Fourth Amendment rights. Similarly, in *Harris v. New York,* 401 U.S. 222 (1971), the Court approved the use of a statement illegally taken in violation of *Miranda* principles to be used to impeach a defendant who told a story different from the version offered in violation of *Miranda.*
12. *Oregon v. Elstad,* 470 U.S. 298 (1985).
13. *Withrow v. Williams,* 507 U.S. 680, 686 (1993).
14. See *United States v. Verdugo-Urquidez,* 494 U.S. 259 (1990).
15. *Elkins v. United States,* 364 U.S. 206 (1960).
16. 367 U.S. 643 (1961).
17. 371 U.S. 471 (1963).
18. Ibid.
19. 468 U.S. 796 (1984).
20. 487 U.S. 533 (1988).
21. 467 U.S. 431 (1984).
22. See *Silverthorne Lumber Co., Inc. v. United States,* 251 U.S. 385 (1920).
23. 487 U.S. 533 (1988).
24. 468 U.S. 796 (1984).

25. *Ohio v. Sincell,* 2002 Ohio 1783; 2002 Ohio App. LEXIS 1656 (2002).

26. *Teal v. State,* 2007 Ga. LEXIS 480 (2007).

27. 308 U.S. 338 (1939).

28. They seemed unaware that they should have been discussing a plea bargain with the prosecutor rather than the police.

29. The *Wong Sun* Court did exclude Toy's confession because of evidentiary reasons unrelated to the Fourth Amendment attenuation issue in the case. The doctrine of attenuation would permit the admission of Toy's confession, but the rule that a confession must be corroborated by some other evidence cannot be met because the only other evidence to corroborate Toy's confession is the heroin, which has been excluded. 371 U.S. 471 (1963).

30. *United States v. Shaw,* 454 F.3d 615, 2006 U.S. App. LEXIS 24257 (6th Cir. 2006).

31. Ibid. at 626.

32. 468 U.S. 897 (1984).

33. 468 U.S. 981 (1984).

34. *United States v. Martin,* 297 F.3d 1308, 1313 (2002).

35. *United States v. Robinson,* 2003 U.S. App. LEXIS 13770 (2003).

36. *United States v. 15324 County Highway East,* 332 F.3d 1070 (2003).

37. 524 U.S. 357 (1998).

38. *Scott* at 363.

39. *Duckworth v. Eagan,* 492 U.S. 195, 208 (1989).

40. *United States v. Leon,* 468 U.S. 897, 920–922 (1984).

41. *Alderman v. United States,* 394 U.S. 165, 174–175 (1969).

42. *Illinois v. Krull,* 480 U.S. 340, 349–350 (1987).

43. *Walder v. United States,* 347 U.S. 62, 65 (1954). A similar principle allows the impeachment of statements taken in violation of *Miranda v. Arizona,* 384 U.S. 436 (1966). See *Harris v. New York,* 401 U.S. 222 (1971).

44. *James v. Illinois,* 493 U.S. 307, 308–309 (1990).

45. In *Arizona v. Evans,* 514 U.S. 1 (1995), a police officer conducted a search following an arrest when the arrest involved "bad" probable cause because of the failure of a clerk to properly remove a warrant notice from a computer system used by police.

46. *United States v. Calandra,* 414 U.S. 338, 349 (1974).

47. 403 U.S. 388 (1971).

48. In *Correctional Services Corporation v. Malesko,* 534 U.S. 61 (2001), the Court noted that it had extended the reach and rationale of *Bivens* on two occasions. In both cases, the Court extended the *Bivens* rationale to provide a cause of action against individual governmental officers who have allegedly acted unconstitutionally. In *Carlson v. Green,* 446 U.S. 14 (1980), the Court permitted the survivor of a deceased federal prisoner to maintain a civil damage suit against federal officers due to unconstitutional conduct, and it allowed a suit where there was no alternative remedy at law for a congressional employee who had allegedly been the victim of discrimination by a U.S. congressman in *Davis v. Passman,* 442 U.S. 228 (1971).

49. See *Webb v. Desan, Warden,* 2007 U.S. App. LEXIS 24005 (3rd Cir. 2007).

50. *Minnesota v. Carter,* 525 U.S. 83, 100 (1998), Justice Kennedy, concurring.

51. *United States v. Padilla,* 508 U.S. 77 (1993).

52. 439 U.S. 128 (1978).

53. 362 U.S. 257 (1960).

54. 448 U.S. 83 (1980).

55. At the time of *Jones v. United States,* 362 U.S. 257 (1960), if a person admitted possession for purposes of filing a motion to suppress in federal court and lost the motion, the individual was deemed to have admitted possessing the object that was the subject of the suppression hearing. This same result could occur in state courts after *Mapp v. Ohio,* 367 U.S. 643 (1961). The criticism was that a prosecutor should not be permitted to allege that a defendant possessed an object criminally while at the same time arguing that he or she did not possess the object for the purpose of claiming the constitutional protections of the Fourth Amendment. This problem was eliminated by the Court's decision in *Simmons v. United States,* 390 U.S. 377 (1968).

56. See *Simmons v. United States,* 390 U.S. 377 (1968).

57. *Brendlin v. California,* 127 S.Ct. 2400 (2007).

58. *United States v. Mosley,* 454 F.3d 249, 253 (3d Cir. 2006).

59. 495 U.S. 91 (1990).

60. Ibid.

61. See *Stoner v. California,* 376 U.S. 483 (1964).

62. 495 U.S. 91 (1990).

63. 525 U.S. 83 (1998).

64. According to Chief Justice Rehnquist, the purely commercial nature of the transaction, the relatively short period of time on the premises, and the lack of any previous connection between Carter and his friend and the householder all lead us to conclude

that Carter's situation is closer to that of one simply permitted on the premises. The Court held that any search that may have occurred did not violate their Fourth Amendment rights. 525 U.S. 83, 91 (1998).

65. 508 U.S. 77 (1993).

66. *United States v. Thomas,* 447 F3d. 1191, 2006 U.S. App. LEXIS 12178 (9th Cir. 2006).

67. *Commonwealth v. Millner,* 585 Pa. 237, 257, 888 A.2d 680, 692, 2005 Pa. LEXIS 3059 (2005).

68. Ibid. at 258, 692.

Part 2

Arrest, Stop and Frisk, and Search Warrant Practice

C H A P T E R   4

Arrest and Seizure of the Person

Learning Objectives

1. Be able to state from memory the legal standard of probable cause.
2. Understand the level of proof necessary to meet the Fourth Amendment standard of probable cause, and offer a fact pattern that supports probable cause to arrest.
3. Recognize the sources of probable cause information, and be able to synthesize these sources to produce probable cause.
4. Identify situations when information that produces probable cause becomes stale, and orally justify the reasons why

a particular situation may indicate stale probable cause.

5. Explain why an arrest warrant is deemed to be a court order, and articulate why a warrant carries the power to make its execution effective.
6. Discriminate between situations that require arrest warrants and those that do not, and identify the reasons justifying the different approaches.
7. Be able to discuss when an arrest inside a suspect's home requires a warrant, and identify situations where a warrantless arrest may be made within the home.

Chapter Outline

Key Terms

Arrest
Arrest in the home
Arrest in third-party home
Exceptions to warrant
Exigent circumstances
Expectation of privacy
Hot pursuit

Neutral and detached judicial official
Probable cause to arrest
Seizure
Stale probable cause
Standing
Warrant to arrest

1. PROBABLE CAUSE ARRESTS: THE LEGAL STANDARD

Although many stop and frisk situations do not escalate to the next level, evidence discovered during a valid stop and frisk may produce probable cause for an arrest. Where the officer's reasonable suspicion has been satisfied, the encounter must end and the detainee be allowed to continue with the prior course of conduct. However, if evidence unearthed during a *Terry* stop and frisk rises to the level of probable cause for an arrest, the officer may effectuate the arrest or make some other disposition of the subject. Probable cause for arrest[1] is said to exist where the officers at the moment of arrest have facts and circumstances available to them that would "warrant a man of reasonable caution in the belief" that an offense has been committed or is being committed. *Carroll v. United States,* 267 U.S. 132, 162 (1925).

2. THE CONCEPT OF PROBABLE CAUSE FOR ARREST

An arrest is a seizure under the Fourth Amendment; an individual person, against his or her will, comes under the total physical control of a governmental agent. There must be either a submission to the will of the law enforcement official or a physical application of force sufficient to put the person in the custody of the officer. "A police officer may make a seizure by a show of authority and without the use of physical force, but there is no seizure without actual submission; otherwise, there is at most an attempted seizure, so far as the Fourth Amendment is concerned."[2] Merely chasing a suspect does not constitute a seizure or an arrest until the individual is physically caught or submits to the lawful authority of the officer. See *Michigan v. Chesternut,* 486 U.S. 567 (1988), and *California v. Hodari D.,* 499 U.S. 621 (1991). In *Hodari D.,* the Court noted that "a police pursuit in attempting to seize a person does not amount to a 'seizure' within the meaning of the Fourth Amendment."[3] To be lawful, probable cause must exist, and the manner of the seizure must be reasonable under the circumstances. The Fourth Amendment provides that "no Warrants shall issue, but upon probable cause," which means that where a court is to issue an arrest warrant, it must make a finding that a strong fact pattern indicates that powerful reasons exist to think a person has committed a particular crime for which taking the person into custody would be reasonable.

3. PLAIN MEANING OF THE FOURTH AMENDMENT

When one reads the Fourth Amendment, a reasonable interpretation with logical inferences would require that a warrant has to be issued in compliance with the dictates of the amendment prior to each and every arrest. Since colonial times, arrests have been made under the common law without the use of warrants, and a warrant is not at present a necessity for felony arrests. In *United States v. Watson,* 423 U.S. 411 (1976), the Court approved of the constitutionality of warrantless arrests, holding that the Fourth Amendment reflected the ancient common-law rule that a law enforcement official had the power to arrest without a warrant for a misdemeanor or felony committed in his presence, as well as for a felony not committed in his presence if there was reasonable ground (probable cause) for making the arrest.

According to *Watson,* a warrant is not generally required even where the officer has adequate time to procure one. By the lesson of history,[4] by legislation passed by the Framers of the Fourth Amendment, and by settled usage,[5] police officers may make warrantless arrests, given the presence of probable cause.

4. PROBABLE CAUSE DEFINED

Although the Fourth Amendment spoke of probable cause, it did not define it or give it any parameters. Probable cause need not rise to the level of proof beyond a reasonable doubt but must be beyond a mere hunch or guess. To establish probable cause, as the Supreme Court noted, "[R]equires only a probability or substantial chance of criminal activity, not an actual showing of such activity."[6] Settled usage of the time (1791) provided content and definition, and later court cases have construed and refined the meaning. Probable cause has been defined as where the facts and circumstances within the officer's knowledge are sufficient in themselves to warrant a prudent person of reasonable caution in believing that a particular person is committing or has committed a particular offense.[7] See *Beck v. Ohio,* 379 U.S. 89 (1964).

As noted in *Beck,* the arresting officer had a picture of the arrestee, knew what he looked like, knew of some of his prior convictions, and had "heard reports" that Beck was running numbers. The Court held that these facts did not rise to probable cause and that the arrest of Beck had been unlawful. The level of belief required to meet probable cause is much more than a mere hunch, as in *Beck,* but falls far below proof sufficient for guilt beyond a reasonable doubt.

In determining whether an officer possesses sufficient evidence to make a warrantless arrest, the Supreme Court of Michigan suggested an inquiry concerning

> whether an officer had probable cause to make an arrest is whether there are any facts which would lead a reasonable person to believe that the suspected person has committed a felony. Secondly, a police officer's belief that a defendant has committed a felony must be based on facts which are present at the moment of the arrest.[8]

The court noted that when courts review probable cause determinations by police, they must analyze whether the facts sufficient to establish probable cause existed at the moment of the arrest that would justify a fair-minded person of reasonable caution and normal intelligence in believing that the person with whom the officer was dealing had committed a felony. All the facts and circumstances known to the officer at the moment of arrest can and should be considered.

In the case the Michigan court had under review against a claim by the defendant that the arresting officers lacked probable cause, the officers knew the defendant had been stalking and threatening the deceased, understood that the smell of gasoline had been detected near the home, and observed that the defendant did not seem upset at news that his girlfriend had died in a fiery blaze. According to the court, the collective information known to the police offered probable cause to arrest for stalking,[9] at a minimum, and probable cause to arrest for murder also may well have existed.

CASE 4.1

Leading Case Brief: The Necessity of Developing Probable Cause for an Arrest

Beck v. Ohio
Supreme Court of the United States
379 U.S. 89 (1964)

Case Facts:

Police officers signaled William Beck to pull over and park his automobile because they suspected that he was involved in gambling. Officers had seen a picture of Beck and knew of his prior reputation as a numbers runner. Although the officers had neither arrest warrant nor search warrant, the officers immediately arrested Beck and conducted a search of his person and of his automobile that revealed nothing indicative of criminal activity. At a nearby police station, a second search of his person revealed an envelope containing a number of clearing house slips "beneath the sock of his leg."

According to testimony, the officers initially decided to stop Beck if they saw him make a "numbers" stop in a bar or tavern. The officers' actual decision to stop Beck was partially based on knowledge that he had a prior record involving gambling, knowledge of his identity from a picture, and the fact that they had "heard reports" that someone reliable had stated that Beck possessed clearing house slips. The officers conducted this individual stop, search, and arrest in the absence of any probable cause or warrant either for a search or an arrest. Even the arresting officer who testified at the trial said no more than that someone (he did not say who) had told him something (he did not say what) about the petitioner being involved in gambling.

The prosecutor charged Beck with possession of clearing house slips in Cleveland Municipal Court. His counsel filed a motion to suppress based on the allegation that the evidence seized from the search of his person incident to his arrest had been seized in violation of his Fourth Amendment rights. The argument that probable cause to arrest was absent was rejected by the court, and a motion to suppress the evidence seized by police was overruled. A guilty verdict followed. An Ohio Court of Appeals affirmed the municipal court conviction and the Supreme Court of Ohio upheld the decision. The United States Supreme Court granted Beck's petition for certiorari.

Legal Issue:

Where police possessed a photograph of a person, where they heard from unnamed and unsubstantiated sources that the person possessed illegal gambling materials, where they knew the person had a reputation for illegal gambling, and where police initiated an arrest based upon such data, has sufficient information been obtained to constitute probable cause to arrest?

The Court's Ruling:

Objective evidence must be possessed by police that would lead a person of reasonable caution in believing that a particular person has committed a particular crime that is sufficient to establish probable cause for an arrest.

Essence of the Court's Rationale:

* * *

The trial court made no findings of fact in this case. The trial judge simply made a conclusory statement: "A lawful arrest has been made, and this was a search incidental to that lawful arrest." The Court of Appeals merely found "no error prejudicial to the appellant." In the Supreme Court of Ohio, Judge Zimmerman's opinion contained a narrative recital which is accurately excerpted in the dissenting opinions filed today. But, putting aside the question of whether this opinion can fairly be called the opinion of the court, such a recital in an appellate opinion is hardly the equivalent of findings made by the trier of the facts. In any event, after giving full scope to the flexibility demanded by "a recognition that conditions and circumstances vary just as do investigative and enforcement techniques," we hold that the arrest of the petitioner cannot on the record before us be squared with the demands of the Fourth and Fourteenth Amendments.

The [factual] record [in this case] is meager, consisting only of the testimony of one of the arresting officers, given at the hearing on the motion to suppress. As to the officer's own knowledge of the petitioner before the arrest, the record shows no more than that the officer "had a police picture of him and knew what he looked like," and that the officer knew that the petitioner had "a record in connection with clearing house and scheme of chance." Beyond that, the officer testified only that he had "information," that he had "heard reports," that "someone specifically did relate that information," and that he "knew who that person was." There is nowhere in the record any indication of what "information" or "reports" the officer had received, or beyond what has been set out above, from what source the "information" and "reports" had come. The officer testified that when he left the station house, "I had in mind looking for [Defendant Beck] in the area of East 115th Street and Beulah, stopping him if I did see him make a stop in that area." But the officer testified to nothing that would indicate that any informer had said that the petitioner could be found at that time and place. And the record does not show that the officers saw the petitioner "stop" before they arrested him, or that they saw, heard, smelled, or otherwise perceived anything else to give them ground for belief that the petitioner had acted or was then acting unlawfully.

No decision of this Court has upheld the constitutional validity of a warrantless arrest with support so scant as this record presents. . . . [T]he record in this case does not contain a single objective fact to support a belief by the officers that the petitioner was engaged in criminal activity at the time they arrested him.

An arrest without a warrant bypasses the safeguards provided by an objective predetermination of probable cause, and substitutes instead the far less reliable procedure of an after-the-event justification for the arrest or search, too likely to be subtly influenced by the familiar shortcomings of hindsight judgment. "Whether or not the requirements of reliability and particularity of the information on which an officer may act are more stringent where an arrest warrant is absent, they surely cannot be less stringent than where an arrest warrant is obtained." [Citation omitted.]

* * *

Where the constitutional validity of an arrest is challenged, it is the function of a court to determine whether the facts available to the officers at the moment of the arrest would "warrant a man of reasonable caution in the belief" that an offense has been committed. *Carroll v. United States,* 267 U.S. 132, 162. If the court is not informed of the facts upon which the arresting officers acted, it cannot properly discharge that function. All the trial court was told in this case was that the officers knew what the petitioner looked like and knew that he had a previous record of arrest or convictions for violations of the clearing house law.

Case Importance:

A mere hunch or suspicion provides insufficient information to create probable cause to arrest.

5. SOURCES OF PROBABLE CAUSE TO ARREST

The information that matures probable cause to arrest may have a variety of sources. The officer may have personally observed the facts creating probable cause, have received information from a fellow officer,[10] have received some or all information from an informant, or a combination of all of these. If an informant supplied the basis for probable cause, courts (and police) generally want to know what facts the informant observed and why the court (and police) should believe the particular informant. In *Draper v. United States,* 358 U.S. 307 (1959) (Case 4.2), an informant of known reliability gave excellent information concerning drug trafficking, and a law enforcement official later corroborated the facts. The information matured probable cause to arrest because of its detail and its reliable source and because a reasonable person would have

CASE 4.2

Leading Case Brief: Developing Probable Cause for Arrest Through an Informant

Draper v. United States
Supreme Court of the United States
358 U.S. 307 (1959)

Case Facts:

A federal narcotics agent with twenty-nine years' experience, Marsh, arrested Draper for possession of heroin as he alighted from a train. The warrantless arrest had been prompted by information given to the agent by an informant, Hereford, who "worked" for the Bureau of Narcotics. Hereford, the "special employee," related to agent Marsh that Draper had gone to Chicago by train to purchase three ounces of heroin and that he would return by train on one of two different mornings. The "special employee" offered a complete physical description of Draper, including minute details of clothing he would be wearing, facts that only a person intimately involved with Draper could know.

On one of the mornings suggested by the informant Hereford, a person matching Draper's description emerged from the Chicago train and rapidly strolled away. Agent Marsh and a police officer arrested Draper based on Hereford's description of Draper, coupled with his visual and personal validation of these significant details. Subsequent to the arrest, Marsh conducted a search of Draper's person that disclosed two envelopes of heroin and a hypodermic needle.

Contending that police lacked probable cause to arrest him as he exited the train, Draper filed a motion to suppress the evidence of heroin based on an alleged illegal arrest under the Fourth Amendment. The trial court held that probable cause for an arrest existed and that the heroin was properly admitted as a search incident to a lawful arrest. At Draper's trial, the prosecutor introduced the drug evidence against Draper, who was convicted of violating federal law by knowingly concealing and transporting narcotic drugs in interstate commerce. The court of appeals affirmed the conviction and the Supreme Court of the United States granted certiorari.

Legal Issue:

Where an informant, known to the police, has given reliable information in past cases, and where the informant offered a detailed description of a suspected criminal and his criminal activities, which were later validated by an agent personally present, does informant's information couple plus the verification of the officer equal probable cause for an arrest?

The Court's Ruling:

While the Court reaffirmed that hearsay evidence could be used in determining produce probable cause, it held that where a reliable informant gives some evidence of criminal wrongdoing and predicts future activity of the suspect, where a police officer can later personally confirm the accuracy of the prior information and link it to the predicted behavior, probable cause will result.

Essence of the Court's Rationale:

* * *

[The Court could not] agree with petitioner's second contention that Marsh's information was insufficient to show probable cause and reasonable grounds to believe that petitioner had violated or was violating the narcotic laws and to justify his arrest without a warrant. The information given to narcotic agent Marsh by "special employee" Hereford may have been hearsay to Marsh, but coming from one employed for that purpose and whose information had always been found accurate and reliable, it is clear that Marsh would have been derelict in his duties had he not pursued it. And when, in pursuing that information, he saw a man, having the exact physical attributes and wearing the precise clothing and carrying the tan zipper bag that Hereford had described, alight from one of the very trains from the very place stated by Hereford and start to walk at a "fast" pace toward the station exit, Marsh had personally verified every facet of the information given him by Hereford except whether petitioner had accomplished his mission and had the three ounces of heroin on his person or in his bag. And surely, with every other bit of Hereford's information being thus personally verified, Marsh had "reasonable grounds" to believe that the remaining unverified bit of Hereford's information— that Draper would have the heroin with him—was likewise true.

> In dealing with probable cause, . . . as the very name implies, we deal with probabilities. These are not technical; they are the factual and practical considerations of everyday life on which reasonable and prudent men, not legal technicians, act.

Brinegar v. United States, supra, at 175. Probable cause exists where

> the facts and circumstances within their [the arresting officers'] knowledge and of which they had reasonably trustworthy information [are] sufficient in themselves to warrant a man of reasonable caution in the belief that an offense has been or is being committed. *Carroll v. United States,* 267 U.S. 132, 162, 45 S.Ct. 280, 288. [(1925).]

We believe that, under the facts and circumstances here, Marsh had probable cause and reasonable grounds to believe that petitioner was committing a violation of the laws of the United States relating to narcotic drugs at the time he arrested him. The arrest was therefore lawful, and the subsequent search and seizure, having been made incident to that lawful arrest, were likewise valid. It follows that petitioner's motion to suppress was properly denied and that the seized heroin was competent evidence lawfully received at the trial.

Affirmed.

Case Importance:

Probable cause to arrest may mature through personal observations of police officers, through information offered by informants, or a combination of informant hearsay and police verification.

arrived at the conclusion that Draper was probably carrying drugs. Probable cause may be established based on the collective knowledge of the officers involved rather than only the knowledge personally obtained by the arresting officer.[11]

Where an informant is involved, developing probable cause for an arrest involves virtually identical legal considerations as those involved in developing probable cause for a search. There needs to be sufficient reason to believe that the information given by the informant equals probable cause, and the informant must be believable as a person. This basic two-pronged test for evaluating an informant's information arose in *Aguilar v. Texas*[12] and was reviewed and altered in *Illinois v. Gates,*[13] when the Court replaced the two-pronged *Aguilar* test with a totality of the circumstances test. Prior to *Gates,* the reliability of an informant was evaluated on two levels: Was there a reason to believe this particular informant, and if the informant was to be believed, did the facts offered by the informant equal probable cause for an arrest or a search? *Gates* lowered the level of reliability demanded of an informant by allowing a weak showing of honesty to be cured by facts showing minute details that would be known only by one close to the situation.

Gates involved the maturing of probable cause for a search of a car and a home based on an anonymous letter in which the informant was unknown and the alleged facts uncorroborated. Police verified some of the information in the anonymous letter but not every detail, and some facts were never corroborated. The letter noted that

Gates and his wife made a living by selling illegal drugs and predicted that Gates would take a plane flight to meet his wife on a particular day. The informant suggested conduct that Gates would follow once he arrived in Florida at his wife's location. While there was no reason to believe the informant, once police verified that the informant knew important details of how Gates' life would unfold, there was a strong reason to believe that the informant was telling the truth and that recreational pharmaceuticals would be found at their home. In upholding the validity of the search warrants involved in *Gates,* the Supreme Court made the future procurement of probable cause for arrest and for search warrants significantly easier and less contestable where an informant's information has been necessary to the development of probable cause.

Even after the *Gates* case, when determining probable cause to arrest based on an informant's information, it remains important to evaluate the informant's trustworthiness and carefully consider what information has been communicated. Under the totality of the circumstances test, the officer needs to make a practical, commonsense determination of whether, considering all the information available, probable cause to arrest exists, while giving due consideration to the informant's information.

As a general rule, probable cause may be based on hearsay statements or declarations contained within a criminal complaint or attached to an affidavit for a warrant, as long as there is a substantial reason for believing that the source of the hearsay evidence is believable and that a factual basis exists for the information. Arrest probable cause may exist following the evaluation of wiretap information obtained pursuant to a federal or state warrant. Research in public records, when combined with other information, may also indicate probable cause to arrest.

Although the majority of arrests occur without a warrant, the existence of probable cause for an arrest remains an absolute prerequisite for a valid seizure of a person. Where the police arrest an individual without a warrant, the Fourth Amendment requires a judicial determination of probable cause within a reasonable time. According to the Court in *Riverside v. McLaughlin,* 500 U.S. 44 (1991), the judicial determination of probable cause must generally be made within forty-eight hours after a warrantless arrest.

6. STALE PROBABLE CAUSE

Where probable cause to arrest exists at a particular point in time, it does not subsequently cease to exist, as a general rule. If police have obtained information that indicates an individual is subject to arrest for a particular crime, the passage of time and continued police effort are most likely to generate more evidence of guilt rather than produce exculpatory evidence. In some cases, however, the original grounds supporting probable cause for arrest could be disproved by subsequent investigation that at the same time turns up wholly new evidence supporting probable cause to arrest a different person. In that type of situation, probable cause could become stale because it was based on information now discredited. The outer time limitation for arrest, once probable cause to arrest has been established, is the passage of the statute of limitations, if any, for the particular crime. Once the statute of limitations has expired, probable cause, in the legal sense, no longer exists, and the person may not be arrested.

Probable cause may become stale because the underlying crime may have been resolved or the reason for arrest no longer exists. For example, in *Arizona v. Evans,* 514 U.S. 1 (1995), a justice of the peace issued an arrest warrant for the defendant, which was duly logged into the police computer. Several days after the justice issued the warrant, the defendant appeared before the judicial official and resolved the outstanding legal matters. The judicial official had the warrant quashed (extinguished) because probable cause had ceased to exist. Phoenix police arrested Evans following a routine traffic stop when a patrol car's computer indicated that there was an outstanding misdemeanor warrant for his arrest. In essence, the probable cause had become stale by the passage of more recent events.[14] A lawful search of his car following his arrest on the outstanding warrant revealed a recreational amount of marijuana. When the police notified the court that Evans had been arrested, the court discovered that the arrest warrant previously had been quashed, and so advised the police. Evans argued that, because his arrest was based on a warrant that had been quashed seventeen days prior to his arrest, the marijuana seized incident to the arrest should be suppressed as the fruit of an unlawful arrest. Although the *Evans* Court failed to expressly reach the issue of whether the arrest was invalid because of stale information, it did determine that the search following the arrest was valid and that the marijuana was properly introduced against Evans. Even though probable cause in *Evans* was considered outdated or stale, in most cases, stale probable cause to arrest does not become a legal issue.

7. ARREST PURSUANT TO A WARRANT

An arrest warrant[15] is a court order directed toward law enforcement officers to take into custody a particularly described individual. For a judicial official to issue an arrest warrant, the judge[16] or magistrate must be personally convinced that probable cause to arrest exists for a specifically described individual. Arrest warrants are often issued when the subject is known and has been indicted but his or her exact location is not known. There is a procedural advantage to arresting a person pursuant to a warrant: If the arrestee later wishes to contest the validity of probable cause, the burden of proof is on the defendant and not on the prosecution. Where a warrantless arrest has occurred without the benefit of a judicial decision, the prosecution must prove arrest probable cause by a preponderance of the evidence.

An arrest warrant typically contains the name of the defendant and/or a clear description from which he or she can be positively identified with reasonable certainty. The warrant should describe the offense for which the defendant has been charged and may have a copy of the complaint or indictment attached to it. The arrest warrant commands the person executing it to seize the person named and bring that individual before the court that issued the warrant, without needless delay. Where a law enforcement officer makes the arrest and does not have a copy of the arrest warrant, the officer should inform the arrestee of as much of the information contained within the warrant as is known, but a failure to inform does not invalidate the arrest or otherwise affect the warrant to arrest. Figure 4.1 shows a warrant for an arrest used in federal courts.

UNITED STATES DISTRICT COURT

District of _____

UNITED STATES OF AMERICA

V.

WARRANT FOR ARREST

Case Number: _____

To: The United States Marshal
    and any Authorized United States Officer

    YOU ARE HEREBY COMMANDED to arrest _____
                                                    Name

and bring him or her forthwith to the nearest magistrate judge to answer a(n)

☐ Indictment   ☐ Information   ☐ Complaint   ☐ Order of court

☐ Pretrial Release   ☐ Probation   ☐ Supervised Release   ☐ Violation Notice
   Violation Petition   Violation Petition   Violation

charging him or her with   (brief description of offense)

☐ in violation of Title _____ United States Code, Section(s) _____

☐ in violation of the conditions of his or her pretrial release imposed by the court.

☐ in violation of the conditions of his or her supervision imposed by the court.

Name of Issuing Officer	Signature of Issuing Officer
Title of Issuing Officer	Date and Location

RETURN

This warrant was received and executed with the arrest of the above-named individual at

DATE RECEIVED	NAME AND TITLE OF ARRESTING OFFICER	SIGNATURE OF ARRESTING OFFICER
DATE OF ARREST		

FIGURE 4.1   Sample Federal Warrant for Arrest.

Following an arrest without a warrant, the arresting officer or another officer should bring the arrested person, without undue delay, before a court of competent jurisdiction for a judicial consideration of probable cause. In *Gerstein v. Pugh,* 420 U.S. 103 (1975), in addressing the Fourth Amendment's prohibition against unreasonable seizures, the Court determined that a police detention of an arrestee requires a prompt judicial determination of probable cause following an arrest made without a warrant. In arrest situations, where police alone have determined probable cause, a judge or magistrate must reconsider whether probable cause exists, and the judge must do so within a reasonable time following the arrest. See *Riverside v. McLaughlin,* 500 U.S. 44 (1991). According to the *Riverside* Court, a reasonable time to be incarcerated on less than a judicial showing of probable cause or a grand jury indictment was forty-eight hours.[20] As a practical matter, charges that support the arrest should be filed by the officer or one acting on behalf of the officer within a reasonable time, but a judicial official should rule on probable cause within the two-day period. The sample form in Figure 4.2 shows what courts use when making a probable cause only determination within the required forty-eight hours.[21]

9. REQUIREMENTS FOR ARRESTS WITHIN THE HOME

The Fourth Amendment has been judicially construed to prohibit a warrantless arrest within one's home unless exigent circumstances, destruction of evidence, hot pursuit, or some other exception applies. In construing the Fourth Amendment, the Court emphasized in *Coolidge v. New Hampshire,* 403 U.S. 443 (1971), the distinction between searches and seizures that take place on a person's property—home or office—and those carried out elsewhere. It is accepted, at least as a matter of principle, that a search or seizure carried out on a suspect's premises without a warrant is per se unreasonable, unless the police can show that it falls within one of a carefully defined set of exceptions based on the presence of "exigent circumstances." *Coolidge* at 474.

In a case in the Second Circuit Court of Appeal, the court reaffirmed its view that a home arrest requires a warrant:

> To be arrested in the home involves not only the invasion attendant to all arrests, but also an invasion of the sanctity of the home. This is simply too substantial an invasion to allow without a warrant, at least in the absence of exigent circumstances, even when it is accomplished under statutory authority and when probable cause is clearly present. *United States v. Reed,* 572 F.2d 412, 423 (CA2 1978)

As noted in *Coolidge* and *Reed,* the expectation of privacy in the home has been so protected from intrusion that even police with probable cause to arrest may not transgress the home boundaries without a warrant or some emergency circumstance.[22] The Court of Appeals for the Fourth Circuit found a violation of the Fourth Amendment when a police officer with probable cause entered the home of the suspect without a warrant to make an arrest. The officer knocked at the door with the result that the suspect answered the door. The officer went inside to complete the arrest after telling the subject that he was under arrest. Absent hot pursuit or exigent circumstances, the arrest was unreasonable because of the lack of a warrant.[23]

[For use with with District Court Rule 5-301,
Magistrate Court Rule 6-203,
Metropolitan Court Rule 7-203 and
Municipal Court Rule 8-202]

STATE OF NEW MEXICO
[COUNTY OF_____]
[CITY OF_____]
_____ COURT   No. _____

[STATE OF NEW MEXICO]
[COUNTY OF _____]
[CITY OF _____]

v.

_____, Defendant

PROBABLE CAUSE DETERMINATION

(For use only if the defendant
has been arrested without a warrant
and has not been released)

Finding of Probable Cause

[ ]   I find that there is a written showing of probable cause to believe that a crime has been committed and that the above named defendant committed it.

It is ordered that the defendant shall be released:
[ ]   on personal recognizance.
[ ]   on the conditions of release set forth in the release order.

Failure to Make Showing of Probable Cause
[ ]   I find that probable cause has not been shown that a crime has been committed and that the above named defendant committed it.
It is therefore ordered that the complaint against the defendant be and the same is hereby dismissed without prejudice and the defendant be immediately discharged from custody.

_____
Date

_____
Judge

Unless the defendant has been released on personal recognizance, the amount of bail set and any conditions of release prescribed by a designee must also be reviewed.
This form is not necessary if the finding of probable cause is endorsed by the judge on the criminal complaint or on a statement of probable cause.

FIGURE 4.2   Judicial Probable Cause Determination Form for Warrantless Arrest.

In *Payton v. New York,*[24] police officers had developed probable cause to arrest Payton for murder, but they entered his home illegally without a warrant. The Court held that the officers needed an arrest warrant to enter the home, and that by entering without a warrant, they had violated Payton's Fourth Amendment rights[25] in warrantlessly seizing evidence. The need for a warrant to make an arrest was reaffirmed in *Kirk v. Louisiana,*[26] where police warrantlessly entered, arrested Kirk, and searched his residence with probable cause to believe that drugs were being sold on the premises. In a per curiam decision, the *Kirk* Court held that a warrantless entry to search and/or arrest requires a warrant or some exception to the warrant requirement; it sent the case back for further proceedings consistent with *Payton v. New York.*[27] (The principle that one may not be lawfully arrested in one's own home without a warrant may not always apply to the arrest of casual visitors within another person's home and does not apply to trespassers who may be found in the home.) Similarly, in *Welsh v. Wisconsin,* 466 U.S. 740 (1984), officers had probable cause to arrest Welsh for driving while intoxicated. Police gained entry to Welsh's home and arrested him in his bed, even though there had been no immediate or continuous pursuit (no hot pursuit) of Welsh from the scene of the crime. The Court held that, under the circumstances of the case, the arrest of Welsh in his own bed was illegal under the Fourth Amendment.

Police may prevent a home occupier from reentering his home where probable cause to search the residence for marijuana exists. Police may prevent reentry until a judge has issued or refused to issue a search warrant. In one case,[28] an estranged wife told police that she knew that her husband had illegal drugs within their trailer home when she asked police to stand nearby while she picked up some of her belongings. She had recently been inside the home and had firsthand knowledge, facts that gave rise to probable cause to search. Police suspected that if the husband reentered the place, he would flush the evidence, so they prevented him from going inside without a police escort. Once police searched the home and found marijuana, probable cause for arrest of the husband existed. Despite the defendant's contention that the police illegally seized his home without a warrant, the Supreme Court held that probable cause did exist to search the trailer home and that it was reasonable police conduct that prevented the occupant from reentering his home while a warrant was being obtained.

10. REQUIREMENTS FOR ARRESTS WITHIN A THIRD PARTY'S HOME

Where police have an arrest warrant for one person but want to look in the home of a second person in an effort to find the first person, generally a warrant or a substitute theory to enter the home is required.[29] This merely restates the general rule that absent exigent circumstances or consent, a home may not be searched without a warrant. In *Steagald v. United States,* 451 U.S. 204 (1981), Drug Enforcement Administration (DEA) agents entered Steagald's home to search for another man without first obtaining a search warrant for Steagald's residence. Although DEA agents possessed a warrant for the individual they wished to arrest, they arrested Steagald after warrantlessly entering his home and after it appeared that he possessed illegal recreational pharmaceuticals and other contraband. The *Steagald* Court held that the entry and search of Steagald's home and the arrest of Steagald were illegal and contrary to the requirements of the Fourth Amendment in the absence of exigent circumstances or consent. To lawfully search Steagald's home for the target of the arrest, law enforcement officials would have had to procure a search warrant for the home.

Possession of an arrest warrant indicates that a judicial official has determined that circumstances reasonably permit the seizing of the person wherever the individual may be located, including within the suspect's home. The arrest warrant carries with it the power to make it effective by using a reasonable level of force, if necessary. Without an arrest warrant, the burden is on the government to demonstrate exigent circumstances that overcome the presumption of unreasonableness and illegality that attach to all warrantless home arrests.

11. SUMMARY

The federal government or a state may take a person into custody where probable cause exists to believe that that person has committed a crime or crimes. Probable cause exists where the facts and circumstances that have been presented or made known to an officer of reasonable caution would reasonably lead that officer to conclude that a crime has been committed or is being committed by a particular person. The concept of probable cause requires only a proper proof or a substantial chance that a particular person has committed a crime. The evidence encompassing probable cause that comes to a law enforcement officer may be from an informant's information, the police officer's observations, a fellow officer's information, a citizen's complaint, or a combination of these sources. Where probable cause to arrest exists, the officer may make the arrest wherever the person may be found except inside that person's own home, where an arrest warrant is probably required, absent the presence of an excusing legal theory. If an arrestee is discovered within the home of a third party, as a general rule, a warrant is required to enter the home of the third party as a way of protecting the rights of privacy belonging to the third party. As a strong general rule, arrest warrants can be issued only by neutral and detached judicial officials when the presence of probable cause to arrest has been demonstrated.

REVIEW EXERCISES AND QUESTIONS

1. What is the legal standard for probable cause to arrest?
2. From what sources may a police officer obtain information that meets the standard of probable cause to arrest?
3. How can the validity of an informant's information be determined? How does a police officer determine whether to believe an informant or to seek additional information to develop probable cause?
4. Does the "totality of the circumstances" test for evaluating informant reliability under *Illinois v. Gates* make the determination of probable cause easier?
5. Why does "stale" probable cause to arrest rarely become an issue? What is the outer limit of probable cause with respect to the passage of time?
6. What is an arrest warrant? What is the procedural advantage of arresting with a warrant over arresting without a warrant?

7. Although the Fourth Amendment appears to require warrants for all seizures, including arrests, why are arrest warrants generally not required where probable cause exists?

8. Assume that a defendant has been warrantlessly arrested within her own home and that she neither invited the officers inside the premises nor was hotly pursued to her home. Under these circumstances, is her arrest valid? Can a prosecutor still prosecute her if the arrest is determined to have been illegal?

HOW WOULD YOU DECIDE?

1. In the Ohio Court of Appeals

As Cabell drove his van with his girlfriend and her children from the trailer home they shared, three unmarked police cruisers forced the vehicle to stop, and police surrounded the van on three sides. Police planned to arrest Cabell for drug trafficking, among other charges. Days prior to the arrest, two confidential informants had notified police that Cabell would be delivering drugs in a specific area of town, and one informant had participated in a police-controlled purchase of drugs from Cabell on March 2, 2005. Police obtained Cabell's address from a database search by using the license plate number of the motor vehicle Cabell used during the earlier drug transaction. On March 3, 2005, informants alerted police that the defendant would be delivering drugs from his van that very day. Police watched Cabell meet another vehicle at a restaurant but observed no drug sales taking place. Continued surveillance for a week revealed no clear drug sales, but police were again informed that Cabell would make a sale on March 10. As the defendant drove away from his home, the police stopped his van and arrested him after a brief foot chase. A search incident to arrest revealed four individually wrapped bags of cocaine, a baggie of marijuana, two cell phones, and some money. The trial court ordered the drugs suppressed on the theory that the officers stopped Cabell for the purpose of arresting him based solely on the tip police received on March 10 and that the tip and the fact that he was predicted to be driving to deliver the drugs between 6 and 7 P.M. were not sufficient to establish probable cause for an arrest. The prosecutor appealed the trial court's ruling that the arrest was illegal on account of an absence of probable cause.

How would you rule on the defendant's contention that his arrest violated the Fourth Amendment because the police officers lacked probable cause to arrest?

The Court's Holding:

The Ohio Court of Appeals reviewed the concept that an arresting officer must have probable cause to arrest at the moment of arrest for the arrest to be considered constitutionally valid. To develop probable cause, an officer must have information that is sufficient and from a reasonably trustworthy source that would allow a person of reasonable prudence to believe that the subject had committed a felony. The sufficiency of the evidence must be measured by the facts and circumstances in each case. The appellate court noted that the arrest occurred when Cabell's vehicle was pinned by three police cars, preventing his movement until he decided to attempt flight.

In rejecting the presence of probable cause to arrest, the appellate court noted that the officers knew only that Cabell had sold drugs to the police informant eight days prior to his arrest; that Cabell had been seen driving his van where the informant said he would be delivering drugs; that Cabell had apparently participated in a drug sale, the details of which were never observed by police; and that Cabell had exited his trailer park and driven down a road. The court discounted the facts of the alleged drug transaction that the police never observed because meeting in a parking lot is consistent with innocent activity. The police knew Cabell was a licensed driver, so the traffic stop was only for the purposes of arresting Cabell and to catch him transporting drugs that the informant stated would be in his possession. The decision to arrest had been made at the time Cabell left his home consistent with the predictions of the informant, and police observed no new evidence of drug selling that would help mature probable cause. The court rejected the earlier sale reported by the informant on March 2 as stale evidence that could not support current probable cause to arrest. The court noted that "appellee's actions of randomly driving around, parking in restaurant parking lots, and talking briefly with others, does not indicate that appellee was acting suspiciously. Appellee's actions between March 2 and March 10 simply did not indicate 'ongoing' criminal activity." Therefore, the arrest was without probable cause, and the search incident to arrest that revealed drugs and phones was similarly unlawful under the Fourth Amendment. The court reversed the convictions. See *State v. Cabell,* 2006 Ohio 4914; 2006 Ohio App. LEXIS 4841 (2006).

HOW WOULD YOU DECIDE?

2. In the Court of Criminal Appeals of Tennessee

Police developed a suspicion that one Scotty Henry was manufacturing methamphetamine in his trailer home, a tip that was based on information they received from a "meth lab hotline." Without probable cause to arrest, two officers identified Henry's residence and walked up on the porch to conduct a "knock and talk" with any person who answered the door. There was an absence of "no trespassing" signs that might have precluded the officers from entering the property. The officers had their badges around their necks when a man identified as Watson answered their knocks and opened the front door all the way. One officer immediately recognized a strong chemical odor. When the officers asked to speak to Henry, Watson indicated that Henry was present inside the home, and Watson invited the officers to enter the home when he stated, "Sure. Come on in." Prior to entering the trailer home, the officers scanned the parts of the interior visible to them and also smelled a chemical odor. The officers recognized the smell as indicating the presence of components needed in the manufacture of methamphetamine. Police arrested Henry, Watson, and others immediately.

The defendant, Henry, sought to suppress the evidence of methamphetamine manufacturing and contended that the search of his home and his arrest were illegal under the Fourth Amendment. The trial court held that the officers had probable cause to perform the warrantless search of his home because the "knock and talk" was lawful. The court observed that Watson appeared to be in control of the home and could give valid consent to enter. Once the door was opened and the officers were invited inside and continued to smell traditional odors associated with meth manufacture and observe chemicals and pill soak, they were lawfully on the premises and could make warrantless arrests based on probable cause. The appellate court observed that the officers possessed experience in methamphetamine lab seizures and were aware of the odors to be expected from a meth lab. The trial court concluded that the officers had lawfully observed a crime being committed that gave probable cause to arrest. Defendant Henry pled guilty to the charges but reserved the right to an appellate challenge concerning whether the officers had probable cause to search his house. Implicit in this reservation is the question concerning whether the officers had the right to lawfully enter the home on Watson's permission immediately prior to the arrests.

How will you rule on the defendant's contention that the officers should not have entered his home without a warrant and that following such a procedure made his arrest unlawful under the Fourth Amendment?

The Court's Holding:

The Court of Criminal Appeals of Tennessee noted that the Constitution of the United States and the Tennessee Constitution protect the homes of people from unreasonable searches and seizures and that the general rule contemplates that homes will not be entered for searches or arrests unless probable cause and a warrant exist. The "knock and talk" procedure has been previously determined to be a lawful approach for which probable cause is not a necessary requirement, and in this case, the occupants had not placed "no trespassing" signs on the property. The officers were lawfully allowed to enter the home because Watson possessed apparent authority over the property sufficient to invite others, including police officers, to enter. Therefore, the officers were lawfully inside the home when they viewed incriminating activity and smelled incriminating odors for which felony probable cause to arrest matured. Citing *Payton v. New York,* 445 U.S. 573, 583–90 (1980), the appellate court agreed that warrantless arrests within a home are generally unreasonable and therefore unlawful, but where the police have been invited to enter the home, no complaint that the officers were not lawfully on the premises can be sustained. In addition, the officers could see some of the methamphetamine production from their vantage point on the front porch. The appellate court rejected Henry's appeal that the arrests were unlawful and that the home had been improperly searched, and the court affirmed the convictions. See *State v. Henry,* 2007 Tenn. Crim. App. LEXIS 302 (2007).

ENDNOTES

1. Probable cause for arrest has been phrased similarly to *Carroll.* In *Beck v. Ohio,* probable cause for an arrest was said to exist if "at the moment the arrest was made . . . the facts and circumstances within [the arresting officers'] knowledge and of which they had reasonably trustworthy information were sufficient to warrant a prudent man in believing that the [suspect] had committed or was committing an offense." 379 U.S. 89 (1964).

2. *Brendlin v. California,* 127 S.Ct. 2400, 2405 (2007).

3. *California v. Hodari D.,* 499 U.S. 621, 626 (1991).

4. "The rule of the common law, that a peace officer or a private citizen may arrest a felon without a warrant, has been generally held by the courts of the states to be in force in cases of felonies punishable by the civil tribunals." See *Kurtz v. Moffitt,* 115 U.S. 487, 504 (1885).

5. Many federal law enforcement officers have been expressly authorized by statute to make felony arrests on probable cause but without a warrant. This is true of United States marshals, 18 U.S.C. § 3053; agents of the Federal Bureau of Investigation, 18 U.S.C. § 3052; the Drug Enforcement Administration, 84 Stat. 1273, 21 U.S.C. § 878; the Secret Service, 18 U.S.C. § 3056(a); and the Customs Service, 26 U.S.C. § 7607.

6. *Illinois v. Gates,* 462 U.S. 213 (1983).

7. In *Carroll v. United States,* 276 U.S. 132 (1925), which offered a definition of probable cause in the context of a bootleg liquor search, the Court stated: "This is to say that the facts and circumstances within their [the police] knowledge and of which they had reasonably trustworthy information were sufficient, in themselves, to warrant a man of reasonable caution in the belief that intoxicating liquor was being transported in the automobile which they stopped and searched." The legal standard for a search is the same level of proof as for an arrest.

8. *Michigan v. Davis,* 660 N.W.2d 67, 69 (2003).

9. *Davis* at 70.

10. *United States v. Perkins,* 994 F.2d 1184 (6th Cir. 1993).

11. See *Collins v. Nagle,* 892 F.2d 489, 495 (6th Cir. 1989).

12. 378 U.S. 108 (1964).

13. 462 U.S. 213 (1983).

14. The case, *Arizona v. Evans,* dealt primarily with the application of the exclusionary rule of the Fourth Amendment, but it serves as an example of stale probable cause.

15. An arrest warrant is court order issued by a neutral and detached judicial official who has determined that probable cause for arrest exists. The warrant directs law enforcement officers to take into custody a particularly described individual for having committed a specifically described crime where the evidence would permit a person of reasonable caution to believe that the described person has committed the crime or crimes.

16. The general rule is that an arrest warrant or search warrant must be issued by a judge or magistrate. See *Coolidge v. New Hampshire,* 403 U.S. 443 (1971). Justice Stewart wrote the lead opinion for the *Coolidge* Court, which invalidated a search warrant because it had not been issued by a neutral and detached judicial official. In the context of a search warrant, in Justice Brennan's dissent in *Horton v. California,* 496 U.S.128 at 148 (1990), he noted that generally, "The Fourth Amendment demands that an individual's possessory interest in property be protected from unreasonable governmental seizures, not just by requiring a showing of probable cause but also by requiring a neutral and detached magistrate to authorize the seizure in advance." Arrest warrants are not required so long as probable cause exists, but where an arrest warrant is to be issued, a member of the judicial branch must make the probable cause determination.

17. See *United States v. Watson,* 423 U.S. 411 (1976), and *Atwater v. City of Lago Vista,* 532 U.S. 318 (2001).

18. 532 U.S. 318 (2001).

19. In *Tennessee v. Garner,* 471 U.S. 1 (1985), the Court held that using deadly force against an apparently unarmed, nondangerous fleeing suspect for whom probable cause existed cannot be justified as reasonable under the Fourth Amendment, unless necessary to prevent an escape from arrest where the officer has probable cause to believe that the suspect poses a significant threat of death or serious physical injury to the officer or others. According to the *Garner* Court, "The use of deadly force to prevent the escape of all felony suspects, whatever the circumstances, is constitutionally unreasonable."

20. When the forty-eight-hour period of custody without a judicial determination of probable cause is violated, the remedy is not clear. In *United States v. Alvarez-Sanchez,* 511 U.S. 350 (1994), the arrestee argued on appeal that his rights were violated, since he had not been given a hearing within forty-eight hours of arrest and had made incriminating statements while being held illegally under *McLaughlin.* The Court held that he had waived the argument by not raising it in the lower courts. Thus, the remedy for a violation of the forty-eight-hour period is not clear at this point, but it would appear that a successful litigant would have to show prejudice.

21. Http://www.supremecourt.nm.org/cgi-bin/ download.cgi/supctforms/dc-criminal.

22. See *Payton v. New York,* 445 U.S. 573 (1980).

23. *Sparing v. Village of Olympia Fields,* 266 F.3d 684, 691 (2001).

24. Ibid.

25. An illegal arrest does not prevent the government from convicting the individual whose rights have been violated. See *Frisbie v. Collins,* 342 U.S. 519 (1952). The effect of the illegal arrest inside the home is that evidence observed or seized within the home as a result of the illegal arrest is suppressed from prosecutorial use at trial for proof of guilt.

26. 536 U.S. 635 (2002).

27. See *Payton v. New York,* 445 U.S. 573 (1980).

28. See *Illinois v. McArthur,* 531 U.S. 326 (2001).

29. See *State v. Brown,* 2004 Wash. App. LEXIS 1748 (Wash. 2004), where the court upheld a lawful entry and arrest of a suspect when where police received permission from a third party to enter the home where the subject had been hiding. The third party had had dominion and control over the home and consented to the police entry.

C H A P T E R 5

The Concept of Stop and Frisk

Learning Objectives

1. Understand the concept of a stop and frisk, and be able to explain why allowing stop and frisk is important to law enforcement officials.
2. Comprehend the *Terry v. Ohio* legal standard that regulates every stop and frisk, and give a clear example of a valid stop and frisk.
3. Recognize why every lawful stop may not allow a frisk of the individual, and be able to generate a hypothetical situation where a stop is lawful and a frisk is illegal.
4. Evaluate the significance of unexplained flight from a police officer, and explain why an officer may have the legal right to stop a fleeing person under such circumstances.
5. Trace the evolution of the stop and frisk concept from its beginning to stops of motor vehicles to the development of the drug courier profile.
6. Articulate the "checklist" that traces the steps an officer should take under the *Terry* standard prior to conducting a "pat-down" search.
7. Describe a hypothetical fact pattern to suggest that under the plain feel doctrine, a deeper search than a mere frisk is permitted.
8. Explain how the stop and frisk concept developed beyond its original beginning involving reasonable suspicion to encounters with persons for whom police have no individualized suspicion.

Chapter Outline

1. Introduction to Stop and Frisk
2. Stop and Frisk
3. The *Terry* Legal Standard
4. Facts Indicating Unusual Conduct
5. Flight upon Seeing an Officer as Unusual Conduct
6. Frisk May Not Always Allow Additional Search
7. *Terry* Stops under a Drug Courier Profile
8. Subject Must Be Aware of Officer's Status
9. Officer Must Have Reason to Believe That the Person May Be Armed and Dangerous
10. Investigation Must Not Dispel the Fear That the Subject May Be Armed and Dangerous
11. The Plain Feel Doctrine
12. Expansion of the Stop and Frisk beyond Its Genesis
13. Expansion of *Terry*-Like Stops to Individuals Not under Suspicion
14. Summary

Key Terms

Drug courier profile	Scope of frisk
Frisk	Stop
Limitations on scope	Stop and identify
Plain feel doctrine	Time limitations on detention
Reasonable basis to suspect	Unexplained flight
Reasonable suspicion	Weapons frisk of automobile

1. INTRODUCTION TO STOP AND FRISK

Every society has individuals whose conduct attracts the attention of the law enforcement community but may or may not involve criminality. Historically, an encounter with a justice official and brief questioning involves the Fourth Amendment if the subject is not free to walk away. The case law appears to recognize three types of police-citizen contact. The first situation has the officer merely exchanging pleasantries with a person, with neither under any obligation to converse with the other, and each free to go on his or her way. Since no seizure has occurred, the Fourth Amendment has no application. In a second situation, where the facts suggest that the officer has an obligation to make some investigation of conduct that could be criminal, a stop and (where the facts indicate some reasonable fear that the individual may be armed) a frisk may be appropriate. In this situation, the jurisprudence of the Fourth Amendment regulates the conduct of an officer who has momentarily made a seizure of a person. The third situation is an arrest; the individual comes under the total physical control of the officer, following the development of probable cause to arrest.

2. STOP AND FRISK

As a legal concept, the stop and frisk doctrine constitutes the least intrusive search that an officer may be permitted to make of a person for whom the officer has some suspicion of criminality. The stop allows a cursory investigation sufficient to determine whether additional steps are appropriate. The frisk, where allowed, permits a police officer to determine whether a person poses a danger to the officer or to other citizens by discerning whether the individual is armed with some sort of weapon. The concept involves several steps, each one dependent on the outcome of the prior step, until the person may be initially searched in a limited fashion by a pat-down of the outer garments. As a general rule, the officer must possess a reasonable suspicion that a person may be armed. This suspicion must be objectively reasonable, judged by the surrounding facts and circumstances. This reasonable suspicion may be negated by an objectively credible explanation offered by the person for his or her "unusual conduct." A stop and frisk involves situations that do not certainly appear criminal but deserve further scrutiny by law enforcement to determine whether criminality exists.

The Fourth Amendment[1] prohibition against unreasonable searches and seizures, as incorporated into the Fourteenth Amendment's Due Process Clause, has been determined to regulate the brief police-citizen encounters in stop and frisk situations, *Terry v. Ohio,* 392 U.S. 1 (1968) (see Case 5.1). When a police officer restrains an individual from walking away, a Fourth Amendment seizure has occurred, and to be lawful, the manner of seizure, its duration, and any subsequent search must be "reasonable." The police officer does not need traditional probable cause for arrest to briefly detain a suspicious person, merely a reasonable suspicion that criminal activity might be afoot. The Supreme Court of the United States held that this limited seizure of the person does not require a warrant and that similarly, where reasonable, a limited search does not necessitate a warrant.

The officer who observes unusual conduct that suggests criminal activity may be happening or has just occurred may detain the person involved and inquire into what he or she has observed. If the explanation does not resolve the concern, and if the officer has reason to fear that the person may be armed, it is permissible to pat down the individual's outer clothing. According to *Terry* and its progeny, the officer is permitted to look for weapons by searching the outer garments of the detainee. If no "weaponlike lump" is discovered and no other evidence of criminality comes to the knowledge of the officer, the individual must be allowed to continue on his or her way.

Prior to *Terry v. Ohio,* police routinely conducted brief investigative encounters with citizens where police observed facts indicating suspicious circumstances. The location of the subject in a high-crime area late at night,[2] the experience of the police officer,[3] attempts at flight upon sight of the officer,[4] and acting strangely[5] are all factors that an officer may use to conclude that a brief investigation is warranted. People can readily explain some of these unusual situations, but other police-citizen encounters dictate additional scrutiny. A brief conversation and sometimes a limited search of the person may dispel any legitimate curiosity; other *Terry* searches produce evidence sufficient for probable cause for arrest. Out of the Court's decision in *Terry* emerged definite and generally clear guidelines for the conduct of stop and frisk searches. Following *Terry,* courts have adapted the stop and frisk rationale to situations involving automobiles and airport detentions.

3. THE *TERRY* LEGAL STANDARD

The *Terry* Court held that wherever and whenever an officer observes unusual conduct that, in light of the officer's experience, leads him or her to reasonably conclude, based upon articulated facts, that criminal activity might be afoot, the officer is permitted to lawfully stop the person and make an inquiry. A reasonable level of force may be used to effectuate the stop if the individual proves resistant. If not in uniform, the law enforcement officer must convey his or her identity. The subject may be briefly questioned about the unusual conduct; if the explanation proves unreasonable, and the officer reasonably believes the person is armed and dangerous, he or she may conduct a limited search of the outer clothing. This search is intended to protect the officer and those in the immediate vicinity from danger or harm.

CASE 5.1

Leading Case Brief: Stops of Suspicious Individuals Can Be Based on Less than Probable Cause

Terry v. Ohio
Supreme Court of the United States
392 U.S. 1 (1968)

Case Facts:

While on routine, nonuniformed patrol, Detective Martin McFadden of the Cleveland Police Department observed two men acting in a strange fashion. One of the men under McFadden's view repeatedly walked partway down one block, peered in a store window, walked a bit further, returned to look in the window a second time, and then retraced his steps to confer with the unknown subject. The second man repeated the conduct of the first and then returned for a conference. This conduct repeated several times until a third man joined them. When the third man left the company of the first two men, they repeated their unusual conduct. Detective McFadden observed all of this activity to the point that it aroused his suspicions.

McFadden, based on his thirty-five years as a police detective, believed that the men were "casing a job, a stick-up" and that the conduct warranted further investigation. When the third man rejoined the first two, McFadden approached the three men, made his identity known to the men, and asked them for their names. When the three mumbled inaudible replies, McFadden grabbed Terry and spun him around so that McFadden could view Chilton and the other man while he conducted a limited search of Terry's outer garments.

The pat-down search revealed to McFadden the fact that Terry possessed a pistol in an inside pocket of an overcoat. Prior to removing Terry's overcoat, McFadden patted only the outer garments and did not reach inside until he felt the "weapon-like" lump. He ordered all three men inside the nearest store, where a further pat-down of the three produced one more weapon.

After he had been charged with carrying a concealed weapon and prior to a trial on the merits, Terry filed a motion to suppress the evidence uncovered by McFadden. He alleged that Officer McFadden had no probable cause for arrest; therefore, the search of his person exceeded the bounds permitted by the Fourth Amendment as applied to the states. The trial court agreed with Terry that probable cause for arrest did not exist but held the opinion that Detective McFadden had the right to pat down the men for his own protection. The trial court held that, under the circumstances, such conduct was reasonable under the Fourth Amendment and refused to suppress the weapon evidence from trial.

Subsequent to the trial court's denial of Terry's pretrial motion to suppress the revolver, Terry elected a bench trial and he was convicted. The Court of Appeals affirmed, and the Supreme Court of Ohio dismissed their appeal on the ground that it involved no "substantial constitutional question." The Supreme Court of the United States granted Terry's petition for certiorari.

Legal Issue:

Where a police officer has observed unusual conduct that led him to reasonably conclude that criminal activity might be afoot or has occurred and that the person with whom he was dealing may be armed and dangerous; where, during the course of the encounter, he identified himself as an officer; and where his fear for his safety remains, may the officer conduct a limited pat-down of the subject's outer clothing in order to discover weapons?

The Court's Ruling:

The Supreme Court balanced the need for an officer to determine whether a suspicious person might be armed against the Fourth Amendment expectation of privacy and decided that a pat-down of outer garments of a subject may be appropriate where objective facts are present.

Essence of the Court's Rationale:

Unquestionably petitioner was entitled to the protection of the Fourth Amendment as he walked down the streets in Cleveland. The question is whether in all the circumstances of this on-the-street encounter, his right to personal security was violated by an unreasonable search and seizure.

We would be less than candid if we did not acknowledge that this question thrusts to the fore difficult and troublesome issues regarding a sensitive area of police activity—issues which have never before been squarely presented to this Court. . . .

On the one hand, it is frequently argued that in dealing with the rapidly unfolding and often dangerous situations on city streets the police are in need of an escalating set of flexible responses, graduated in relation to the amount of information they possess. For this purpose it is urged that distinctions should be made between a "stop" and an "arrest" (or a "seizure" of a person), and between a "frisk" and a "search." Thus, it is argued, the police should be allowed to "stop" a person and detain him briefly for questioning upon suspicion that he may be connected with criminal activity. Upon suspicion that the person may be armed, the police should have the power to "frisk" him for weapons. If the "stop" and the "frisk" give rise to probable cause to believe that the suspect has committed a crime, then the police should be empowered to make a formal "arrest," and a full incident "search" of the person. This scene is justified in part upon the notion that a "stop" and a "frisk" amount to a mere "minor inconvenience and petty indignity," which can properly be imposed upon the citizen in the interest of effective law enforcement on the basis of a police officer's suspicion.

On the other side the argument is made that the authority of the police must be strictly circumscribed by the law of arrest and search as it has developed to date in the traditional jurisprudence of the Fourth Amendment. It is contended with some force that there is not—and cannot be—a variety of police activity which does not depend solely upon the voluntary cooperation of the citizen and yet which stops short of an arrest based upon probable cause to make such an arrest. The heart of the Fourth Amendment, the argument runs, is a severe requirement of specific justification for any intrusion upon protected personal security, coupled with a highly developed system of judicial controls to enforce upon the agents of the State the commands of the Constitution. Acquiescence by the

court in the compulsion inherent in the field interrogation practices at issue here, it is urged, would constitute an abdication of judicial control over, and indeed an encouragement of, substantial interference with liberty and personal security by police officers whose judgment is necessarily colored by their primary involvement in "the often competitive enterprise of ferreting out crime." *Johnson v. United States*, 333 U.S. 10, 14, 68 S.Ct. 367, 369 (1948). This, it is argued, can only serve to exacerbate police-community tensions in the crowded centers of our Nation's cities.

* * *

In this case there can be no question, then, that Officer McFadden "seized" petitioner and subjected him to a "search" of his clothing. We must decide whether at that point it was reasonable for Officer McFadden to have interfered with petitioner's personal security as he did. And in determining whether the seizure and search were "unreasonable" our inquiry is a dual one—whether the officer's action was justified at its inception, and whether it was reasonably related in scope to the circumstances which justified the interference in the first place.

* * *

The sole justification of the search in the present situation is the protection of the police officer and others nearby, and it must therefore be confined in scope to an intrusion reasonably designed to discover guns, knives, clubs, or other hidden instruments for the assault of the police officer.

The scope of the search in this case presents no serious problem in light of these standards. Officer McFadden patted down the outer clothing of petitioner and his two companions. He did not place his hands in their pockets or under the outer surface of their garments until he had felt weapons, and then he merely reached for and removed the guns. He never did invade . . . [the third gentleman's] person beyond the outer surfaces of his clothes, since he discovered nothing in his pat down which might have been a weapon. Officer McFadden confined his search strictly to what was minimally necessary to learn whether the men were armed and to disarm them once he discovered the weapons. He did not conduct a general exploratory search for whatever evidence of criminal activity he might find.

* * *

(continued)

We conclude that the revolver seized from Terry was properly admitted in evidence against him. At the time he seized petitioner and searched him for weapons, Officer McFadden had reasonable grounds to believe the petitioner was armed and dangerous, and it was necessary for the protection of himself and others to take swift measures to discover the true facts and neutralize the threat of harm if it materialized. The policeman carefully restricted his search to what was appropriate to the discovery of the particular items which he sought. Each case of this sort will, of course, have to be decided on its own facts. We merely hold today that where a police officer observes unusual conduct which leads him reasonably to conclude in light of his experience that criminal activity may be afoot and that the persons with whom he is dealing may be armed and presently dangerous; where in the course of investigating this behavior he identifies himself as a policeman and makes reasonable inquiries; and where nothing in the initial stages of the encounter serves to dispel his reasonable fear for his own or others' safety, he is entitled for the protection of himself and others in the area to conduct a carefully limited search of the outer clothing of such persons in an attempt to discover weapons which might be used to assault him. Such a search is a reasonable search under the Fourth Amendment, and any weapons seized may be properly introduced in evidence against the person from whom they were taken. *Affirmed.*

Case Importance:

Consistent with the Fourth Amendment, police officers may stop suspicious persons, ask brief questions, and if they suspect that a person might be armed, conduct limited warrantless searches. The result keeps police officers more secure and protects the public and the rights of individuals by without violating the Constitution.

Chief Justice Warren, writing for the majority, stated the Court's essential holding in *Terry:*

> We merely hold today that, where a police officer observes unusual conduct which leads him reasonably to conclude in light of his experience that criminal activity may be afoot and that the persons with whom he is dealing may be armed and presently dangerous, where, in the course of investigating this behavior, he identifies himself as a policeman and makes reasonable inquiries, and where nothing in the initial stages of the encounter serves to dispel his reasonable fear for his own or others' safety, he is entitled for the protection of himself and others in the area to conduct a carefully limited search of the outer clothing of such persons in an attempt to discover weapons which might be used to assault him. 392 U.S. 1, 30.

The *Terry* Court determined that a stop and frisk can be legitimately conducted on less evidence than is required for probable cause for arrest or for a traditional search of a house or motor vehicle. Consistent with the reasonableness requirement of the Fourth Amendment, the search is restricted to tactics designed to discover weapons. Even though a stop and frisk requires only "reasonable suspicion" as justification, in situations where the pat-down reveals a lump or bulge that could reasonably be construed as a weapon, the officer may reach inside the clothing. Some weapons are easily discerned, but other lumps within clothing do not lend themselves to quick determination. In *United States v. Campbell,* 178 F.3d 345 (1999), the Court approved a search within a pocket where a police officer removed a bulge from a bank robbery suspect. Contained within the bulge were $1,400 in cash, a gold cardboard jewelry box containing some gold chain, and some change. The Court felt that the money could have been hiding a weapon. However, if an officer concludes that the object felt through the clothing could not reasonably be construed as a weapon, further searching cannot proceed. In *Minnesota v. Dickerson,* 508 U.S. 366 (1993), the Court held that a police officer cannot manipulate an object (crack cocaine) from outside a suspect's pants pocket to discern the identity of the pocket's contents. The officer never entertained the thought that the lump was a weapon and did not immediately recognize it as rock cocaine. As a general rule, where the protective search goes beyond what is necessary to determine whether the suspect is armed, the search cannot be valid under *Terry,* and its fruits should be suppressed.[6]

In a companion case to *Terry, Sibron v. New York,*[7] where the facts were held not sufficient to allow a frisk, the Court held that evidence obtained from the frisk had been obtained in violation of the Fourth Amendment as applied to the states. In *Sibron,* which had facts some what similar to those in *Terry,* a uniformed police officer observed Sibron from four o'clock in the afternoon until midnight. Sibron conversed with known narcotics addicts, but the officer did not observe any transfer or sale of drugs or see anything approaching illegality.

Late in the evening, Sibron entered a restaurant. The officer observed Sibron speak with three more known addicts inside the restaurant. Once again, nothing was overheard, and nothing was seen to pass between Sibron and the addicts. Sibron sat down and ordered pie and coffee, and as he was eating, the officer approached him and told him to come outside. Once outside, the officer said to Sibron, "You know what I am after." According to the officer, Sibron "mumbled something and reached into his pocket." At the same time, the officer put his hand into the same pocket, and together they removed several glassine envelopes containing heroin. At no time did the officer state that he was fearful of Mr. Sibron or believed that Sibron might be armed and dangerous.

When Sibron's case reached the Supreme Court of the United States, his contention that the officer's search of his person was unreasonable under the circumstances prevailed. The distinction between the *Terry* case and Sibron's situation turns on the issue of whether the officer could have developed a reason to suspect Sibron of criminal activity and to have concluded that Sibron might be armed and dangerous. No evidence pointed to any reasonable suspicion of criminal activity by Sibron, and there was no reason to believe that he was armed. Therefore, the search by the officer was illegal under the Fourth Amendment, and the evidence of heroin possession should have been suppressed from his trial.

4. FACTS INDICATING UNUSUAL CONDUCT

The facts that generate a police officer's reasonable basis to suspect criminal activity may be derived from the officer's personal observation, from informant information, from a dispatcher message, or from a combination of two or more sources. In *Terry v. Ohio,* the police detective observed two men apparently "casing" a store by repeatedly walking past the store window and conferring with each other. This conduct demanded some inquiry by the detective and allowed him to briefly stop the two men for questioning. Personal observation of furtive and evasive behavior by a passenger following a routine traffic stop can create a reasonable basis to suspect criminal behavior. According to the Florida Court of Appeals in *Brown v. State,* 2004 Fla. App. LEXIS 254 (2004), police officers could justify a frisk of a passenger where his evasive movements while in the vehicle suggested that he might be trying to hide something and that he might be armed. A police officer may also obtain information from an informant, as happened in *Adams v. Williams,* 407 U.S. 143 (1972), where the officer received information from a reliable informant[8] that a man was armed, selling drugs, and sitting in an automobile late at night. The officer located the car and asked the occupant to step outside, but the subject rolled down the window instead. The noncompliance, along with the validation of the person's presence and the suggestion that the car's occupant was armed, gave rise to unusual conduct that met the *Terry* standard of reasonable basis to suspect criminal activity. Information giving rise to "reasonable basis to suspect" may come from more than one source. In *Alabama v. White,* 496 U.S. 325 (1990) (Case 5.2), the Court approved the stop of a moving automobile on the stop and frisk rationale where the police obtained information from an anonymous informant and verified some of the information by personal observation. The anonymous caller predicted what conduct a person living in an apartment building would pursue upon leaving the apartment and what car the individual would be driving. A prediction that the driver would head to a local motel to sell drugs seemed to be true when the apartment dweller entered the described car and drove toward the motel where the drug deal was to be consummated. The telephone tip, coupled with the officers' verification of some of the facts, along with the occurrence of the predicted behavior, proved sufficient to meet the *Terry* standard and justify a brief motor vehicle stop and inquiry by police. Thus, the stop and frisk standard of proof may be met by virtue of information supplied by an informant alone or may be combined with personal observations of the officer to reach the proper level of proof.

Facts indicating unusual conduct must be objectively present prior to conducting a *Terry*-type stop of a person or a motor vehicle, or the seizures violate the Fourth Amendment. In *Delaware v. Prouse,* 440 U.S. 648 (1979), an officer testified he made a traffic stop after he "had observed neither traffic or equipment violations nor any suspicious activity, and that he made the stop only in order to check the driver's license and registration."[9] The officer lacked any objective evidence that pointed toward criminality of any of the car's occupants or knowledge that met the standard of reasonable basis to suspect that criminal activity might be occurring. Despite the fact that the officer discovered marijuana in the car, there was no reason to stop the vehicle and to speak with the driver or with passenger Prouse, and the conviction was reversed. In 2007, the Court reaffirmed that automobiles cannot be stopped unless the *Terry* minimal standard has been satisfied or the higher standard of probable cause exists.[10]

Representative of a fact situation that aroused suspicion from personal observations by the officer but failed to meet the *Terry* standard of reasonable basis to suspect criminal activity occurred in a Missouri case. One morning, a police officer noticed a truck drive up and park in a shopping center at 12:30 A.M. on a side of the center where no entrances to the stores were located. The shopping center had not experienced any recent elevated criminal activity. The light from streetlights was sufficient to enable the officer to keep the truck under surveillance at all times, and the officer observed that the driver did nothing unusual. When the driver started the vehicle and drove away, the officer stopped the truck and found that the driver was under

CASE 5.2

Leading Case Brief: *Terry* Standard Can Be Met by Informant and Can Apply to Automobile Stops

Alabama v. White
Supreme Court of the United States
496 U.S. 325 (1990)

Case Facts:

Officers in the Montgomery, Alabama, Police Department received an anonymous telephone tip that respondent Vanessa White would be leaving a named apartment building at a particular time in a uniquely described vehicle that had a broken right taillight lens. Further the caller said that White would be going to Dobey's Motel and would be in possession of an ounce of cocaine. Two officers immediately proceeded to the apartment building, saw a vehicle matching the caller's description, observed White as she left the building and entered the vehicle, and followed her along the most direct route to the motel. Although the police did not observe White take anything from the apartment to her vehicle, they decided to stop her vehicle just short of the motel. Corporal Davis asked her to step to the rear of her car, where he informed her that she had been stopped because she was suspected of carrying cocaine in the vehicle. He asked if they could look for cocaine, and White indicated her consent. The officers found a locked brown attaché case in the car and, upon request, respondent provided the combination to the lock. The officers found marijuana in the attaché case and placed respondent under arrest. In a search incident to arrest, cocaine was found in her purse.

The prosecution charged White with possession of marijuana and cocaine. The trial court rejected her motion to suppress evidence, and she pled guilty, reserving the right to appeal the legality of the stop and search of her automobile and the search incident to arrest.

The Court of Criminal Appeals of Alabama reversed her conviction on possession charges, holding that the trial court should have suppressed the marijuana and cocaine because the officers did not have the reasonable suspicion necessary under *Terry v.*

Ohio, 392 U.S. 1 (1968), to justify the investigatory stop of the vehicle. The Supreme Court of Alabama denied the government's petition for certiorari. The Supreme Court of the United States granted certiorari to the State of Alabama.

Legal Issue:

May an anonymous telephone tip alleging criminal activity, when substantially corroborated by observations by police officers, produce "reasonable basis to suspect criminal activity" sufficient to make an investigatory stop of a person in a moving motor vehicle?

The Court's Ruling:

An anonymous telephone tip that police are able to partially corroborate is sufficient evidence to allow a *Terry*-type automobile stop for a brief inquiry; it does not, without more information, rise to the level of probable cause to arrest or to search.

Essence of the Court's Rationale:

[The Supreme Court in] *Adams v. Williams*, 407 U.S. 143 (1972), sustained a *Terry* stop and frisk [of a motorist in a parked automobile] undertaken on the basis of a tip given in person by a known informant, who had provided information in the past. We concluded that, while the unverified tip may have been insufficient to support an arrest or search warrant, the information carried sufficient "indicia of reliability" to justify a forcible stop. We did not address the issue of anonymous tips in *Adams*, except to say that "[t]his is a stronger case than obtains in the case of an anonymous telephone tip," *id.*, at 146.

[Similarly, the Court in] *Illinois v. Gates*, 462 U.S. 213 (1983), dealt with an anonymous tip in the

(continued)

probable cause context. The Court there abandoned the "two-pronged test" of *Aguilar v. Texas,* 378 U.S. 108 (1964), and *Spinelli v. United States,* 393 U.S. 410 (1969), in favor of a "totality of circumstances" approach to determining whether an informant's tip establishes probable cause. *Gates* made clear, however, that those factors that had been considered critical under *Aguilar* and *Spinelli*—an informant's "veracity," "reliability," and "basis of knowledge"—remain "highly relevant in determining the value of his report." 462 U.S., at 230. These factors are also relevant in the reasonable suspicion context, although allowance must be made in applying them for the lesser showing required to meet that standard.

The opinion in *Gates* recognized that an anonymous tip alone seldom demonstrates the informant's basis of knowledge or veracity inasmuch as ordinary citizens generally do not provide extensive recitations of the basis of their everyday observations and given that the veracity of persons supplying anonymous tips is "by hypothesis largely unknown, and unknowable."

* * *

As there was in *Gates,* however, in this case there is more than the tip itself. The tip was not as detailed, and the corroboration was not as complete, as in *Gates,* but the required degree of suspicion was likewise not as high.

* * *

Reasonable suspicion [required under *Terry*] is a less demanding standard than probable cause not only in the sense that reasonable suspicion can be established with information that is different in quantity or content than that required to establish probable cause, but also in the sense that reasonable suspicion can arise from information that is less reliable than that required to show probable cause. . . . Thus, if a tip has a relatively low degree of reliability, more information will be required to establish the requisite quantum of suspicion than would be required if the tip were more reliable. . . . Contrary to the court below, we conclude that when the officers stopped respondent, the anonymous tip had been sufficiently corroborated to furnish reasonable suspicion that respondent was engaged in criminal activity and that the investigative stop therefore did not violate the Fourth Amendment.

It is true that not every detail mentioned by the tipster was verified, such as the name of the woman leaving the building or the precise apartment from which she left; but the officers did corroborate that a woman left the 235 building and got into the particular vehicle that was described by the caller. With respect to the time of departure predicted by the informant, Corporal Davis testified that the caller gave a particular time when the woman would be leaving, but he did not state what the time was. He did testify that, after the call, he and his partner proceeded to the Lynwood Terrace Apartments to put the 235 building under surveillance. Given the fact that the officers proceeded to the indicated address immediately after the call and that respondent emerged not too long thereafter, it appears from the record before us that respondent's departure from the building was within the time frame predicted by the caller. [The Court felt that the prediction of her destination was sufficiently corroborated by her act of driving toward the described motel.]

* * *

The Court's opinion in *Gates* gave credit to the proposition that because an informant is shown to be right about some things, he is probably right about other facts that he has alleged, including the claim that the object of the tip is engaged in criminal activity. [*Illinois v. Gates*] 462 U.S., at 244. Thus, it is not unreasonable to conclude in this case that the independent corroboration by the police of significant aspects of the informer's predictions imparted some degree of reliability to the other allegations made by the caller.

* * *

When significant aspects of the caller's predictions were verified, there was reason to believe not only that the caller was honest but also that he was well informed, at least well enough to justify the stop.

Although it is a close case, we conclude that under the totality of circumstances the anonymous tip, as corroborated, exhibited sufficient indicia of reliability to justify the investigatory stop of respondent's car. We therefore reverse the judgment of the Court of Criminal Appeals of Alabama and remand for further proceedings not inconsistent with this opinion.

So ordered.

Case Importance:

The reasoning in this case allows police to stop individuals, whether on foot or while driving automobiles, when an informant has given some information that does not rise to the level of probable cause to search or to arrest but where sufficient suspicion of criminal activity has been raised by a person who has special information, partially verified by police, that is not generally available to everyone.

the influence of alcohol. According to trial testimony, the officer stated that he just wanted to get a name in case some crime had been committed. In reversing the conviction for driving while under the influence of alcohol, the appellate court agreed with the defendant's pretrial and trial contentions made during a motion to suppress the evidence of intoxication. The court held that the officer lacked any articulable and reasonable suspicion that could be construed as consistent with *Terry* that the truck or driver may have offended the law, and he should not have stopped the defendant.[11]

Merely being in a high-crime area with a bulge in one's pants does not rise to the level of reasonable basis to suspect criminal activity. In a Maryland case, while cruising in an unmarked car, officers noticed a man standing on the street who looked at them; the officers concluded that a bulge in the man's pants could be a gun. One officer approached the man and initiated a pat-down but started at the waist and did not initially direct his focus at the bulge. When the officer discovered a smaller, until then unknown, bulge that contained drugs, he placed the subject in custody and completed a full search, incident to arrest. In evaluating the reasonable basis to suspect standard under the totality of the circumstances, the appellate court held that the officers failed to possess sufficient evidence to meet the *Terry* standard authorizing an initial stop.[12]

5. FLIGHT UPON SEEING AN OFFICER AS UNUSUAL CONDUCT

Mere flight upon seeing a police officer alone may not be unusual conduct that might be indicative of crime. However, flight upon sight *plus* other factors may give an officer the sufficient level of reasonable suspicion necessary for a *Terry* stop. In *Michigan v. Chesternut,* 486 U.S. 567 (1988), while observing the approach of a police car on routine patrol, Chesternut began to run in the opposite direction. The police followed him "to see where he was going"; after catching up with him and driving alongside him for a short distance, they observed him discarding a number of packets. Believing that the packets contained drugs, the police alighted from the cruiser, examined them, and concluded that they contained narcotics. The police arrested Chesternut. According to the Court, any determination concerning whether police behavior amounts to a seizure implicating the Fourth Amendment must take into account "all of the circumstances surrounding the incident" in each individual case. Thus, flight plus questionable conduct permitted the police to make a stop under the *Terry* standard.

Flight alone would not be sufficiently suspicious, but almost any added factor seems to meet the *Terry* standard. In *Illinois v. Wardlow,* 528 U.S. 119 (2000), the subject took flight upon seeing a caravan of police cars converging on a Chicago street in an area known for heavy drug trafficking. He was holding an opaque plastic shopping bag and, upon spotting the police, began to run away. Officers caught the subject and discovered a revolver during a stop and pat-down of his person and plastic bag. Ultimately, the Supreme Court upheld the stop of the suspect under *Terry* because the otherwise innocent flight upon seeing the police was accompanied by another factor: presence in an area with high drug crimes. The *Wardlow* Court noted that "the determination of reasonable suspicion must be based on common sense judgments and inferences about human behavior."[13] In essence, flight alone probably would not be sufficient to conduct a stop of a person, but where it is accompanied by almost any other action of a suspicious nature, an officer may make a lawful *Terry* stop of the person without running afoul of the Fourth Amendment.

State courts have generally followed the *Wardlow* rationale in permitting stop and frisk where unexplained flight occurs. A citizen complaint that a specifically described individual possessed a handgun at a particular street intersection, coupled with that individual's flight upon seeing an officer approach, can be sufficient to warrant a stop and frisk. In a Pennsylvania case, the court ruled that a complaint about a handgun, coupled with the initial encounter between the suspect and the officer, could not justify a stop. However, that same information, added to the subject's flight upon the officer's approach, justified the stop and the subsequent frisk that revealed the concealed weapon.[14]

In the District of Columbia, in a situation where a man had been flagging down cars in the largest open-air drug market for marijuana sales in the District and yelling, "Hey, hey, right here, right here," police investigated the man's behavior. As police observed, the subject continued to wave his arms at cars as they drove past him, behavior that caused police officers to conclude that he was attempting to sell recreational pharmacueticals. When the subject observed police, he stopped hailing cars and immediately walked away from police. Four Zip-Lock bags of marijuana were found in his immediate vicinity when police managed to get the subject to stop. His conduct and his flight upon identifying police officers was sufficient to justify police intervention for a *Terry* investigative stop.[15]

6. FRISK MAY NOT ALWAYS ALLOW ADDITIONAL SEARCH

Judicial clarifications on stop and frisk where courts disagree with law enforcement officials are limited in comparison with decisions approving police pat-downs. In *Sibron v. New York,* 392 U.S. 40 (1968), a companion case to *Terry* noted earlier in this chapter, the Court held that reasonable basis to suspect was not reached where an officer watched a known drug addict talk to several other known addicts over a period of several hours, did not see anything given to him, and did not overhear any conversation that would indicate criminality. Similarly, a pat-down of a bar patron for weapons during the execution of a search warrant for the premises was improper; there was no individualized suspicion that a particular patron or anyone was armed.[16] Some searches conducted after a lawful *Terry* stop may exceed permissible bounds. A Florida court of appeal held that an officer had no authority to look inside a box of cigarettes taken from a frisked participant at a fight scene. Since the officer had no reason to suspect that a knife or gun was hidden inside the cigarette box, the court held that looking inside the cigarette box exceeded the scope of searches permissible under the Fourth Amendment.[17]

Because a stop may not justify a frisk, and a frisk may not justify a more intrusive search, a police officer must have the proper quantum of evidence before proceeding to the next step under the *Terry* rationale. Demonstrative of this principle, the officer in *Alexander v. Florida,* 616 So. 2d 540 (1993), stopped the defendant because a reliable informant had told the officer that a specific car had some cocaine inside it. Following a stop of the vehicle, the officer conducted a pat-down of the driver and discovered a hard, cylindrical object two or three inches long and a half inch in diameter in the area of his pants crotch. When the officer finally obtained the object, it proved to contain cocaine. The court of appeals reversed conviction based on the evidence obtained from the stop and frisk search and seizure on the theory that removal of the object was unreasonable, since the officer had no information that the object might be a weapon. According to the court:

> Assuming that the informant's tip, that he had seen a large amount of cocaine in the car driven by Alexander, provided reasonable suspicion that a crime was being committed, thereby justifying a stop of the vehicle, neither the facts nor the law supports the remainder of the trial court's finding, that the pat-down search was justified because the informant's tip gave the officer "probable cause to believe that defendant may have been armed and dangerous" because he was engaged in a drug transaction involving a large quantity of narcotics and a large sum of money. 616 So.2d 540, 541, 542.

Thus, the officer's conduct failed to meet the requirements for a search under the stop and frisk rationale.

In a slightly different context, a Florida court overturned a conviction based on a failed stop and frisk. The police initiated the encounter when a bicyclist, in an area known for narcotics dealing, leaned toward the interior of an automobile and reached inside. No exchange was observed, but the officer recognized the bicyclist as a purchaser of drugs on prior occasions. Police attempted to stop the bicyclist, who took flight. Ultimately, the officers caught him after a short foot chase. Opening his hand, they found a baggie containing a trace of cocaine. The Florida Court of Appeals reversed the conviction of the defendant on the basis that the initial detention was not valid. According to the court:

> A stop is not warranted solely upon an officer's observation of a black male in a high-crime district leaning into the window of a white man's car stopped in the middle of the street who walks away upon seeing an officer approach. *Winters v. State,* 578 So.2d 5 (Fla. 2d DCA 1991). Nor is a stop warranted where the defendant engages in such activity while in the presence of known drug dealers. [Citations omitted.] Thus, the fact that the appellant had merely been present at other drug transactions does not raise the basis for the officers' suspicion to the level required for detention under the stop and frisk law. *Shackelford v. Florida,* 579 So. 2d 306, 307 (1991).

Although not all courts would follow the logic as applied to the facts in the foregoing cases, the rationale points out that police officers need to be aware that the facts necessary to justify the initial stop must be more than a mere hunch, that not all stops will mature into pat-down searches, and that even fewer will allow a deeper search once the officer is reasonably satisfied that the individual is not armed.

7. *TERRY* STOPS UNDER A DRUG COURIER PROFILE

If a person fits the "drug courier profile," under the *Terry* rationale, a brief stop of the person and a brief investigation have been held to be appropriate. In *Florida v. Royer,* 460 U.S. 491 (1983) (see Case 5.3), the defendant, an airline passenger, attracted the

CASE 5.3

Leading Case Brief: The Drug Courier Profile Is an Acceptable *Terry* Standard; Unreasonable Detentions Produce Excludable Evidence

Florida v. Royer
Supreme Court of the United States
460 U.S. 491 (1983)

Case Facts:

After purchasing a one-way airline ticket to New York City at Miami International Airport under an assumed name and checking his two suitcases bearing identification tags with the same assumed name, Mark Royer went to the concourse leading to the airline boarding area. Unknown to Royer, two detectives used a "drug courier profile" to isolate Royer from other passengers traveling to New York. The detectives asked to see his airline ticket and some identification. The ticket bore the name of "Holt" and not Royer. After listening to Royer offer a brief explanation, they suggested that Royer accompany them to a small room. At this point the detectives told Mr Royer that they suspected that he was transporting contraband drugs.

Royer's airline ticket, boarding pass, and driver's license remained in the possession of the detectives. Royer appeared to voluntarily walk with the officers to the room. One of the detectives used Royer's luggage claim checks to obtain the luggage.

When asked if he would give consent to a search of the luggage, Royer did not verbally agree, but offered a key and unlocked one suitcase that he did not open. One detective opened that suitcase, revealing a quantity of marijuana. When asked if the detectives could open the second suitcase, Royer explained it was all right with him if they opened it. One of the detectives forcibly opened the second item of luggage, disclosing more marijuana. Approximately fifteen minutes had elapsed from the time the detectives initially stopped Royer until his arrest upon the discovery of the contraband.

Prior to his trial for possession of marijuana, Royer filed a motion to suppress the marijuana, alleging that the officers detained him too long under the stop and frisk theory. He pled no contest to the drug possession charge while reserving his right to appeal the denial of his Fourth Amendment claim.

The Florida District Court of Appeal held that Royer had been involuntarily confined within the small room without probable cause and that the involuntary detention had exceeded the limited time of restraint permitted by *Terry v. Ohio*. The United States Supreme Court granted certiorari.

Legal Issue:

Where government officials detain an airline passenger for fifteen minutes, remove him with his ticket and identification to an interrogation room, and retrieve his luggage from an airline on the basis that he fits a "drug courier profile," does such conduct exceed the time limits of the stop and frisk doctrine?

The Court's Ruling:

Under the stop and frisk doctrine, a stop must be brief and last only as long as necessary to resolve the suspicion. If officers continue a stop of a person beyond the time that is considered reasonable under the circumstances, evidence seized as a result cannot be admitted at trial to prove guilt.

Essence of the Court's Rationale:

* * *

II

Some preliminary observations are in order. First, it is unquestioned that, without a warrant to search Royer's luggage and in the absence of probable cause and exigent circumstances, the validity of the search depended on Royer's purported consent.

* * *

Second, law enforcement officers do not violate the Fourth Amendment by merely approaching an individual on the street or in another public place, by asking him if he is willing to answer some questions, by putting questions to him if the person is willing to listen, or by offering in evidence in a criminal prosecution his voluntary answers to such questions. *Terry v. Ohio,* 392 U.S. at 31, 32–33.

* * *

He may not be detained even momentarily without reasonable, objective grounds for doing so; and his refusal to listen or answer does not, without more, furnish those grounds. *United States v. Mendenhall,* supra, at 556 (opinion of Stewart, J.). If there is no detention—no seizure within the meaning of the Fourth Amendment—then no constitutional rights have been infringed.

Third, it is also clear that not all seizures of the person must be justified by probable cause to arrest for a crime. Prior to *Terry v. Ohio, supra,* any restraint on the person amounting to a seizure for the purposes of the Fourth Amendment was invalid unless justified by probable cause. *Dunaway v. New York, supra,* at 207–209. Terry created a limited exception to this general rule: certain seizures are justifiable under the Fourth Amendment if there is articulable suspicion that a person has committed or is about to commit a crime.

* * *

Fourth, *Terry* and its progeny nevertheless created only limited exceptions to the general rule that seizures of the person require probable cause to arrest. Detentions may be "investigative," yet violative of the Fourth Amendment absent probable cause. In the name of investigating a person who is no more than suspected of criminal activity, the police may not carry out a full search of the person or of his automobile or other effects. Nor may the police seek to verify their suspicions by means that approach the conditions of arrest.

III

The State proffers three reasons for holding that when Royer consented to the search of his luggage, he was not being illegally detained. First, it is submitted that the entire encounter was consensual and hence Royer was not being held against his will at all. We find this submission untenable. Asking for and examining Royer's ticket and his driver's license were no doubt permissible in themselves, but when the officers identified themselves as narcotics agents, told Royer that he was suspected of transporting narcotics, and asked him to accompany them to the police room, while retaining his ticket and driver's license and without indicating in any way that he was free to depart, Royer was effectively seized for the purposes of the Fourth Amendment.

* * *

Second, the State submits that if Royer was seized, there existed reasonable, articulated suspicion to justify a temporary detention and that the limits of a *Terry*-type stop were never exceeded. We agree with the State that when the officers discovered that Royer was traveling under an assumed name, this fact, and the facts already known to the officers—paying cash for a one-way ticket, the mode of checking the two bags, and Royer's appearance and conduct in general—were adequate grounds for suspecting Royer of carrying drugs and for temporarily detaining him and his luggage while they attempted to verify or dispel their suspicions in a manner that did not exceed the limits of an investigative detention. . . . We have concluded, however, that at the time Royer produced the key to his suitcase, the detention to which he was then subjected was a more serious intrusion on his personal liberty than is allowable on mere suspicion of criminal activity.

* * *

What had begun as a consensual inquiry in a public place had escalated into an investigatory procedure in a police interrogation room, where the police, unsatisfied with previous explanations, sought to confirm their suspicions. The officers had Royer's ticket, they had his identification, and they had seized his luggage. Royer was never informed that he was free to board his plane if he so chose, and he reasonably believed that he was being detained. At least as of that moment, any consensual aspects of the encounter had evaporated, and we cannot fault the Florida Court of Appeal for concluding that *Terry v. Ohio* and the cases following it did not justify the restraint to which Royer was then subjected. As a practical matter, Royer was under arrest. Consistent with this conclusion, the State conceded in the Florida courts that Royer would not have been free to leave the interrogation room had he asked to do so.

* * *

(continued)

Because we affirm the Florida Court of Appeal's conclusion that Royer was being illegally detained when he consented to the search of his luggage, we agree that the consent was tainted by the illegality and was ineffective to justify the search. The judgment of the Florida Court of Appeal is accordingly *Affirmed.*

Case Importance:

The Court recognized that under a "drug courier profile" seemingly random facts could be analyzed to meet the reasonable suspicion standard for a stop and frisk. When the duration of a stop and frisk exceeds what is reasonable, any evidence produced must be excluded from a criminal trial.

attention of drug enforcement agents because of his appearance, mannerisms, luggage, and actions, and by his purchase of a one-way airline ticket—all hallmarks of the drug courier profile. the agents properly detained him to ask questions but exceeded the length of time that was considered reasonable under the circumstances. Similarly, in *United States v. Sokolow,* 490 U.S. 1 (1989), the defendant met the drug courier profile by paying cash for a plane ticket from Hawaii to Florida, traveling under a name that did not match his phone number, staying in a drug source city for less than forty-eight hours, appearing nervous during the trip, and having no checked luggage. When met at the Honolulu airport by police, the defendant and his girlfriend were briefly detained so that a drug-sniffing dog could check their carry-on luggage. Two warrants were later issued to search both bags to which the dog alerted. Ultimately, this stop and frisk sniff of the bags by the dog was held to be appropriate, and the conviction was reinstated by the Supreme Court of the United States.

Under the drug courier profile theory of stop and frisk, a person may be detained briefly, without probable cause to arrest, but police curtailment of his or her liberty must be supported at least by a reasonable and articulable suspicion that the person seized may be engaged in criminal activity. The principle allows a brief encounter because of the drug courier profile but does not permit a lengthy detention of the person or luggage unless probable cause for arrest or search of the luggage quickly matures. In *United States v. Place,* 462 U.S. 696 (1983), police officers believed that Place met the drug courier profile and sought additional information from him. Following Place's brief initial encounter with the law enforcement officers at New York's La Guardia Airport, officers requested permission to search his luggage. When Place refused to grant consent, they removed his luggage to a secure area to await a search until police procured a warrant. The agents then took the luggage to Kennedy Airport, where it was subjected to a "sniff test" by a trained narcotics dog, which reacted positively to one of the suitcases. At this point, ninety minutes had elapsed since the seizure of the luggage. At some time later, the warrant arrived, and agents executed it, revealing cocaine.

The trial court admitted the drug evidence against Place, but the court of appeals reversed on the ground that the time limits of a *Terry* investigative stop had been exceeded. The Supreme Court affirmed the reversal of the conviction. The Court held that where an officer reasonably believes that a person carries luggage that contains narcotics, a brief seizure of the luggage may be justified under the dictates of *Terry.* Where police seize personal articles, the time limitations applicable to detentions of people apply to investigative detentions of a person's property. Thus, in

Place's situation, the seizure of his luggage became unreasonable at some point during the ninety minutes. The Court noted that the agents had sufficient time to have a dog ready to sniff the luggage when it arrived in New York, since they knew when and where the plane would land.

Ultimately, the Supreme Court of the United States upheld the reversal of Place's conviction because of the illegal search of the luggage. Police did not have probable cause to arrest Place or to search his luggage until the dog alerted. By that time, the length of detention of the luggage under the *Terry* standard had become unreasonable under the Fourth Amendment. The lesson of *Place* allows police to follow a drug courier profile while making brief stops to gain additional information, but the detention must be both brief and reasonable unless probable cause to arrest or to search the person or luggage develops. If the initial encounter does not resolve the officer's suspicions, but no additional evidence surfaces, the subject must be allowed to continue his or her journey.

8.   SUBJECT MUST BE AWARE OF OFFICER'S STATUS

The *Terry* standard requires that the person being stopped know that he or she is dealing with a law enforcement officer. In most situations, the identity is readily apparent by virtue of the officer's uniform. However, in the original *Terry* case, the detective was in plain clothes and needed to identify himself as a police officer. Once the individual has knowledge that the person is a police officer, submission to authority should be a reasonable approach rather than flight, which could be understandable if the person were not an officer. The person stopped has no duty to submit to alleged authority if he or she does not know the status of the officer.

9.   OFFICER MUST HAVE REASON TO BELIEVE THAT THE PERSON MAY BE ARMED AND DANGEROUS

The circumstances faced by the officer must give rise to the idea that the person with whom she or he is dealing may be armed and dangerous, according to the *Terry* standard. A situation where a robbery may be under way (*Terry*) suggests that the perpetrator might be armed, whereas a person who has passed an airport security checkpoint prior to boarding could not reasonably be believed to be armed. See *Florida v. Royer,* 460 U.S. 491 (1983). In *Michigan v. Long,* 463 U.S. 1032 (1983), the Court held that the *Terry* rationale does not restrict a pat-down search of the person of a detained suspect, even when the detainee is under the control of the officer and could not gain access to a weapon. The *Long* Court concluded it was reasonable under *Terry* to allow officers to conduct an area search of the passenger compartment of a vehicle to uncover weapons, as long as the officers possess an articulable and objectively reasonable belief that the suspect was potentially dangerous. In a slightly different situation, *New York v. Reyes,* 651 N.Y.S.2d 431 (1996), pursuant to a specific citizen complaint, an officer conducted a pat-down of a person who had a gun. The officer approached and noticed a bulge in the person's front coat pocket, tapped the bulge, felt something hard, and, believing that it was a gun, properly pulled out a package of drugs. Similarly, a police officer may order the driver of a lawfully stopped car to exit the car and submit to a pat-down, if given a reasonable suspicion that the driver may be armed and dangerous. See *Pennsylvania v. Mimms,* 434 U.S. 106 (1977). Consistent with *Mimms,* an officer may order passengers from a stopped vehicle and perform a pat-down upon reasonable suspicion that they may be armed and dangerous. See *Maryland v. Wilson,* 519 U.S. 408 (1997).

As a general rule, the officer's fear that the person may be armed and dangerous must be reasonable under the circumstances. In *New York v. Hill,* 1999 N.Y. App. Div. LEXIS 7469 (1999), the court held that police acted lawfully when they stopped two men they encountered late at night at a location where several vehicles had recently been burglarized. The officer engaged one of the subjects in a conversation and observed a bulge in the front pocket of his jacket. The officer conducted a pat-down of the front of the jacket. He discovered several cassette tapes in the front pocket and continued the pat-down until he felt something hard near the small of the defendant's back, which turned out to be a gun. Prior to the pat-down, the defendant provided straightforward answers to the police officer's questions about where he was going, where he had been, and the identity of his companion. The court held that the information possessed by the police officer may have provided, at most, an unfounded suspicion that criminal activity was afoot, thereby activating the common-law right to inquire. The court ruled that the pat-down violated the Fourth Amendment. The police officer's authority to pat down or frisk a defendant is dependent on the right to stop and detain, which authority is activated only by a reasonable suspicion of criminality, which the *Hill* court found lacking.

The reality of the reasonable belief that an individual may be armed and dangerous has a rather low threshold; only rarely is evidence suppressed because of an unreasonable fear that the person may be armed and dangerous. In *Michigan v. Summers,* 452 U.S. 692 (1981), the Court approved the detention of a man who was leaving a home that was the subject of a warrant-based search. The Court based its rationale on whether it was reasonable to detain someone who had a connection with the home and who might have been involved in the suspected criminality within the home. According to the Court, three police interests were furthered by the detention: preventing flight in the event incriminating evidence was found, minimizing risk of harm to the officers, and facilitating an orderly search through cooperation of the occupants. Note that in *Summers* there was barely any thought that the individual might have been armed, yet the detention gained Court approval. However, Summers had a greater and more significant connection to the house being searched than a bar patron who merely happened to be on the premises when a search of the bar occurred.

The Court reaffirmed the *Summers* rationale in a recent case where police were searching a home for a known gang member. According to the Court in *Muehler v. Mena,* 544 U.S. 93 (2005), if police have some suspicion that an occupant of a home might assist the target of a warrant-based home search, the occupant can be searched for weapons, handcuffed for several hours, and kept on the premises without violating the Fourth Amendment.

Demonstrative of how minimal the fear may be that a subject may be armed is the case of one of the New York World Trade Center bombing conspirators. In

United States v. El-Gabrowny, S.D.N.Y., 825 F. Supp. 38 (1993), the court denied a motion to suppress evidence obtained by officers in a pat-down search of one of the defendants.[18] Officers were executing a search warrant of the defendant's apartment when he approached them with his hands in his pockets. One officer removed the defendant's hands from the pockets and proceeded with a pat-down search. The officer discovered and removed a yellow envelope that was folded and fastened with rubber bands. It proved to contain forged and altered passports and birth certificates. The court held that the search was reasonable to ensure the officers' safety, despite the absence of any fear that the packet was a weapon.

As shown in the case law, courts take different approaches in analyzing when a situation appears to indicate that criminality might be afoot and the subjects involved may be armed and dangerous. Predicting the outcome of a particular set of circumstances under the stop and frisk doctrine can be a risky proposition because of the varying interpretations courts have given to substantially similar situations.

10. INVESTIGATION MUST NOT DISPEL THE FEAR THAT THE SUBJECT MAY BE ARMED AND DANGEROUS

Although the original *Terry* case held that, prior to conducting a pat-down, the officer must have a reasonable belief that the subject was armed and dangerous, many court cases construing this requirement have not been as demanding as the original case. In fact, the person on whom police would like to conduct a pat-down need not be personally believed to be armed; it is only necessary that an individual in a similar position might be armed. As mentioned earlier, in *Michigan v. Summers,* 452 U.S. 692 (1981), the Court approved a seizure of a man for whom there was no reason to believe that he was armed; he merely had connections to a home that was being searched pursuant to a warrant.

Suspicion of drug trafficking allows police to stop automobiles and trucks for brief investigations where there is reason to suspect criminal activity but no individualized suspicion that the person may be armed and dangerous. See *United States v. Sharpe,* 470 U.S. 675 (1985). In *Sharpe,* a Drug Enforcement Administration (DEA) officer followed an overloaded pickup truck with a camper shell that appeared to be traveling in tandem with a car. The truck was so overloaded that it did not sway or move up or down when encountering bumps in the road. The agent followed the vehicles for twenty miles and decided to make a *Terry* investigatory stop in concert with local police. The DEA agent walked to the rear of the truck, where he smelled marijuana, and opened the rear of the camper, which revealed bales of it. The Supreme Court believed that the *Terry* standard for a stop had been met. As the Court stated in footnote 3 of *Sharpe:*

> Agent Cooke had observed the vehicles traveling in tandem for 20 miles in an area near the coast known to be frequented by drug traffickers. Cooke testified that pickup trucks with camper shells were often used to transport large quantities of marihuana. Savage's pickup truck appeared to be heavily loaded, and the windows of the camper were covered with a quilted bed-sheet material, rather than curtains. Finally, both vehicles took evasive actions and started speeding as soon as Officer

Thrasher began following them in his marked car. Perhaps none of these facts, standing alone, would give rise to a reasonable suspicion; but taken together as appraised by an experienced law enforcement officer, they provided clear justification to stop the vehicles and pursue a limited investigation.

Although the Supreme Court appeared to have little difficulty in making a decision in *Sharpe* to approve the stop and frisk of the truck, the officer in the field must put the discrete facts together to determine whether the *Terry* standard has been met and whether additional information may be required prior to making a stop.

11. THE PLAIN FEEL DOCTRINE

In making a frisk, an officer may feel objects that are not likely to be weapons but may indicate criminal activity. In *Minnesota v. Dickerson,* 508 U.S. 366 (1993), the Court expanded the scope of a *Terry* stop and frisk by permitting the officer to reach inside the clothing of a detainee if the officer reasonably believed, by the feel of the object, it constituted seizable material. In *Dickerson,* the subject had been detained on suspicion of drug possession. The pat-down conducted by an officer revealed a small lump, and the officer determined that it was crack cocaine wrapped in cellophane because the officer manipulated the object between his thumb and index finger. According to the Court in *Dickerson,* the officer went beyond the allowable search permitted by *Terry,* and the evidence should have been suppressed. Had the officer merely felt an object whose criminal identity was readily apparent, the pat-down would have been permissible; manipulating the object was a greater search than allowed by *Terry.* However, *Dickerson* recognized a new area of seizable property under *Terry* that did not exist previously. This expansion of *Terry* has been variously referred to as the "plain touch" or the "plain feel" doctrine.

Many state courts have followed *Dickerson* in allowing officers to extend the scope of a search when an object's identity has been discovered during a pat-down. In a Texas drug investigation, an officer frisked the suspect for weapons but felt a large amount of cash in the pants pocket. The officer justified the frisk of the outer clothing on the theory that drug dealers are often armed with guns and other weapons, but the suspect argued that the scope of the frisk proved too extensive. The court upheld the frisk since the officer had testified that he immediately recognized that the bulge was currency from the way it felt, creating the justification for going in the pocket to retrieve it. In upholding the search, the Texas court quoted *Minnesota v. Dickerson,* stating, "if a police officer lawfully pats down a suspect's outer clothing and feels an object whose contour or mass makes its identity immediately apparent, there has been no invasion of the suspect's privacy beyond that already authorized by the officer's search for weapons."[19] The court distinguished the facts in its case from those of the *Dickerson* case: in *Dickerson,* the officer manipulated the contents of the pocket, and in the Texas case, the officer did not manipulate the currency. He instantly knew the identity of the bulge by its feel.[20]

Other courts have taken a different approach to the plain feel doctrine when determining whether an officer has been able to feel contraband by a pat-down of the outer clothing. The split of authority permits some courts to approve entry into pockets of clothing when the officer testified merely that the identity of the lamp was immediately apparent. Other jurisdictions will not accept the officer's bare conclusion. In *Rice v. State*,[21] an Arkansas case, an officer had cause to frisk an individual for weapons and gained his consent for the pat-down. Although the officer knew from experience that the person with whom he was dealing had carried weapons in the past, he testified that, based on the his experience, he felt something in the person's coat pocket that he knew was crack cocaine. The state court of appeals reversed the conviction, based on the proposition that other courts have "held that a police officer's generalized statement that the incriminatory nature of the contraband was readily apparent was insufficient to establish that fact for purposes of the plain-feel exception where the officer did not testify concerning specific facts establishing his ability to recognize crack cocaine by touch."[22] Presumably, had the officer offered a detailed explanation of why and how he knew by feel that the contents of the pocket contained crack cocaine, admission of the evidence would have been upheld upon appeal.

12. EXPANSION OF THE STOP AND FRISK BEYOND ITS GENESIS

The Supreme Court of the United States and other courts began to approve stops in situations where there was no belief that the individual person was armed or dangerous. Courts have approved short seizures of luggage where police have reasonable basis to suspect that criminal activity might be ongoing. Where police seize luggage on less than probable cause, the allowable length of the detention of the personal articles has been construed to follow the same standards as the stop of a person. See *Florida v. Royer*, 460 U.S. 491 (1983) (see Case 5.3). In such a situation, the initial stop and subsequent seizure must actually be of a temporary nature and exist no longer than reasonably necessary to effectuate the purpose. Where the seizure extends longer than reasonably required, the seizure may be declared unreasonable and the evidence suppressed.[23]

The Court extended the stop and frisk rationale to cover the situation where police lawfully detained an automobile and possessed an articulate fear that the occupant might obtain a weapon while searching for his driver's license. See *Michigan v. Long*, 463 U.S. 1032 (1983). Two police officers noticed a vehicle driving erratically and at an excessive rate of speed in a rural area late at night. After the officers saw the car go off the road and into a ditch, they stopped to investigate. Long, the driver, met the officers at the rear of the car and seemed to be under the influence of some intoxicant. When Long began walking toward the open door of the car to obtain the vehicle registration, the officers followed him and saw a hunting knife on the floorboard of the driver's side of the car. The officers then stopped the respondent and subjected him to a pat-down search, which revealed no weapons, but one of the officers noticed what appeared to be a baggie of marijuana protruding from under the armrest of the seat. The officers also conducted a limited weapons search of the interior of the auto. The *Long* Court approved this "*Terry* pat-down" of the passenger compartment of the vehicle because of a reasonable suspicion that the driver might gain immediate control of a weapon.

However, not every encounter between a police officer and an individual gives the officer the right to detain and frisk. In *Kolender v. Lawson,* 461 U.S. 352 (1983), police stopped and arrested a person who had no identification. The individual was walking alone and did not appear about to commit a crime. Pursuant to a California statute, any person who loiters or wanders about the streets must identify himself or herself to police upon request and account for his or her presence, even in the absence of any reasonable basis to suspect criminal activity. Failure to provide a "credible and reliable" identification when asked to "stop and identify" could result in an arrest for violating the statute. The Supreme Court of the United States determined that the law was unconstitutionally vague on its face within the meaning of the Due Process Clause of the Fourteenth Amendment. Thus, a person is not subject to stop, arrest, or search for merely walking or loitering without appropriate identification; some reasonable basis to suspect individual criminal activity must be demonstrably present in order to justify a stop and frisk. Similarly, an officer may not stop a motor vehicle when there is no reasonable basis to suspect that the driver is committing any type of criminal activity. In *Delaware v. Prouse,* 440 U.S. 468 (1979), the court disapproved a stop of Prouse's automobile for no reason. The officer had randomly decided to stop the car to check the vehicle's registration and had no individualized suspicion of criminal activity. This practice ran afoul of the Fourth Amendment and the *Terry* line of cases requiring individualized suspicion of criminal activity.[24]

In what appears to be an expansion of the *Terry* rationale, where reasonable basis to suspect criminal activity exists, an officer may make an arrest where a subject refuses to offer identification if state law requires that a person identify himself or herself. In a Nevada case,[25] police received a phone call reporting that a man was engaged in an assault on a woman inside a red and silver pickup truck on a particular road. When a dispatched officer arrived on the scene, he observed the truck and a man outside talking to a woman sitting inside the truck. Vehicle skid marks appeared in the gravel behind the pickup truck. After informing the subject that he was investigating a report of a fight or disturbance and then observing that the pickup truck's driver appeared to be intoxicated, he asked the man to identify himself with a driver's license or other written identification. The driver refused to offer identification and following the officer's eleventh request for identification, the officer concluded that the refusal to identify during a stop and frisk demonstrated a willful violation of Nevada law and arrested the subject. The Supreme Court upheld the validity of the arrest by holding that a state law requiring a suspect to disclose his name in the course of a valid *Terry* stop is consistent with Fourth Amendment prohibitions against unreasonable searches and seizures. The Court viewed the request for identification as a reasonable balance of the intrusion on the individual's Fourth Amendment interests against the legitimate needs of governmental law enforcement. The Court noted, "The principles of *Terry* permit a State to require a suspect to disclose his name in the course of a *Terry* stop."[26] Although the original *Terry* case did not deal with the requirement of identification, a state is free to make it a requirement where there is reasonable basis to suspect an individual of criminal activity.

13. EXPANSION OF *TERRY*-LIKE STOPS TO INDIVIDUALS NOT UNDER SUSPICION

A decade ago, the Supreme Court arguably retreated from requiring individualized suspicion in situations similar to a stop and frisk. In *Maryland v. Wilson,* 519 U.S. 408 (1997), a police officer who had validly stopped the vehicle in which Wilson was a passenger ordered Wilson to exit the automobile. As Wilson complied, some crack cocaine fell to the ground in full view of the officer. Prior to his trial, Wilson argued that the officer's act of ordering him out of the car constituted an unreasonable seizure, since he was not suspected of any wrongdoing at that time. Ultimately, the Supreme Court held that the reasonableness of a seizure depends on a balance between the needs of the public interest and the individual's right to personal security free from arbitrary interference by law enforcement officials. The Court noted that traffic stops are dangerous to police officers because drivers or passengers may assault officers. The added safety to police compared with the relatively small inconvenience of exiting a motor vehicle means that requiring a passenger to exit is reasonable during a routine traffic stop, even where there is no suspicion of individual wrongdoing.[27]

Although the Court does not require individualized suspicion to force an occupant to leave a vehicle that has been lawfully stopped, the Court recently held that when an officer stops a motor vehicle, the officer has seized everyone in the vehicle. The validity of the stop depends upon the information the police officer possesses at the moment prior to the seizure. In *Brendlin v. California,*[28] officers stopped a vehicle to check its registration but lacked any reason to believe that it or its operation offended the law. One officer recognized Brendlin as a parole violator and arrested him. Police soon discovered other evidence of criminality that resulted in some criminal convictions involving methamphetamine manufacturing. The Supreme Court vacated the convictions based on the Fourth Amendment violation of Brendlin's rights because the police lacked even the *Terry* minimun level of reasonable suspicion to support the stop of the motor vehicle.

In cases where police have no individualized suspicion, they are free to enter into discussions with individuals of their choosing without meeting the *Terry* stop standard. This suspicionless inquiry has been determined not to constitute a seizure under the Fourth Amendment or a *Terry* stop under the stop and frisk standard. In one instance, police entered an interstate bus to talk with passengers on the bus during a stop. In *United States v. Drayton,* 536 U.S. 194 (2002), two police officers stationed themselves one at each end of the aisle of a bus, while the third officer began talking to passengers concerning transportation of drugs and guns. First appearances would indicate that the persons on the bus were not free to leave and effectively had been seized since police officers blocked both means of egress. However, passengers were in fact free to enter or leave the bus, but the officers did not inform them of this freedom. When an officer spoke to passenger Drayton and requested permission to pat him down, Drayton consented. The officer discovered bulky items on his inner thighs where drug smugglers normally carry contraband. Drayton and his traveling companion were arrested, tried, and convicted of drug offenses, but a federal court of appeals reversed the convictions. The Supreme Court reversed the court of appeals and ruled that the men had never been seized and were free to go at any time until the point of arrest. According to the Court, police officers do not violate the Fourth Amendment's prohibition of unreasonable seizures merely by approaching individuals on the street or in other public places and putting questions to them if they are willing to listen. The fact that Drayton, who the Court noted was free to leave, consented to a search of his person ended his argument that he had been improperly seized under the Fourth Amendment.

14. SUMMARY

The Fourth Amendment permits seizures of persons on less than probable cause for the purpose of briefly investigating human behavior that might be criminal. A police officer must possess a reasonable basis to suspect that criminal activity might be happening or about to happen. When this standard has been met, the officer has the legal authority to detain a person and briefly ask reasonable questions. If the answers would satisfy the reasonable officer, the forced encounter ends, and the individual becomes free to leave without being subject to a pat-down. On the other hand, when the answers fail to satisfy a reasonable officer and the officer has a reasonable suspicion, based on articulable facts, that the individual might be armed and dangerous, the officer may decide to conduct a pat-down of the subject's outer clothing for the purpose of determining whether the person is armed. The unusual conduct may be observed by the officer, be reported by an informant, or be based on a combination of the officer's personal knowledge and the informant's information. Criminal profiles using typical factors that might indicate that criminal behavior has been or is occurring may give rise to a stop and frisk situation. Such criminal profiles help identify persons involved in drug smuggling at airports, on highways, and in bus stations. During a lawful pat-down, if the officer feels objects, the possession of which offends the criminal law, the officer may remove them from the subject and use the evidence in a prosecution. The stop and frisk standard of *Terry v. Ohio* is based on a lesser level of proof than the concept of probable cause to arrest or probable cause to search.

REVIEW EXERCISES AND QUESTIONS

1. According to *Terry v. Ohio,* what factors must a police officer consider prior to conducting a valid stop? What additional factors must be considered for a valid frisk?

2. What sources of information may an officer use to develop the proper "reasonable basis to suspect criminal activity" sufficient for a stop and frisk?

3. Assume that a person observed a police officer nearby and immediately began to run in the opposite direction. What additional factors might have to be present before a police officer could initiate a stop followed by a frisk? Is flight upon seeing an officer sufficient?

4. What must an officer do when the initial encounter with a suspicious subject is clarified by a verbal discussion sufficient to end the officer's suspicion that criminal activity might have been about to occur? May the officer always conduct a frisk?

5. Explain what is meant by "drug courier profile" and why it gives rise to "reasonable suspicion" when the standard has been satisfied.

6. Describe what has been called the "plain feel" doctrine. Can it be used to justify an extended intrusion of a detainee's inner clothing? What about a situation where a police officer has justifiably frisked a known felon and felt a gun cartridge on his person during the pat-down. Felons are not permitted to possess ammunition. Pursuant to the plain feel doctrine, could an officer recognize something in a defendant's pocket as powder cocaine based on his training and experience as a narcotics officer? Consult *United States v. McGlown,* 150 Fed. Appx. 462; 2005 U.S. App. LEXIS 21827 (6th Cir. 2005).

7. Suppose that an officer on a college campus observed an individual who was doing stretching exercises under a streetlight and, upon noticing the officer, started running in the opposite direction down a jogging trail. Should this type of activity allow a police officer to make a stop of the jogger? Would a person's flight upon seeing a police officer allow the officer to stop if it appeared that the person had initiated his or her jogging routine in a high-crime area? Would it matter if the jogging were in the evening? What other factors could you add that might allow a stop? Do other factors that might be present have to be considered when a subject flees upon observing a police officer?

8. The stop and frisk concept has been extended to justify stops of persons who are not expected to be armed and to "frisks" of motor vehicle interiors. Give an example of a *Terry*-type limited search that does not involve a suspicion that a subject may be armed and dangerous.

9. Consider the case where a motorist had been lawfully detained for two misdemeanor traffic violations. The officer called for a K-9 unit (within seven minutes after the stop) to conduct a sniff scan of the stopped vehicle when the officer noticed heavily tinted windows, a strong air freshener odor, and some false identification given in response to requests. The officer felt that he possessed a *Terry* level of articulable suspicion that the occupants were possibly in violation of a narcotics law, based on the observed facts. The K-9 officer and dog arrived and finished the sniff scan within twenty-four minutes of the original stop. Was the articulable suspicion sufficient for a *Terry* stop? Did the officers detain the motorists too long based on reasonable suspicion? Would this case be controlled by *Florida v. Royer,* as mentioned in this chapter? See *State v. Ofori,* 170 Md. App. 211, 906 A.2d 1089, 2006 Md. App. LEXIS 151 (2006).

HOW WOULD YOU DECIDE?

1. In the United States Court of Appeals for the District of Columbia Circuit

The appellant contended that evidence of his being felon in possession of a firearm should have been suppressed because the officers did not have "reasonable suspicion" sufficient to stop him or to conduct a frisk of his clothing.

Following a radio dispatch involving an attempted unauthorized use of a motor vehicle, four nonuniformed police officers in an unmarked car went to the area where the crime had occurred. Police arrived within minutes of receiving the radio call. Observing a group of four men, all of whom wore clothing matching the description of the suspect, the officers pulled into the gas station where the men were standing. As the plainclothes officers approached the group, police observed the defendant walking away from the others while holding the right side of his waistband, as if he were hiding or holding a firearm. The situation appeared unusual, given that the group was aware that the approaching men were police

officers. One of the officers heard defendant Goddard state that he had a gun. Two officers got control of the defendant and handcuffed him prior to conducting a *Terry* pat-down, which revealed a gun in the defendant's waistband. The federal district court refused to suppress the gun evidence because the stop occurred close to the earlier reported attempted crime and the four men loosely met the description of the suspect given by the original victim. Defendant Goddard pled guilty, but he reserved his right to raise the gun suppression issue on appeal by contending that he should have been neither stopped nor frisked.

How would you rule on the defendant's contention that the police officer had no lawful right to stop him or to conduct the frisk of his clothing that revealed the firearm?

The Court's Holding:

The United States Court of Appeals for the District of Columbia Circuit determined that there were two issues to be determined: when the stop actually occurred, and whether the officer conducting the frisk had reasonable suspicion at the time of the pat-down.

In deciding when a stop has occurred, the court noted that such conduct as a threatening presence of several officers, the display of a weapon, the demeanor of the officer, the time and place of the encounter, or some physical touching of the subject by police may indicate that a stop had occurred. In this case, the men roughly matched the description of the person who had attempted to use a motor vehicle without permission, so the stop of defendant Goddard met the reasonable suspicion standard,

especially since he was trying to leave the group and was somewhat furtive in his actions and demeanor. The court held that the stop occurred when one of the officers yelled, "Gun," and directed their attention to Goddard, while they ordered another man to return to the original group. In *United States v. Brown,* 357 U.S. App. D.C. 339, 334 F.3d 1161, 1167 (D.C. Cir. 2003), the Court of Appeals held that furtive movements in response to police presence may create reasonable suspicion. In this case, Goddard had previously declared that he possessed a gun, giving the officers ample grounds for the *Terry* stop and for the immediate frisk. The Court of Appeals upheld the conviction based on the proper stop and frisk. See *United States v. Goddard,* 2007 U.S. App. LEXIS 14828 (D.C. Cir. 2007).

HOW WOULD YOU DECIDE?

2. In the Supreme Court of Wyoming

Police stopped defendant Barch as he was driving through Wyoming because his vehicle failed to display a front license plate. The officer had some concerns because Barch appeared nervous, was unclear about his travel plans, and exhibited a hurried demeanor. Barch did not know where in Denver or the surrounding area his friends actually lived, and the officer discovered that Barch had been unemployed for a period of time. After Barch obtained his front plate from the car's trunk, the officer prepared a warning ticket and returned his driver's license, even though the officer noticed a quantity of dried food in the trunk in opaque containers. The officer had earlier radioed another officer with a drug-sniffing dog to stop past the site but had told Barch that he was free to go. When the K-9 unit arrived, the original officer requested permission to search the car for drugs, but Barch refused, whereupon the K-9 unit officer had the dog sniff the defendant's car, revealing the presence of illegal drugs. Barch should have been free to go because all the other details had been completed.

When the dog alerted to marijuana, police arrested Barch and conducted a drug search of the car. The defendant pled guilty to drug charges, reserving the right to contest the Fourth Amendment issues of whether there was a reasonable basis to suspect criminal activity sufficient to justify the extended detention once the traffic stop had ended. Since the trial court refused to suppress the drug evidence, Barch entered a conditional plea of

guilty to one count of possession with intent to deliver a controlled substance, reserving his right to appeal the legality of the detention under the *Terry* standard of reasonable suspicion.

How would you rule on the defendant's contention that his continued detention after the traffic stop was concluded was illegal because the officers did not have a reasonable suspicion sufficient to extend the detention beyond the traffic stop?

The Court's Holding:

The Supreme Court of Wyoming reversed the trial court decision to admit the marijuana because it believed that the police officers did not have an articulable suspicion that Barch or his conduct was offending the law, which would have allowed the officers to detain him for the drug-sniffing dog to take a scan of his car. The court noted that it would employ "a dual inquiry for evaluating the reasonableness of an investigatory stop: (1) whether the officer's actions were justified at the inception; and (2) whether it was reasonably related in scope to the circumstances that justified the interference in the first instance." Barch conceded that the initial stop was lawful, but the court had to determine whether the extended detention could be consistent with the "reasonable suspicion" standard of *Terry v. Ohio*. The court noted that often people refer to the south suburbs of Denver as South Denver, that motorists are often nervious when stopped by police, and that his dried food did not elevate any suspicion. Any suspicion created by Barch could, according to the court, not justify Barch's continued detention once the traffic stop was concluded and he had been told that he was free to leave the scene. The fact that Barch had been unemployed for a time did not indicate that he was a criminal or add to any suspicion. Therefore, the Supreme Court of Wyoming reversed the trial court and permitted Barch to withdraw his guilty plea. See *Barch v. State,* 2004 WY 79; 92 P.3d 828; 2004 Wyo. LEXIS 104 (2004).

ENDNOTES

1. Amendment Four (1791). The right of the people to be secure in their persons, houses, papers, and effects, against unreasonable searches and seizures, shall not be violated, and no warrants shall issue, but upon probable cause, supported by Oath or affirmation, and particularly describing the place to be searched, and the persons or things to be seized.
2. See *Adams v. Williams,* 407 U.S. 143 (1972).
3. See *Terry v. Ohio,* 392 U.S. 1 (1968).
4. See *Illinois v. Wardlow,* 528 U.S. 119 (2000).
5. Ibid.
6. See *Florida v. J.L.,* 529 U.S. 266 (2000). In this case, an anonymous informant conveyed news to police that a specifically described young male, wearing a plaid shirt, was standing at a particular bus stop and illegally carrying a concealed firearm. The Court held that an uncorroborated tip from an unknown informant could not justify a frisk.
7. 392 U.S. 40 (1968).
8. There must be objective reasons to believe an informant. An anonymous phone tip to police from a concerned citizen that indicated criminality may be sufficient to permit a frisk. In *United States v. Pleas,* 2007 U.S. Dist. LEXIS 76237 (2007), an telephone informant directed police to investigate whether a specifically described man possessed a concealed weapon. The caller had called police several days earlier about the same man and problem and her sister had been threatened by the subject. A detailed description covering race, general appearance, hair style, a first name, and a possible last name gave police reasonable suspicion to approach and frisk. The anonymous caller could be believed based on making a second complaint and the detail of her description supplied sufficient reliability to allow officers to approach and frisk.
9. *Delaware v. Prouse,* 440 U.S. 648, 650 (1979).
10. See *Brendlin v. California,* 127 S. Ct. 2400, 168 L. Ed. 2d 132, 2007 U.S. LEXIS 7897 (2007). Police may set up roadblocks without any individualized suspicion as an exception to the general rule requiring at least a reasonable basis to suspect criminal activity. See *Michigan v. Sitz,* 496 U.S. 444 (1990), where the Court allowed the Michigan State Police to check motorists for alcohol impairment.
11. *Missouri v. Schmutz,* 100 S.W.3d 876, 880, 881 (2003).
12. *Ransome v. Maryland,* 373 Md. 99, 108, 109; 816 A.2d 901, 905, 906 (2003).
13. 528 U.S. at 124.
14. *In the Interest of D.M.,* 566 Pa. 445; 781 A.2d 1161 (2001).
15. See *Howard v. United States,* 2007 D.C. App. LEXIS 247 (2007).
16. See *Ybarra v. Illinois,* 444 U.S. 85 (1979). The Court determined that a *Terry*-type frisk of all patrons of a bar for which a search warrant had been issued was unreasonable, since no individualized suspicion existed for any particular patron. Police conducted a pat-down of the customers and returned to make a more extensive search on Ybarra by reaching inside his clothing when there was no reason to suspect him of any wrongdoing.
17. *Harford v. State,* 816 So. 2d 789 (Fla. 2002).
18. The Second Circuit Court of Appeals upheld the eventual conviction of El-Gabrowny, including, by implication, the search of El-Gabrowny's clothing prior to arrest in *United States v. El-Gabrowny,* 189 F.3d 88, 1999 U.S. App. LEXIS 18926 (CA2 1999).
19. 508 U.S. 366 at 375.
20. *Carmouche v. State,* 10 S.W.3d 323 (Tex. Crim. App. 2000).
21. 219 S.W.3d 672; 2005 Ark. App. LEXIS 890 (2005).
22. Ibid. at 675.

23. *United States v. Place,* 462 U.S. 696, 709, 710 (1983).

24. Not all seizures require "individual suspicion" despite the *Terry* requirement. In *Michigan v. Sitz,* 496 U.S. 444 (1990), the Court upheld the use of "sobriety checkpoints" where the stop was extremely brief, officers stopped every vehicle, and the intrusion was outweighed by the state's interest in reducing drunken driving. Such stops did not involve any individualized suspicion of any particular driver but served as a screen to find impaired motor vehicle operators.

25. *Hiibel v. Sixth Judicial District Court of Nevada,* 542 U.S. 960 (2004).

26. Ibid. at 187.

27. See *Wyoming v. Houghton,* 526 U.S. 295 (1999), where the Court noted that a passenger is often engaged in a common enterprise with the same goals as the driver of a vehicle and shares a reduced expectation of privacy while traveling in a motor vehicle. To require the passenger to exit the vehicle is reasonable under the circumstances.

28. *Brendlin v. California,* ___ U.S. ___, No. 06–8120 (2007).

C H A P T E R   6

Obtaining and Using Search Warrants: Practice, Execution, and Return

Learning Objectives

1. Know and be able to articulate the definition of probable cause to search.
2. Understand why the Fourth Amendment requires specificity in describing property to be seized, and give an example of a description of personal property that would meet the specificity requirements.
3. Be able to explain what a search warrant is and what powers it gives to a police officer.
4. Explain how warrants for electronic eavesdropping or wiretapping can be obtained.
5. Describe some of the challenges of establishing probable cause using informant testimony and information.
6. List two of the factors that are considered under the "totality of the circumstances" test used in determining

the value of an informant's information.
7. Trace the process followed by a police officer from an initial investigation to obtaining a search warrant.
8. Distinguish between the requirement of knock and announce and the reality that it may not be necessary, and give an example where the knock and announce requirement may be excused.
9. Analyze the factors that determine the scope of a search, and give an example where the type of object would dictate the scope of the search.
10. Explain why probable cause to search can become stale, and offer a clear example where probable cause has ceased to exist through the passage of time.

Chapter Outline

1. The Fourth Amendment: Probable Cause to Search
2. Specificity of Search: Particularity of Description
3. Requirement of a Warrant: Physical Searches
4. Requirement of a Warrant: Electronic Eavesdropping
5. Sources of Probable Cause: The Informant
6. Informant Probable Cause: The Totality of the Circumstances Test
7. Sources of Probable Cause: Police Officers and Others
8. The Affidavit for a Warrant: Written or Electronic
9. The Search Warrant: A Court Order
10. Fourth Amendment: Knock and Announce Requirement and Permissible Detention of Persons Present

Key Terms

Affidavit for a warrant
Knock and announce
Particularity of description
Probable cause
Scope of search

Stale probable cause
Totality of the circumstances test
Two-pronged test
Warrant

1. THE FOURTH AMENDMENT: PROBABLE CAUSE TO SEARCH

"The right of the people to be secure in their persons, houses, papers, and effects, against unreasonable searches and seizures, shall not be violated, and no warrants shall issue, but upon probable cause."[1] The language of the Fourth Amendment describes rights possessed by people, but it does not define all its terms, and it is not self-enforcing. While basically describing some sort of a right of privacy, it does so without mentioning the word *privacy*. As a general rule, we are guaranteed the right to keep objects and personal effects from governmental inquiry and scrutiny unless there are powerful reasons for the government to intrude on our personal lives. When governmental agents believe there are indications of criminal wrongdoing, procedures have evolved to test the validity of the reasons and to allow searches and seizures in many cases where the governmental need outweighs our right to expect, for lack of a better term, our right of privacy. According to *Carroll v. United States,* 267 U.S. 132, 162 (1925), in a case involving transportation of untaxed alcoholic beverages, probable cause to search existed when police officers possessed "facts and circumstances within their knowledge and of which they had reasonably trustworthy information [that those facts] were sufficient, in themselves, to warrant a man of reasonable caution in the belief that intoxicating liquor was being transported in the automobile which they stopped and searched."[2]

With some exceptions,[3] probable cause must exist before any search may lawfully occur, whether the search is pursuant to a warrant or otherwise. To paraphrase *Carroll v. United States,* 267 U.S. 132, 162 (1925), probable cause has been said to exist when the facts and circumstances within the officers' knowledge are sufficient to warrant a person of reasonable prudence in the belief that contraband or evidence of a crime will be found in a particular place or on a particular person. This standard of belief rises above a mere hunch but falls far short of proof beyond a reasonable doubt. Probable cause is based on an objective standard and not on the subjective belief of the particular police officer. While a police officer may believe that probable cause to search exists, further steps are required prior to making a search. Some searches may be conducted with probable cause but without a warrant; the general rule, however, is that warrantless searches inside a home are presumed to be unreasonable, in violation of the Fourth Amendment.[4]

CASE 6.1

Leading Case Brief: The Legal Standard of Probable Cause to Search

Carroll v. United States
Supreme Court of the United States
267 U.S. 132 (1925)

Case Facts:

Evidence presented in a federal court in Michigan convicted George Carroll and John Kiro for transporting intoxicating liquor, in violation of the National Prohibition Act. The defendants appealed their convictions, and the Supreme Court of the United States granted certiorari. Carroll and Kiro alleged that the search and seizure of their motor vehicle was in violation of their rights under the Fourth Amendment. A motion to suppress the evidence was made by the defendants that all the liquor seized be returned to the defendant. This motion was denied.

Carroll and a friend of his had made an earlier attempt to sell intoxicating liquors to law enforcement agents, but because the identity of law enforcement agents may have become known to Carroll, the sale was never completed. During this encounter, the law enforcement agents observed Carroll's physical characteristics, the make and model of his motor vehicle, and the identity of one of his associates. Carroll had a reputation as a bootlegger who sold and trafficked in distilled spirits in violation of federal law. A month or so later, the same agents observed the Oldsmobile roadster containing Carroll and John Kiro headed eastward from Grand Rapids, Michigan, toward Detroit, a well-known liquor smuggling route. Officers followed but lost sight of the vehicle. Two months later, officers spotted the same vehicle traveling westward toward Grand Rapids and were successful in stopping it. With the reputation as bootleggers that Carroll and Kiro possessed, the fact that they were using the same Oldsmobile that was used in the aborted earlier sale, the fact that they were driving the same vehicle seen several months earlier traveling along the smuggling route, and the fact that they were once again traveling along a liquor-trafficking

highway route gave the officers probable cause to stop the automobile. The same facts generated probable cause to believe that the motor vehicle contained contraband. A warrantless search of the motor vehicle revealed sixty-eight bottles of intoxicating liquor carried in violation of federal law. The officers were not anticipating that Carroll and Kiro would be driving down the highway at that time, but when they observed them in the same car, they believed they were carrying liquor, and as a result the officers made the stop, search, seizure, and arrest of Carroll and Kiro.

Legal Issue:

Where a person has a reputation for illegal activity of a specific type and has attempted to commit a crime involving a federal officer, and where the same government agent observes the person apparently plying his trade openly, does such conduct meet the standard of probable cause to search under the Fourth Amendment?

The Court's Ruling:

The justices concluded that the amount of evidence known to the officers allowed them to conclude that seizable materials were hidden within the automobile.

Essence of the Court's Rationale:

* * *

Finally, was there probable cause? In *The Apollon*, 9 Wheat. 362, the question was whether the seizure of a French vessel at a particular place was upon probable cause that she was there for the purpose of smuggling.

(continued)

In this discussion, Mr. Justice Story, who delivered the judgment of the Court, said (page 374):

> It has been very justly observed at the bar that the Court is bound to take notice of public facts and geographical positions, and that this remote part of the country has been infested, at different periods, by smugglers, is a matter of general notoriety, and may be gathered from the public documents of the government.

We know in this way that Grand Rapids is about 152 miles from Detroit, and that Detroit and its neighborhood along the Detroit River, which is the International Boundary, is one of the most active centers for introducing illegally into this country spirituous liquors for distribution into the interior. It is obvious from the evidence that the prohibition agents were engaged in a regular patrol along the important highways from Detroit to Grand Rapids to stop and seize liquor carried in automobiles. They knew or had convincing evidence to make them believe that the Carroll boys, as they called them, were so-called "bootleggers" in Grand Rapids, i.e., that they were engaged in plying the unlawful trade of selling such liquor in that city. The officers had soon after noted their going from Grand Rapids half way to Detroit, and attempted to follow them to that city to see where they went, but they escaped observation. Two months later, these officers suddenly met the same men on their way westward, presumably from Detroit. The partners in the original combination to sell liquor in Grand Rapids were together in the same automobile they had been in the night when they tried to furnish the whisky to the officers which was thus identified as part of the firm equipment. They were coming from the direction of the great source of supply for their stock to Grand Rapids, where they plied their trade. That the officers, when they saw the defendants, believed that they were carrying liquor we can have no doubt, and we think it is equally clear that they had reasonable cause for thinking so. Emphasis is put by defendants' counsel on the statement made by one of the officers that they were not looking for defendants at the particular time when they appeared. We do not perceive that it has any weight. As soon as they did appear, the officers were entitled to use their reasoning faculties upon all the facts of which they had previous knowledge in respect to the defendants.

The necessity for probable cause in justifying seizures on land or sea, in making arrests without warrant for past felonies, and in malicious prosecution and false imprisonment cases has led to frequent definition of the phrase. In *Stacey v. Emery,* 97 U. S. 642, 645, a suit for damages for seizure by a collector, this Court defined probable cause as follows:

> If the facts and circumstances before the officer are such as to warrant a man of prudence and caution in believing that the offense has been committed, it is sufficient.

* * *

> [I]t is clear the officers here had justification for the search and seizure. This is to say that the facts and circumstances within their knowledge and of which they had reasonably trustworthy information were sufficient, in themselves, to warrant a man of reasonable caution in the belief that intoxicating liquor was being transported in the automobile which they stopped and searched.

* * *

The judgment is Affirmed.

Case Importance:

The level of proof contained in this case offers a benchmark with which to measure the amount of evidence needed to establish probable cause to search. Probable cause exists when the facts and circumstances presented to a person of reasonable caution would lead that person to conclude that seizable property will be found at a particular place or on a particular person.

Since the Fourth Amendment protects against unreasonable searches and seizures, reasonable searches are permitted. As a general rule, where a judicial official has issued a search warrant, the search conducted pursuant to it is presumed to be reasonable. Case law permits warrantless searches of motor vehicles given probable cause to search on the theory that such searches are reasonable under the circumstances. Similarly, an open field, where there is little or no expectation of privacy, may be searched without a warrant, whether or not probable cause exists.[5] As exceptions to the general rule, searches incident to arrest, searches based on consent, inventory searches, and emergency searches may be conducted without warrants.

When determining whether evidence reaches the level of probable cause, police officers must carefully weigh the facts of each case. To establish probable cause for a search of the house of a suspected methamphetamine manufacturer, police gathered information that a particularly described person had purchased denatured alcohol and two thousand books of matches and was suspected of stealing four boxes of cold medicine containing pseudoephedrine. Later evidence disclosed that a person matching the suspect's description often purchased quantities of cold medicine containing pseudoephedrine and Coleman stove fuel at a convenience store. When an officer questioned the suspect outside his home, he noticed a gas can modified in a manner that is often used as a hydrogen chloride gas generator as part of the methamphetamine cooking process. An Alaska court held that the evidence was sufficient to warrant a person of reasonable caution to believe that seizable property would be found on the particular property occupied by the suspect, and the search warrant that had been issued was properly based on probable cause.[6]

In a different drug case, one court concluded that where an officer had stopped an automobile and smelled a strong odor of ether, a substance used in the production of methamphetamine, the smell of ether alone did not give probable cause to search the vehicle. The reviewing court noted that an odor of ether did give a reason for additional investigation, but the level of proof failed to reach probable cause to search.[7]

2. SPECIFICITY OF SEARCH: PARTICULARITY OF DESCRIPTION

Under the Fourth Amendment, to obtain a search warrant, the person applying for a warrant must include sufficient specificity when describing the object to be seized and specifically describe its location. The specificity of description requirement can be satisfied where "the description is such that the officer with a search warrant can with reasonable effort ascertain and identify the place intended."[8] One court held that a warrant to search a specified computer for child pornography applied to allow a search of all computers within the defendant's home that were under his control.[9] A warrant for which the supporting documentation indicates probable cause to search the garage and the area of the home used for business purposes is specific enough to allow a search of the entire building.[10] In a case[11] where police officers obtained and executed a search warrant for a search of a described person, as well as premises known as "2603 Park Avenue third floor apartment," for drugs was held to be sufficiently specific, even though, unknown to officers, there was more than one apartment on the third floor. Minor errors in a warrant's description of real property are not normally fatal to the validity of a search warrant. For example, one court upheld as properly specific a description of a rural trailer home where the warrant contained some errors but the remaining description was sufficiently detailed to direct law enforcement officials to search the proper structure.[12] Where a building or real estate is the subject of the search, proper description such as the mailing address and its location at the corner of specific streets is generally specific enough to withstand a court challenge to the validity of the search. A description of an object needs to be as specific as possible; it need not be perfect, just sufficiently detailed, given the nature of the object of the search.

Obviously, a serial number would not be expected for a search for a quantity of drugs, and gambling records do not allow precise description, but a search for a stolen firearm might well include a serial number, caliber, type of weapon, and manufacturer.

Figure 6.1 shows the federal warrant form that is used when the probable cause has been based on an affidavit.[13]

3. REQUIREMENT OF A WARRANT: PHYSICAL SEARCHES

To conduct a legal search, absent some well-defined exception, a search warrant from a neutral and detached judicial official is required under the dictates of the Fourth Amendment. In addition, as a practical matter, where a search is conducted pursuant to a warrant, the warrant assures the individual whose property is being searched or being seized of the lawful authority of the law enforcement officer, the need to search, and the limits of the officer's power to search. The procedure to obtain a warrant to search must begin with a police officer making a determination, based on facts and circumstances known to the officer, that probable cause exists. The officer, sometimes with assistance from a prosecutor's office, prepares an affidavit for a search warrant in which the operative facts and details are recited. The officer (affiant) must swear that the facts are true as far as he or she knows. Since the Fourth Amendment requires specificity concerning the object and location of the search, detailed information proves essential in the process of obtaining a search warrant. If an informant has been used to establish or help establish probable cause, the facts elicited from that person are recounted, along with reasons the judge should believe the informant's conclusions. The role of the judge is not to "rubber-stamp" the conclusions of police but to exercise independent judgment in rendering a decision concerning the existence of probable cause. If the judge concurs with police that probable cause exists to believe that seizable property will be found at a particularly described place or on a particular person, he or she will sign a warrant to search. The search warrant issued by a neutral and detached judicial official upon a finding of probable cause is a court order to law enforcement officials to search and seize specifically described and located property and return the property to the court. The warrant form in Figure 6.2 illustrates how a federal search warrant appears when the probable cause is received upon an oral statement.[14]

4. REQUIREMENT OF A WARRANT: ELECTRONIC EAVESDROPPING

As a general rule, to wiretap or electronically eavesdrop on private conversations, a state or federal law enforcement officer must obtain a warrant. Warrants to conduct electronic eavesdropping are based on the same standard of probable cause that is required to enter a home or an office. Under the Federal Wiretap Act,[15] people are prohibited from intentionally intercepting, using, or disclosing any wire or other communications unless the intercept is done according to the requirements of the federal law. The statute does note that nothing contained within the law is to be construed to affect or limit the federal government's acquisition of foreign intelligence information from international or foreign communications facilities.

AO 93   (Rev. 12/03) Search Warrant

UNITED STATES DISTRICT COURT

District of _____

In the Matter of the Search of
(Name, address or bried description of person or property to be searched)

SEARCH WARRANT

Case Number: _____

TO: _____ and any Authorized Officer of the United States

Affidavit(s) having been made before me by _____ who has reason to believe
                                                        Affiant

that ☐ on the person of, or ☐ on the premises known as (name, description and/or location)

in the _____ District of _____ there is now
concealed a certain person or property, namely (describe the person or property)

I am satisfied that the affidavit(s) and any record testimony establish probable cause to believe that the person or property so described
is now concealed on the person or premises above-described and establish grounds for the issuance of this warrant.

        YOU ARE HEREBY COMMANDED to search on or before _____
                                                                            Date

(not to exceed 10 days) the person or place named above for the person or property specified, serving this warrant and making the
search   ☐ in the daytime — 6:00 AM to 10:00 P.M.   ☐ at anytime in the day or night as I find reasonable cause has been
established and if the person or property be found there to seize same, leaving a copy of this warrant and receipt for ther person
or property taken, and prepare a written inventory of the person or property seized and promptly return this warrant to
                                            _____ as required by law.
        U.S. Magistrate Judge (Rule 41(f)(4))

_____   at   _____
Date and Time Issued   City and State

_____   _____
Name and Title of Judge   Signature of Judge

FIGURE 6.1   Typical Example of a Search Warrant Form Used in Federal Courts.

UNITED STATES DISTRICT COURT

District of _____

In the Matter of the Search of
(Name, address or brief description of person or property to be searched)

SEARCH WARRANT UPON ORAL TESTIMONY

Case Number: _____

TO: _____ and any Authorized Officer of the United States

Sworn oral testimony has been communicated to me by _____
                                                                                        Affiant

that   ☐   on the person of,   or   ☐   on the premises known as (name, description and/or location)

in the _____ District of _____ there is now
concealed a certain person or property, namely (describe the person or property)

I am satisfied that the circumstances are such as to make it reasonable to dispense with a written affidavit and that there is probable cause to believe that the property or person so described is concealed on the person or premises above described and that grounds for application for issuance of the search warrant exist as communicated orally to me in a sworn statement which has been recorded electronically, stenographically, or in long-hand and upon the return of the warrant, will be transcribed, certified as accurate and attached hereto.

YOU ARE HEREBY COMMANDED to search on or before _____
                                                                                                    Date

the person or place named above for the person or property specified, serving this warrant and making the search   ☐ in the day-time — 6:00 AM to 10:00 PM   ☐ at anytime in the day or night as I find reasonable cause has been established and if the person or property be found there to seize same, leaving a copy of this warrant and receipt for the person or property taken, and prepare a written inventory of the person or property seized and promptly return this warrant to _____
                                                                                                    U.S. Magistrate Judge (Rule 41(f)(4))

as required by law.

_____ at _____
Date and Time Issued   City and State

_____   _____
Name and Title of Judge   Signature of Judge

I certify that on _____ at _____
                                                    Date   Time

_____ orally authorized the
Judge

issuance and execution of a search warrant conforming to all the foregoing terms.

_____   _____   _____
Name of affiant   Signature of affiant   Exact time warrant

FIGURE 6.2   Federal Court Form for a Search Warrant upon Oral Testimony.

For specified criminal violations of federal law, the attorney general of the United States or a deputy properly designated may apply for an order that authorizes the interception of wire or oral communications. The statute also authorizes the principal prosecuting attorney in any state or any subdivision of that state to apply to a judge in that state to obtain an electronic search warrant, provided state law allows electronic eavesdropping.[16] Every affidavit for an electronic warrant under federal law must be made in writing and under oath to a judge of competent jurisdiction, and it must include the statutory authority under which the applicant is requesting an electronic warrant. As is the case in standard warrant practice, the applicant must offer a complete statement of the facts and circumstances that justify a probable cause to issue a warrant for electronic eavesdropping. Details of the suspected offense must be included in the particular description of the nature and location from which the electronic communication is desired.

Like traditional warrants, the application for an electronic intercept warrant must include a specific description of the type of communications to be seized and the identity of the person believed to be committing the offense or offenses. According to the statute, the applicant for the warrant must explain why other methods of obtaining the evidence have not worked or will not work as a prerequisite to obtaining a warrant. Warrants are good for a reasonable time when physical objects are to be seized, and the federal wiretap act application asks the length of time that the intercept will have to be maintained and whether the intercept should cease at the first moment the evidence has been obtained or be continued to obtain additional data. According to the statute, when the applicant has met all the requirements, the judge is permitted to enter an ex parte order that authorizes the interception of wire, oral, or electronic indications within the jurisdiction of that particular court. The judge's approval of the search warrant must be based on a determination that probable cause exists to believe that a person has committed or is committing a crime, that there's probable cause for believing that criminal communications will be intercepted, and that normal methods of investigating had failed or will not work under the circumstances.[17]

Upon the judge's approval, the warrant will issue, identifying the communications the government wants to intercept, the nature and location of the facilities where the interceptions are expected, a description of the communications expected to be intercepted, the identity of the agency authorized to intercept the communication, and the period of time during which the wiretap or other interception may be made,[18] not to exceed thirty days.[19]

The Federal Wiretap Act contains its own version of the exclusionary rule in § 2515. Where wire or oral communications have been intercepted in violation of the law, the evidence cannot be admitted in any trial, hearing, or other proceeding, including any court, grand jury, or other legislative or regulatory body in the United States, a state, or a political subdivision of a state.

The intent of the statute regulating eavesdropping was to mirror, as closely as circumstances permit, the procedures that are used for ordinary physical warrants. It attempts to assure that wiretapping and electronic eavesdropping are carefully monitored and not used unless other methods of collecting evidence have been tried and failed or would never have worked. One obvious reason for limiting electronic eavesdropping is that other persons who are not targets will have their conversations monitored as a natural consequence of gaining information from the target of the investigation.

After the September 11, 2001, terrorist attacks on the United States, the federal government initiated a variety of steps directed toward discovering what potential future terrorists might be planning. Consistent with this effort, federal agencies allegedly began collecting data through a variety of eavesdropping techniques. President George W. Bush authorized the National Security Agency to begin counterterrorism operations directed at surveillance of suspected terrorist organizations. A program that came to be known as the Terrorist Surveillance Program (TSP) intercepted communications without warrants to eavesdrop on e-mail and telephone conversations where one of the parties was located outside the United States and one of the parties was believed to be linked with the terrorist organization al Qaeda.[20] Several organizations sued the federal government, contending they were victims of this warrantless wiretapping, and succeeded in obtaining an injunction from a federal district court based on their injuries.[21] The plaintiffs alleged several causes of action based on the First Amendment, the Fourth Amendment, the Administrative Procedures Act, and the Foreign Intelligence Surveillance Act (FISA), among others. On appeal, the case was reversed because of a lack of jurisdiction based on the fact that none of the plaintiffs had standing to sue.[22] There may or may not have been merit to the plaintiffs' allegations, but they failed to prove individual injury occurred; therefore, the federal courts had no jurisdiction to hear the cause of action.

In another action,[23] the United States brought criminal charges against one Muhamed Mubayyid for crimes relating to the collection of federal taxes. The defendant and others brought an action to compel the federal government to disclose or provide an ex parte review of materials seized under FISA. The federal district court concluded that it was unnecessary to disclose details of the surveillance to properly determine the legality of the surveillance. The federal judge upheld the granting of the surveillance order by the Foreign Intelligence Surveillance Court because all of the FISA court procedures were properly met. In this case, the court reached the merits of the FISA surveillance and determined that federal law had been followed and upheld the admissibility of the evidence that had been unearthed by exploiting the surveillance.

In dealing with electronic surveillance under a variety of federal statutes and programs, adversely affected litigants will continue to fight an uphill battle, whether they are thrown out of court based on jurisdictional grounds, on the merits, or are frustrated due to the invocation of the state secrets privilege that belongs to the federal government. There is always the possibility that Congress might change some of the statutes or roll back some of the governmental privilege that relates to secrecy where foreign terrorist interdiction operations are ongoing.

5. SOURCES OF PROBABLE CAUSE: THE INFORMANT

Where the foundation of probable cause rests on information from an informant, earlier case law from the Supreme Court of the United States suggested that police and judges use a two-pronged test[24] to determine whether that information demonstrated probable cause. The police officers in *Aguilar v. Texas*[25] obtained a warrant based on a defective affidavit in which they swore that they had "received reliable information from a credible person and do believe that heroin, marijuana, barbiturates" were located within a residence. The *Aguilar* Court noted that the officers failed to state facts or circumstances from which the magistrate could have independently concluded that probable cause existed, *and* they neglected to offer any evidence that could have given credibility to the informant's conclusion that drugs were located in a particular place. To establish probable cause from using an informant, the two-pronged test had to be met, or police risked obtaining a defective warrant.

Under the *Aguilar* test, an informant's veracity and reliability had to be determined prior to a finding that the informant's information supplied probable cause. The police had to prove that the informant was a believable person. An informant might be believed to be truthful if he or she had given reliable information in the past or had implicated himself or herself in a crime by conveying the information to the police. The believability of a local priest, mayor, or another police officer, as an informant would probably not be questioned. The second prong required police to present facts to the judge or magistrate that demonstrate the informant possessed a basis from which one could reasonably conclude that probable cause existed.

In summary, to demonstrate probable cause based on an informant's information, the police must establish the basis of knowledge of the informant. First, police must understand the particular means by which the informant came by the information; second, supporting facts must prove either the veracity of the informant or the specific reliability of the information in the particular case. Unacceptable facts were bald and unilluminating conclusions offered by an informant that were not supported by the facts he or she provided.[26] For judicial approval, the police officer must include some of the underlying circumstances that would allow the judicial official to independently assess the validity of the informant's conclusions.

6. INFORMANT PROBABLE CAUSE: THE TOTALITY OF THE CIRCUMSTANCES TEST

In attempting to follow the dictates of *Aguilar*, state courts generated significant litigation centering on application of aspects of the two-pronged test. Subsequent to deciding *Aguilar*, the Court reaffirmed the two-pronged test in *Spinelli v. United States*, 393 U.S. 410 (1969). In *Spinelli*, officers investigating interstate gambling relied partly on information supplied by an informant and partly on personal investigation. In preparing the affidavit for a search warrant of Spinelli's apartment, the officers neglected to state facts that could have permitted the magistrate to independently conclude that the informant was reliable. The Court held that the officers did not state facts that would lead one to believe that probable cause existed, and they failed to state facts that supported the reliability of the informant. On the face of the affidavit, the officers should have noted why they concluded that the informant should be believed. In overturning the search pursuant to the warrant, the Court reaffirmed the continued validity of the *Aguilar* decision.

Convinced that the *Aguilar* test was not being applied properly in a number of cases, and revisiting the issue of informant production of probable cause, the Court overruled the *Aguilar* two-pronged test in *Illinois v. Gates,* 462 U.S. 213 (1983), and adopted a totality of the circumstances test (Case 6.2). Under the totality of the circumstances approach, a judge must look at the information offered by the informant and consider all relevant information, including facts supporting the believability and truthfulness of the informant, in reaching a decision. The *Gates* Court noted that under the totality of the circumstances analysis, "a deficiency in one may be compensated for, in determining the overall reliability of a tip, by a strong showing as to the other, or by some other indicia of reliability."[27] What the Court was attempting to avoid was a mechanical application of the two-pronged test. Under the totality of the circumstances test, if an informant had no past record of reliability or honesty but gave a detailed account of facts that indicated probable cause, the wealth of detail should overcome the lack of a proven record of honesty. Following *Gates,* a judicial officer may look at all the evidence pointing toward probable cause and come to a determination, without having to satisfy unrealistic pigeonhole standards. An informant's evidence may meet the probable cause standard by virtue of a past record as an informant, the extensive detail of the information conveyed, the surrounding circumstances, or any combination of these.

Although *Gates* abandoned strict adherence to the two-pronged test in determining informant-based probable cause under the Fourth Amendment, some state jurisdictions continued to apply the old *Aguilar* rule, requiring a reason to believe the informant and dictating close scrutiny of whether the substance of what the informant offered equaled probable cause. In an effort to bury the *Aguilar* two-pronged test, the Supreme Court reaffirmed the *Gates* decision and the demise of the two-pronged test in *Massachusetts v. Upton,* 466 U.S. 727 (1984).

In *Upton,* the state court had continued to interpret the Fourth Amendment as requiring the two-pronged test of *Aguilar* in determining whether an informant's information equaled probable cause. According to the *Upton* Court:

> Prior to *Gates,* the Fourth Amendment was understood by many courts to require strict satisfaction of a "two-pronged test" whenever an [informant helps supply probable cause] . . . in the particular case. The Massachusetts court apparently viewed *Gates* as merely adding a new wrinkle to this two-pronged test: where an informant's veracity and/or basis of knowledge are not sufficiently clear, substantial corroboration of the tip may save an otherwise invalid warrant.
>
> > We do not view the *Gates* opinion as decreeing a standardless "totality of the circumstances" test. The informant's veracity and basis of his knowledge are still important but, where the tip is adequately corroborated, they are not elements indispensible [*sic*] to finding of probable cause. It seems that, in a given case, the corroboration may be so strong as to satisfy probable cause in the absence of any other showing of the informant's "veracity" and any direct statement of the "basis of [his] knowledge." 390 Mass. At 568, 458 N.E.2d at 721.
>
> We think that the Supreme Judicial Court of Massachusetts misunderstood our decision in *Gates.* We did not merely refine or qualify the "two-pronged test." We

CASE 6.2

Leading Case Brief: Reliability of Informant's Information Will Be Judged on the Totality of the Circumstances

Illinois v. Gates
Supreme Court of the United States
462 U.S. 213 (1983)

Case Facts:

On May 3, 1978, the police received an unsolicited and anonymous letter alleging that Mr. and Mrs. Gates were selling drugs and possessed a quantity of drugs worth over $100,000 in the basement of their dwelling. Police received the following letter:

> This letter is to inform you that you have a couple in your town who strictly make their living on selling drugs. They are Sue and Lance Gates, they live on Greenway, off Bloomingdale Rd. in the condominiums. Most of their buys are done in Florida. Sue his wife drives their car to Florida, where she leaves it to be loaded up with drugs, then Lance flys [*sic*] down and drives it back. Sue flys [*sic*] back after she drops the car off in Florida. May 3 she is driving down there again and Lance will be flying down in a few days to drive it back. At the time Lance drives the car back he has the trunk loaded with over $100,000.00 in drugs. Presently they have over $100,000.00 worth of drugs in their basement.
>
> They brag about the fact they never have to work, and make their entire living on pushers.
>
> I guarantee if you watch them carefully you will make a big catch. They are friends with some big drug dealers, who visit their house often.
> Lance & Susan Gates
> Greenway

After some preliminary inquiries, police contacted an informant and discovered that Lance Gates had an airplane reservation to Florida near the date mentioned in the anonymous letter. Bloomingdale police contacted the Drug Enforcement Administration, which observed Lance Gates. The DEA surveillance disclosed that Lance Gates took a flight to Florida, stayed overnight in a motel room registered in his wife's name, and left the following morning with a woman in a car bearing an Illinois license plate issued to Lance Gates. The automobile started north on an interstate highway used by travelers to the Bloomingdale area. Numerous facts mentioned in the letter were corroborated by state and federal agents. On this basis, the police procured search warrants for the condo and the Gates' cars. Police recovered quantities of drugs.

The Gates appealed their drug convictions on the ground that the informant's information was not properly corroborated and probable cause did not exist.

Legal Issue:

When probable cause is based on an informant, must the two-pronged test of *Aguilar v. Texas* always be met?

The Court's Ruling:

In reviewing the way the two-pronged test operated, the Court determined that the better way to evaluate probable cause based on an informant was to consider the totality of the circumstances.

Essence of the Court's Rationale:

The Illinois Supreme Court concluded—and we are inclined to agree—that, standing alone, the anonymous letter sent to the Bloomingdale Police Department would not provide the basis for a magistrate's determination that there was probable cause to believe contraband would be found in the Gates' car and home. The letter provides virtually nothing from which one might conclude that its author is either honest or his information reliable; likewise, the letter gives absolutely no indication of the basis for the writer's predictions regarding the Gates' criminal activities. Something more was

(continued)

required, then, before a magistrate could conclude that there was probable cause to believe that contraband would be found in the Gates' home and car. See *Aguilar v. Texas*, 378 U.S. 108, 109, n.1 (1964); *Nathanson v. United States*, 190 U.S. 41 (1933).

* * *

We agree with the Illinois Supreme Court that an informant's "veracity," "reliability" and "basis of knowledge" are all highly relevant in determining the value of his report. We do not agree, however, that these elements should be understood as entirely separate and independent requirements to be rigidly exacted in every case, which the opinion of the Supreme Court of Illinois would imply. Rather, as detailed below, they should be understood simply as closely intertwined issues that may usefully illuminate the common-sense, practical question whether there is "probable cause" to believe that contraband or evidence is located in a particular place.

* * *

Moreover, the "two-pronged test" directs analysis into two largely independent channels—the informant's "veracity" or "reliability" and his "basis of knowledge." There are persuasive arguments against according these two elements such independent status. Instead, they are better understood as relevant considerations in the totality of circumstances analysis that traditionally has guided probable cause determinations: a deficiency in one may be compensated for, in determining the overall reliability of a tip, by a strong showing as to the other, or by some other indicia of reliability. [Citations omitted.]

* * *

[W]e conclude that it is wiser to abandon the "two-pronged test" established by our decisions in *Aguilar* and *Spinelli*. In its place we reaffirm the totality of the circumstances analysis that traditionally has informed probable cause determinations. The task of the issuing magistrate is simply to make a practical, common-sense decision whether, given all the circumstances set forth in the affidavit before him, including the "veracity" and "basis of knowledge" of persons supplying hearsay information, there is a fair probability that contraband or evidence of a crime will be found in a particular place. And the duty of a reviewing court is simply to ensure that the magistrate had a "substantial basis for . . . conclud[ing]" that probable cause existed. We are convinced that this flexible, easily applied standard will better achieve the accommodation of public and private interests that the Fourth Amendment requires than does the approach that has developed from *Aguilar* and *Spinelli*.

Reversed.

Case Importance:

By overruling the cases that supported the two-pronged test for measuring probable cause when based on an informant, the Court allowed a wider consideration of relevant facts in making a determination of probable cause. When some facts are so strong and other factors are weak, probable cause may logically still be determined.

rejected it as hypertechnical and divorced from "the factual and practical considerations of everyday life on which reasonable and prudent men, not legal technicians, act." Quoting *Brinegar v. United States*, 338 U.S. at 175 (1949).[28]

Consistent with principles of federalism, state courts relying on their individual state constitutional provisions are free to continue to use the two-pronged test to determine probable cause, but they can no longer use the test as determinative for probable cause under the Fourth Amendment.

7. SOURCES OF PROBABLE CAUSE: POLICE OFFICERS AND OTHERS

In a large number of cases, the evidence presented to the judicial official in an affidavit for a search warrant comes from the personal observation of police officers and the reports of other officers. Since courts assume that a sworn affidavit of personal knowledge offered by a police officer contains true information, the problems associated with the use of anonymous or questionable informants do not arise. Where the text of the affidavit for a search warrant includes information provided by fellow officers, the credibility of those officers does not come into question unless factually incredible evidence has been included. Generally, the judge need only consider the information contained within the affidavit to make an informed judgment concerning whether the facts support the existence of probable cause. If the judge determines from the affidavit that probable cause exists, he or she signs the warrant authorizing the search of a particularly described premises or person.

8. THE AFFIDAVIT FOR A WARRANT: WRITTEN OR ELECTRONIC

A search warrant will not be issued until the judge or magistrate has considered the facts contained within the written affidavit presented by the police and determined that probable cause exists to believe that seizable property will be found in a particular place. In addition to a description of why probable cause exists, the affidavit must particularly describe the place,[29] person, or property to be searched or the object to be seized. In most jurisdictions, the affiant must state the offense to which the seized property is believed to relate. The judicial official may agree with the officer's probable cause conclusions and sign the paper warrant. Alternatively, the judge or magistrate may require additional evidence before being convinced that probable cause exists. If the evidence must be added to the affidavit, generally it must be provided in writing as an amended affidavit or as an addendum to the original.

Some jurisdictions allow warrants to be issued upon sworn oral testimony taken by the judicial official over the telephone or by electronic transmission via fax or computer. With the growth of the Internet and the ease of communication facilitated by that medium, the number of jurisdictions permitting oral electronic warrants will increase as states update their rules of criminal procedure. One state permits the affidavit for a search warrant to be based on sworn testimony offered to the judge communicated by telephone or other electronic means. The person requesting the warrant by the affidavit must prepare a duplicate original of the affidavit and read it to the judge or magistrate verbatim. The judge or magistrate takes down the wording on paper for judicial consideration. In a situation where the judicial official is satisfied that probable cause exists, the official can direct that the applicant for the warrant sign the judicial official's signature on the face of the warrant that has been prepared by the affiant at the remote location.[30] The state of Georgia provides: "Search warrant applications heard by video conference shall be conducted in a manner to ensure that the judge conducting the hearing has visual and audible contact with all affiants and witnesses giving testimony."[31] The Georgia judge hearing a video conference application for a search warrant is required to administer oaths by means of the electronic video connection.[32] Additional rules exist for the return to the court of the documents once they have been reduced to the written form. Alternatively, a police officer may submit an affidavit by electronic means to the judge or magistrate. The magistrate orally places the police officer under oath, and the affidavit for the warrant is sent to the magistrate or judge by electronic means. If the judicial official agrees that probable cause exists, the judge or magistrate signs the warrant, noting the time and date of issuance, and indicates that the affidavit was sworn over the phone. An electronic transmission of the documents has the same effect as the original documents.[33] These newer methods of sending affidavits and issuing warrants take advantage of modern means of communication but do not change the standards that must be met with an affidavit or with a warrant.

Federal judges and federal magistrate judges have the power to issue search warrants based on either paper affidavits or a request by telephone or other means. According to Rule 41 of the Federal Rules of Criminal Procedure, "A magistrate judge may issue a warrant based on information communicated by telephone or other appropriate means, including facsimile transmission." The judge must place the applicant under oath, make an accurate record of the conversation with a proper recording device, and file the transcript with the court clerk.

9. THE SEARCH WARRANT: A COURT ORDER

A warrant is a court order issued by a neutral and detached judicial official and directed to a law enforcement official that recites the material facts alleged in the affidavit and carefully describes the place to be searched and particularly describes the objects to be seized. The warrant is a court order that commands the officer to search the place or person or described property and to bring any items seized to the court. The warrant requires the person or persons in control of the particular premises to allow the search to be conducted, and there is no legal right to impede the search or the searchers. Since a warrant is a lawful court order, no one possesses any right to resist the execution of a search warrant, but there is no duty to affirmatively assist in the search. The officer or officers executing the warrant give the person in control of the premises a copy of the warrant and, later, a list or inventory of items seized. If no one is present, the inventory is affixed to the premises that have been searched.

Police officers must follow several rules and requirements during the execution of the warrant. The warrant must be executed within a reasonable time or within the time limits dictated by state law[34] if it specifies a time limit. A warrant executed later than what is considered as reasonable or as specified is invalid and does not produce good evidence. The general preference for executions of warrants is that they be served during daytime hours, but most jurisdictions allow requests for night executions. Significantly, most states do not invalidate a night search, whether or not it had been requested pursuant to state law.

10. FOURTH AMENDMENT: KNOCK AND ANNOUNCE REQUIREMENT AND PERMISSIBLE DETENTION OF PERSONS PRESENT

The Supreme Court determined in *Wilson v. Arkansas* that the Fourth Amendment contains a "knock and announce" requirement that must be followed before forcing entry pursuant to a search warrant's execution. The knock and announce principle may be ignored if following it would subject the officers to greater danger.[35] In fact, some state laws allow the affiant to request approval in the affidavit for a nonconsensual entry where the officer has reason to believe that a knock and announce procedure will pose a greater danger to the officers executing the warrant. Nonconsensual or dynamic entries to execute search warrants have been approved[36] by the United States Supreme Court as consistent with the Fourth Amendment. A violation of the knock and announce requirement normally does not result in the suppression of evidence, even where police admit that they failed to comply with the knock and announce requirement. In *Hudson v. Michigan,* police had a warrant to search for guns and drugs at the defendant's home but waited only three to five seconds after announcing their purpose and intention.[37] The prosecution admitted that it did not follow the law with respect to knock and announce, but the Supreme Court indicated that suppression of evidence was not the remedy and exclusion could not be premised on violation of the Fourth Amendment. In *Hudson,* the police would have inevitably obtained the guns lawfully, even if they had not announced their presence, so the Court determined not to use the suppression of evidence as a remedy for a violation of the knock and announce requirement. The reality in this situation is that even though there is a knock and announce requirement in the Fourth Amendment, it is not normally enforced and does not affect the admission of evidence.

In addition to the general knock and announce requirement, police may detain persons who are present or who come to the premises during the execution of the search warrant.[38] Police officers may detain persons connected to the place of search, but they may not search the persons[39] of the seized individuals unless some other legal theory permits a search or searches. In some situations, when police have probable cause and are awaiting the arrival of a search warrant, they may prohibit unaccompanied reentry to premises by the occupant. Such brief seizure of the property until a judge issued a warrant has been deemed reasonable under the Fourth Amendment.[40] In an investigation into a gang-related shooting, the Supreme Court approved the handcuff detention in a garage of persons found on the premises being searched by police officers.[41] During a two- to three-hour search of a home where guns and drugs were the target of a warrant-based search, occupants of the home could be lawfully restrained in handcuffs in their own home without violating the Fourth Amendment. The officer's use of force in the form of handcuffs was reasonable because the warrant included a search for weapons, a wanted gang member lived on the premises, and in a dangerous situation, it minimized the danger to the police officers.

11. SCOPE OF SEARCH

The extent of a search, or its scope as it is often called, is dictated by the size and type of object that is the goal of the search, as well as the location where the search is to occur. Obviously, powdered recreational pharmaceuticals might be hidden in any location; thus, a warrant ordering the search and seizure of drugs would allow police officers to search virtually anywhere in a motor vehicle or residence. On the other hand, because a larger object such as a computer or a rifle could not be stored in an automobile console or a bathroom medicine chest in a residence, a search for such an object in those areas exceeds the lawful scope of the search. As Justice

CASE 6.3

Leading Case Brief: Exclusionary Rule Does Not Apply to Violations of Knock and Announce Principle

Hudson v. Michigan
Supreme Court of the United States
587 U.S. 586 (2006)

Case Facts:

Police obtained a warrant that authorized a search for drugs and guns at Hudson's home. They uncovered large amounts of drugs and some firearms. In addition, Hudson possessed rock cocaine on his person. In the location where he had been sitting, police discovered a loaded firearm lodged between the cushion and armrest of his chair. The prosecutor charged Hudson under state law with unlawful drug and firearm possession.

The prosecution admitted that, in executing the search warrant, the police violated the Fourth Amendment's requirement of "knock and announce" since they waited only three to five seconds after announcing before they forced their way into Hudson's abode. Prior to trial, defendant Hudson filed a motion to suppress all evidence seized from his home on the ground that police conduct violated his Fourth Amendment rights. The state trial court granted his motion to suppress. The Michigan Court of Appeals reversed because it felt suppression was not the proper remedy. The Supreme Court granted certiorari.

Legal Issue:

Although the Fourth Amendment has a recognized knock and announce requirement, in executing a search warrant, does the failure to follow approved knock and announce directives require that all evidence seized during the search be suppressed from the guilt phase of a trial?

The Court's Ruling:

The evidence of drug and gun possession should have been admitted at his trial because the knock and announce requirement was not a but-for case for obtaining the evidence; it would have been obtained in any event, and suppression takes too high a social cost.

Essence of the Court's Rationale:

II

The common-law principle that law enforcement officers must announce their presence and provide residents an opportunity to open the door is an ancient one. See *Wilson v. Arkansas,* 514 U.S. 927, 931-932, 115 S. Ct. 1914, 131 L. Ed. 2d 976 (1995). Since 1917, when Congress passed the Espionage Act, this traditional protection has been part of federal statutory law, see 40 Stat. 229, and is currently codified at 18 U.S.C. § 3109. . . . [I]n *Wilson,* we were asked whether the rule was also a command of the Fourth Amendment. Tracing its origins in our English legal heritage, 514 U.S. , at 931-936, 115 S. Ct. 1914, 131 L. Ed. 2d 976, we concluded that it was.

We recognized that the new constitutional rule we had announced is not easily applied. *Wilson* and cases following it have noted the many situations in which it is not necessary to knock and announce. . . . It is not necessary when "circumstances presen[t] a threat of physical violence," or if there is "reason to believe that evidence would likely be destroyed if advance notice were given," id., at 936, 115 S. Ct. 1914, 131 L. Ed. 2d 976, or [*2163] if knocking and announcing would be "futile," *Richards v. Wisconsin,* 520 U.S. 385, 394, 117 S. Ct. 1416, 137 L. Ed. 2d 615 (1997). We require only that police "have a reasonable suspicion . . . under the particular circumstances" that one of these grounds for failing to knock and announce exists, and we have acknowledged that "[t]his showing is not high." *Ibid.*

When the knock-and-announce rule does apply, it is not easy to determine precisely what officers must do. How many seconds' wait are too few? Our "reasonable wait time" standard [Citation omitted.] is necessarily vague.

* * *

III A

* * *

Suppression of evidence, however, has always been our last resort, not our first impulse. The exclusionary rule generates "substantial social costs," *United States v. Leon,* 468 U.S. 897, 907, 104 S. Ct. 3405, 82 L. Ed. 2d 677 (1984), which sometimes include setting the guilty free and the dangerous at large.

* * *

In this case, of course, the constitutional violation of an illegal manner of entry was not a but-for cause of obtaining the evidence. Whether that preliminary misstep had occurred or not, the police would have executed the warrant they had obtained, and would have discovered the gun and drugs inside the house. But even if the illegal entry here could be characterized as a but-for cause of discovering what was inside, we have "never held that evidence is 'fruit of the poisonous tree' simply because 'it would not have come to light but for the illegal actions of the police.'" *Segura v. United States,* 468 U.S. 796, 815, 104 S. Ct. 3380, 82 L. Ed. 2d 599 (1984).

* * *

Until a valid warrant has issued, citizens are entitled to shield "their persons, houses, papers, and effects," United States Const., Amdt. 4, from the government's scrutiny. Exclusion of the evidence obtained by a warrantless search vindicates that entitlement. The interests protected by the knock-and-announce requirement are quite different—and do not include the shielding of potential evidence from the government's eyes.

* * *

What the knock-and-announce rule has never protected, however, is one's interest in preventing the government from seeing or taking evidence described in a warrant. Since the interests that *were* violated in this case have nothing to do with the seizure of the evidence, the exclusionary rule is inapplicable.

* * *

[The Court rejected Hudson's contention that without suppression there would be no deterrence to police conduct. The Court noted that civil suits would be one remedy despite Hudson's assertion that no attorney would want to take a civil case based on a knock and announce violation.]

In sum, the social costs of applying the exclusionary rule to knock-and-announce violations are considerable; the incentive to such violations is minimal to begin with, and the extant deterrences against them are substantial—incomparably greater than the factors deterring warrantless entries when *Mapp* [*v. Ohio*] was decided. Resort to the massive remedy of suppressing evidence of guilt is unjustified.

[The Court affirmed the Michigan Court of Appeals holding that the evidence should not be suppressed.]

Case Importance:

Following this case, police have very little incentive to adhere to the requirements of the knock and announce principle that is part of the Fourth Amendment. It remains to be seen whether the possibility of civil suits will keep police officers from conducting more unannounced entries under the Fourth Amendment.

Stevens explained the concept of the scope of a lawful search in the context of a container search:

> The scope of a warrantless search of an automobile thus is not defined by the nature of the container in which the contraband is secreted. Rather, it is defined by the object of the search and the places in which there is probable cause to believe that it may be found. Just as probable cause to believe that a stolen lawnmower may be found in a garage will not support a warrant to search an upstairs bedroom, probable cause to believe that undocumented aliens are being transported in a van will not justify a warrantless search of a suitcase. *United States v. Ross,* 456 U.S. 798, 824 (1982).

Generally, once the object of the search has been described, the scope of the search is limited to areas and places where that object might reasonably be located. To search in areas where the object might not reasonably be located could constitute an unreasonable search under the Fourth Amendment and result in the object being excluded from use in evidence at trial.

12. THE RETURN OF THE WARRANT

In serving a warrant, the officer shows a copy of the original warrant to the person whose property is about to be searched to give that person notice of what property the police may legally seize. The serving officer gives the person whose property had been searched a receipt for the property being taken or should leave a copy of the inventory at the scene if no one is home at the time of the search.[42] The return occurs when the officer delivers the warrant and the property to the custody of the court or the issuing judicial official, along with a written inventory of the property seized pursuant to the warrant. Generally, a judge has a copy of the inventory delivered to the person from whom the property has been seized when the judge receives a request. Until the property is returned to the rightful possessor, the property seized is safely stored for use as evidence by the court that issued the warrant or by the law enforcement agency that served the warrant.[43] Figure 6.3 shows a sample return of inventory that is representative of the information contained on the return form transmitted to the court that issued the warrant.[44]

13. STALE PROBABLE CAUSE

Although warrants are valid for a reasonable time or for a set period of time, the problem of stale probable cause may undercut the validity of a warrant-based search conducted after probable cause has ceased to exist. The objects of many searches possess ready mobility, so that what is true today is not necessarily true later. A seller of recreational pharmaceuticals must turn over the inventory rather than hoard or store the product. Where the police have presented probable cause to believe that a particular home contains illegal drugs, the situation may change within a short time, so that probable cause quickly becomes stale.[45] One court held that probable cause was not stale when the probable cause information concerning child pornography sent by e-mail attachment was seven months old. The court noted that recipients of child pornography rarely delete pictures, so the suspected photographs were probably still on the defendant's home computer.[46] Probable cause to believe that a stolen forty-ton punch press has been installed in an industrial building remains for quite some time, since the press is not readily movable without obvious expenditure of observable effort. Similarly, business records required for everyday transactions at an ongoing commercial enterprise are not likely to be moved between the time probable cause matures and the time the warrant is executed. In these and similar situations, stale probable cause should not pose a problem for law enforcement or the prosecution.

Whether probable cause continues to exist must be determined by an examination of the facts of each case.[47] Staleness cannot be determined by any mechanical

RETURN AND INVENTORY

I received the attached Search Warrant on _____, _____, and executed it on the _____ day of _____, _____, at _____ [a.m.] [p.m.]. I searched the person or premises described in the Warrant and I left a copy of the Warrant with

_____

_____

(name the person searched or owner at the place of search) together with a copy of the inventory for the items seized.

The following is an inventory of property taken pursuant to the warrant: *(attach separate inventory if necessary)*

_____

_____

_____

This inventory was made in the presence of _____ *(name of applicant for the search warrant)* and _____ *(name of owner of premises or property). (If not available, name of other credible person witnessing the inventory.)*

This inventory is a true and detailed account of all the property taken pursuant to the Warrant.

                                  _____
                                    Signature of Officer

                                    _____
                                    Signature of Owner of

Property or Other Witness

Return made this _____ day of _____, _____, at _____ [a.m.] [p.m.].

                              _____
                              (Judge) (Clerk)

After careful search, I could not find at the place or on the person described, the property described in this warrant.

                              _____
                              Officer

                              _____
                              Date

FIGURE 6.3 Example of Return and Inventory Report Form following Execution of a Warrant.

formula such as the passage of time alone. Whether a tip equaling probable cause may be said to be stale depends on the nature of the tip and when it is used to procure a warrant. A tip about repetitive and continued criminal behavior may last for an extended period, especially when some of the conduct may be readily observable. The lapse of time is least important when the suspected criminal activity is continuing in nature and when the property or contraband is not likely to be destroyed, consumed, or dissipated.

14. WARRANTLESS SEARCHES: EXCEPTIONS TO THE GENERAL RULE

As an exception to the general rule requiring warrants to conduct searches, police may conduct searches without warrants on abandoned property or on property where no one has a legitimate expectation of privacy. When one throws away a soft drink can containing a sample of fingerprints, vacates a motel room and leaves behind incriminating evidence[48] in a trash can, or takes the license plates from a vehicle and leaves with no intent to have anything to do with the car in the future, such conduct indicates that the property has been abandoned. Property where no one presently possesses any expectation of privacy or has any rights under the Fourth Amendment is subject to search and seizure at any time without probable cause and/or a warrant.

Even property over which a person possesses a general right of privacy may be searched without a warrant in some circumstances. In *United States v. Dunn,* 480 U.S. 294 (1987), the Supreme Court reaffirmed the doctrine that an occupier of fenced farm land does not have an expectation of privacy in fenced but otherwise open fields unless steps are taken to keep people out of the area or to keep others from observing the fields directly (see Case 1.5).

Demonstrative of the principle that no one has privacy rights in abandoned property is the case of *California v. Greenwood,* 486 U.S. 35 (1988), where the Court approved a warrantless police search of residential trash canisters that had been placed near the public street for a private trash hauler to pick up. A high volume of vehicle and pedestrian traffic around the residence had caused Greenwood's neighbors to complain to police that he might be dealing in recreational pharmaceuticals. Without a warrant, the police arranged for the private trash collector to pick up Greenwood's waste in an empty truck and to deliver the contents to the police. Inspection of the truck's contents indicated the presence and probable use of illegal drugs at the residence.

The police used the trash evidence as part of the basis for developing probable cause to search Greenwood's residence. A judge issued a search warrant, and the subsequent search revealed illegal drugs. The *Greenwood* Court approved the warrantless search of the trash on the theory that the act of placing the trash for pickup indicated that the occupants had abandoned the property and possessed no Fourth Amendment expectation of privacy[49] in connection with the contents of the trash container.

15. SUMMARY

For a law enforcement official to conduct a search, the officer must have probable cause. Court cases have determined that probable cause exists where the facts and circumstances that have been presented to an officer of reasonable caution lead the officer to reasonably conclude that seizable property will be found on a particular person or in a particular place. The place or the person who is the subject of a search must be particularly described, and the object that is the goal of a search must also be carefully and particularly described. As a general rule, a warrant is required to search a home or a business unless there is consent or some other reasonable excuse. Where electronic surveillance may prove useful to law enforcement agents, as a strong general rule, a warrant is required to make the seizure reasonable and lawful. Probable cause to search may come from an informant, a police officer's personal observations, a fellow officer, a complaining witness, or a combination of these sources. Where an informant's data must serve as the basis for probable cause, there must be sufficient reason to believe that the informant is telling the truth and that the substance of what the informant relates equals probable cause.

Where a warrant is to be used, police or the prosecutor's office prepares an affidavit for a search warrant that details the facts and circumstances that the government believes constitutes probable cause to search. Where a neutral and detached judicial official agrees with the law enforcement official that probable cause to search exists, the judicial official signs a prepared document that serves as a search warrant. As a general rule, the search warrant must be served within a statutory designated time period or within a reasonable time if no statutory time applies.

When police officers serve a search warrant, they must do so in a reasonable manner. Case law interpreting concepts of reasonableness holds that the Fourth Amendment includes a knock and announce requirement. The officers need to indicate their presence at the location of the search and indicate that they are law enforcement officers who are prepared to conduct a search. Where the situation indicates that a knock and announce would dramatically enhance the risk to the police officers, this requirement may be excused.

The object of the search dictates the physical locations in a home or on a person where law enforcement officials may search. If an object could not be hidden within a particular location, it is deemed unreasonable for an officer to search that location. Once the property that is the subject of the search has been discovered, the search must end and a return made to the court that issued the warrant. As a general rule, an inventory of the object or objects seized is left with person or persons who were present at the place of the search, and an inventory is returned to the court that issued the search warrant.

REVIEW EXERCISES AND QUESTIONS

1. Give the narrative legal standard known as probable cause to search.
2. Since the Fourth Amendment requires specificity when describing things to be seized, what would be a good description of a quantity of marijuana? Of a pistol?
3. A police officer has suspicions that a person had been using illegal drugs. A judge issued a search warrant for the search of his home. The police officer overheard conversations of the defendant that could be interpreted in more than one way. The police officer's affidavit for the search warrant indicated that the defendant had engaged in acts that were indicative of drug activity, and the officer's drug dog alerted to abandoned drug packaging that defendant had discarded. This evidence was included in the affidavit. Do you think probable cause to search the defendant's home was established? Why or why not? See *People v. Martinez*, 2007 NY Slip Op 3480 (2007).
4. What are some of the basic steps that a federal law enforcement official must take to secure a warrant for electronic eavesdropping?

5. Explain how the totality of the circumstances test used to determine informant credibility operates (see Case 6.2).

6. Why can it be stated that police officers really do not need to comply with the knock and announce requirement of the Fourth Amendment? Explain.

7. Explain how probable cause can become stale, even though this will not be a problem in most cases.

8. How does the type of evidence being sought determine the scope of the search permitted?

HOW WOULD YOU DECIDE?

1. In the Supreme Court of the United States

Ms. Wilson made a series of sales of illegal recreational pharmaceuticals to undercover agents working with the Arkansas State Police. One of these informants arranged to purchase some marijuana and, at the consummation of the sale, Wilson threatened to kill the informant if she was found to be working for the police.

Law enforcement agents applied for and obtained warrants for search of Wilson's home, as well as an arrest warrant for Wilson. When the police arrived to execute the search and arrest warrants, Wilson's front door was unlocked and wide open, but entry was blocked by a screen door. The police did not knock and announce their presence but opened the screen door and entered the residence while identifying themselves as police officers. In plain view, the officers discovered a virtual pharmacy of drugs: marijuana, methamphetamine, Valium, and narcotics paraphernalia. Police found a gun and ammunition. They also found Wilson in her bathroom, flushing marijuana down the toilet.

Defendant Wilson filed a motion to suppress because the officer failed to knock and announce as is required under the Fourth Amendment. The trial court convicted her, and she brought her case to the Supreme Court. She alleges that her Fourth Amendment rights were violated because the officer failed to knock and announce, and the evidence found pursuant to the warrant should have been suppressed from her drug and weapons trial.

How would you rule on the defendant's contentions that if police officers fail to properly knock and announce, that the evidence discovered should be suppressed under the exclusionary rule?

The Court's Holding:

[The Court reviewed the purpose of the Fourth Amendment and considered other cases where evidence had been suppressed.]

Although the common law generally protected a man's house as "his castle of defence and asylum," 3 W. Blackstone, Commentaries 288 (hereinafter Blackstone), common law courts long have held that,

> when the King is party, the sheriff (if the doors be not open) may break the party's house, either to arrest him, or to do other execution of the K[ing]'s process, if otherwise he cannot enter. *Semayne's Case*, 5 Co.Rep. 91a, 91b, 77 Eng.Rep. 194, 195 (K.B. 1603).

To this rule, however, common law courts appended an important qualification:

> But before he breaks it, he ought to signify the cause of his coming, and to make request to open doors. . . . for the law without a default in the owner abhors the destruction or breaking of any house (which is for the habitation and safety of man) by which great damage and inconvenience might ensue to the party, when no default is in him; for perhaps he did not know of the process, of which, if he had notice, it is to be presumed that he would obey it. . . . *Ibid.* 77 Eng.Rep. at 195–196.

* * *

The common law "knock and announce" principle was woven quickly into the fabric of early American law. Most of the States that ratified the Fourth Amendment had enacted constitutional provisions or statutes generally incorporating English common law, see, e.g., N.J.Const. of 1776, § 22, in 5 Federal and State Constitutions 2598 (F. Thorpe ed. 1909) ("[T]he common law of England . . . shall still remain in force, until [it] shall be altered by a future law of the Legislature"). . . . [Other examples omitted.]

This is not to say, of course, that every entry must be preceded by an announcement. The Fourth Amendment's flexible requirement of reasonableness should not be read to mandate a rigid rule of announcement that ignores countervailing law enforcement interests. As even petitioner concedes, the common law principle of announcement was never stated as an inflexible rule requiring announcement under all circumstances.

* * *

[The Court held that the knock and announce requirement was a part of the Fourth Amendment, but the Court did not suggest any remedy for breaking the Fourth Amendment in this case.]

The judgment of the Arkansas Supreme Court is reversed, and the case is remanded for further proceedings not inconsistent with this opinion. See *Wilson v. Arkansas*, 514 U.S. 927 (1995).

HOW WOULD YOU DECIDE?

2. *In the Court of Criminal Appeals of Alabama*

Citizens informed police that some men were attempting to break into a house. The break-in suspects told law enforcement officers that the owners of the targeted home stored large quantities of marijuana inside the residence, and they were attempting to steal it. Police obtained a search warrant that covered all vehicles, people, and buildings located on or within defendant's residence where the marijuana was believed to be stored. In executing the warrant, police found more than five pounds of marijuana. The trial court did not initially suppress the evidence but did suppress after reading the defendant's brief on the motion to suppress. On appeal, the state contended that the trial court erred in granting defendant's motion to suppress based on the trial court's determination that there was no probable cause for the search since it had been based on the unreliable, unverified information from a confidential informant. The informant described how he regularly purchased an ounce of marijuana weekly from the defendant over a period of time.

How would you rule on the defendant's contention that there was no probable cause to believe that seizable property would be found in the defendant's home because the informant's evidence was not proven to be reliable and believable, and that the evidence should be suppressed?

The Court's Holding:

[The court reviewed the requirements for probable cause for a search when the basis depends on an informant and looked at *Illinois v. Gates* (Case 6.2) and the totality of the circumstances test for determining when probable cause exists when it is based on an informant's story.]

This Court has previously stated:

"'The present test for determining whether an informant's tip establishes probable cause is the flexible totality-of-the-circumstances test of *Illinois v. Gates* [Citations omitted]. The two prongs of the test of *Aguilar v. Texas* [Citations omitted] and *Spinelli v. United States* [Citations omitted] involving informant's veracity or reliability and his basis of knowledge, "are better understood as relevant considerations in the totality of circumstances analysis that traditionally has guided probable cause determinations: a deficiency in one may be compensated for, in determining the overall reliability of a tip, by a strong showing as to the other, or by some other indicia of reliability." *Gates* [Citations omitted]. . . . Probable cause involves "a practical, common sense decision whether, given all the circumstances, . . . including the 'veracity' and 'basis of knowledge' of persons supplying hearsay information, there is a fair probability that contraband or evidence of a crime will be found in a particular place." *Gates* [Citations omitted].

Pugh v. State, 493 So. 2d 388, 392 (Ala. Cr. App. 1985), aff'd, 493 So. 2d 393 (Ala. 1986).

[The court noted that a prosecutor is not required to show that an informant has proven to be accurate any number of times and that every informant has to start with his or her first time as an informant. The informant admitted to purchasing marijuana numerous times over a fairly recent period of time, his own crimes, which should bolster his credibility. Additionally, the informant had purchased drugs recently, so the probable cause could not be considered stale.]

Here, we believe that the trial court incorrectly determined that the search warrant authorized an unconstitutional "general search" for all drugs in Jenkins's apartment. We recognize that

"[g]eneral exploratory searches and seizures, with or without a warrant, can never be justified and are forbidden and condemned. *Marron v. United States,* 275 U.S. 192, 48 S. Ct. 74, 72 L. Ed. 231, Treas. Dec. 42528 (1927). The specific command of the Fourth Amendment to the Constitution of the United States is that no warrants shall issue except those 'particularly describing the . . . things to be seized.'

"However, the description of things to be seized contained in the warrant under review is not so broad that the authorization constitutes a general exploratory search. Certainly, 'an otherwise unobjectionable description of the objects to be seized is defective if it is broader than can be justified by the probable cause upon which the warrant is based.' *Vonderahe v. Howland,* 508 F.2d 364 (9th Cir. 1974); W. LaFave, 2 Search and Seizure, Section 4.6, n. 11 (1978) (hereinafter Search).

"However, a less precise description is required of property which is, because of its particular character, contraband.

"'If the purpose of the search is to find a specific item of property, it should be so particularly described in the warrant as to preclude the possibility of the officer seizing the wrong property; whereas, on the other hand, if the purpose is to seize not a specific property, but any property of a specified character, which by reason of its character is illicit or contraband, a specific particular description of the property is unnecessary and it may be described generally as to its nature or character.'"

"2 Search, p. 101, citing *People v. Schmidt,* 172 Colo. 285, 473 P.2d 698 (1970)."

Palmer v. State, 426 So. 2d 950, 952 (Ala. Crim. App. 1983).

Thus, in the instant case, the search warrant sufficiently described that law-enforcement officers were authorized. [The court held that the warrant was valid.] See *State v. Jenkins,* 2007 Ala. Crim. App. LEXIS 89 (2007).

ENDNOTES

1. Amendment Four, United States Constitution.
2. Probable cause may be said to exist when the facts and circumstances that have been presented to an officer of reasonable caution would cause the officer to conclude that seizable property would be found in a particular place or on a particular person.
3. Exceptions to the requirement of probable cause include brief stop and frisks under *Terry v. Ohio,* 392 U.S. 1 (1968); sweeps of real estate under *Maryland v. Buie,* 494 U.S. 325 (1990); and brief sobriety stops of motorists under *Michigan v. Sitz,* 496 U.S. 444 (1990).
4. *Coolidge v. New Hampshire,* 403 U.S. 443 (1971).
5. See *United States v. Dunn,* 480 U.S. 294, 1987 U. S. LEXIS 1057 (1987), where the Court permitted officers to enter private land for the purposes of a drug investigation and held that Fourth Amendment protections could not be extended from the house to include the area surrounding a farm barn. See also *Hester v. United States,* 265 U.S. 57 (1924), where federal officials were permitted to enter private land without a warrant and without probable cause.
6. See *Moore v. State* 2007 Alas. App. LEXIS 133 (2007).
7. See *State v. Ibarra,* 282 Kan. 530, 2006 Kan. LEXIS 719 (2006).
8. *Steele v. United States,* 267 U.S. 498, 503 (1925).
9. *State v. Foran,* 2006 Conn. Super. LEXIS 3007 (2006).

10. Ibid. According to the *Steele* Court and stated with approval, "A warrant was applied for to search any building or rooms connected or used in connection with the garage, or the basement or subcellar beneath the same. It is quite evident that the elevator of the garage connected it with every floor and room in the building, and was intended to be used with it."

11. *Maryland v. Garrison,* 480 U.S. 79 (1987).

12. See *Galin v. State,* 262 Ark. 485, 1988 Ark. LEXIS 1835 (Ark. 1977).

13. http://www.uscourts.gov/forms/AO093.pdf, September 13, 2007.

14. http://www.uscourts.gov/forms/AO093a.pdf, September 13, 2007.

15. 18 U.S.C. § 2511.

16. 18 U.S.C. § 2516.

17. 18 U.S.C. § 2518(3).

18. 18 U.S.C. § 2518(4).

19. 18 U.S.C. § 2518(5).

20. Gonzales, Attorney General. "Press Briefing by Attorney General Gonzales and General Michael Hayden, Principal Deputy Director for National Intelligence." December 19, 2005; United States Government, November 29, 2007, http://www.whitehouse.gov/news/releases/2005/12/print/20051219-1.html.

21. *ACLU v. Nat'l Sec. Agency/Central Sec. Serv.,* 438 F.2d 754, 2006 U.S. Dist. LEXIS 57338 (E.D Mich. 2006).

22. *American Civil Liberties Union, et al. v. National Security Agency, et al.,* 493 F.3d 644, 2007 U.S. App. LEXIS 16149 (6th Cir. 2007).

23. *United States v. Muhamed Mubayyid,* 2007 U.S. Dist. LEXIS 81807 (D. Mass. 2007).

24. The two-pronged test was developed in *Aguilar v. Texas,* 378 U.S. 108 (1964), and refined somewhat in *Spinelli v. United States,* 393 U.S. 410 (1969), before being dropped by the Court in *Illinois v. Gates,* 462 U.S. 213 (1983).

25. 378 U.S. 108 (1964).

26. For a more detailed explanation of the history of the two-pronged test, see *Aguilar v. Texas,* 378 U.S. 108 (1964), and *Spinelli v. United States,* 393 U.S. 410 (1969). The two-pronged test was officially overruled in *Illinois v. Gates,* 462 U.S. 213 (1983), but courts still look to both factors in determining the value of an informant's information.

27. *Gates* at 233.

28. 466 U.S. 727 at 731, 732.

29. Specificity concerning the place to be searched is a requirement under the Fourth Amendment according to the Court in *Maryland v. Garrison,* 480 U.S. 79, 84 (1987), where Justice Stevens, writing for the Court, stated:

> The Warrant Clause of the Fourth Amendment categorically prohibits the issuance of any warrant except one "particularly describing the place to be searched and the persons or things to be seized." The manifest purpose of this particularity requirement was to prevent general searches. By limiting the authorization to search to the specific areas and things for which there is probable cause to search, the requirement ensures that the search will be carefully tailored to its justifications, and will not take on the character of the wide-ranging exploratory searches the Framers intended to prohibit.

30. Rule 41(c)(2), North Dakota Rules of Criminal Procedure.

31. O.C.G.A § 17-5-21.1(b). Issuance of search warrants by video conference (2007).

32. Ibid. (c).

33. Rule 41(c)(3), North Dakota Rules of Criminal Procedure.

34. Demonstrative of the time limit is the Ohio Revised Code, Section 2933.24, which requires the search to be completed within three days of the issuance of the warrant. Other states have similar statutes.

35. See *Wilson v. Arkansas,* 514 U.S. 927 (1995), where the Court held that the Fourth Amendment included the knock and announce requirement because of common-law practice. However, the Court also held that a search and seizure in a dwelling might be reasonable without a prior announcement because of the circumstances of a reasonable belief of enhanced peril if done openly. This issue will be litigated on a case-by-case basis.

36. Ibid.

37. 547 U.S. 586, 126 S.Ct. 2159 (2006).

38. See *Michigan v. Summers,* 452 U.S. 692 (1981).

39. See *Ybarra v. Illinois,* 444 U.S. 85 (1979).

40. See *Illinois v. McArthur,* 531 U.S. 326 (2001).

41. See *Muehler v. Mena,* 544 U.S. 93 (2005).

42. Rule 41(d), North Dakota Rules of Criminal Procedure.

43. Rule 41(D), Ohio Rules of Criminal Procedure.

44. Adapted from a Warrant Packet from the Supreme Court of New Mexico. See http://www.supreme-court.nm.org/cgi-bin/download.cgi/supctforms/dc-criminal.

45. Continuing enterprises may keep probable cause from becoming stale. See, e.g., *United States v. Greany,* 929 F.2d 523, 525 (9th Cir. 1991), where two-year-old information relating to an ongoing marijuana operation was not deemed stale, and *Rivera v. United States,* 928 F.2d 592, 602 (2d Cir. 1991), where that court noted that in drug-trafficking cases involving repeated conduct, information may be months old and not stale.

46. *Commonwealth v. Gomolekoff,* 2006 PA Super 301, 2006 Pa. Super LEXIS 3538 (2006).

47. *United States v. Webster,* 734 F.2d 1048, 1056 (5th Cir. 1984).

48. See *Abel v. United States,* 362 U.S. 217 (1960), where the Court held that Abel had abandoned papers by placing them in a trash can in his motel room, which he later vacated, never to return.

49. A case could be made that Greenwood had an expectation of privacy under California law and case law. In *People v. Krivda,* 5 Cal.3d 357, 486 P.2d 1262 (1971), the California Supreme Court previously held that warrantless trash searches violate the Fourth Amendment and the California constitution. Following *Krivda,* the California constitution was altered to bar the suppression of illegally seized evidence, but *Krivda* continued to allow suppression under the United States Constitution. Thus, one could have reasonably possessed an expectation of privacy in California trash.

Part **3**

Searching Persons and Property

Searches and Seizures: Houses, Places, Persons, and Vehicles

Learning Objectives

1. Evaluate and describe why a person has the greatest expectation of privacy under the Fourth Amendment within that person's own home.
2. Be able to explain why police officers generally need a warrant to make an arrest within a suspect's home.
3. Evaluate and articulate the rationale that holds that a thermal image scan for escaping heat from the outside of a home constitutes a search, whereas having a drug dog sniff near luggage to detect escaping odors is not considered a search.
4. Justify why a search incident to a lawful arrest does not require an additional or separate showing of probable cause to search.
5. Be able to explain how the plain view doctrine operates, and give a concrete example.
6. Understand the concept of consent searches, and be able to explain how the totality of the circumstances test used to determine whether a person has given free and voluntary consent.
7. Articulate the rationale why most motor vehicles can be searched with probable cause in the absence of a warrant.
8. Explain how the nature of the object of a motor vehicle search informs the officer as to the scope of the constitutionally permissible search, and give an example of an object that limits where an officer might lawfully search.
9. List the three reasons suggested by the Supreme Court for allowing warrantless inventory searches of motor vehicles that have been lawfully seized.
10. Explain why no Fourth Amendment expectation of privacy exists in a forfeited vehicle.

Chapter Outline

1. Searches of Houses
2. Warrant to Search and Arrest inside the Home
3. Modern Technology and Warrantless Home Searches: Thermal Imaging Searches
4. Search Incident to Arrest
5. Search Incident to Arrest: No Warrant Requirement
6. General Scope of the Search Incident to Arrest
7. Inventory of Arrestee's Property
8. Traditional Requirements for the Plain View Doctrine
9. Inadvertent Discovery: No Longer Required
10. Officer Needs to Be Lawfully Present
11. The Plain Feel and Plain Smell Doctine
12. Searches Based on Consent
13. Searches of Motor Vehicles
14. Vehicle Searches Generally Do Not Require Warrants

Key Terms

Consent search
Infrared scan
Inventory search: motor vehicle
Inventory search: possessions
Plain feel search
Plain view seizure
Scope of search: home

Scope of search: motor vehicle
Search for arrestee
Search incident to arrest
Thermal imaging
Vehicle forfeiture search
Warrant exception for vehicles
Warrant requirement for house

1. SEARCHES OF HOUSES

In 1604, an English court made the now-famous observation that "the house of every one is to him as his castle and fortress, as well for his defence against injury and violence, as for his repose." *Semayne's Case,* 5 Co.Rep. 91a, 91b, 195, 77 Eng.Rep. 194, 195 (K.B.).[1]

In his *Commentaries on the Laws of England,* William Blackstone noted that

> the law of England has so particular and tender a regard to the immunity of a man's house that it stiles it his castle, and will never suffer it to be violated with impunity, agreeing herein with the sentiments of [ancient] Rome. . . . For this reason no doors can in general be broken open to execute any civil process, though, in criminal causes, the public safety supersedes the private. *Commentaries on the Laws of England* 223 (1765–1769)[2]

Since the Framers of the Fourth Amendment understood much of the legal philosophy of the English and had shared many recent abusive experiences, one of the reasons for adopting the Fourth Amendment was the security of one's home. Consistent with the British view, it would be reasonable to expect that the place where one resides should have a great level of protection from governmental intrusion. A strong general rule has developed through case law that a private home shall not be entered by a governmental agent without a search or arrest warrant that allows the intrusion.[3] Subject to a few limited exceptions, the question of whether a warrantless search of a home is reasonable and, therefore, constitutional must be answered with a strong no. When the police officer displays a properly drawn search warrant, the occupier is on notice that proper procedure has been followed and that the officer has carefully delineated authority to search in a particular place while looking for particularly described objects. A warrant is a court order directed to an officer or officers to perform a search for particular objects and to seize them if they are discovered. The home occupier has no right to resist the lawful probing of a police officer or officers when they operate pursuant to a search warrant.

Where the Fourth Amendment has been interpreted to allow for a departure from the warrant requirement, there has usually been an exigency making an intrusion into a dwelling imperative to the health or safety of the police and/or community. For example, in *Warden v. Hayden,* 387 U.S. 294 (1967), police were permitted to follow a suspect into a private dwelling without a warrant under the theory of "hot pursuit"; in *Michigan v. Tyler,* 436 U.S. 499 (1978), the Court approved a building search by law enforcement officials because the structure was burning and there was a dire need for official action; and in *Maryland v. Buie,* 494 U.S. 325 (1990), police were permitted to warrantlessly sweep the house to make sure there were no other suspects present who might harm them.

2. WARRANT TO SEARCH AND ARREST INSIDE THE HOME

Demonstrative of the concept that police officers and other law enforcement personnel may not enter a private residence without an arrest or search warrant is the case of *Payton v. New York,* 445 U.S. 573 (1980) (see Case 7.1). Police officers developed probable cause that Payton had committed murder of a gas station attendant. Several officers went to Payton's apartment for the purpose of arresting him, but they failed to obtain either a search warrant or an arrest warrant, although there was probable cause for his arrest. When neither Payton nor anyone else responded to the officers' repeated knocks on the door, the officers summoned assistance and brought down the door with a crowbar. When it became obvious that no one was home, police seized a .30-caliber shell casing that was later linked to the murder and was admitted against Payton at his homicide trial.

In rejecting Payton's motion to suppress the shell casing taken from his apartment, the trial judge cited two theories justifying the warrantless intrusion. The trial court held that exigent circumstances (an emergency) excused the officers' failure to announce their presence prior to entry and that New York law permitted the warrantless probable cause entry into the apartment. Exigent circumstances were not argued as justification for the warrantless entry into Payton's residence. New York appellate courts upheld the admission of evidence, but the Supreme Court of the United States reversed Payton's conviction.

The *Payton* Court noted, "Unreasonable searches or seizures conducted without any warrant at all are condemned by the plain language of the first clause of the Amendment."[4] According to the Court, the language of the Fourth Amendment applies equally to seizures of persons as to seizures of property, and a basic principle of the Fourth Amendment dictates that searches and seizures inside a home without a warrant are presumptively unreasonable. The purpose of the decision was not to protect the person of the suspect but to protect his home from entry in the absence of a judicial finding of probable cause. Because there was no proof of exigent circumstances for the arrest of Payton and because warrantless arrests inside the home are presumptively illegal, the Court reversed Payton's conviction.

CASE 7.1

Leading Case Brief: Arrest Within the Arrestee's Home Generally Requires a Warrant

Payton v. New York
Supreme Court of the United States
445 U.S. 573 (1980).

Case Facts:

New York detectives gathered evidence sufficient to establish probable cause to believe that Theodore Payton had murdered the manager of a gas station several days earlier. Without a warrant for search or arrest, six officers went to the apartment rented by Payton. Although the sound of music could be heard playing from inside the apartment, no one answered the door. Eventually officers broke into the apartment but found no one home. In plain view, the officers observed a .30-caliber shell casing, which they seized and which the trial court later admitted into evidence at Payton's murder trial. The trial judge believed that the warrantless and forcible entry was authorized by New York law and that the shell had been lawfully seized. The trial resulted in a verdict of guilty. The Appellate Division and the New York Court of Appeals affirmed the admission of evidence and the verdict. Neither court relied on exigent, or emergency, circumstances for its decision.

Payton applied for a writ of certiorari from the Supreme Court of the United States and offered the argument that under the Fourth Amendment, a warrant to enter a home should be required in order to arrest or seize a person, unless there are exigent circumstances present. The Supreme Court of the United States granted certiorari to hear the case.

Legal Issue:

Must law enforcement agents possess either a search warrant or an arrest warrant to make a lawful arrest inside a suspect's home or to search a suspect's home, absent exigent circumstances?

The Court's Ruling:

The Fourth Amendment requires police to have probable cause and obtain a warrant to arrest a person within his or her own home, unless a clear and immediate emergency exists.

Essence of the Court's Rationale:

* * *

It is familiar history that indiscriminate searches and seizures conducted under the authority of "general warrants" were the immediate evils that motivated the framing and adoption of the Fourth Amendment. Indeed, as originally proposed in the House of Representatives, the draft contained only one clause, which directly imposed limitations on the issuance of warrants, but imposed no express restrictions on warrantless searches or seizures. As it was ultimately adopted, however, the Amendment contained two separate clauses, the first protecting the basic right to be free from unreasonable searches and seizures and the second requiring that warrants be particular and supported by probable cause. The Amendment provides:

> The right of the people to be secure in their persons, houses, papers, and effects, against unreasonable searches and seizures, shall not be violated, and no Warrants shall issue, but upon probable cause, supported by Oath or affirmation, and particularly describing the place to be searched, and the persons or things to be seized.

It is thus perfectly clear that the evil the Amendment was designed to prevent was broader than the abuse of a general warrant. Unreasonable searches or seizures conducted without any warrant at all are condemned by the plain language of the first clause of the Amendment.

The simple language of the Amendment applies equally to seizures of persons and to seizures of property. Our analysis in this case may therefore properly commence with rules that have been well established in Fourth Amendment litigation involving tangible items. As the Court reiterated just a few years ago, the "physical entry of the home is the chief evil against which the wording of the Fourth Amendment is directed." *United States v. United States District Court*, 407 U.S. 297, 313. And we have long adhered to the view that the warrant procedure minimizes the danger of needless intrusions of that sort.

It is a "basic principle of Fourth Amendment law" that searches and seizures inside a home without a warrant are presumptively unreasonable.

* * *

The Fourth Amendment protects the individual's privacy in a variety of settings. In none is the zone of privacy more clearly defined than when bounded by the unambiguous physical dimensions of an individual's home—a zone that finds its roots in clear and specific constitutional terms: "The right of the people to be secure in their . . . houses . . . shall not be violated." That language unequivocally establishes the proposition that,

[a]t the very core [of the Fourth Amendment] stands the right of a man to retreat into his own home and there be free from unreasonable governmental intrusion. *Silverman v. United States*, 365 U.S. 505, 511.

In terms that apply equally to seizures of property and to seizures of persons, the Fourth Amendment has drawn a firm line at the entrance to the house. Absent exigent circumstances, that threshold may not reasonably be crossed without a warrant.

* * *

[W]e note the State's suggestion that only a search warrant based on probable cause to believe the suspect is at home at a given time can adequately protect the privacy interests at stake, and since such a warrant requirement is manifestly impractical, there need be no warrant of any kind. We find this ingenious argument unpersuasive. It is true that an arrest warrant requirement may afford less protection than a search warrant requirement, but it will suffice to interpose the magistrate's determination of probable cause between the zealous officer and the citizen. If there is sufficient evidence of a citizen's participation in a felony to persuade a judicial officer that his arrest is justified, it is constitutionally reasonable to require him to open his doors to the officers of the law. Thus, for Fourth Amendment purposes, an arrest warrant founded on probable cause implicitly carries with it the limited authority to enter a dwelling in which the suspect lives when there is reason to believe the suspect is within.

Because no arrest warrant was obtained in either of these cases, the judgments must be reversed and the cases remanded to the New York Court of Appeals for further proceedings not inconsistent with this opinion.

It is so ordered.

Case Importance:

A person may expect the greatest level of privacy in his or her private home, which, absent rare exceptions, legally cannot be breached by police officers unless a judicial official has issued a warrant for an arrest or a search.

Payton stands for the age-old principle that a man's home is his castle and should not have its walls breached by the government in the absence of some clear emergency unless the government agent possesses a warrant to arrest or to search the private premises.

The Supreme Court reaffirmed the rationale of *Payton* in *Kirk v. Louisiana*, 536 U.S. 635 (2002), where police arrested the defendant without a warrant after entering his place of residence. After law enforcement officials observed drug purchases made out of Kirk's apartment and arrested a customer, they knocked on the door of the apartment and arrested defendant Kirk. A search incident to arrest revealed cocaine and money. Citing *Payton v. New York*[5] and its well-settled theory that, absent exigent or emergency circumstances, police may not enter a private dwelling without an arrest or search warrant, the Supreme Court reversed Kirk's conviction of possession of cocaine with intent to distribute.

Even though a man's home may be his castle, neither the home nor all the surrounding objects are beyond being searched under proper circumstances. Where police officers possess a warrant to search a particular home, the warrant may extend to include vehicles parked within the structure and those parked nearby if the objects of the search warrant could be hidden within the vehicle or vehicles. Since the goals of a search might be frustrated if vehicles are not searched and because vehicles can be used as storage areas, a vehicle on searched premises should be treated and searched just like other personal effects found on the searched premises that could contain the contraband or evidence. In a Michigan case, the officers searched a vehicle located on the premises and partially on the driveway as part of their search of the home. When the searching officers found drugs within the vehicle, the defendant moved to suppress the drugs from trial, alleging an unreasonable search and seizure under the Fourth Amendment. In approving a vehicle search, at least where the police had a search warrant for the home and found the vehicle on the searched premises, a Michigan court of appeals noted, "Although Michigan has not ruled on the precise issue raised by defendant, nearly all jurisdictions that have decided the question have held a search warrant for 'premises' authorizes the search of all automobiles found on the premises."[6] Part of the rationale for allowing a search anywhere on the premises where the object could have been physically hidden has, as its basis, some language from the Supreme Court in *United States v. Ross*.[7] In permitting the search of a motor vehicle for which probable cause existed, the *Ross* Court noted:

> A lawful search of fixed premises generally extends to the entire area in which the object of the search may be found and is not limited by the possibility that separate acts of entry or opening may be required to complete the search. Thus, a warrant that authorizes an officer to search a home for illegal weapons also provides authority to open closets, chests, drawers, and containers in which the weapon might be found. . . . A warrant to search a vehicle would support a search of every part of the vehicle that might contain the object of the search.[8]

By analogy, if the object could be hidden within the car on the premises, the car should be treated just like a medicine chest or a closet.

While police and other law enforcement agents may not enter private premises in the absence of a warrant to arrest or to search, mere presence on private apartment property does not give an individual an expectation of privacy while inside the property. In *Minnesota v. Carter,* 525 U.S. 83 (1998), an officer observed Carter and some associates dividing cocaine into separate containers. The officer was looking through a street-level window, which contained a gap in the curtains. Upon observing sufficient information for probable cause to search the apartment, the officer procured a warrant and searched the apartment. The Supreme Court held that Carter had no expectation of privacy within the apartment because he did not live there, he had not stayed there overnight, and he was using the apartment only for the purposes of a commercial drug trade. Had the officers immediately entered the apartment without a warrant, at first blush it would seem like Carter could make an argument similar to that made by Payton and with it succeed in having the cocaine evidence suppressed. The difference here was that Carter had an insufficient connection to the apartment to claim a right of privacy under the Fourth Amendment, whereas Payton lived in his apartment and possessed a traditional expectation of privacy, which the Court recognized.

If Carter could have been lawfully arrested inside an apartment without a warrant because of insufficient expectation of privacy, some additional connection to real estate should arguably create an expectation of privacy close to that observed in *Payton v. New York*. The case of *Minnesota v. Olson*, 495 U.S. 91 (1990), provides a suitable benchmark for the minimum connection to property sufficient to produce an expectation of privacy under the Fourth Amendment. In *Olson*, police developed probable cause for Olson's arrest and discovered that he was believed to be in a particular home where he had been staying. Without permission or a warrant but with probable cause for arrest, police entered the home and arrested Olson. During a subsequent interrogation, Olson made an inculpatory statement, which he argued should have been suppressed from his trial.

Prior to trial, the trial court refused to suppress Olson's statement on the ground that he possessed no expectation of privacy at another person's home. The Minnesota Supreme Court reversed[9] the conviction because it believed that Olson had an expectation of privacy, even though he was never left alone in the home or given a key. The Supreme Court of the United States affirmed the Minnesota court because it believed that Olson had a sufficient connection to the property to have an expectation of privacy and, secondarily, there existed no emergency exception to allow the warrantless arrest within the home.

3. MODERN TECHNOLOGY AND WARRANTLESS HOME SEARCHES: THERMAL IMAGING SEARCHES

While physical intrusions into the home have historically been the focus of Fourth Amendment litigation, new methods to search humans, buildings, homes, and cars have recently been developed. In *Kyllo v. United States*, 533 U.S. 27 (2001) (Case 7.2), federal agents had become suspicious that marijuana was being cultivated with the use of high-intensity lamps in Kyllo's residence. To determine whether the high-intensity lamps were actually being used, federal agents conducted an infrared scan, creating a thermal image of the outside of the home that could measure heat emanating from the interior. The scan of Kyllo's home took only a brief time to complete and was performed from across the street from the front of the house. The infrared scan showed that the roof over the garage and a sidewall of the home were relatively hot compared with the rest of the home and substantially warmer than neighboring homes subjected to thermal imaging. The information from the scan, along with other evidence, produced probable cause for a search warrant. Evidence obtained from the search warrant was used against Kyllo at his trial for growing marijuana. The court of appeals affirmed the conviction, but the Supreme Court of the United States reversed.

Because the agents did not enter the home in any form or fashion, it would seem that there was no search of Kyllo's home. In a case involving a similar principle,

CASE 7.2

Leading Case Brief: Thermal Imaging Search of Home's Heat Signature Requires Warrant

Kyllo v. United States
Supreme Court of the United States
533 U.S. 27 (2001).

Case Facts:

An agent of the United States Department of the Interior developed suspicions that Danny Kyllo might have been growing and might continue to grow marijuana in one apartment of a triplex in Florence, Oregon. Indoor cultivation of marijuana typically requires high-intensity lamps that substitute for sunlight and create a warmer atmosphere than is usually kept in private homes. In an effort to measure the amount of excess heat that might be escaping from Kyllo's place of residence, the agent from the Department of the Interior, associated with another law enforcement agent, procured an Agema Thermovision 210 thermal imaging scanner to scan Kyllo's home. The image produced by the scanner portrayed shades of gray that represented relative temperatures of the residence. White portions of the image indicated warm surfaces; black portions indicated cold surfaces. The agents performed the scan from across the street from Kyllo's home and from an automobile and did not invade the home in any way. The machine read escaping heat and did not intrude into the home. The scan revealed that Kyllo's garage roof and the side wall were relatively hot compared to the rest of his home and substantially warmer than the signature offered by neighboring residential units.

The scan was done without a warrant and not under circumstances indicating an emergency, but it produced sufficient evidence to permit a federal judicial official to issue a warrant for a traditional search of Kyllo's home. The search pursuant to the warrant disclosed more than a hundred marijuana plants growing inside the home.

Kyllo tendered a conditional guilty plea, reserving his right to appeal the search and seizure issue. The Ninth Circuit Court of Appeal remanded the case for a determination concerning the intrusiveness of the imaging machinery. The District Court found that the Agema 210 was not a device that intruded into the inside of a home, it did not show people or activity within the home, and it did not reveal intimate human conduct. The Ninth Circuit subsequently found that there had been no violation of the Fourth Amendment in the original scan of the home and that the warrant had been properly issued.

The Court upheld the conviction.

The Supreme Court granted certiorari to Kyllo's petition for review of the decision of the Ninth Circuit Court of Appeal.

Legal Issue:

Where police make a warrantless scan of the exterior of a home using nonintrusive imaging devices that read only heat emanated from a residential structure, does such practice constitute a search of a home for which a warrant is traditionally required under the Fourth Amendment?

The Court's Ruling:

* * *

II

The Fourth Amendment provides that "[t]he right of the people to be secure in their persons, houses, papers, and effects, against unreasonable searches and seizures, shall not be violated." "At the very core" of the Fourth Amendment "stands the right of a man to retreat into his own home and there be free from unreasonable governmental intrusion." *Silverman v. United States,* 365 U.S. 505, 511 (1961). With few exceptions, the question whether a warrantless search of a home is reasonable and hence constitutional must be answered no. See *Illinois v. Rodriguez*, 497 U.S. 177, 181 (1990); *Payton v. New York*, 445 U.S. 573, 586 (1980).

* * *

In assessing when a search is not a search, we have applied somewhat in reverse the principle first enunciated in *Katz v. United States*, 389 U.S. 347 (1967). Katz involved eavesdropping by means of an electronic listening device placed on the outside of a telephone booth—a location not within the catalog ("persons, houses, papers, and effects") that the Fourth Amendment protects against unreasonable searches. We held that the Fourth Amendment nonetheless protected Katz from the warrantless eavesdropping because he "justifiably relied" upon the privacy of the telephone booth. *Id.* at 353. As Justice Harlan's oft-quoted concurrence described it, a Fourth Amendment search occurs when the government violates a subjective expectation of privacy that society recognizes as reasonable. See *id.* at 361. We have subsequently applied this principle to hold that a Fourth Amendment search does not occur—even when the explicitly protected location of a house is concerned—unless "the individual manifested a subjective expectation of privacy in the object of the challenged search," and "society [is] willing to recognize that expectation as reasonable." [Citation omitted.].

[The government argued that the conviction should be upheld, since the imaging detected only heat that radiated from the residence and was not an intrusive search of the interior of the home. The Court rejected the mechanical analysis, since more sophisticated equipment in the near future may be capable of "looking" inside the home without any physical intrusion. The Court rejected the government contention that the imaging of the home met constitutional standards, since it did not detect private activities occurring in private areas of the home. Additionally, were the Court to enter the labyrinth of determining which activities within the home deserve "private" protection, the door would have been opened to endless litigation.]

We have said that the Fourth Amendment draws "a firm line at the entrance to the house," *Payton*, 445 U.S. at 590. That line, we think, must be not only firm, but also bright—which requires clear specification of those methods of surveillance that require a warrant.

While it is certainly possible to conclude from the videotape of the thermal imaging that occurred in this case that no "significant" compromise of the homeowner's privacy has occurred, we must take the long view, from the original meaning of the Fourth Amendment forward.

The Fourth Amendment is to be construed in the light of what was deemed an unreasonable search and seizure when it was adopted, and in a manner which will conserve public interests as well as the interests and rights of individual citizens. *Carroll v. United States*, 267 U.S. 132, 149 (1925).

Where, as here, the Government uses a device that is not in general public use, to explore details of the home that would previously have been unknowable without physical intrusion, the surveillance is a "search" and is presumptively unreasonable without a warrant.

Since we hold the Thermovision imaging to have been an unlawful search, it will remain for the District Court to determine whether, without the evidence it provided, the search warrant issued in this case was supported by probable cause—and if not, whether there is any other basis for supporting admission of the evidence that the search pursuant to the warrant produced.

* * *

The judgment of the Court of Appeals is reversed; the case is remanded for further proceedings consistent with this opinion.
It is so ordered.

Essence of the Court's Rationale:

Although the thermal imaging device allowed police to view only heat that had escaped from the home, the Court believed that the technology had the ability to observe details of life inside the home for which a warrant was normally required.

Case Importance:

The Court recognized that a distinction could be drawn between a dog sniff of luggage that searched only the air outside the luggage and an image assembled by an imaging device that could reveal details from inside a private home; the former was not a search, and the latter qualified as a Fourth Amendment search for which a warrant is generally required.

a luggage sniff by a drug-locating dog had been determined not to be a search of the interior of the luggage, since the dog reacted only to odors outside the luggage.[10] On those grounds, the government could certainly argue that there was no search of the interior of the home and that the only evidence collected from the infrared scan was heat that had escaped from within the home, which the agents collected and measured from the outside with thermal imaging equipment. Kyllo contended that the process constituted a search because details of his private life within the home became observable to the government because of the use of advanced technology to obtain evidence previously unknowable without a physical intrusion.

Justice Scalia, writing for the *Kyllo* Court in reversing the lower federal courts, noted:

> Where, as here, the Government uses a device that is not in general public use, to explore details of the home that would previously have been unknowable without physical intrusion, the surveillance is a "search" and is presumptively unreasonable without a warrant.
>
> Since we hold the Thermovision imaging to have been an unlawful search, it will remain for the District Court to determine whether, without the evidence it provided, the search warrant issued in this case was supported by probable cause— and if not, whether there is any other basis for supporting admission of the evidence that the search pursuant to the warrant produced.[11]

Even with newer technology that would allow the government access to information emanating from a home, the Supreme Court of the United States has seen fit to return to the philosophy and jurisprudence of the early Fourth Amendment. The Court, by giving protection to those individuals within homes and buildings who possess an expectation of privacy that society is prepared to recognize, gives effect to the original intent of the Framers of the Fourth Amendment. At that time, no one would have envisioned that a law enforcement official would be able to discern the interior of the house without looking in a window or walking through the entrance. Future developments in emerging technologies that use sound waves or backscatter x-ray imaging to penetrate a home, personal property, or a nonconsenting person presumably will run afoul of the *Kyllo* case and similar reasoning.

4. SEARCH INCIDENT TO ARREST

A search incident to a lawful arrest is a traditional exception to the warrant requirement of the Fourth Amendment. The arrest consists of a law enforcement officer taking physical control over a person and determining where, when, and how the person moves from or stays in a particular location. When an arrest is made, courts have universally considered it permissible for the arresting officer to search the person of the arrestee. In addition, a search may be made of the area within the immediate dominion and control of the arrestee. The search incident to arrest has been determined as reasonable under the Fourth Amendment because the privacy interest protected by that constitutional guarantee is subordinated to legitimate and paramount governmental concerns. Courts have also considered it entirely reasonable for the arresting officer to seize any evidence of criminality on the arrestee's person to prevent its concealment and/or destruction.[12] There are two historical ratio-nales[13] for allowing the search incident to arrest exception to the search warrant requirement: the need to disarm the suspect to take him into custody and the necessity of preserving evidence for later use at trial.

A search incident to a lawful arrest would, by its definition, appear to require a valid arrest as a foundation for conducting a search following an arrest. In *Knowles v. Iowa,* 525 U.S. 113 (1998), a police officer conducted a search of a motor vehicle's interior with probable cause to arrest the driver but without making the actual arrest. The Supreme Court held that the search was invalid under the Fourth Amendment since there was no other rationale to justify the vehicle search other than a search incident to an arrest, and there had never been a valid arrest on which to base the subsequent vehicle search. The clear lesson from *Knowles* is that an actual arrest is a necessary step prior to conducting a search incident to an arrest. Similarly, in a Wisconsin case,[14] a police officer developed probable cause to arrest a suspect for drug-related offenses and eventually searched the interior of the subject's automobile. At the time of the motor vehicle search, the officer had neglected to place the subject under arrest. The trial court determined that the search of the vehicle was invalid and unreasonable because case interpretations of the Fourth Amendment require that a search incident to lawful arrest must occur after a lawful arrest. Since the officer failed to arrest the subject, his car could not be lawfully searched incident to an arrest that had yet to occur. However, in an earlier case, *Rawlings v. Kentucky,*[15] the Court noted that where probable cause to arrest existed, a search incident to arrest that briefly preceded the actual arrest could be considered reasonable so long as the formal arrest followed quickly on the heels of the search.

5. SEARCH INCIDENT TO ARREST: NO WARRANT REQUIREMENT

A search incident to a lawful arrest has been recognized as an exception to the warrant requirement since 1914 and by actual practice prior to that time.[16] See *Weeks v. United States,* 232 U.S. 383. Whereas the *Weeks* Court approved of warrantless searches of the arrestee's person and effects, the Court expanded the scope of the search incident to arrest in *Marron v. United States,* 275 U.S. 192 (1927). There the Court enlarged the permitted scope of a search incident to an arrest to include personal effects not described in a search warrant but seized on the premises. The *Marron* Court asserted that the police authority to search incident to arrest includes all parts of the premises used for the unlawful purpose. The Court subsequently approved of an expanded warrantless search incident to arrest in *United States v. Rabinowitz,* 339 U.S. 56 (1950), where the police were permitted to search the entire premises that the suspect occupied at the time of the arrest. The police obtained a warrant for Rabinowitz's arrest, but they did not procure a search warrant. When they arrested him in his place of business, they searched not only his person but also the desk, safe, and file cabinets; they also seized 573 forged postage stamps as incident to arrest. The Court approved the search of the business premises without a warrant as incident to the warrant-based arrest. The rule derived from *Rabinowitz,* later overruled, allowed the complete warrantless search of business premises based on an arrest and could easily be applied to private homes.

6. GENERAL SCOPE OF THE SEARCH INCIDENT TO ARREST

Although *Rabinowitz* authorized an extensive search following arrest, the virtually unlimited search permitted there has subsequently seen restriction. In more recent cases, the Court significantly reduced the scope of the search incident to arrest. In *Chimel v. California,* 395 U.S. 752 (1969), the Court reconsidered the extensive searches approved in *Rabinowitz* and *Marron* and effectively overruled the *Rabinowitz* and *Marron* approval of extensive searches incident to arrest.

The *Chimel* police went to the defendant's home to arrest him pursuant to a warrant, but they had to wait for the defendant to arrive home from work. Mrs. Chimel allowed the officers to enter the home and wait for her husband. When Chimel arrived, police arrested him and conducted a warrantless search of his home. Accompanied by Chimel's wife, the officers looked through the entire three-bedroom house, including the attic, the garage, and a small workshop. The officers directed her to open drawers and to physically move contents of the drawers from side to side so that they might view any items that would have come from the burglary of which Chimel had been accused. The search revealed primarily coins but also several medals, tokens, and a few other objects. The entire search took less than an hour. The *Chimel* Court rejected the extensive scope of the search and held that the search conducted by the officers was unreasonable under the Fourth Amendment. To meet the requirements of the Fourth Amendment, the Court redefined the extent of a search incident to an arrest by limiting it to the area under the defendant's immediate dominion and control. The portions of the home that remained beyond Chimel's immediate control should not have been searched as incident to the arrest.

Chimel continued to recognize the principle that an arrest that occurs within a home allows search of portions of the home that would not be permissible if the individual had been arrested on a public street. Under *Chimel,* an object, indicative of criminality, that comes into view during a search incident to arrest where the search has been appropriately limited in scope may be seized without a warrant. In the absence of any additional suspicion following an in-home arrest, police officers are permitted a limited search beyond the person of the arrestee. This ancillary search includes looking into closets, cabinets, and other spaces immediately adjoining the place the arrestee occupies following the arrest. This additional search is justified because a weapon could be stored nearby, a confederate might exit a closet and attempt to frustrate arrest, or some other hidden danger could present harm to the officers or others within the home. This area around the arrestee has often been known as the "lunge area," the area from which an arrestee might abruptly grab a weapon or destroy evidence. The search should be limited to the area into which an arrestee might reach. As a practical matter, the lunge area encompasses the area within the arrestee's immediate dominion and control, but it generally would not include a basement,[17] an attic, or a separate room of the home inaccessible to the arrestee. According to the general rule, where police are lawfully searching incident to arrest, an object that comes into view that is indicative of criminality may be seized without a warrant.

Demonstrative of a search incident to a lawful arrest is a recent Texas case where police arrested the driver of a motor vehicle for making an unlawful lane change, an offense that was subject to arrest under Texas law.[18] The driver also smelled of marijuana smoke and had glassy red eyes. The officer searched the driver's person, including his pockets, and discovered several cards, including a credit union debit card, a high school identification card, and some discount cards for retail stores, all in the name of a different person. The additional evidence eventually implicated the defendant in an armed robbery, and he argued that the search that revealed the cards was unreasonable. The Texas trial court and the appellate court determined that the search of the interior pockets of the defendant was simply the type of search permitted incident to a lawful arrest. The court noted that a search incident to arrest allowed a more extensive search than would have been allowed if the search had been only a stop and frisk pat-down.

A search incident to a valid arrest has often been called a full search of the person; it is not limited to a frisk of the suspect's outer clothing and removal of such weapons as the arresting officer may reasonably believe the suspect has in his possession. The absence of probable fruits or further evidence of the particular crime for which the arrest is made does not narrow the permissible scope of the search. The officer not only may frisk the individual but also is entitled to conduct a complete search of the person, a complete search of clothing, and a complete search of the effects with the arrestee. Naturally, the search must be reasonable in the manner in which the officer conducts the quest. Clearly, an individual cannot be forced to completely disrobe on a public street corner to facilitate a clothing search without violating the Fourth Amendment's requirement that searches be reasonable. Similarly, a body cavity or other extensive personal search must have additional justification beyond the usual probable cause to arrest.

7. INVENTORY OF ARRESTEE'S PROPERTY

Police may lawfully search an arrestee's personal property that he or she possessed at the time of the arrest. This search may include purses and wallets as well as jackets and other clothing that may be on the person of the arrestee or in an automobile in which the arrestee had recently been riding. The property of an arrestee who has been removed from his vehicle is generally subject to search. In a Florida case,[19] the subject had been arrested for an ordinance violation, and police had searched his person, revealing marijuana. Immediately after his arrest, officers searched the interior of the arrestee's motor vehicle and a container that held marijuana roaches and a bag of marijuana. Since the officers released the vehicle to a friend of the arrestee, the defendant argued that the police did not conduct a true inventory because they did not tow the vehicle and gave it to a friend of the defendant. The appellate court approved the search because the trend has been to allow a search of a motor vehicle's interior following an arrest as a matter of course. The court noted, "Arrest for an ordinance violation, even though it is neither a felony or misdemeanor arrest, can be the basis for a lawful search of a vehicle incident to that arrest."[20] An Alaska court refused to suppress drug evidence taken from a search of the arrestee's property.[21] The court permitted the search of the console in an arrestee's motor vehicle because the center console was unlocked, it was an item immediately associated with driver's person, and it was within the arrestee's immediate dominion and control at the time of the arrest.

Searching an arrestee's property, whether clothing, luggage, or motor vehicle, based on an inventory policy also produces admissible evidence. In a Texas case[22] where the defendant had been arrested for failure to display a front license plate and not having a valid driver's license, officers searched the defendant's pickup truck to reveal methamphetamine and a loaded revolver. The search was based on an inventory search requirement of the local police department, and the officers followed the policy for inventory searches appropriately. As a result, the drugs and firearm were properly admitted against the defendant.

8. TRADITIONAL REQUIREMENTS FOR THE PLAIN VIEW DOCTRINE

The "plain view" doctrine is an exception to the warrant requirement for a search, but standing alone, the doctrine does not allow an officer to immediately enter private premises to effectuate a seizure. As a general rule, law enforcement officials may make warrantless seizures of evidence in plain view when the officer observes the object of the seizure from a lawful vantage point, the incriminating nature of the object or its clear connection to crime is immediately apparent, and the officer can acquire dominion over and control of the object without a violation of the Fourth Amendment.

An object subject to police seizure may present itself during a search for some different object, a stop and frisk, a routine traffic stop, hot pursuit, or at any other time when a law enforcement officer lawfully observes evidence indicative of criminality. Under this legal theory, police may be permitted to seize an object without a warrant where the officer is lawfully in a position to view it, if the object's incriminating character is clearly and immediately apparent, and if the police have a lawful right of access to the item. The legal theory behind the plain view doctrine is that

> if contraband is left in open view and is observed by a police officer from a lawful vantage point, there has been no invasion of a legitimate expectation of privacy, and thus no "search" within the meaning of the Fourth Amendment—or at least no search independent of the initial intrusion that gave the officers their vantage point. *Minnesota v. Dickerson,* 508 U.S. 366, 375 (1993)

The usual legal standards for a valid plain view seizure as described in *Coolidge v. New Hampshire,* 403 U.S. 443 (1971), required that the police officer observed the seizable evidence from a position the officer had a lawful right to occupy, that the officer's discovery was unexpected or inadvertent, and that the incriminating nature of the evidence was clearly apparent to the officer. This final requirement merely restates the necessity of probable cause to seize the evidence. Under *Coolidge,* if the officer expected to find a particular item of evidence at a particular place, the "discovery" of the evidence could not be sustained under the plain view doctrine because of the absence of inadvertent discovery.

In a classic case in which the plain view had application, in the early morning hours a police officer observed a vehicle traveling at about ninety miles per hour in a forty-five-miles-per-hour zone with a flat tire and sparks coming from the rim of the tire wheel. The officer made a probable cause stop of the vehicle, and the driver subsequently opened the driver's door and fell out of the car onto the road. When one officer smelled a strong odor of marijuana coming from the vehicle, he looked inside the passenger compartment and observed plastic baggies containing what the officer recognized as marijuana. The appellate courts upheld the seizure under the plain view theory, since the officers had a lawful vantage point outside the vehicle, the nature of the object clearly offended the law, and in a vehicle context, they were lawfully allowed to enter the premises and make a seizure.[23]

9. INADVERTENT DISCOVERY: NO LONGER REQUIRED

Subsequent to the *Coolidge* plain view doctrine case, police officers were permitted to seize evidence if they were lawfully on the premises and discovered evidence that had not been anticipated but was clearly indicative of criminal activity. The reality, of course, was that officers legitimately on the premises would pretend to inadvertently discover evidence they expected to discover but for which they lacked probable cause. The fact that probable cause did not exist for the expected objects meant that the affidavit could not have mentioned such evidence and the warrant would not have included a description of the evidence.

Almost twenty years later, the Supreme Court reexamined the legal elements of the plain view doctrine in *Horton v. California*, 496 U.S. 128 (1990) (Case 7.3). In *Horton*, police determined that there was probable cause to search Horton's residence for the proceeds of a robbery and weapons used in the robbery. Police obtained a search warrant that covered the proceeds of the robbery but did not mention a handgun that police believed would probably be present. The search revealed a handgun but no evidence of the robbery proceeds. The Supreme Court held that even if the discovery of the handgun was expected and not inadvertent, the evidence was properly seizable under the plain view doctrine. According to the Court, inadvertent discovery no longer was a requirement for use of the plain view doctrine.

10. OFFICER NEEDS TO BE LAWFULLY PRESENT

Following *Horton*, the requirements for the use of the plain view doctrine dictate that the officer is lawfully on the premises or at a lawful vantage point, that probable cause for seizure is clearly apparent, and that the officer has a lawful method of gaining access to the seizable property.

The evidence must be clearly visible and not in a location where the officer must manipulate or minutely examine it to determine whether the property is seizable. If the officer needs to move the property to find a serial number to determine whether the property was stolen[24] or needs to open a container to observe the incriminating item, such conduct constitutes a separate search and cannot meet the

CASE 7.3

Leading Case Brief: The Plain View Doctrine No Longer Requires Inadvertent Discovery

Horton v. California
Supreme Court of the United States
496 U.S. 128 (1990)

Case Facts:

A California trial court convicted Horton of an armed robbery of the treasurer of the San Jose Coin Club. As the victim, Wallaker, entered his garage, two masked men, one armed with an Uzi submachine gun, attacked him. One of the robbers used an electrical stun gun that rendered the victim unable to resist. As the robbers carried on a fairly open conversation between themselves, they bound and handcuffed Wallaker. The victim recognized petitioner Horton's distinctive voice; another witness observed the robbers leaving the scene of the crime and was able to add some corroboration to the identification. Additional evidence disclosed that Horton had gained knowledge that Wallaker possessed a large quantity of cash and jewelry because Horton had attended a coin show where Wallaker had done business.

After an initial investigation, police obtained a warrant to search Horton's residence for the proceeds of the robbery. The affidavit for the search warrant described weapons as well as proceeds of the robbery as objects of the proposed search, but the warrant mentioned only robbery proceeds, including three specifically described rings. During the execution of the warrant, police seized an Uzi submachine gun, a .38-caliber revolver, two stun guns, a handcuff key, and several other items. The officer conducting the search admitted searching not only for the rings but for other evidence connecting Horton to the crime. Some of the seized evidence was not discovered "inadvertently" since police expected to find some of the seized materials.

Horton alleged that the warrant had been defective since it did not have sufficient specificity to mention the firearms that the police fully expected to find. The trial court refused to suppress the evidence, and a jury convicted Horton. He appealed with no success to the California Court of Appeals. Subsequently, the Supreme Court of California denied review.

Since the application of the plain view exception to the warrant requirement had been construed by the California courts to not require inadvertence in discovery under the plain view doctrine, the Supreme Court of the United States granted certiorari.

Legal Issue:

Is warrantless seizure of criminal evidence in plain view prohibited by the Fourth Amendment if the discovery of the evidence was expected, even though the item was not listed on a search warrant?

The Court's Ruling:

The justices determined that the earlier version of the plain view doctrine that required that evidence to be inadvertently discovered was not required under the plain view doctrine if the evidence seized is clearly indicative of crime under the facts of the case, even if police expected to find some of the evidence.

Essence of the Court's Rationale:

In this case we revisit an issue that was considered, but not conclusively resolved, in *Coolidge v. New Hampshire,* 403 U.S. 443 (1971): Whether the warrantless search of evidence of crime in plain view is prohibited by the Fourth Amendment if the discovery of the evidence was not inadvertent. We conclude that even though inadvertence is a characteristic of most legitimate "plain view" seizures, it is not a necessary condition.

I

* * *

The criteria that generally guide "plain view" seizures were set forth in *Coolidge v. New Hampshire,* 403 U.S. 443 (1971). The Court held that the seizure of two automobiles parked in plain view on the defendant's driveway in the course of arresting the defendant violate the Fourth Amendment. . . . The State endeavored to justify the seizure of the automobiles, and their subsequent search at the police station, on four different grounds, including the "plain view" doctrine. The scope of that doctrine as it had developed in earlier cases was fairly summarized in these three paragraphs from Justice Stewart's opinion:

It is well established that under certain circumstances the police may seize evidence in plain view without a warrant. But it is important to keep in mind that, in the vast majority of cases, *any* evidence seized by the police will be in plain view, at least at the moment of seizure. The problem with the 'plain view' doctrine has been to identify the circumstances in which plain view has legal significance rather than being simply the normal concomitant of any search, legal or illegal.

* * *

Justice Stewart then described the two limitations on the doctrine that he found implicit in its rationale: First, "that plain view *alone* is never enough to justify the warrantless seizure of evidence," and second, "that the discovery of evidence in plain view must be inadvertent."

* * *

It is, of course, an essential predicate to any valid warrantless seizure of incriminating evidence that the officer did not violate the Fourth Amendment in arriving at the place from which the evidence could be plainly viewed. There are, moreover, two additional conditions that must be satisfied to justify the warrantless seizure. First, not only must the item be in plain view, its incriminating character must also be "immediately apparent." Thus, in *Coolidge,* the cars were obviously in plain view, but their probative value remained uncertain until after the interiors were swept and examined microscopically. Second, not only must the officer be lawfully located in a place from which the object can be plainly seen, but he or she must also have a lawful right of access to the object itself. . . . In all events, we are satisfied that the absence of inadvertence was not essential to the Court's rejection of the State's "plain view" argument in *Coolidge.*

III

Justice Stewart concluded that the inadvertence requirement was necessary to avoid a violation of the express constitutional requirement that a valid warrant must particularly describe the things to be seized. He explained:

The rationale of the exception to the warrant requirement, as just stated, is that a plain-view seizure will not turn an initially valid (and therefore limited) search into a "general" one, while the inconvenience of procuring a warrant to cover an inadvertent discovery is great. But where the discovery is anticipated, where the police know in advance the location of the evidence and intend to seize it, the situation is altogether different. The requirement of a warrant to seize imposes no inconvenience whatever, or at least none which is constitutionally cognizable in a legal system that regards warrantless searches as "per se unreasonable" in the absence of "exigent circumstances."

If the initial intrusion is bottomed upon a warrant that fails to mention a particular object, though the police know its location and intent to seize it, then there is a violation of the express constitutional requirement of "Warrants . . . particularly describing . . . [the] things to be seized." 403 U.S., at 469–471.

We find two flaws in this reasoning. First, evenhanded law enforcement is best achieved by the application of objective standards of conduct, rather than standards that depend upon the subjective state of mind of the officer. The fact that an officer is interested in an item of evidence and fully expects to find it in the course of a search should not invalidate its seizure if the search is confined in area and duration by the terms of a warrant or a valid exception to the warrant requirement.

* * *

Second, the suggestion that the inadvertence requirement is necessary to prevent the police from conducting general searches, or from converting specific warrants into general warrants, is not persuasive because that interest is already served by the requirements that no warrant issue unless it "particularly describ[es] the place to be searched and the persons

(continued)

or things to be seized," see *Maryland v. Garrison*, 480 U.S. 79, 84 (1987); and that a warrantless search be circumscribed by the exigencies which justify its initiation. See, *e.g., Maryland v. Buie*, 494 U.S. 325, 332–334 (1990); *Mincey v. Arizona*, 437 U.S. 385, 393 (1978). Scrupulous adherence to these requirements serves the interests in limiting the area and duration of the search that the inadvertence requirement inadequately protects. Once those commands have been satisfied and the officer has a lawful right of access, however, no additional Fourth Amendment interest is furthered by requiring that the discovery of evidence be inadvertent.
[Affirmed.]

Case Importance:

The plain view doctrine allows officers to seize any evidence indicative of criminality that is observed during a valid search if the officers occupied an area they were legally permitted to occupy. This decision makes the plain view doctrine easier to apply.

dictates of the plain view doctrine. Demonstrative of the proposition that the property and its seizable qualities must be clearly visible to the officer is *Arizona v. Hicks*, 480 U.S. 321 (1987), where police were lawfully on the premises following reports of a shooting. One of the officers noticed some expensive stereo components that looked out of place in such a squalid apartment and concluded that they might have been stolen. The officer moved the components to see their serial numbers and recorded them for future use. The equipment later proved to be stolen property, but the *Hicks* Court concluded that the warrant that had been issued on the basis of the serial numbers had been improperly obtained by virtue of the officer's warrantless search for the serial numbers. In effect, the plain view doctrine requires the relevancy of the evidence to be readily apparent prior to seizure, and even a warrantless search for serial numbers could not be justified under the plain view doctrine.

Although the evidence must be in plain view, the officer can lawfully take a position that permits the best vantage point. For example, in *California v. Ciraolo*, 476 U.S. 207 (1986), following reports from neighbors that Ciraolo was cultivating marijuana in his backyard, police boarded an aircraft to search the yard from a lawful altitude. Officers observed marijuana growing inside the defendant's yard behind a privacy fence. Officers expected to find marijuana growing in the backyard plot and the discovery was not inadvertent, but the Court upheld the search, even though *Ciraolo* was decided four years prior to *Horton*. So long as the place or position that the officer takes is a lawful one, the observation can properly be the basis for the use of the plain view doctrine.

11. THE PLAIN FEEL AND PLAIN SMELL DOCTRINE

Under the stop and frisk doctrine, police officers often discover items that are not reasonably considered weapon-like lumps but that, to a trained and experienced officer, seem likely to be contraband. Consider the situation in which an officer touches what seems to be contraband during an otherwise lawful pat-down. Such a search may allow the officer to enter the inner clothing if he or she has felt an object whose contour or mass makes its identity immediately apparent. Under these circumstances, there has been no illegal invasion of the suspect's privacy beyond that already authorized by the search for weapons under a stop and frisk.

In *Minnesota v. Dickerson*, 508 U.S. 366 (1993), a police officer was conducting a lawful stop and frisk. As he patted down a suspect who had been lawfully seized, the officer felt what he thought was a rock of crack cocaine, a determination he made only after manipulating it between his thumb and index finger. The Supreme Court agreed that a plain feel doctrine allows a seizure under the circumstances where a police officer lawfully patted down a suspect's outer clothing and felt an object whose contour or mass makes its identity as contraband immediately apparent. The *Dickerson* Court recognized there would have been no invasion of the suspect's privacy beyond that already authorized by the officer's search for weapons. If the object reasonably seems to be contraband, the seizure by the officer would be justified by the same practical considerations that inhere in the plain view context. Justice White, writing the lead opinion in *Dickerson,* held that the officer's manipulation of the object in the subject's pants constituted a search beyond the stop and frisk and the cocaine was not lawfully seized following the plain feel doctrine. A seizure would be permitted only where the lawful touch allowed the officer to instantly develop a reasonable belief that the object offended the law.

Where police officers smell odors that through their training indicate criminality, whether that smell odor is marijuana smoke or ether that might indicate the manufacture of methamphetamine, the odor may give rise to a reasonable basis to suspect criminal activity. In any event, odors dictate additional investigation and response. In an Ohio case,[25] an officer had stopped a motorist for running a red light and smelled a strong odor of marijuana coming from the interior of the motor vehicle. The vehicle's interior lights came on when the officer asked the driver to step from the vehicle, and the illumination from the interior light revealed in the ashtray of the car a cellophane wrapper that contained rock cocaine. Following his arrest, the defendant contended that the officer did not have probable cause to arrest or to search his motor vehicle based on the odor of marijuana. The trial court and the appellate court agreed that smelling marijuana by a person trained to recognize the odor was sufficient to establish probable cause to search the motor vehicle. In this situation, the odor of marijuana detected by a police officer who occupied a physical position outside the stopped vehicle gave rise to probable cause. In a similar situation, Maryland police officer stopped a defendant for speeding and smelled evidence of burned marijuana coming from the motor vehicle.[26] When a search revealed no marijuana in the interior of the car, the officer searched the trunk and discovered six and a half pounds of marijuana. The trial court and the Maryland Court of Special Appeals agreed that the smell of burnt marijuana provided probable cause to search the motor vehicle's interior as well as the trunk.

12. SEARCHES BASED ON CONSENT

Where law enforcement officials wish to search a particular area for which no probable cause exists or where probable cause may exist but the officer does not have a required search warrant, searching may be possible by the use of the theory of consent. Like many personal constitutional rights, the Fourth Amendment guarantees can be waived if the parties involved follow appropriate steps.

The first requirement in acquiring consent dictates that the *proper person* give consent. This person must have sole dominion and control over the property or must share dominion and control with another person or persons. Apartment dwellers may not own the real estate, but they have dominion and control over the property at the moment, and can grant consent. Personal property generally falls into the same set of rules. The person possessing dominion and control over the subject property may give consent to search a car, backpack, shoulder bag, purse, or other container. In a Minnesota case, a driver of an automobile gave consent to a police officer to search the vehicle, which had been stopped for having a broken headlight. The officer searched the locked trunk area and opened a passenger's suitcase, revealing controlled substances. According to the appellate court, the results of the search should have been suppressed from admission into evidence because the prosecution failed to demonstrate that the third-party driver of the vehicle had dominion and control over the property or shared common authority over the suitcases. The appellate court took the position that a driver's consent to search a motor vehicle should not be construed automatically to extend to property owned and controlled by passengers if the passengers were present and available to grant or withhold consent to the search of their property.[27] Even though Fourth Amendment rights are generally considered personal and cannot be asserted vicariously, some jurisdictions allow vicarious waiver and would enable allow a driver to consent to a search of the passenger's belongings under the foregoing circumstances[28] because of a reduced expectation of privacy in motor vehicles.

Sometimes a person purports to have dominion and control over the property, especially real estate, but the individual is being untruthful or the police are relying on reasonable appearances. In *Illinois v. Rodriguez,* 497 U.S. 177 (1990), Rodriguez' former girlfriend used her key to allow police to enter an apartment to arrest Rodriguez, who had drugs in plain view. The woman represented that the apartment was "ours" and that she had clothes and furniture there. The general rule is that a warrantless entry is valid when based on the consent of a third party if the police reasonably believe that the third party possesses common dominion and control over the premises.[29] The *Rodriguez* Court held, essentially, that if police had a good faith reasonable belief that the individual with the key possessed dominion and control, that fact could support a consent search if all the other components were present.

The second requirement under the Fourth Amendment for a valid consent to search is that the consent is given freely and voluntarily. Voluntariness is a question of fact to be determined from all the circumstances surrounding the situation, but knowledge of the right to refuse consent is not an absolute requirement.[30] The factors to be considered include the level of education and general intelligence of the consenting party, the coerciveness of the circumstances, whether the individual was under arrest, whether the person knew about the right to refuse to grant consent, whether the police indicated a search would be conducted anyway, and whether police falsely stated that they possessed a warrant. Although these factors are not exclusive, they demonstrate the usual considerations that courts use in determining whether consent was voluntarily given.

Where a question arises concerning the validity of a consent search, the prosecution must demonstrate that the proper person gave consent and that it was given freely and voluntarily under the totality of the circumstances. Demonstrative of these principles is *Schneckloth v. Bustamonte,* 412 U.S. 218 (1973), where police lawfully stopped a vehicle during the early morning hours. The driver had no license, and most of the six men in the vehicle had no identification. Officers requested permission from the car owner's brother, Alcala, to search the car. A police backup unit arrived with more officers, creating a slightly coercive atmosphere. As the proper person to give consent, Alcala agreed to allow a search of the vehicle. Criminal charges eventually resulted against passenger Bustamonte, who contended that the evidence seized had been discovered during an illegal search involving a lack of consent.

The driver apparently did not possess dominion and control over the vehicle because Alcala, the owner's brother, made decisions involving the car's operation. The real issue involved whether Alcala gave a free and voluntary consent under the totality of the circumstances. Alcala's educational level was not known, but he appeared to be of normal intelligence. There was no indication that anyone was initially threatened with arrest or that the numbers of officers present indicated an excessively coercive atmosphere. Under the circumstances, the Supreme Court upheld the conviction and ruled that the consent had been freely and voluntarily offered by the proper person.[31]

Clearly the proper person or party must give consent, but sometimes two individuals possess shared dominion and control over real or personal property. When both are not present, the person who is present and who has shared dominion and control may give consent to search. Although two people may share control over the property when both are present, when one is absent, control over the property falls to the one individual who is present. A different rule applies where two people share a dominion and control over property and are both present when police officers request consent to conduct a search. If one person refuses to grant consent while the other is willing to give consent, the consent of one over the objection of the other fails to give lawful consent for police to conduct a search. In a recent Georgia case, the wife was willing to allow police to search their marital home, and the husband objected to the search and refused to give his consent. Police entered the premises anyway. This initial search revealed evidence that was used to procure a search warrant that was used to conduct a more extensive search of the home, which revealed some drug possession offenses that had been committed by the husband. A majority of the justices on the Supreme Court of the United States decided that consent to enter a private home would not exist for a guest if one resident invited the social guest into the home while the other resident commanded the guest not to enter the home. If consent to enter the home would not exist for a social guest when both parties are present and disagree, there cannot be valid consent for police to conduct a search of the home where the disagreement is obvious.[32] On the other hand, if two persons possess shared dominion and control over property and only one is present, that person may give valid consent for a search to law enforcement officials. The only remaining issue would be whether the consent was given freely and voluntarily by the remaining person.

If police request permission to search personal property where two or more individuals possess dominion and control over the property, consent of those present is

CASE 7.4

Leading Case Brief: Consent Search Requires Agreement by the Proper Parties Present to Grant Valid Consent

Georgia v. Randolph
Supreme Court of the United States
547 U.S. 103 (2006)

Case Facts:

In late May 2001, Scott Randolph and his wife separated when she left the marital home to reside in Canada. At this time, she removed some of her personal possessions and took their son for a time to her parents' home. In early July, she returned to the residence but harmony did not ensue because their tumultuous relationship continued at its former pace. After some specific marital strife, Mrs. Randolph phoned police to report the domestic dispute and indicated to police that respondent Randolph had removed their son from the premises.

Mrs. Randolph informed police that her husband's drug abuse had harmed the marriage relationship. One police officer accompanied Jane Randolph to retrieve her child from where her husband had taken the son. Upon her return to the family home with a police officer, she renewed her allegations of her husband's drug abuse and current drug possession. Following a police request for consent to search the marital home, Jane Randolph agreed to permit a consent search of their shared residence, but her husband, who was present, refused to grant consent. Pursuant to directions offered by the wife, police initiated a cursory search of the home and recovered a drinking straw with a residue believed to contain cocaine powder.

Subsequently, police executed a search warrant based on the wife's information and the straw containing the cocaine powder. The search of the marital home revealed additional evidence of drug possession that resulted in the indictment of Mr. Randolph for possession of cocaine. His motion to suppress was denied by the trial court on the ground that the wife of the defendant possessed shared dominion and control over the marital residence and could grant a legally sufficient consent to search the premises.

The Court of Appeals of Georgia reversed the trial court on the theory that the consent to conduct a warrantless search of a residence given by one lawful occupant is not valid when another occupant who is physically present refuses to grant consent. The Supreme Court of Georgia upheld the Court of Appeals by distinguishing an earlier federal case, *United States v. Matlock,* 415 U.S. 164 (1974), that permitted one occupant to consent to a search of commonly occupied property when the other occupant was absent at the time of the consent request. The Supreme Court of the United States granted certiorari.

Legal Issue:

If one of two co-occupants of residential property grants consent to search commonly held property when an equal cotenant refuses to grant consent, can police conduct a proper consent search consistent with the Fourth Amendment?

The Court's Ruling:

The justices determined that where two persons share dominion and control over property and both are present, the consent of one cotenant over the objection of the other does not constitute proper consent under the Fourth Amendment.

Essence of the Court's Rationale:

* * *

The Fourth Amendment recognizes a valid warrantless entry and search of premises when police obtain the voluntary consent of an occupant who shares, or is reasonably believed to share, authority over the area in common with a co-occupant who later objects to the use of evidence so obtained. *Illinois v. Rodriguez,*

497 U.S. 177 (1990); *United States v. Matlock,* 415 U.S. 164 (1974). . . .

* * *

II

To the Fourth Amendment rule ordinarily prohibiting the warrantless entry of a person's house as unreasonable *per se, Payton v. New York,* 445 U.S. 573, 586 (1980); *Coolidge v. New Hampshire,* 403 U.S. 443, 454–455 (1971), one "jealously and carefully drawn" exception, *Jones v. United States,* 357 U.S. 493, 499 (1958), recognizes the validity of searches with the voluntary consent of an individual possessing authority, *Rodriguez,* 497 U.S., at 181. . . . None of our co-occupant consent-to-search cases, however, has presented the further fact of a second occupant physically present and refusing permission to search, and later moving to suppress evidence so obtained. The significance of such a refusal turns on the underpinnings of the co-occupant consent rule, as recognized since *Matlock.*

A

The defendant in that case was arrested in the yard of a house where he lived with a Mrs. Graff and several of her relatives, and was detained in a squad car parked nearby. When the police went to the door, Mrs. Graff admitted them and consented to a search of the house. In resolving the defendant's objection to use of the evidence taken in the warrantless search, we said that "the consent of one who possesses common authority over premises or effects is valid as against the absent, nonconsenting person with whom that authority is shared." Id., at 170. Consistent with our prior understanding that Fourth Amendment rights are not limited by the law of property, we explained that the third party's "common authority" is not synonymous with a technical property interest:

* * *

B

Matlock's example of common understanding is readily apparent. When someone comes to the door of a domestic dwelling with a baby at her hip, as Mrs. Graff did, she shows that she belongs there, and that fact standing alone is enough to tell a law enforcement officer or any other visitor that if she occupies the place along with others, she probably lives there subject to the assumption tenants usually make about their common authority when they share quarters. They understand that any one of them may admit visitors, with the consequence that a guest obnoxious to one may nevertheless be admitted in his absence by another.

* * *

C

* * *

To begin with, it is fair to say that a caller standing at the door of shared premises would have no confidence that one occupant's invitation was a sufficiently good reason to enter when a fellow tenant stood there saying, "stay out." Without some very good reason, no sensible person would go inside under those conditions.

* * *

E

There are two loose ends, the first being the explanation given in *Matlock* for the constitutional sufficiency of a co-tenant's consent to enter and search: it "rests . . . on mutual use of the property by persons generally having joint access or control for most purposes, so that it is reasonable to recognize that any of the co-inhabitants has the right to permit the inspection in his own right. . . ." 415 U.S., at 171, n. 7. If *Matlock*'s co-tenant is giving permission "in his own right," how can his "own right" be eliminated by another tenant's objection? The answer appears in the very footnote from which the quoted statement is taken: the "right" to admit the police to which *Matlock* refers is not an enduring and enforceable ownership right as understood by the private law of property, but is instead the authority recognized by customary social usage as having a substantial bearing on Fourth Amendment reasonableness in specific circumstances. Thus, to ask whether the consenting tenant has the right to admit the police when a physically present fellow tenant objects is not to question whether some property right may be divested by the mere objection of another. It is, rather, the question whether customary social understanding accords the consenting tenant authority powerful enough to prevail over the co-tenant's objection.

* * *

III

This case invites a straightforward application of the rule that a physically present inhabitant's express

(continued)

refusal of consent to a police search is dispositive as to him, regardless of the consent of a fellow occupant. Scott Randolph's refusal is clear, and nothing in the record justifies the search on grounds independent of Janet Randolph's consent.

* * *

The judgment of the Supreme Court of Georgia is therefore affirmed.

Case Importance:

To have proper Fourth Amendment consent to search property where two individuals share dominion and control over the property and both are present, consent by both parties is required under the Fourth Amendment.

required to validate a warrantless search. Alternatively, if two persons were traveling with one piece of luggage that they shared and one of the two individuals left to use a restroom, police could lawfully ask the person remaining with the luggage for permission to search its contents.

Assuming the proper party voluntarily and freely grants consent, the person may offer a complete or limited right to search with respect to the length of the search or its scope. Once given, consent may be withdrawn at any time. If police exceed the scope of the consent, items seized in violation of the limitations may be excluded from use as evidence. The scope of consent may be informed by the object of the search. In *Florida v. Jimeno,* 500 U.S. 248 (1991), a police officer informed a motorist that the officer had reason to believe that the automobile contained narcotics. The officer explained that the driver did not have to consent to a search of the car. After the driver stated that he had nothing to hide, he granted the officer permission to search the automobile. When a folded brown bag in the car proved to contain cocaine, the driver contended that his consent did not extend to the closed paper bag. Although Jimeno had success in the Florida state courts, the Supreme Court held that the consent covered the paper bag. Justice Rehnquist, writing for the Court, held that consent to search for drugs allowed the officer to open and look into any containers within the car that could reasonably conceal drugs.

Where the consenting party gave a free and voluntary consent to search property under that party's control, and police do not exceed the bounds of the consent given, any evidence seized may be used in court unless excluded for evidentiary reasons unrelated to the Fourth Amendment. Consent to search for an object or material extends to any place where the property may be hidden or stored within reasonable bounds.

13. SEARCHES OF MOTOR VEHICLES

The mobile nature of motor vehicles dictates that search and seizure issues under the Fourth Amendment take a different route than those for homes and buildings. Naturally, most motor vehicles are mobile and could pass through a court's jurisdiction before a warrant could be obtained. All motor vehicles have windows, and arguably persons inside have a lower expectation of privacy for themselves and for personal items they place within the interior of the vehicle. Motor vehicles, as well as their operators, have been subject to extensive regulation by the states almost from their introduction as a self-powered means of conveyance. Court interpretation of the right to be secure against unreasonable searches in one's papers and effects when they are contained within a motor vehicle indicates that a person has a reduced expectation of privacy[33] in a motor vehicle.

Despite a diminished level of Fourth Amendment protection for motor vehicles, the general rule requires that, prior to a search, the governmental agent has probable cause. Although the level of privacy is reduced in a motor vehicle, the level of probable cause remains identical to that for any other search where evidence of criminality is being sought. Probable cause may mature because of a police officer's observations, reports from other officers, information from informants, or a combination of all these factors. For example, in *Carroll v. United States,* 267 U.S. 132 (1925), police officers had convincing evidence that the Carrolls were transporting illegal liquor in violation of federal law because the men had offered illegal liquor to the officers at an earlier time. When the officers identified the Carrolls traveling along the same route frequented by illegal bootleggers, in the same car, they possessed probable cause to stop and search the vehicle.[34] Under the Court's interpretation of *Carroll,* the presence of probable cause permitted the officers to search the vehicle without a warrant.

14. VEHICLE SEARCHES GENERALLY DO NOT REQUIRE WARRANTS

The Fourth Amendment speaks of no warrants being issued except upon probable cause, and a literal reading of the amendment might indicate that a warrant would be required for a search of a motor vehicle. The reality is that the Supreme Court has determined that a warrant is not a usual requirement of a vehicle search. The operative difficulty with motor vehicles revolves around their inherent mobility and the fact that a court has a limited jurisdiction in which its search warrant may be executed. A court in California cannot issue a warrant that would be valid in Nevada—whether to search a building or an automobile. If a police officer possessed probable cause, wished to search a motor vehicle, and needed a warrant, the vehicle could leave the jurisdiction. Alternatively, an officer could seize the vehicle and immobilize it until a warrant had been procured, but a warrantless seizure would still run afoul of the literal meaning of the Fourth Amendment. Since the Fourth Amendment requires a reasonable approach to searches and seizures, one could contend that an immediate search with probable cause would be more reasonable and less of an inconvenience to the driver and occupants than immobilizing the vehicle while other officers procure a search warrant. According to the Court in *Chambers v. Maroney,* 399 U.S. 42 (1970), where the police possessed probable cause to stop a car matching the description of a robbery getaway vehicle, the Court approved an immediate warrantless search of that car. According to the *Chambers* Court:

[A]n immediate search is constitutionally permissible. Arguably, because of the preference for a magistrate's judgment, only the immobilization of the car should be permitted until a search warrant is obtained; arguably, only the "lesser" intrusion is permissible until the magistrate authorizes the "greater." But which is the "greater" and which the "lesser" intrusion is itself a debatable question, and the answer may depend on a variety of circumstances. For constitutional purposes, we see no difference between, on the one hand, seizing and holding a car before presenting the probable cause issue to a magistrate and, on the other hand, carrying out an immediate search without a warrant. Given probable cause to search, either course is reasonable under the Fourth Amendment. *Chambers v. Maroney,* 399 U.S. 42, 52 (1970).

Following *Chambers,* which built on the doctrine of *Carroll,* where police have probable cause to search a motor vehicle, the search may be conducted immediately[35] so long as good probable cause exists at the time of the search. In support of the concept, the Supreme Court, in *Maryland v. Dyson,* 527 U.S. 465 (1999), in a *per curiam* opinion reaffirmed that a search warrant generally is not a requirement for a vehicle search. It noted that a vehicle search is not unreasonable if based on facts that would have justified the issuance of a warrant, even though a warrant was never obtained. In most situations, the officers may obtain a warrant prior to making a motor vehicle search, but the warrant is not generally required, provided probable cause exists. Essentially, where a motor vehicle is involved, the officer has the choice to conduct a search with or without a warrant; either course has been determined to be reasonable, given the presence of probable cause.

Although most searches of motor vehicles do not require warrants,[36] in *Coolidge v. New Hampshire,* 403 U.S. 443 (1971), the Court identified a situation wherein a search warrant was required for a motor vehicle. Although the facts in *Coolidge* were unique and the case may stand only for a situation exactly on point with *Coolidge,* the case has not been overruled and remains good law. In *Coolidge,* the police suspected the defendant of murder, the defendant had no control over the car, and there were no exigent or emergency circumstances that justified an immediate warrantless search. The *Coolidge* Court invalidated the searches of the automobile because a valid warrant had not been obtained prior to the police search of the car. The Court distinguished this case from *Carroll v. United States* (the *Carroll* doctrine) by noting that the defendant had ample time to destroy any evidence in his car, he had no access at the time of search, and the car was not capable of going anywhere, unlike the *Carroll* automobile, which was actually being driven at the time it was seized. One concept that arises from *Coolidge* is that automobiles that cannot be moved under their own power may require a search warrant or some recognized exception to the warrant requirement in order to be lawfully searched. Most assuredly, law enforcement officers should consider to protect the admissibility of evidence in motor vehicles that are not readily mobile.

15. SCOPE OF MOTOR VEHICLE SEARCH

Given the existence of probable cause to search a vehicle, the police need to determine the extent of the lawful search permitted. Clearly, probable cause to search a car does not, without significantly more evidence, justify a search of the driver's home, especially without a warrant. The general rule on the scope of a search dictates that the area of the automobile to be searched depends upon the nature of the object that is the goal of the search. For example, if the police had probable cause to search a car for a stolen desktop computer system, a look in the trunk of the vehicle would be appropriate, but sifting through the ashtray near the driver's seat would not reveal a computer and would be an unreasonable search. Following similar logic, given probable cause to search for recreational pharmaceuticals, a search virtually anywhere in the vehicle would be reasonable, since drugs may be hidden in any small or large area of the car. In one case,[37] a detainee gave permission to a police officer to enter the detainee's vehicle for the purpose of retrieving the detainee's pistol permit, and the officer smelled a strong odor of marijuana from within the vehicle. This amount of evidence gave the officer probable cause to search the interior of the vehicle to isolate any drugs that might be present. In this case, the officer opened a vinyl bag that was designed to store CDs but smelled of marijuana and contained the drug. A reviewing court reversed the trial court's decision to suppress the marijuana evidence because it felt that probable cause to search for drugs existed once the officer smelled marijuana coming from the interior of the car and that any argument that the search exceeded the consent to obtain the pistol permit failed. Given probable cause to search a motor vehicle, police may search in any location in the vehicle where the object of the search might reasonably be located.

16. LIMITED VEHICLE SEARCHES ON LESS THAN PROBABLE CAUSE

In addition to complete motor vehicle searches based on probable cause, a governmental agent may make limited warrantless searches of moving vehicles in the absence of any probable cause where the government is searching for evidence of alcohol impairment by car and truck drivers. In *Michigan v. Sitz*, 496 U.S. 444 (1990), the Court gave approval to the practice of stopping all vehicles passing through a checkpoint as a way to screen for alcohol-impaired drivers. Following this plan, the police made limited roadside seizures in the absence of probable cause and in the absence of any individualized suspicion of intoxication or impairment. The *Sitz* Court approved the brief seizures by balancing the state's interest in reducing impaired driving against the minimal intrusion upon members of the motoring public who were briefly stopped. The Court determined that the short stop to discern sobriety was reasonable under the Fourth Amendment.

Limited motor vehicle searches based on less than probable cause do have their limitations, as the Court noted in the *City of Indianapolis v. Edmond*.[38] Indianapolis police operated various vehicle checkpoints designed to interdict unlawful drug users and traffickers. At each roadblock, the police stopped a predetermined number of motor vehicles and did not base the stops on any individualized suspicion. Police advised each driver that the purpose of the stop involved checking the license and registration and looking for signs of impairment or drug use. Police conducted a look-see into each vehicle from the outside of the car. The primary focus of the program was general criminal drug interdiction and not brief stops to detect alcohol impairment. The Supreme Court of the United States agreed with the Court of Appeals that the drug interdiction program of stopping motorists on the highway failed to meet the requirements of the Fourth Amendment because the program's focus was general criminal law enforcement and did not have the narrow purpose and focus of the situation in the *Michigan v. Sitz* case. As was noted in the syllabus to the case, the Supreme Court never has approved any roadblock program with the primary purpose of detecting evidence of usual and typical criminal wrongdoing.

A search that is initially based on the *Terry v. Ohio* standard of reasonable basis to suspect that criminal activity may be afoot allows a limited search. If an officer has some reason to suspect that a lawfully detained driver may have either drugs or illegal weapons inside the motor vehicle but lacks the level of proof known as probable cause, the officer may peer inside the vehicle to satisfy his or her objective curiosity. For example, an officer discovered a person parked in a car in a remote area who made furtive movements as the officer approached the car and had no rational explanation of why he was parked where he was at 3:30 in the morning. The subject appeared nervous and uncomfortable. After securing the detainee, the officer looked inside the windows of the vehicle and saw a syringe and a piece of aluminum foil that indicated probable cause that drug usage had occurred or was occurring. The initial cursory search the officer made, based on the reasonable basis to suspect standard, permitted the limited initial search but matured into probable cause to search the car for drugs. The court in this case permitted the admission of the drugs against the defendant.[39]

Limited searches of persons, cars, and effects may be initiated on less than probable cause where there is reasonable basis to suspect criminal activity but insufficient evidence for the officer to have probable cause to believe that a crime has been committed and that evidence will be found in a particular place or on a particular person.

17. VEHICLE INVENTORY SEARCHES

Some vehicle searches may follow valid arrests of the driver or passenger under the theory of search incident to arrest,[40] other warrantless searches may be justified under an inventory search theory.[41] In a search incident to arrest in a motor vehicle, officers are permitted to search the interior of the vehicle wherever the arrestee might reasonably grab or lunge to obtain a weapon or destroy evidence. The inventory search[42] stands on a different theoretical basis and is designed to "protect an owner's property while it is in the custody of the police, to insure against [false] claims of lost, stolen, or vandalized property, and to guard the police from danger";[43] it also is intended to protect property custodians from any dangerous substance or ordinance that might be transported to a property room from an impounded vehicle. The Supreme Court approved inventory searches in *Colorado v. Bertine,* 479 U.S. 367 (1987), where the search parameters were directed by a written policy. Where an automobile has been lawfully impounded, courts generally uphold inventory searches as reasonable, even in the absence of search probable cause.

An inventory search of a motor vehicle requires that the police agency have and follow an inventory search policy. In the absence of a policy regulating this process, individual officers would have unlimited discretion, and a particular inventory search could evolve into a ruse for conducting a general search. The policy regulating inventory searches must be designed to produce an inventory rather than permitting the inventory officer so much latitude that no standards exist. The absence of a policy on inventory searches or a defective policy can create difficulties for the prosecution. In *Florida v. Wells,* 495 U.S. 1 (1990), an arrested driver gave police permission to open the trunk of his impounded car. An inventory search of the car revealed marijuana within a suitcase. The *Wells* Court approved the state court decision holding that the evidence should have been suppressed on the grounds that the Florida Highway Patrol possessed no governing standards covering the opening of closed containers found within motor vehicles. A search of this nature was not deemed reasonable under the Fourth Amendment.

Clear examples of the appropriate use of an inventory search theory occur when, after traffic accidents, the vehicles need to be removed from the roadway for safety reasons. When police officers conduct an inventory search with a view to securing valuables, the basic reasonableness of such a search becomes obvious. In an Arkansas case, a woman had a one-car accident with a rollover of the vehicle, and her injuries dictated hospitalization and her removal from the scene of the accident. The police engaged a wrecker service to remove the vehicle from the accident location and conducted an inventory search prior to the car being towed. According to the police officer on the scene, the written policy of the police was to impound a vehicle involved in an accident if it would otherwise have been left unattended on or near the roadway. The inventory search disclosed some recreational quantities of marijuana and methamphetamine. According to the court of appeals, the trial court properly refused to suppress the evidence, citing the reasonableness of the inventory policy, even where the officer may have possessed a secondary investigatory motive.[44]

18. PLAIN VIEW DOCTRINE AND MOTOR VEHICLE SEARCHES

In the context of motor vehicle stops, police officers frequently have occasion to lawfully view the interior of motor vehicles. As a general rule, so long as the traffic stop is determined to be lawful, the officer is in a position to lawfully observe evidence in plain view that is seizable if its criminal nature is clearly obvious. In one case,[45] police officers stopped the defendant's vehicle because of an inoperable taillight. As the officers approached the vehicle, they observed a firearm in plain view, which led them to remove both occupants from the vehicle. In due course, the officers determined that the defendant was a felon and that his possession of a gun and some ammunition constituted new crimes. The trial court refused to suppress evidence of the gun because it had been found in plain view. The Court of Appeals for the 11th Circuit agreed with the trial court that the plain view doctrine permitted the gun to be seized and introduced in evidence because the officers had made a lawful traffic stop and were occupying a lawful position when they first observed the gun.

As long as the officer occupies a lawful position within or near a motor vehicle and observes objects that, under the circumstances, indicate criminality, the plain view doctrine allows the officer to immediately seize the offending object. In a Pennsylvania case,[46] an undercover officer purchased Xanax prescription drugs from a suspect and asked if he could supply her with more of the drug. After the officer handed the suspect additional marked money, the suspect entered a motor vehicle, apparently to obtain additional pills. Backup officers were notified to check out the motor vehicle, at which point the defendant shoved an amber container under the seat cushion on the driver's side. The amber pill bottle proved to contain prescription drugs and, as police officers opened the door to the motor vehicle, the officers observed additional bottles containing prescription drugs. According to the reviewing court, when the officers, who had probable cause to arrest the driver, approached the motor vehicle, they observed, in plain view, the amber bottle of pills being hidden by the defendant, and the officers occupied a position next to the car that they were lawfully permitted to occupy. The officers maintained that same lawful position when the car door was opened, and they observed more drugs in plain view inside a pocket in the door. The Supreme Court of Pennsylvania upheld the admission of pills from all locations in the car on the theory that the plain view doctrine applied and that there was no violation of the Fourth Amendment under the circumstances.

19. SCOPE OF SEARCH OF CONTAINERS WITHIN MOTOR VEHICLES

Where containers are not associated with motor vehicles, individuals possess a Fourth Amendment right to expect that governmental agents will not look through luggage, backpacks, grocery bags, and similar articles without probable cause and without a warrant unless special circumstances exist.[47] Different rules have developed when the same containers are stowed or hidden in motor vehicles. When police encounter luggage and similar containers within motor vehicles, the jurisprudence has followed a complicated path as courts struggled to produce coherent, consistent, and unified rationales consistent with the Fourth Amendment.

In *Carroll v. United States,* 267 U.S. 132 (1925), the Court approved a general search of the vehicle on probable cause that it held untaxed liquor in some sort of container or containers. Consistent with *Carroll* was *United States v. Ross,* 456 U.S. 798 (1982), where the Court gave approval to a probable cause warrantless search of the interior of a car, its trunk, a closed brown paper bag, and a zippered leather pouch. In *Ross,* the police had probable cause to believe that Ross had been selling drugs from the car and that additional drugs were contained within the car, with the exact location unknown. The *Ross* Court allowed a search anywhere within the automobile where drugs might reasonably be hidden, which naturally included a search of any containers.

When the police do not have probable cause to search an entire vehicle, but only a container, a different rule has been applied, but it is not current law.[48] In *Arkansas v. Sanders,* 442 U.S. 753 (1979), the police, acting on an informant's information that Sanders, upon arriving at an airport, would be carrying a green suitcase containing marijuana, placed him under surveillance. When Sanders placed a green suitcase in the trunk of a taxi, police stopped the vehicle, opened the unlocked suitcase, and discovered marijuana. The police conducted the vehicle search without a warrant,[49] based on the justification of the *Carroll* vehicle doctrine permitting warrantless searches of vehicles on probable cause. Since there was probable cause for not only the vehicle stop and search but probable cause to search the luggage, the connection of the luggage to the vehicle seemed sufficient to allow a warrantless search of the luggage under the *Carroll* doctrine. The Supreme Court disagreed on the legality of the search, holding that in the absence of exigent circumstances, police are required to obtain a warrant before searching for recreational pharmaceuticals in luggage taken from an automobile properly stopped and searched. In *Sanders,* the probable cause extended only to the luggage, and merely touching a motor vehicle with luggage did not turn the search into a *Carroll* search, for which no warrant would have been required. The Court made a distinction between a probable cause search of an automobile that coincidentally turned up a container and a similar search of a container that coincidentally ended up in an automobile. Thus, at the time of *Sanders,* the evidence had to be suppressed, since police needed a warrant to search luggage taken from a motor vehicle.

That theory changed when the Court decided *United States v. Ross,* 456 U.S. 798 (1982), where the Court held that given probable cause to search a container within a motor vehicle, no warrant was required to conduct the search. To the extent that *Ross* was inconsistent with *Sanders* and similar cases, the Court seems to have overruled that line of cases and substituted the rule of *Ross.* The Court reasoned that where a home search has been authorized, a search for a small object includes looking inside containers and closets. Therefore, where a vehicle search for an easily hidden object is appropriate, looking inside containers, as in a house search, should be reasonable.

The problem with the court cases centered on the concept that a search of luggage or other container would be illegal if conducted without a warrant where probable cause extended only to a search of the luggage, but the same piece of luggage could be lawfully searched without a warrant if encountered inside a vehicle during a search as in *Ross.* The Supreme Court attempted to clarify the case law so that Fourth Amendment protections would not turn on the happenstance of the location of the luggage at the time probable cause matures. As the *Ross* Court stated:

> When a legitimate search is under way, and when its purpose and its limits have been precisely defined, nice distinctions between closets, drawers, and containers, in the case of a home, or between glove compartments, upholstered seats, trunks, and wrapped packages, in the case of a vehicle, must give way to the interest in the prompt and efficient completion of the task at hand. *Ross* at 821

The newer theory applied where there was probable cause to search the automobile, but it did not clearly address a situation where there was probable cause to search only a particularly described container within the vehicle, as was the case in *Arkansas v. Sanders.*

In *California v. Acevedo,* 500 U.S. 565 (1991), police made a controlled delivery of drugs to an apartment (see Case 7.5). Acevedo arrived, entered, and exited the apartment quickly while carrying a brown paper bag of the size delivered to the apartment. With probable cause to search the bag but not the car, police waited until Acevedo placed the bag within his automobile and drove away. Police stopped him and conducted a warrantless search of the brown paper bag. The police followed the search practice, which transgressed the outdated theory of *Sanders,* by searching a container because it had come in contact with a motor vehicle.

To provide one rule for searches of containers discovered in automobiles, the *Acevedo* Court held that the police may search an automobile and the containers

CASE 7.5

Leading Case Brief: Where Probable Cause Exists to Search a Vehicle, Police May Search Anywhere the Object Might Reasonably be Hidden, Including Containers

California v. Acevedo
Supreme Court of the United States
500 U.S. 565 (1991)

Case Facts:

A federal drug enforcement agent in Hawaii told Santa Ana, California, police that the government had seized drugs from the Federal Express system. Federal agents sealed the package and had it sent to the Santa Ana police department, which, with the cooperation of the local Federal Express office, delivered the drugs to one J. R. Daza. He immediately drove to his apartment where he took the drug package inside.

While Daza was still under law enforcement observation, Charles Acevedo arrived at the Daza's address, entered Daza's apartment, and left after a ten-minute visit. Police observed that he carried a brown paper bag of the same size as the marijuana shipped from Hawaii and that he placed it in the trunk of a Honda. As he drove away, officers stopped his car and conducted a warrantless search limited to the contents of the brown bag. The search disclosed a quantity of marijuana.

Acevedo lost a motion to suppress the marijuana and pled guilty but reserved his right to appeal the denial of his claim that the bag had been illegally searched. The California Court of Appeal reversed the trial court with the conclusion that although the police had probable cause to believe that the bag contained drugs, opening the bag required a warrant. According to the Court of Appeal, once the bag was inside the car, a separate expectation of privacy existed.

The California Court of Appeal reasoned that the case was controlled by *United States v. Chadwick* (1977), where officers were permitted to seize a container for which probable cause existed but the search failed because officers did not obtain a needed warrant to open the container. The Supreme Court of California rejected the government's petition for review in Acevedo's case.

The Supreme Court of the United States granted certiorari for the purpose of clarifying search and seizure law applicable to a closed container in an automobile.

Legal Issue:

Where probable cause exists for the search of a container within an automobile and where there is no probable cause to search the entire vehicle, may police stop the car, seize the container, and search it without a warrant?

The Court's Ruling:

The Justices decided that where probable cause exists to search a container that has been placed in a motor vehicle, police may stop the vehicle and search the container without a warrant without violating the Fourth Amendment.

Essence of the Court's Rationale:

* * *

II

* * *

In *United States v. Ross,* 456 U.S. 798, decided in 1982, we held that a warrantless search of an automobile under the *Carroll* doctrine [motor vehicle can be searched based on probable cause only] could include a search of a container or package found inside the car when such a search was supported by probable cause. . . . In *Ross,* therefore, we clarified the scope of the *Carroll* doctrine as properly including a "probing search" of compartments and containers within the automobile so long as the search is supported by probable cause.

In addition to this clarification, *Ross* distinguished the *Carroll* doctrine from the separate rule that governed the search of closed containers. The Court had announced this separate rule, unique to luggage and other closed packages, bags, and containers, in *United States v. Chadwick,* 433 U.S. 1 (1977). In *Chadwick,* federal narcotics agents had probable cause to believe that a 200-pound double-locked footlocker contained marijuana. [Police seized and opened the locker once it had been placed in an automobile trunk.] . . . [T]he United States urged that the search of movable luggage could be considered analogous to the search of an automobile. 433 U.S., at 11–12. The Court rejected this argument because, it reasoned, a person expects more privacy in his luggage and personal effects than he does in his automobile.

In *Arkansas v. Sanders,* 442 U.S. 753 (1979), the Court extended *Chadwick*'s rule to apply to a suitcase actually being transported in the trunk of a car. [In Sanders, police stopped a taxi and warrantlessly searched luggage for which they had probable cause.] . . . Although the Court had applied the *Carroll* doctrine to searches of integral parts of the automobile itself (indeed, in *Carroll,* contraband whiskey was in the upholstery of the seats, *see* 267 U.S., at 136), it did not extend the doctrine to the warrantless search of personal luggage "merely because it was located in an automobile lawfully stopped by the police." Again, the *Sanders* majority stressed the heightened privacy expectation in personal luggage and concluded that the presence of luggage in an automobile did not diminish the owner's expectation of privacy in his personal items.

In *Ross,* the Court endeavored to distinguish between *Carroll,* which governed the *Ross* automobile search, and *Chadwick,* which governed the *Sanders* automobile search. It held that the *Carroll* doctrine covered searches of automobiles when the police had probable cause to search an entire vehicle but that the *Chadwick* doctrine governed searches of luggage when the officers had probable cause to search only a container within the vehicle. Thus, in a *Ross* situation, the police could conduct a reasonable search under the Fourth Amendment without obtaining a warrant, whereas in a *Sanders* situation, the police had to obtain a warrant before they searched.

* * *

III

* * *

The Court in *Ross* rejected *Chadwick*'s distinction between containers and cars. . . . It also recognized that it was arguable that the same exigent circumstances that permit a warrantless search of an automobile would justify the warrantless search of a movable container. In deference to the rule of *Chadwick* and *Sanders,* however, the Court put that question to one side. . . . We now must decide the question deferred in *Ross:* whether the Fourth Amendment requires the police to obtain a warrant to open the sack in a movable vehicle simply because they lack probable cause to search the entire car. We conclude that it does not.

IV

* * *

To the extent that the *Chadwick-Sanders* rule protects privacy, its protection is minimal. Law enforcement officers may seize a container and hold it until they obtain a search warrant. *Chadwick,* 433 U.S. at 13.

Since the police, by hypothesis, have probable cause to seize the property, we can assume that a warrant will be routinely forthcoming in the overwhelming majority of cases.

And the police often will be able to search containers without a warrant, despite the *Chadwick-Sanders* rule, as a search incident to a lawful arrest. In *New York v. Belton,* 453 U.S. 454 (1981), the Court said:

> [W]e hold that when a policeman has made a lawful custodial arrest of the occupant of an automobile, he may, as a contemporaneous incident of that arrest, search the passenger compartment of that automobile.

It follows from this conclusion that the police may also examine the contents of any containers found within the passenger compartment. *Id.,* at 460.

* * *

In light of the minimal protection to privacy afforded by the *Chadwick-Sanders* rule, and our serious doubt whether that rule substantially serves privacy

(continued)

interests, we now hold that the Fourth Amendment does not compel a separate treatment for an automobile search that extends only to a container within the vehicle.

* * *

VI

* * *

In the case before us, the police had probable cause to believe that the paper bag in the automobile's trunk contained marijuana. That probable cause now allows a warrantless search of the paper bag. The facts in the record reveal that the police did not have probable cause to believe that contraband was hidden in any other part of the automobile and a search of the entire vehicle would have been without probable cause and unreasonable under the Fourth Amendment.

* * *

We . . . interpret *Carroll* as providing one rule to govern all automobile searches. The police may search an automobile and the containers within it where they have probable cause to believe contraband or evidence is contained.

The judgment of the California Court of Appeal is reversed and the case is remanded to that court for further proceedings not inconsistent with this opinion. **It is so ordered.**

Case Importance:

Police do not need a warrant to search a vehicle where they have probable cause to search only within a container inside the vehicle. The Fourth Amendment allows police to search anywhere within a motor vehicle, including containers, where the object of the search may be reasonably hidden, so long as probable cause to search for the item exists.

within it where they have probable cause to believe contraband or evidence is contained somewhere within the motor vehicle. Under this view, the search of the luggage in *United States v. Chadwick* would have been lawful in the absence of a warrant, and the search of the luggage in *Arkansas v. Sanders* would have produced lawfully seized evidence.

20. SEARCHES FOLLOWING VEHICLE FORFEITURES

In some cases, a state government may possess a complete right of ownership of a car[50] and not merely a right under the Fourth Amendment to search it. Where a motor vehicle's status allows it to be seized as forfeitable contraband, no warrant is required prior to taking control of the vehicle and searching the interior. In *Florida v. White,* 526 U.S. 559 (1999), police officers observed White using his car to deliver cocaine on three separate occasions, thus developing probable cause to believe that the automobile was subject to forfeiture under Florida law. Several months later, police had probable cause to arrest White on charges unrelated to his cocaine dealing. During the arrest process, police noticed the car, which they believed was subject to forfeiture, and immediately, without a warrant, seized the vehicle.[51] The Supreme Court of the United States reversed the Florida Supreme Court's holding that a warrant was required under the Fourth Amendment to seize the car. According to the *White* Court, since there was probable cause to believe that the car was contraband, having been used in a drug delivery, and since it was mobile and in a public place, the vehicle could be reasonably seized without a warrant under the Fourth Amendment as interpreted by the *Carroll* doctrine.

21. OTHER THEORIES OF VEHICLE SEARCHES AND SEIZURES

The Fourth Amendment allows officials to conduct warrantless searches of motor vehicles based on probable cause to search, pursuant to an inventory search, incident to lawful arrest, based on consent, and to a limited extent, at sobriety checkpoints. Limited searches are permitted under the stop and frisk rationale where police officers possess reasonable basis to suspect that criminal activity might be afoot. Automobile inventory searches require the law enforcement agency to have and routinely follow a written inventory policy. Exigent circumstances might allow a vehicle search where life was clearly at risk.

Searches of motor vehicles following a lawful arrest[52] of the driver or a passenger follow the general rules for searches incident to arrest.[53] The primary goal of such a search is to remove any weapons an arrestee might gain control of. Where the arrest occurs while a driver is seated, the area inside the passenger compartment may be searched, since the arrestee might be able to grab a gun or other weapon or destroy evidence. Naturally, the driver's person may be searched following an arrest within a motor vehicle.

Limited motor vehicle searches have been approved on less than probable cause where the state was attempting to detect alcohol-impaired drivers. In *Michigan v. Sitz,* 496 U.S. 444 (1990), the Supreme Court approved a police plan in which automobile drivers were stopped briefly while officers attempted to observe traits that indicated impairment. The *Sitz* Court held that although such stops were Fourth Amendment seizures, they constituted reasonable seizures when balanced between the state's grave and legitimate interest in curbing drunken driving and the minimal intrusion on and inconvenience for the motorist. According to the Court, sobriety checkpoints are reasonable where all the motorists are briefly screened for alcohol use and only those who appear impaired are subject to additional inquiry.

If an effort to detect drinking drivers passed muster under the Fourth Amendment on less than probable cause or reasonable basis to suspect criminal activity, it would seem as if the interdiction of a drug-carrying or drug-using motorist might win court approval. In *Indianapolis v. Edmond,* 531 U.S. 32 (2000), the Court ruled against the practice of setting up roadblocks on public highways so that police could inspect the interiors of automobiles and observe drivers while a drug-sniffing dog walked around the vehicle. The locations where automobiles would be stopped were marked by highway signs. Police practice involved stopping a group of cars and allowing all others to proceed while the officers processed the stopped vehicles. There was no particular reason to stop any car. The officers conducted each stop in the same manner until and unless particularized suspicion developed. The officers possessed no discretion to stop any vehicle out of sequence.

In failing to approve the practice in *Edmond,* the Court distinguished *Michigan v. Sitz* on the ground that the program in *Sitz* was

> clearly aimed at reducing the immediate hazard posed by the presence of drunk drivers on the highways, and there was an obvious connection between the imperative of highway safety and the law enforcement practice at issue. The gravity of the drunk driving problem and the magnitude of the State's interest in getting drunk

drivers off the road weighed heavily in our determination that the program was constitutional. *Michigan v. Sitz,* 496 U.S. 444, 451 (1990)

The stop in *Sitz* was quite brief, the carnage on highways from impaired drivers was well documented, and the Court felt the stop at the checkpoint was reasonable under the Fourth Amendment. In contrast, in *Edmond* the primary purpose was the interdiction of narcotics and other illegal drugs and the arrest of drug offenders. Such a goal was more of a general crime-fighting activity; if the drug stops were upheld, roadside stops could be considered for other types of crime. Since the primary purpose involved a general interest in crime control, the Court declined to suspend the general requirement of individualized suspicion normally required to seize a person.

While receiving mixed reviews in the drug and alcohol context, the roadblock screen has constitutional vitality in some other limited contexts, especially where an emergency dictates that reasonable police practice requires some minimal scrutiny of vehicles leaving an area. In a Massachusetts case, after three o'clock in the morning, police received numerous 911 calls concerning a series of multiple gunshots from a cul-de-sac and found fifty or more people milling about. Since some of the individuals were attempting to leave the area in vehicles, the police decided to take a look at each vehicle passing out of the cul-de-sac. During the brief questioning of each occupant, an officer noticed a firearm in one of the vehicles, eventually arrested the occupants, and charged one with illegal possession of a firearm. When the subject filed a motion to suppress the evidence, the court noted that, although normally articulable suspicion is required to make a vehicle stop, on some occasions the intrusion is limited and serves a crucial public need that cannot be easily met in any other manner. The court held that the initial stop and intrusion were reasonable, given that the police knew a crime had been committed but possessed no individually particularized suspicion. The reasonableness required a balancing of the public interest against the right of a person to be free from arbitrary seizure by law enforcement personnel. In upholding the brief stop, the court of appeals noted that "the facts indicate this was a deliberate emergency police effort to apprehend one or more fleeing suspects as to whom the police had no physical description, no information as to their number, and indeed no indication as to whether they were fleeing on foot or by vehicle."[54]

22. SUMMARY

Fourth Amendment case decisions have determined that persons residing in private residences have the greatest expectation of privacy under the Fourth Amendment, even though the Fourth Amendment does not mention the concept of privacy. As a strong general rule, the search of a home requires a search warrant based on probable cause, unless some other legal theory provides an excuse or other justification. The use of thermal imaging devices cannot be used to help develop probable cause to search a residence. Consent and emergency circumstances are two exceptions to the warrant requirement that allow warrantless searches of homes. In a similar fashion, an arrest warrant is generally required to make a lawful arrest within the home of the arrestee. Individuals who live within a residence clearly have an expectation of privacy, as do other persons who are permitted to stay or sleep overnight.

Individuals for whom probable cause to arrest exists may be arrested outside the home without a warrant, and arrestees may be searched incident to the arrest. The scope of a search incident to arrest includes the person of the arrestee and the area within that person's immediate dominion and control. Personal property on an arrestee or near an arrestee may be searched without probable cause and without a warrant immediately following a lawful arrest.

Objects that are in plain view and observed by an officer who lawfully occupies the position from which contraband or other seizable evidence has been observed may be seized without a warrant. Seizable objects that are expected to be found pursuant to a search warrant but were not listed as seizable property on the warrant may be seized, even though the discovery was not inadvertent. Evidence that may be smelled by an officer who is lawfully on the premises may be seized, provided the smell indicated criminality. Officers who are conducting frisks and feel objects for which the nature of the incriminating property is immediately apparent may lawfully seize those objects.

Where probable cause does not exist, a search may be based on consent of the person who holds dominion and control over the property. Where the person gives consent, based on the totality of circumstances test, and where the consent has been freely and voluntarily given, police officers may conduct searches within the scope of the consent.

Motor vehicle searches generally do not require warrants but do require the presence of probable cause to search. The mobility of motor vehicles that enables them to move through other jurisdictions makes obtaining warrants in some cases difficult. Given probable cause, a motor vehicle and its containers may be searched, limited only by the scope dictated by the type of object that is the goal of the search. Court decisions have permitted brief stops of motor vehicles for sobriety checks of drivers but have stopped short of permitting roadway stops for general criminal investigation.

REVIEW EXERCISES AND QUESTIONS

1. Why is a warrant generally necessary to lawfully arrest a person who is residing within his or her own home?

2. Where police officers have a search warrant for a particular home for small objects and drugs, can the search extend to motor vehicles that are inside an attached garage and to motor vehicles that are parked in front of the attached garage?

3. Assume that law enforcement officials developed information that individuals were growing marijuana inside a suburban home, but they did not have probable cause to obtain a search warrant. If the officers used a thermal imaging device that could detect and interpret heat signatures coming from the home that indicated excessive heat escaping from the home, could this information be combined with other information to obtain a warrant based on probable cause to search? Why or why not? See *Kyllo v. United States*, 533 U.S. 27 (2001).

4. Explain the scope of a search of a person incident to that person's lawful arrest. Should any incriminating evidence that was discovered during the search be suppressed if the search turns out to have been unlawful? Why or why not?

5. Why is conducting a search of an arrestee's personal property appropriate following an arrest? Does an inventory search of an arrestee's property require a search warrant?

6. What are the requirements for use of the plain view doctrine? Give an example.

7. Assume that a police officer conducted a lawful stop and frisk. In conducting the frisk, the officer felt what reasonably seemed to be a package of cigarettes in the subject's top shirt pocket. Will the plain feel doctrine that is related to the plain view doctrine allow the officer to reach inside the shirt pocket, retrieve the cigarette pack, and look inside the pack for incriminating evidence? Why or why not?

8. In conducting a lawful consent search of a person or of that person's motor vehicle, the proper person must be asked to give consent, and it must be given freely and voluntarily. Who is the proper person to give consent? What factors are considered in determining whether the consent has been freely and voluntarily given?

9. Do searches of motor vehicles generally require search warrants in addition to probable cause?

10. If police have probable cause to search a motor vehicle, may the search extend, in all cases, to every possible place in a motor vehicle where anything could have been hidden? What factor determines the scope of a motor vehicle search?

HOW WOULD YOU DECIDE?

1. In the Supreme Court of Pennsylvania

Defendant Adam Pakacki was convicted of possession of drug paraphernalia [a marijuana pipe] following his apprehension by State Trooper Keppel. Reports of a shooting cause police to investigate the area where the defendant was discovered and his name and description had been given as a potential suspect. The state trooper, who had been driving a marked cruiser along a country road, called to Pakacki to come over to where the officer was located. As the officer engaged Pakacki, he asked him if he had any weapons, drugs, or needles. Fearing that Pakacki might be armed and dangerous, the officer conducted a frisk for weapons. The officer smelled some marijuana odor coming from the defendant and felt what he believed was a marijuana pipe. The defendant was asked if it indeed was a marijuana pipe, and he replied in the affirmative. The trial court refused to grant Pakacki's request for suppression of a marijuana pipe based on his contention that the seizure of the pipe was not lawful under the plain feel doctrine. The defendant further complained that the *Miranda* warnings should have been given before he was asked any questions. Pakacki appealed to Superior Court, which reversed his conviction based on its determination that the incriminating nature of the marijuana pipe could not have been immediately apparent to the officer and the reason the officer asked the question of the defendant was to confirm his suspicions concerning what he had felt. The prosecutor appealed the reversal of the conviction and requested that the original trial court verdict be reinstated.

How would you rule on the defendant's contention that the plain feel doctrine could not support the search and seizure of the marijuana pipe because the police officer was uncertain concerning the identity of what he felt?

The Court's Holding

[In the Supreme Court of Pennsylvania, the prosecution contended that Pakacki was not in custody for *Miranda* purposes when the officer asked the question about the identity of what he felt during the pat-down. If he was not in custody, according to the prosecution, *Miranda* did not apply, and the inquiry by the officer was appropriate. The defendant argued that his statement to the officer admitting that the pipe was a marijuana pipe should have been suppressed because the search was unlawful and the plain feel doctrine should not apply since the officer did not know exactly what he had felt.]

In determining whether appellee was in custody, we note that "Fourth Amendment jurisprudence has led to the development of three categories of interactions between citizens and the police. The first of these is a "mere encounter" (or request for information) which need not be supported by any level of suspicion, but carries no official compulsion to stop or to respond. See *Florida v. Royer,* 460 U.S. 491, 103 S. Ct. 1319, 75 L. Ed. 2d 229 (1983); *Florida v. Bostick,* 501 U.S. 429, 111 S. Ct. 2382, 115 L. Ed. 2d 389 (1991). The second, an "investigative detention" must be supported by a reasonable suspicion; it subjects a suspect to a stop and a period of detention, but does not involve such coercive conditions as to constitute the functional equivalent of an arrest. See *Berkemer v. McCarty,* 468 U.S. 420, 104 S. Ct. 3138, 82 L. Ed. 2d 317 (1984); *Terry v. Ohio,* 392 U.S. 1, 88 S. Ct. 1868, 20 L. Ed. 2d 889 (1968). Finally, an arrest or "custodial detention" must be supported by probable cause. See *Dunaway v. New York,* 442 U.S. 200, 99 S. Ct. 2248, 60 L. Ed. 2d 824 (1979).

The key difference between an investigative detention and a custodial one is that the latter "involve[s] such coercive conditions as to constitute the functional equivalent of an arrest." *Id.,* at 1047. In determining whether an encounter with the police is custodial, "[t]he standard . . . is an objective one, with due consideration given to the reasonable impression conveyed to the person interrogated rather than the strictly subjective view of the troopers or the person being seized . . ." and "must be determined with reference to the totality of the circumstances." *Commonwealth v. Edmiston,* 535 Pa. 210, 634 A.2d 1078, 1085–86 (Pa. 1993). Not every detention is custodial for Miranda purposes, and the situation here was an investigation based on reasonable suspicion, as delineated by *Terry.* In a *Terry* situation, the officer possesses reasonable suspicion that criminal activity is afoot, and is thereby justified in briefly detaining the suspect in order to investigate. See *Commonwealth v. E.M.,* 558 Pa. 16, 735 A.2d 654, 659 (Pa. 1999) (officer may conduct brief investigatory stop of individual if officer observes unusual conduct which leads him to reasonably conclude, in light of his experience, that criminal activity may be afoot). If, during this stop, the officer observes conduct which leads him to believe the suspect may be armed and dangerous, the officer may pat down the suspect's outer garments for weapons. *Id.* If no weapons are found, the suspect is free to leave if the officer concludes he is not involved in any criminal activity.

[The Court held that the defendant was not in custody at the time the police frisked him.]

* * *

The Commonwealth further challenges the Superior Court's holding that the trooper violated the plain feel doctrine because the incriminating nature of the marijuana pipe was not immediately apparent, as evidenced by the trooper's question to appellee concerning the nature of the object.

Under the plain feel doctrine,

a police officer may seize non-threatening contraband detected through the officer's sense of touch during a Terry frisk if the officer is lawfully in a position to detect the presence of contraband, the incriminating nature of the contraband is immediately apparent from its tactile impression and the officer has a lawful right of access to the object. Dickerson, 508 U.S. at 373–75. [T]he plain feel doctrine is only applicable where the officer conducting the frisk feels an object whose mass or contour makes its criminal character immediately apparent. Immediately apparent means that the officer readily perceives, without further exploration or searching, that what he is feeling is contraband. If, after feeling the object, the officer lacks probable cause to believe that the object is contraband without conducting some further search, the immediately apparent requirement has not been met and the plain feel doctrine cannot justify the seizure of the object.

Commonwealth v. Stevenson, 560 Pa. 345, 744 A.2d 1261, 1265 (Pa. 2000) (citations and parallel citation omitted).

[The Supreme Court noted that the officer did not manipulate the pipe with his hands; he seemed to know what is was by its feel.]

* * *

Having reviewed the record, we conclude it supports this factual finding by the suppression court. Trooper Keppel, having five years' experience as a state trooper, noticed the smell of marijuana coming from appellee as he approached him. During the lawful pat-down, the trooper felt an object which he knew from his experience in law enforcement to be a marijuana pipe. Under the totality of the circumstances, the incriminating nature of the pipe was immediately apparent to Trooper Keppel, who had a lawful right of access to it. Based on these facts, no additional testimony was necessary to describe the pipe, and the Superior Court erred in concluding the nature of the contraband was not immediately apparent to the trooper. Accordingly, we reverse the order vacating appellee's judgment of sentence, and we reinstate the judgment of sentence.

Order reversed; judgment of sentence reinstated. See *Commonwealth v. Pakachki,* 587 Pa. 511, 901 A.2d 983, 2006 Pa. LEXIS 1274 (2006).

HOW WOULD YOU DECIDE?

2. *In the Superior Court of Pennsylvania.*

In a homicide case in Pennsylvania, the deceased's sister gave police a description of the vehicle that the killer drove. A police officer identified a vehicle that makes the description given by the victim's sister and initiated a traffic stop, because, among other reasons, the registration sticker on the vehicle's license plate indicated that it had expired and the vehicle could not be legally operated on the public highways of Pennsylvania. When the subject told the officer that he did not have the required vehicle insurance, the officer impounded a motor vehicle and initiated an inventory search pursuant to the police department's inventory policy. Evidence indicated that the inventory search followed the department's inventory policy and that under the circumstances presented by this case, the officers in the department would have routinely conducted an inventory of an impounded vehicle. The inventory search revealed a firearm in the vehicle that the subject could not lawfully possess. At a later time, after the defendant was in custody, he confessed to being the person who committed the homicide at issue in this case. The firearm and the defendant's confession to murder made following his arrest were introduced against him at his murder trial. The Court of Common Pleas of Allegheny County refused to suppress either the firearm or confession and both contributed to the guilty verdict of first-degree murder.

How would you rule on the defendant's contention that the inventory search was illegal because he should not have been stopped and his vehicle should not have been impounded in the first instance?

The Court's Holding

[The reviewing court considered the facts in the case in considered the arguments that the defendant offered in support of the proposition that he had been illegally stopped by the police officer. The court also reviews the facts that led to the inventory search that revealed the illegally possessed firearm that prompted the arrest of the defendant.]

Appellant seeks to suppress the evidence of the gun and his confession based on (1) the illegal inventory search and (2) the illegal traffic stop of his vehicle.

* * *

Appellant argues that because Officer Hilley was following his car at Detective Logan's request and intended to pull him over regardless of whether or not he was in violation of the Code, this renders the stop somehow illegal. We have to look at the facts as they are, not what they might have been; Officer Hilley's testimony is clear that he saw appellant's expired registration sticker prior to pulling the vehicle over. Appellant does not contest the fact that an expired registration is a violation of the Motor Vehicle Code. Therefore, the stop was valid.

* * *

Next, we consider appellant's argument that the impoundment of his vehicle and subsequent inventory search were unlawful and the evidence should have been suppressed. Inventory searches are a well-defined exception to the search warrant requirement. *Colorado v. Bertine,* 479 U.S. 367, 107 S. Ct. 738, 93 L. Ed. 2d 739 (1987); *Commonwealth v. Nace,* 524 Pa. 323, 327, 571 A.2d 1389, 1391 (1990), *cert. denied,* 498 U.S. 966, 111 S. Ct. 426, 112 L. Ed. 2d 411 (1990).

"The purpose of an inventory search is not to uncover criminal evidence. Rather, it is designed to safeguard seized items in order to benefit both the police and the defendant." [Citations omitted.] Inventory searches serve one or more of the following purposes: (1) to protect the owner's property while it remains in police custody; (2) to protect the police against claims or disputes over lost or stolen property; (3) to protect the police from potential danger; and (4) to assist the police in determining whether the vehicle was stolen and then abandoned. *See South Dakota v. Opperman,* 428 U.S. 364, 369, 96 S. Ct. 3092, 49 L. Ed. 2d 1000 (1976).

* * *

In determining whether a proper inventory search has occurred, the first inquiry is whether the police have lawfully impounded the automobile, *i.e.,* have lawful custody of the automobile. *Opperman,* 428 U.S. at 368, 96 S.Ct. 3092. The authority of the police to impound vehicles derives from the police's reasonable community care-taking functions. *Id.* Such functions include removing disabled or damaged vehicles from the highway, impounding automobiles which violate parking ordinances (thereby jeopardizing public safety and efficient traffic flow), and protecting the community's safety. *Id.* at 368–369, 376 n.10, 96 S.Ct. 3092.

The second inquiry is whether the police have conducted a reasonable inventory search. *Id.* at 370, 96 S. Ct. 3092. An inventory search is reasonable if it is conducted pursuant to reasonable standard police procedures and in good faith and not for the sole purpose of investigation. *See Bertine,* 479 U.S. at 374, 107 S.Ct. 738, 93 L. Ed. 2d 739 ("reasonable police regulations relating to inventory procedures of automobiles administered in good faith satisfy the Fourth Amendment, even though courts might as a matter of hindsight be able to devise equally reasonable rules requiring a different procedure").

* * *

At the suppression hearing in January 2000, the validity of the inventory search conducted pursuant to City of Pittsburgh Police Department procedures was raised and extensively discussed. Appellant argued that the impounding of the vehicle for lack of registration and insurance was not covered by the relevant police standard order, and therefore the inventory search was not proper procedure. The trial court resolved the issue as follows:

The subsequent search of the vehicle was also proper. It was made pursuant to the policy of the Pittsburgh Police regarding inventory searches. It was not disputed that [appellant]'s vehicle did not have a current registration and that it did not carry insurance. It was also not disputed that the vehicle was stopped in an area where parking was not permitted on either side of the street. The officer could not permit [appellant] to move the vehicle; department policy prohibited the officer from moving it himself and it could not be left where it was because parking was not permitted in that area. The only course left to the officer was the one he followed, the towing of the vehicle. Since it was going to be towed, department policy required that an inventory search be conducted. It was during this lawful search that the weapon, which gave the officer probable cause to arrest [appellant], was found.

The second requirement, that the inventory search be conducted in accordance with a reasonable, standard policy, was also met. The officer explained that the department policy was that whenever a vehicle is seized the seizing officer is to conduct a search of the entire vehicle to identify its contents.

* * *

We find no evidence to support appellant's contention. Officer Hilley testified that appellant's vehicle was stopped in the middle of the roadway such that it constituted a traffic hazard; that the particular street on which appellant's vehicle was stopped did not permit parking on either side; and that there was a great amount of snow on the road, preventing appellant from pulling onto the sidewalk so as not to interfere with traffic. Officer Hilley also testified that in the case of a recovery of a stolen vehicle, the owner is notified and given an opportunity to come and claim it; however, department policy in the case of an unregistered/uninsured vehicle is to impound it if it cannot be legally parked. Officers are not permitted to move an unregistered/uninsured vehicle to a safe area where it can be legally parked. In impounding appellant's vehicle and conducting the required inventory search, Officer Hilley was merely following established departmental policy; the search was not designed to uncover evidence of a crime. Affirmed. [the conviction.] See *Commonwealth v. Henley,* 2006 PA Super 276, 909 A.2d 352, 2006 Pa. Super. LEXIS 3054 (2006).

ENDNOTES

1. *Wilson v. Layne,* 526 U.S. 603, 609 (1999), Chief Justice Rehnquist quoting *Semayne's Case* as cited internally, above.
2. Ibid. at 610.
3. See *Payton v. New York,* 445 U.S. 573 (1980), where the Court held that a warrant was a requirement to validly arrest within the subject's home unless special circumstances were present. According to Justice Stevens, "Unreasonable searches or seizures conducted without any warrant at all are condemned by the plain language of the first clause of the Amendment." 445 U.S. 573, 584.
4. *Payton v. New York,* 445 U.S. 573, 585 (1980).
5. 445 U.S. 573 (1980).
6. *Michigan v. Jones,* 249 Mich. 131, 137; 640 N.W.2d 898, 900, 901 (2002).
7. 456 U.S. 798 (1982).
8. Ibid. at 821.
9. 436 N.W.2d 92 (1989).
10. See *United States v. Place,* 462 U.S. 696 at 707 (1983).
11. *Kyllo v. United States,* 533 U.S. 27, 40 (2001).
12. *Chimel v. California,* 395 U.S. 752 at 762–763 (1969).
13. In *United States v. Robinson,* 414 U.S. 218 at 234 (1973), the Court approved the full search of a driver of an automobile for whom probable cause to arrest existed. Immediately following the arrest, the officer conducted a search of the inner pockets and personal effects of the arrestee and discovered heroin. The *Robinson* Court quoted then Associate Judge Cardozo of the New York Court of Appeals as he explained the justification of a search incident to arrest. Cardozo stated, "The peace officer empowered to arrest must be empowered to disarm. If he may disarm, he may search, lest a weapon be concealed. The search being lawful, he retains what he finds if connected with the crime." *People v. Chiagles,* 237 N.Y. 193, 197; 142 N.E. 583, 584 (1923).
14. See *State v. O'Neal,* 148 Wn.2d 564, 62 P.3d 489, 2003 Wash. LEXIS 71 (2003).
15. 448 U.S. 98, 100 S. Ct. 2556, 65 L. Ed. 2d 633, 1980 U.S. LEXIS 142 (1980). Accord, *United States v. Powell,* 483 F.3d 836, 2007 U.S. App. LEXIS 8690 (2007).
16. In *Payton v. New York,* 445 U.S. 573 at 610 (1980), the Court quoted with approval an early Massachusetts case, *Rohan v. Swain,* 59 Mass. 281 at 282 (1851), which upheld the practice of warrantless arrests:

    > It has been sometimes contended that an arrest . . . without a warrant, was a violation of the great fundamental principles of our national and state constitutions, forbidding unreasonable searches and arrests except by warrant founded upon a complaint made under oath. . . . They do not conflict with the authority of constables or other peace officers . . . to arrest without warrant those who have committed felonies. The public safety, and the due apprehension of criminals, charged with heinous offences, imperiously require that such arrests should be made without warrant by officers of the law.

17. Some searches may be permissible following an arrest within the home that are not necessarily incident to arrest as the term is now understood. In *Maryland v. Buie,* 494 U.S. 325 (1990), the Court approved of a properly limited protective sweep of the rooms in conjunction with an in-home arrest when the searching officer possessed a reasonable belief based on specific and articulable facts that the area to be swept could harbor an individual posing a danger to those on the arrest scene. The justification for such an extensive sweep is decidedly not automatic; the sweep may be conducted only when justified by a reasonable suspicion on behalf of the officers.
18. See *Collins v. State,* 2006 Tex. App. LEXIS 7410 (2006).
19. See *State v. Waller,* 918 So. 2d 363, 2005 Fla. App. LEXIS 21143 (2005).
20. Ibid., 367.
21. See *Crawford v. State,* 138 P.3d 254; 2006 Alas. LEXIS 91 (2006).
22. See *Obregon v. State,* 2007 Tex. App. LEXIS 6282 (2007).
23. *Pennsylvania v. Ballard,* 2002 PA Super 283; 806 A.2d 889, 892 (2002).
24. See *Arizona v. Hicks,* 480 U.S. 321 (1987).
25. See *State v. Thompson,* 2007 Ohio 4296, 2007 Ohio App. LEXIS 3839 (2007).
26. See *Wilson v. State,* 174 Md. App. 434, 921 A.2d 881, 2007 Md. App. LEXIS 67 (2007).

27. *Minnesota v. Frank,* 650 N.W.2d 213 (2002), and see *Brown v. Florida,* 7879 So.2d 1021, 1021, 1023 (Fla. Dist. Ct. App. 2001), where a driver's consent to search a vehicle did not extend to personal items like purses and backpacks.

28. See *United States v. Navarro,* 169 F.3d 228, 230 (5th Cir. 1999), and *Wisconsin v. Matejka,* 241 Wis.2d 52; 621 N.W.2d 891 (2001); cert. denied 532 U.S. 1058 (2001). Note: In *Wyoming v. Houghton,* 526 U.S. 295 (1999), the Court approved of the search of a woman passenger's purse, but the distinction involved the presence of probable cause to search rather than consent to search.

29. *Illinois v. Rodriguez,* 497 U.S. 177, 182–189 (1990).

30. The Court in *Schneckloth v. Bustamonte,* 412 U.S. 218, 226, 227 (1973), held that knowledge of the right to refuse to grant consent was not essential to offering valid consent; it was but one of several factors in the totality of the circumstances test.

31. When a court decides whether to suppress evidence, an important question is which person possesses standing to contest an alleged illegal search and seizure. Normally, only a person with an expectation of privacy as recognized by Fourth Amendment case law will be permitted to argue the merits of a motion to suppress. Applying modern standing rules of *Rakas v. Illinois,* 439 U.S. 128 (1978), to *Schneckloth v. Bustamonte,* the passenger, Bustamonte, who was eventually prosecuted, might not have any expectation of privacy since he did not own or lease the vehicle. Under such circumstances, the passenger would not have any legal right to contest the validity of the search and seizure.

32. See *Georgia v. Randolph,* 547 U.S. 103 (2006).

33. The Fourth Amendment by its words does not speak of a right of privacy being guaranteed to individuals, but the amendment has been interpreted over the years as giving some level of privacy that varies with the fact situation and location. For some discussion of privacy and the Fourth Amendment in two different contexts, consult Justice Scalia's opinion in *Wyoming v. Houghton,* 526 U.S. 295 (1999), and Justice White's lead opinion in *California v. Greenwood,* 486 U.S. 35 (1988).

34. In enforcing the Fourth Amendment's prohibition against unreasonable searches and seizures, the Court has insisted upon probable cause as a minimum requirement for a reasonable search permitted by the Constitution. As a general rule, it has also required the judgment of a magistrate on the probable cause issue and the issuance of a warrant before a search is made. Only where an emergency exists and in a few other exceptional situations, the judgment of the police as to probable cause may serve as a sufficient authority for a warrantless search. *Carroll* held that a search warrant was unnecessary where there is probable cause to search an automobile stopped on the highway, where the car is movable and the car's contents may never be found again if a warrant must be obtained. Hence, an immediate search is constitutionally permissible.

35. There is no requirement that police procure a search warrant for a motor vehicle even where there is ample time to do so. In a per curiam opinion in *Pennsylvania v. Labron,* 518 U.S. 938 (1996), the Court clearly rejected the Pennsylvania Supreme Court's attempt to require police to obtain vehicle search warrants where time permits.

36. In a per curiam opinion the Court stated in *Maryland v. Dyson,* 527 U.S. 465, 467 (1999), "We made this clear in *United States v. Ross,* 456 U.S. 798 (1982), when we said that in cases where there was probable cause to search a vehicle `a search is not unreasonable if based on facts that would justify the issuance of a warrant, even though a warrant has not been actually obtained.'"

37. See *State v. Black,* 2006 Ala. Crim. App. LEXIS 171 (2006).

38. 531 U.S. 32, 121 S. Ct. 447, 148 L. Ed. 2d 333, 2000 United States LEXIS 8084 (2000).

39. See *Camp v. State,* 2007 Ala. Crim. App. LEXIS 72 (2007).

40. For examples of searches incident to arrest of drivers of motor vehicles, see *United States v. Robinson,* 414 U.S. 218 (1973), and *Gustafson v. Florida,* 414 U.S. 260 (1973).

41. In many situations, probable cause for a search, the justification for an inventory search, and consent may all coexist, giving a prosecutor several legal theories on which to argue in favor of admission of the evidence. Where one theory allows admission, the evidence will generally be admitted.

42. An inventory search may be conducted after an automobile has been lawfully impounded, as occurred in *Florida v. White,* 526 U.S. 559 (1999), where the officers, conducting a routine inventory search, discovered illegal drugs within the automobile.

43. *Benson v. State,* 342 Ark. 684, 30 S.W.3d 731 (2000).

44. *Bratton v. Arkansas,* 77 Ark. App. 174; 72 S.W.3d 522 (2002).

45. See *United States v. Mackley,* 149 Fed. Appx. 874; 2005 U.S. App. LEXIS 19391 (2005).

46. See *Commonwealth v. McCree,* 924 A.2d 621; 2007 Pa. LEXIS 1197 (2007).

47. Emergency situations, airport searches, consent searches, school searches, border searches, postarrest searches, and some stop and frisk situations may allow an officer to search personal belongings as exceptions to the general rule that probable cause and warrants are necessary.

48. The current law is expressed by *United States v. Ross,* 456 U.S. 798 (1982). The *Ross* Court concluded that officers who have legitimately stopped an automobile and who possess probable cause that seizable matter is concealed somewhere within the vehicle may conduct a warrantless search of the vehicle that is as thorough as a judge or magistrate could have authorized by warrant, even though no warrant has been obtained.

49. The *Sanders* police would have been on notice that a search of a piece of luggage generally required a warrant in addition to probable cause. In *United States v. Chadwick,* 433 U.S. 1 (1977), with probable cause but without a warrant, police seized and opened a piece of luggage that had traveled from San Diego to Boston on a train. The *Chadwick* defendants had just placed the luggage in the trunk of a car. In substance, the *Chadwick* Court held that the warrant clause of the Fourth Amendment required a warrant to search luggage absent exigent circumstances or some other exception and that merely touching a car with the luggage did not trigger the *Carroll* doctrine.

50. Justice Thomas explained, "The Florida Contraband Forfeiture Act [Florida Contraband Forfeiture Act, Fla. Stat. § 932.701 *et seq.* (1997)] provides that certain forms of contraband, including motor vehicles used in violation of the Act's provisions, may be seized and potentially forfeited." *Florida v. White,* 526 U.S. 559, 561 (1999).

51. White also developed other troubles subsequent to his arrest when the police subjected his forfeited vehicle to an inventory search that revealed two rocks of crack cocaine. The inventory search could have been justified as a routine inventory search for which neither probable cause nor a warrant would be required. An alternative manner of justifying the search finds no expectation of privacy in the automobile for White, since, at the time of the search, it belonged to the government of Florida under the forfeiture law. See Florida Contraband Forfeiture Act, Fla. Stat. § 932.701 *et seq.* (1997).

52. The basis for a search of a motor vehicle following an arrest of the driver requires an actual arrest of the driver. In *Knowles v. Iowa,* 525 U.S. 113 (1998), where a police officer possessed probable cause to arrest but issued only a citation and then searched the automobile because the officer *could* have arrested Knowles, the Court held the search to be unreasonable under the Fourth Amendment.

53. For a case detailing the scope of a search incident to an arrest involving a motor vehicle, consult *United States v. Robinson,* 414 U.S. 218 (1973).

54. *Commonwealth v. Grant,* 57 Mass. App. Ct. 334, 339; 783 N.E.2d 455, 459, 460 (2003).

C H A P T E R   8

Special Problem Searches: Administrative, Inventory, School, Airport, Work, Border, and National Security Searches

Learning Objectives

1. Understand and be able to describe the different needs that support administrative, inventory, airport, school, and work searches.
2. Articulate the justification for searches under the common law "police" powers of states and local jurisdictions.
3. Be able to explain what the term *closely regulated* means in relation to industry or business, and give three examples.
4. Analyze and explain why the Supreme Court originally did not require administrative search warrants for ordinary homes but later determined that warrants were generally required for administrative searches of private residences.
5. Distinguish between administrative probable cause and traditional criminal probable cause, and be able to give two examples of each.
6. Describe the three rationales that courts use to hold that proof of

traditional criminal probable cause is not required to make inventory searches reasonable under the Fourth Amendment.
7. Articulate the rationales the Supreme Court used to determine that in order to make inventory searches reasonable, police agencies must have a written inventory search policy that must be routinely followed.
8. Be able to explain the circumstances under which public school students may be searched for violating school rules or violating the criminal law.
9. Identify the basis for warrantless and suspicionless searches of airport passengers and their baggage.
10. Describe why border searches stand on a completely different basis than other traditional searches designed to uncover criminality.

Chapter Outline

1. Introduction to Administrative, Special Needs, Inventory, School, Airport, and Work Searches
2. Administrative Searches
3. Administrative Searches of Ordinary Businesses and Industries
4. Administrative Searches of Closely Regulated Industries

Key Terms

Administrative probable cause
Administrative search: business
Administrative search: home
Airport passenger search
Closely (heavily) regulated industry
Emergency administrative search
FISA searches
Functional equivalent of international border

International border search
Inventory search: motor vehicle
Inventory search: personal property
Inventory search policy
Private employer search
Reasonable basis to suspect
Reduced expectation of privacy: juveniles
Suspicionless public school search
Suspicionless workplace search

1. INTRODUCTION TO ADMINISTRATIVE, SPECIAL NEEDS, INVENTORY, SCHOOL, AIRPORT, AND WORK SEARCHES

In a variety of contexts, local, state, and federal governmental agencies possess informational needs that can be met by searches that do not necessarily have as their primary goal the discovery of criminal activity. The Fourth Amendment to the Constitution grants to individuals the right to be free from unreasonable searches and seizures, not to be free from all searches and seizures. It follows from this that a government may be relatively free to conduct any type of search so long as it is deemed to be reasonable under the circumstances. For example, when necessary to implement social programs and structure public policy, governments may conduct searches and request information in ways that do not offend the Fourth Amendment. In a variety of contexts, a branch of government that is attempting to promote a policy, promote social interests, protect property and society, or accomplish a variety of goals expected of governments conducts what have been described as "special needs" searches. However, in pursuing some special needs searches where Fourth Amendment interests are clearly implicated, the nature of particular searches may dictate the use of warrants.

Special needs searches include searches of houses for zoning compliance, scrutiny of ordinary businesses for fire and safety issues, and searches of closely regulated industries. Some of the special needs searches may require warrants; others do not because of the nature of the search or the need for immediacy. Searches of pervasively or closely regulated industries and businesses may not require search warrant and may not require probable cause because conducting these businesses requires a relinquishment of some Fourth Amendment protections. In all cases of administrative searches, emergency or exigent circumstances will excuse the procurement of the warrant that might have otherwise been necessary.

The Supreme Court has upheld warrantless special needs searches in a variety of contexts. For example, in *Veronia School District 47J v. Acton,*[1] the Court approved a warrantless special needs search to randomly test student athletes for drugs in specified circumstances. Similarly, administrative suspicionless and warrantless drug tests were permitted for United States Customs Service employees who were seeking promotions or lateral transfers to specified positions, according to the majority in *Treasury Employees v. Von Raab.*[2] Because railroad operations involve risks to many people, the Court approved warrantless and suspicionless drug and alcohol tests for privately employed railroad workers involved in train accidents or found to be violating specific safety regulations.[3]

Warrantless inspections of the physical property of "closely regulated" businesses, even in the absence of any suspicion, such as automobile recyclers, were approved by the Court in *New York v. Burger.*[4] Special needs searches that are warrantless and suspicionless have limitations, however, at least in the medical arena. In *Ferguson v. City of Charleston,* pregnant women were tested for drugs against their will to determine whether they had injected illegal drugs prior to obtaining obstetrical care at South Carolina hospitals. Patients who tested positive were subject to arrest and prosecution. The Supreme Court found that the testing constituted an unreasonable search when done by the hospitals for the purposes of law enforcement and violated the Fourth Amendment prohibition against unreasonable searches and seizures.[5] Similarly, the City of Indianapolis had a program involving suspicionless stopping of motorists to determine if they had used or were using illegal drugs, like a sobriety checkpoint.[6] The Supreme Court overturned the plan, despite the city's argument that its secondary purpose of keeping drug- and alcohol-impaired motorists off of the road and verifying licenses and registrations should make the stops reasonable. The Court focused on the primary purpose—catching criminals—and held that since the main reason for the roadblocks was not road safety but criminal interdiction, the plan could not square with the Fourth Amendment. In striking down the Indianapolis plan, the Court noted, "While reasonableness under the Fourth Amendment is predominantly an objective inquiry, our special needs and administrative search cases demonstrate that purpose is often relevant when suspicionless intrusions pursuant to a general scheme are at issue."[7] In this case, the stops and searches were more than mere administrative stops and were unreasonable because they could not be justified on general criminal detection principles.

Inventory searches occur when a governmental agency must take custody of personal property for which it retains a level of responsibility for safekeeping. Where an individual has been arrested and police take control of an automobile, impounding it to keep it from harm and other damage may be reasonable. In addition, the contents of the automobile may include valuables for which a police agency might have responsibility. It is generally considered reasonable, so long as the law enforcement agency has an inventory search policy and routinely follows it, to conduct an inventory of the automobile to assure the security of any of its contents. If by some chance evidence of criminality appears, such evidence is usually admissible in court. An inventory search may also be applied to personal property taken from an arrestee, such as a purse, wallet, backpack, or similar item. Once again, it is generally considered reasonable to catalog the contents of these items and to secure them until they are returned to the individual. Paramount justifications for inventory search are the protection of property, the protection of police from dangerous items or ordnance, and the protection of police against false claims of loss while the property is not in the owner's possession.

The protection of schoolchildren provides the justification for a variety of school-based special needs searches of both student property and students personally. A large percentage of legal cases involving searches of school-age children concern drug use and sale in public schools. While the United States Supreme Court has held that children possess Fourth Amendment rights, case law is also very clear that children do not enjoy the exact same Fourth Amendment rights as adults. Courts on many levels have approved the search of persons, purses, backpacks, and lockers for items that offend the criminal law and/or for evidence that school rules have been broken. In many instances, individual suspicion that a particular student has transgressed the law or violated school rules may allow search of that student and/or his or her possessions. In other contexts involving secondary school athletes and students involved in extracurricular activities, suspicionless drug testing has been approved as meeting the reasonableness standard under the Fourth Amendment.

Special needs searches include workplace searches of individuals, whether conducted by a private employer or a state or federal government agency. In some cases, the government agency requires employees desiring transfers or promotions to submit to a drug-screening test, despite the absence of any individualized suspicion. In the context of private employers who may be required by the federal government or a state government to conduct drug searches of their employees, suspicionless testing has been approved. The general rationale involves weighing the employees' expectation of privacy against the significant needs of the government for a drug-free workplace and for the private employer who must meet government-mandated drug testing guidelines. In situations where a government employee may be required to carry a firearm and/or deal with drug interdiction, suspicionless testing has been mandated. Federal regulations require that operators of instrumentalities of interstate commerce, such as railroads, are subject to drug testing following an accident involving a specified level of property damage. As a general rule, many of these workplace drug-testing searches have been upheld as reasonable under the Fourth Amendment.

Various types of searches involving airline passengers, crew, and other workers have received court approval as special needs searches. For the past several decades, persons wishing to board domestic commercial airliners have been forced to choose between submitting to a personal and baggage search prior to boarding and finding an alternate means of transportation. Searches of passenger baggage, both carry-on and checked, have been based on either a consent theory or an administrative search basis. Following the events of September 11, 2001, extensive new types and levels of airport searches have either been initiated or loom on the horizon, including deeper personal screening and enhanced chemical and hazardous material screening.

International border searches may be considered within the special needs search category because the requirements of national sovereignty allow extreme scrutiny over items entering or leaving the United States. As a means of enforcing the international boundary, persons crossing a border of the United States possess diminished Fourth Amendment rights and may be searched for any reason without a showing of probable cause. Searches at an international border and its functional equivalent, an international airport, are generally subject to identical rules concerning searches. As a person moves inland from a border, Fourth Amendment rights begin to have full application. Permanent stations along the major highways leading to and from the border allow government agents to scrutinize traffic passing through the choke point and stop individuals who appear not to be entitled to be in the United States. Roving patrols near the border have been allowed to make stops based on reasonable suspicion that a person, a person's possessions, or a vehicle's content offends the law. In conducting a special needs stop and search, federal border officials possess much leeway in their activity, but their overall conduct inside the United States remains subject to the Fourth Amendment concept of reasonableness.

Some types of special needs searches are not covered in this chapter. Parolees and probationers, as a condition of their release, can be required to submit to searches based on a lower standard than that traditionally required by the Fourth Amendment. Persons in prisons have reduced expectations of privacy and are subject to search at any time. Special needs searches mentioned in this chapter are, therefore, not exclusive, and a variety of others are beyond the scope of this book.

2. ADMINISTRATIVE SEARCHES

The states and the federal government are empowered with the authority to promote the general welfare, public health, and safety. This power frequently has been called the "police" power, not in its traditional law enforcement fashion but to denote a government's power to promote and ensure the common good of society. The Fourth Amendment limitation against unreasonable searches and seizures has been held to apply to commercial structures used in business and industry. The expectation of privacy in commercial operations includes protection against criminal investigatory searches and also searches designed to implement and enforce social regulatory schemes.[8] These social objectives range from protecting water supplies, to preventing conditions that could cause a conflagration, to ensuring worker safety in commerce, industry, and transportation. If a governmental administrative search encompasses a secondary desire to procure evidence of criminal activity, such a search is generally valid so long as the facts and circumstances justify a proper administrative search. However, when the searching individual may have the authority to conduct both administrative searches and criminal investigative searches, care must be exercised to assure that an administrative search has not been conducted by reliance on or exercise of law enforcement powers.[9]

Probable cause is generally required for administrative searches, although in some contexts such as food service inspections or welfare compliance inspections, warrants may not be required. Where an administrative search requires a warrant, it must be based on a special category of probable cause called administrative probable cause. It is a reduced or watered-down level of probable cause and was described in *Camara v. Municipal Court* when dealing with housing inspections as:

> "probable cause" to issue a warrant to inspect must exist if reasonable legislative or administrative standards for conducting an area inspection are satisfied with respect to a particular dwelling. Such standards, which will vary with the municipal program being enforced, may be based upon the passage of time, the nature of the building (e.g., a multi-family apartment house) or the condition of the entire area, but they do not necessarily depend upon specific knowledge of the condition of the particular dwelling.[10]

While the Supreme Court has not had occasion to rule on significant new challenges to administrative searches in recent years, the principles pertaining to these searches are fairly well known, and litigants have probed most of the parameters. Numerous cased have clearly indicated that administrative searches are regulated by the Fourth Amendment.[11]

3. ADMINISTRATIVE SEARCHES OF ORDINARY BUSINESSES AND INDUSTRIES

Fourth Amendment expectations of privacy in business or commercial settings differ from those in a personal residence or in an automobile in that there is a reduced level of privacy that society is prepared to recognize as reasonable. Businesses invite customers to visit parts of their premises, and manufacturing entities sometimes have thousands of employees who enter the physical plant each day. Many commercial operations are subject by law to certain inspections for health and safety, and the managers understand that agents of the government will enter the property on occasion. These factors do not, however, mean that a warrant to inspect or search is not required; most operators of businesses can choose to require governmental inspectors to possess warrants[12] prior to gaining admission. The fact that a business entity has the right to insist on a warrant in most cases, however, does not mean that most businesses will require a warrant prior to governmental entry for inspection.

4. ADMINISTRATIVE SEARCHES OF CLOSELY REGULATED INDUSTRIES

While most businesses may be searched only with a warrant, absent consent, one category of commerce is subject to inspection without warrant. Businesses or industries classified as closely regulated industries possess a diminished expectation of privacy over all or some of their operations. A primary example of a closely regulated industry is the manufacture, transport, and sale of intoxicating spirits. In *Colonnade Catering Corporation v. United States,*[13] the Court noted that in England and its colonies, which later became the United States, inspectors were permitted to enter brewing houses and similar establishments upon request and without a warrant. Subsequent federal law allowed officials without a warrant to enter and inspect distilling premises and those of companies that imported spirits. The sale and disposition of firearms, while not traditionally regulated as pervasively as alcohol, has been held to be an example of a closely regulated industry. In *United States v. Biswell,*[14] the Court allowed as reasonable under the Fourth Amendment a warrantless inspection of a federally licensed firearm dealer under the theory that the law authorizing the inspection would constitute only a limited threat to the pawnshop operator's expectation of privacy. The *Biswell* Court noted:

> When a dealer chooses to engage in this pervasively regulated business and to accept a federal license, he does so with the knowledge that his business records, firearms, and ammunition will be subject to effective inspection. 406 U.S. 311, 316 (1972)

The general rule that has emerged appears to indicate that persons and corporate entities engaged in pervasively or closely regulated businesses and industries have a reduced level of Fourth Amendment protections.

5. ORDINARY COMMERCIAL BUSINESS: SEARCH WARRANT REQUIRED

Although some businesses might seem to fall into the category of closely regulated industries because of federal or state safety requirements, not every business has to submit to warrantless inspections. For example, in *Marshall v. Barlow's, Inc.,* 436 U.S. 307 (1978), federal inspectors attempted to make a warrantless inspection of Barlow's company, an electrical and plumbing business. Barlow refused to allow the Occupational Safety and Health Administration (OSHA) inspector into private areas of the firm and sued the federal government for injunctive relief from warrantless OSHA inspections. The trial court held that a warrant for the type of search involved here was necessary, absent consent, under the Fourth Amendment and that the OSHA statutory authorization for warrantless inspection was unconstitutional. Barlow may have had an expectation of privacy in his business that was reduced somewhat by virtue of inviting employees onto his property. According to the *Barlow's* Court:

> The owner of a business has not, by the necessary utilization of employees in his operation, thrown open the areas where employees alone are permitted to the warrantless scrutiny of Government agents. *Barlow's* at 315

The Court proved unwilling to allow governmental inspection of businesses in the absence of warrant or consent where the businesses were not traditionally pervasively regulated under traditional and long-standing legislative formulations. Precisely what causes a line of business to be known as a closely regulated industry may be discerned on a case-by-case basis. Coal mining has been found to fit the pattern,[15] as have businesses dealing in firearms[16] and alcohol.[17]

Some businesses that would not seem to qualify as closely regulated operations may still fall into the category. In Virginia, the manufacture and sale of goat cheese is on the list of closely regulated industries because each cheese entity makes food products for human consumption. In at least two cases,[18] farmers were convicted of refusing to allow commonwealth health inspectors to search their respective premises to look for violations of the health code. The Virginia courts appear to rely on three factors to determine whether a particular business or industry qualifies as closely regulated. According to an intermediate Virginia court, the commonwealth must have a substantial interest that informs the regulatory scheme under which the inspection will be made, the warrantless inspection must be necessary to advance the regulatory scheme, and the inspection program must advise or give notice to the owner or operator of the commercial or business premises that the search complies with the law and has a defined scope that will not be exceeded.[19]

In a final decision in 2006, the Court of Appeals, Virginia's top court, upheld the characterization of this type of business as closely regulated when it noted, "The Commonwealth likewise has a substantial interest in protecting the health of its citizens by regulating its food supply."[20] The fundamental need to inspect under the Commonwealth's inspection program, as the court noted, "can only be furthered by unannounced inspections."[21]

While constructing a list of the types of businesses covered under pervasive or close regulation it may be impossible, it is arguable that as enhanced governmental regulation occurs, more fields may be seen as closely regulated industries with a diminished expectation of privacy.

6. ADMINISTRATIVE SEARCHES OF HOMES: NO WARRANT ORIGINALLY REQUIRED

An appropriate starting point to consider administrative searches of residences and private homes is *Frank v. Maryland,*[22] where the Supreme Court upheld a criminal conviction that resulted from the refusal by a dwelling's occupier to permit a warrantless inspection of private residential premises. Prompted by a citizen complaint, the government desired to conduct a warrantless inspection to ascertain whether a public nuisance involving rats existed. When the occupier persisted in refusing to allow warrantless admission, an arrest for refusal to allow an inspection followed. The city code provided as follows:

> Whenever the Commissioner of Health shall have cause to suspect that a nuisance exists in any house, cellar, or enclosure, he may demand entry therein in the day time, and if the owner or occupier shall refuse or delay to open the same and admit a free examination, he shall forfeit and pay for every such refusal the sum of Twenty Dollars. § 120 of Art. 12 of the Baltimore City Code. *Frank v. Maryland* at 361

A trial court found Frank guilty of violating the Baltimore health code. When the case arrived at the Supreme Court of the United States, the Court upheld the statute authorizing a warrantless arrest[23] for refusing to allow the inspectors access to the home. It noted a long history of warrantless housing inspections, and modern requirements of health and sanitation dictate that due process has not been violated by the provision for warrantless admission to a private home upon a complaint.

The lesson of *Frank* was that searches of private premises for administrative purposes did not require a warrant and that a refusal to allow entry might be followed by criminal legal proceedings. The only method to determine whether a governmental agent could lawfully enter involved risking a criminal prosecution. The *Frank* Court felt that the Fourth Amendment was designed to have primary effect when criminal investigations were involved. Consequently, the Court held that the privacy interests under *Frank* "touch[ed] at most upon the periphery of the important interests safeguarded by the Fourteenth Amendment's protection against official intrusion."[24] For those reasons, as an exception to the usual requirements of a warrant, no warrant was required to conduct a residential inspection.

7. A CHANGE IN REQUIREMENTS: SEARCHES OF PRIVATE PREMISES REQUIRE WARRANTS

The Supreme Court indicated a significant change in direction when it decided *Camara v. Municipal Court* (see Case 8.1).[25] A housing inspector repeatedly had been refused entrance to private premises following a complaint that the commercial leasehold was being used for private residential purposes. Camara sued the district court in Superior Court for a writ of prohibition of enforcement of the municipal code but had no success in the California court system. The *Camara* Court held that the interests at stake when the government desired to enforce zoning restrictions were different from those when the Court decided *Frank v. Maryland*. Instead of believing that privacy interests being protected were peripheral to the Fourth Amendment protections, the *Camara* Court determined that the privacy interests were quite a bit more important than in *Frank*. Warrantless administrative searches cannot be justified, according to the Court, on the grounds that they make minimal demands on occupants. The Court stated:

> [W]e hold that administrative searches of the kind at issue here are significant intrusions upon the interests protected by the Fourth Amendment, that such searches, when authorized and conducted without a warrant procedure, lack the traditional safeguards which the Fourth Amendment guarantees to the individual, and that the reasons put forth in *Frank v. Maryland* and in other cases for upholding these warrantless searches are insufficient to justify so substantial a weakening of the Fourth Amendment's protections. *Camara v. Municipal Court,* 387 U.S. 523 at 534

The *Camara* Court allowed a "watered-down" version of probable cause to be sufficient for procuring an administrative warrant. Clearly, criminal probable cause would be a difficult standard to meet in the administrative setting, so the Court indicated

CASE 8.1

Leading Case Brief: Entry to Private Residential Premises Requires an Administrative Warrant

Camara v. Municipal Court
Supreme Court of the United States
387 U.S. 523 (1967)

Case Facts:

After receiving a complaint, an inspector of the San Francisco Division of Housing Inspection attempted to enter the first floor of an apartment building, where apartment living was not allowed. The building manager had informed the inspector that the appellant was using the street–level premises as a personal residence in contravention of the building's occupancy permit. When the inspector confronted Camara with a request to inspect the premises, he refused to permit the inspection unless the housing inspector possessed a search warrant.

Acting on the same complaint, the building inspector returned to attempt a search without a warrant and requested admission to the building, and Camara maintained his original position. Following local protocol, the inspector caused a citation to be mailed requesting. Camara to appear at the district attorney's office. When the appellant ignored this request, two inspectors visited the appellant a third time to inform him of his duty under Section 503 of the municipal code.

Sec. 503. RIGHT TO ENTER BUILDING. Authorized employees of the City departments or City agencies, so far as may be necessary for the performance of their duties, shall, upon presentation of proper credentials, have the right to enter, at reasonable times, any building, structure, or premises in the City to perform any duty imposed upon them by the Municipal Code.

When Camara refused to permit the two inspectors to enter the premises, prosecutors filed a complaint charging him with refusing to permit a lawful warrantless inspection of his premises in violation of Section 503. Camara brought an action in Superior Court alleging that he had been charged criminally for violating

the San Francisco Housing Code by refusing to permit a warrantless search of his residence. He requested that the Superior Court issue a writ of prohibition to the criminal court because the authorization of warrantless searches permitted by the ordinance was unconstitutional on its face. The Superior Court refused, a position that continued through the California state court system, resulting in a writ of certiorari being issued by the Supreme Court of the United States.

Legal Issue:

Consistent with the Fourth Amendment, and absent an emergency or other exception to the warrant requirement, may the occupier of real property require that a government possess a warrant permitting entry where the purpose is an administrative search?

The Court's Ruling:

Since significant privacy interests are attached to residential dwellings, the Court determined that a governmental agent must have a warrant to enter private residential premises or possess some other reasonable basis to enter in the absence of a warrant.

Essence of the Court's Rationale:

I

* * *

In *Frank v. State of Maryland,* this Court upheld the conviction of one who refused to permit a warrantless inspection of private premises for the purposes of locating and abating a suspected public nuisance . . . the *Frank* [*v. Maryland*] opinion has generally been interpreted as carving out an additional exception to the rule that [warrants are generally required for searches under the Fourth Amendment].

To the *Frank* majority, municipal fire, health, and housing inspection programs touch at most upon the periphery of the important interests safeguarded by the Fourteenth Amendment's protection against official intrusions, 359 U.S. at 367, because the inspections are merely to determine whether physical conditions exist which do not comply with minimum standards prescribed in local regulatory ordinances. . . .

We may agree that a routine inspection of the physical condition of private property is a less hostile intrusion than the typical policeman's search for the fruits and instrumentalities of crime. For this reason alone, *Frank* differed from the great bulk of Fourth Amendment cases which have been considered by this Court. But we cannot agree that the Fourth Amendment interests at stake in these inspection cases are merely "peripheral." It is surely anomalous to say that the individual and his private property are fully protected by the Fourth Amendment only when the individual is suspected of criminal behavior. For instance, even the most law-abiding citizen has a very tangible interest in limiting the circumstances under which the sanctity of his home may be broken by official authority, for the possibility of criminal entry under the guise of official sanction is a serious threat to personal and family security.

* * *

The *Frank* majority suggested, and appellee reasserts, two other justifications for permitting administrative health and safety inspections without a warrant. First, it is argued that these inspections are "designed to make the least possible demand on the individual occupant." . . . In addition, the argument proceeds, the warrant process could not function effectively in this field. The decision to inspect an entire municipal area is based upon legislative or administrative assessment of broad factors such as the area's age and condition. Unless the magistrate is to review such policy matters, he must issue a "rubber stamp" warrant which provides no protection at all to the property owner.

In our opinion, these arguments unduly discount the purposes behind the warrant machinery contemplated by the Fourth Amendment. Under the present system when the inspector demands entry the occupant has no way of knowing whether enforcement of the municipal code involved requires inspection of his premises, no way of knowing the lawful limits of the inspector's power to search, and

no way of knowing whether the inspector himself is acting under proper authorization. These are questions which may be reviewed by a neutral magistrate without any reassessment of the basic agency decision to canvass an area. Yet only by refusing entry and risking a criminal conviction can the occupant at present challenge the inspector's decision to search. And even if the occupant possesses sufficient fortitude to take this risk, as appellant did here, he may never learn any more about the reason for the inspection than that the law generally allows housing inspectors to gain entry. The practical effect of this system is to leave the occupant subject to the discretion of the official in the field. This is precisely the discretion to invade private property which we have consistently circumscribed by a requirement that a disinterested party warrant the need to search.

The final justification suggested for warrantless administrative searches is that the public interest demands such a rule: it is vigorously argued that the health and safety of entire urban populations is dependent upon enforcement of minimum fire, housing, and sanitation standards, and that the only effective means of enforcing such code is by routine systematized inspection of all physical structures. [However], the question is not . . . whether these inspections may be made, but whether they may be made without a warrant. . . .

It has nowhere been urged that fire, health, and housing code inspection programs could not achieve their goals within the confines of a reasonable search warrant requirement. Thus, we do not find the public need argument dispositive.

In summary, we hold that administrative searches of the kind at issue here are significant intrusions upon the interests protected by the Fourth Amendment, that such searches when authorized and conducted without a warrant procedure lack the traditional safeguards which the Fourth Amendment guarantees to the individual. . . .

* * *

II

* * *

[The city argued that the inspection process would not work if it had to show probable cause for each structure it wished to inspect. The Court noted that all

(continued)

interested parties agreed that inspections were essential to enforcement of municipal codes. The Court found that area inspections were also necessary to enforce building codes and that probable cause need not be limited to one structure but could be an area-wide probable cause.]

* * *

Having concluded that the area inspection is a "reasonable" search of private property within the meaning of the Fourth Amendment, it is obvious that "probable cause" to issue a warrant to inspect must exist if reasonable legislative or administrative standards for conducting an area inspection are satisfied with respect to a particular dwelling. Such standards, which will vary with the municipal program being enforced, may be based upon the passage of time, the nature of the building (e.g., a multi-family apartment house) or the condition of the entire area, but they do not necessarily depend upon specific knowledge of the condition of the particular dwelling. It has been suggested that so to vary the probable cause test from the standard applied in criminal cases would be to authorize a "synthetic search warrant" and thereby, to lessen the overall protections of the Fourth Amendment. But we do not agree. The warrant procedure is designed to guarantee that a decision to search private property is justified by a reasonable governmental interest. But reasonableness is still the ultimate standard. If a valid public interest justifies the intrusion contemplated, then there is probable cause to issue a suitably restricted search warrant. . . . [The use of this procedure] neither endangers time-honored doctrines applicable to criminal investigations nor makes a nullity of the probable cause requirement in this area. It merely gives full recognition to the competing public and private interests here at stake. . . .

III

Since our holding emphasizes the controlling standard of reasonableness nothing we say today is intended to foreclose prompt inspections, even without a warrant, that the law has traditionally upheld in emergency situations. [Citations omitted. The deleted citations refer to cases dealing with particular emergency situations: seizure of unwholesome food, compulsory smallpox vaccination, health quarantine, and summary destruction of tubercular cattle.] On the other hand, in the case of most routine area inspections, there is no compelling urgency to inspect at a particular time or on a particular day. Moreover, most citizens allow inspections of their property without a warrant. Thus, as a practical matter and in light of the Fourth Amendment's requirement that a warrant specify the property to be searched, it seems likely that warrants should normally be sought only after entry is refused unless there has been a citizen complaint or there is other satisfactory reason for securing immediate entry.

* * *

The judgment is vacated, and the case is remanded for further proceedings not inconsistent with this opinion.
It is so ordered.

Case Importance:

The Court reconsidered earlier Fourth Amendment interpretations concerning whether a warrant was required for residential entry by government officials and determined that the privacy in a home was an important and central Fourth Amendment protection for which a warrant was necessary. The Court reaffirmed that a person's home is where he or she may expect the greatest privacy from governmental intrusion, whether the person is home, away, or suspected of a crime.

that administrative inspections must meet a special standard of probable cause fitting this type of intrusion. According to the Court:

"[P]robable cause" to issue a warrant to inspect must exist if reasonable legislative or administrative standards for conducting an area inspection are satisfied with respect to a particular dwelling. Such standards, which will vary with the municipal program being enforced, may be based upon the passage of time, the nature of the building (e.g., a multi-family apartment house), or the condition of the entire area, but they will not necessarily depend upon specific knowledge of the condition of the particular dwelling. *Camara v. Municipal Court*, 387 U.S. 523 at 538

In a companion case to *Camara, See v. City of Seattle,* 387 U.S. 541 (1967), government administrative inspectors wanted to gain entry to inspect a warehouse. The Court held that they were required to procure a warrant to gain entry to a commercial warehouse because the Fourth Amendment protections extended to commercial locations. According to the Court's rationale, the defendant in the case, See, had been improperly convicted of violating a local ordinance that made it a crime to refuse to allow a warrantless entry by a fire inspector. The words of the Seattle ordinance empowered fire inspectors to conduct routine inspections without probable cause and without a warrant. The *See* Court held that "administrative entry, without consent, upon the portions of commercial premises which are not open to the public may only be compelled through prosecution or physical force within the framework of a warrant procedure."[26] *See* extended similar *Camara* residential protection under the Fourth Amendment to business and business buildings.

In a later case, Justice O'Connor echoed the standards for administrative probable cause and the issuance of an administrative warrant when she stated:

> [T]he appropriate standard for administrative searches is not probable cause in its traditional meaning. Instead, an administrative warrant can be obtained if there is a showing that reasonable legislative or administrative standards for conducting an inspection are satisfied. *O'Connor v. Ortega,* 480 U.S. 709, 723 (1987)

The administrative probable cause criterion, while using the identical language of criminal probable cause, in practice has proven to be a lower standard and fairly easy to meet. Administrative probable cause may mature because of complaints by citizens, employees within an industry, or labor unions or by observations derived from routine governmental activities. When courts are faced with a request for an administrative warrant, they must weigh the governmental need to search against the reasonable expectation of privacy and will normally issue warrants, practically as a mere formality.

As is the case with traditional searches under the Fourth Amendment, there are exceptions to the administrative warrant. The clearest case arises when the occupier of premises gives free and voluntary consent for the administrative search. The standards for judging whether the property occupier has rendered valid consent are arguably cloudy, but better judgment requires that the "totality of the circumstances" test, as illustrated in *Schneckloth v. Bustamonte,*[27] be used as a clear benchmark. Under the *Schneckloth* standard of the "totality of the circumstances" for determining voluntariness, the government need not prove that the person possessed knowledge of the right to refuse consent.

In addition to the consent theory, exigent circumstances or emergency situations permit warrantless administrative searches and seizures. The *Camara* Court clearly contemplated continued used of emergency administrative searches when it observed:

> . . . [N]othing we say today is intended to foreclose prompt inspections, even without a warrant, that the law has traditionally upheld in emergency situations. *Camara v. Municipal Court,* 387 U.S. 523, 539

Demonstrative of this principle, the Court noted with approval searches and seizures of unwholesome food, compulsory smallpox vaccination, health quarantines, and summary destruction of tubercular cattle.

In applying an emergency rationale for some administrative searches, the Sixth Circuit approved a search that firefighters conducted following a residential fire that involved some exigencies or potential emergencies.[28] Firefighters had been called to extinguish a residential fire but remained on the scene after the fire was extinguished. The fire investigators checked for water damage that might cause electrical shorts or structural damage and checked for the dangers of carbon monoxide. While conducting these checks during the first hour after the fire had been extinguished, firefighters encountered some commercial fireworks explosives stored in a basement room in plain view. The homeowner lacked the proper licenses to possess those particular fireworks under federal law. According to *Camara* and later cases, the federal district judge noted that the caselaw seemed to require some exigent circumstance to allow a warrantless search but determined that seeping water might cause other damage or danger, and potential electrical short-circuit problems met the definition of an emergency or exigency. On appeal, the Sixth Circuit referred to *Michigan v. Clifford* where Justice Powell noted that:

> [t]he aftermath of a fire often presents exigencies that will not tolerate the delay necessary to obtain a warrant or to secure the owner's consent to inspect fire-damaged premises. . . . [T]he warrant requirement does not apply in such cases. For example, an immediate threat that the blaze might rekindle presents an exigency that would justify a warrantless and nonconsensual post-fire investigation.[29]

The Sixth Circuit Court of Appeal upheld the conviction and the decision of the trial judge that exigent circumstances permitted the search of the home for hidden dangers. The Court of Appeals particularly found that the firefighter decision to survey for hidden electrical damage and dangers justified the search of rooms that may have not clearly been affected by the fire. In most cases, an administrative search significantly later after a fire has been extinguished would have required an administrative search warrant, but in this case, the firefighters had never left the scene and were investigating potential hazards to the home occupiers following the fire, which allowed the court to recognize the exigent or emergency circumstances exception to administrative searches.

8. ADMINISTRATIVE SEARCHES: REASONABLE UNDER THE FOURTH AMENDMENT

To summarize, administrative searches trigger Fourth Amendment concerns and, in the absence of consent or other exception, generally require warrants based on probable cause. The quantum of proof necessary to constitute administrative probable cause has been reduced to the point that extreme specificity concerning either the reasons for the search or the precise place to be searched proves to be an easy burden to meet. The relaxed standards under probable cause are justified, since the administrative search is directed not toward the uncovering of criminal wrongdoing but toward furthering the health, safety, and welfare regulations of municipalities, the states, and the federal government.

9. INVENTORY SEARCHES: PROBABLE CAUSE NOT REQUIRED

An inventory search is a special type of search under the Fourth Amendment because it does not require, as its basis, the finding of probable cause. The inventory search is considered reasonable in the absence of probable cause because other rationales beyond finding evidence of crime support its use. When property lawfully comes into the hands of law enforcement personnel, they are under a duty of safekeeping the property until it is returned to the rightful possessor. As is often the case, property comes to the police within different types of containers. A purse or backpack may contain valuable personal property, a car may hold hidden treasures or stolen property, and these types of personal property may hide harmful ordnance, noxious gases, and other dangerous items. Once a person and property come under the dominion and control of the police, it is reasonable under the Fourth Amendment to inventory, catalog, and securely store the property. During this process, if additional evidence of the possessor's criminality becomes evident, generally this evidence may be used in a criminal trial. Since the police are not looking for evidence of crime but inadvertently stumble upon it while conducting a reasonable inventory, there should be no constitutional impediment to its use. The inventory search occurs most frequently when motor vehicles are involved or individuals have been arrested while in possession of personal property and accoutrements.

10. VEHICLE INVENTORY SEARCHES

Some vehicle searches may follow valid arrests of the driver or a passenger in accordance with the theory of search incident to arrest,[30] and other warrantless searches may be justified under an inventory search theory. The inventory search[31] stands on a different footing and is designed to protect the property of the arrestee from loss and the police from false claims of loss, as well as protect police and property custodians from any dangerous substance or ordnance that might be within a motor vehicle. Inventory searches have been approved in several cases, including *South Dakota v. Opperman*[32] and *Colorado v. Bertine*[33] (Case 8.2), where the search parameters were directed by a written policy. Where motor vehicles have been lawfully impounded, the Court approved the use of inventory searches as reasonable responses, even in the absence of probable cause.

In *Opperman,* the defendant had parked his car where it was unlawful to do so, and in due course police had it towed to an impound lot. Since the automobile contained some personal items, the officer who noticed the valuables had the car unlocked and, using a standard inventory form pursuant to the department's normal procedure, initiated an inventory. The officer discovered some marijuana in addition to some valuables. After the trial court refused to suppress the criminal evidence

CASE 8.2

Leading Case Brief: Inventory Search Policies May Give Officers Some Discretion as to Whether to Search and to the Extent of a Search

Colorado v. Bertine
Supreme Court of the United States
479 U.S. 367 (1987)

Case Facts:

A Boulder, Colorado, police officer possessing probable cause arrested Bertine for operating a motor vehicle under the influence of alcohol. The officer called for a tow truck to remove Bertine's motor vehicle and, pursuant to a written policy, conducted an immediate inventory search of the contents of the motor vehicle. The policy required the officer to follow standard procedures for impounding vehicles and mandated a detailed inventory involving the opening of containers and the listing of all contents. Inside the vehicle, the officer discovered a backpack that contained various controlled substances, money, and cocaine paraphernalia. The officer did not have probable cause to search the motor vehicle and its contents at the time of the inventory. The search conducted by the officer followed local police department requirements for a detailed inspection and inventory of all impounded vehicles but gave the officer on the scene discretion concerning whether to impound a vehicle.

Although the search was "somewhat slipshod" in the manner in which it was conducted, the trial court held that neither the inventory search policy nor the inventory search violated the dictates of the Fourth Amendment. Interestingly, the trial court held that the inventory search as conducted in this case *violated relevant portions of the State of Colorado constitution*. With a slight twist in legal theory, the Supreme Court of Colorado upheld the trial court decision but based the affirmation and the exclusion of evidence on the Fourth Amendment rather than on the Colorado state constitution. The Supreme Court of the United States granted Colorado's petition for a writ of certiorari.

Legal Issue:

Consistent with the Fourth Amendment, where police officers have some limited discretion pursuant to a departmental inventory search policy of either conducting an inventory search of an impounded vehicle and its contents or not impounding the vehicle, does such discretion leave the inventory search policy without sufficient standards?

The Court's Ruling:

An inventory policy may give police some discretion both as to when to conduct an inventory and as to the extent of the search necessary to produce the inventory without violating the reasonableness standard of the Fourth Amendment.

Essence of the Court's Rationale:

* * *

[A]n inventory search may be "reasonable" under the Fourth Amendment even though it is not conducted pursuant to warrant based upon probable cause. In *[South Dakota v.] Opperman* [428 U.S. 364 (1976)], this Court assessed the reasonableness of an inventory search of the glove compartment in an abandoned automobile impounded by the police. We found that inventory procedures serve to protect an owner's property while it is in the custody of the police, to insure against claims of lost, stolen, or vandalized property, and to guard the police from danger.

* * *

In our more recent decision, *[Illinois v.] Lafayette* [462 U.S. 640 (1983)], a police officer conducted an inventory search of the contents of a shoulder bag in the possession of an individual being taken into custody. [In *Lafayette*, the officer who took the defendant's backpack could have placed it entirely inside a property bag rather than conducting an inventory of the contents, including drugs.] In deciding whether this search was reasonable, we recognized that the search served legitimate governmental interests similar to those identified in *Opperman*. [In *Opperman*, police towed a car that had valuables clearly visible for the purposes of safekeeping of the vehicle and conducted a reasonable inventory search.] We determined that those interests outweighed the individual's Fourth Amendment interests and upheld the search.

* * *

In the present case, as in *Opperman* and *Lafayette*, there was no showing that the police, who were following standardized procedures, acted in bad faith or for the sole purpose of investigation. In addition, the governmental interests justifying the inventory searches in *Opperman* and *Lafayette* are nearly the same as those which obtain here. In each case, the police were potentially responsible for the property taken into their custody. By securing the property, the police protected the property from unauthorized interference. Knowledge of the precise nature of the property helped guard against claims of theft, vandalism, or negligence. Such knowledge also helped to avert any danger to police or others that may have been posed by the property.

* * *

The Supreme Court of Colorado also expressed the view that the search in this case was unreasonable because Bertine's van was towed to a secure, lighted facility and because Bertine himself could have been offered the opportunity to make other arrangements for the safekeeping of his property. But the security of the storage facility does not completely eliminate the need for inventorying; the police may still wish to protect themselves or the owners of the lot against false claims of theft or dangerous instrumentalities.

* * *

Bertine finally argues that the inventory search of his van was unconstitutional because departmental regulations gave the police officers discretion to choose between impounding his van and parking and locking it in a public parking place. The Supreme Court of Colorado did not rely on this argument in reaching its conclusion, and we reject it. Nothing in *Opperman* or *Lafayette* prohibits the exercise of police discretion so long as that discretion is exercised according to standard criteria and on the basis of something other than suspicion of evidence of criminal activity. Here, the discretion afforded the Boulder police was exercised in light of standardized criteria, related to the feasibility and appropriateness of parking and locking a vehicle rather than impounding it. There was no showing that the police chose to impound Bertine's van in order to investigate suspected criminal activity.

While both *Opperman* and *Lafayette* are distinguishable from the present case on their facts, we think that the principles enunciated in those cases govern the present one. The judgment of the Supreme Court of Colorado is therefore ***Reversed.***

Case Importance:

Inventory search policies that are routinely followed and that give police officers some discretion are permissible and consistent with the Fourth Amendment. A policy may give an officer some limited discretion in whether to make an inventory search and in the way the search is performed without violating the Fourth Amendment. The Court reaffirmed that inventory searches are reasonable when police conduct searches by following a police department policy governing such searches.

because it considered the search reasonable, the Supreme Court of Colorado reversed the conviction, concluding that the evidence had been obtained in violation of the Fourth Amendment prohibition against unreasonable searches and seizures. The Supreme Court of the United States reversed the decision of the Supreme Court of Colorado and found that the inventory search met reasonable standards under the Fourth Amendment as regulated by the police department's inventory search policy.[34]

According to the Court, the police procedures followed in *Opperman* did not involve an unreasonable search in violation of the Fourth Amendment. The Court noted that there is a diminished expectation of privacy in a motor vehicle and that police departments for many years have followed standard inventory policies when securing valuables taken into custody. The Court noted:

> When vehicles are impounded, local police departments generally follow a routine practice of securing and inventorying the automobiles' contents. These procedures developed in response to three distinct needs: the protection of the owner's property while it remains in police custody; the protection of the police against claims or disputes over lost or stolen property; and the protection of the police from potential danger. The practice has been viewed as essential to respond to incidents of theft or vandalism. [Internal citations omitted.] *Opperman* at 369

The *Opperman* Court approved the concept of the inventory search, which had been used by many police departments in many states. The principle was followed in *Colorado v. Bertine* (Case 8.2),[35] where a police officer arrested a driver for driving under the influence of alcohol. Inside the vehicle, the officer could observe visible personal property, presumably belonging to the driver or owner of the car. While waiting for a tow truck, and in accordance with local procedures, the backup officer inventoried the van's contents.[36] He opened a closed backpack in which he found containers of controlled substances, cocaine paraphernalia, and a large amount of cash. The officer was acting in good faith and attempting to follow his department's policy under the circumstances. The Supreme Court upheld the admission of the articles into evidence in *Bertine* because the police were operating their inventory search in an objectively reasonable manner for the purpose of protecting valuables and protecting police officers from harm.[37]

11. INVENTORY SEARCHES OF MOTOR VEHICLES: WRITTEN POLICY REQUIRED

An inventory search of a motor vehicle requires the police agency to have and follow an inventory search policy. In the absence of a policy regulating this process, individual officers would have unlimited discretion, and a particular inventory search could evolve into a ruse for conducting a general search. The policy regulating inventory searches must be designed to produce an inventory rather than permitting the inventory officer so much latitude that no standards exist.

Consistent with other vehicle inventory search cases is *Florida v. Wells,*[38] where an arrested driver gave police permission to open the trunk of his impounded car. An inventory search of the car revealed marijuana within a suitcase. The *Wells* Court approved the state court decision holding that the evidence should have been suppressed on the ground that the Florida Highway Patrol had no written governing standards or policy about opening closed containers found within motor vehicles. In the absence of an inventory policy, the officer could search wherever he desired, which could turn an inventory search into general snooping without any purpose or rationale. Without a written inventory search policy, a police search based on an inventory theory is deemed unreasonable, and the evidence seized is generally excluded from court. The *Wells* Court ruled that the evidence of drug possession should have been excluded from Wells' trial.

Under the vehicle inventory theory, performing a valid search requires the particular law enforcement agency to have a clear inventory search policy that police routinely follow. The policy must contain general guidelines for police practice and can allow a police officer some discretion concerning the scope of the search. Situations that may be fatal to inventory searches are the absence of an inventory policy, a failure to routinely follow the policy, or a policy that gives the inventory officer virtually unbridled discretion in the scope of the search.

12. INVENTORY SEARCHES OF PERSONAL PROPERTY

Although inventory searches usually develop where police have lawfully impounded a motor vehicle, the legal principle is not so limited. The principle has been applied to search the effects of an arrestee who was being booked into jail following his arrest. In *Illinois v. Lafayette,*[39] a police officer responding to a dispatch about a disturbance at a movie theater found Lafayette in an altercation with the manager. The officer arrested Lafayette for disturbing the peace, handcuffed him, and took him to the police station, along with a purse-type shoulder bag. Lafayette's shoulder bag arrived with him at the booking area inside the police station. The booking officer conducted an inventory search of all of Lafayette's personal possessions, including his bag. The inventory search revealed some cigarettes removed by Lafayette from the bag, and the officer found some amphetamine tablets within the packaging normally surrounding cigarettes. The presence of the drugs resulted in a charge of violating the Illinois Controlled Substance Act. The officer searched Lafayette's belongings as a result of the department's standard procedure to inventory everything brought to the jail by a person under arrest.

The trial court ordered suppression of drug evidence recovered from Lafayette's shoulder bag because it rejected the theory that the station house search could be justified as a search incident to arrest. Since the search had not happened contemporaneously with the arrest, it could not qualify as a search incident to an arrest. A state appellate court determined that the evidence should have been suppressed under Fourth Amendment principles because a greater privacy interest existed in personal items like purses and bags; therefore, the station house procedure could not qualify as a valid inventory search. The Supreme Court granted certiorari and reversed the state court. As the *Lafayette* Court stated the issue:

> The question here is whether, consistent with the Fourth Amendment, it is reasonable for police to search the personal effects of a person under lawful arrest as part of the routine administrative procedure at a police station house incident to booking and jailing the suspect. *Lafayette* at 644

According to the Court, since an inventory search is merely an incidental administrative step during the booking process that follows arrest, it constitutes a reasonable search under the Fourth Amendment. In determining whether Lafayette's rights under the Fourth Amendment were violated, the Court found it necessary to balance the intrusion on the rights of the arrestee against any legitimate governmental interests. The arrestee would rather have personal property remain unsearched and undisturbed to protect his privacy. On the other hand, it is not unheard of that individuals working within police departments have stolen property belonging to arrested persons. Sometimes arrestees make false claims about lost property. Arrested persons have also been known to injure themselves and other inmates or police with belts, knives, drugs, or other items brought into jail. Dangerous instrumentalities, including blades and chemical weapons, have been discovered within innocent-looking articles taken from arrested persons. When the interest of the individual's privacy is weighed against the needs and desires of the government to maintain a secure jail, courts have arrived at the inescapable conclusion that it is quite appropriate to conduct inventory searches of personal property under the circumstances, and such searches appear to be reasonable under the Fourth Amendment,[40] according to the *Lafayette* Court.

13. SCHOOL SEARCHES MUST BE BASED ON FOURTH AMENDMENT REASONABLENESS

The Fourth Amendment has been held applicable in cases where public school officials conduct searches and where law enforcement officials conduct searches in public and private schools. Children as well as adults have rights under the Fourth Amendment, but their rights have been deemed to be more limited than those of adults. Searches of children in school may fall into a variety of categories, since the goals of school officials differ according to the program being implemented. The goal of a search may be to discover recreational pharmaceuticals in a student's locker, purse, or backpack; other types of searches may be much more intrusive, such as where the school system desires to ensure that student leaders and athletes remain drug-free. The standards for reasonable suspicion[41] are normally a prerequisite to a search of the personal property of the public school student, but in many cases there is no individualized suspicion prior to a urine test for an athlete. Depending on how student lockers are assigned, a student may or may not have an expectation of privacy in the locker itself. If at the time of the assignment it is made clear to the student that the school is not relinquishing authority over the interior of the locker, the student may have no expectation of privacy unless there is a container within the locker, such as a personal backpack. On the other hand, if the locker has been granted to or rented to the student as a private place to store school-related items, the student may retain an expectation of privacy under the Fourth Amendment. If school authorities allow a drug-sniffing dog under the control of the police to walk down school hallways, this approach does not constitute a search[42] because the animal is detecting odors outside a particular locker and not searching inside the locker.

In an early test of the Fourth Amendment involving public school students, the Court held that a student could be searched by school officials (government employees) where there were reasonable grounds for believing that the student's possessions violated either a school rule or the law.[43] In *New Jersey v. T.L.O.*,[44] a student had been under suspicion for smoking tobacco in the school rest room. A principal eventually searched the student's purse on the theory that she possessed tobacco; that search did disclose tobacco, and a later, deeper search revealed marijuana, rolling paper, money, and a customer list. Following juvenile proceedings, the case was eventually heard by the Supreme Court of the United States to determine whether the search was reasonable under the circumstances.

The *T.L.O.* Court suggested a two-step approach that it would consider: first, whether the search was justified at its inception and, second, whether the search as actually conducted was reasonably related in scope to the circumstances that justified the interference in the first place. Since there had been a credible accusation that the student had been smoking in the rest room, the school official possessed sufficient suspicion to conduct a search of the student's purse. The items that were initially disclosed suggested the need for a deeper inquiry. The results from this case include the concept that school officials need not obtain a warrant before searching a student and that a school official's search of a student is justified where there are reasonable grounds for suspecting that the search will turn up evidence that the student has transgressed either the law or the rules of the school. Reasonable suspicion and reasonable grounds appear to be synonymous terms supporting the threshold of public school searches.

14. PUBLIC SCHOOL DRUG SEARCHES: DRUG TESTING OF ATHLETES

In a case involving no individualized suspicion, a school system decided to implement drug tests for all students who participated in interscholastic athletics.[45] In Oregon, Vernonia School District 47J determined that all athletes desiring to participate in a sport must submit to a drug test at the beginning of the season before playing. At a subsequent time, 10 percent of all athletes would be selected for random drug testing. In no case was there a requirement of individualized suspicion of drug use prior to testing. When one student's parents refused to consent to drug screening, the school prohibited him from participating in sports. The family filed suit, alleging a violation of the Fourth Amendment as applied to the states through the Fourteenth Amendment's Due Process Clause.

When the case reached the Supreme Court in *Vernonia School District 47J v. Acton*,[46] the Court first determined that personal drug screening constituted a search under the Fourth Amendment. The Court then had to determine whether the school district was operating in a reasonable fashion with respect to the drug tests by balancing the students' expectation of privacy against the needs of the school system. According to the Court, drug use had expanded within the school system, and students had become more unruly. In addition, it was believed that allowing participation in sports by students under the influence of drugs could result in increased injuries or even death. The *Acton* Court considered that public school students have some reduced expectation of privacy because they can be required to be vaccinated and to take school physicals prior to admission. The Court also looked at the privacy measures built into the drug tests; urine could be collected without a teacher actually watching the student produce it. The Court considered the need to reduce drug usage and the school's reasonable attempts under this policy to have drug-free athletes. On balance, the *Acton* Court concluded that the school district's policy was reasonable under the Fourth Amendment.[47] While public school students do possess a reasonable expectation of privacy, that privacy can be reduced where students wish to play sports, an activity that makes them role models. Students who do not wish to play sports generally are under no duty to submit to any sort of drug screen or test.

15. PUBLIC SCHOOL DRUG SEARCHES: SUSPICIONLESS TESTING OF NONATHLETES

Following *Acton*, public school districts had authority to screen sports participants for drug use and abuse, even in the absence of any individualized suspicion. In a later decision, the Court approved an extension of *Acton* to all middle and high school students whose districts required a drug test prior to engaging in any extracurricular activity. The Tecumseh, Oklahoma, School District adopted a drug policy that required students who were interested in participating in extracurricular activities to consent to urinalysis. The actual practice of the school district had been to test all the athletes engaging in competitive sports, but the policy allowed the district to test other individuals involved in extracurricular activities. Pursuant to the drug-testing policy, covered students were required to take a drug test before beginning an extracurricular activity and while participating in that activity; covered students also had to agree to be tested at any time when facts that created a reasonable suspicion of drug use.

In *Board of Education v. Earls*[48] (Case 8.3), several students and their parents brought a legal action against the school district under 42 U.S.C. Sec. 1983, alleging that their civil rights had been violated by the drug-testing policy and that the policy violated their rights under the Fourth Amendment. The students argued that while it might be reasonable to test school athletes, as in *Acton*, it was not reasonable to require suspicionless testing for other activities when the school district had failed to identify any special need or problem common to students engaged in nonathletic extracurricular activities. The federal district court found for the school district because the judge felt that a certain history of drug abuse in the school system created a legitimate cause for concern and could be effectively addressed by testing the students involved in extracurricular activities. The Court of Appeals for the Tenth Circuit reversed because it believed that the school district failed to show a serious drug problem among nonathletes engaged in extracurricular activities. The Supreme Court granted certiorari to consider the reasonableness of testing such students under the circumstances.

The Supreme Court, in *Earls*, cited *Delaware v. Prouse*[49] and noted that it generally determines the reasonableness of a search and seizure by balancing the nature of the intrusion against the individual's privacy with the promotion of reasonable government interests, but that the Fourth Amendment does not always require an individual level of suspicion. The respondent schoolchildren argued that they possessed a stronger interest in privacy than athletes because they did not have to disrobe in front of fellow participants. This argument did not have much effect on the majority of the Court, which observed that undressing in close proximity to fellow students is a frequent part of some nonathletic extracurricular activities and that any related distinction was not a cornerstone of the Court's decision in *Acton*.[50] Additionally, the Court noted that the sole outcome of a failed drug test was a limitation on that student's participation in extracurricular activities. Justice Thomas,

CASE 8.3

Leading Case Brief: Suspicionless Drug Testing for Public School Students Involved in Extracurricular Activity Permitted

Board of Education v. Earls
Supreme Court of the United States
536 U.S. 822 (2002)

Case Facts:

The Tecumseh, Oklahoma, School District adopted a policy that required all middle and high school students and parents to consent to urinalysis drug testing to participate in any extracurricular activity. In actual practice, the school board did not apply drug testing except for competitive extracurricular activities sponsored by the state sanctioning body. Several high school students who objected to the drug-testing policy filed suit in a federal district court, alleging that under 42 U.S.C. Sec. 1983 they were eligible for equitable relief, and they contended that the policy violated their rights guaranteed by the Fourth Amendment.

The district court believed that the case *Vernonia School Dist. 47J v. Acton,* 515 United States 646 (1995), controlled because of similarities in the drug-testing policy. In *Vernonia,* the Supreme Court of the United States upheld the drug testing of school athletes in the absence of any individual suspicion. Thus, the district court granted summary judgment in favor of the Tecumseh, Oklahoma, School District. The student plaintiffs appealed to the Court of Appeal for the Tenth Circuit, which disagreed with the lower court and found in favor of the students, holding that the drug-testing policy violated the Fourth Amendment. According to the Court of Appeal, a school district must demonstrate some identifiable drug abuse before imposing a suspicionless drug-testing program. The Court held that the Tecumseh, Oklahoma, School District had failed to show a drug problem among students participating in the competitive extracurricular activities offered by the school system.

The Supreme Court of the United States granted the school district's petition for certiorari.

Legal Issue:

Does the school district policy requiring student parental consent for suspicionless drug testing of all those who wish to participate in extracurricular competitive activities violate the Fourth Amendment prohibition against unreasonable searches and seizures?

The Court's Ruling:

After conducting a fact-specific balancing of the level of the intrusion of the Fourth Amendment rights of schoolchildren who participated in extracurricular activities against the promotion of legitimate government interests, the Court determined that suspicionless drug searches based on required student and parental consent did not violate the Fourth Amendment.

Essence of the Court's Rationale:

* * *

II

The Fourth Amendment to the United States Constitution protects "[t]he right of the people to be secure in their persons, houses, papers, and effects, against unreasonable searches and seizures." Searches by public school officials, such as the collection of urine samples, implicate Fourth Amendment interests. See *Vernonia* [*School Dist. v. Acton,* 515 U.S. 646], at 652; cf. *New Jersey v. T.L.O.,* 469 U.S. 325, 334 (1985). We must therefore review the School District's Policy for "reasonableness," which is the touchstone of the constitutionality of a governmental search.

(continued)

* * *

Given that the School District's Policy is not in any way related to the conduct of criminal investigations, respondents [the students] do not contend that the School District requires probable cause before testing students for drug use. Respondents instead argue that drug testing must be based at least on some level of individualized suspicion. It is true that we generally determine the reasonableness of a search by balancing the nature of the intrusion on the individual's privacy against the promotion of legitimate governmental interests. But we have long held that "the Fourth Amendment imposes no irreducible requirement of [individualized] suspicion." *United States v. Martinez-Fuerte,* 428 U.S. 543, 561 (1976).

* * *

Significantly, this Court has previously held that "special needs" inhere in the public school context. See *Vernonia, supra,* at 653; *T.L.O., supra,* at 339–340. While schoolchildren do not shed their constitutional rights when they enter the schoolhouse, see *Tinker v. Des Moines Independent Community School Dist.,* 393 U.S. 503, 506 (1969), Fourth Amendment rights . . . are different in public schools than elsewhere; the "reasonableness" inquiry cannot disregard the schools' custodial and tutelary responsibility for children. *Vernonia, supra,* at 656.

In particular, a finding of individualized suspicion may not be necessary when a school conducts drug testing.

In *Vernonia,* this Court held that the suspicionless drug testing of athletes was constitutional. The Court, however, did not simply authorize all school drug testing, but rather conducted a fact-specific balancing of the intrusion on the children's Fourth Amendment rights against the promotion of legitimate governmental interests. Applying the principles of *Vernonia* to the somewhat different facts of this case, we conclude that Tecumseh's Policy is also constitutional.

* * *

A student's privacy interest is limited in a public school environment where the State is responsible for maintaining discipline, health, and safety. Schoolchildren are routinely required to submit to physical examinations and vaccinations against disease. Securing order in the school environment sometimes requires that students be subjected to greater controls than those appropriate for adults. See *T.L.O., supra,* at

350 (Powell, J., concurring) ("Without first establishing discipline and maintaining order, teachers cannot begin to educate their students. And apart from education, the school has the obligation to protect pupils from mistreatment by other children, and also to protect teachers themselves from violence by the few students whose conduct in recent years has prompted national concern").

Respondents argue that because children participating in nonathletic extracurricular activities are not subject to regular physicals and communal undress, they have a stronger expectation of privacy than the athletes tested in Vernonia. See Brief for Respondents 18–20. This distinction, however, was not essential to our decision in Vernonia, which depended primarily upon the school's custodial responsibility and authority.

In any event, students who participate in competitive extracurricular activities voluntarily subject themselves to many of the same intrusions on their privacy as do athletes. Some of these clubs and activities require occasional off-campus travel and communal undress. All of them have their own rules and requirements for participating students that do not apply to the student body as a whole. For example, each of the competitive extracurricular activities governed by the Policy must abide by the rules of the Oklahoma Secondary Schools Activities Association, and a faculty sponsor monitors the students for compliance with the various rules dictated by the clubs and activities. This regulation of extracurricular activities further diminishes the expectation of privacy among schoolchildren. *Cf. Vernonia, supra,* at 657 ("Somewhat like adults who choose to participate in a closely regulated industry, students who voluntarily participate in school athletics have reason to expect intrusions upon normal rights and privileges, including privacy." (internal quotation marks omitted.)) We therefore conclude that the students affected by this Policy have a limited expectation of privacy.

B

Next, we consider the character of the intrusion imposed by the Policy. Urination is "an excretory function traditionally shielded by great privacy." *Skinner,* 489 U.S. at 626.

* * *

Under the Policy, a faculty monitor waits outside the closed restroom stall for the student to produce a sample and must listen for the normal sounds of urination in order to guard against tampered specimens and to insure an accurate chain of custody.

* * *

Moreover, the test results are not turned over to any law enforcement authority. Nor do the test results here lead to the imposition of discipline or have any academic consequences. Rather, the only consequence of a failed drug test is to limit the student's privilege of participating in extracurricular activities. Indeed, a student may test positive for drugs twice and still be allowed to participate in extracurricular activities.

* * *

Given the minimally intrusive nature of the sample collection and the limited uses to which the test results are put, we conclude that the invasion of students' privacy is not significant. . . . Additionally, the School District in this case has presented specific evidence of drug use at Tecumseh schools. Teachers testified that they had seen students who appeared to be under the influence of drugs and that they had heard students speaking openly about using drugs.

* * *

Given the nationwide epidemic of drug use and the evidence of increased drug use in Tecumseh schools, it was entirely reasonable for the School District to enact this particular drug testing policy.

* * *

Finally, we find that testing students who participate in extracurricular activities is a reasonably effective means of addressing the School District's legitimate concerns in preventing, deterring, and detecting drug use. While in *Vernonia* there might have been a closer fit between the testing of athletes and the trial court's finding that the drug problem was "fueled by the 'role model' effect of athletes' drug use," such a finding was not essential to the holding. *Vernonia* did not require the school to test the group of students most likely to use drugs, but rather considered the constitutionality of the program in the context of the public school's custodial responsibilities. Evaluating the Policy in this context, we conclude that the drug testing of Tecumseh students who participate in extracurricular activities effectively serves the School District's interest in protecting the safety and health of its students.

III

Within the limits of the Fourth Amendment, local school boards must assess the desirability of drug testing schoolchildren. In upholding the constitutionality of the Policy, we express no opinion as to its wisdom. Rather, we hold only that Tecumseh's Policy is a reasonable means of furthering the School District's important interest in preventing and deterring drug use among its schoolchildren. Accordingly, we reverse the judgment of the Court of Appeals.

It is so ordered.

Case Importance:

Under the Fourth Amendment, public school officials have significant discretion to require students who wish to participate in any activity beyond the required school attendance to consent to suspicionless drug testing as a precondition to participation in extracurricular activities or programs. The drug testing under these circumstances does not violate the Fourth Amendment.

writing for the Court, stated, "Given the minimally intrusive nature of the sample collection and the limited uses to which the test results are put, we conclude that the invasion of students' privacy is not significant."[51] The Court essentially found that a school system's interest in assuring a safe and drug-free educational experience outweighed an individual student's Fourth Amendment right to privacy. Consequently, the *Earls* Court reversed the court of appeals by rejecting its view that the Fourth Amendment prohibited drug testing under the circumstances; it also upheld the right of a school district to require consent to submit to a drug test as a prerequisite for participation in extracurricular activities.

When *Acton* and *Earls* are considered together, public schools may initiate drug-testing policies covering every student who steps forward to become involved in any optional school activity. The drug policy need not focus on individual suspicion in requiring testing and may appropriately involve random decisions on which students to subject to a test. These tests are, arguably, based somewhat on the consent of the parent or guardian and the consent of the student, since a prior agreement to submit to the drug-testing program remains an essential precursor to participation in an extracurricular activity. The Court has approved drug testing as a reasonable approach, consistent with the Fourth Amendment, to the perceived national problem of drug abuse by schoolchildren. As of the current state of jurisprudence, unconsented drug screening of all public school children does not appear reasonable under the Fourth Amendment.

16. GOVERNMENT SEARCHES IN THE WORKPLACE

While diminished expectations of privacy may inure to schoolchildren, the same reduced constitutional expectations have not traditionally applied to adults in the workplace. In recent years, to implement national policies to assure a drug-free workplace, both the private sector and governments at various levels have created plans and developed other programs to prevent drug-using prospective employees from being hired and to remove drug-using employees from service. As a general rule, the private sector is not regulated by the rules dictated by the Fourth Amendment. The same cannot be said for governmental employers, whether state or federal, because the Fourth Amendment has full impact on governments and adults generally have full Fourth Amendment rights. For a government program involving searches and seizures to pass constitutional muster, the search program must be reasonable given the circumstances. In evaluating the constitutionality of governmental personnel workplace searches, courts tend to use a weighing process whereby the interests of individuals are balanced against the needs of the governmental employer. If a plan involving search and seizure for government employees is to gain judicial approval, courts must determine that the search or seizure contemplated is objectively reasonable.

In an early case of suspicionless employee searches by the federal government, *National Treasury Employees Union v. Von Raab,*[52] the Customs Service, which assists in enforcing drug laws involving smuggling, embarked upon a plan requiring urine tests of selected employees seeking transfer or promotion to positions directly involved in drug interdiction or requiring the employee to carry a firearm or to deal with classified material. The results of the testing were not to be used in criminal prosecutions, but adverse results could affect employment and curtail opportunities for advancement. The labor union representing some of the employees filed suit alleging that the drug tests required for employees violated the guarantees of the Fourth Amendment against unlawful searches and seizures. The *Von Raab* Court considered the interests at stake and determined a warrant procedure was not a constitutional requirement. The Court evaluated the needs of the government, balanced those needs against the employees' loss of privacy, and concluded that the equities favored the government. The testing program contained general guidelines sufficient to alert employees when testing might occur and to guide the testing process to ensure that reasonable standards would be met. The government position appeared to gain added justification when the Court noted that a warrant procedure in this area would dissipate precious government assets. According to the Court, it is reasonable for employees who apply for promotion to particular positions to be tested for drug use in the absence of a requirement of probable cause or some level of individualized suspicion. From the thrust of the *Von Raab* decision, it is clear that governmental units may conduct drug tests on less than individualized suspicion so long as the government makes the case that its operations require drug-free employees.

17. GOVERNMENT-MANDATED PRIVATE EMPLOYER SEARCHES

Whereas *Von Raab* directly involved governmental workplace searches, the federal government decided to take additional steps toward a drug-free workplace for many American workers. The federal government moved to require some private employers to conduct searches of their employees pursuant to federal law or administrative regulation. Under some of these programs, the government required private employers to conduct drug tests on employees under certain conditions.

In one program, the Federal Railroad Safety Act of 1970 authorized the secretary of transportation to set standards for all areas of railroad safety. Because there had been some drug- or alcohol-related accidents, the secretary promulgated regulations that required certain private railroad employees to be tested for drugs or alcohol subsequent to reportable major train accidents. Both blood and urine samples were required to meet the goals of the drug-testing program. Employees who refused to provide samples were not eligible to work in their particular positions for nine months, but individual employees could request a hearing concerning the merits of their refusal to give the requested samples of body fluids. If an employee declined to give a blood sample, the regulations allowed the railroad corporation to presume drug impairment. All the drug tests were to be administered in the absence of probable cause to believe that an employee was under the influence of drugs or alcohol.

The Railway Labor Executives' Association and various of its member labor organizations brought suit because they believed that required searches and seizures on less than probable cause constituted a violation of railroad employees' rights under the Fourth Amendment.[53] The trial court granted summary judgment for the government, but the court of appeals reversed on the authority that the Fourth Amendment required individualized suspicion prior to drug or alcohol testing. The Supreme Court of the United States accepted the case and reinstated the trial court decision in favor of the government.

The Court determined that the Fourth Amendment applied to railroad workers who might be detained and required, for all practical purposes, to give a blood or urine sample. Although railroad workers are, for the most part, private employees, the Court determined that since the government required the use of drug tests, the railroads were acting in the position of the government, and for that reason the workers possessed Fourth Amendment protections. According to the Court, when intrusions are made into the body for the purposes of gathering body fluids, such conduct constitutes a search. The next aspect of the case that the Court was required to consider involved a determination of whether such intrusion could be deemed reasonable under the circumstances. The *Skinner* Court analyzed the practicalities of the situation and determined that a warrant system would not be feasible in this context because in the length of time it would take to procure a warrant to search body fluids, much of the evidence would be carried away from the body in the normal elimination process. The Court also determined that any requirement of individualized suspicion would frustrate the goals of determining drug or alcohol impairment. The *Skinner* Court held:

> We conclude that the compelling Government interests served by the FRA's [Federal Railroad Administration's] regulations would be significantly hindered if railroads were required to point to specific facts giving rise to a reasonable suspicion of impairment before testing a given employee. In view of our conclusion that, on the present record, the toxicological testing contemplated by the regulations is not an undue infringement on the justifiable expectations of privacy of covered employees, the Government's compelling interests outweigh privacy concerns. *Skinner v. Railway Labor Executives' Association,* 489 U.S. 602, 633 (1989) (Case 8.4)

The essence of the decision turns on the fact that safety in railroad operations is of such paramount importance to the government, to business, and to the general public that a search of those employees constitutes a reasonable approach under the Fourth Amendment, even in the absence of individualized suspicion and a warrant. The principle of this case may easily be taken to other areas of transportation, as well as to other businesses where there has been extensive federal government regulation.

18. AIRPORT, SUBWAY, AND TRANSPORTATION SEARCHES: GENERALLY FOUNDED ON THEORY OF CONSENT

For the past several decades, airplane hijacking and terrorist activity have dictated that persons boarding scheduled commercial aircraft within and departing from or to the United States be subjected to searches. In promoting aviation safety, the searches involved personal passenger screening, complete with searches of checked baggage and carry-on luggage. The routine search of luggage and passengers has been upheld as reasonable under the circumstances. As Judge Friendly noted in upholding the constitutionality of airline passenger searches:

> When the risk is the jeopardy to hundreds of human lives and millions of dollars of property inherent in the pirating or blowing up of a large airplane, that danger alone meets the test of reasonableness, so long as the search is conducted in good faith for the purpose of preventing hijacking or like damage, and with reasonable scope, and the passenger has been given advance notice of his liability to such a search, so that he can avoid it by choosing not to travel by air. *United States v. Edwards,* 498 F.2d 496, 500 (CA2 1974)

CASE 8.4

Leading Case Brief: Government-Required Private Searches by Employers Is Constitutional in Some Situations

Skinner v. Railway Labor Executives' Association
Supreme Court of the United States
489 U.S. 602 (1989)

Case Facts:

Congress granted the Secretary of Transportation power under the Federal Railroad Safety Act of 1970 to prescribe rules and regulations for all areas of railroad safety. The secretary determined that alcohol and drug abuse by railway employees posed an ongoing threat to railway safety. The secretary instituted regulations that permitted blood and urine tests for employees who were on the job when specified railway events and accidents occurred. In addition, the Federal Railroad Administration (FRA) adopted regulations to allow railroad companies to administer breath and urine tests to employees who violate specified safety rules, even in the absence of an accident. These blood, urine, and breath tests were to be administered without any individualized suspicion of alcohol or drug impairment. If an employee refused to participate in the tests, that employee could not perform regulated work for the railroad for nine months.

In the present case, the specific portions of the regulations required toxicological testing of blood and urine following every "major train accident" and after all "impact accidents" involving a reportable human injury. The results of the tests were to be given to the employees involved and the railroad.

The respondents, the Railway Labor Executives' Association and several labor unions, brought suit to enjoin the FRA's regulation on Fourth Amendment (and other) grounds.

The federal district court granted summary judgment on behalf of the petitioner railroad employee organizations, but the Court of Appeals for the Ninth Circuit reversed the trial court. The theory behind the reversal concerned the emergencies involving accident situations required swift testing without the requirement of a warrant. In addition, the Court of Appeals held that "accommodation of railroad employees' privacy interest with the significant safety

concerns of the government did not require adherence to a probable cause requirement." The Court of Appeals did not require the government to have any particularized suspicion or probable cause prior to testing any railroad employee.

The Supreme Court granted certiorari to consider the Fourth Amendment issues.

Legal Issue:

Where governmental regulations require testing of certain privately employed workers' body fluids and breath without either probable cause or particularized suspicion in an industry where impairment by drugs may have catastrophic consequences, does such a search violate the Fourth Amendment?

The Court's Ruling:

The Supreme Court found that the Fourth Amendment had application but that a government requiring a private employer to test its employees for drug usage was a minimal intrusion when conducted in a medical facility and that it did not violate the lessened Fourth Amendment expectation of privacy of private railroad workers.

Essence of the Court's Rationale:

* * *

We granted the Government's petition for a writ of certiorari to consider whether the regulations invalidated by the Court of Appeals violate the Fourth Amendment. We now reverse.

* * *

Our precedents teach that where, as here, the Government seeks to obtain physical evidence from a

(continued)

person, the Fourth Amendment may be relevant at several levels.

* * *

We have long recognized that a "compelled intrusio[n] into the body for blood to be analyzed for alcohol content" must be deemed a Fourth Amendment search. See *Schmerber v. California,* 384 U.S. 757, 767–768 (1966).

* * *

Unlike the blood-testing procedure at issue in *Schmerber,* the procedures prescribed by the FRA regulations for collecting and testing urine samples do not entail a surgical intrusion into the body. It is not disputed, however, that chemical analysis of urine, like that of blood, can reveal a host of private medical facts about an employee, including whether she is epileptic, pregnant, or diabetic. Nor can it be disputed that the process of collecting the sample to be tested, which may in some cases involve visual or aural monitoring of the act of urination, itself implicates privacy interests.

* * *

To hold that the Fourth Amendment is applicable to the drug and alcohol testing prescribed by the FRA regulations is only to begin the inquiry into the standards governing such intrusions.

* * *

The Government's interest in regulating the conduct of railroad employees to ensure safety, like its supervision of probationers or regulated industries, or its operation of a government office, school, or prison, "likewise presents 'special needs' beyond normal law enforcement that may justify departures from the usual warrant and probable-cause requirements." *Griffin v. Wisconsin,* 483 U.S. at 875.

* * *

An essential purpose of a warrant requirement is to protect privacy interests by assuring citizens subject to a search or seizure that such intrusions are not the random or arbitrary acts of government agents. A warrant assures the citizen that the intrusion is authorized by law, and that it is narrowly limited in its objectives and scope. [Citations omitted.] A warrant also provides the detached scrutiny of a neutral magistrate, and thus ensures an objective determination whether an intrusion is justified in any given case. See *United States v. Chadwick, supra,* 433 U.S., at 9. In the present context, however, a warrant would do little to

further these aims. Both the circumstances justifying toxicological testing and the permissible limits of such intrusions are defined narrowly and specifically in the regulations that authorize them, and doubtless are well known to covered employees.

* * *

By and large, intrusions on privacy under the FRA regulations are limited. To the extent transportation and like restrictions are necessary to procure the requisite blood, breath, and urine samples for testing, this interference alone is minimal given the employment context in which it takes place.

* * *

The breath tests authorized by Subpart D of the regulations are even less intrusive than the blood tests prescribed by Subpart C. Unlike blood tests, breath tests do not require piercing the skin and may be conducted safely outside a hospital environment and with a minimum of inconvenience or embarrassment. Further, breath tests reveal the level of alcohol in the employee's bloodstream and nothing more.

* * *

A more difficult question is presented by urine tests. Like breath tests, urine tests are not invasive of the body and, under the regulations, may not be used as an occasion for inquiring into private facts unrelated to alcohol or drug use. We recognize, however, that the procedures for collecting the necessary samples, which require employees to perform an excretory function traditionally shielded by great privacy, raise concerns not implicated by blood or breath tests. While we would not characterize these additional privacy concerns as minimal in most contexts, we note that the regulations endeavor to reduce the intrusiveness of the collection process. The regulations do not require that samples be furnished under the direct observation of a monitor, despite the desirability of such a procedure to ensure the integrity of the sample.

* * *

We do not suggest, of course, that the interest in bodily security enjoyed by those employed in a regulated industry must always be considered minimal. Here, however, the covered employees have long been a principal focus of regulatory concern. As the dissenting judge below noted:

"[t]he reason is obvious. An idle locomotive, sitting in the roundhouse, is harmless. It becomes lethal when operated negligently by persons who are under the influence of alcohol or drugs." 839 F.2d, at 593.

Though some of the privacy interests implicated by the toxicological testing at issue reasonably might be viewed as significant in other contexts, logic and history show that a diminished expectation of privacy attaches to information relating to the physical condition of covered employees and to this reasonable means of procuring such information. We conclude, therefore, that the testing procedures contemplated by Subparts C and D pose only limited threats to the justifiable expectations of privacy of covered employees. By contrast, the government interest in testing without a showing of individualized suspicion is compelling. Employees subject to the tests discharge duties fraught with such risks of injury to others that even a momentary lapse of attention can have disastrous consequences.

* * *

We conclude that the compelling government interests served by the FRA's regulations would be significantly hindered if railroads were required to point to specific facts giving rise to a reasonable suspicion of impairment before testing a given employee. In view of our conclusion that, on the present record, the toxicological testing contemplated by the regulations is not an undue infringement on the justifiable expectations of privacy of covered employees, the Government's compelling interests outweigh privacy concerns.

* * *

Alcohol and drug tests conducted in reliance on the authority of Subpart D cannot be viewed as private action outside the reach of the Fourth Amendment. Because the testing procedures mandated or authorized by Subparts C and D effect searches of the person, they must meet the Fourth Amendment's reasonableness requirement. In light of the limited discretion exercised by the railroad employers under the regulations, the surpassing safety interests served by toxicological tests in this context, and the diminished expectation of privacy that attaches to information pertaining to the fitness of covered employees, we believe that it is reasonable to conduct such tests in the absence of a warrant or reasonable suspicion that any particular employee may be impaired. We hold that the alcohol and drug tests contemplated by Subparts C and D of the FRA's regulations are reasonable within the meaning of the Fourth Amendment.

The judgment of the Court of Appeals is accordingly reversed.

Case Importance:

In special needs searches, where a statute or regulation provides the broad authority to conduct searches and where employees have been subject to a strong regulatory history, requiring drug screening without individualized suspicion or production of a warrant does not violate the reasonable expectation of privacy of the covered workers, given the compelling governmental interest in safety. This theory can be applied to similar work situations involving significant governmental regulation to allow warrantless and suspicionless searches.

Similarly, the Ninth Circuit in *United States v. Davis* held that airport security measures must meet the standard of reasonableness requirements under the Fourth Amendment. The court noted:

> An airport screening search is reasonable if: (1) it is no more extensive or intensive than necessary, in light of current technology, to detect weapons or explosives; (2) it is confined in good faith to that purpose; and (3) passengers may avoid the search by electing not to fly. 482 F.2d 893, 913 (CA9 1973)

Until recent changes in federal law,[54] much airport scrutiny and most passenger searches were conducted by employees of the airlines following federal directives. For the foreseeable future searches of airline passengers and flight crews will be conducted by employees of the federal government and a few contract screeners in small airports. When private companies conducted the screening mandated by the federal government, it was possible to view the searches as being conducted by private nongovernmental corporations, which, arguably, would not implicate the Fourth Amendment. The better view involves conceding that the Fourth Amendment has application because the federal government mandated passenger screening. However, each search may be deemed as consensual, since a person can avoid any search by deciding not to board an aircraft. Once a person gives consent by placing bags or carry-on luggage on the screening devices, generally the consent cannot be withdrawn. With the federal government takeover of passenger screening and baggage searching, an administrative search or consent theory should remain a valid justification for upholding reasonable airport searches.

With the present policy of screening airport passengers as they enter boarding concourses and with the posting of written notices that all baggage, personal effects, and persons are subject to search at any time after a person passes a certain point in the airport concourse, these searches fall under a consent theory or an administrative search rationale[55] under the Fourth Amendment. Passengers who have entered the airport but have not passed beyond security screening will generally not be deemed to have consented to give up their Fourth Amendment rights. Consent may be obtained with visible warnings to all persons who might enter an airport that their entry and transit beyond a particular point signifies consent to search by governmental agents. Airport security and search and seizure implications will undoubtedly be further litigated in the years to come as significant changes and alterations in Fourth Amendment jurisprudence evolve.

Following the 2004 and 2005 terrorist attacks in Madrid and Moscow and attempts in London, the government of New York City initiated a program to search some subway passengers who were carrying parcels large enough to conceal explosives.[56] The New York Container Inspection Program was designed to deter terrorists from carrying out plans and, to a smaller extent, to uncover any plans prior to implementation. Under the plan:

> the NYPD establishes daily inspection checkpoints at selected subway facilities. A "checkpoint" consists of a group of uniformed police officers standing at a folding table near the row of turnstiles disgorging onto the train platform. At the table, officers search the bags of a portion of subway riders entering the station.[57]

The overall operations are random concerning site selection, and persons selected are chosen by a supervisor as every fifth or tenth person, depending on passenger traffic and the staffing levels at a particular location. Police explain the program and indicate that it is voluntary, but a selected person must submit or leave the subway system. The officers possess virtually no discretion concerning how to search or which person to detain and search.

Several aggrieved subway riders filed a suit alleging, among other causes of action, that the search protocol violated their Fourth and Fourteenth Amendments and sought a declaratory judgment and an injunction. The district court held a two-day trial and found the New York City program constitutional and consistent with the special needs exception to the Fourth Amendment.[58]

On appeal, the Second Circuit found that the New York program met constitutional standards by analyzing the unique situation faced by society. A special need for the searches was established by the government as a method of deterring terrorists, and the container inspection protocol served as the method of implementing the deterrence of terrorists. The court considered the searches reasonable since they only targeted parcels large enough to hide explosives, the searches are minimally intrusive, and the individuals were free to leave the subway area without being searched. Thus, after a full evaluation, the Court of Appeals held

> that the Program is reasonable, and therefore constitutional, because (1) preventing a terrorist attack on the subway is a special need; (2) that need is weighty; (3) the Program is a reasonably effective deterrent; and (4) even though the searches intrude on a full privacy interest, they do so to a minimal degree.[59]

The limitations with respect to special needs searches, when the alternative to deterrent searches may be catastrophic terrorist damage, have yet to be determined. It appears that courts will recognize a special needs search where significant lives or property damage may be at stake and the program sufficiently addresses the danger in a way that seeks to diminish the threat.

19. BORDER SEARCHES: SOVEREIGNTY AND THE FOURTH AMENDMENT

Governmental agents' searches at the international borders of the United States are deemed to be reasonable because the federal government has the right to control the items that leave or enter the nation. These searches, which may occur at the border or at its functional equivalent, do not require probable cause or reasonable suspicion, and a warrant is not necessary. It overstates the case to say that nobody has any Fourth Amendment rights at the border, but it is rather close. Obviously, a strip search may not be conducted in a public place near the border, and body cavity searches require additional justification. While most border crossings and searches are rather swift, the duration of detention may be lengthy where there is suspicion that a person is a smuggler. In *United States v. Montoya de Hernandez,*[60] the subject was detained for about sixteen hours as a suspected alimentary canal drug smuggler. Suspicion arose due to the nature of her current travel plans and past travel patterns, all of which pointed to her as a probable drug smuggler. Medical personnel eventually retrieved cocaine during a rectal search pursuant to a warrant.

In addition to actual border searches, the federal government may set up fairly fixed checkpoints on roads leading to and from the border areas. At these locations, vehicles moving through the area are subjected to an intermediate level of scrutiny. The officers may ask routine questions of the occupants and evaluate their responses to determine if additional inquiries should be pursued. The questioning at the checkpoints may be conducted in the absence of any individualized suspicion of any occupant of a motor vehicle, but a more intrusive search requires probable cause or some other legal justification.

Since fixed borders and fixed checkpoints on major highways can easily be bypassed by determined individuals, courts have deemed reasonable the practice of roving patrols and stops by federal officials.[61] However, where governmental officials patrol border areas, the officers may stop vehicles only if they possess specific articulable facts and couple those facts with rational inferences, giving rise to reasonable suspicion that the vehicles may contain illegal aliens[62] or contraband items. Subsequent to a stop, federal officials may ask the driver and any passengers about their citizenship and whether the individuals are in the United States lawfully. Any additional detention or deeper search beyond the plain view requires either consent or probable cause.

The standard of reasonable suspicion sufficient to stop vehicles near the border was originally borrowed from the stop and frisk line of cases beginning with *Terry v. Ohio.*[63] The Supreme Court reaffirmed this legal theory in 2002 in *United States v. Arvizu,*[64] a case in which a border patrol agent developed reasonable suspicion to believe that Arvizu was engaged in illegal trafficking in drugs. According to the Court, when an officer engages in the process of determining reasonable suspicion, the officer should consider the totality of the circumstances in reaching a conclusion. Arvizu, the driver of a minivan, was making every effort to avoid any federal officer by driving back roads in a remote part of southeastern Arizona, specifically avoiding all checkpoints. Border patrol agents moved to intercept the suspicious vehicle. As Arvizu passed the officer's vehicle on the side of the road, he did not react to the officer the way local people usually did, which seemed odd. Instead of waving, the driver's posture was stiff, and he clearly avoided looking at the officer's vehicle. The children, riding in the heavily loaded minivan, had their feet on top of some cargo where their feet should have been. Since the driver took a route typical of a person who wished to avoid the Immigration Service officers in the area, the officer could look at the totality of the circumstances to conclude that reasonable basis to suspect criminal activity existed. This justified the initial stop of the vehicle in *Arvizu.*

In summary, when a person crosses the international border leading to or from the United States, no suspicion is required to conduct a search of the person or his or her belongings. More intimate personal searches involving body cavities require probable cause and a court order. At permanent checkpoints, officers may stop vehicles in the absence of individualized suspicion and visually observe the occupants of the vehicle. Only where probable cause matures, consent is granted, or some other theory allows a search may a search of a vehicle or of a person be considered lawful. Where the government observes suspicious individuals at some distance from the border, probable cause will allow a stop and search, but a vehicle may be stopped on less than probable cause, using the stop and frisk standard of reasonable basis to suspect criminal activity.

20. NATIONAL SECURITY AND ANTITERRORISM SEARCHES

In a variety of contexts and in numerous situations since the Middle Eastern Muslim terrorist attacks on the United States on September 11, 2001, Congress passed and the president signed a variety of legislative acts designed to enhance the internal security of the United States by giving additional tools and powers to federal law enforcement agencies. Consistent with these developments, Congress strengthened the Foreign Intelligence Surveillance Act (FISA)[65] to allow enhanced electronic gathering of foreign intelligence that might affect the United States. Electronic surveillance included the interception of wire, electronic, or radio communications that can be initiated by the president of the United States giving the attorney general permission to apply to a special FISA court for warrants to intercept foreign intelligence. The application for the warrant must include information that essentially provides the special FISA court with probable cause, has procedures for minimizing intrusion on innocent persons,[66] and details the activity that the federal agents desire to monitor or to intercept. When the FISA court issues the warrant, it must, among other requirements, indicate that the "target of the electronic surveillance is a foreign power or agent of a foreign power" and that "each of the facilities or places at which the electronic surveillance is directed is being used, or is about to be used, by a foreign power or an agent of a foreign power."[67] The order permitting electronic eavesdropping also requires that common carriers such as telephone companies and Internet service providers assist the federal agents in accomplishing the goals of the warrant.[68] In emergency situations, the government may initiate the surveillance and apply for the warrant to the FISA court within seventy-two hours for a warrant that has retroactive effect.[69]

The intention of Congress in enacting the FISA statute was to allow the federal government to gather foreign intelligence that included information that concerned national security or might harm the ability of the United States to protect the nation against a real or potential attack by foreign powers or foreign operatives. Such information could include sabotage or clandestine intelligence gathering, harm to the defense or security of the United States, or intelligence that might affect conducting United States foreign affairs. While targeted at foreigners, the electronic surveillance could certainly involve United States citizens who might be working for a foreign power against the interests of our national government.[70]

FISA initiated a process whereby the federal government could, in a more clandestine manner than traditional searches obtained from federal district courts, obtain warrants for electronic surveillance that basically met the federal constitutional requirements but provided a quicker and more streamlined procedure for obtaining the warrants. In another part of the federal code, 50 USCS § 1821, Congress made provisions for physical searches of foreign agents and their operatives. According to § 1821,

> "Physical search" means any physical intrusion within the United States into premises or property (including examination of the interior of property by technical means) that is intended to result in a seizure, reproduction, inspection, or alteration of information, material, or property, under circumstances in which a person has a reasonable expectation of privacy and a warrant would be required for law enforcement purposes.

Similar to ordinary physical intrusion warrants, federal agents had to apply to the FISA court for an order that approved the physical search following approval by the attorney general. Among other requirements, the application for the FISA warrant had to include a recitation of the authority under which the warrant was being sought and a statement of the facts and circumstances that justified the intrusion and search and affirmed that the purpose of the intrusion was to gain foreign intelligence information.[71] Where the judge determines that the application was authorized by the president and a federal official had applied for the warrant with the approval of the attorney general, the FISA judge may issue the warrant where the judge believes that foreign intelligence is being sought from a foreign power or an operative of a foreign poser and that the premises are owned or controlled by a foreign power or its agents.[72]

In one case[73] where the federal agents had complied with the requirements of FISA, as it then existed, and obtained an authorization to conduct a search of a home, federal agents conducted a physical search of a future defendant's private premises. Under the Foreign Intelligence Surveillance Act, the FISA court later authorized the FBI to conduct electronic surveillance of the defendant's residential telephone and fax lines. The federal district court refused to suppress the evidence or to apply the Fourth Amendment's exclusionary rule. In a prosecution for allegedly assisting the terrorist organization, Hamas, the defendant urged the trial court to suppress some evidence, materials, and documents the federal government obtained pursuant to the FISA search. As a general rule, where illegal searches have been conducted by government agents, the exclusionary rule has application to deter the future conduct of other officers who may be faced with similar motivations to not adhere to the Fourth Amendment. The trial judge refused to apply the exclusionary rule in this case, due to the philosophy of the FISA statutory process that outlines the procedures for conducting physical searches against agents of foreign powers. The judge believed that under the circumstances, no deterrent effect on law enforcement would be gained by excluding the evidence seized from the home pursuant to the FISA warrant. The judge, however, did conclude that the search was a reasonable one that squared with the requirements of the Fourth Amendment. As the judge noted:

> To be sure, FISA now governs the process for obtaining authorization for foreign intelligence physical searches in circumstances similar to the ones here, but that was not the case when the FBI searched Ashqar's [defendant's] residence. Accordingly, the FBI search, which complied with the procedures that were properly in place at the time of the search, falls within the foreign intelligence exception to the Fourth Amendment's general warrant requirement and the search, [and] . . . was reasonable in light of the FISA court's findings.[74]

Using similar legal theories, Fourth Amendment issues have been litigated over electronic eavesdropping by the National Security Agency (NSA) on electronic messages between terrorist organizations and their sympathizers who exchange information by e-mail, fax, and telephone. The president of the United States acknowledged the existence of a program that the NSA carried into operation. As the Sixth Circuit Court of Appeal noted,

> Sometime after the September 11, 2001, terrorist attacks, President Bush authorized the NSA to begin a counter-terrorism operation that has come to be known as the Terrorist Surveillance Program ("TSP"). Although the specifics remain undisclosed, it has been publicly acknowledged that the TSP includes the interception

(i.e., wiretapping), without warrants, of telephone and email communications where one party to the communication is located outside the United States. . . .[75]

Numerous plaintiffs in Michigan sued for a permanent injunction to prevent future warrantless interceptions, alleging, among other wrongs, that the government use of the ongoing interception program violated their First Amendment and Fourth Amendment rights because they felt that they were the type of persons whose communications were probably being warrantlessly intercepted. The NSA refused to reveal whether any of the plaintiffs had been the subjects of the surveillance, citing the State Secrets Doctrine[76] that contended that the information was privileged and could not be released. Even though the information that would have demonstrated the personal injury that each plaintiff may have suffered could not be forced to be given to the plaintiffs, the federal district court held that the Fourth Amendment had to be interpreted as demanding that all interceptions require warrants prior to making an interception and granted the injunction against the NSA from continuing the program. The injunction was not enforced pending the appeal.

On cross appeals by both parties to the Sixth Circuit, the court held that the injunction was improper because it found that no plaintiff could prove standing to sue the NSA, meaning that no individual plaintiff could prove that he or she had been personally injured or directly affected by the government's admitted program of intercepting international communications. No plaintiff could prove an individual injury because the NSA invoked the State Secrets Doctrine that prevented any plaintiff from discovering that the person had experienced an individual wrong. As the appeals court noted, "the plaintiffs do not—and because of the State Secrets Doctrine cannot—produce any evidence that any of their own communications have ever been intercepted by the NSA, under the TSP [Terrorist Surveillance Program], or without warrants."[77] The court also considered that where one of the plaintiffs alleged that he was afraid to communicate because of harm that could come to him in the future, such an allegation does not preclude that a plaintiff has standing to sue in an action for a declaratory judgment and an injunction. The court rejected the fear of harm to self or to the person with whom the person might be communicating in a foreign land as sufficient to demonstrate a real "injury in fact" and rejected any individual standing to litigate the issues. Ultimately, the Court of Appeals vacated the district court's injunction against the NSA and remanded the case to the district court with orders to dismiss the case.

Searches that produce evidence under the Foreign Intelligence Surveillance Act may be admissible against criminal defendants, even thought the primary goal of the act was to facilitate national security through the collection of foreign intelligence. The United States PATRIOT Act provided amendments to FISA in 2001 to allow interceptions where a "significant purpose of the surveillance is to obtain foreign intelligence information"[78] rather than when the purpose was purely foreign intelligence gathering. The interpretation that logically could be given to the changes brought by the PATRIOT Act to FISA is that evidence gathered for national security purposes should be usable in domestic criminal cases.

In *United States v. Ning Wen*,[79] a criminal prosecution for providing technology with currently useful characteristics to China without the required export license, the federal government procured evidence through a FISA wiretap that had been approved by the special FISA Court. Wen argued that the district court should have suppressed evidence from his criminal trial because evidence gathered for international security purposes should not be admitted in a domestic criminal court case. In Wen's case, the international investigation apparently did not result in any findings, but the information gathered was given to domestic federal prosecutors so that they could charge Wen under federal law. According to the Court of Appeals, the exclusionary rule designed to enforce the Fourth Amendment is to be used to assure respect for the Constitution and not to assure compliance with federal statutes or regulations. In this case, the evidence was lawfully gathered, and the standards that allowed the collection of the data were properly followed. In addition, the FISA statute does not require exclusion of evidence obtained pursuant to its terms.[80] Where Congress wanted to exclude evidence gathered pursuant to statute, it provided explicit terms governing exclusion.[81] The Appeals Court went further and noted:

> [T]here is scant support for suppression even when a particular intercept is unreasonable under the Fourth Amendment. For each intercept must be authorized by a warrant from a federal district judge. See 50 U.S.C. § 1803(a). This brings into play the rule of *United States v. Leon,* 468 U.S. 897, 104 S. Ct. 3405, 82 L. Ed. 2d 677 (1984), that the exclusionary rule must not be applied to evidence seized on the authority of a warrant, even if the warrant turns out to be defective (say, because not supported by probable cause), unless the affidavit supporting the warrant was false or misleading, or probable cause was so transparently missing that "no reasonably well trained officer [would] rely on the warrant." *Id.* at 923.[82]

The Wen case did not go to the Supreme Court and appears to represent the current state of admissibility of evidence seized pursuant to the various antiterrorism statutes and the way the federal government operates under FISA and the PATRIOT Act. Therefore, it appears that where evidence has been seized or intercepted by the federal government in its ongoing effort to secure the nation's safety from foreign terrorists and terrorism, in a manner that complies with the relevant statute, the evidence will be admissible in domestic criminal courts in the United States.

In August 2007, Congress enacted legislation, the Protect America Act of 2007 (PAA), that permitted the federal government to eavesdrop on e-mails, telephone conversations, and other electronic communication involving a source in the United States and a foreign destination, provided the foreign destination involves a person the government has reason to monitor. Until the act expired in February 2008,[83] it provided a legal framework for the surveillance that the federal government previously conducted without warrants. Prior to the Protect America Act, the federal government arguably needed search warrants approved by the FISA Court to eavesdrop on phone conversations and e-mail communications that originated or terminated within the United States. The law gave the attorney general of the United States with the director of national security the authority to approve the initiation of international surveillance rather than the FISA Court, but the act contemplated that the

FISA court would review and approve the procedures that the federal government followed after the surveillance has been conducted.[84] Under the PAA, if a resident of the United States became a primary target of federal eavesdropping, the law required that government agents procure a warrant from the FISA Court. Even though the Protect America Act has expired, President Bush has pushed for its restoration and for the act to become a permanent tool in the arsenal in the fight against international terrorism.[85] Congress and the executive branch failed to agree on provisions that would grant retroactive immunity from civil suit to telecommunication companies that cooperated with the government in making the intercepts under the PAA. Without this immunity, President Bush was not willing to have the PAA restored and has challenged Congress to reconsider its position.

21. SUMMARY

Special needs searches encompass administrative searches, inventory searches, airport searches, and some workplace searches where the search has been mandated by a government regulator or by a legislature. Administrative searches are based on the police power that is inherent to any organized government. The searches are designed not to discover criminal wrongdoing but to enforce civil governmental programs, such as zoning, fire, and safety rules, among other goals. Although administrative searches originally did not require the use of an administrative search warrant and were enforced by criminal penalties upon refusal, present Supreme Court interpretations contemplate the use of administrative warrants where the occupier of property refuses to allow a government official to enter the premises, provided that administrative probable cause can be demonstrated. Administrative probable cause, based on a lower standard than criminal probable cause, may be based upon the passage of time or the condition of an entire area or vary with the type of governmental program being enforced.

Searches of ordinary commercial and business establishments may require administrative warrants where consent is not forthcoming from the property occupier. However, closely regulated industries that have been historically heavily regulated by governments, such as the manufacture, transportation, and storage of explosives, alcohol, and firearms, may be searched without probable cause and without a warrant. The theory is that by engaging in businesses and industries that have a history of close regulation, persons entering that business possess a reduced expectation of privacy.

Inventory searches of motor vehicles that lawfully come into law enforcement officials' possession do not require probable cause to search. Case law indicates that such warrantless searches are reasonable to protect police from false claims of theft, protect property of those who have been arrested, and protect police from harboring noxious or dangerous chemicals or explosives or ordnance taken from arrestees or their property. To make a lawful inventory search of seized motor vehicles, a police agency must have a written inventory search policy that it routinely follows. Inventory searches of arrestees' personal property is generally permitted, even in the absence of probable cause to search, although most departments have written regulations that cover postbooking searches of property.

Searches of public schoolchildren and their property are regulated by the Fourth Amendment, but schoolchildren may be searched on less than probable cause. Where there is a reasonable suspicion to believe that a public school child possesses contraband or has broken a school rule involving possession of particular objects, school officials may search that person. Where school policy requires that parents consent to random drug tests for students who have stepped forward from the main student body to play sports or other extracurricular activities, those students may be searched pursuant to the policy. The extracurricular activity student searches need not be based on reasonable suspicion and may be conducted pursuant to a random, suspicionless decision to test.

The federal government may require suspicionless tests for workers who are involved in some types of private employment and in public employment. Private employment testing mandated by the federal government is covered by the Fourth Amendment and must meet a standard of reasonableness even in the absence of a warrant. Federal employees can be subjected to warrantless drug testing where their employment involves carrying weapons or other sensitive positions, such as drug interdiction. Promotion and lateral transfers for some government employees may lawfully trigger suspicionless drug testing that is consistent with the Fourth Amendment.

REVIEW EXERCISES AND QUESTIONS

1. What are some examples of special needs searches that fall under the category of administrative searches?

2. Why did the Supreme Court decide that administrative searches of residential property generally require a warrant or some other exception to a warrant before a government agent may conduct a search?

3. What is the difference in the warrant requirement for ordinary businesses and those businesses or industries classified as "closely regulated" businesses or industries?

4. Explain why a warrantless inventory search that is not based on probable cause is usually considered reasonable under the Fourth Amendment.

5. Consider the following situation: Police officers properly stopped a defendant's car and properly arrested him when he admitted to operating a vehicle with a suspended driver's license. The police proceeded to search the car for evidence of ownership, in accordance with a claimed departmental policy of performing such searches of cars that were being impounded, and found large quantities of cocaine. The prosecution argued that that the cocaine was admissible as having been found in plain sight during a legal inventory search. For an inventory search to be legal, the prosecutor must produce a copy of the police department's written inventory policy pursuant to which the search was conducted. No evidence of the existence of the policy was ever entered in evidence. Should the evidence of the cocaine be admitted against the defendant? Why or why not? See *Commonwealth v. Silva,* 61 Mass. App. Ct. 28, 807 N.E.2d 170; 2004 Mass. App. LEXIS 441 (2004).

6. Under what circumstances may public school officials search the personal effects of public school students? What is the legal standard that public school officials must meet to allow a search?

7. Airport passenger searches are generally conducted without a warrant and in the absence of probable cause. How can these searches be justified under the Fourth Amendment?

8. Has legislation under the FOREIGN INTELLIGENCE SURVEILLANCE ACT and the PATRIOT Act amendments given the federal government too much power to initiate eavesdropping without proper court oversight? Why or why not?

HOW WOULD YOU DECIDE?

1. In the United States Court of Appeals for the Ninth Circuit

While on routine patrol, a Kansas state trooper pulled over Robert J. Herrera to conduct an inspection of his pickup truck. The police officer believed that he was acting lawfully pursuant to a Kansas regulatory scheme that allows the police to conduct random inspections of some classes of commercial vehicles. Herrera's pickup truck did not qualify as a commercial vehicle that could be subjected to such inspections. Although the Fourth Amendment has been interpreted to allow warrantless administrative inspections of pervasively or closely regulated businesses in some instances, the searches generally require that the person have some notice that he or she is conducting the type of business that is subject to warrantless, suspicionless searches. Herrera's truck was not a commercial vehicle under state law because it weighed 10,000 pounds and commercial vehicles started at 10,001 pounds and heavier.

After stopping Herrera, the officer arrested him for failure to carry proof of insurance and conducted an inventory search of the vehicle. During that inventory search, the police officer recovered twenty-three kilograms of cocaine hidden among cargo in the truck's cargo bed.

Herrera filed a motion to suppress the drug evidence, as well as his admissions of guilt that he made to police after the officer stopped his truck. Among other theories, the government attempted to justify the warrantless stop as an administrative warrantless stop permitted under state law regulating stops of motor carriers. After the district court denied Herrera's motion to suppress, he entered a guilty plea to the drug charges, but reserved his right to appeal the trial court's denial of his suppression motion.

How would you rule on the defendant's contention that his drugs should have been excluded from admission against him because he should never have been stopped because he was not a participant in a heavily regulated industry and his truck failed to meet the standards of a commercial vehicle?

The Court's Holding:

"The Fourth Amendment's prohibition against unreasonable searches [still] applies to administrative inspections of private commercial property." *Donovan v. Dewey,* 452

U.S. 594, 598, 101 S. Ct. 2534, 69 L. Ed. 2d 262 (1981). But under the Fourth Amendment, an administrative search is very different from a search based upon individualized suspicion.

> A regulatory search . . . does not require probable cause as defined traditionally by the courts. In general, probable cause, and the less stringent standard of reasonable suspicion, require *particularized* suspicion—that is, the officer must have some articulable basis to believe that the individual to be searched or seized has committed or is committing a crime. In contrast, a regulatory search is justified if the state's interest in ensuring that a class of regulated persons is obeying the law outweighs the intrusiveness of a program of searches or seizures of those persons. *Seslar,* 996 F.2d at 1061

The Supreme Court has further distinguished a regulatory search of commercial property from "searches of private homes, which generally must be conducted pursuant to a warrant in order to be reasonable," holding that "legislative schemes authorizing warrantless administrative searches of commercial property do not necessarily violate the Fourth Amendment." *Donovan,* 452 U.S. at 598. The Court has recognized that the "expectation of privacy in commercial premises . . . is different from, and indeed less than, a similar expectation in an individual's home. This expectation is particularly attenuated in commercial property employed in 'closely regulated' industries."

* * *

[The Court of Appeals noted that operators of closely regulated businesses have a reduced Fourth Amendment expectation of privacy so that where the privacy interests of those involved have been recognized as weakened and the government's interests have been enhanced, a warrantless inspection may be reasonable under the Fourth Amendment.]

This warrantless inspection, however, even in the context of a pervasively regulated business, is deemed reasonable only so long as three criteria are met: First, there must be a "substantial" government interest that informs the regulatory scheme pursuant to which the inspection is made.

Second, the warrantless inspections must be necessary to further the regulatory scheme. . . . Finally, the statute's inspection program, in terms of the certainty and regularity of its application, must provide a constitutionally adequate substitute for a warrant. In other words, the regulatory statute must perform the two basic functions of a warrant: it must advise the owner of the commercial premises that the search is being made pursuant to the law and has a properly defined scope, and it must limit the discretion of the inspecting officers.

* * *

The problem this case presents is that Herrera's truck did not fall within Kansas's definition of a commer-

cial vehicle subject to these random regulatory seizures and searches. Herrera was not engaging in a closely regulated industry and, thus, would not have had any reason to know that his truck could be subject to a random inspection.

[The ruling of the appellate court noted that Herrera's truck was not subject to a regulatory search because it did not meet the regulatory scheme. The officer's stop of the truck was unreasonable under the Fourth Amendment and the evidence should have been suppressed. The Court of Appeal sent the case back to the trial court with instructions to vacate his conviction and sentence.] See *United States v. Herrera,* 444 F.3d 1238, 2006 U.S. App. LEXIS 9830 (9th Cir. 2006).

HOW WOULD YOU DECIDE?

2. In the Appeals Court of Massachusetts

A police officer driving a cruiser happened to run a computer check of the license plate of a vehicle that caught his attention, a light purple Dodge cargo van, that was headed into the Dunkin' Donuts lot a few vehicles in front of his cruiser. After the officer had completed his purchase at the Dunkin' Donuts drive-through window, he noticed the computer report indicated that the defendant, who was the registered owner of the van, had a suspended license. Suspecting that the driver of the van might be the registered owner, the officer initiated a stop of the vehicle to check the status of the driver. Defendant and a passenger, who had an outstanding warrant, were immediately arrested. The police arranged to tow defendant's vehicle. Pursuant to a departmental inventory search policy, the police searched the van. The police inventory policy was silent concerning what to do with closed but unlocked containers that police might find during an inventory search. Among the items on the floor of the cargo area were a crumpled Dunkin' Donuts bag that contained marijuana and a laundry bag that contained baggies. The officer opened the Dunkin' Donuts bag before there was any indication that it was anything more than trash on the floor of the van and opened the laundry bag in the same manner.

The trial court motion judge refused to suppress the evidence discovered inside the van, taking the position that when both occupants were arrested, the impoundment of the van and the inventory search were both

appropriate and did not offend Massachusetts law or the Fourth Amendment.

How would you rule on the defendant's contention that the inventory that police conducted violated the Fourth Amendment since it failed to adequately guide the officers in conducting an inventory search where unlocked and unlockable containers were involved?

The Court's Holding:

[The appellate court noted that the inventory policy on which the officers relied permitted the officers to tow the van from a heavily traveled road to police custody, where the inventory occurred. The appellate court observed that]

Officer Fucci picked up the paper bag, which had no "volume or weight," and "opened it." Inside, he found a small clear plastic baggie containing a green leafy substance that was later shown to be marijuana. Fucci handed the substance to Officer DeMoura and continued his inventory of the vehicle. In the course of that search, he also found a nylon laundry bag secured by a drawstring. He opened the bag and discovered shoes, clothing and some empty glassine baggies. Fucci turned the baggies over to Officer DeMoura.[86]

* * *

The propriety of the discovery of the marijuana and the glassine baggies turns on whether the written inventory policy at issue impermissibly leaves to the discretion of a police officer the decision of whether to open closed but unlocked containers, such as the Dunkin' Donuts bag and the nylon laundry bag. Preliminarily, we observe that the stop of the van, the arrests of its occupants, and the impoundment of the vehicle were constitutionally proper. Officer DeMoura's discovery that the license of the van's registered owner had been suspended did not involve a search in the constitutional sense. See *Commonwealth v. Starr,* 55 Mass. App. Ct. 590, 592–594, 773 N.E.2d 981 (2002) (operator of motor vehicle has no reasonable expectation of privacy in number plate required by law to be displayed conspicuously on vehicle). "While random police stops of motor vehicles to check licenses and registrations violate the Fourth Amendment [to the United States Constitution], see *Delaware v. Prouse,* 440 U.S. 648, 59 L. Ed. 2d 660, 99 S. Ct. 1391 (1979), random computer *checks* of number plates do not." Id. at 594 (emphasis in original). Once Officer DeMoura learned that the registered owner's license to operate was under suspension, he had an objective basis for stopping the vehicle and requesting that its operator produce his license.

[The appellate court reviewed the inventory policy and noted that it prohibited, generally, the opening of locked areas of a vehicle. Whether the discovery of the marijuana and the glassine baggies was proper must be based on whether the written inventory policy fails to address what to do with closed but unlocked or unlockable containers by leaving it to the discretion of a police officer. The lack of direction and complete discretion concerning the Dunkin' Donuts bag and the nylon laundry bag meant that the inventory policy was lacking in standards and direction.]

* * *

The propriety of the discovery of the marijuana and the glassine baggies turns on whether the written inventory policy at issue impermissibly leaves to the discretion of a police officer the decision whether to open closed but unlocked containers, such as the Dunkin' Donuts bag and the nylon laundry bag.

* * *

We find unpersuasive the Commonwealth's argument that the Bridgewater police department's written inventory policy, requiring that the passenger area of a vehicle be "thoroughly examined" and all personal property be removed and secured at the police station, necessitated opening the Dunkin' Donuts bag to determine whether it contained personal property, as opposed to trash.

* * *

Even broadly read, the Bridgewater police department's inventory policy fails to require the police to open closed containers. As in *Commonwealth v. Rostad,* 410 Mass. 618, 622, 574 N.E.2d 381 (1991), the inventory policy at issue is not explicit or obvious enough to guard against the possibility that police officers would exercise discretion with respect to whether to open closed containers, such as the nylon bag or the Dunkin' Donuts bag, as part of their inventory search. Here, the inventory procedure did not authorize opening of closed but unlocked containers at all.

[The appeals court reversed Muckle's conviction by reversing the trial court's decision because the inventory policy was unclear and gave too much discretion to police.] See *Commonwealth v. Muckle,* 61 Mass. App. Ct. 678; 814 N.E.2d 7; 2004 Mass. App. LEXIS 947 (2004).

ENDNOTES

1. 515 U.S. 646 (1995).
2. 489 U.S. 656 (1989).
3. See *Skinner v. Railway Labor Executives' Association,* 489 U.S. 602, 617 (1989).
4. 482 U.S. 691 (1987).
5. 532 U.S. 67 (2001).
6. See *City of Indianapolis v. Edmond,* 531 U.S. 32 (2000).
7. Ibid. at 47.
8. *New York v. Burger,* 482 U.S. 691, 699 (1987).
9. A Massachusetts court held that a police officer acting like an administrative searcher, who did not have criminal probable cause, illegally searched the subject's tack room where the subject stored leather horse harnesses and saddles. The cocaine he discovered should have been excluded from evidence,

since the officer had crossed over from conducting an administrative search to executing a criminal search, which required a warrant or a substitute for a warrant. See *Commonwealth v. Rosenthal*, 52 Mass. App. Ct. 707; 755 N.E.2d 817 (2001).

10. *Camara v. Municipal Court*, 387 U.S. 523, 538 (1967).

11. *Michigan v. Tyler*, 436 U.S. 499, 501 (1978); *Skinner v. Railway Labor Executives' Association*, 489 U.S. 602, 617 (1989), and *New Jersey v. T.L.O*, 469 U.S. 325, 333 (1985).

12. See *Marshall v. Barlow's Inc.*, 436 U.S. 307 (1978).

13. 397 U.S. 72 (1970).

14. 406 U.S. 311 (1972).

15. *Donovan v. Dewey*, 452 U.S. 594 (1981).

16. *United States v. Biswell*, 406 U.S. 311 (1972).

17. *Colonnade Catering Corporation v. United States*, 397 U.S. 72 (1970).

18. See *Hill v. Commonwealth*, 47 Va. App. 442, 624 S.E.2d 666, 2006 Va. App. LEXIS 16 (2006), and *Solem v. Courter*, 57 Va. Cir. 143, 2001 Va. Cir. LEXIS 326 (2001).

19. *Hill* at 453.

20. *Hill v. Commonwealth*, 47 Va. App. 442, 444 (2006).

21. Ibid. 445.

22. 359 U.S. 360 (1959).

23. At this time, the Fourth Amendment had not yet been incorporated into the Due Process Clause of the Fourteenth Amendment, so *Frank* was argued under due process protected by the Fourteenth Amendment. See *Mapp v. Ohio*, 367 U.S. 643 (1961).

24. *Frank v. Maryland*, 359 U.S. 360, 367 (1959).

25. 387 U.S. 523 (1967).

26. *See v. City of Seattle*, 387 U.S. 541, 546 (1967).

27. 412 U.S. 218 (1973). In determining whether a free and voluntary consent has been given under the "totality of the circumstances" test, a variety of factors have been considered. The factors "taken into account have included the youth of the accused, *e.g., Haley v. Ohio*, 332 U.S. 596; his lack of education, *e.g., Payne v. Arkansas*, 356 U.S. 560; or his low intelligence, *e.g., Fikes v. Alabama*, 352 U.S. 191; the lack of any advice to the accused of his constitutional rights, *e.g., Davis v. North Carolina*, 384 U.S. 737; the length of detention, *e.g., Chambers v. Florida, supra;* the repeated and prolonged nature of the questioning, *e.g., Ashcraft v. Tennessee*, 322 U.S. 143; and the use of physical punishment such as the deprivation of food or sleep, *e.g., Reck v. Pate*, 367 U.S. 433." *Schneckloth* at 226.

28. *United States v. Buckmaster*, 485 F.3d 873, 2007 U.S. App. LEXIS 10776 (6th Cir. 2007).

29. *Michigan v. Clifford*, 464 U.S. 287, 293 (1984).

30. For examples of searches incident to arrest of drivers of motor vehicles, see *United States v. Robinson*, 414 U.S. 218 (1973), and *Gustafson v. Florida*, 414 U.S. 260 (1973).

31. An inventory search may be conducted after an automobile has been lawfully impounded, as occurred in *Florida v. White*, 526 U.S. 559 (1999), where the officers, conducting a routine inventory search, discovered illegal drugs within the automobile.

32. 428 U.S. 364 (1976).

33. 479 U.S. 367 (1987).

34. *South Dakota v. Opperman*, 428 U.S. 364, 375 (1976).

35. 479 U.S. 367 (1987).

36. Ibid. at 369.

37. Ibid. at 376.

38. 495 U.S. 1 (1990).

39. 462 U.S. 604 (1983).

40. *Illinois v. Lafayette*, 462 U.S. 604, 648 (1983).

41. See *New Jersey v. T.L.O.*, 469 U.S. 325 (1985).

42. A "sniff test" by a trained narcotics dog is not considered to be a search within the meaning of the Fourth Amendment because it does not require physical intrusion of the object being sniffed, and it does not expose anything other than the contraband items. *United States v. Place*, 46102 U.S. 696, 706–707 (1983).

43. See *New Jersey v. T.L.O.*, 469 U.S. 325 (1985).

44. Ibid.

45. *Vernonia School Dist. 47J v. Acton*, 515 U.S. 646 (1995).

46. Ibid.

47. *Vernonia School District 47J v. Acton*, 515 U.S. 646, 665 (1995).

48. 536 U.S. 822 (2002).

49. 440 U.S. 648 (1978). According to the *Prouse* Court, "[T]he permissibility of a particular law enforcement practice is judged by balancing its intrusion on the individual's Fourth Amendment interests against its promotion of legitimate governmental interests." *Prouse* at 654.

50. *Vernonia School District 47J v. Acton*, 515 U.S. 646 (1995).

51. *Board of Education v. Earls*, 536 U.S. 822, 834 (2002).

52. 489 U.S. 656 (1989).

53. See *Skinner v. Railway Labor Executives' Associations,* 489 U.S. 602 (1989).

54. On November 19, 2001, President Bush signed the Aviation and Transportation Security Act, which established a new Transportation Security Administration under the control of the Department of Transportation. The Transportation Security Administration at present has authority for searching and screening airline passengers and passenger property in the United States. In a few airports, companies under contract with the Transportation Security Administration conduct passenger screening. See Public Law 107-71, 107th Congress.

55. See *United States v. de los Santos Ferrer,* 999 F.2d 7, 9 (1st Cir. 1993), where passenger airport searches were characterized as being administrative searches conducted for limited and exigent purposes.

56. *MacWade v. Kelly,* 460 F.3d 260 (2nd Cir. 2006).

57. Ibid. at 264.

58. *MacWade v. Kelly,* 2005 U.S. Dist. LEXIS 39695 (S.D.N.Y. 2005). The special needs exception covers extraordinary circumstances where ordinary law enforcement use of warrants and probable cause are impractical or impossible and a court is permitted to weigh the competing interests and the Fourth Amendment in place of the intent of the Framers of the Fourth Amendment.

59. *MacWade v. Kelly,* 460 F.3d 260, 275 (2nd Cir. 2006).

60. 473 U.S. 531 (1985).

61. See *United States v. Brignoni-Ponce,* 422 U.S. 873 (1975).

62. *Almeida-Sanchez v. United States,* 413 U.S. 266 (1973).

63. 392 U.S. 1 (1968).

64. 534 U.S. 266 (2002).

65. 50 USCS § 1801

66. Ibid. (h) "Minimization procedures," with respect to electronic surveillance, means (1) specific procedures, which shall be adopted by the Attorney General, that are reasonably designed in light of the purpose and technique of the particular surveillance, to minimize the acquisition and retention, and prohibit the dissemination, of nonpublicly available information concerning unconsenting United States persons consistent with the need of the United States to obtain, produce, and disseminate foreign intelligence information.

67. 50 USCS § 1805(a)(3)(A) and (B).

68. 50 USCS § 1805(c).

69. 50 USCS § 1805(f).

70. 50 USCS § 1801(e).

71. 50 USCS § 1823.

72. 50 USCS § 1824.

73. *United States v. Marzook, Salah and Ashqar,* 435 F. Supp.2d 778 (2006).

74. Ibid. at 794.

75. *ACLU v. NSA,* 2007 U.S. App. LEXIS 16149, 2007 FED App. 0253P (6th Cir. 2007).

76. Ibid. Footnote 2. According to the Sixth Circuit Court of Appeals, "The State Secrets Doctrine has two applications: a rule of evidentiary privilege, see *United States v. Reynolds,* 345 U.S. 1, 10, 73 S. Ct. 528, 97 L. Ed. 727 (1953), and a rule of non-justiciability, see *Tenet v. Doe,* 544 U.S. 1, 9, 125 S. Ct. 1230, 161 L. Ed. 2d 82 (2005). The present case implicates only the rule of state secrets evidentiary privilege. The rule of non-justiciability applies when the subject matter of the lawsuit is itself a state secret, so the claim cannot survive.

77. *ACLU v. NSA,* 2007 United States App. LEXIS 16149, 2007 FED App. 0253P (6th Cir. 2007).

78. 50 U.S.C. § 1804(a)(7)(B).

79. *United States v. Ning Wen,* 471 F.3d. 777, 2006 U.S. App. LEXIS 30613 (7th Cir. Wis 2006). Rehearing denied by *United States v. Wen,* 2007 U.S. App. LEXIS 5279 (7th Cir. Wis., Feb. 21, 2007).

80. See 50 U.S.C. §§ 1801 et seq.

81. The *Wen* Court noted, "Legislation may provide for enforcement via exclusion; Title III of the Omnibus Crime *Control and Safe* Streets Act of 1968, the principal statute regulating domestic wiretaps, does just that. See 18 U.S.C. § 2518(10)(a); *United States v. Donovan,* 429 U.S. 413, 97 S. Ct. 658, 50 L. Ed. 2d 652 (1977)."

82. *United States v. Ning Wen,* 471 F.3d. 777, 2006 U.S. App. LEXIS 30613 (7th Cir. Wis. 2006).

83. Protect America Act of 2007, Sec. 6(c).

84. http://www.nytimes.com/2007/08/06/washington/ 06nsa.html?ei=5065&en=4e05f95a4b60ac78&ex= 1187064000&partner=MYWAY&pagewanted=print 9 (August 6, 2007).

85. http://www.whitehouse.gov/news/releases/2007/ 09/20070919.html (March 4, 2008).

86. *Commonwealth v. Muckle,* 61 Mass. App. Ct. 678, 680, 681,814 N.E.2d 7, 10; 2004 Mass. App. LEXIS 947 (2004).

CHAPTER 9

Searches of Open Fields and Abandoned Property

Learning Objectives

1. Understand of what kind of property meets the definition of an open field.
2. Understand the definition of the curtilage and why there is a greater expectation of privacy within the curtilage.
3. Be able to give the rationale that supports the lack of Fourth Amendment privacy in an open field.
4. Know that the term, *open field,* may include any occupied or undeveloped area outside of the curtilage.
5. Examine why there is no expectation of privacy under the Fourth Amendment with respect to an abandoned property.

6. Understand why abandoned property may be seized by the police without a warrant or other reason and why a prosecutor can use the evidence in court without violating the Fourth Amendment.
7. Know that proof of abandonment of property negates any contention that the property has been illegally seized under the Fourth Amendment.
8. Be able to explain the effect that police misconduct may have on the admission in court of abandoned personal property.

Chapter Outline

1. Introduction to Open Fields: No Expectation of Privacy
2. Genesis of the Open Fields Doctrine: The *Hester* Case
3. The *Dunn* Case and Refining the Concept of the Curtilage
4. Expectation of Privacy and Abandoned Property

5. General Proof of Intent to Abandon
6. Abandonment of Personal Property
7. Abandonment of Motor Vehicles
8. Police Misconduct and Abandonment of Personal Property
9. Abandonment of Real Property, Land, Home, and Motel
10. Summary of Abandonment

Key Terms

Abandonment
Curtilage
Intent to abandon
Open fields doctrine

Personal property
Real property
Voluntary abandonment

1. INTRODUCTION TO OPEN FIELDS: NO EXPECTATION OF PRIVACY

The Fourth Amendment guarantee against unreasonable searches and seizures, which also guarantees that people will be secure in their persons, houses, and effects, does not generally extend to what has been described in legal terms as an open field. As the Supreme Court noted in *Oliver v. United States,* "[N]o expectation of privacy legitimately attaches to open fields."[1] Precisely what qualifies as an open field has been subject to significant litigation and does not necessarily meet the English language version of an open field, but the Supreme Court stated that "thickly wooded area nonetheless may be an open field as that term is used in construing the Fourth Amendment."[2] According to some courts, an open field can include fields that are enclosed by fences, such as horse fences, cattle fences, or barbed-wire fences. A field on which a barn is located may also be considered an open field, although the barn presents different Fourth Amendment search and seizure issues. An open field could also include a field in which crops have been planted, whether those crops are short or sufficiently tall to obscure an ordinary view of the field. Farm fields that have been posted with "no trespassing" signs and fields with fences with locks on the gates or fences topped with barbed wire qualify as open fields with respect to the Fourth Amendment. If police officers enter a field under such circumstances that the entry would be a trespass to land, the illegal entry does not mean that any evidence seized must be suppressed because there is generally no expectation of privacy under the Fourth Amendment in an open field. Since police may enter an open field on foot, they may also fly over an open field or overfly a curtilage with a fixed-wing aircraft or helicopter, so long as they are flying within lawfully navigable airspace.[3]

2. GENESIS OF THE OPEN FIELDS DOCTRINE: THE *HESTER* CASE

The starting point for the open fields doctrine begins with the case of *Hester v. United States* (Case 9.1) that arose in 1919 when federal agents charged with enforcing revenue laws encountered Hester and an associate dealing with whiskey on which the agents believed the taxes had not been paid. The agents trespassed on land belonging to Hester's father to be in a position to observe an illegal transaction between Hester and another man. According to the officers, Hester was transferring some untaxed whiskey to the customer, and it appeared that Hester retained possession of an amount of untaxed whiskey. According to the Court of Appeals:

> The evidence indisputably shows that the defendant was seen to hand what was supposed to be a bottle of spirits to one Henderson, who ran off and broke the bottle, and that the defendant also was seen to take a jug supposed to contain a gallon of spirits from an automobile, and run away with and break the jug, scattering the contents on the ground. Two revenue officers testified that the contents of the jug, which they judged of from that on the ground, and the remnants in broken particles of glass, consisted of blockade whisky. One of the witnesses testified he knew it when he saw it, and the other witness referred to it as "new corn liquor," "untax-paid liquor—blockade liquor." Still it is manifest, from a careful review of the entire testimony, that the witnesses used the words "blockade" and "untax-paid"

CASE 9.1

Leading Case Brief: No Fourth Amendment Expectation of Privacy Exists in an Open Field

Hester v. United States
Supreme Court of the United States
265 U.S. 57 (1924)

Case Facts:

A grand jury indicted Charlie Hester, who was then convicted of concealing untaxed distilled spirits in violation of federal revenue laws. Agents of the government walked toward the house where Hester lived with his father. Agents saw a man named Henderson drive toward the Hester house. Agents concealed themselves from view of the home when they saw Hester come out and hand Henderson a quart bottle. Hester got an alarm that something was amiss, went to a car parked nearby, and took a gallon jug from it, and he and Henderson ran away from where the agents were located. One of the officers pursued the two men, and fired a pistol that caused Hester to drop his jug. Although broken, the jug contained about a quart of its illegal contents. Henderson tossed his bottle as well, but federal agents recovered it. The jug and bottle contained what the officers, as experts in illegal spirits, recognized as moonshine whiskey. The other officer entered the Hester home, but after being told there was no whiskey there, left the home. In the yard, he then discovered a jar that had been thrown out of the home and broken, and the jar contained additional non-taxpaid whiskey.

The officers possessed no warrant for either a search or an arrest, so Hester argued that the evidence should be suppressed under the exclusionary rule and that by the agents taking the incriminating property, he was being forced to incriminate himself. The government did not contest the fact that the officers were on Hester's father's land.

The case came to the Supreme Court from the Court of Appeal for the Fourth Circuit, which had reversed the District Court on the ground the prosecutor failed to prove that the tax had not been paid.

Constitutional issues were argued in the Supreme Court.

Legal Issue:

Did the revenue officers make an illegal Fourth Amendment seizure of the jug and bottle and their contents when they trespassed on private land and recovered them from the ground where the defendant tossed them during flight?

The Court's Ruling:

There was no Fourth Amendment seizure since the agents took possession of the property after it had been abandoned by the defendant in an open field and had become property of no one.

Essence of the Court's Rationale:

The officers had no warrant for search or arrest, and it is contended that this made their evidence inadmissible, it being assumed, on the strength of the pursuing officer's saying that he supposed they were on Hester's land, that such was the fact. It is obvious that even if there had been a trespass, the above testimony was not obtained by an illegal search or seizure. The defendant's own acts, and those of his associates, disclosed the jug, the jar and the bottle—and there was no seizure in the sense of the law when the officers examined the contents of each after it had been abandoned. This evidence was not obtained by the entry into the house and it is immaterial to discuss that. The suggestion that the defendant was compelled to give evidence against himself does not require an answer. The only shadow of a ground for bringing up the case is drawn from the hypothesis that the examination of the vessels took place upon Hester's father's land.

(continued)

As to that, it is enough to say that, apart from the justification, the special protection accorded by the Fourth Amendment to the people in their "persons, houses, papers, and effects," is not extended to the open fields. The distinction between the latter and the house is as old as the common law. 4 Bl. Comm. 223, 225, 226.

Case Importance:

Abandoned property is the property of no one, and no person has a Fourth Amendment right in property of which he or she does not own or have possession. Special protections under the Fourth Amendment do not extend to property found or abandoned in open fields.

as synonymous terms for untax-paid spirits. This was the only suggestion in the evidence indicating that the spirits was not tax-paid.[4]

The Court of Appeals reversed the trial court's guilty verdict on the basis of a failure of the government's evidence to reach the burden of proof. When Hester's case reached the Supreme Court of the United States, different issues were argued; the sufficiency of the evidence that was crucial to the Court of Appeals decision seemed not to be the determining factors for the Supreme Court. The Court took the view that the evidence of possession of untaxed spirits was properly admissible because the federal agents had not conducted an illegal search and seizure by entering on the Hester property. The *Hester* Court determined that there was no expectation of privacy in an open field or in the abandoned containers in which the untaxed spirits were seized. Writing for the Court, Justice Holmes held the opinion that the special protections that the Fourth Amendment offered to people in their "persons, houses, papers, and effects" does not extend to an open field. With respect to the whiskey found in the broken containers, the Court noted that "there was no seizure in the sense of the law when the officers examined the contents of each after it had been abandoned."[5]

While the Supreme Court in the *Hester* case determined that there was no expectation of privacy in an open field, later court cases provide a definition and limitations concerning what type of property qualifies for treatment as an open field. In *Hester,* the property appears to involve a house that was some distance from the public road with fences on some parcels of the property, while other areas of the property do not appear to have been fenced.

In a similar fashion, in *Oliver v. United States,*[6] police received information that Oliver was growing marijuana on his farm, and they went to investigate. Without a warrant, they drove up to his farm and on past his house to a locked gate on which a "no trespassing" sign had been affixed. They walked around the gate and passed a barn and a camper and eventually found a marijuana patch more than a mile from Oliver's farmhouse. Kentucky State Police eventually arrested Oliver for manufacturing a controlled substance. The trial court conducted a pretrial hearing and suppressed evidence of the discovery of the marihuana field. Applying *Katz v. United States,* 389 U.S. 347, 357 (1967), the court found that the petitioner had a reasonable expectation that the field would remain private because he "had done all that could be expected of him to assert his privacy in the area of farm that was searched."[7] Oliver had posted the "no trespassing" signs around his farm and had locked the gate at his central entrance to the farm. In addition, access to the property was limited; the marijuana growing area was secluded and could not be seen from any public vantage point. The trial court ordered the evidence of marijuana manufacturing suppressed, citing the defendant's reasonable expectation of privacy under the Fourth Amendment. The Court of Appeals for the Sixth Circuit reversed the trial court on the basis that a property owner's common-law right to keep trespassers from intruding upon a person's land was insufficiently linked to a reasonable expectation of privacy that would warrant the Fourth Amendment's protection. The Court of Appeals sided with the *Hester* case and approved the continued use of the open fields doctrine, reaffirming the position that no expectation of privacy can reasonably be enjoyed in an open field.

The *Oliver*[8] Supreme Court cited the *Hester* case with the words of Justice Holmes: "[The] special protection accorded by the Fourth Amendment to the people in their 'persons, houses, papers, and effects,' is not extended to the open fields. The distinction between the latter and the house is as old as the common law" (*Hester v. United States,* 265 U.S., at 59. n. 6). According to *Oliver* Court, the Fourth Amendment has been interpreted to focus on a constitutionally protected view of what constitutes a socially reasonable expectation of privacy and not a subjective individual right of privacy. The only right of privacy under the Fourth Amendment is one that society is prepared to recognize as reasonable. The Court reaffirmed the validity of *Hester* by noting that, "an individual may not legitimately demand privacy for activities conducted out of doors in fields, except in the area immediately surrounding the home."[9] An open field fails to offer privacy for intimate activities that would be sheltered from public view if they occurred within a home. The Court found no social interest in privacy in most open fields that are devoted to agriculture or other aspects of farming or property classified as vacant land. For those reasons the *Oliver* court determined that there was no Fourth Amendment expectation of privacy in an open field, whether it was fenced, remote, locked, or inaccessible except by viewing it from the air. In many significant respects, the farm in *Oliver* was quite similar to the *Hester* farm, and the legal rationales proved quite similar, so the Supreme Court affirmed the lower court decision that the evidence could be used against Oliver in his trial for manufacturing marijuana.

While *Hester* and *Oliver* taught the lesson of what constitutes an open field, the Court in *Dunn v. United States* (Case 9.2) offered some additional suggestions about the limits of privacy in an, open field. Dunn's dwelling house had a surrounding fence that enclosed the area, known to the common law as the curtilage, where he could reasonably expect privacy under the Fourth Amendment. As a general principle of the common law, a person's home provides some reasonable expectation of privacy while the occupiers are inside the area that would commonly be fenced. Outside the area close to the home and beyond the area that might reasonably be fenced surrounding the home, land could legally be considered an open field, where the privacy of the owner or occupier of the field does not exist.

To give some additional clarity to the concept of the curtilage and the expectation of privacy that a home occupier might expect while remaining within the curtilage, the same general level of privacy that a person could expect within the home can be expected within the curtilage. Obviously, when neighbors or passers-by can observe the area from a lawful vantage point, the expectation of privacy that a home occupier might expect is somewhat reduced. In a North Carolina prosecution, *State v. Reed,*[10] a burglary and sex offense case, a police officer initiated a conversation with the suspect on his patio, which was connected directly to his house. The officer wanted the suspect to give a DNA sample, which the suspect refused. The suspect smoked a cigarette that he later flicked away to a pile of trash located on his residential patio. Without the defendant's knowledge, the officer carefully flipped the cigarette butt off the patio into a grassy common area outside the curtilage, where he later retrieved it for analysis. The defendant contended that the DNA evidence from the cigarette butt should not have been introduced at his trial because the evidence was taken from inside his curtilage, where he had an expectation of privacy. The prosecution argued that the defendant had abandoned the cigarette butt by discarding it and therefore lost his expectation of privacy in the cigarette remains. The reviewing court granted the defendant a new trial based on the officer's illegal seizure of the cigarette butt from within the curtilage of the defendant's home, where he possessed an expectation of privacy.

3. THE *DUNN* CASE AND REFINING THE CONCEPT OF THE CURTILAGE

While the *Hester* and *Oliver* cases taught and reaffirmed the lesson of what an open field is, the Court in *Dunn v. United States*[11] offered additional suggestions concerning the limits of an open field that indirectly explained the curtilage. Since the Fourth Amendment mentioned houses in its text as being places that are protected against unreasonable searches, and open fields have been interpreted as not offering any expectation of privacy, the extent of the house privacy expectation and the concept of where an open field begins presented challenges for court determination. A dwelling house that had a surrounding fence that enclosed the area, known as the common-law curtilage, provided the home occupier some expectation of privacy in the home and its immediate surroundings. However, the land deemed to be outside the area that would commonly be fenced around the home could be considered an open field.

In *Dunn v. United States*[12] (Case 9.2), drug enforcement officers initiated an investigation because Dunn had purchased precursor chemicals used to make illegal recreational pharmaceuticals such as amphetamine. After officers observed Dunn place the chemicals in a barn on his farm, the agents warrantlessly entered the farm through open fields and, in the process, climbed over some fences that secured the perimeter of the farm. As they approached the barn, officers smelled phenylacetic acid, a precursor chemical to phenylacetone, and heard a motor running inside the structure. The officers shined a flashlight into cracks in the barn and peered inside, where they observed what appeared to be a drug laboratory. Officers obtained a search warrant and returned to seize drug-making chemicals and paraphernalia that eventually convicted Dunn on several federal drug-manufacturing charges. The barn was approximately sixty yards away from the house and outside the traditional limits of the curtilage, if a fence had existed. The Supreme Court of the United States upheld Dunn's conviction on the theory that the officers had not violated any legitimate Fourth Amendment expectation of privacy that he may have possessed because the

CASE 9.2

Leading Case Brief: An Open Field May Include Buildings Not Used with the Dwelling House

United States v. Dunn
Supreme Court of the United States
480 U.S. 294 (1987)

Case Facts:

The Drug Enforcement Administration (DEA) discovered that respondent Dunn and another defendant appeared to be in the process of manufacturing amphetamine and phenylacetone in a barn on Dunn's property. In addition, it appeared that Dunn was in possession of amphetamine tablets with intent to distribute. With the goal of ascertaining the truth and developing probable cause for a search warrant, DEA agents entered respondent's 198-acre ranch. The agents crossed a perimeter fence and an interior fence, where they were able to detect an odor of phenylacetic acid emanating from the barn. The officers proceeded to the larger barn, which required crossing Dunn's barbed-wire fence and his wooden fence.

When in front of one of the barn's entrances, the officers peered inside the barn and observed what seemed to be a phenylacetone laboratory. The officers returned twice more but never entered the barn prior to executing a search warrant issued on the basis of their observations. An additional source of probable cause, on which the judge who issued the search warrant relied, arose from two locating beepers originally legally installed in cans of the precursor chemicals that ended up at the ranch.

Although the District Court refused to suppress the evidence seized pursuant to the search warrant, the Court of Appeals concluded that the warrant had been based on the agents' illegal entry on the respondent's property. Following a variety of appellate maneuvers, the Supreme Court granted certiorari to consider the issue of whether respondent had an expectation of privacy in fields outside the curtilage of his ranch home sufficient to prevent officers from walking in his field to look at his barn interior. (At common law the curtilage included the area around a

dwelling house that might actually be fenced or could reasonably be fenced but was not actually fenced.)

Legal Issue:

Where a barn and other outbuildings are located in a field beyond the curtilage of a home, does the occupier of the land have an expectation of privacy in those fields absent a special effort to prevent observation or walking through the fields?

The Court's Ruling:

Where a building rests within a field outside the curtilage of a home and is not fenced so as to enclose the home and where police have information that the building was not being used intimately with the dwelling home, the occupier of the land has no expectation of privacy in the field. Generally speaking, there is little Fourth Amendment expectation of privacy in an open field, even if it is fenced.

Essence of the Court's Rationale:

* * *

II

The curtilage concept originated at common law to extend to the area immediately surrounding a dwelling house the same protection under the law of burglary as was afforded the house itself. The concept plays a part, however, in interpreting the reach of the Fourth Amendment. *Hester v. United States,* 265 U.S. 57, 59 (1924), held that the Fourth Amendment's protection accorded "persons, houses, papers and effects" did not extend to the open fields, the Court

(continued)

observing that the distinction between a person's house and open fields "is as old as the common law. 4 Bl. Comm. 223, 225, 226."

* * *

Drawing upon the Court's own cases and the cumulative experience of the lower courts that have grappled with the task of defining the extent of a home's curtilage, we believe that curtilage questions should be resolved with particular reference to four factors: the proximity of the area claimed to be curtilage to the home, whether the area is included within an enclosure surrounding the home, the nature of the uses to which the area is put, and the steps taken by the resident to protect the area from observation by people passing by. [Citations omitted.]

* * *

First. The record discloses that the barn was located 50 yards from the fence surrounding the house, and 60 yards from the house itself. Standing in isolation, this substantial distance supports no inference that the barn should be treated as an adjunct of the house.

Second. It is also significant that respondent's barn did not lie within the area surrounding the house that was enclosed by a fence. We noted in *Oliver, supra,* that

> "for most homes, the boundaries of the curtilage will be clearly marked; and the conception defining the curtilage—as the area around the home to which the activity of home life extends—is a familiar one easily understood from our daily experience." 466 U.S., at 182, n. 12.

Viewing the physical layout of respondent's ranch in its entirety, see 782 F.2d, at 1228, it is plain that the fence surrounding the residence serves to demark a specific area of land immediately adjacent to the house that is readily identifiable as part and parcel of the house. Conversely, the barn—the front portion itself enclosed by a fence—and the area immediately surrounding it, stands out as a distinct portion of respondent's ranch, quite separate from the residence.

Third. It is especially significant that the law enforcement officials possessed objective data indicating that the barn was not being used for intimate activities of the home. The aerial photographs showed that the truck Carpenter had been driving that contained the container of phenylacetic acid was backed up to the barn, "apparently," in the words of the

Court of Appeals, "for the unloading of its contents." 674 F.2d, at 1096. When on respondent's property, the officers' suspicion was further directed toward the barn because of "a very strong odor" of phenylacetic acid. App. 165. As the DEA agent approached the barn, he "could hear a motor running, like a pump motor of some sort . . ." *Id.,* at 17. Furthermore, the officers detected an "extremely strong" odor of phenylacetic acid coming from a small crack in the wall of the barn. *Ibid.* Finally, as the officers were standing in front of the barn, immediately prior to looking into its interior through the netting material, "the smell was very, very strong . . . [and the officers] could hear the motor running very loudly." *Id.,* at 18. When considered together, the above facts indicated to the officers that the use to which the barn was being put could not fairly be characterized as so associated with the activities and privacies of domestic life that the officers should have deemed the barn as part of respondent's home.

Fourth. Respondent did little to protect the barn area from observation by those standing in the open fields. Nothing in the record suggests that the various interior fences on respondent's property had any function other than that of the typical ranch fence; the fences were designed and constructed to corral livestock, not to prevent persons from observing what lay inside the enclosed areas.

III

* * *

Oliver reaffirmed the precept, established in *Hester,* that an open field is neither a "house" nor an "effect," and, therefore,

> "the government's intrusion upon the open fields is not one of the 'unreasonable searches' proscribed by the text of the Fourth Amendment." 466 U.S., at 177.

The Court expressly rejected the argument that the erection of fences on an open field—at least of the variety involved in those cases and in the present case—creates a constitutionally protected privacy interest. *Id.,* at 182–193.

"[T]he term 'open fields' may include any unoccupied or undeveloped area outside of the curtilage. An open field need be neither 'open' nor a 'field' as those terms are used in common speech." *Id.* at 180, n. 11

* * *

Under *Oliver* and *Hester,* there is no constitutional difference between police observations conducted while in a public place and while standing in the open fields.

* * *

The officers lawfully viewed the interior of respondent's barn, and their observations were properly considered by the Magistrate in issuing a search warrant for respondent's premises. Accordingly, the judgment of the Court of Appeals is reversed.

Case Importance:

Under the Fourth Amendment, an open field, even if fenced, is neither a house nor an effect for which an expectation of privacy is reasonable to expect unless the occupier of the property takes extraordinary efforts to prevent observation by other persons.

barn was located in an open field beyond the scope of the curtilage and the police officers had merely walked through an area of the farm where Dunn had no expectation of privacy. Dunn had taken no special action to secure the farm fields beyond farm fencing, and he had taken no steps to secure the barn from prying eyes. In addition, the officers possessed objective knowledge that demonstrated the barn was not being used for intimate activities associated with the home. Had the barn been extremely close to the house within or encroaching on the curtilage, Dunn might have had a stronger argument about an expectation of privacy.

In more modern usage, the curtilage would include the backyard of a suburban house that might encompass a barbecue or picnic area, a deck, and a hot tub or a swimming pool. On some small suburban lots, concrete block walls or wood fences might provide privacy and indicate the extent of the curtilage. The Supreme Court of Georgia referred to the curtilage as encompassing the grounds of a particular address and including its gardens, barns, and buildings.[13] Chief Justice Burger, in explaining the basis for the curtilage expectation of privacy, noted, "The protection afforded the curtilage is essentially a protection of families and personal privacy in an area intimately linked to the home, both physically and psychologically, where privacy expectations are most heightened."[14] In explaining the curtilage, the United States Supreme Court "recognized that the Fourth Amendment protects the curtilage of a house and that the extent of the curtilage is determined by factors that bear upon whether an individual reasonably may expect that the area in question should be treated as the home itself."[15]

After the *Hester* case and most especially following the *Dunn* case, the open fields doctrine demonstrated that, as a strong general rule, no one has an expectation of privacy in land that is not used intimately in conjunction with a dwelling house. No warrant is needed to search an open field, and any evidence discovered will be admissible against a person who owns or controls the open field unless some rule of evidence requires its exclusion.

4. EXPECTATION OF PRIVACY AND ABANDONED PROPERTY

As a general rule, a person who has given up any claim to ownership or possession of real property or personal property has no claim to any right or expectation of privacy with respect to that property. "There is a very long line of caselaw establishing the principle that police may freely seize and search abandoned items, such as items thrown from vehicles during a police chase, items placed in trash containers, or items dropped by a pedestrian while fleeing from the police."[16] As one court noted, "An expectation of privacy is the threshold standing requirement that a defendant must establish before a court can proceed with any Fourth Amendment analysis."[17] A person who abandons property becomes a legal stranger to the property and, for Fourth Amendment purposes, has no future legal interest concerning what is done to or with the property.

Demonstrative of this consequences of abandonment is a case[18] where a female driver of a vehicle called police to have them remove from her car a man she did not know who would not leave. When police arrived, they required the subject to exit the motor vehicle and conducted a frisk of the intoxicated subject. Although police discovered no weapon, they observed a firearm on the floorboard of the vehicle where the subject had been sitting. The subject faced the situation that if he exited the car with a concealed weapon, the police would find it during a frisk but if he left it the vehicle, police would probably see it there and connect him to it. If he kept it on his person, he could make Fourth Amendment arguments for suppression if the search had errors, but if he left it in the vehicle, his Fourth Amendment rights in the gun were extinguished by virtue of his abandonment of the property. The trial court admitted the gun against him because he had abandoned it in the car.

When a person determines that personal property has no future use and ends his or her connection to it, it becomes the property of no one until a new owner or possessor asserts some level of property interest in it. Individuals who abandon personal property and have no present connection to it have no reason to complain if a police officer takes a look at it, picks it up, or carefully examines the object, even if it may implicate persons in crime.[19] For example, in a federal prosecution in Maryland,[20] the police received the defendant's girlfriend's permission to search their home, including the attic. When police discovered a gun case that had been in the attic, they removed it from the premises without a complaint from the girlfriend. When the police questioned the defendant about ownership of the gun case and its contents, he denied that he was the owner, and the police opened the case to reveal a rifle that was later used in evidence against him. According to the suppression judge, when the defendant disclaimed any ownership to the gun case and its contents, he abandoned any standing to contest the legality of the police search of the gun case. The court cited with approval a First Circuit Court of Appeal case that noted:

> One who abandons ownership forfeits any entitlement to rights of privacy in the abandoned property . . . and one who disclaims ownership is likely to be found to have abandoned ownership. . . . Phrased another way, disclaiming ownership is tantamount to declaring indifference, and thus negates the existence of any privacy concern in a container's contents.[21]

The appellate court upheld the trial court's admission of the firearm because the defendant had abandoned ownership and had no complaint concerning the search of the gun case and admission into evidence of its contents. In another firearm case,[22] an arrestee attempted to transfer ownership of his personal property to his girlfriend because he was a convicted felon and some of his personal property included firearms that he was not eligible to own. When police conducted a warrantless search of his leased apartment with the assistance of a landlord, they may have violated his girlfriend's Fourth Amendment rights, but they did not infringe upon his Fourth Amendment rights in the personal property because he had by a letter to his girlfriend abandoned ownership of the firearms and had also indicated that he had no intention of returning to the apartment he once shared with his girlfriend.

With respect to real property, although a person may be still listed as the owner of record, it is still possible to abandon the property and intend to have no future connection to it. With real property, this might be evidenced by vacating the property with no intention to return, failing to pay property tax on it combined with leaving the property without a future intent to deal with it at any time, vacating the premises and returning the key to the landlord or motel operator, or failing to pay rent on a motel room. Similarly, a person who enters an abandoned house for the purposes of dividing or distributing drugs and does not live there does not generally have an expectation of privacy within the residence. In one case,[23] police entered a dilapidated residential structure that had no doors, had a window broken out, and had no utility service. Inside they found a brick of cocaine and marijuana hidden in a ripped and dirty couch. Police did not violate any Fourth Amendment privacy expectation of an interloper who was in the house when police approached him on the second floor of the house. The defendant tossed an object that contained a controlled substance, which the officers retrieved. The appellate court ruled that the defendant interloper possessed no reasonable expectation of privacy in the abandoned residence on either the first or second floor because he was a mere squatter in an abandoned building.

However, using an alias in sending a package containing drugs through an express company fails to indicate an abandonment of the package under the Fourth Amendment.[24] In one case, the defendant, who had concerns over a package of drugs he wanted delivered by an express company, made four or five phone calls to the express company concerning the location of the package with reference to its tracking number. Conduct demonstrating an intention not to abandon included obtaining a tracking number that allowed the defendant to use the Internet to follow the package's progress toward its destination, which objectively demonstrated a continuing interest in the parcel. The phone calls and other information made the shipping company suspicious, so an employee called police, who warrantlessly opened the package, revealing marijuana. The trial court suppressed the marijuana on the theory that using an alias did not in itself indicate abandonment since most courts that have ruled on the subject indicate that using an alias does not reduce one's expectation of privacy in a package, especially since the defendant clearly indicated a continuing interest in the package. The defendant retained an expectation of privacy in the package because his conduct and concern for the package did not indicate abandonment.

5. GENERAL PROOF OF INTENT TO ABANDON

As a strong general rule, abandoned property may be seized by police, and the prosecution can use the property for evidentiary purposes. For property to be abandoned, there must be proof that the owner or possessor intended to give up all title,[25] interest, claim, and/or right to possess. Whether property has truly been abandoned with the proper intention is generally determined by looking at the surrounding circumstances under which it appeared the property was abandoned. Merely giving property to another person to hold or store does not indicate an intent to abandon the property,[26] but leaving property with no intention to return to the property may indicate abandonment. When police contend that personal property has been abandoned, the "determination is made based on the objective facts available to the officers at the time they recovered the evidence, taking into account the totality of the circumstances."[27]

In cases involving personal property, the human conduct of placing an article on a trash can, throwing property out of a car window, or leaving the remains of a meal at a restaurant may be so obvious that no long analysis is required. The simple act of placing articles in a personal trash can and leaving the trash can at the curb of one's residence generally indicates an intention to abandon the contents.[28] An Alaska court noted that it would find it difficult to reach any conclusion other than that the person who placed trash in a curb receptacle intended to abandon the contents.[29] An intention to abandon a motor vehicle can be seen where an individual left his car unattended in a public place, transferred the paper title to a different person, and told another person in a letter that he had no intention to return for the vehicle.[30] Merely transferring the title of an automobile to a second person can indicate the intent to abandon the vehicle.[31] A defendant indicated an intention to abandon mail that police seized from a Mail Boxes, Etc. store that the defendant had not retrieved for longer than a year and had made no rental payment on the box for more than a year.[32] However, where police stopped a woman driving a rental car and she walked away from it, the conduct was ambiguous of an intention to abandon the car or to abandon her suitcase inside the rental car's trunk.[33] The car had been rented but the driver was not authorized to drive the car by the rental company, and the company wanted the police to impound the car. The woman was told that she could ride with police but that her belongings would have to be searched prior to placing them in the police cruiser. She declined and walked away with her personal items and a rolling suitcase. The drugs found in the trunk of the rental car had to be suppressed because she did not abandon the vehicle; it was taken from her.

A court may hold that an abandonment of personal property has occurred even where a defendant did not exhibit the intent to abandon the property when the property initially became separated from the defendant. In a California armed robbery case,[34] the defendant dropped his cell phone at the scene of the crime, and police eventually recovered it. Although it was locked in a way that prevented its use, police opened it to gain the serial number as a way of finding the identity of the subscriber-robber. The defendant wanted to contest the search for the serial number and suppress its fruits. In support of his continued expectation of privacy in the cell phone and the serial number, he contended that he did not abandon the phone or intend to discard it, but that he accidentally dropped it during the robbery. The trial court determined that he had abandoned his cell phone because at trial the defendant's own testimony established that he made a conscious decision not to reclaim his phone once he knew he had lost it at the scene of the robbery. His intent to abandon need not have occurred at the exact moment the defendant dropped the phone, but the intent to abandon did occur subsequently, and that intention sufficiently supported the legal concept of abandonment. With his abandonment, any expectation of privacy vanished.

To demonstrate that a person lacked an expectation of privacy in discarded property, courts require the prosecution to offer proof of a defendant's intention to abandon, tested by the totality of the circumstances. Abandonment is not determined exclusively by a property rights analysis, but the intention to abandon may be inferred from word, acts, and deeds that indicate the person has given up sufficient interest in the property to no longer have an expectation of privacy in it.

6. ABANDONMENT OF PERSONAL PROPERTY

In addition to an intention to abandon property, there must be actual abandonment sufficient to indicate that the defendant has no intention of dealing with the property in the future. In many cases, a suspect with whom the police would like to talk runs or walks away and drops or discards drugs or other objects that the subject would not want to possess while speaking with the police. A suspect faces a problem because by retaining the drugs, gun, or other contraband, there is the probability that possessing the evidence will be incriminating. Alternatively, the suspect who discards the property generally gives up any Fourth Amendment expectation of privacy in the discarded item and cannot successfully argue for suppression of evidence that he or she had previously abandoned.

In one case[35] police officers observed a subject who had been riding a bicycle lean inside a motor vehicle in a manner that suggested a drug sale might be taking place. When subject observed police approaching, he attempted to ride his bicycle away in another direction, refusing a police command to stop. During his flight, he threw a black bag he had been carrying under a parked car. Police eventually gained control over the bicycle rider and arrested him once they retrieved the bag and discovered cocaine inside. The trial court convicted the defendant, but he appealed, contending that he should have been allowed to suppress the evidence of drug possession found in his discarded black bag. He argued that the police had no right to stop him and that the cocaine was the fruit of an illegal stop. The appellate court considered the facts and determined that the defendant abandoned the bag and its contents during the chase and prior to the time he was stopped, so he had no expectation of privacy in the bag at the time the officers opened it. The cocaine had been properly admitted against the defendant because he had abandoned the bag and any expectation of privacy.

In a similar situation,[36] police officers observed two individuals in the process of walking away from an abandoned house that had boarded windows. The two individuals began walking in opposite directions. The area was known for drug use and trafficking, and there were many abandoned houses that facilitated drug transactions. When one of the officers ordered one of the men to stop, he ignored the command and walked to a parked car, where he crouched partially out of sight of the officer. When the officer told the subject to show his hands, he made a gesture as if he were throwing something away from his person. Once the officer had handcuffed the subject, he noticed two small bags on the ground nearby that later analysis revealed contained marijuana and cocaine. The drugs were admitted against the defendant at his trial over his objection that he had been illegally stopped. The trial court noted that he had not been seized until he stopped and that he had abandoned the two bags prior to being in custody. In affirming the trial court decision, the appellate court noted that abandoned property can be properly seized without a warrant and that the defendant could not assert any Fourth Amendment claim involving property he had clearly abandoned.

Proof of abandonment negates any contention that the property had been illegally seized or that a search of the property was unlawful. In a different case,[37] an interstate Greyhound bus passenger denied that a piece of luggage bearing his name belonged to him. Police were interested in the luggage because a drug-sniffing dog had alerted to the bag while it rested in the belly of the interstate bus. In cooperation with the Greyhound Bus Company, a police officer wearing a company uniform announced that the bus had mechanical problems, the passengers would have to switch to another bus, and each passenger would have to claim his or her luggage. One passenger picked up the suspect baggage and its name tag matched the name on the passenger ticket. The police officer asked the passenger why a drug dog alerted to his blue bag, but the passenger stated, "That's not my bag." He later repeated that the bag did not belong to him. The trial court admitted the twelve pounds of heroin against the defendant over his objection. On appeal, he argued that the police officer disguised as a bus employee illegally seized him when he was ordered to leave the bus and claim his baggage, that he did not voluntarily abandon his bag, and that his bag should not have been warrantlessly searched. The appellate court rejected the defendant's argument that he had been seized when the officer wearing bus company attire ordered the passengers to exit the bus and claim their baggage. According to the court, the test to be used to determine abandonment is whether

> ". . . [T]he defendant has retained any reasonable expectation of privacy in the property." *United States v. Hernandez,* 7 F.3d 944, 947 (10th Cir. 1993). "Abandonment is akin to the issue of standing because a defendant lacks standing to complain of an illegal search or seizure of property which has been abandoned." *Garzon,* 119 F.3d at 1449.[38]

In this case, the abandonment was voluntary, and it was not made due to an illegal Fourth Amendment seizure of his person. Because of his abandonment of his suitcase, the heroin was properly admitted against him, according to the court of appeals.

Police may use deception to get a person to abandon personal property or other evidence when the subject may not realize that he or she is actually abandoning anything. In an Iowa case, *State v. Christian,*[39] police invited the suspect to an arranged fake job interview for the purpose of obtaining his DNA sample. During the intererview, the suspect was offered and accepted a drink from a bottle of water, and he ate a piece of cake with a fork supplied by police. The defendant was none the wiser and left both the bottle of water and the fork at the interview site. Police collected the water bottle and fork and subjected them to DNA analysis, the results of which linked the defendant to a sexual assault. The court determined that no error occurred when the DNA evidence was used against the defendant in the sexual assault case because the defendant had voluntarily abandoned the materials containing his DNA profile when he left the items at the "job interview." According to the court, determining if a person voluntarily abandoned property considers whether the person intended to abandon the property, a fact that can be discerned from words, acts, or other objective facts. In this case, the defendant brought other articles, including paperwork, to the meeting and left with the paperwork, indicating that he took what he wanted from the meeting and left what he no longer wanted, which included the water bottle, the cake fork, and his DNA sample. The reviewing court approved the admission of the DNA results into evidence despite the defendant's assertion that the seizure was illegal under the Fourth Amendment because he had not intended to abandon DNA.

7. ABANDONMENT OF MOTOR VEHICLES

Courts apply the same constitutional procedures in cases where owners, possessors, renters, and other individuals in control of motor vehicles exhibit conduct that indicates a desire to abandon the vehicle for the future. There may be some limitations on the expectation of privacy in a motor vehicle that many states recognize when the occupant or passenger does not own or lease the vehicle.[40] When a person who has control over a motor vehicle determines that he or she will abandon the vehicle and the conduct of the person demonstrates a permanent abandonment of the vehicle and its contents, that individual will possess an expectation of privacy neither in the vehicle nor in any of the vehicle's contents. In some states, courts will not find a voluntary abandonment if police misconduct prompted the person in control of the vehicle to abandon it. In such cases, the courts will continue to recognize an expectation of privacy in the vehicle and its contents.

A New York case[41] demonstrates the legal effects of abandoning a motor vehicle on a defendant's efforts to suppress evidence under the Fourth Amendment. Rochester police responded to a 911 call that involved a suspicious person sitting at a motor vehicle that was specifically described as to its identity and location. When police located the car, a license plate check indicated that the registered owner had an outstanding warrant for his arrest. As one officer approached the motor vehicle, the defendant left the car unlocked with the key remaining in the ignition and walked into the street. The conversation with the officer involved information that the subject was not the owner of the car, that he did not know the location of the owner, and that he did not possess a driver's license. At this point, the officer determined to impound the car and initiated an inventory search that disclosed a baggie containing crack cocaine. Prior to the trial for possession of crack cocaine, the defendant attempted to suppress the evidence that police found in the motor vehicle. The court determined, among other things, that the defendant had no expectation of privacy in the motor vehicle because he had effectively and voluntarily abandoned it without any observable police misconduct. The trial court noted that:

> . . . [O]nce he exited and walked away from the automobile, defendant effectively abandoned it. By leaving the car door unlocked and the key in the ignition, defendant left the car vacant on the street, available for any passer-by to enter and drive the car away. Because he had no driver's license, defendant was not in a position to drive the car away himself. Having walked away from the car under these circumstances, defendant waived any legitimate expectation of privacy in the vehicle he might otherwise have had.[42]

Under the circumstances, the trial court refused to suppress the crack cocaine and held that it was admissible against the defendant.

Exiting a motor vehicle with no intention to return to the vehicle may constitute legal abandonment and eliminate any expectation of privacy regarding the vehicle. One court determined that the defendant abandoned his motor vehicle where police initially attempted stop the defendant's van due to a broken taillight, but the van driver accelerated, which caused the officer to give chase.[43] At a point near the end of the chase, the defendant van driver turned in to a residential driveway and bailed out of the van while the vehicle was still moving in excess of thirty miles per hour, with the result that the van crashed into a house. The driver of the van left the scene of the crash, but police captured him several blocks away. Pursuant to police policy, the van was impounded, and eventually an inventory search revealed a pistol hidden within the van. The trial court admitted the pistol against the defendant over his objection that he had not abandoned the van and had left it only temporarily. On appeal, the court noted that a defendant abandons his property when he discards it, and in this case proof of abandonment was evident when he

> jumped from the van while it was still moving. He left it crashed into a garage with the lights on, the door open, and the keys in the ignition. He never tried to return to the van and was apprehended several blocks away. Although he may not have wanted to relinquish his legal interests, he certainly shed the van when it served his more immediate interest of escape. He also admitted that he fled from the van because he did not want to be connected with the gun inside.[44]

The Court of Appeals upheld the admission of the pistol into evidence based on the fact that the defendant abandoned both the pistol and the van.

8. POLICE MISCONDUCT AND ABANDONMENT OF PERSONAL PROPERTY

In some jurisdictions, police misconduct prior to a suspect's abandonment of property may destroy the voluntariness of the abandonment; in most jurisdictions, if police misconduct coexists with abandonment, the court treats the two issues as separate concepts and may allow the admission of the evidence. Where police illegally arrest or attempt to wrongfully arrest a subject and the subject abandons property, the abandonment may not be considered as voluntary and the evidence will be suppressed.

In a Florida case,[45] a police officer lawfully stopped a motor vehicle that turned in front of the officer's cruiser, based on a failure to properly use a turn signal. The officer had to slow his vehicle to avoid being hit by the turning vehicle. During the stop, one officer determined to give a ticket to the front-seat passenger, who was not wearing a seatbelt following the stop of the motor vehicle. When the officer, for no objective reason, believed that the passenger gave a false name, the officer decided to arrest the passenger. Following police directions, the passenger placed his hands on the roof of the car but suddenly bolted away and ran from the police officer. During his moments of freedom, the subject abandoned a firearm that resulted in his prosecution for being a felon in possession of a firearm. Since the officer never observed whether the passenger used the seatbelt while the car was in operation, he had no reason whatsoever to issue a citation or to seize the passenger for giving a false name. Additionally, it was not a crime to give a false name to a police officer because, in this case, it did not occur during a lawful detention. Because the defendant should not have been seized, and his detention was unlawful, the court rejected the government's argument that the gun had been properly introduced against the defendant because he had abandoned it. According to the appellate court, the illegality of the police arrest caused the defendant to throw down the gun, and it should have been suppressed from his trial. This case demonstrates that some jurisdictions consider the legality of police conduct in determining whether the abandonment of evidence was the result of an illegal police act or whether it was an act of free will, unmotivated by police misconduct.

There is little chance for police misconduct that may relate to a claim of abandonment until a person has been physically seized or has submitted to police authority. Abandonment made prior to custody is generally considered to have been done voluntarily. In *Campbell v. State*,[46] the defendant tossed his gun under a car when a police spotlight illuminated him as he stood in a residential front yard. In Indiana, property abandoned due to police misconduct is generally not admissible. Police came over to question him concerning his conduct and discovered the tossed gun. The defendant alleged that he had been illegally seized when the spotlight hit him. If he were seized at the time that the spotlight illuminated him and there was no legitimate reason to make a seizure, then illegal police conduct caused him to abandon the gun and it should be suppressed, as in the prior case. However, if the defendant was not seized at that time, no illegal police conduct made the defendant abandon the gun, and it should be admissible against him for having a concealed weapon without a permit. In Indiana, a person is seized when, by means of physical force or a show of authority, a police officer has in some way restrained the liberty of a citizen. Earlier case law on the federal level demonstrated that the shining of a light, without more, does not constitute a seizure. Other states have held that a spotlight on a car, combined with blocking the defendant's car, constitutes a Fourth Amendment seizure. The Indiana court held that the mere shining of a flashlight on a subject, without more, does not constitute a seizure, so the defendant's abandonment of his firearm was not done in response to illegal police conduct. Since the gun was abandoned, the police properly seized it, and the gun could properly be admitted in evidence against the defendant.

Where police make mistakes and do not have a reason to seize a person, property abandoned property prior to apprehension may still be admissible where the police conduct was generally reasonable. In a recent federal prosecution for being a felon in possession of a firearm,[47] police officers wrongfully chased a subject because they thought he was somebody else. The subject walked away from the officers and then added speed to run from the nonuniformed officers, who eventually captured the subject who was the wrong person. The police officers had neither probable cause nor reasonable suspicion to seize the defendant, but one officer genuinely, but erroneously, believed that the defendant was a person who was subject to arrest. During his flight from the police, the defendant discarded an assault rifle and some ammunition magazines that the prosecution introduced at the defendant's trial. The reviewing court approved the trial court use of the firearm and ammunition magazines because they were obtained due to voluntary abandonment that preceded the police illegality of wrongfully seizing the defendant's person.

9. ABANDONMENT OF REAL PROPERTY, LAND, HOME, AND MOTEL

Abandonment of real property occurs if the defendant intended to abandon the property and actually abandoned the property, and the abandonment was not based on police misconduct. Abandonment is often considered to be a matter of intent that can be inferred from words that a defendant spoke, acts done, or from other objective evidence of conduct.

In a Texas case,[48] the defendant rented a motel room for a one-day period, but his conduct created concern among the hotel staff that he might be on drugs. The defendant paid cash, and because of the defendant's prior conduct during an earlier motel stay, the motel staff contacted police. When the police arrived, the staff directed them to the defendant's hotel room to talk to him. The defendant refused to consent to search of his motel room while the officers spoke with him. For some reason, the defendant called the front desk to tell them he was checking out immediately, and he drove away from the motel. With the permission of the motel staff following his oral checkout, police officers searched his room and discovered cocaine. The trial court refused to suppress the cocaine evidence, despite the defendant's contention that he did not make an oral checkout and did not abandon his motel room because he had paid for it for a full day. The trial court believed the motel staff that he had checked out, partly because he left the electronic door card key on the inside of the motel room. The appellate court viewed the evidence in the light most favorable to the trial court's determination that the defendant had abandoned the motel room, and the appellate court found that there was no police misconduct that wrongfully would have induced the defendant's abandonment of his motel room. The evidence supported the conclusion that the defendant's actions demonstrated a voluntary abandonment of the hotel room and that the trial court properly admitted the cocaine against the defendant.

The intention to abandon occupancy of a motel room is a contested fact in many criminal cases, and the resolution of abandonment issues determines the admissibility of evidence from the room. In *United States v. Mitchell*,[49] the defendant had rented a motel room and paid for it in advance but checked out, according to motel employees, prior to the expiration of the rental period. The defendant denied checking out and vacating the room, and her conduct of retaining the door key indicated that she felt she still had rights to the motel room. When asked, the motel staff told state police that the subject had checked out and left in a vehicle. A warrantless search of the motel room revealed papers and personal items, including a pile of clothing on the closet floor, that could indicate the defendant intended to return and had not abandoned the room and its contents. From the defendant's motel room, police officials seized stolen United States mail, a check printer, chemical bleaching solution, and other evidence that the trial court permitted to be introduced against the defendant at her trial for possessing stolen mail. The trial court found the defendant's version of renting the motel room and the time of her checkout not believable and chose to believe the motel staff, holding that she had abandoned her motel room prior to the warrantless government search and seizure. The appellate court upheld the trial court decision that because she had abandoned the room and its contents, she had no remaining expectation of privacy.

10. SUMMARY OF ABANDONMENT

When a defendant abandons property, generally the defendant must have an intention to abandon the property and exhibit conduct that indicates that he or she wishes nothing further to do with the property. The intention and the act are often intertwined and in some cases may be difficult to separate, but abandonment is often the question of fact to be determined by looking at the totality of the circumstances. Words, acts, and conduct may indicate that a defendant wants no further connection with a piece of personal property or with real property. A disclaimer of ownership of property suffices as a general indication of either abandonment or of never having possessed any connection with the property in question. Where a suspect disclaims ownership of a piece of luggage, a quantity of drugs, a package, or a firearm, generally there is no expectation of privacy in the property over which ownership has been denied. As a general rule, a subject must have voluntarily abandoned property and not have been prompted to abandon property by virtue of police misconduct. Courts often strain to separate abandonment that occurs prior to police misconduct from police violations of a suspect's rights. As a general rule, courts generally admit evidence that was abandoned prior to a constitutional violation. If the abandonment coexists with police misconduct involving seizure of a person, many courts will suppress the evidence of the abandoned property because of law enforcement errors involving the Fourth Amendment.

REVIEW EXERCISES AND QUESTIONS

1. Police received information that a man named Jones was growing marijuana on the edge of a cornfield on one of his farms. The information appeared to be from a reliable source, and police wanted to check it out prior to obtaining a search or arrest warrant.

One evening two officers, without a warrant, walked past Jones' home and near his hot tub at the back of the house, on a dirt road that had been posted with no trespassing signs. When the officers reached the area in question, they found marijuana plants ready for harvest. The officers would like to use the evidence of marijuana manufacturing against Jones. Explain whether the officers have or have not violated Jones' Fourth Amendment rights by the way they discovered the marijuana plants.

2. Why have courts determined that there is little expectation of privacy in an open field?

3. In the case *United States v. Dunn* (Case 9.2), would the outcome of the case have been different if Dunn's barn had been located immediately behind his house and if family members regularly used a hot tub in the barn? In this altered fact pattern, Mrs. Dunn used a room in the downstairs area of the barn for her quilting hobby. Would the Court have ruled the same way?

4. In many cases involving abandoned personal property, a defendant is under some strain and motivation to throw away property that might be indicative of criminal activity. On the assumption that abandonment must be a voluntary act, when a suspect discards crack cocaine during a police chase, does such conduct indicate voluntary or involuntary abandonment of the drugs? Explain.

5. Construct a scenario or fact pattern in which a defendant will be deemed to have voluntarily abandoned a motor vehicle and have no remaining Fourth Amendment expectation of privacy in the vehicle or its contents.

6. As a general rule, for property to be considered abandoned, the abandonment must have been done freely and voluntarily. A criminal who inadvertently misplaces a cell phone or forgets to finish a cookie and leaves it, partially eaten, at a crime scene has not consciously or intentionally abandoned the property. Can lost or misplaced property qualify as "abandoned" property for purposes of admission into evidence under the Fourth Amendment?

7. Can police misconduct have any effect on the admissibility into evidence of property that a defendant abandoned, where the abandonment was directly related to or prompted by police misconduct? Explain.

HOW WOULD YOU DECIDE?

1. In the United States Court of Appeals for the Eighth Circuit

Police drug interdiction officers were working the bus station in Omaha, Nebraska, and noticed that when the bags were removed from the bus, one blue bag remained that appeared to have no identification. Edward Deshawn Hawkins gave an attendant a claim check and removed the bag to the taxi stand area outside the bus terminal, where he met a traveling companion. Hawkins left to hail a taxi. Police officers approached the companion and asked him a few questions concerning the blue travel bag, but he denied ownership and said it belonged to his brother. When Hawkins returned, he gave a false name to the police officer and stated that he just carried the bag outside for a person he just met, who was inside the bus station. When Hawkins continued to deny ownership and any possessory right in the bag, police officers opened it and discovered a liquid in a container that appeared to be phencyclidine or PCP, a drug of abuse. At Hawkins' trial for drug possession and transportation of phencyclidine, the district judge refused to grant his motion to suppress the evidence. Hawkins contended that he was a bailee of the bag, and he was protesting that the police should not open the bag because he had, as bailee, some sort of expectation of privacy. He appealed his conviction to the appropriate federal court of appeals.

How would you rule on the defendant's contention that he should be able to suppress the evidence of PCP, even though he denied owning or possessing the travel bag in which the drug was found?

The Court's Holding:

[The court reviewed the facts in the case and considered the defendant's connection to the travel bag. His alleged position as a bailee of the property did not enhance his argument concerning his alleged Fourth Amendment expectation of privacy. The court found that any expectation of privacy that Hawkins may have had in the bag was forfeited by his abandonment of it.]

"When a person abandons his [property], his expectation of privacy in the property is so eroded that he no longer has standing to challenge a search of the luggage on Fourth Amendment grounds." *United States v. Liu,* 180 F.3d 957, 960 (8th Cir. 1999). A warrantless search of abandoned property does not involve a constitutional violation, because "any expectation of privacy in the item searched is forfeited upon its abandonment." *United States v. Chandler,* 197 F.3d 1198, 1200 (8th Cir. 1999) (quoting *United States v. Tugwell,* 125 F.3d 600, 602 (8th Cir. 1997)). We are to consider the totality of evidence when determining whether property has been abandoned, focusing on two principal factors: whether the defendant has claimed or denied ownership of the item, and whether the defendant physically relinquished it. *United States v. James,* 353 F.3d 606, 616 (8th Cir. 2003). The government bears the burden of showing property has been abandoned. *Id.*

The totality of circumstances indicates Hawkins abandoned any interest he had in the bag. When the officers approached Hawkins's companion, he stated the bag belonged to his brother who had just reentered the terminal. When Hawkins returned, however, he stated he did not have any luggage and had merely carried the bag to the front of the terminal for an unidentified person who Hawkins purportedly met in the terminal. When directly asked about the bag, Hawkins consistently

denied that he owned it. Even as Hawkins exhibited some concern about the bag as he learned the police wanted to search it, he continued to deny he owned it. These circumstances would lead reasonable officers to believe that Hawkins abandoned his interest in the bag.

* * *

Even assuming the truth of Hawkins's claim that he brought the bag out for some stranger in the terminal, any interest he had in the bag evaporated when his duties as bailee were over. Hawkins told the police that he carried the bag out at the request of this unidentified person, but there is no evidence that Hawkins agreed to stand guard over the bag. Indeed, Hawkins indicated to the police that he did not have time to identify the true owner because he was waiting for a ride, presumably to leave the area without the bag. Hawkins cannot now assert interests when his conduct at the scene suggested to officers that he no longer had any interest in the bag. At the time of the search, Hawkins had no remaining privacy interest as either owner or bailee of the bag, and thus cannot prevail on a challenge to the search of it.

We thus affirm the denial of Hawkins's motion to suppress.

See *United States v. Hawkins,* 116 Fed. Appx. 776, 2004 U.S. App. LEXIS 24671 (8th Cir. 2004).

HOW WOULD YOU DECIDE?

2. United States District Court for the Eastern District of Missouri

Police stopped defendant Travis Norman after he drove over a highway lane divider, an act that constituted a moving traffic violation. The stop of defendant Norman's car was based on a legitimate moving violation and could not have been considered a pretextual stop. The police officer involved had been following Norman for the purpose of waiting until he committed a traffic violation and then had plans to stop him if and when a violation occurred. Upon being stopped, defendant Norman fled the scene of the traffic stop on foot and, while fleeing, discarded a bag of crack cocaine that was retrieved by the police officer. Law enforcement officers arrested Norman for possession of a controlled substance. As incident to his arrest, the car from which he fled was searched, revealing another bag of cocaine that police

seized. The United States magistrate recommended that Travis Norman's motion to suppress be denied by the district judge. Norman's attorney filed objections to the magistrate's recommendation.

How would you rule on the defendant's contention that the evidence he discarded and was found in his car be suppressed from his upcoming drug trial?

The Court's Holding:

Defendant has filed written objections to the Report and Recommendation arguing that Judge Mummert's Report and Recommendation is against the weight of the evidence and the law.

* * *

Defendant presumably objects to the entire Report and Recommendation since no specific finding or conclusion is presented. Further, defendant presents no specific authority for his position, rather, he generally argues, in his motion to suppress, that his constitutional rights would be violated without suppression.

* * *

Defendant does not attack the credibility of the witnesses who testified at the hearing. Defendant also did not present any evidence to controvert the testimony of the witnesses. The Report and Recommendation submitted by Judge Mummert clearly and accurately sets forth the facts from the testimony of these witnesses.

Defendant, in objecting to Judge Mummert's recommendation, states that Judge Mummert's ruling was against the weight of the evidence and law. Defendant incorporates by reference all arguments he made in his Motion to Suppress Evidence and Statements, with no specific objections as to Judge Mummert's conclusions.

As the testimony established, defendant was stopped for the traffic violation of crossing over a lane divider on November 24, 2004 by Officer Hart. Officer Hart had been following defendant at the time in order to stop him if he violated a traffic law. After being stopped, defendant fled and, while fleeing, discarded a bag of crack cocaine that was retrieved by Officer Taylor. Defendant was arrested for possession of a controlled substance. His car was searched incident to this arrest. A bag of cocaine was discovered and seized.

The traffic stop was not pretextual. "It is well established, however, that any traffic violation, no matter how minor, provides an officer with probable cause to stop the driver of the vehicle." *United States v. Pereira-Munoz,* 59 F.3d 788, 791 (8th Cir. 1995). Furthermore, defendant abandoned the crack cocaine while he was fleeing from the police and a warrantless search of the abandoned property does not violate the Fourth Amendment. *United States v. Segars,* 31 F.3d 655, 658 (8th Cir. 1945). The search of defendant's vehicle incident to his arrest and the seizure of the cocaine were proper. *United States v. Fladten,* 230 F.3d 1083, 1085–86 (8th Cir. 2000).

See *United States v. Norman,* No. 4:05CR745 HEA (ED MO 2006).

ENDNOTES

1. 466 U.S. 170, 179 (1984).
2. Ibid., 181.
3. See *California v. Ciraolo,* 476 U.S. 207 (1986), and *Florida v. Riley,* 488 U.S. 445 (1989).
4. *Hester v. United States,* 284 F. 487, 488 (1922).
5. Ibid. at 58.
6. 466 U.S. 170 (1984).
7. Ibid. at 173.
8. Ibid. at 222.
9. Ibid. at 224.
10. 641 S.E.2d 320, 2007 N.C. App. LEXIS 474 (2007).
11. 480 U.S. 294, 1987 U.S. LEXIS 1057 (1987).
12. Ibid.
13. See *Gordon v. State,* 277 Ga. App. 247, 249 626 S.E.2d 214, 215, 2006 Ga. App. LEXIS 53 (2006).
14. *California v. Ciraolo,* 476 U.S. 207, 213 (1986).
15. *United States v. Dunn,* 480 U.S. 294, 300 (1987), citing *United States v. Oliver,* 466 U.S. 170, 180 (1984).
16. *State v. Dubose,* 164 Ohio App. 3d 698, 707, 708, 2005 Ohio 6602, 843 N.E.2d 1222, 1230, 2005 Ohio App. LEXIS 5928 (2005).
17. *United States v. Samboy,* 433 F.3d 154, 161 (1st Cir. 2005).
18. *United States v. Whitsett,* 207 Fed. Appx. 723, 2006 U.S. App. LEXIS 30635 (7th Cir. 2006).
19. See *United States v. Denny,* 441 F.3d 1220, 2006 U.S. App. LEXIS 7565 (2006), where a subject who denied that drugs in a bag on a train seat were his and had the drugs introduced against him because he had abandoned the drugs.
20. *United States v. McCurdy,* 480 F. Supp.2d 380 (2007).
21. Ibid., at 391, (2007), citing *United States v. Zapata,* 18 F.3d 971, 978 (1st Cir. 1994).
22. See *United States v. Stevenson,* 396 F.3d 538, 2005 U.S. App. LEXIS 1558 (4th Cir. 2005).
23. See *State v. Linton,* 356 N.J. Super. 255, 812 A.2d 382; 2002 N.J. Super. LEXIS 510 (2002).
24. See *People v. Pereira,* 150 Cal. App. 4th 1106, 58 Cal. Rptr. 3d 847, 2007 Cal. App. LEXIS 756 (2007).
25. A Louisiana court stated the legal title requirement slightly differently when it noted! "Abandonment for purposes of the Fourth Amendment differs from

abandonment in property law; . . . the analysis examines the individual's reasonable expectation of privacy, not his property interest in the item." *State v. Stephens,* 917 So. 2d 667, 673, 2005 La. App. LEXIS 2565 (2005).

26. *United States v. James,* 353 F.3d 606, 616 (8th Cir. 2003).

27. *United States v. Simpson,* 439 F3d 490, 494 (8th Cir. 2006), quoting *United States v. Hoey,* 983 F.2d 890, 892–93 (8th Cir. 1993).

28. See *California v. Greenwood,* 486 U.S. 35 (1988), where the Court failed to find any expectation of privacy under the Fourth Amendment when a homeowner placed his trash at the curb for normal refuse collection.

29. *State v. Beltz,* 160 P.3d 154; 2007 Alas. App. LEXIS 126 (2007).

30. *People v. Sutherland,* 223 Ill. 2d 187; 860 N.E.2d 178; 2006 Ill. LEXIS 1650 (2006).

31. See 1 *W. LaFave, Search & Seizure* § 2.5(a), at 649–50 (4th ed. 2004).

32. See *United States v. Thomas,* 451 F.3d 543, 546 (2006), where federal agents seized mail from a private mailbox, which the defendant had abandoned.

33. See *United States v. Eden,* 190 Fed. Appx. 416, 2006 U.S. App. LEXIS 16337 (6th Cir. 2006). Drivers of rental cars who are not listed as drivers may have no expectation of privacy in the car in some states.

34. *People v. Daggs,* 133 Cal. App. 4th 361, 365, 34 Cal. Rptr. 3d 649, 652, 2005 Cal. App. LEXIS 1589 (2005).

35. See *Wilson v. State,* 825 N.E.2d 49, 2005 Ind. App. LEXIS 558 (2005).

36. See *Gooch v. State,* 834 N.E.2d 1052; 2005 Ind. App. LEXIS 1799 (2005).

37. See *United States v. Ojeda-Ramos,* 455 F.3d 1178; 2006 U.S. App. LEXIS 19175 (10th Cir. 2006).

38. Ibid., 1187.

39. 2006 Iowa App. LEXIS 1031 (2006).

40. See *Rakas v. Illinois,* 439 U.S. 128 (1978).

41. *People v. Majors,* 2007 NY Slip Op 27024, 15 Misc. 3d 239, 828 N.Y.S.2d 866, 2007 N.Y. Misc. LEXIS 146 (2007).

42. Ibid. 15 Misc. 3d 239, 241.

43. *People v. Michigan,* 2007 Mich. App. LEXIS 456 (2007).

44. Ibid.

45. *Cooks v, State,* 901 So. 2d 963, 964, 2005 Fla. App. LEXIS 6768 (2005).

46. 841 N.E.2d 624, 2006 Ind. App. LEXIS 131 (2006).

47. See *United States v. Simpson,* 439 F.3d 490, 494, 495, 2006 U.S. App. LEXIS 4934 (8th Cir. 2006).

48. See *Antes v. State,* 2007 Tex. App. LEXIS 276 (2007).

49. 429 F.3d 952, 2005 U.S. App. LEXIS 25106 (10th Cir. 2005).

Part 4

Miranda Warnings, Confessions, and Identification Procedures

C H A P T E R   1 0

Miranda *Principles: Fifth and Sixth Amendment Influences on Police Practice*

Learning Objectives

1. Explain the Supreme Court's rationale for determining that police must offer warnings of constitutional rights when they want to interrogate persons in custody.
2. Be able to articulate the constitutional rationale for the *Miranda* warnings.
3. Describe police interrogation techniques that were common practice prior to the case of *Miranda v. Arizona*.
4. Define the two prerequisites or triggering events that need to be present before police must administer the *Miranda* warnings.
5. Orally offer the substance of the *Miranda* warnings that must be offered to detainees police wish to interrogate.

6. Articulate when police must cease questioning, if already initiated, and explain the circumstances when police may not start interrogation.
7. Describe the concept referred to as the "functional equivalent" of interrogation under *Miranda.*
8. Offer two emergency situations, called exigent circumstances, that may permit interrogation of a subject in cases where the *Miranda* warnings would otherwise have to be read to the suspect prior to questioning.
9. Explain two ways that a person subject to the *Miranda* warnings may properly waive his or her rights and agree to talk with police.

Chapter Outline

1. Introduction to *Miranda* Warnings
2. The Basis for the Warnings
3. The Road to *Miranda*
4. The Case of *Miranda v. Arizona*
5. Prerequisites for *Miranda* Warnings
6. Substance of the Warnings
7. Delivering the *Miranda* Warnings
8. When *Miranda* Warnings Are Required: The Triggering Events
9. When Interrogation Must Cease
10. Necessary Condition for *Miranda* Warnings: Custody
11. Necessary Condition for *Miranda* Warnings: Interrogation

12. *Miranda* Interrogation: The Functional Equivalent
13. Exigent Circumstance Exception to *Miranda* Interrogation
14. Right to Counsel under *Miranda* Is Personal to Arrestee
15. Procedure for Waiver of *Miranda* Protection
16. Congressional Challenge to the *Miranda* Warnings
17. *Miranda* Warnings: Required by the Constitution
18. Summary

Key Terms

Constitutional requirement for warning
Custody
Emergency exception
Functional equivalent of interrogation
Impeachment use of *Miranda*
Interrogation
Miranda warning

Misdemeanor warning
Necessary conditions for warning
Public safety exception
Right to counsel
Right to remain silent
Separate offense interrogation
Waiver

1. INTRODUCTION TO *MIRANDA* WARNINGS

Under our adversarial system of criminal justice, a defendant generally need not offer evidence that might help prove the government's case. The Fifth Amendment privilege against self-incrimination allows an accused to remain silent, and in support of this right, the teaching of *Miranda v. Arizona,* 384 U.S. 436 (1966), requires police to advise a person in custody that he or she does not have an affirmative duty to speak with representatives of the government and that he or she may remain silent. Whether an accused has been charged in state or federal court, he or she has no obligation to assist the prosecution. Many individuals who become defendants are unaware of their right to remain silent and are similarly ignorant of other important constitutional rights possessed by persons under United States jurisdiction. As a result of constitutional requirements and from a concern that trained police officers might overcome an individual's reluctance to speak with them, judicial decisions have required law enforcement agents to offer a minimum measure of legal advice to those who come into police custody and whom the police wish to interrogate. The legal advice should be calculated to alert an arrestee not only that he or she has the right of silence and the right to consult with an attorney but also that legal counsel will be made available free of charge to those who might have difficulty hiring an attorney. For a review of the warnings, see Figure 10.1. The warnings must be administered in a manner the arrestee can understand, and *Miranda* must be given whether the suspect is in custody for a felony or misdemeanor.

Miranda Warning

1. Your have the right to remain silent.
2. Anything you do say can and will be used against you in a court of law.
3. You have the right to talk to a lawyer and have him or her present with you while you are being questioned.
4. If you cannot afford to hire an attorney, one will be appointed to represent you before any questioning.
5. You can decide at any time to exercise these legal rights and not answer any questions or not make any statements.

Waiver

Do you understand these rights as I have explained them to you?
Having these rights in mind, do you wish to talk to me now?

FIGURE 10.1   Sample of Typical *Miranda* Warning Form.

2. THE BASIS FOR THE WARNINGS

Under the Constitution of the United States, Amendment Five,[1] no person can be required to become a "witness against himself" unless the person freely and voluntarily decides to testify or otherwise offer adverse evidence. If an individual is ignorant of the right or is overreached by law enforcement officials, the right may be lost. Prior to 1966, officers could pressure a person in custody to tell police the facts in criminal cases, and arrestees often confessed due to overwhelming pressure. According to *Miranda v. Arizona*,[2] police violence and the "third degree" flourished in numerous places in the 1930s and in some places thereafter (see Case 10.1).

Reportedly, some police resorted to physical brutality, beating, hanging, and protracted isolation from friends and relatives to obtain confessions.[3] Such activity, designed to make a person confess and become a witness against himself or herself, transgressed the guarantee of the Fifth Amendment.[4]

Originally, the Fifth Amendment limited federal law enforcement practice and had no application against the states. While many state constitutions offered identical protections from compelled testimonial self-incrimination, state courts did not always enforce the guarantee equitably in criminal prosecutions. When the Supreme Court decided *Malloy v. Hogan*,[5] state and federal criminal procedure became identical with respect to protections against self-incrimination under the Fifth Amendment. *Malloy* determined that the Fifth Amendment's privilege against self-incrimination was incorporated into the Due Process Clause of the Fourteenth Amendment and was enforceable against the states. Police practices developed that partially undercut the self-incrimination guarantee by careful use of psychology and other methods that produced confessions without physical violence or threat. Police manuals of the pre-*Miranda* era taught psychological tactics that could break down a suspect's will to resist, such as keeping the arrestee isolated in unfamiliar surroundings, having the officers alone with the individual and in total control, appearing to want only specific details since guilt was to be assumed, and giving the arrestee logical reasons for having committed the crime. Although not everyone succumbed to these practices, for many people, the totality of police tactics had the effect of wearing them down to the point that some even confessed to crimes they had not committed.

3. THE ROAD TO *MIRANDA*

An example of the problems surrounding police interrogation is provided by the case of *Escobedo v. Illinois*, 378 U.S. 478 (1964), where Escobedo had been arrested and interrogated for a homicide. His attorney succeeded in having him released, but police rearrested him and kept him away from family, friends, and his attorney. His attorney arrived at the police station and observed Escobedo but was prevented from talking to him despite Escobedo's clear, repeated requests.[6] At no time was Escobedo warned about his right under the Constitution to remain silent. During the interrogation, he remained handcuffed in a standing position, and he stated that he was nervous, upset, and agitated, since he had not slept well for more than a week. A Spanish-speaking officer played Escobedo against another suspect and told him that he could go home if he implicated the other suspect in the crime. After

CASE 10.1

Leading Case Brief: Police Custodial Interrogation Requires Warnings to Subject

Miranda v. Arizona
Supreme Court of the United States
384 U.S. 436 (1966)

Case Facts:

Phoenix police arrested Ernesto Miranda at his home on March 13, 1963, and removed him to the police station. After the complaining witness identified Miranda, police questioned him for two hours. Miranda and the police emerged from the room with a signed confession in which Miranda acknowledged that he had voluntarily confessed with complete knowledge that his statement could be used against him in court.

Miranda's attorney objected to the admission of his confession on the ground that the confession was obtained in violation of Miranda's Fifth Amendment right to remain silent. The officers recounted Miranda's confession and related the specifics under which it had been obtained. The trial court admitted the confession into evidence over Miranda's continued objection. The trial court found Miranda guilty of kidnapping and rape, and the court sentenced him to twenty to thirty years on each count, with the sentences to be served concurrently.

The Supreme Court of Arizona held that none of Miranda's constitutional rights had been violated and affirmed his conviction. The court relied heavily on the admitted fact that Miranda had not specifically requested the assistance of counsel. [Several other cases were consolidated with the *Miranda* case.]

Legal Issue:

Where police desire to interrogate an arrestee, must police warn the subject of the right to remain silent under the Fifth Amendment, of the right to have the assistance of counsel under the Sixth Amendment prior to beginning any interrogation, and of the fact that what the person says may be used against that person?

The Court's Ruling:

Whenever a person is taken into police custody and police desire to question that individual, police must warn the subject of the right to counsel, that the right to counsel exists presently, that the person has the right of silence and does not have to speak with police officers, and that if the individual speaks, what he or she says may be used against them in a court of law. The warning helps enforce the Fifth Amendment privilege against self-incrimination by using the Sixth Amendment right to counsel to assist the arrestee in making an informed decision.

Essence of the Court's Rationale:

Our holding will be spelled out with some specificity in the pages which follow but briefly stated it is this: the prosecution may not use statements, whether exculpatory or inculpatory, stemming from custodial interrogation of the defendant unless it demonstrates the use of procedural safeguards effective to secure the privilege against self-incrimination. By custodial interrogation, we mean questioning initiated by law enforcement officers after a person has been taken into custody or otherwise deprived of his freedom of action in any significant way. As for the procedural safeguards to be employed, unless other fully effective means are devised to inform accused persons of their right of silence and to assure a continuous opportunity to exercise it, the following measures are required. Prior to any questioning, the person must be warned that he has a right to remain silent, that any statement he does make may be used as evidence against him, and that he has a right to the presence of an attorney, either retained or appointed. The defendant may waive effectuation of these rights, provided the waiver is made voluntarily, knowingly and intelligently. If, however, he indicates in any manner and at any stage of the process that he wishes to consult with an attorney before speaking there can be no questioning. Likewise, if the individual is alone and indicates in any manner that he does not wish to be interrogated, the police may not question him. The mere fact that he may have answered some questions or volunteered some statements on his own does not deprive him of the right to refrain from answering any further inquiries until he has consulted with an attorney and thereafter consents to be questioned.

I

The constitutional issue we decide in each of these cases is the admissibility of statements obtained from a defendant questioned while in custody or otherwise deprived of his freedom of action in any significant way. In each, the defendant was questioned by police officers, detectives, or a prosecuting attorney in a room in which he was cut off from the outside world. In none of these cases was the defendant given a full and effective warning of his rights at the outset of the interrogation process. In all the cases, the questioning elicited oral admission, and in three of them, signed statements as well which were admitted at their trials. They all thus share salient features—incommunicado interrogation of individuals in a police-dominated atmosphere, resulting in self-incriminating statements without full warnings of constitutional rights.

An understanding of the nature and setting of this in-custody interrogation is essential to our decisions today. The difficulty in depicting what transpires at such interrogations stems from the fact that in this country they have largely taken place incommunicado. From extensive factual studies undertaken in the early 1930's, including the famous *Wickersham Report to Congress by a Presidential Commission,* it is clear that police violence and the "third degree" flourished at that time. In a series of cases decided by this Court long after these studies, the police resorted to physical brutality—beating, hanging, whipping—and to sustained and protracted questioning incommunicado in order to extort confessions. The Commission on Civil Rights in 1961 found much evidence to indicate that "some policemen still resort to physical force to obtain confessions," 1961 *Comm'n on Civil Rights Rep. Justice,* pt. 5, 17. The use of physical brutality and violence is not, unfortunately, relegated to the past or to any part of the country. Only recently in Kings County, New York, the police brutally beat, kicked and placed lighted cigarette butts on the back of a potential witness under interrogation for the purpose of securing a statement incriminating a third party.

* * *

At the outset, if a person in custody is to be subjected to interrogation, he must first be informed in clear and unequivocal terms that he has the right to remain silent. For those unaware of the privilege, the warning is needed simply to make them aware of it— the threshold requirement for an intelligent decision as to its exercise. More important, such a warning is an absolute prerequisite in overcoming the inherent pressures of the interrogation atmosphere. It is not just the subnormal or woefully ignorant who succumb to an interrogatory's imprecations, whether implied or expressly stated, that the interrogation will continue until a confession is obtained or that silence in the fact of accusation is itself damning and will bode ill when presented to a jury. Further, the warning will show the individual that his interrogators are prepared to recognize his privilege should he choose to exercise it.

* * *

The warning of the right to remain silent must be accompanied by the explanation that anything said can and will be used against the individual in court. This warning is needed in order to make him aware not only of the privilege, but also of the consequences of forgoing it. It is only through an awareness of these consequences that there can be any assurance of real understanding and intelligent exercise of the privilege. Moreover, this warning may serve to make the individual more acutely aware that he is faced with a phase of the adversary system—that he is not in the presence of persons acting solely in his interest.

* * *

In order to fully apprise a person interrogated of the extent of his rights under this system, then, it is necessary to warn him not only that he has the right to consult with an attorney, but also that if he is indigent a lawyer will be appointed to represent him. Without this additional warning, the admonition of the right to consult with counsel would often be understood as meaning only that he can consult with a lawyer if he has one or has the funds to obtain one. The warning of a right to counsel would be hollow if not couched in terms that would convey to the indigent—the person most often subjected to interrogation—the knowledge

(continued)

that he too has a right to have counsel present. As with the warnings of the right to remain silent and of the general right to counsel, only by effective and express explanation to the indigent of this right can there be assurance that he was truly in a position to exercise it.

Once warnings have been given, the subsequent procedure is clear. If the individual indicates in any manner, at any time prior to or during questioning, that he wishes to remain silent, the interrogation must cease. At this point he has shown that he intends to exercise his Fifth Amendment privilege; any statement taken after the person invokes his privilege cannot be other than the product of compulsion, subtle or otherwise. Without the right to cut off questioning, the setting of in-custody interrogation operates on the individual to overcome free choice in producing a statement after the privilege has been once invoked. If the individual states that he wants an attorney, the interrogation must cease until an attorney is present.

At that time, the individual must have an opportunity to confer with the attorney and to have him present during any subsequent questioning. If the individual cannot obtain an attorney and he indicates that he wants one before speaking to police, they must respect his decision to remain silent.

* * *

[The Court reversed Miranda's conviction.]

Case Importance:

There is a virtual presumption that where an arrestee speaks with police in the absence of a proper warning of rights that the person's decision to speak with police has been involuntary and that the police may have coerced the individual. In the absence of the warning and a clear waiver of the rights mentioned within the warning, the words of the arrestee will not be admitted in court against the person to prove guilt.

Escobedo noted some involvement in the homicide, officers moved to obtain the details that further implicated him.

Escobedo alleged that his right to remain silent under the Fifth Amendment and his right to an attorney under the Sixth Amendment had been violated by techniques the police used. When the Supreme Court decided the case, it ruled in Escobedo's favor and held that where an investigation is no longer a general inquiry into an unsolved crime but has begun to focus on a particular suspect, where the suspect has been taken into police custody and the police carry out a process of interrogations that lends itself to eliciting incriminating statements, where the suspect has requested and been denied an opportunity to consult with his lawyer, and where the police have not effectively warned the suspect of his or her absolute constitutional right to remain silent, the accused has been denied "the assistance of counsel" in violation of the Sixth Amendment. In *Escobedo v. Illinois,*[7] the Court held that no statement elicited by the police during the interrogation should have been used against him at his criminal trial. The Court stopped short of requiring police to affirmatively warn all persons interrogated while in custody of their constitutional rights, but that appeared to be the direction in which it was moving.

4. THE CASE OF *MIRANDA v. ARIZONA*

In *Miranda v. Arizona,*[8] (Case 10.1), the police took Ernesto Miranda into custody, kept him in an unfamiliar atmosphere, and subjected him to traditional police practices designed to get him to confess to the crime for which he had been arrested. Miranda, who had some mental problems, had been described as an indigent Mexican and as a seriously disturbed individual with pronounced sexual fantasies. None of the police practices involved overt physical coercion, disingenuous psychological games, or unusual tricks to gain a confession. However, the police *did not* inform Miranda that he had a right to remain silent and that he possessed a privilege against self-incrimination, that he could have an attorney to advise him, and that if he was too poor to pay for legal advice, the assistance of legal counsel would be free of charge. The *Miranda* Court felt that the presence of counsel, in Miranda's case, would have provided the adequate protection necessary to make the police interrogation conform to the dictates of the privilege against self-incrimination. Counsel's presence with Miranda would have ensured that statements made in the government-controlled interrogation atmosphere were not the product of compulsion.

In deciding *Miranda,* the Court resorted to "rule-making" by holding that an individual held for interrogation must be clearly informed by police that he or she has the right to consult a lawyer and be represented by the lawyer during interrogation. The person must be told that anything he or she says can be used as evidence. The Court noted that the warning under *Miranda* was an absolute prerequisite to interrogation.[9] According to the Court, it would not accept any circumstantial evidence that the person may have been aware of the right against self-incrimination. The Court believed that only through such a warning would there be ascertainable assurance that an accused would be aware of this right. Following the *Miranda* decision, if an individual who is in police custody indicates that the assistance of counsel is desired before any interrogation occurs, the police cannot rationally ignore or deny this request on the basis that the individual does not have or cannot afford a retained attorney. After the warnings have been given, when an arrestee indicates that he or she would like to remain silent, or at any time indicates that he or she wants to remain silent thereafter, or requests the assistance of legal counsel, according to the *Miranda* Court, interrogation must cease immediately.

5. PREREQUISITES FOR *MIRANDA* WARNINGS

Subsequent to the Court's *Miranda* decision, all law enforcement agencies were required to carefully advise every detainee of the constitutional rights under the Fifth and Sixth Amendments at any time police contemplated questioning a person in custody. While the original *Miranda* case dealt with a felony, a later decision[10] extended the right to be apprised of constitutional rights to misdemeanant detainees for whom interrogation is desired.

In *Berkemer v. McCarty,*[11] police had made a traffic stop for suspicion of misdemeanor driving under the influence of alcohol or drugs. While McCarty was detained and under the control of law enforcement officials, police questioned him concerning the details of his offense in hopes of obtaining evidence to be used against him. At no point in this sequence of events did the police inform McCarty that he had a right to remain silent, to consult with an attorney, and to have an attorney appointed for him if he could not afford one. During the police stop, McCarty offered incriminating evidence, which the prosecutor later introduced against him in court. The *McCarty* Court held that the *Miranda* warnings had to be given to misdemeanor suspects in custody whom the police wished to interrogate. But the Court held that persons who have been detained during a traffic stop are not "in custody" for *Miranda* purposes unless the stop results in an arrest.[12] Following *McCarty*, *Miranda* warnings must be given to all individuals prior to custodial interrogation, whether the offense investigated is a felony or a misdemeanor and regardless of the educational level or legal understanding of the arrestee. The warnings need not be offered if interrogation is not contemplated or in situations where custody does not exist at the time the question is uttered.

However, most traffic stops are considered to be exceptions to the requirements under *Miranda* because they are generally fairly brief, occur in public view, and do not typically generate the control associated with the necessity of offering a *Miranda* warning. Clearly a motorist can be said to be in the custody of a police officer at a traffic stop, but the custody is not considered the type of custody that the *Miranda* warnings were designed to address. Unless and until the traffic stop results in an arrest and the officer desires to interrogate the driver, the necessity of offering the *Miranda* warnings does not exist because the roadside detention and interrogation is not considered to be custody for *Miranda* purposes.[13]

6. SUBSTANCE OF THE WARNINGS

According to the *Miranda* Court, several warnings must be given to a person who is in custody and whom police officers would like to interrogate. The individual must be first informed in clear and unequivocal terms that he or she has the right to remain silent. Without this information, the person in custody might be unaware of the legal right not to speak. This warning seems to be an absolute prerequisite to overcoming the inherent pressure to talk that accompanies the interrogation atmosphere of an arrest. Second, the individual must be told that anything that is communicated to police may be used against him or her in a court of law. This advice is necessary to create awareness not only of the right to silence but also of the consequences of deciding to forgo it by speaking to law enforcement personnel. Third, the arrestee must be informed of the right to consult with an attorney; otherwise, the circumstances surrounding an in-custody interrogation can often overcome the will of an individual who has only been told about the right to remain silent and of the potential use of information if he or she chooses to speak. With the assistance of an attorney, there is much less likelihood that the police will attempt any level of coercion, and if any does occur, the attorney may testify about that fact. Fourth, the police must inform the arrestee that if he or she cannot afford an attorney, one will be appointed prior to any questioning. The information concerning free legal advice may prove to be very important for many individuals who lack financial resources. In the absence of this knowledge, an arrestee might otherwise understand that a right to legal counsel exists only for those who can afford to pay for the service. If these four basic warnings are not properly offered by law enforcement personnel to an individual who has been subjected to custodial interrogation, any evidence that the individual might convey, though offered voluntarily under traditional analysis, will be excluded from the prosecution's case in chief.

7. DELIVERING THE *MIRANDA* WARNINGS

In an effort to properly comply with the *Miranda* requirements, police officers often resort to reading the warnings from a printed form or card. Problems arise when officers administer the warnings in less than perfect order or, in some cases, with less than textbook clarity.[14] As a matter of routine practice, many police departments follow the oral warning with a written warning containing a check sheet to be signed by the person in custody. The sheet indicates whether the person understood the advisement of rights, desired to waive the warnings or to take advantage of them, wished to remain silent, and/or desired to consult with an attorney.

One of the difficulties with reading the *Miranda* warnings involves the circumstances under which they are typically administered. An oral warning sometimes must be given during an unsettled street scene or a domestic disturbance, situations that are less than ideal for conveying information. Although there must be a fairly clear administration of the warnings, some deviation from the original language has been upheld as appropriate. In *Duckworth v. Eagan,*[15] the Supreme Court approved a warning[16] given in a confusing manner in which the officer stated that the arrestee had the right to an attorney if and when he went to court. The warning first indicated that there was the right to counsel but then removed the essence of the guarantee when the arrestee was told that the police had no way to give him an attorney. Even though the language was less than a model of clarity and could imply that an attorney was not available immediately, the Court held that it met the minimum standards under *Miranda*.

8. WHEN *MIRANDA* WARNINGS ARE REQUIRED: THE TRIGGERING EVENTS

As a general rule, law enforcement officials possess no affirmative duty to warn any person of constitutional rights until the officer places the individual in custody and intends to initiate questioning. Thus, the triggering factors that give rise to the necessity of offering the *Miranda* warnings are governmental custody coupled with interrogation. However, interrogation concerning name, address, and related matters are not considered covered by the warnings otherwise required. As a general rule, if custody exists and interrogation occurs, any statement made by the subject in response to a police question prior to the administration of proper warnings cannot be admitted in evidence against defendant for proof of guilt. For example, in *Oregon v. Elstad,*[17] prior to giving the proper warnings, police lawfully arrested Elstad, asked an incriminating question, and received an incriminating response. Elstad's immediate answer, including the incriminating statements, was suppressed from his trial. Since police had an arrest warrant for Elstad and an officer was in his bedroom at the time the officer asked an incriminating question and received an answer, Elstad was in custody while the officer interrogated him in violation of the principles of *Miranda*. Subsequent statements at the police station that Elstad made after he had been given the *Miranda* warnings were properly admitted at his burglary trial.[18] However, the court suppressed the answers to questions in the bedroom.

However, when police intentionally fail to offer the *Miranda* warnings in a question-first technique, with the goal of obtaining an excludable admission or confession that will lead to admissible evidence, the later evidence following a proper reading of *Miranda* will be excluded from trial. In *Missouri v. Seibert* (Case 10.2), police questioned one of the defendants while in police custody prior to giving any *Miranda* warning. Both custody and interrogation occurred under circumstances calling for mandatory warnings. The police were hoping to obtain an inadmissible confession and then, after some time passed, offer the *Miranda* warnings and attempt to obtain the same confession that they felt should be admissible. Once the person had confessed prior to *Miranda*, the theory was that the person would feel as if no harm could be done to the case by making a repeat confession, since the earlier, unwarned confession had been made to police. In the *Seibert* case, the arrestee repeated her unwarned confession after she had been *Mirandized*, and the trial court allowed the second confession to be used against the defendant. The Supreme Court held that reciting the warnings after intentionally obtaining an unwarned confession failed to comply with the philosophy of the original *Miranda* case. The second confession should not have been admitted against the defendant because police were trying to thwart *Miranda*'s design of reducing the risk that an involuntary confession would be admitted. The use of successive interrogations designed to produce confessions failed to support a conclusion that giving the warnings in that manner could serve their purpose under *Miranda* (Case 10.2).

Some evidence taken in violation of *Miranda* may have utility for impeachment purposes if the defendant were to offer testimony from the witness stand that directly conflicted with earlier non-*Mirandized* statements.[19] In such a situation, the prosecution may introduce the illegally obtained statements solely to attempt to impeach the defendant and not for proof of guilt.

Once the warnings have been properly administered, the subject may choose to assert the rights under *Miranda* or may decide to waive the rights to silence and/or counsel. A waiver may be oral, written, or both, but the essence of a waiver is that the arrestee understands the significance of the rights being relinquished and the consequences that may flow from that decision. If the arrestee has been taken to a police station, the written waiver is most commonly used; a street waiver typically takes an oral form.

9. WHEN INTERROGATION MUST CEASE

During the encounter with police, if the arrestee indicates in any manner and at any time that he or she no further desire to be interrogated, the police inquiry must immediately cease, according to the Court in *Edwards v. Arizona*.[20] The police are not allowed to try to change the arrestee's mind; they must respect the right to silence until the arrestee has consulted an attorney and indicates a desire to speak to the police. In *Edwards*, the defendant asserted his right to speak with an attorney, and the initial interrogation ended. The next morning, when two detectives arrived at the jail, the detention officer in charge told Edwards that he "had" to speak with officers who wanted to talk to him. Eventually, Edwards implicated himself in criminal activities. The Court held that the admission into evidence of Edwards' confession given to the two detectives violated his rights under the Fifth and Fourteenth Amendments as construed in *Miranda v. Arizona*. According to *Miranda*, if the

CASE 10.2

Leading Case Brief: Attempts to Avoid *Miranda* Warnings Produce Bad Evidence

Missouri v. Seibert
Supreme Court of the United States
542 U.S. 600 (2004)

Case Facts:

Defendant-respondent Seibert feared that charges of neglect would be brought against her when her twelve-year-old son, who suffered from cerebral palsy, died in his sleep in her trailer home. Seibert listened to a plan offered by two of her sons and their friends to burn the family's trailer home to conceal the circumstances of the death of her impaired son. The plan contemplated that Donald, an unrelated mentally ill eighteen-year-old living with the family, was to be left to die in the fire, in order to avoid the appearance that the defendant-respondent's son had been unattended. Donald perished in the fire, according to plan. Following a short investigation, police arrested Seibert, but intentionally failed to read her the rights to which she was entitled under *Miranda v. Arizona*, 384 U.S. 436, 16 L. Ed. 2d 694, 86 S. Ct. 1602 (1966). At the police station, one of the officers interrogated her for thirty to forty minutes, obtaining an unwarned confession that the plan was for Donald to die in the fire. As part of a scheme derived from police training manuals, the officer gave the defendant-respondent a twenty-minute break, after which he returned and offered the *Miranda* warnings to her and obtained a signed *Miranda* waiver. The officer resumed questioning by confronting Seibert with her prewarning statements and managed to influence her to repeat the earlier unwarned confession. Prior to trial, Seibert filed a motion to suppress both her prewarned and postwarned statements. The interrogating officer testified that he made an intentional decision to withhold *Miranda* warnings, question her first, then give the warnings, and then repeat the questions to her until he received a repeat of the unwarned confession.

In ruling on the motion to suppress, the trial court held that the confession taken in violation of *Miranda* was inadmissible. However, the judge ruled that the second, post-*Miranda* statement/confession should be admitted in evidence with the result that Seibert was convicted of second-degree murder. The Missouri Supreme Court disagreed with the trial court and held that, because the interrogation was nearly continuous, the second confession, which was clearly the product of the invalid first statement, should have been suppressed. The Supreme Court of the United States granted certiorari.

Legal Issue:

May police officers, consistent with the requirements of the *Miranda* warnings, conduct custodial interrogation until a confession is obtained and then offer the warnings with the hope that the original, unwarned confession will be repeated?

The Court's Ruling:

Attempts to evade the constitutional requirements of the *Miranda* warnings by careful interrogation or other plans will not be acceptable to the Court and will result in evidence being excluded.

Essence of the Court's Rationale:

* * *

[W]e hold that a statement repeated after a warning in such circumstances is inadmissible.

* * *

In *Miranda,* we explained that the "voluntariness doctrine in the state cases . . . encompasses all interrogation practices which are likely to exert such pressure upon an individual as to disable him from making a free and rational choice," *id.* at 464–465, 16 L. Ed. 2d

(continued)

694, 86 S. Ct. 1602. We appreciated the difficulty of judicial enquiry *post hoc* into the circumstances of a police interrogation, *Dickerson v. United States,* 530 U.S. 428, 444, 147 L. Ed. 2d 405, 120 S. Ct. 2326 (2000), and recognized that "the coercion inherent in custodial interrogation blurs the line between voluntary and involuntary statements, and thus heightens the risk" that the privilege against self-incrimination will not be observed, *id.,* at 435, 147 L. Ed. 2d 405, 120 S. Ct. 2326. Hence our concern that the "traditional totality-of-the-circumstances" test posed an "unacceptably great" risk that involuntary custodial confessions would escape detection. *Id.,* at 442, 147 L. Ed. 2d 405, 120 S. Ct. 2326.

* * *

There are those, of course, who preferred the old way of doing things, giving no warnings and litigating the voluntariness of any statement in nearly every instance. In the aftermath of *Miranda,* Congress even passed a statute seeking to restore that old regime, 18 U.S.C. § 3501, although the Act lay dormant for years until finally invoked and challenged in *Dickerson v. United States, supra. Dickerson* reaffirmed *Miranda* and held that its constitutional character prevailed against the statute.

* * *

When a confession so obtained is offered and challenged, attention must be paid to the conflicting objects of *Miranda* and question-first. *Miranda* addressed "interrogation practices . . . likely . . . to disable [an individual] from making a free and rational choice" about speaking, 384 U.S., at 464–465, 16 L. Ed. 2d 694, 86 S. Ct. 1602, and held that a suspect must be "adequately and effectively" advised of the choice the Constitution guarantees, *id.,* at 467, 16 L. Ed. 2d 694, 86 S. Ct. 1602. The object of question-first is to render *Miranda* warnings ineffective by waiting for a particularly opportune time to give them, after the suspect has already confessed.

* * *

The threshold issue when interrogators question first and warn later is thus whether it would be reasonable to find that in these circumstances the warnings could function "effectively" as *Miranda* requires. Could the warnings effectively advise the suspect that he had a real choice about giving an admissible statement at that juncture? Could they reasonably convey

that he could choose to stop talking even if he had talked earlier? For unless the warnings could place a suspect who has just been interrogated in a position to make such an informed choice, there is no practical justification for accepting the formal warnings as compliance with *Miranda,* or for treating the second stage of interrogation as distinct from the first, unwarned and inadmissible segment.

* * *

The unwarned interrogation was conducted in the station house, and the questioning was systematic, exhaustive, and managed with psychological skill. When the police were finished there was little, if anything, of incriminating potential left unsaid. The warned phase of questioning proceeded after a pause of only 15 to 20 minutes, in the same place as the unwarned segment. When the same officer who had conducted the first phase recited the *Miranda* warnings, he said nothing to counter the probable misimpression that the advice that anything Seibert said could be used against her also applied to the details of the inculpatory statement previously elicited. In particular, the police did not advise that her prior statement could not be used.

* * *

VI

Strategists dedicated to draining the substance out of *Miranda* cannot accomplish by training instructions what *Dickerson* held Congress could not do by statute. Because the question-first tactic effectively threatens to thwart *Miranda*'s purpose of reducing the risk that a coerced confession would be admitted, and because the facts here do not reasonably support a conclusion that the warnings given could have served their purpose, Seibert's postwarning statements are inadmissible. [The Supreme Court of the United States held that] [t]he judgment of the Supreme Court of Missouri is affirmed.

Case Importance:

In a prior case, *Dickerson v. United States,* 530 U.S. 428, (2000), the Court determined that the *Miranda* warnings were required by the federal Constitution. The Court stressed and reaffirmed that the guarantees of the Constitution cannot be evaded by skilful police interrogation designed to avoid the philosophy and the requirements of the *Miranda* warnings.

accused indicates a wish to remain silent, the interrogation must cease; if he requests counsel, the interrogation must cease until an attorney is present. The Court decided that where an accused has expressed the desire to deal with the police only through counsel, he or she is not subject to further interrogation by the authorities until counsel has been made available, unless the arrestee personally initiates further communication, exchanges, or conversations with the law enforcement officers.

Interrogation with custody has been permitted where an arrestee has not requested an attorney and has not clearly noted his or her desire to remain silent, or where the arrestee has made an ambiguous reference to counsel insufficient to invoke the prohibition against further questioning. Nothing in *Edwards* requires furnishing counsel to a suspect who consents to answer questions without the assistance of a lawyer. Where an arrestee indicated only a desire to stand on the Fifth Amendment privilege against self-incrimination and has not requested to speak with a lawyer, police may inquire if he or she wants to answer questions after they have waited a significant amount of time. Police must inquire concerning crimes *unrelated to the crime for which the person is in custody,* and police must offer the *Miranda* warnings a second time.[21]

Even where police attempt to question an arrestee about additional crimes *unrelated* to the reason for initial custody and the arrestee has previously invoked the right to counsel protections under *Miranda,* such questioning runs afoul of *Arizona v. Roberson.*[22] In *Roberson,* the arrestee indicated that he did not wish to speak with police and wanted an attorney. Three days later, while the defendant was still in custody, a different police officer approached him, advised him of his rights, and obtained a confession for a crime for which Roberson was not then under arrest. Since Roberson had indicated that he wished to speak only to a lawyer and not to police, that wish should have been respected under the *Edwards* rule. The *Roberson* Court held that the confession for the second crime should have been excluded from admission at his trial for the second offense.

However, when the arrestee has not refused to speak with police or asserted his or her right to silence and has not requested to speak with an attorney but has been to court on different charges, police may ask if the arrestee is willing to waive *Miranda* rights and speak with police concerning criminal matters unrelated to the reason the defendant was in court. An accused's invocation of his or her Sixth Amendment right to counsel during a judicial proceeding does not constitute an invocation of the *Miranda*-derived right to counsel emanating from the Fifth Amendment's guarantee against compelled self-incrimination.[23] Under these circumstances, the *Edwards* rule does not apply.

Since *Miranda* warnings are necessary only where both custody *and* interrogation are present, if police merely make an arrest with no immediate design of interrogation, there is no absolute need to offer *Miranda* warnings. Similarly, where a question directed to a person clearly not in custody might elicit an incriminating response, no *Miranda* warning is essential, since the person is free to leave and free to disregard the question. Some situations involving both custody and interrogation do not require a *Miranda* warning where the element of coercion does not exist. If, for example, the police place a plainclothes officer with an arrestee within a jail cell and the arrestee is unaware that the person with whom he or she is speaking is a police officer, no *Miranda* warnings are necessary, provided the plainclothes officer does not actually question the arrestee about the crime for which he or she is in custody.[24]

In *Perkins,* police placed an undercover officer in a cell with Perkins, who was incarcerated on charges unrelated to homicide. The undercover officer engaged in small talk and banter until the two men began to talk of their criminal careers. Perkins made damaging admissions about a homicide, which he readily admitted committing. According to the Court, the prosecution could use Perkins' admissions against him because there was no chance of coercion or overreaching by the government, since Perkins was unaware of the status of his cellmate. The *Perkins* Court held that "an undercover law enforcement officer posing as a fellow inmate need not give *Miranda* warnings to an incarcerated suspect before asking questions that may elicit an incriminating response."[25]

10. NECESSARY CONDITION FOR *MIRANDA* WARNINGS: CUSTODY

To determine when *Miranda* warnings become mandatory, an understanding of the legal definition of custody proves essential. Although the concept of custody would appear to be quite clear, court definitions have failed to provide a complete model of clarity.[26] In *Miranda,* the Court considered custody to exist when the individual had been restrained of his freedom of movement in any significant manner or otherwise deprived of freedom of action in any significant way. While a formal arrest clearly meets this standard, other situations with murky fact patterns fail to offer a bright line for determination. In *California v. Beheler,*[27] a suspect with information about a homicide had responded to a police invitation to discuss the matter at the station house. At the interview and prior to offering any *Miranda* warning, police informed Beheler that they believed he had been involved in the crime. During the discussion, Beheler admitted his presence and some participation in the homicide, at which point the police informed him of his *Miranda* rights. Although Beheler was released without charge at that time, he contended that he had been in actual custody at the time of his inculpatory statements. The Court ultimately stated that as "a determination of whether a suspect is 'in custody' for purposes of receiving *Miranda* protection, the ultimate inquiry is simply whether there is a 'formal arrest or restraint on freedom of movement.'"[28] Applying this standard, Beheler was not in custody when he voluntarily met with and spoke to the investigators. The key to *Beheler* may have been that he was freely permitted to leave at the end of the questioning, indicating a lack of custody.

In another case with similar but not identical facts, when federal agents notified an elderly suspect that they would like to discuss some matters with him, the suspect suggested that they talk in a conference room that he controlled. The federal agents rejected the conference room location and insisted on driving with the suspect to the local FBI headquarters. Once inside the government conference room, they failed to tell the subject that he was not under arrest and that he was free to leave at any time. The interview lasted approximately four hours, during which the government agents failed to give the suspect breaks from the discussion even to call his wife, as was his custom due to ill health. The officers did not want him to call home because it might have interfered with the interview. When the agents were satisfied by what they had learned and ended the discussions, the subject wanted to drive his car home, but officers accompanied him to his office and on the trip to his home. The trial court ordered suppression of the evidence discovered from the interview on the ground that, under the circumstances, no reasonable person would have felt free to have ended the interview and walked out the door. According to the judge, the *Miranda* warnings should have been given because the suspect had been interrogated while in custody.[29]

Although an arrest accompanied with the use of handcuffs while the subject is under the complete control of an officer would indicate that custody exists, other situations similar to *Beheler* may not be so clear, even when the individual freely leaves the police station following an interview. In *Thompson v. Keohane*,[30] police asked a murder suspect to voluntarily come to the station to answer some questions. At their headquarters, several Alaska state troopers interrogated Thompson for two hours. Thompson's ex-wife had been missing for a while, and the police had been notified of a suspicious death of a woman. The police had invited Thompson to come to headquarters and discuss the case, but they did not tell him that he was a prime suspect. Thompson was not given any *Miranda* warnings, and he was told he was free to leave at any time while or after talking with police. Police told him that he was a suspect in a murder, and Thompson subsequently admitted killing his ex-wife. He was allowed to leave the station because he was not under arrest. Following his conviction for murder, he contended that he had been in custody during the interrogation and that his confession should have been excluded from evidence because his rights under *Miranda* had been violated. According to the *Thompson* Court, for custody purposes,

> Two discrete inquiries are essential to the determination: first, what were the circumstances surrounding the interrogation; and second, given those circumstances, would a reasonable person have felt he or she was not at liberty to terminate the interrogation and leave. *Thompson* at 112

Most individuals would consider themselves in custody following a confession to murder, and most police officers would not allow such a person to leave the police station, but Thompson appeared not to be in custody, and *Miranda* may not have been required.[31]

In some situations, an individual may believe that the police have taken custody when, in fact, they have made no such decision.[32] In such a case, "a person who honestly but unreasonably believes he is in custody is subject to the same coercive pressures as one whose belief is reasonable; this suggests that such persons also are entitled to warnings."[33] Alternatively, a detainee may feel free to leave when, in reality, police would not permit the individual to leave if an attempt were to be made. Another view of when custody exists focuses on the point in time when a reasonable officer would believe that custody has been taken of the individual, but this view does not appear to be the controlling opinion.

More recently, a federal court of appeal offered additional factors to consider in making a determination of whether a person is in custody and should be given the *Miranda* warnings.[34] This court took the position that the question of custody should be driven by what a reasonable person in the suspect's position would believe with respect to custody. The court considered several factors to determine the issue of custody. In consideration of the first factor, the court noted that the search of the defendant's home was by warrant, occurred early in the morning, and included interrogation. The second factor that pointed toward custody was the presence of eight officers in the defendant's home. The police confronting the defendant with an unholstered gun in his bedroom indicated that police did not expect the defendant to be leaving soon. A factor indicating custody involved the way the police controlled all aspects of what occurred within the home, including where the defendant could locate in the home, when his girlfriend showered, and when she went to work. The fact that the police interrogated the subject in excess of one and a half hours indicated his lack of freedom to leave the premises. Finally, custody could be indicated by the coercive statements made by some of the police that invited cooperation while avoiding offering the *Miranda* warnings during interrogation.

11. NECESSARY CONDITION FOR *MIRANDA* WARNINGS: INTERROGATION

The second factor to be considered in determining whether *Miranda* warnings need to be administered is whether police officers have initiated interrogation. Most interrogation takes the form of the officer asking direct questions and the arrestee answering, refusing to answer, or being evasive. While the existence of interrogation can generally be discerned from the conduct of the participants, the act of interrogation may not always be interrogatory sentences. Subtle communication may disguise a question, making it appear to be a declarative sentence, where the pressure is on the subject to make a response. If, in the presence of the arrestee, police officers talk among themselves about the case at hand and make derogatory remarks about the crime, the suspect, or the manner in which the crime was committed, the arrestee may be prompted or feel obligated to say something that could be incriminating. If police reasonably expected a response under the circumstances, many courts will hold that the act of speaking in the presence of the arrestee constitutes the functional equivalent of interrogation and a violation of the principles of *Miranda*. In a slightly different context, police may not interrogate a person who is in custody, obtain an unwarned confession, and then read the warnings, in hopes of having the subject repeat an earlier admission or confession that would now follow the *Miranda* warnings.

12. *MIRANDA* INTERROGATION: THE FUNCTIONAL EQUIVALENT

Interrogation may take many forms and may be so subtle that the one being interrogated may not always be aware that questioning is actually happening. In *Rhode Island v. Innis* (Case 10.3),[35] the Court held that the term *interrogation,* for *Miranda* purposes, not only includes direct and unequivocal questions but also encompasses "any words or actions on the part of the police (other than those normally attendant to arrest and custody) that the police should know are reasonably likely to elicit an incriminating response from the suspect."[36] In *Innis,* the police officers were talking

CASE 10.3

Leading Case Brief: Creative Conduct by Police Officers May Constitute Custodial Interrogation

Rhode Island v. Innis
Supreme Court of the United States
446 U.S. 291 (1980)

Case Facts:

Following a dispatch to pick up a fare, a Providence, Rhode Island, taxicab driver's body was discovered. A day later, another taxicab driver reported that he had been robbed at gunpoint by a man wielding a sawed-off shotgun. At the police station, the taxi driver noticed a photograph of Innis on the mug board and identified him as the robber. Police initiated a search in the area where the taxi driver robbery occurred.

A police officer discovered Innis walking on the public street, placed him under arrest, and read him the standard *Miranda* warnings. While waiting for backup officers, the arresting officer did not converse with Innis. Subsequently, a police captain read the *Miranda* warnings to Innis a second time. Innis indicated that he wished to speak with an attorney, so the police ceased efforts to interrogate him and began to transport Innis to the police station.

Three officers rode with Innis to the central station. The police captain instructed the officers not to question Innis or intimidate or coerce him in any way. En route to the jail, two officers conversed about what a tragedy it would be if one of the children from the handicapped children's school near the point of arrest happened to find a loaded shotgun and it would be too bad if a little girl would pick up the gun and harm herself.

Patrolman Gleckman later testified at Innis's trial:

A. At this point, I was talking back and forth with Patrolman McKenna stating that I frequent this area while on patrol [and that, because a school for handicapped children is located nearby] there's a lot of handicapped children running around in this area, and God forbid one of them might find a weapon with shells and they might hurt themselves. App. 43–44.

Officer Gleckman also said that, in the conversation with Officer McKenna, he intimated that it would be a tragedy if some little girl would find the gun and accidentally kill herself.

Innis interrupted the conversation of McKenna and Gleckman and told them that he would reveal where he had hidden the missing shotgun if they would return to the scene of his arrest. Upon arrival, the police captain, read the *Miranda* rights to Innis again. Innis noted that he wanted to show the police the gun because of the danger to the handicapped schoolchildren. He pointed out the shotgun under some rocks by the side of the road.

The prosecutor introduced the shotgun as evidence after the trial court refused Innis' efforts to suppress the shotgun under *Miranda.* Following the return of a guilty verdict, Innis filed a successful appeal based on the alleged *Miranda* violation. The Rhode Island Supreme Court agreed with his contention concerning the *Miranda* violation and reversed his conviction. According to the Court, the police officers in the vehicle had "interrogated" the respondent without a valid waiver of his right to counsel when they spoke in front of him. The Rhode Island Supreme Court believed that Innis had been subjected to "subtle coercion" that was the functional equivalent of interrogation.

The Supreme Court of the United States granted certiorari to address the meaning of *interrogation* under *Miranda v. Arizona,* 440 U.S. 934.

Legal Issue:

If police officers discuss an arrestee's case where the arrestee can hear the police and the officers' conversation has not been specially tailored to motivate or coerce the arrestee to speak on the facts of the case, is

(continued)

such conduct by police officers the functional equivalent of interrogation under *Miranda*?

The Court's Ruling:

The officer's conversation did not involve interrogation. The Court could find no reason to believe that the officers were talking between themselves with an intention to get the arrestee to incriminate himself and the officers had no special knowledge of any special sensitivities of the arrestee. Therefore, their conversation was not determined to be the functional equivalent of interrogation.

Essence of the Court's Rationale:

* * *

II

In the present case, the parties are in agreement that the respondent was fully informed of his *Miranda* rights, and that he invoked his *Miranda* right to counsel when he told Captain Leyden that he wished to consult with a lawyer. It is also uncontested that the respondent was "in custody" while being transported to the police station.

The issue, therefore, is whether the respondent was "interrogated" by the police officers in violation of the respondent's undisputed right under *Miranda* to remain silent until he had consulted with a lawyer. In resolving this issue, we first define the term "interrogation" under *Miranda* before turning to a consideration of the facts of this case.

A

The starting point for defining "interrogation" in this context is, of course, the Court's *Miranda* opinion. There the Court observed that,

> [b]y custodial interrogation, we mean *questioning* initiated by law enforcement officers after a person has been taken into custody or otherwise deprived of his freedom of action in any significant way. *Id.* At 44 (emphasis added).

This passage and other references throughout the opinion to "questioning" might suggest that the *Miranda* rules were to apply only to those police interrogation practices that involve express questioning of a defendant while in custody.

* * *

The Court in *Miranda* also included in its survey of interrogation practices the use of psychological ploys, such as to "postulate" "the guilt of the subject," to "minimize the moral seriousness of the offense," and "to cast blame on the victim or on society." It is clear that these techniques of persuasion, no less than express questioning, were thought, in a custodial setting, to amount to interrogation.

* * *

We conclude that the *Miranda* safeguards come into play whenever a person in custody is subjected to either express questioning or its functional equivalent. That is to say, the term "interrogation" under *Miranda* refers not only to express questioning, but also to any words or actions on the part of the police (other than those normally attendant to arrest and custody) that the police should know are reasonably likely to elicit an incriminating response from the suspect. The latter portion of this definition focuses primarily upon the perceptions of the suspect, rather than the intent of the police.

* * *

Moreover, it cannot be fairly concluded that the respondent was subjected to the "functional equivalent" of questioning. It cannot be said, in short, that Patrolmen Gleckman and McKenna should have known that their conversation was reasonably likely to elicit an incriminating response from the respondent. There is nothing in the record to suggest that the officers were aware that the respondent was peculiarly susceptible to an appeal to his conscience concerning the safety of handicapped children. Nor is there anything in the record to suggest that the police knew that the respondent was unusually disoriented or upset at the time of his arrest.

* * *

It is our view, therefore, that the respondent was not subjected by the police to words or actions that the police should have known were reasonably likely to elicit an incriminating response from him.

* * *

For the reasons stated, the judgment of the Supreme Court of Rhode Island is vacated, and the case is remanded to that court for further proceedings not inconsistent with this opinion.

Case Importance:

The *Innis* litigation indicated that interrogation can include speech by police officers that does not seem to constitute questioning and may involve sentences that do not have a question mark at the end. Police conduct constitutes interrogation or its functional equivalent where police intend it to motivate an arrestee to make incriminating conversation that the police desire to hear.

among themselves but in front of an arrestee concerning the missing firearm belonging to the arrestee. One of the officers stated that quite a few handicapped children were running around and playing near the crime scene because a school for such children was nearby. The officer noted, "God forbid one of them might find a weapon with shells and they might hurt themselves."[37] Innis told the officers to turn the car around and that he would show them the location of the gun. A practice that the police reasonably should know is likely to motivate a suspect to make an incriminating response has the same legal effect as overt interrogation. In the *Innis* case, the Court clearly indicated that the definition of interrogation focuses on the reasonable intentions of the police rather than on the individual in custody. For example, if two police officers were to speak with each other in front of an arrestee and comment that if one of them had been arrested, he certainly would have denied guilt or explained his innocence, courts would probably hold that the arrestee had been interrogated under *Miranda.* However, merely asking a subject prior to a pat-down whether he had any sharp objects that could hurt the officer does not constitute custodial interrogation under *Miranda,* even if it produces incriminating verbal or physical evidence. Since the officers' question serves the noncriminal purpose of officer safety, it falls squarely within the class of questions that typically accompany arrest and custody.[38] Police conduct constitutes interrogation or its functional equivalent where it is intended to motivate an arrestee to initiate conversation that the police desire to hear.[39]

Thus the Court held that a practice that the police should understand would be likely or is intended to provoke an incriminating response from an arrestee amounts to custodial interrogation. In *Nix v. Williams,* 467 U.S. 431 (1984), an officer who knew a mental patient was deeply religious did not interrogate in the usual sense. He played upon the sensitivities of the arrestee to get the prisoner to tell him where a murdered girl's body was located in order to give her a proper burial. While in the police cruiser, one office suggested that with the snow coming that night and the passage of time, even the arrestee might not be able to locate the girl's body later, a fact that would deprive the parents of a proper Christian burial for the body. The Supreme Court held this approach to constitute the functional equivalent of interrogation under *Miranda,* which required suppression of his words, but determined that the physical evidence of the girl's body and her personal items would have been inevitably discovered and were properly admitted against defendant Williams.

Private, nongovernmental questioning and conversation do not implicate the protective warnings of *Miranda.* In one case, interrogation did not occur for *Miranda* purposes where a wife, in the presence of an officer, was allowed to speak with her husband, who was under arrest for murder of their son. In *Arizona v. Mauro,*[40] police had arrested Mauro following his confession to the murder of his own son. Subsequent to receiving his *Miranda* warnings, he told the officers he did not wish to speak further until he had seen an attorney. With some reluctance, police allowed his wife to speak with Mauro in the presence of a police officer and in full view of an operating tape recorder. Mauro answered his wife's questions concerning why he had killed their son. The information on the audio recording and related police testimony was properly admitted at his murder trial despite Mauro's contention that the tape recording constituted custodial interrogation. Although the police might have expected that some incriminating information might be elicited between husband and wife, the police officers were not conducting an interrogation, even though they openly recorded the conversation. The Court refused to follow language from *Innis,* where the Court stated that interrogation includes a "practice that the police should know is reasonably likely to evoke an incriminating response from a suspect."[41] Crucial to the Court's decision in *Mauro* was the fact that the police did not conduct the interrogation; Mauro's spouse questioned him about his role in the death of their son.

In a similar manner in a 2007 case involving drugs and firearms, *United States v. Kimbrough,*[42] police arrested a son who lived with his mother and who had been sitting on a basement bed, apparently dividing cocaine on a plate with a razor blade. Police brought the son into the presence of his mother at her home. The *Miranda* warnings had not been completed when the mother began to interrogate her own son concerning drugs and guns. The police stood by as the mother asked questions without direction or involvement by the police and listened as he gave incriminating information to his mother that the police duly noted. The federal district court ordered the incriminating answers suppressed from defendant Kimbrough's trial because the judge concluded that the mother's involvement in the questioning of her son was the same as official police custodial interrogation. However, on the prosecution's appeal, the Court of Appeals reversed and held that the son's statements were not the result of express police interrogation and did not qualify as a functional equivalent of police questioning. The statements made to his mother in front of police officers should be admitted against defendant Kimbrough, when and if the case proceeded to trial.

13. EXIGENT CIRCUMSTANCE EXCEPTION TO *MIRANDA* INTERROGATION

Although the Court initially required that *Miranda* warnings be offered in every situation in which law enforcement officials desired to conduct custodial interrogation of an arrestee, the Court recognized a public safety or emergency exception. In *New York v. Quarles,*[43] the officer had reason, based on a complaint, to believe that the arrestee had hidden a loaded gun near the officer, which could have been used to harm the officer or the public. Presumably, the arrestee could have lunged to gain dominion and control of the gun, or a confederate could have acquired it and attempted to harm the officer or frustrate the arrest. Under the circumstances, the *Quarles* Court held that the officer was free to inquire about the weapon prior to offering any *Miranda* warning and that the prosecution was permitted to introduce both the weapon and the oral answers against the defendant. In contrast to the usual requirements, due to the emergency situation, the *Quarles* Court permitted the admission of the words and the gun despite the absence of *Miranda* warnings prior to custodial interrogation.

Under *Quarles,* the rule emerged that where an immediate danger to the safety of the public or a police officer appeared to exist, police can delay offering the *Miranda* warnings and may question the suspect in an effort to alleviate the imminent danger. The questions asked should be directed toward discovery of a dangerous weapon and must be reasonably directed to ending a police or public danger rather than focused on the collection of evidence. Emergencies could conceivably include the location of explosives, the location of a kidnapping victim, discovery of poisons directed at the public, or other terror-type situations in which time is crucial to life and health. The exact limits of the public safety exception to *Miranda* have not been fully developed in state and federal litigation, and the Supreme Court of the United States has not accepted a second case concerning the doctrine. Since the number of public safety exception cases remains small, the full development of this doctrine will be a long time coming. Notwithstanding the failure to offer the *Miranda* warnings where the public safety exception has application, verbal and physical evidence obtained by delaying the *Miranda* warnings will be admissible at trial against an arrestee and will not normally be subject to evidentiary exclusion.

A New Jersey court reviewed the requirements of a public safety emergency and found that the doctrine had some limitations. In *New Jersey v. Stephenson,*[44] police had been called to a motel room occupied by a single person who had been reported threatening others with a firearm. When the subject allowed police to enter the motel room, they patted him down, with negative results. One of the officers asked about the location of the gun, which prompted an obvious nervous demeanor on the part of the subject. The officers noted that the subject appeared to be looking for a way to leave the motel room. At this point the officers handcuffed him but told him that he was not under arrest. When the officers told him that they would get a warrant to search the room, the suspect gestured toward a dresser and stated that a gun was inside. Upon finding the gun, the police placed him under arrest and advised him of his *Miranda* rights. The court of appeals held that the public safety exception under the *Quarles* case did not apply to a situation where the public was in no immediate danger and the police faced no unusual danger, since they had the situation well under control. The appeals court rejected the admission of the firearm into evidence, since the court felt that the police were in the process of gathering information for a prosecution instead of acting to protect themselves or the public from an immediate danger.[45]

14. RIGHT TO COUNSEL UNDER *MIRANDA* IS PERSONAL TO ARRESTEE

The *Miranda*-derived right to counsel is personal to the accused and cannot be asserted by a family member or even the arrestee's attorney. In *Moran v. Burbine,*[46] the police arrested Burbine on a burglary charge but quickly focused on him as a possible homicide suspect wanted in another jurisdiction. Burbine's sister, who was unaware that police suspected Burbine of murder, arranged for a public defender to render legal assistance for her brother on the burglary charge. When the attorney phoned the police, they informed her that Burbine would not be interrogated on the burglary charge that evening. Significantly, the police did not tell the attorney that another jurisdiction's law enforcement officials were planning to question Burbine about the homicide. Burbine did not know that he was represented by counsel.

When the police from the second jurisdiction orally gave him new *Miranda* warnings, Burbine waived his rights and also signed three written warning acknowledgments. Subsequently, Burbine signed three incriminating statements admitting to the murder. Burbine was unaware of his sister's efforts to retain counsel and of the attorney's telephone call to police, but at no time did he request an attorney.

Following his conviction for murder, Burbine appealed, contending that his rights under *Miranda* and his right to due process had been violated by the police practice. The Supreme Court held that police deception of the defendant's attorney—by not telling her that her client was a homicide suspect and by actively misinforming her that her client would not be interrogated that evening—did not violate the protections of *Miranda*. Similarly, when the police did not inform the suspect that his attorney wished to speak with him, such subterfuge did not affect the voluntariness of his statements to police or alter his lack of desire to have an attorney present. The *Burbine* Court held that the trial court ruled correctly by allowing the confessions into evidence and that Burbine had waived his right to counsel and his Fifth Amendment privilege against self-incrimination. Requiring police to inform arrestees that an attorney wishes to consult with them would create an inappropriate shift in the careful balance struck in *Miranda* between the needs of law enforcement and the constitutional protections accruing to the accused.

The *Burbine* Court clearly held that the constitutional rights enforced by *Miranda* are personal to the accused and cannot be asserted by a family member, an attorney, or any other individual.

15. PROCEDURE FOR WAIVER OF *MIRANDA* PROTECTION

In order to relinquish the protections offered by *Miranda,* an individual may indicate the decision to waive *Miranda* rights by an oral statement, a written statement, or both, or by other unambiguous conduct. In *Miranda v. Arizona,* the Court held that a suspect's waiver of the Fifth Amendment privilege against self-incrimination is valid only if it is made voluntarily, knowingly, and intelligently. In determining the standards for a *Miranda* waiver, the Court in *Moran v. Burbine* held that a two-step approach was required:

> First, the relinquishment of the right must have been voluntary in the sense that it was the product of a free and deliberate choice, rather than intimidation, coercion, or deception. Second, the waiver must have been made with a full awareness of both the nature of the right being abandoned and the consequences of the decision to abandon it. 475 U.S. 412, at 421 (1975)

Waivers are not effective unless there are both particular and systemic assurances that the coercive pressures of custody were not the inducing cause. In determining whether a defendant has chosen to give up his *Miranda* rights, courts look to all the attendant circumstances. In *Miranda,* the Court noted that the rules for custodial interrogation did not include any change from prior practice when an arrestee volunteered statements. A waiver may exist where the arrestee initiated the conversation with police or requested that an officer come to the cell and speak with the arrestee, or where the arrestee confessed without any intervention by police. For example, in *Colorado v. Connelly,* 479 U.S. 157 (1986), Connelly walked up to a police officer and confessed to murder; after being advised of his *Miranda* warnings and indicating that he understood them, he stated that he still wished to talk about the murder. The Court approved Connelly's waiver by affirmative conduct and by voluntary consent. The Court did not suggest that the officer should have stopped Connelly and warned him under *Miranda* before allowing him to continue his confession to murder. However, once the officer had heard sufficient information to deny the subject permission to freely leave, asking a substantive question about the crime would run counter to *Miranda* principles because the subject would then be in custody.

Typically, investigators prefer to obtain a written statement of waiver, but during the initial phases of an investigation such practice may prove difficult, and the lack of a written waiver is not fatal to admissibility.[47] If an arrestee purportedly makes a valid waiver and subsequently denies so doing, a heavy burden of proof rests with the government to demonstrate that the decision to waive the constitutional rights was made knowingly and intelligently.[48]

A waiver of the *Miranda* warnings may be implied rather than expressed in many contexts. If arrestees fail to state that they are waiving their rights but do so by words and/or conduct and begin talking to police, sometimes asking officers questions and generally engaging them in conversation, a waiver under *Miranda* may exist. As a general rule, a valid waiver cannot be inferred from the silence of an arrestee after warnings are given or deduced from the fact that the arrestee eventually offered a confession. As the Court stated in *Carnley v. Cochran:*

> Presuming waiver from a silent record is impermissible. The record must show, or there must be an allegation and evidence which show, that an accused was offered counsel but intelligently and understandingly rejected the offer. Anything less is not waiver. 369 U.S. 506, 516 (1962)

Moreover, where in-custody interrogation is involved, there is no room for the contention that the privilege is waived if the individual answers some questions or gives some information on his own prior to invoking his right to remain silent when interrogated. In most cases, if law enforcement officers did not violate an arrestee's constitutional rights or practice coercion, an individual's personal motivation to waive the protections of *Miranda* to make an admission or a confession does not create an involuntary confession. A confession has not been received in violation of *Miranda* and is not considered coerced even if it has been prompted by a mental illness,[49] a desire to please family members, or an overwhelming religious experience.[50] On issues of alleged waiver of *Miranda* rights, the prosecution has the burden of proof by a preponderance of the evidence.[51]

A prosecutor may not successfully argue that a person who was never read the *Miranda* warnings nevertheless properly understood them and has effectively waived any claims under the *Miranda doctrine.* According to the *Miranda* Court,

> a warning is an absolute prerequisite in overcoming the inherent pressures of the interrogation atmosphere. It is not just the subnormal or woefully ignorant who succumb to an interrogator's imprecations, whether implied or expressly stated, that the interrogation will continue until a confession is obtained or that silence in the face of accusation is itself damning and will bode ill when presented to a jury.[52]

Such language appears to close the door to any prosecutor making the argument that the warnings, in a specific situation, were unnecessary, given the arrestee's education or experience.

16. CONGRESSIONAL CHALLENGE TO THE *MIRANDA* WARNINGS

From the initial decision in *Miranda v. Arizona,* members of Congress, among others, were neither happy with the result nor willing to allow a guilty person to go free because of a police officer's defective warning. In the wake of that decision, Congress enacted 18 U.S.C. § 3501,[53] which provided that the admissibility of such statements taken in violation of the *Miranda* warnings should turn only on whether they were voluntarily made and not be thrown out of court because of a defective *Miranda* warning. Under Section 3501, Congress directed federal courts to determine if the confession or other inculpatory statements were voluntarily made, according to traditional analysis, taking into consideration the time when the suspect made a confession, whether the suspect had been warned of the use of his or her statement, whether the individual had been made aware of the right to counsel, and whether counsel was present when the statement was made. According to congressional intent, if the statement or confession were made voluntarily, then such evidence should be admitted in federal courts, even if the *Miranda* warnings had never been offered. In other words, the evidence should be admitted if voluntarily offered where there was an absence of coerciveness. The design of Congress was to override the Court's decision in *Miranda v. Arizona* and replace it with the traditional voluntariness of confession standard[54] rather than follow *Miranda*'s conclusive presumption of coerciveness and exclusion where the warnings had not been given properly.

17. *MIRANDA* WARNINGS: REQUIRED BY THE CONSTITUTION

In *Dickerson v. United States,* 530 U.S. 428 (2000) (Case 10.4), the Supreme Court determined that the case of *Miranda v. Arizona* was of constitutional dimension, which meant that the decision could not be nullified or overturned by an act of Congress. It is a rule of constitutional construction that if a decision of the Supreme Court has as its basis the interpretation of the Constitution, the Congress cannot tell the Court that a different meaning must be used. In the United States, the Supreme Court is the final arbiter of what the Constitution means and how it may be interpreted. Even before

CASE 10.4

Leading Case Brief: *Miranda* Warnings Are Required under the Constitution

Dickerson v. United States
Supreme Court of the United States
530 U.S. 428 (2000)

Case Facts:

Subsequent to the decision of *Miranda v. Arizona,* law enforcement officials were required to read to persons in custody warnings against self-incrimination and to advise concerning the availability of the right to counsel as well as to inform the person that if the individual spoke, the information could be used against the person in court. The Supreme Court required these warnings if police planned to attempt to interrogate an arrestee. A breach of the warning process followed by incriminating statements resulted in otherwise voluntary statements being excluded for proof of guilt in state and federal criminal trials. Displeased with the *Miranda* warning requirement, Congress enacted 18 U.S.C. § 3501, which, in essence, made the admissibility of statements taken in violation of the *Miranda* warnings turn solely on whether they were made freely and voluntarily under traditional understandings of the words.

Dickerson, under indictment for bank robbery and allied crimes, filed a petition to suppress incriminating statements he made following a custodial, non-*Mirandized* interrogation. The trial court granted his motion and ruled that his statements would be excluded from trial; the prosecution appealed to the Court of Appeal for the Fourth Circuit, citing the requirements of 18 U.S.C. § 3501. In reversing the trial court, the Court of Appeal conceded that petitioner had not received proper *Miranda* warnings but held that Section 3501 was satisfied because his statement was voluntary and not the product of duress. It concluded that *Miranda* was not a constitutionally required holding, and that Congress could by statute have the final say on the admissibility question by overruling the Supreme Court by statutory law.

Legal Issue:

Was the original decision of *Miranda v. Arizona* mandating warnings of the rights of silence and of counsel, of constitutional dimension and required by the United States Constitution and, therefore, not susceptible of being overturned by legislation passed by the United States Congress?

The Court's Ruling:

The Supreme Court determined that the Constitution requires the *Miranda* warnings in order to give force and effect to the Fifth Amendment privilege against self-incrimination. The original *Miranda* decision applied to a state case, and unless the *Miranda* decision was required by the Constitution, the Supreme Court would have been powerless to make the ruling since it has no supervisory power over state courts.

Essence of the Court's Rationale:

* * *

In *Miranda,* we noted that the advent of modern custodial police interrogation brought with it an increased concern about confessions obtained by coercion. Because custodial police interrogation, by its very nature, isolates and pressures the individual, we stated that,

> [e]ven without employing brutality, the "third degree" or [other] specific stratagems, . . . custodial interrogation exacts a heavy toll on individual liberty and trades on the weakness of individuals. *Id.* at 455.

(continued)

We concluded that the coercion inherent in custodial interrogation blurs the line between voluntary and involuntary statements, and thus heightens the risk that an individual will not be "accorded his privilege under the Fifth Amendment . . . not to be compelled to incriminate himself." Accordingly, we laid down "concrete constitutional guidelines for law enforcement agencies and courts to follow." Those guidelines established that the admissibility in evidence of any statement given during custodial interrogation of a suspect would depend on whether the police provided the suspect with four warnings. These warnings (which have come to be known colloquially as "*Miranda* rights") are:

a suspect has the right to remain silent, that anything he says can be used against him in a court of law, that he has the right to the presence of an attorney, and that if he cannot afford an attorney one will be appointed for him prior to any questioning if he so desires. *Id.* at 479.

Two years after *Miranda* was decided, Congress enacted Sec. 3501. That section provides, in relevant part:

(a) In any criminal prosecution brought by the United States or by the District of Columbia, a confession . . . shall be admissible in evidence if it is voluntarily given. Before such confession is received in evidence, the trial judge shall, out of the presence of the jury, determine any issue as to voluntariness. If the trial judge determines that the confession was voluntarily made it shall be admitted in evidence and the trial judge shall permit the jury to hear relevant evidence on the issue of voluntariness and shall instruct the jury to give such weight to the confession as the jury feels it deserves under all the circumstances.

(b) The trial judge in determining the issue of voluntariness shall take into consideration all the circumstances surrounding the giving of the confession, including (1) the time elapsing between arrest and arraignment of the defendant making the confession, if it was made after arrest and before arraignment, (2) whether such defendant knew the nature of the offense with which he was charged or of which he was suspected at the time of making the confession, (3) whether or not such defendant was advised or knew that he was not required to make any statement and that any such statement could be used against him, (4) whether

or not such defendant had been advised prior to questioning of his right to the assistance of counsel, and (5) whether or not such defendant was without the assistance of counsel when questioned and when giving such confession.

The presence or absence of any of the above-mentioned factors to be taken into consideration by the judge need not be conclusive on the issue of voluntariness of the confession.

Given Sec. 3501's express designation of voluntariness as the touchstone of admissibility, its omission of any warning requirement, and the instruction for trial courts to consider a nonexclusive list of factors relevant to the circumstances of a confession, we agree with the Court of Appeals that Congress intended by its enactment to overrule *Miranda*. . . . Because of the obvious conflict between our decision in *Miranda* and Sec. 3501, we must address whether Congress has constitutional authority to thus supersede *Miranda*. If Congress has such authority, Sec. 3501's "totality of the circumstances" approach must prevail over *Miranda*'s requirement of warnings; if not, that section must yield to *Miranda*'s more specific requirements.

* * *

Congress may not legislatively supersede our decisions interpreting and applying the Constitution. This case therefore turns on whether the *Miranda* Court announced a constitutional rule or merely exercised its supervisory authority to regulate evidence in the absence of congressional direction.

* * *

We disagree with the Court of Appeals' conclusion, although we concede that there is language in some of our opinions that supports the view taken by that court. But first and foremost of the factors on the other side—that *Miranda* is a constitutional decision—is that both *Miranda* and two of its companion cases applied the rule to proceedings in state courts—to wit, Arizona, California, and New York. Since that time, we have consistently applied *Miranda*'s rule to prosecutions arising in state courts. It is beyond dispute that we do not hold a supervisory power over the courts of the several States.

The *Miranda* opinion itself begins by stating that the Court granted certiorari

to explore some facets of the problems . . . of applying the privilege against self-incrimination to in-custody interrogation, and to give concrete *constitutional guidelines for law enforcement agencies and courts to follow.* 384 U.S. at 441–442 (emphasis added).

In fact, the majority opinion is replete with statements indicating that the majority thought it was announcing a constitutional rule. Indeed, the Court's ultimate conclusion was that the unwarned confessions obtained in the four cases before the Court in *Miranda* "were obtained from the defendant under circumstances that did not meet constitutional standards for protection of the privilege."

* * *

In sum, we conclude that *Miranda* announced a constitutional rule that Congress may not supersede legislatively. Following the rule of *stare decisis,* we decline to overrule *Miranda* ourselves. The judgment of the Court of Appeals is therefore
Reversed.

Case Importance:

This court decision enshrines the *Miranda* warnings in American federal and state criminal procedure for the foreseeable future because the Court believes that the result is dictated by the Constitution, and longstanding practice makes a reversal in the future unlikely.

the Court gave the definitive answer in *Dickerson,* every trial court ignored the congressional statute purporting to supersede *Miranda.* For the first time, the *Dickerson* case held that the federal statute passed to overturn the *Miranda* case was of no force and effect and was actually unconstitutional.

In the case involving an alleged bank robbery, one Dickerson had been interrogated and made incriminating statements at an FBI field office, at which time he was in custody and had not received the traditional *Miranda* warnings. He filed a motion to suppress his statements, and the trial court granted the motion. The United States attorney appealed this decision, which suppressed evidence voluntarily taken but taken in violation of *Miranda* and that ignored the statute, to the Court of Appeals for the Fourth Circuit. That court reversed the trial court decision and concluded that despite the lack of *Miranda* warning, the statements should be admitted against Dickerson, since his statements had been voluntarily given consistent with 18 U.S.C. § 3501. The court of appeals based its decision on a determination that Section 3501 superseded the decision of *Miranda v. Arizona* and that the *Miranda* decision was not of constitutional dimension and, therefore, could be overruled by an act of Congress.[55]

When the Supreme Court decided to hear the case, it noted that it possessed supervisory authority over the federal courts and could use that authority to prescribe rules of evidence and procedure that are binding in federal tribunals. But the Court noted that it possessed no supervisory authority over state and local courts. The Court observed that Congress may not supersede court decisions interpreting and applying the Constitution and that the *Dickerson* case turned on whether the *Miranda* decision announced a constitutional rule or merely served as an example of the Court's exercise of its supervisory authority to regulate the admission of evidence in federal courts. The Supreme Court held that since *Miranda* and its companion cases applied the *Miranda* warnings to state courts and that the Court has no general supervisory authority over state courts, and that since the United States Supreme Court's authority over state courts is limited to enforcing the commands of the United States Constitution, the *Miranda* decision must have been of constitutional dimension. According to the

Dickerson Court, the *Miranda* decision and its requirements could not be overturned by an act of Congress because the Supreme Court had announced a rule of procedure required by the United States Constitution when it decided the case of *Miranda v. Arizona*. Thus the congressional attempt to overturn the rule of *Miranda* and substitute it with a traditional standard of voluntariness ended with a strong reaffirmation of the principles and practice that have grown up around the case of *Miranda v. Arizona*.

18. SUMMARY

Although every person is presumed to know the law, when a person is arrested and becomes subject to interrogation, this presumption no longer applies, and law enforcement officers must present warnings to those in custody. The warnings were believed necessary so that law enforcement agents would be less likely to overcome or overreach the will of the person in police custody. The warnings must convey that the individual has a right to remain silent and a right to an attorney and that if the individual chooses to speak with police, anything said may be used against him or her in a court of law. If a person wishes to speak and later decides not to speak further, the request will be respected. If the person in custody would like to speak with an attorney, one will be made available before any questioning and will be available without cost if the person cannot afford legal representation. While there may be questions concerning precisely when a person enters police custody and questions of precisely what constitutes interrogation, where both custody and interrogation are present, the *Miranda* warnings must be offered to the individual or any evidence obtained will not be affirmatively admissible against the arrestee. Where a person in custody wishes to exercise the right of silence, the right to consult legal counsel, or both, interrogation must cease until the individual, by conduct, indicates a wish to speak further. Failure to respect the constitutional rights of the arrestee will result in excludable evidence. An exception to the *Miranda* warnings exists in the context of an emergency where safety of the officer or other individuals nearby may be compromised if the warnings are given prior to immediate interrogation.

REVIEW EXERCISES AND QUESTIONS

1. What factors appear to have led the Supreme Court of the United States to decide the case, *Miranda v. Arizona,* that requires police to offer legal warnings to persons in custody?

2. What rights must police include in their warnings to persons under arrest in order to comply with the requirements under the *Miranda* case?

3. Consider the situation where a police officer has stopped a motorist for a traffic violation and has asked questions related to the observed offense. Must the officer offer the motorist the *Miranda* warnings under most situations? If the motorist responded to the officer's roadside questions, should the answers be suppressed from a criminal trial? Why or why not? See *State v. Djisheff,* 2006 Ohio 6201, 2006 Ohio App. LEXIS 6155 (2006).

4. What are the two triggering events or situations that mandate that a police officer must offer a subject the *Miranda* warnings?

5. A detained person may be interrogated by an officer who does not actually ask questions of the detained person but who talks in full view and within the

hearing range of the detainee. Give an example of such a situation where a court would probably rule that interrogation has taken place.

6. Assume that police have lawfully detained a person and that an officer has read the *Miranda* warnings to that person. What are two ways that the detainee may waive rights under *Miranda* and choose to submit to police questions?

HOW WOULD YOU DECIDE?

1. In the Court of Appeals of Ohio

A police officer noticed that a truck was speeding at about 70 mph in a 55 mph zone that transitioned into a 45 mph zone. After the standard police lights were initiated, defendant Jesse Smith pulled to the side of the road, and the officer began his investigation into speeding and driving under the influence or alcohol. Smith was not free to leave the scene and was under the officer's control when the officer asked him if he had been drinking. Smith answered in the affirmative, a fact that was used against him at his trial. The officer asked detailed questions of Smith to obtain information confirming or dispelling the officer's suspicions that Smith may have had too much alcohol to be driving legally. The officer reported that Smith's speech was not exactly normal and that he could smell alcohol coming from Smith's mouth. Smith contended that the officer should have offered him *Miranda* warnings prior to asking him questions because he was in the officer's custody and not free to leave and he was interrogated contrary to the rules set forth in *Miranda v. Arizona.* In addition, Smith contended the failure of his attorney to attempt to suppress his answer that he had been drinking constituted ineffective assistance of counsel because an attorney should attempt to suppress information taken in violation of *Miranda.*

The trial court convicted Smith of operating a vehicle while under the influence of alcohol, for which it sentenced Smith to a fine and jail time.

How would you rule on the defendant's contention that his rights under Miranda were violated because the officer interrogated him during a traffic stop while he was in the officer's custody and his attorney failed to attempt to suppress Smith's answers to the police officer's questions?

The Court's Holding:

The appellate court rejected Smith's contention that his attorney had been ineffective as his lawyer because a traffic stop is an exception to the custodial interrogation that triggers the need for a *Miranda* warning. In *Berkemer v. McCarty,* 468 U.S. 420 (1984), the Supreme Court of the United States determined that a traffic stop was not generally a seizure for which a *Miranda* warning was typically a necessity. The appeals court in Smith's case noted:

> According to the *McCarty* Court, the traffic stop exception to *Miranda* is constitutionally valid because a traffic stop is temporary, brief, public and substantially less police-dominated than the type of interrogation at issue in Miranda itself, especially where only one officer is present. *McCarty,* 468 U.S. at 437–439. The Court stated that although a traffic stop curtails freedom of movement by the detainee and imposes some pressure to answer questions, the pressure does not sufficiently impair the privilege against self-incrimination to warrant a *Miranda* warning. Id. at 421.
>
> Consequently, the officer can ask the detained motorist a moderate number of questions in an attempt to obtain information confirming or dispelling the officer's suspicions. Id. at 439. The *McCarty* Court concluded that the roadside questioning of a motorist detained pursuant to a routine traffic stop is not a custodial interrogation. Id. at 421. Thus, the officer in that case was permitted to ask the detained motorist if he had been drinking without providing Miranda warnings, even where the motorist was not free to go until the officer finished his traffic investigation. Id.[56]

Thus, the Ohio court of appeals ruled that a *Miranda* warning is not needed at a typical traffic stop because an encounter with a police officer during a stop was not generally coercive enough to require the warnings contemplated by the *Miranda* case. Additionally, there could be no winning argument of ineffective assistance of counsel when a defense attorney failed to attempt to suppress evidence that would clearly have been admissible. The court of appeals affirmed Jesse Smith's conviction for driving under the influence of alcohol. See *State v. Smith,* 2007 Ohio App. LEXIS 2981 (2007).

HOW WOULD YOU DECIDE?

2. In the Court of Appeals of Georgia

A police officer made a lawful traffic stop of the defendant, Daniel Lopez, who admitted that he did not have a driver's license. The passengers in the car remained at the scene. Following the arrest of Lopez, the officer placed him in a police vehicle and conducted a search of Lopez' car. Police found several baggies of cocaine in the car, as well as some marijuana. The officer returned to the police cruiser to inform Lopez that he was also being arrested for possession of cocaine because none of his friends admitted owning the drug. At this point:

> Lopez interrupted the officer and said, "[t]hat cocaine is mine. I don't want my home boys to get in trouble for my cocaine." A few minutes later, and without any additional statement being made by the officer, Lopez continued and said, "I have the [gumption] to sell it [and] I've got the [gumption] to go to jail for it."[57]

Over his objection, the trial court admitted the statement of Lopez against him at his bench trial for drug possession. Lopez contended that his admissions concerning cocaine ownership should have been suppressed because he had not been given his *Miranda* warnings and was under arrest and in custody for driving without a license. Lopez argued that when the officer informed him about the cocaine, the officer expected a response so the officer was actually interrogating him by giving him the information. The trial to the judge resulted in several convictions.

How would you rule on the defendant's contention that he was in custody and was interrogated in violation of the principles of* Miranda *when the officer informed him that he was being arrested for drug possession?

The Court's Holding:

The trial court admitted Lopez' statement against him at his trial for drug possession over his objection that his admissions concerning drug ownership should have been suppressed because he had not been given his *Miranda* warnings and was under arrest and in custody for driving without a license.

On appeal, Lopez claimed that he was really being interrogated by the officer because he believed that the officer was threatening to arrest his passenger friends for drug possession unless Lopez confessed to possessing the recreational pharmaceuticals. The court of appeals found that:

> Lopez's statements were spontaneous and voluntary. The officer did not threaten to arrest anyone other than Lopez for possession of cocaine. Instead, he merely informed Lopez that he was being arrested for possession because the cocaine was found in his vehicle and none of the passengers claimed ownership.[58]

In refusing to hold that the officer's statement informing Lopez of his additional arrest constituted interrogation under *Miranda,* the court of appeals held that the statements were freely and voluntarily given and that the officer was merely informing Lopez of the reason for his additional arrest. The court noted that the concept of interrogation can be extended only to words or deeds that an officer could reasonably understand would have been likely to cause Lopez to make an incriminating statement. In this case, the officer was merely informing Lopez of some developments in the investigation. The court of appeal affirmed defendant Lopez' convictions on the drug charges. See *Lopez v. State,* 2007 Ga. App. LEXIS 429, 2007 Fulton County D. Rep. 1358 (2007).

ENDNOTES

1. Amendment Five: "No person . . . shall be *compelled in any criminal case to be a witness against himself,* nor be deprived of life, liberty, or property, without due process of law; . . ." (emphasis added).

2. 385 U.S. 436 (1966).

3. See *Brown v. Mississippi,* 297 U.S. 278 (1936), for an especially egregious case of in-custody interrogation that totally transgressed any constitutional boundary, even though at that time the Fifth Amendment did not apply against the states, and the Court decided the case on due process grounds of the Fourteenth Amendment.

4. The Fifth Amendment did not originally apply against the states but only limited the federal government. Following *Malloy v. Hogan,* 378 U.S. 1 (1964), the amendment had the same effect on the states. As Justice Brennan stated in the lead opinion, "We hold today that the Fifth Amendment's exception from compulsory self-incrimination is also protected by the Fourteenth Amendment against abridgment by the States."

5. 378 U.S. 1 (1964).

6. The right to request counsel under *Miranda* is personal to the arrestee and cannot be asserted by any third party or even a family member. An attorney has no right to demand to see a "client" where a "client" has not asked to be represented by an attorney. See *Moran v. Burbine,* 475 U.S. 412 (1986).

7. 378 U.S. 478 (1964).

8. 384 U.S. 436 (1966).

9. The Court required that the warning be given to everyone who was subject to custodial interrogation. In *Miranda v. Arizona,* 384 U.S. at 468, the Court stated, "[A] warning is an absolute prerequisite in overcoming the inherent pressures of the interrogation atmosphere. It is not just the subnormal or woefully ignorant who succumb to an interrogator's imprecations, whether implied or expressly stated, that the interrogation will continue until a confession is obtained or that silence in the face of accusation is itself damning, and will bode ill when presented to a jury." And at 384 U.S. 471, 472, the *Miranda* Court stated, "No amount of circumstantial evidence that the person may have been aware of this right will suffice to stand in its stead."

10. 468 U.S. 420 (1984).

11. Ibid.

12. Ibid. at 440.

13. See *State v. Smith,* 2007 Ohio 3182, 2007 Ohio App. LEXIS 2981 (2007).

14. A rigid reading of the warnings as suggested in *Miranda* is not absolutely required to meet the warning requirements. In *California v. Prysock,* 453 U.S. 355 (1981), the Court held that *Miranda* warnings need not be a virtual incantation of the precise language contained in the original opinion.

15. 492 U.S. 195 (1989).

16. The marginally defective warning approved by the Court as minimally adequate in *Duckworth v. Eagan,* 492 U.S. 195 at 198 (1989), did not add to the clarity of how the warnings should be administered. The *Duckworth* warning is as follows: "You have the right to remain silent. Anything you say can be used against you in court. You have a right to talk to a lawyer for advice before we ask you any questions, and to have him with you during questioning. You have this right to the advice and presence of a lawyer even if you cannot afford to hire one. *We have no way of giving you a lawyer, but one will be appointed for you, if you wish, if and when you go to court.* If you wish to answer questions now without a lawyer present, you have the right to stop answering questions at any time. You also have the right to stop answering at any time until you've talked to a lawyer" (emphasis added). The *Duckworth* Court noted that the warning actually given touched all the bases required by *Miranda,* since the subject had been substantially given a warning that alerted him to his rights to silence, counsel, and the effects if he chose to speak. So long as the warnings offered contain the essentials of the right to silence and the right to counsel (free if the subject is indigent), the *Miranda* requirements have been satisfied.

17. 470 U.S. 298 (1985).

18. *Wong Sun v. United States,* 371 U.S. 471 (1963), held that where a person's Fourth Amendment rights have been violated by police, evidence obtained directly or indirectly from exploitation of the illegal search or seizure cannot be introduced to prove guilt at a criminal trial. This principle involved an extension of *Mapp v. Ohio,* 367 U.S. 643 (1961) (which excluded evidence illegally seized by police

from state trials) to evidence that can be called derivative of the original wrongdoing by law enforcement agents. The police are not permitted to benefit from wrongdoing and are placed in the same evidentiary position as if no wrongdoing had occurred. Note that *Mapp* and *Wong Sun* involved violations of the United States Constitution, not transgressions of a prophylactic or remedial legal rule developed by the Court like the *Miranda* warnings. The waters get more murky since in *Dickerson v. United States,* 530 U.S. 428 (2000), the Court held that the *Miranda* warnings were of constitutional dimension and were required by the Constitution. The *Dickerson* case may require the Court to revisit *Elstad* in the future because such conduct may violate the Constitution.

19. See *Harris v. New York,* 401 U.S. 222 (1971).
20. 451 U.S. 477 (1981).
21. *Michigan v. Moseley,* 423 U.S. 96 at 106, 107 (1975).
22. 486 U.S. 675 (1988).
23. See *McNeil v. Wisconsin,* 501 U.S. 171 (1991).
24. See *Illinois v. Perkins,* 496 U.S. 292 (1990).
25. Ibid. at 300.
26. Custody, for *Miranda* purposes, has not been deemed to occur when a traffic stop has been made, even though the driver is not free to leave and is under the control of the police officer. *Berkemer v. McCarty,* 468 U.S. 420 (1984). Stopping a car is a Fourth Amendment "seizure," but the driver is not considered in custody according to *Delaware v. Prouse,* 440 U.S. 648 (1979).
27. 463 U.S. 1121 (1983).
28. *California v. Beheler,* 464 U.S. 1121 at 1125 (1983). In a case similar to *Beheler, Oregon v. Mathiason,* 429 U.S. 492 (1977), the subject agreed to meet with police at the patrol office. After they informed him that he was a suspect in a burglary and falsely told him that his fingerprints were found at the scene, Mathiason confessed but was not held at that time. The Supreme Court held in *Mathiason* that "a noncustodial situation is not converted to one in which *Miranda* applies simply because a reviewing court concludes that, even in the absence of any formal arrest or restraint on freedom of movement, the questioning took place in a 'coercive environment.'" 429 U.S. at 495.
29. *United States v. Fisher,* 215 F. Supp.2d 1212, 1216, 1217 (2002).
30. 516 U.S. 99 (1995).
31. The Court in *Thompson* sent the case back to the lower courts for a determination of whether, under

the two-step test, outlined earlier here, Thompson was really in custody. 516 U.S. 99 at 117 (1995).
32. See *Oregon v. Mathiason,* 429 U.S. 492 (1977), where the defendant had been invited to the police station for discussions concerning a burglary. The police initially told Mathiason that he was not under arrest and allowed him to leave the station following his interview, where he made inculpatory statements. The Court held that Mathiason was not in custody or otherwise deprived of his freedom of action in any significant way, and it approved the trial court's admission of his police station statement.
33. *Oregon v. Mathiason,* 429 U.S. 492, 496 (1977), Justice Marshall, dissenting.
34. *United States v. Mittel-Carey,* 2007 U.S. App. LEXIS 16396 (1st Cir. 2007).
35. 446 U.S. 291 (1980).
36. *Innis* at 301.
37. Ibid. at 316.
38. *Oregon v. Cunningham,* 179 Ore. App. 498; 40 P.3d 535 (2002).
39. Not all unwarned custodial interrogation by police will be suppressed from introduction at trial. Questions asked of an arrestee that are for record-keeping purposes, that are routine booking questions, and that request biographical data necessary for booking or pretrial purposes are exempt from exclusion under *Miranda.* See *Pennsylvania v. Muniz,* 496 U.S. 582 at 601 (1990). Also consider *New York v. Quarles,* 467 U.S. 649 (1984), which permitted an emergency interrogation from which evidence was not suppressed. Illegally seized evidence under *Miranda* may be used for impeachment purposes in some situations, according to *New York v. Harris,* 401 U.S. 222 (1971).
40. 481 U.S. 520 (1987).
41. *Innis* at 301.
42. 477 F.3d 144, 2007 U.S. App. LEXIS 3488 (4th Cir. 2007).
43. 467 U.S. 649 (1984).
44. 350 N.J. Super 517; 796 A.2d 274 (2002).
45. See *Minnesota v. Caldwell,* 639 N.W.2d 64 (2002), where a gun was admitted under the public safety exception, since it was believed to be in a public place. See also *Allen v. Roe,* 305 F.3d 1046 (9th Cir. 2002), where the court approved the admission of a firearm believed to be located in a public area when officers questioned the suspect prior to offering *Miranda* warnings.
46. 475 U.S. 412 (1986).

47. According to the Court in *North Carolina v. Butler*, 441 U.S. 369 (1979), the absence of a written *Miranda* waiver of rights is not necessarily determinative of waiver. As the *Butler* Court stated, "An express written or oral statement of waiver of the right to remain silent or of the right to counsel is usually strong proof of the validity of that waiver, but is not inevitably either necessary or sufficient to establish waiver."
48. Ibid.
49. See *Colorado v. Connelly*, 479 U.S. 157 (1986).
50. Ibid.
51. Ibid.
52. *Miranda v. Arizona*, 384 U.S. 436, 468 (1966).
53. 18 U.S.C. § 3501 provides, among other things, that: "(a) In any criminal prosecution brought by the United States or by the District of Columbia, a confession shall be admissible in evidence if it is voluntarily given. Before such confession is received in evidence, the trial judge shall, out of the presence of the jury, determine any issue as to voluntariness. If the trial judge determines that the confession was voluntarily made it shall be admitted in evidence and the trial judge shall permit the jury to hear relevant evidence on the issue of voluntariness and shall instruct the jury to give such weight to the confession as the jury feels it deserves under all the circumstances."
54. The Supreme Court agreed with the Court of Appeals for the Fourth Circuit that the Congress intended to overrule *Miranda*. In *Dickerson v. United States*, 530 U.S. 428 at 436 (2000), the Court noted, "Given § 3501's express designation of voluntariness as the touchstone of admissibility, its omission of any warning requirement, and the instruction for trial courts to consider a nonexclusive list of factors relevant to the circumstances of a confession, we agree with the Court of Appeals that Congress intended by its enactment to overrule *Miranda*."
55. *Dickerson v. United States*, 166 F.3d 667 (4th Cir.1999).
56. *State v. Smith*, 2007 Ohio App. LEXIS 2981 (2007).
57. *Lopez v. State*, 2007 Ga. App. LEXIS 429; 2007 Fulton County D. Rep. 1358 (2007).
58. Ibid.

CHAPTER 11

Confession and the Privilege against Self-Incrimination

Learning Objectives

1. Analyze and be able to explain the original intent of the Framers of the Fifth Amendment privilege against self-incrimination.
2. Give examples of evidence that would be admissible under the Fifth Amendment and evidence that may be excluded from admission under the Fifth Amendment.
3. Detail the changes brought to the Fifth Amendment by its incorporation into the Fourteenth Amendment's Due Process Clause.
4. Evaluate and be able to explain why nontestimonial evidence is not excluded by the Fifth Amendment's privilege against self-incrimination.
5. Be able to discriminate between situations where the privilege against self-incrimination may be asserted and where the privilege has no application.
6. Describe a hypothetical situation where an individual should successfully contend that the privilege against self-incrimination has application and should exclude evidence.
7. Describe why a prosecutor may neither call a defendant to the witness stand nor make adverse comments to the jury if a defendant chooses not to testify.
8. Analyze why use immunity granted by the prosecution is coextensive with the

protections of the Fifth Amendment against self-incrimination, and be able to describe the limitations of use immunity.
9. Articulate the rationale why an immunized witness may not properly assert the privilege against self-incrimination at a trial or at a grand jury proceeding dealing with the grant of immunity.
10. Be able to discuss how the Fifth Amendment privilege may be waived and be able to explain the substance of the rights that are being given up by a waiver of this privilege.
11. Be able to describe the limitations that the privilege against self-incrimination places on modern police interrogation practices.
12. Be able to explain the theory that personal motivations directed toward giving a confession do not prevent the admissibility of a confession, so long as police have not overreached the individual.
13. Explain why an involuntary confession cannot be used for impeachment or other purposes at a criminal trial but a confession received only in violation of the *Miranda* warnings may be used for impeachment.

Chapter Outline

Key Terms

Adverse prosecutorial comment
Blood alcohol tests
Due Process Clause of the Fourteenth Amendment
Fifth Amendment privilege
Impeachment use of confession
Involuntary confession
Nontestimonial evidence

Physical compulsion
Right assertable against government
Testimonial evidence
Totality of the circumstances test
Transactional immunity
Use immunity
Voluntary confession
Waiver of privilege

1. INTRODUCTION TO THE FIFTH AMENDMENT PRIVILEGE

Amendment Five

No person shall be . . . compelled in any criminal case to be a witness against himself. . . .

The Fifth Amendment provides a guarantee that a person shall not have to offer assistance in making a conviction by becoming a witness against himself or herself, but case law has determined that an individual may have to offer nontestimonial evidence that may have the effect of assisting the government in the case against that individual. Although originally not intended to limit the states, the Fifth Amendment has been held to apply to state criminal practice through the Due Process Clause of the Fourteenth Amendment. The Fifth Amendment helps assure reliability and truthfulness of evidence, since compelled evidence may be based on coercion and lack of free will and be motivated to remove or end coercion or torture. Since the amendment guarantees that a person shall not have to self-incriminate, the prohibition against use of coerced evidence helps to enforce that right not to be overreached into giving damaging evidence. Where testimonial evidence has been obtained in violation of the Fifth Amendment, it will be excluded from use at trial, a fact that removes any police incentive to obtain such evidence in violation of the Constitution. In addition to removing physical or psychological motivations to coerce a defendant, the Fifth Amendment forces the prosecution to obtain damaging evidence from sources external to the defendant in order to obtain a conviction.

2. ORIGINAL INTENT AND THE FIFTH AMENDMENT

As originally contemplated by the Framers of the Bill of Rights, the Fifth Amendment privilege against self-incrimination[1] allowed a person to refuse to divulge any evidence that could assist the federal government in prosecuting that individual. It was not clear whether the privilege merely prevented words from being extracted from the individual or whether other means of obtaining information of an incriminating nature might be included within the protection. Justice Thomas suggested that the Fifth Amendment may have originally possessed a broader meaning than that currently in vogue with the Supreme Court. In his concurring opinion in *United States v. Hubbell,* he noted:

> The Fifth Amendment provides that "[n]o person . . . shall be compelled in any criminal case to be a witness against himself." The key word at issue in this case is "witness." The Court's opinion, relying on prior cases, essentially defines "witness" as a person who provides testimony, and thus restricts the Fifth Amendment's ban to only those communications "that are 'testimonial' in character." None of this Court's cases, however, has undertaken an analysis of the meaning of the term at the time of the founding. A review of that period reveals substantial support for the view that the term "witness" meant a person who gives or furnishes evidence, a broader meaning than that which our case law currently ascribes to the term. 530 U.S. 27, 49–50 (2000).

Although, according to Justice Thomas, the Framers of the Fifth Amendment may have intended to include a prohibition against general production of incriminating evidence, case law and recent precedent have restricted the privilege to cover only testimonial evidence, as a general rule. Since the Fifth Amendment originally applied only against the federal government, the protection against self-incrimination had application only when the federal government attempted to require an individual to give incriminating information. As originally conceived, the Fifth Amendment failed to offer any protection to a person when a state official requested documentary or physical evidence of an incriminating nature. Prior to a 1964 case,[2] protection from self-incrimination in state courts depended upon state constitutional law, state statutory law, and state judicial interpretations of that law and was completely independent of federal law.

3. PRIVILEGE AGAINST SELF-INCRIMINATION: EXCLUDABLE EVIDENCE

Evidence obtained in violation of the Fifth Amendment is generally excluded from affirmative use in criminal trials. Since a person need not serve as a "witness against himself," judicial construction illuminating and explaining the phrase proves crucial. The privilege provides protection for an accused from being required to actually testify against himself or herself as a witness or otherwise give evidence that is testimonial or communicative in nature. According to the Court in *Doe v. United States:*

> [I]n order to be testimonial, an accused's communication must itself, explicitly or implicitly, relate a factual assertion or disclose information. Only then is a person compelled to be a "witness" against himself. *Doe v. United States,* 487 U.S. 201, 210 (1988)

A state violates the privilege against self-incrimination when it obtains evidence against a defendant through efforts that force the defendant to divulge adverse information. The privilege is violated where a state gains evidence by

> the cruel, simple expedient of compelling it from his own mouth. . . . In sum, the privilege is fulfilled only when the person is guaranteed the right "to remain silent unless he chooses to speak in the unfettered exercise of his own will." *Miranda v. Arizona,* 384 U.S. 436, 460 (1966)

And in *Culombe v. Connecticut,* the Court suggested the proper inquiry for determining the voluntariness of a confession:

> Is the confession the product of an essentially free and unconstrained choice by its maker? If it is, if he has willed to confess, it may be used against him. If it is not, if his will has been overborne and his capacity for self-determination critically impaired, the use of his confession offends due process. 367 U.S. 568, 602 (1961)

The essence of the privilege is that if a person wishes to testify, it should be due to the personal decision of the defendant, freely made and not motivated by mental or physical coercion on behalf of the government. There is a requirement that a government "which proposes to convict and punish an individual produce the evidence against him by the independent labor of its officers"[3] rather than devise a method of extracting the appropriate evidence personally from a defendant by overreaching his or her mind and will.

4. THE FOURTEENTH AMENDMENT ALTERATIONS

Following the Civil War, the United States adopted the Fourteenth Amendment (1868), which, among other things, required the states to grant procedural due process to all persons.[4] In a nutshell, procedural due process requires that the state governments treat all individuals with fundamental fairness. The framers of this amendment did not envision that it might encompass most of the guarantees of the first eight amendments. Similarly, the precise extent of fundamental fairness included in due process was not delineated in the amendment, but the concept has been amplified and described more fully by court decisions subsequent to its adoption.

5. REQUIRED PRODUCTION OF NONTESTIMONIAL EVIDENCE AND THE FIFTH AMENDMENT

Although involuntary confessions should not be admitted in court,[5] the government may compel the production of other types of evidence that, though not testimonial, helps the prosecution gain convictions. The privilege against self-incrimination protects a defendant from being compelled to testify against himself or herself or otherwise provide the prosecution with evidence of a testimonial or communicative nature, but not from being compelled by the state to produce real or physical evidence. To be testimonial, the communication must, explicitly or implicitly, relate a factual assertion or disclose similar information.

The Fifth Amendment does not insulate an individual from being forced to divulge business records when the person is a mere custodian. In *Bellis v. United States,*[6] the Court noted:

> It has long been established, of course, that the Fifth Amendment privilege against compulsory self-incrimination protects an individual from compelled production of his personal papers and effects as well as compelled oral testimony. In *Boyd v. United States,* 116 U.S. 616 (1886), we held that "any forcible and compulsory extortion of a man's own testimony or of his private papers to be used as evidence to convict him of crime" would violate the Fifth Amendment privilege. *Id.* at 630; see also *id.* at 633–635; *Wilson v. United States,* 221 U.S. 361, 377 (1911)

However, in *Bellis,* the custodian of the records for a law firm could not successfully invoke a personal Fifth Amendment privilege against incrimination in common law firm records, since they were not his personal papers but collective papers of the firm and had to be divulged when requested by a federal grand jury.

In *Schmerber v. California* (Case 11.1),[7] the Court upheld the introduction of evidence of intoxication taken from a suspected alcohol-impaired driver by a doctor at the request of a police officer (see Case 8.1). The motorist contended that the use of his blood violated his Fifth Amendment privilege against self-incrimination because it effectively made him a witness against himself, but the Court rejected that argument. According to the Court, the Fifth Amendment provides protection to an accused "only from being compelled to testify against himself, or otherwise provide the State with evidence of a testimonial or communicative nature." According to *Schmerber:*

> [B]oth federal and state courts have usually held that it [Fifth Amendment privilege against self-incrimination] offers no protection against compulsion to submit to fingerprinting, photographing, or measurements, to write or speak for identification, to appear in court, to stand, to assume a stance, to walk, or to make a particular gesture. The distinction which has emerged, often expressed in different ways, is that the privilege is a bar against compelling "communications" or "testimony," but that compulsion which makes a suspect or accused the source of "real or physical evidence" does not violate it. *Schmerber v. California,* 384 U.S. at 764 (1966)

CASE 11.1

Leading Case Brief: Self-Incrimination and Physical Evidence from the Defendant

Schmerber v. California
Supreme Court of the United States
384 U.S. 757 (1966)

Case Facts:

A police officer arrested Schmerber at a hospital while he was being treated for injuries suffered in an accident in the automobile he had been driving. At the direction of a police officer, a hospital doctor took a blood sample from petitioner's body at the hospital. The chemical analysis of his blood revealed a blood alcohol level indicative of intoxication. The report of his blood alcohol level was admitted in evidence at his trial. The Los Angeles Municipal Court convicted petitioner Schmerber of driving an automobile while under the influence of alcohol.

At the trial, Schmerber's attorney objected to trial court use of the analysis of the blood evidence on the ground that the blood had been withdrawn despite his refusal to consent to the test. Through counsel, Schmerber contended that the withdrawal of the blood and the acceptance of the analysis as evidence denied him the exercise of his constitutional rights against self-incrimination under the Fifth Amendment and his rights under several different provisions of the United States Constitution. The Appellate Department of the California Superior Court rejected these contentions and affirmed the conviction. The Supreme Court of the United States granted certiorari to consider the constitutional arguments offered by Mr. Schmerber.

Legal Issue:

Does the medically appropriate extraction of bodily fluids from a person against the will of the individual and the subsequent use of the evidence against that person violate the Fifth Amendment privilege against self-incrimination?

The Court's Ruling:

The Court determined that allowing the introduction of a defendant's blood alcohol reading in a driving under the influence case did not violate the Fifth Amendment privilege against self-incrimination because the evidence was not testimonial in nature but was proof of a physical fact.

Essence of the Court's Rationale:

We therefore must now decide whether the withdrawal of the blood and admission in evidence of the analysis involved in this case violated petitioner's privilege. We hold that the privilege protects an accused only from being compelled to testify against himself, or otherwise provide the State with evidence of a testimonial or communicative nature, and that the withdrawal of blood and use of the analysis in question in this case did not involve compulsion to these ends. It could not be denied that in requiring petitioner to submit to the withdrawal and chemical analysis of his blood, the State compelled him to submit to an attempt to discover evidence that might be used to prosecute him for a criminal offense. He submitted only after the police officer rejected his objection and directed the physician to proceed. The officer's direction to the physician to administer the test over petitioner's objection constituted compulsion for the purpose of the privilege. The critical question, then, is whether petitioner was thus compelled "to be a witness against himself."

* * *

It is clear that the protection of the [Fifth Amendment] privilege [against self-incrimination] reaches an accused's communications, whatever form they might take, and the compulsion of responses which are also communications, for example, compliance with a subpoena to produce one's papers. *Boyd v. United States,* 116 U.S. 616. On the other hand, both federal and state courts have usually held that it offers no protection against compulsion to submit to fingerprinting, photographing, or measurements, to write or speak for identification, to appear in court, to stand, to assume a stance, to walk, or to make a particular gesture. The distinction which has emerged, often expressed in different ways, is that the privilege is a bar against compelling "communications" or "testimony," but that compulsion which makes a suspect or accused the source of "real or physical evidence" does not violate it.

Case Importance:

The Schmerber decision reaffirmed the concept that unless a defendant has been forced to offer testimony or evidence that is close to testimony, proof of physical facts, even if they come from a defendant, has not violated the Fifth Amendment privilege.

Justice Stevens noted in *United States v. Hubbell* that Justice Holmes had concluded that there existed a significant difference between using duress to compel testimony from a witness and requiring that person to engage in activity that could lead to incrimination.[8] In essence, the *Schmerber* Court held that mere physical evidence, though it may communicate information, is not considered testimonial and is not prohibited under the Fifth Amendment.

The *Schmerber* Court was on solid ground with an earlier case, *Holt v. United States,*[9] where Justice Holmes dismissed an argument that the Fifth Amendment privilege against self-incrimination would be violated by requiring a defendant to put on an article of clothing for identification purposes. Justice Holmes noted that

> the prohibition of compelling a man in a criminal court to be witness against himself is a prohibition of the use of physical or moral compulsion to extort communications from him, not an exclusion of his body as evidence when it may be material. 218 U.S. at 252

The wearing of clothing, while it could harm a defendant's case, was not considered "testimonial" and thus did not constitute a violation of the Fifth Amendment.

In a case in which the legal theory was consistent with *Schmerber,* the Supreme Court held that the Fifth Amendment did not offer protection to a grand jury witness who had been ordered to give a voice sample for comparison purposes. In *United States v. Dionisio,*[10] a trial court mandated that Dionisio make a voice recording for use by the prosecutor in a grand jury proceeding. Dionisio refused on the ground, among others, that to offer a sample of his voice would violate his Fifth Amendment privilege against self-incrimination because the sample might be used against him in a criminal prosecution. The *Dionisio* Court rejected his Fifth Amendment argument with the conclusion that prior cases have uniformly rejected the contention that the compelled display of identifiable physical characteristics infringes on the privilege against compelled testimonial self-incrimination.

Under *Schmerber, Dionisio,* and numerous other cases, it has become clear that physical attributes such as fingerprints, weight, height, tone of speech, manner of handwriting, walking characteristics, general body stance, content of blood or other bodily fluids, and general appearance are not testimonially communicative and, as such, are not subject to Fifth Amendment privilege self-incrimination claims. While performing a particular act may provide nontestimonial incriminating evidence, a criminal suspect may be compelled to put on a shirt, *Holt v. United States,* 218 U.S. 245 (1910); to provide a blood sample, *Schmerber,* or a handwriting example, *Gilbert v. California,*

388 U.S. 263 (1967); and to make a recording of his voice, *United States v. Wade,* 388 U.S. 218 (1967). The act of exhibiting such physical characteristics is not the same as a sworn communication by a witness that relates either express or implied assertions of fact or belief.

Consistent with case law, the prosecution may force a person to exhibit his or her body and the extent of his or her motor skills while under suspicion for driving under the influence of alcohol. In *Pennsylvania v. Muniz,*[11] police videotaped a motorist attempting to perform various diagnostic tests for intoxication and later used the video in court in an attempt to demonstrate impairment. The Court approved the introduction of portions of the recording that revealed only the physical manner in which his speech was constructed and demonstrated the defendant's lack of muscular coordination without revealing any testimonial components of those responses.

In a similar fashion, a defendant has no right to prevent a prosecutor from commenting to a jury that the defendant, while under suspicion of driving while under the influence of alcohol, refused to take a Breathalyzer test following his arrest. In *South Dakota v. Neville,* 459 U.S. 553 (1983), the trial court granted Neville's motion to suppress, and the prosecution eventually appealed to the Supreme Court of the United States. According to the Court, the admission into evidence of a defendant's refusal to submit to a blood alcohol test would not have violated Neville's Fifth Amendment privilege against self-incrimination. According to the Court, a refusal to take such a test, after a police officer has lawfully requested it, is not an act coerced by the officer, and thus is not protected by the Fifth Amendment privilege against self-incrimination as applied to the states through the Due Process Clause of the Fourteenth Amendment.

6. ASSERTION OF THE PRIVILEGE AGAINST SELF-INCRIMINATION

The privilege against self-incrimination has been determined to benefit only real human beings and does not apply to corporations or other artificial business entities. Where a witness offers testimony that would tend to incriminate, he or she may not retroactively assert the privilege so as to render the previously offered testimony useless; the privilege has been deemed to have been waived by conduct. The privilege is personal to the person who asserts it, and it generally cannot be asserted by one person on behalf of another. An individual who is asked or has been subpoenaed to give evidence against another individual may not invoke the first individual's Fifth Amendment privilege to prevent giving evidence against the other person. A defendant who is awaiting sentencing may assert the privilege if called to testify against a second individual, since that evidence might adversely affect the sentence ultimately imposed.[12] Because the Fifth Amendment does not apply outside the United States, as a general rule, an individual may not successfully invoke the privilege not to testify when that evidence might tend to incriminate the individual solely in a foreign nation.[13]

7. PRIVILEGE AGAINST SELF-INCRIMINATION ASSERTABLE IN A VARIETY OF CONTEXTS

While the privilege against self-incrimination is often viewed as available only at a criminal trial, the application of the privilege is not so limited, and its assertion may properly occur in a variety of contexts. The privilege may be asserted anytime a police officer asks questions of an individual, whether or not that person is in custody. A person may refuse to testify on Fifth Amendment grounds when called as a witness in a grand jury proceeding where the answers might tend to incriminate the witness. Since legislative bodies have power to compel witness attendance, if an individual is asked a question for which the answer might be incriminating, refusal under the Fifth Amendment has been held to be appropriate. In essence, whenever a government or its agents demand or request that an individual offer evidence of a testimonial nature that might either directly incriminate or indirectly lead to other evidence that would incriminate, any person may refuse to testify on Fifth Amendment grounds.[14]

8. PROSECUTION COMMENT ON DEFENDANT'S USE OF FIFTH AMENDMENT

When a defendant does not offer evidence but probably has such knowledge, he or she may be relying on the Fifth Amendment privilege. A failure to explain evidence or to personally present a defense cannot be rendered especially costly by allowing a prosecutor to adversely comment on the failure of the defendant to take the witness stand. To allow a prosecutor to comment on a defendant's use of the Fifth Amendment would render the privilege against self-incrimination somewhat illusory. In *Griffin v. California,*[15] the defendant chose not to testify in his capital murder trial, and the judge instructed the jury not to draw any inference of guilt or innocence from this failure. The prosecutor reminded the jury that the defendant knew things that he was not telling the jury and invited the jury to consider the failure to testify against the defendant. The Supreme Court reversed the conviction with the observation that the Fifth Amendment forbids adverse comment by the prosecution on the accused's silence and on instructions from the judge concerning the silence of the accused that indicate that silence may be evidence of guilt.

9. AN EQUIVALENT SUBSTITUTE FOR THE FIFTH AMENDMENT PRIVILEGE: IMMUNITY

Where a prosecutor determines that the importance of obtaining evidence or testimony to assist in one prosecution outweighs the loss that accrues to society when a different guilty party goes free, a grant of immunity to that individual may be appropriate. In such a case, the prosecution may require a person to give evidence that might tend to convict or be a link in a chain of evidence that might result in a successful prosecution. To successfully require an individual to offer evidence that might provide a link toward a conviction, the prosecution must offer some type of immunity. The level or scope of the immunity must be coextensive with the protections offered by the privilege against self-incrimination. As a general rule, use immunity is the minimal level of immunity that replaces the same level of protection originally offered by the Fifth Amendment's privilege against self-incrimination. As Chief Justice Rehnquist noted in *Braswell v. United States,* "Testimony obtained pursuant to a grant of statutory use immunity may be used neither directly nor derivatively."[16]

Use immunity means that the prosecution will not take evidence offered by a witness or defendant and use it affirmatively against the individual and will not use the evidence as a link in a chain to discover additional evidence related to the original evidence. Since this level of immunity merely replaces the guarantee under the Fifth Amendment with an equal level of protection, once it is given, the prosecution may require the witness to answer questions that could otherwise be barred by the assertion of the privilege against self-incrimination.[17] A more extensive immunity, transactional immunity, may be offered by a prosecutor in most jurisdictions as an added inducement to get a reluctant witness testify. The essence of transactional immunity is that the prosecution gives up any legal right to prosecute the immunized witness for any crime that is covered by the grant of immunity so long as the witness cooperates to the full extent of any agreement with the prosecutor. Naturally, a potential defendant-witness would prefer a grant of transactional immunity as opposed to mere use immunity, but the grant of use immunity fully grants the same legal protection as is covered by the Fifth Amendment privilege against self-incrimination.

10. WAIVER OF THE FIFTH AMENDMENT PRIVILEGE

Like most constitutional rights, the Fifth Amendment privilege against self-incrimination is a waivable right, and a waiver is effective, provided it is properly accomplished. The most obvious waiver of the Fifth Amendment privilege occurs in the context of the *Miranda* warning, where the individual either orally or in writing agrees to talk with police and understands that what he or she says may be used in a court of law. A defendant may waive the privilege by voluntarily taking the witness stand at the trial, where the witness testifies fully and is subject to cross-examination.[18] A waiver of the Fifth Amendment privilege may occur where a defendant seeks out a police officer and freely offers a confession to criminal activity, provided the defendant's waiver has been made voluntarily, knowingly, and intelligently.[19]

The concept that a waiver of the Fifth Amendment privilege must have been made "voluntarily, knowingly, and intelligently" does not mean that a defendant understands every legal nuance and effect of the decision to waive the privilege. For example, in *Connecticut v. Barrett,* the arrestee indicated a willingness to talk about his crimes with police but did not want to make any written statement.[20] According to the Supreme Court, the *Barrett* trial court held that the arrestee's decision was a voluntary waiver of constitutional protections and that there was no evidence of threats, trickery, or other police overreaching. Waiver is generally a question of fact to be resolved during pretrial legal proceedings, subject to appeal following conviction.

In determining whether a defendant has properly waived the Fifth Amendment privilege against self-incrimination and has voluntarily given a confession, courts often evaluate the voluntariness of the statement by the use of a test that considers the totality of the circumstances.[21] When deciding the admissibility of a confession, courts often consider the subject's age, education, and level of sobriety; the circumstances of the *Miranda* warning; the subject's prior experience with police and the criminal justice system; the length and circumstances of any interrogation; threats made by officials, if any; promises made; and any other factors that could produce an involuntary confession.[22]

In one allegation of an involuntary confession, the defendant had been charged with assault of his minor child. According to police, following *Miranda* warnings, the defendant waived his Fifth Amendment privilege against self-incrimination and admitted committing the assault. As part of his argument against use of his confession, he contended that his statements had been taken involuntarily, since at the time they were given he was suffering from the effects of lack of sleep and was not thinking clearly due to the influence of recent marijuana use. The trial court had admitted the confession into evidence following a pretrial hearing. According to the reviewing court, the defendant's age and education did not contribute to an involuntary confession, and a psychological evaluation demonstrated a normal understanding of social situations. The court rejected the defendant's contention of involuntariness, even though he alleged that he was unable to understand his *Miranda* rights because he was of low-average intelligence and had completed only six years of formal education. In negating one of the defendant's contentions, a prosecution expert offered evidence that the defendant's cognitive functioning was not significantly impaired by either marijuana or lack of sleep. In support of a voluntary waiver, the court noted that the defendant had prior criminal justice experience, since he had been arrested on other occasions and seemed to understand what he faced in the present situation. The reviewing court evaluated the manner of the interrogation and concluded that the length, tactics, and methods the police employed were not likely to produce and did not produce an involuntary confession. According to the appellate court, giving due consideration to all the factors, the trial court was correct in allowing it to be admitted against the defendant.[23] Although each case is determined on its unique fact pattern, most courts consider all relevant information under a totality of the circumstances test to determine whether a defendant's Fifth Amendment right not to self-incriminate has been violated.

Waiver of the Fifth Amendment privilege against self-incrimination in one context may not constitute a waiver of the privilege for all jurisdictions and for all potential causes of action. In a Minnesota case, a witness pled guilty to murder and testified against another defendant, waiving her Fifth Amendment privilege at the trial. When the state wanted her to testify against a different defendant in the same criminal case, she refused, and the trial court held her in contempt of court. The judge took the position that the earlier testimony indicated a waiver of her privilege concerning the case and her involvement in it. The refusing witness feared a possibility of a federal prosecution and based her refusal to testify on the ground that she had remaining concerns about criminal liability. The court of appeal agreed that where the courts of one jurisdiction attempt to compel testimony from a witness that could be used by a different jurisdiction in a subsequent proceeding, the witness possesses a Fifth Amendment privilege that can be asserted, even if it has been waived in an earlier proceeding.[24]

11. CONFESSION PRACTICE PRIOR TO THE WARREN COURT REVOLUTION

In an old case involving state racial discrimination and brutality, *Brown v. Mississippi*,[25] the Court determined that brutal beatings directed and conducted by a state cannot be used to coerce a confession from a defendant without violating the defendant's right to due process of law under the Fourteenth Amendment. In *Brown,* the suspects were subjected to extensive physical torture, including hanging and repeated whipping, to the point that they made involuntary confessions to law enforcement officials. Since the free will of the defendants had been broken by torture, there were two reasons not to admit their confessions: First of all, no one could be sure that the confessions were true and accurate, since the defendants had been coerced into offering them; second, fundamental fairness prohibited the use of the confessions due to the methods used to extract them. The lesson of *Brown* suggested that where the defendant's free exercise of discretion in giving a confession has been eliminated, the resulting confession, whether truthful or not, cannot be used against the defendant. In a state court, any confession extracted from a defendant, even if truthful, should not be introduced in evidence, since the process of extraction failed to comport with the fundamental fairness required under due process of law. While *Brown* was not decided on Fifth Amendment grounds because the amendment had not then been deemed to apply to state government actions, the basis for excluding the use of coerced confessions can be traced to the rationale behind the privilege against self-incrimination.

Demonstrative of the due process principle prohibiting the use of involuntary confessions is the case of *Payne v. Arkansas,* 356 U.S. 560 (1958), where a retarded man had been convicted in an Arkansas state court of first-degree murder. Over his objection at his trial, the prosecution introduced a confession, which the defendant alleged had been improperly taken. He had been arrested and placed in a cell for two days without access to friends, family, or legal counsel; he had been given very little food during a forty-hour period; and a mob had gathered outside the jail. The defendant confessed after being told that the chief of police would try to keep the mob from coming and getting him if he would tell the police the whole story. Several police officers entered the room with a court reporter, and several local businessmen were present when the defendant gave his confession.

According to the *Payne* Court, the use in a state criminal trial of a defendant's confession obtained by coercion, whether physical or mental, has been forbidden under decisions interpreting the Fourteenth Amendment. The confession was motivated by the defendant's fear that a mob might end his life and that law enforcement might do little or nothing to prevent it unless he cooperated by offering an acceptable confession. The Court found that torture of either the mind or body can affect free will, since the will is influenced as much by fear as by force. Upon a finding of involuntariness of the confession, the Supreme Court reversed the conviction on due process grounds.

In determining whether a confession has been given freely and voluntarily, courts typically look to see if the defendant's will was overborne by the circumstances. Factors to consider include both the characteristics of the accused and the details of the interrogation under a totality of the circumstances test. See *Schneckloth v. Bustamonte,* 412 U.S. 218 (1973). Some of the factors the Court has taken into account in the past have included the youth of the accused, *Haley v. Ohio,* 332 U.S. 596 (1948); lack of education, *Payne v. Arkansas,* 356 U.S. 560 (1958); low intelligence, *Fikes v. Alabama,* 352 U.S. 191 (1957); the lack of any advice to the accused regarding his constitutional rights, *Davis v. North Carolina,* 384 U.S. 737 (1966); the length of detention, *Chambers v. Florida,* 309 U.S. 227 (1940); the repeated and prolonged nature of the questioning, *Ashcraft v. Tennessee,* 322 U.S. 143 (1944); and the use of physical punishment such as the deprivation of food or sleep, *Reck v. Pate,* 367 U.S. 433 (1961). The Court in *Culombe v. Connecticut,* 367 U.S. 568 (1961), phrased a test for voluntariness of a confession as follows:

> The ultimate test remains that which has been the only clearly established test in Anglo-American courts for two hundred years: the test of voluntariness. Is the confession the product of an essentially free and unconstrained choice by its maker? If it is, if he has willed to confess, it may be used against him. If it is not, if his will has been overborne and his capacity for self-determination critically impaired, the use of his confession offends due process.

During the years when the Court adjudicated coerced confession cases prior to determining that the self-incrimination clause of the Fifth Amendment applied to the states, due process proved to be the constitutional vehicle of choice. As court membership changed over the years and as novel constitutional changes became accepted, the court moved toward incorporating various parts of the Bill of Rights into the Due Process Clause of the Fourteenth Amendment. In various cases, arguments were made that suggested that due process must include an exclusion of evidence if illegally seized, a prohibition against double jeopardy, and a right to a grand jury indictment in a serious state case, among others. Some rights arguably might be essential to criminal justice, while others might be desirable but not absolutely essential. Over the years, the Court evaluated those rights and incorporated most, though not all, of the rights from the first eight amendments into the Fourteenth Amendment and made them applicable to the states.

12. EVOLUTION OF INTERROGATION AND CONFESSION UNDER THE WARREN COURT

Following *Brown* and *Payne,* the Court decided *Malloy v. Hogan,*[26] where it held that the privilege against self-incrimination contained within the Fifth Amendment should provide protection against a state that was seeking to force an individual to give criminal evidence against himself. In *Malloy,* the previously convicted defendant had been called to testify before a referee concerning his gambling and other activities, which he refused to do on grounds that the answers might tend to incriminate him. Since the Fifth Amendment offered him no protection at that time, he was committed to jail until he would agree to testify. Following the denial of his state court application for a writ of habeas corpus, the case eventually reached the Supreme Court. According to the holding of the *Malloy* Court, "[T]he Fourteenth Amendment guaranteed the petitioner the protection of the Fifth Amendment's privilege against self-incrimination."[27] The Due Process Clause operated as if the federal Fifth Amendment privilege against self-incrimination had been written within the words "due process."

The *Malloy* Court determined that in enforcing the concept of due process in state cases, the Fifth Amendment privilege against self-incrimination must be read as part and parcel of the Fourteenth Amendment's guarantee of due process. Therefore, in meeting the constitutional requirement of voluntariness under a "totality of the circumstances" test, an admissible confession must be the result of the defendant's free and voluntary decision, unfettered by coercion, whether physical or mental. Factors that courts consider in making a determination concerning whether a particular confession has been properly offered involve the treatment of the individual by law enforcement officials. The length of the time of interrogation and manner of questioning, including rest periods for food, personal essentials, and sleep, are considered in evaluating the voluntariness of a confession. The number of interrogators who have repeatedly "worked" on the defendant in an effort to "whipsaw" him or her into an untenable position must also be weighed. Age, level of education, intelligence, and emotional health are additional elements to consider in specific cases to determine whether a particular individual has made a proper confession.

13. MODERN EVOLUTION OF INTERROGATION AND CONFESSION

The process of defining the scope of the privilege against self-incrimination involved numerous court cases and was not completely orderly. Clearly, any concept of due process must include a prohibition of physical and mental torture designed to break a person's will to produce a coerced confession. In a case in which the plaintiff claimed a violation of civil rights based on an alleged Fifth Amendment violation, the Court determined that where an officer, in the absence of *Miranda* warnings, was merely asking questions of a severely injured suspect while he was receiving hospital treatment, such conduct did not constitute a violation of the Fifth Amendment. The suspect was never prosecuted, and his incriminating statements were never used against him. There was no evidence that the officer was trying to coerce the suspect. According to the Court, the suspect "was no more compelled to be a witness against himself than an immunized witness is forced to testify on pain of contempt."[28] In addition, jurisprudence has determined that the privilege against self-incrimination is not violated by the use of many traditional identification procedures, such as being forced to stand in a lineup, to wear a particular piece of clothing, to utter the words allegedly spoken by the criminal, to make a voice recording, and to give blood, hair, or fingernail samples.[29] Although such identification procedures may communicate potentially incriminating evidence, courts have determined that the processes are not communicative in a testimonial nature and, therefore, are not regulated or prohibited by the Fifth Amendment privilege.

14. PERSONAL MOTIVATIONS FOR CONFESSION IRRELEVANT

Under current interpretation, if an arrestee decides to make a confession, internal personal motivations are generally not factors to take into consideration where the law enforcement personnel have not improperly created the stimulus to confess. In *Colorado v. Connelly* (Case 11.2),[30] the defendant approached a police officer and confessed to a homicide. While the confession appeared to be the result of a personal decision, an existing mental illness created the motivation to confess.[31] According to the defendant's physician, the mental disease produced "voices" that told the defendant

CASE 11.2

Leading Case Brief: Personal Motivations Do Not Produce Involuntary Confessions

Colorado v. Connelly
Supreme Court of the United States
479 U.S. 157 (1986)

Case Facts:

Connelly approached a uniformed off-duty Denver police officer, Patrick Anderson, stated that he had committed a murder, and indicated a desire to discuss the situation. The officer advised Connelly of his right under *Miranda* to remain silent and informed him that anything he said could be used against him in court. Connelly indicated that he had come all the way from Boston to confess to the murder and that he understood his rights and wanted to talk. When Officer Anderson asked if Connelly had been drinking or taking drugs, Connelly replied in the negative but added that he had previously been admitted as a mental patient in several hospitals.

Subsequent to a second warning of the right to remain silent and the arrival of a homicide detective, the officer warned Connelly for the third time. Connelly indicated that he was the person responsible for the murder of Mary Ann Junta, a young girl who had been killed in Denver. Connelly was taken to headquarters, told his story to another officer, and led the police to the location of the homicide. During the entire encounter with officers and during the confessions, Connelly appeared clear-headed and normal in all respects.

Connelly began giving confused answers during an interview with a public defender. He noted that "voices" had told him to return to Denver and the "voices" had directed his confession. Convinced that the confessions were involuntary due to the defendant's mental state, the public defender filed a motion to suppress the confessions as not being freely and voluntarily given.

At a motion to suppress hearing, a psychiatrist testified that Connelly suffered from schizophrenia and was in a psychotic state the day prior to the confession. Such diagnosis indicated that the disease interfered with respondent's volitional abilities and impaired his capacity to make free and rational choices.

The trial court ordered that the statements to police be suppressed because they had been given involuntarily. The state Supreme Court agreed and held that the correct test for admissibility was "whether the statements are 'the product of a rational intellect and a free will.'" According to the court, the capacity for proper judgment and free choice may be overcome by mental illness as well as other factors. The Supreme Court of the United States granted certiorari.

Legal Issue:

Where a person with a history of mental illness confesses to a police officer following an appropriate warning of his Fifth Amendment privilege against self-incrimination, must the confession be suppressed as involuntarily given where the police have not coerced the individual in any way?

The Court's Ruling:

The Court reversed the top state court and ruled that a confession that has not been motivated by official police conduct, regardless of the defendant's internal motivations, does not violate the Fifth Amendment privilege against self-incrimination even if the confession was not the product of a rational intellect and free will.

Essence of the Court's Rationale:

* * *

The Due Process Clause of the Fourteenth Amendment provides that no State shall "deprive any person of life, liberty, or property, without due process of law." Just

(continued)

last Term, in *Miller v. Fenton,* 474 U.S. 104 (1985), we held that by virtue of the Due Process Clause

> certain interrogation techniques, either in isolation or as applied to the unique characteristics of a particular suspect, are so offensive to a civilized system of justice that they must be condemned.

Indeed, coercive government misconduct was the catalyst for this Court's seminal confession case, *Brown v. Mississippi,* 297 U.S. 278 (1936). In that case, police officers extracted confessions from the accused through brutal torture. The Court had little difficulty concluding that even though the Fifth Amendment did not at that time apply to the States, the actions of the police were "revolting to the sense of justice." *Id.,* at 286. The Court has retained this due process focus, even after holding, in *Malloy v. Hogan,* 378 U.S. 1 (1964), that the Fifth Amendment privilege against compulsory self-incrimination applies to the States.

Thus the cases considered by this Court over the 50 years since *Brown v. Mississippi* have focused upon the crucial element of police overreaching. While each confession case has turned on its own set of factors justifying the conclusion that police conduct was oppressive, all have contained a substantial element of coercive police conduct. Absent police conduct causally related to the confession, there is simply no basis for concluding that any state actor has deprived a criminal defendant of due process of law.

* * *

We have previously cautioned against expanding "currently applicable exclusionary rules by erecting additional barriers to placing truthful and probative evidence before state juries . . ." *Lego v. Twomey,* 404 U.S. 477, 488–489 (1972). We abide by that counsel now. "[T]he central purpose of a criminal trial is to decide the factual question of the defendant's guilt or innocence," *Delaware v. Van Arsdall,* 475 U.S. 673, 681 (1986), and while we have previously held that exclusion of evidence may be necessary to protect constitutional guarantees, both the necessity for the collateral inquiry and the exclusion of evidence deflect a criminal trial from its basic purpose. Respondent would now have us require sweeping inquiries into the state of mind of a criminal defendant who has confessed, inquiries quite divorced from any coercion brought to bear on the defendant by the State. We think the Constitution rightly leaves this sort of inquiry to be resolved by state laws governing the admission of evidence and erects no standard of its own in this area.

Case Importance:

The Supreme Court of the United States reaffirmed the principle under the Fifth and Fourteenth Amendments that for a confession to have been involuntarily taken, government action must have improperly coerced or otherwise wrongfully influenced a defendant to confess. Private motivations to confess do not create official coerciveness that would suppress a subject's confession.

either to make a confession or to commit suicide. Connelly may not have possessed an entirely free will regarding whether or not to make a confession and may have confessed due to personal internal motivations. Since the police dealt with him properly, warned him under *Miranda,* and did not otherwise motivate him to offer a confession, whatever personal motivation Connelly may have possessed had no effect on police conduct. *Connelly* stands for the proposition that so long as police do not illegally coerce physically or otherwise mentally motivate an individual to confess, the confession will not be excludable under grounds of a Fifth Amendment violation.

15. INVOLUNTARY CONFESSION NOT AVAILABLE FOR PROOF OF GUILT

An involuntary confession is not admissible against a defendant in a state court by virtue of the Due Process Clause of the Fourteenth Amendment.[32] Similarly, an involuntary confession should be excluded from a federal criminal trial based on the Fifth Amendment's Due Process Clause. To determine whether a confession has been voluntarily offered or involuntarily extracted, courts must examine the totality of the circumstances.[33] A trial court might consider the physical condition under which an arrestee has been held, the age of the defendant, whether the defendant has seen friends or family, and whether the arrestee consulted with an attorney and received sufficient sleep, food, water, and access to toilet facilities. It would be essential to determine whether threats of harm have been made and whether physical harm has occurred to the arrestee. Upon the evaluation of the factors under the totality of the circumstances test, a trial judge should render a ruling concerning the admissibility of the confession.

If the evidence shows that a confession has been made freely, voluntarily, and without duress, compulsion, or coercion, it should be admitted against the defendant. Where a court makes a determination that a confession has been involuntarily taken, the court should refuse to allow the introduction of that confession in evidence. From an appellate perspective, once an involuntary confession has been admitted for consideration as evidence in a trial court, analysis under the harmless error rule determines the resolution of the appeal. Under this standard, if an appellate court determines that the use of the involuntary confession had no effect on the outcome of the case, the resulting conviction will not be disturbed. On the other hand, if an appellate court cannot say that, beyond a reasonable doubt, the admission of the involuntary confession had no effect on the outcome, then the criminal case should be reversed.[34]

In *Arizona v. Fulminante,* 499 U.S. 279 (1991), the prosecution used the defendant's confession against him in a murder prosecution (Case 11.3). The defendant was serving time in a federal prison but was having a rough time of it because it was rumored among the other prisoners that he was a child murderer. Another federal prisoner, working with police, offered to protect Fulminante if he could hear the whole story about the killing of the child. In exchange for security within prison, Fulminante confessed to the government's agent and subsequently to the government agent's wife. The state prosecutor used the prison confession against Fulminante in a successful state murder prosecution. On appeal, the Supreme Court reversed the conviction. The coerced confession should not have been introduced in court because the manner in which it was obtained violated the Due Process Clause of the Fourteenth Amendment, and the Court held that the harmless error standard had not been met.

16. INVOLUNTARY CONFESSION NOT AVAILABLE FOR IMPEACHMENT

An involuntary confession, while illegally obtained, cannot be used for impeachment purposes. Assume that a defendant has given a confession that has been determined to have been obtained by virtue of physical or mental coercion. There is no way to discern whether the coerced confession possessed any reliability or truth. In addition, there is also the desire that the police must obey the law while enforcing the law and the fact that our society and culture might well be undermined as much from illegal police investigatory tools as from criminals themselves.[35] We might exclude an illegally obtained confession from the case in chief of the prosecution on federal constitutional grounds, but we also would have to exclude it from use as impeachment evidence because we have no way of determining its truthfulness.

CASE 11.3

Leading Case Brief: Police Coerced Confessions Are Inadmissible for Any Purpose

Arizona v. Fulminante
Supreme Court of the United States
499 U.S. 279 (1991)

Case Facts:

After Fulminante's eleven-year-old stepdaughter was murdered in Arizona, he emerged as a prime suspect in her murder due to a series of inconsistent statements he made to police and to the effect of other evidence. Even when the victim's body was discovered, police remained unable to develop sufficient evidence to successfully prosecute Fulminante for the homicide of his stepdaughter. Later, a federal court convicted Fulminante on an unrelated crime and he served time in a federal correctional facility. During this incarceration, some inmates began to give him a rough time because of the rumor that he was a child murderer and rapist-molester. Sarivola, an inmate and a former police officer working undercover for the Federal Bureau of Investigation, pretended to befriend Fulminante and offered "protection" from other inmates on the condition that Fulminante tell Sarivola the complete story of the child killing. After Fulminante admitted his sexual assault of the victim, he confessed to murder and then related to Sarivola significant details concerning the girl's death. Following Fulminante's release from prison, for unknown reasons, he repeated the substance of his original confession to Sarivola's future wife, Donna. Both this confession to the girl's death and the earlier prison confession were introduced at Fulminante's subsequent trial for the murder of his stepdaughter. The prosecution obtained a capital conviction and a death penalty for Fulminante. On appeal, Fulminante contended that the prison confession was involuntarily obtained by a government agent and should not have been introduced against him at trial.

Legal Issue:

Where a confession has been illegally coerced from a suspect by a police operative in violation of the Fifth Amendment and admitted in evidence against the accused, on appellate review should courts apply the harmless error analysis concerning the admissibility of the confession?

The Court's Ruling:

The Court determined that the prison confession had been extracted in violation of the Fifth Amendment's self-incrimination provision and should not have been admitted at the murder trial. Since the Court could not determine whether the admission of the first confession had no effect on the verdict, a new trial resulted.

Essence of the Court's Rationale:

Although the question is a close one, we agree with the Arizona Supreme Court's conclusion that Fulminante's confession was coerced. The Arizona Supreme Court found a credible threat of physical violence unless Fulminante confessed. Our cases have made clear that a finding of coercion need not depend upon actual violence by a government agent; a credible threat is sufficient.

* * *

The Court has repeatedly stressed that the view that the admission of a coerced confession can be harmless error because of the other evidence to support the verdict is "an impermissible doctrine," *Lynumn v. Illinois,* 372 U.S. 528, 537 (1963); for "the admission in evidence, over objection, of the coerced confession vitiates the judgment because it violates the Due Process Clause of the Fourteenth Amendment."

* * *

[S]ome coerced confessions may be untrustworthy. *Jackson v. Denno,* 378 U.S., at 385–386; *Spano v. New York,* 360 U.S., at 320. Consequently, admission of coerced confession may distort the truth-seeking function of the trial upon which the majority focuses. More importantly, however, the use of coerced confessions, "whether true or false," is forbidden

because the methods used to extract them offend an underlying principle in the enforcement of our criminal law: that ours is an accusatorial and not an inquisitorial system—a system in which the State must establish guilt by evidence independently and freely secured and may not by coercion prove its charge against an accused out of his own mouth, *Rogers v. Richmond*, 365 U.S., at 540–541.

* * *

[On the merits, the Supreme Court determined that the burden of demonstrating that the admission of the prison confession rested with the prosecution and that it had not proved beyond a reasonable doubt that the admission of the first confession had no influence on the jury's verdict. The Court upheld the ordering of a new trial to Fulminante.]

Case Importance:

Fulminante determined that the issue of whether a new trial must be granted when a coerced confession has been improperly admitted against a defendant turns on whether the erroneous admission of the confession had any effect on the outcome of the trial. The case reinforced the concept that coerced confessions taken in violation of the Fifth Amendment as applied to the states through the Due Process Clause of the Fourteenth Amendment cannot be admitted against a defendant for any purpose.

A confession obtained in violation of the Constitution stands on different grounds than one taken after a defective *Miranda* warning; the confession following *Miranda* may well be truthful but inadmissible only on *Miranda* grounds.

17. VIOLATION OF *MIRANDA:* USE OF CONFESSION FOR IMPEACHMENT PURPOSES

The Fifth Amendment privilege against self-incrimination cannot be fully understood without reference to the landmark case, *Miranda v. Arizona*.[36] The Court in *Miranda* held that anytime a person is in law enforcement custody and an officer intends to conduct any interrogation, the arrestee must be told of the right to speak with counsel prior to questioning, that there exists no requirement that the individual speak with the officer, and that anything the person does say may be used against him or her in a court of law. If the dictates of *Miranda* are not met, the evidence thereby obtained will not be admissible in court for purposes of proving guilt. The exclusion is virtually absolute, despite the strong chance that any statement offered was given without violation of the Fifth Amendment privilege against self-incrimination. As the *Miranda* Court noted, the warnings were required and a waiver of rights necessary as a prerequisite to the admission of any statement made by a person in custody. The *Miranda* prohibition does not depend on proof of a Fifth Amendment violation; the evidence is excluded because of the chance that the statement was not voluntarily offered by the arrestee.

Where a confession has been taken in violation of *Miranda*, but not under duress or coercion, the confession can be used for impeachment purposes,[37] so long as there is no allegation of involuntariness. Impeachment use of a "bad" *Miranda* confession may be admissible in a case where a defendant has taken the witness stand and offered a story that is materially inconsistent from the original. The confession presumably offers accurate evidence, since it was given by the subject's free decision and is excludable from the prosecution's case only due to the *Miranda* violation. If impeachment use of voluntary confessions taken in violation of *Miranda* were not permitted, the shield provided by *Miranda* would be altered into a license to commit defense perjury.[38] In such a case, the defendant would possess little worry that earlier contrary evidence from the defendant's own mouth might be used to impeach.

18. SUMMARY

The Fifth Amendment provides that a person shall not have to offer evidence that would help a prosecutor gain a conviction against the same person or to otherwise give testimonial evidence that could tend to incriminate that individual. The same guarantee extends to cover state and local criminal prosecutions. Courts exclude evidence obtained through police coercion or torture from introduction against the person from whom it was extracted. The essence of the privilege is that if a defendant or an ordinary witness decides to testify and offer incriminating evidence, the decision should be freely and voluntarily made and not be prompted by prior mental or physical coercion.

The assertion of a Fifth Amendment privilege is generally available at any time in any sort of proceeding and carries protection beyond criminal tribunals. As a general rule, the prosecutor may not emphasize a defendant's assertion of the privilege during a criminal trial. Use immunity gives a witness the same protection as the Fifth Amendment, so a prosecutor may give immunity to a witness whom the prosecutor wants to testify against a defendant. Any witness or defendant may waive the protections of the Fifth Amendment and agree to testify in a criminal or other proceeding.

Police are required to offer warnings containing information about the Fifth Amendment whenever they have a person in custody and desire to interrogate that individual, but the Fifth Amendment privilege does not extend to using it to refuse to participate in an in-person lineup or other identification procedure. A confession taken in violation of the *Miranda* warnings may be used for impeachment purposes in some situations. However, when an interrogation violates the Fifth Amendment, producing an involuntary confession, such a confession cannot be used to prove guilt or for impeachment purposes.

REVIEW EXERCISES AND QUESTIONS

1. In what type of context is the Fifth Amendment privilege against self-incrimination assertable? Only in criminal trials? In other contexts?

2. In a criminal case, the defendant determined that it would be in his best interests to not give testimony during the defense portion of the trial. Obviously, a defendant knows some information that the prosecutor does not know. May the prosecutor argue to the jury that the defendant has information that he has refused to share with the trial jury? Why or why not?

3. The prosecutor may give immunity to a witness whose testimony would otherwise subject the witness to potential criminal prosecution. Why is granting immunity of sufficient importance and effect that the prosecutor may force the witness to offer incriminating information at a criminal trial or at a grand jury proceeding?

4. If the prosecution alleges that a defendant has waived her privilege against self-incrimination, what are some of the factors that a judge might properly consider to make a determination concerning a waiver?

5. Consider a situation where a mentally unstable individual sought out police to confess to a homicide. The officer did not question the individual and merely listened to the story. The decision to confess to police appeared to have been motivated by some mental problems, coupled with a recent religious experience. Once the individual consulted with a court-appointed attorney, the defense lawyer wanted the confession suppressed from trial use. Should such a confession be suppressed? Why or why not?

HOW WOULD YOU DECIDE?

1. In the Court of Criminal Appeals of Alabama

The prosecution had evidence that James Ben Brownfield Jr. had savagely beaten his sister and her grandson to death with a hammer and attempted to set fire to the house. Subsequent to the first series of crimes, police believe Brownfield drove to the house where his brother-in-law lived and savagely beat him with the same hammer and stabbed him with a knife. Following defendant's arrest for the crimes, he made a videotaped confession to the police. The prosecution planned to introduce Brownfield's confession, made after *Miranda* warnings, against him during the prosecution's case. The defendant contended that the confession had been involuntarily taken because he had ingested seven or eight Zanax pills before the commission of the murders and had been using methamphetamine for two weeks prior to the murders. A defense expert testified that the defendant appeared to be in a "drug soup" when observed on the confession videotape. The expert noted additionally that the defendant was in a "highly suggestive state and assimilated information and details relayed to him during the interrogations as his own memories." Defendant Brownfield contended that because of his prior drug use, his mind and free will had been overreached by professional police officers. Law enforcement officers testified that when the defendant made his confession, he appeared to be coherent, did not appear to be under the influence of drugs, and seemed to understand his constitutional rights. Police asserted that they offered defendant Brownfield no threats or inducements to get him to confess. Law enforcement officials indicated that the defendant was not told that it would be better for him to confess or make a statement so that the police would go easy on him. The trial court allowed the confession to be introduced against the defendant.

How would you rule on the defendant's contention that his confession was involuntarily taken and should have been excluded from his homicide trial?

The Court's Holding:

The Court of Criminal Appeals of Alabama held that strong precedent existed to exclude a confession or other inculpatory statement as involuntary if it had been coerced through force or induced by an express or implied promise of leniency. To admit a confession as voluntary, a defendant must have possessed the capacity to exercise an independent free will under the "totality of the circumstances." In this case, to exclude the confession, defendant Brownfield would have had to have demonstrated that "his mind was substantially impaired when the confession was made." The Court of Criminal Appeals of Alabama agreed with the trial court decision that based on the conflicting evidence, the defendant was not intoxicated at the time of the murders, at the time of his arrest, or at the time he made his statements to the authorities, so the confession was voluntarily made and properly admitted. The appellate court felt that evidence of overreaching did not exist and evidence of impairment of the defendant was lacking, so the trial court properly allowed the use of the confession. See *Brownfield v. State,* 2007 Ala. Crim. App. LEXIS 79 (2007).

HOW WOULD YOU DECIDE?

2. In the Court of Appeal of California

A jury convicted Clifton Terrell Jr. of murder arising from a robbery on the streets of San Francisco. The facts indicated that Terrell and an accomplice approached a couple with the intention of committing robbery but the male victim proved uncooperative and scuffled with the defendant, with the result that the defendant's gun went off, killing the victim. Defendant Terrell stated to police that when he snatched the woman's purse, the male victim ran up to him and grabbed the gun, causing it to fire. After the police arrested the defendant and took him to an interrogation room, he confessed to the homicide and other robberies. However, police had not properly followed *Miranda* procedure when they continued to interrogate him after he indicated that he did not want to talk to them. Although the interrogation had been videotaped, the prosecution did not oppose the defendant's motion to suppress the evidence of the confession to police. Following his jailhouse confession, the defendant asked to make a telephone call to his mother, at which time he basically repeated his confession to her, which the police duly recorded. The trial court found that Terrell's confession to the police was inadmissible to prove guilt because police continued to question the defendant after he invoked his right to remain silent. The court further held that the confession was involuntary using the following reasoning:

"You have an 18-year-old who is obviously very concerned and worried about the death penalty that is discussed. Police say they can't make any promises, but they will speak to the District Attorney, tell them that he cooperated and he felt sorry. And they said that after he first said he didn't want to talk unless he thought it would do him some good. So . . . under the facts of this case . . . I do think it is an involuntary confession." 141 Cal. App. 4th 1371, 1382 (2006).

The court ruled against the defendant's first confession because it was not elicited by police in the course of a proper custodial interrogation but upheld the use of the confession to his mother because the defendant initiated the call on his own volition without prompting or influence by the police. The trial court permitted the prosecutor to use the confession given by defendant Terrell to his mother because it was not elicited by police in the course of the illegal custodial interrogation. The defendant contended on appeal that the confession given to his mother should have been excluded from the prosecutor's use at trial.

How will you rule on the defendant's contention that his confession given to his mother on the telephone was illegally obtained in violation of his* Miranda *right not to speak with police?

The Court's Holding:

The court determined that it was completely defendant Terrill's idea to call his mother and that there was no police conduct that motivated him to make the call and to share his information with his mother concerning the crimes for which he stood accused. The fact that the police did not tell the defendant that his calls would be recorded or that they might be listing to his conversation does not make his confession to his mother any less voluntary. The court felt that his motivation in speaking to his mother was completely different from any motivation he may have had to confess to the police. Terrill admitted that it was his decision alone concerning what to say to his mother and two other family members. Therefore, this confession that he made to his mother that was recorded by police was properly and completely admissible at the defendant's trial since there was no government coercion or police prompting that would have altered the content of this phone call. In addition, the telephone conversation with his mother did not occur under conditions that could be considered custodial interrogation or even its functional equivalent. See *People v. Terrell*, 141 Cal. App. 4th 1371 (2006).

ENDNOTES

1. Amendment Five: "*No person . . . shall be compelled in any criminal case to be a witness against himself,* nor be deprived of life, liberty, or property, without due process of law; nor shall private property be taken for public use, without just compensation" (emphasis added).

2. See *Malloy v. Hogan*, 378 U.S. 1 (1964), where the Court held that the Fifth Amendment privilege against self-incrimination should be applied to state criminal prosecutions through the Due Process Clause of the Fourteenth Amendment.

3. *Culombe v. Connecticut*, 367 U.S. 568, 581–582 (1961).

4. Amendment Fourteen: ". . . nor shall any State *deprive any person of life, liberty, or property, without due process of law;* nor deny to any person within its jurisdiction the equal protection of the laws" (emphasis added).

5. In *Arizona v. Fulminante,* 499 U.S. 279 (1991), where an involuntary confession had been introduced against Fulminante, the Court held that a coerced confession admitted in court would not automatically result in a reversal and new trial. The resolution of a case involving a coerced confession should turn on an evaluation of the "harmless error" standard that would reverse a conviction unless it could be said beyond a reasonable doubt that the outcome would not be different without the admission of the coerced confession. The Court reversed Fulminante's conviction. See also *Chapman v. California,* 386 U.S. 18 (1967), where the Court rejected the position "that all federal constitutional errors in the course of a criminal trial require reversal. We held that the Fifth Amendment violation of prosecutorial comment upon the defendant's failure to testify would not require reversal of the conviction if the State could show 'beyond a reasonable doubt that the error complained of did not contribute to the verdict obtained.'" 386 U.S. at 24.

6. 417 U.S. 85 (1974).

7. 384 U.S. 757 (1966).

8. 530 U.S. 27, 35–36 (2000).

9. 218 U.S. 245 (1910).

10. 410 U.S. 1 (1973).

11. 496 U.S. 582 (1990).

12. *Estelle v. Smith,* 451 U.S. 454, 463 (1981).

13. *United States v. Balsys,* 524 U.S. 666 (1998).

14. If either use immunity or transactional immunity has been accorded to the witness at a grand jury session, legislative hearing, or similar proceeding, no Fifth Amendment privilege remains, and the witness must testify in response to questions.

15. 380 U.S. 609 (1965).

16. 487 U.S. 99, 117 (1988).

17. See *Kastigar v. United States,* 406 U.S. 441 (1972).

18. *Powell v. Texas,* 492 U.S. 680, 684 (1989).

19. See *Colorado v. Spring,* 479 U.S. 564, 572 (1987).

20. 479 U.S. 523, 527 (1987).

21. *Montana v. Loh,* 275 Mont. 460, 475; 914 P.2d 592, 601 (1996).

22. *Montana v. Campbell,* 278 Mont. 236; 924 P.2d 1304, 1307, 1308 (1996).

23. *Montana v. Hoffman,* 314 Mont. 155, 162, 163; 64 P.3d 1013, 1018 (2003).

24. See *In re Contempt of Ecklund,* 636 N.W.2d 585, 589, 590 (2001). For a case with the same outcome based on a similar legal rationale, see also *Martin v. Flanagan,* 259 Conn. 487; 789 A.2d 979 (2001).

25. 297 U.S. 278 (1936).

26. 378 U.S. 1 (1964).

27. *Malloy* at 3.

28. *Chavez v. Martinez,* 538 U.S. 760 (2003).

29. See, generally, *Schmerber v. California,* 384 U.S. 757 (1966).

30. 479 U.S. 157 (1986).

31. When Connelly spoke with police, he denied any drug use or that he had been drinking. Connelly did mention that in the past he had been a mental patient in several mental hospitals. Connelly told police that his conscience had been bothering him following the homicide.

32. See *Arizona v. Fulminante,* 499 U.S. 279 (1991).

33. In making a determination under the totality of the circumstances test, Justice Stewart in *Schneckloth v. Bustamonte,* 412 U.S. 218, 226 (1973), offered some suggestions of factors the Court has considered in past cases. "Some of the factors taken into account have included the youth of the accused, *e.g., Haley v. Ohio,* 332 U.S. 596; his lack of education, *e.g., Payne v. Arkansas,* 356 U.S. 560; or his low intelligence, *e.g., Fikes v. Alabama,* 352 U.S. 191; the lack of any advice to the accused of his constitutional rights, *e.g., Davis v. North Carolina,* 384 U.S. 737; the length of detention, *e.g., Chambers v. Florida* [309 U.S. 227]; the repeated and prolonged nature of the questioning, *e.g., Ashcraft v. Tennessee,* 322 U.S. 143; and the use of physical punishment such as the deprivation of food or sleep, *e.g., Reck v. Pate,* 367 U.S. 433.

34. *Arizona v. Fulminante,* 499 U.S. 279 (1991).

35. See *Blackburn v. Alabama,* 361 U.S. 199, 206 (1960).

36. 394 U.S. 436 (1966).

37. See *Harris v. New York,* 401 U.S. 222, 225 (1971).

38. Ibid. at 226.

Part 5

Pretrial and Trial Criminal Procedure and Appellate Practice

Pretrial Criminal Process: Pretrial Motions, Identification Process, Preliminary Hearing, Bail, Right to Counsel, Speedy Trial, and Double Jeopardy

Learning Objectives

1. Be able to explain why there is a right to the presence of legal counsel at some types of identification procedures but not at other procedures.
2. List the identification procedures that permit the presence of counsel and those for which there is no right to counsel.
3. Understand and describe the events that give rise to the right to have legal counsel at an identification procedure.
4. List and be able to apply the five-factors test from the case of *Neil v. Biggers* that courts use to determine the accuracy of eyewitness identification.

5. Be able to explain why a defendant has the right to counsel at a preliminary hearing.
6. Articulate the purposes of pretrial bail and the justification for allowing bail to many defendants.
7. Comprehend and be able to apply the *Barker v. Wingo* four-factors test used to determine whether the constitutional right to a speedy trial has been violated.
8. Be able to explain the concept of jeopardy and double jeopardy, and offer an example of a prosecution that would violate the constitutional provision protecting against being tried twice for the same crime.

Chapter Outline

1. Pretrial Motions
2. Identification Procedures: Introduction
3. Due Process and the Right to Counsel at Identification Procedures
4. Sixth Amendment Right to Counsel at Lineups
5. Right to Counsel during Identification: Limitations

6. Photographic Arrays: No Sixth Amendment Right to Counsel
7. Due Process Concerns: Suggestiveness of Identification
8. Accurate Eyewitness Identification: The *Neil* Five-Factors Test
9. Current Application of Identification Procedures

Key Terms

Arraignment
Attachment of jeopardy
Bail provision of Eighth Amendment
Bailable offense
Blockburger test for double jeopardy
Collateral estoppel
Determination of bail amount
Dual sovereignty
Excessive bail
Factors used in determining bail
First hearing
Misdemeanor bail
Neal five-factors test
Preliminary hearing

Pretrial detention
Pretrial motions
Probable cause only hearing
Probable cause to arrest
Rationale for bail
Rationale for double jeopardy
Remedy for violation of speedy trial
Requirements to claim double jeopardy
Right to counsel at a lineup
Right to counsel at preliminary hearing
Sixth Amendment right to a speedy trial
Speedy trial: *Barker* factors to consider
Statutory right to a speedy trial

1. PRETRIAL MOTIONS

From the initiation of a criminal case until the matter is resolved, whether by plea or by trial, various issues that affect both the prosecution and the defense positions arise that must be resolved by the trial judge. These issues range from constitutional objections by the defense to controversial items of evidence that the prosecution desires to introduce at the trial. Motions to reduce the amount of bail may result in the defendant being granted an affordable level of bail. Claims that involve questions concerning the jurisdiction of the court[1] or venue concerns should be resolved prior to trial, but allegations that the court lacks jurisdiction may be raised at any time in the criminal justice process. A pretrial motion to change the venue, the place where the trial will be held, may prove crucial to a fair trial for a defendant where local pretrial publicity may have polluted the jury pool or led prospective jurors to draw some conclusions in a case that has a high publicity value. Motions to suppress evidence under the Fourth Amendment, allegations that the right to a speedy trial has been denied, and allegations that holding a trial will violate double jeopardy guarantees need to be resolved prior to trial in order to foster an orderly and smooth presentation of the evidence. In fact, speedy trial and double jeopardy issues generally must be raised during the pretrial phase, or they will be considered waived by the defendant because the very issues they seek to address might make a trial unnecessary. Where there is concern about the competency of a defendant to stand trial or an issue related to an insanity defense, pretrial motions for mental exams related to these issues are of paramount importance so that decisions may be made prior to the start of a trial. Where a variety of pretrial motions have not been resolved, either party to the lawsuit may file a motion for a continuance that will delay the start of the criminal trial. Where there is an allegation that a confession has not been freely given under standards of voluntariness, a motion to exclude the confession may result in a dismissal of the case if the prosecution's case has been anchored on the use of the questioned confession. Evidentiary questions that turn on the resolution of an evidentiary privilege such as the husband-wife marital testimonial privilege or a doctor-patient privilege may be best resolved prior to trial in a way that promotes the orderly presentation of the evidence. Under *Brady v. Maryland,* 373 U.S. 83 (1963), when the defense requests evidence from the prosecution of an exculpatory nature, the prosecution generally must reveal whatever evidence it possesses that meets the request. When a prosecutor fails to deliver what has been called *Brady* material, the defense may file a pretrial motion to compel the prosecution to comply with the *Brady* request. To prevent unfair prejudice to multiple defendants who face multiple counts, some of which may be related and some of which may not be related, defendant may petition the court in a pretrial motion to sever the charges into separate trials or to separate codefendants into individual trials. Motions to sever defendants or charges generally must be made prior to the beginning of a trial, or they will be deemed to have been waived.

Pretrial motions that are considered mandatory must be made at the appropriate time prior to trial, or they are generally considered to have been waived. In most situations, the pretrial motions that are made by either the defense or the prosecution are designed to promote the orderly progress and resolution of the criminal trial. On occasion, issues that could and should have been resolved at the pretrial stage arise during the trial and a court is forced to deal with them. Usually these are issues that were not apparent to either the prosecution or the defense prior to the beginning of trial or that changed circumstances have brought into the forefront in a way that requires the trial judge to deal with them during trial.

2. IDENTIFICATION PROCEDURES: INTRODUCTION

Screening the potentially guilty from the rest of society has been a problem of long standing without absolutely clear solutions that guarantee accuracy with reasonable certainty. Although a variety of methods of identification are available, a witness identification of the human body with a focus on the face has been a traditional avenue to discriminate the guilty from the innocent. We make discriminations on identity based on gender, race, skin color, eye color, height, and weight, as well as tone of voice and linguistic characteristics. Fingerprinting, blood typing, and DNA matching have been added to the traditional ways of discerning identity. Newer types of biometric measures are just now making their way to the forefront of identity screening. Measuring and identifying the blood vessel patterns on the human retina and using mathematical ratios and formulas to measure the face and head are among the most modern methods of what is claimed to be foolproof identification. Some of the newest methods will eventually become widely used in the law enforcement community, but even though the technology may be quite accurate, the expense of such advanced scientific measures may limit their application in the near term. The admissibility of scientific identity testing, assuming that the data have been obtained with due concern for appropriate criminal procedure, generally rests more with the law of evidence than with substantive criminal procedure.[2]

3. DUE PROCESS AND THE RIGHT TO COUNSEL AT IDENTIFICATION PROCEDURES

In most instances, traditional witness identification, with procedures based on fairly settled law, will be the path followed by most police departments and prosecutors. Most of the larger issues concerning identification procedures have been litigated years ago to the point that prosecutors, the defense bar, and the law enforcement community have fairly clear directives concerning the appropriateness of specific procedures. Issues surrounding the right to counsel during lineup procedures under the Sixth Amendment remain clear and are not subject to much dispute. The appropriateness and practice of conducting pre-indictment and pre-information interrogation in the absence of legal counsel are well known. Due process concerns involving suggestiveness or steering have been detailed in a variety of court cases to the point of fairly clear certainty, if proper procedures are followed, that a criminal case will not be reversed for errors in this area. However, an appellate court should reverse a conviction based partially or wholly on eyewitness identification where the pretrial identification procedure "was so impermissibly suggestive as to give rise to a very substantial likelihood of irreparable misidentification."[3]

The legal standards involving identification procedures have seen little activity in the United States Supreme Court over the last several years, and future major changes are unlikely to be forthcoming. Commentators have criticized the identification process as creating potential for error in too many cases,[4] but judges and courts have not proven to be particularly amenable to change, even when faced with scientific studies challenging the correctness or reliability of eyewitness identification.

Proper identification of criminal suspects involves inquiry concerning whether the suspect possesses a right to counsel and whether the identification procedure meets the standards of due process. Although the identification of a suspect may be one step toward a conviction, the Fifth Amendment privilege against compelled testimonial self-incrimination has been held not to be implicated when a witness views a suspect. Some suspects may refuse to participate in a lineup because identification may provide a step toward an eventual guilty verdict, but there is no constitutional basis for a suspect to refuse to participate in a lineup. In *United States v. Wade,* the defendant contended that by forcing him to take part in an in-person lineup, the government violated his Fifth Amendment privilege against self-incrimination.[5] The *Wade* Court rejected the suggestion by noting that the Fifth Amendment privilege protects a defendant from being required to testify against himself or herself and not from exhibiting himself or herself to potential eyewitnesses.[6]

Consistent with due process considerations, identification procedures include showing a single suspect to a witness, conducting a traditional lineup, having a witness look through the "mug book" or a computer-generated modern version, and conducting a photographic array of suspects. In all the identification processes, there must be no "steering" of the witness with a view to identifying a particular person as the criminal.

4. SIXTH AMENDMENT RIGHT TO COUNSEL AT LINEUPS

Court decisions have held that suspects may be entitled to the Sixth Amendment right to the assistance of legal counsel when a lineup is being conducted by law enforcement agents. Past decisions indicate that legal counsel is required at all "critical stages" of the criminal justice process where substantial rights of an accused may be compromised. Some identifications occur in the absence of counsel but under circumstances that have court approval. A failure to follow the rules and regulations developed through case law may culminate in a conviction ultimately being overturned or in the refusal of a court to allow a witness to offer an identification. The most clear-cut situation for the right to counsel exists when there is a post-indictment or post-information in-person lineup. According to the Court in *United States v. Wade,*[7] when an arrestee has been formally charged with a crime, an in-person lineup constitutes a critical stage of the criminal justice process, during which the suspect has a constitutional right to the assistance of counsel. In *Wade,* the Court quoted one commentator who observed:

> [t]he influence of improper suggestion upon identifying witnesses probably accounts for more miscarriages of justice than any other single factor—perhaps it is responsible for more such errors than all other factors combined. Wall, *Eyewitness Identification in Criminal Cases* 26

Justice Brennan indicated concern with eyewitness identification procedures when he cautioned in *Wade* at 229:

> Suggestion can be created intentionally or unintentionally in many subtle ways. And the dangers for the suspect are particularly grave when the witness' opportunity for observation was insubstantial, and thus his susceptibility to suggestion the greatest.

Brennan continued to emphasize his concern for requiring reliable eyewitness identification procedures when he quoted from a legal encyclopedia:

> [i]t is a matter of common experience that, once a witness has picked out the accused at the line-up, he is not likely to go back on his word later on, so that, in practice, the issue of identity may (in the absence of other relevant evidence) for all practical purposes be determined there and then, before the trial. Williams Hammelmann, Identification Parades, Part I, [1963] *Crim.L.Rev.* 479, 482. *Wade* at 229.

The *Wade* Court indicated that in many cases the witness identification of a suspect as the guilty party may effectively conclude a criminal case and seal the fate of the accused, whether guilty or not. Once an eyewitness has selected a particular person as the guilty party and the government has taken clear steps to prosecute, the eyewitness is unlikely to recant the identification at a later time due to personal and institutional pressures.

According to the *Wade* Court, a major factor in the miscarriage of justice has traditionally been the degree of suggestion inherent in the manner in which the government presents the arrestee to the witness for the purpose of identification. Writing for the majority, Justice Brennan cited cases of questionable identification procedures in which one suspect had been identified by a witness where the suspect was the only person of Asian heritage in the lineup, a case where a tall suspect had been placed with short participants, and where a young suspect had been placed in a lineup array with older men.[8] Suggestive identification procedures create the potential for impermissibly "steering" eyewitnesses toward identifying a particular suspect and producing a due process violation.

The *Wade* case determined that the Sixth Amendment right to counsel extends to a person under an indictment or otherwise formally charged[9] with a criminal offense who is placed in an in-person lineup. An attorney may offer corrective suggestions concerning lineup procedures that will assist the police in conducting a proper identification. Naturally, law enforcement personnel have no interest in identifying the wrong person and should cooperate with an arrestee's counsel. In the absence of counsel, a variety of wrongs could occur, and the suspect would be powerless to contest their occurrence even if the arrestee became aware of them. Witnesses may be unaware of subtle steering in the making of an identification, and the suspect might be completely ignorant of undue suggestiveness in whatever form it might take. Other lineup participants have no particular interest in protesting an improper lineup, since they are not targets of the identification procedure. Thus, where a suspect is represented by counsel and errors in procedure appear about to develop, the attorney may request that corrective measures be taken prior to irreparable misidentification.[10]

In a companion case to *Wade, Gilbert v. California,* the defendant had been required to participate in a postindictment in-person lineup without the presence of his attorney. Because there were so many witnesses to Gilbert's alleged crimes, the lineup proceedings occurred in an auditorium with bright lights shining on the participants so that they could not observe the witnesses. Nearly one hundred witnesses gathered in the auditorium, where presumably they were able to talk with each other and observe identifications made by fellow witnesses. During the guilt phase of his capital murder trial, Gilbert sought to elicit confirmation from some of these eyewitnesses that they had made earlier identifications of him at the auditorium lineup, thus indicating that the identification procedure occurred without his attorney being present. The *Gilbert* Court vacated the sentence of death, since it held:

> The admission of the in-court identifications without first determining that they were not tainted by the illegal lineup but were of independent origin was constitutional error. *United States v. Wade, supra.* We there held that a postindictment pretrial

lineup at which the accused is exhibited to identifying witnesses is a critical stage of the criminal prosecution; that police conduct of such a lineup without notice to, and in the absence of, his counsel denies the accused his Sixth Amendment right to counsel and calls in question the admissibility at trial of the in-court identifications of the accused by witnesses who attended the lineup. *Gilbert* at 273.

From the *Wade* and *Gilbert* cases, a clear rule has emerged that post-indictment or post-information in-person lineups require the presence of counsel, absent waiver, or the evidence concerning the lineup will, at a minimum, be excluded from trial.

5. RIGHT TO COUNSEL DURING IDENTIFICATION: LIMITATIONS

A reading of the *Wade* and *Gilbert* cases would seem to indicate that the Supreme Court of the United States was moving in the direction of mandating the presence of counsel at all identification procedures. It could be argued that counsel would have to be supplied for every individual arrested by police if any witness identification process was contemplated. However, the Court backed away from the *Wade* holding a bit when it determined that the Sixth Amendment right to counsel during the identification process does not apply in every conceivable context. In *Kirby v. Illinois,*[11] the Court required that formal adversarial proceedings beyond a bare arrest have to be initiated before the right to counsel matured at witness lineup identification procedures. The defendants in *Kirby* had been arrested for robbery but had not been formally charged. While Kirby was in custody, police allowed the victim to enter a holding room and make an identification by merely observing Kirby and another defendant, who were the lone occupants. According to the Court, Kirby and his companion had no right to counsel for purposes of identification, since they had not been indicted, had not had an information filed against them, were not being arraigned or subjected to a preliminary hearing, and were not facing a clear decision by the state to prosecute. The rule that emerged requires the presence of counsel when an information has been filed or an indictment returned, but no federal constitutional right to counsel exists for a person who has been merely arrested when police want to subject him or her to an identification process.

6. PHOTOGRAPHIC ARRAYS: NO SIXTH AMENDMENT RIGHT TO COUNSEL

The use of a still photographic array for identification purposes, even where the subject has been indicted or a prosecution has otherwise been initiated, does not require the presence of counsel, according to *United States v. Ash.*[12] According to the Court, an arrestee or defendant has no Sixth Amendment right to counsel at a photographic array, no matter when it occurs, because the procedure is not one at which the accused requires "aid in coping with legal problems or assistance in meeting his adversary."[13] Were legal counsel required at each and every photo array, as a practical matter, an attorney would have to participate every time a witness looked at a mug book or computer display of photographs, even if the target was on the run and had never been captured. In the pretrial context, the attorney's role is to assist the defendant in dealing with legal questions and to suggest solutions where unfair practices or conditions appear. Where a defendant is not present, as in a police presentation of a photographic array to eyewitnesses, "no possibility arises that the accused might be misled by his lack of familiarity with the law or overpowered by his professional adversary."[14] Since a photographic array does not involve an actual defendant-witness confrontation similar to a trial, the assistance of an attorney is not constitutionally mandated. However, impermissible "steering," suggestive photograph selection, and the repeated presence of only the suspect's picture in a series of photographic arrays collectively remain as potential problems for an accused for which a remedy may prove illusory.

In dealing with photographic arrays, the Supreme Court was not willing to further extend the right to counsel under the Sixth Amendment, even though potential prejudice to a particular defendant might arise from improper conduct of law enforcement officials. The Court noted that photographic identifications were not the only part of a criminal prosecution where an unfair prosecutor might fail to follow due process requirements. According to Justice Blackmun, writing for the Court in *Ash:*

> Evidence favorable to the accused may be withheld; testimony of witnesses may be manipulated; the results of laboratory tests may be contrived. In many ways, the prosecutor, by accident or by design, may improperly subvert the trial. The primary safeguard against abuses of this kind is the ethical responsibility of the prosecutor, who, as so often has been said, may "strike hard blows," but not "foul ones." *Berger v. United States,* 295 U.S. 78, 88 (1935); *Brady v. Maryland,* 373 U.S. 83, 87–88 (1963). If that safeguard fails, review remains available under due process standards. See *Giglio v. United States,* 405 U.S. 150 (1972). *Ash* at 320

The Court trusted that most prosecutors would properly follow the law, and in cases where the prosecution failed to accord due process to a defendant at a non-adversarial photographic array, a defendant's legal counsel should be able to ferret out the wrongdoing and ultimately achieve justice. However, a practical problem, never addressed by the Court, exists where the wrongdoing never becomes apparent through pretrial discovery or from cross-examination during trial, instead remaining hidden to wreak its unconstitutional wrong on an unknowing defendant's case.

7. DUE PROCESS CONCERNS: SUGGESTIVENESS OF IDENTIFICATION

Consistent with due process considerations, all identification procedures should be constructed in a neutral manner with a view to producing a reliable and accurate identification. Where impermissible steering, directing, or suggesting transpires, the accuracy of the result comes into question. While a witness ideally may be offered several choices of photographs or of persons in a lineup, on occasion a formal lineup or photographic array is impractical, and other techniques must be substituted. Sometimes a suspect quickly enters police custody, virtually at the crime scene, and is subjected to a return to the scene for an immediate identification or exclusion from further police interest. If a victim cannot travel to the location of the suspect, the suspect may be brought to the victim without violating the suspect's due process rights or right to counsel. However, such a procedure becomes improper where adversarial proceedings have been initiated and the defendant has appeared at a preliminary hearing without counsel. An identification by a witness who observed the defendant alone at the preliminary hearing should have been excluded from the subsequent trial due to a violation not of due process but of the Sixth Amendment right to counsel.[15]

Exigent or emergency circumstances permit identification by witnesses where practical necessities dictate the rapid use of creative identification procedures despite the risks of suggestiveness. In *Stovall v. Denno,*[16] police brought an arrested homicide suspect to the hospital bedside of a victim whose health was precarious. The victim was permitted to identify the unrepresented suspect as the killer of her husband, despite the suggestiveness inherent in the one-on-one encounter. According to the *Stovall* Court, such practice was appropriate under the circumstances of the case: a sole suspect, a critically injured victim, and a need for identification. The teaching of *Stovall* illustrates that there are identifications in which counsel need not be present and the use of a formal lineup is not required so long as there is no significant chance of irreparable misidentification of the suspect.

Improper suggestiveness may violate the Due Process Clause of the Fourteenth Amendment in a situation where successive lineups were conducted and where the only common individual to all of them happened to be the defendant. In *Foster v. California,*[17] the defendant was initially placed in a lineup of three men. The defendant was nearly six feet tall, and the other two men in the lineup were significantly shorter, a fact that gave rise to an impermissible steering argument. One of the eyewitnesses to the case said that he "thought" Foster was one of the guilty men but was not positive. After speaking to Foster and hearing his voice, the eyewitness was not any more secure in his identification, even after meeting with him one-on-one in a room. A week or so later, the police arranged for the eyewitness to view another lineup involving five men. Foster was the only person in the second lineup who had appeared in the first lineup. The witness made a certain identification of Foster following the second lineup. The *Foster* Court reversed and remanded the case. According to *Foster,* successive positioning in repeated lineups clearly violated due process and could not be lawfully conducted as a general rule. In many respects, the result in *Foster* was required if the Court followed its prior *Wade* decision because *Wade* had held that lineups are a critical stage of the criminal justice process and that judged by the totality of the circumstances, an identification procedure cannot be allowed to stand where the procedures were unnecessarily suggestive and conducive to irreparable mistaken identification.

8. ACCURATE EYEWITNESS IDENTIFICATION: THE *NEIL* FIVE-FACTORS TEST

Whether or not counsel is required, the identification process must produce reliable and reasonably accurate identification. In an effort to determine the appropriate standard for proper eyewitness identification procedures, the Court clarified *Stovall v. Denno* by adopting a more specific test in *Neil v. Biggers* (Case 12.1).[18] In developing the "totality of the circumstances" test, the Court listed five factors as a guideline to

CASE 12.1

Leading Case: The Five-Factor Test to Meet Due Process Standards in Identification

Neil v. Biggers
Supreme Court of the United States
409 U.S. 188 (1972)

Case Facts:

A Tennessee trial court convicted Biggers of rape based on the victim's visual and voice identification of him. According to the victim, the rape began at her home where the victim initially managed to observe the attacker's face as it was illuminated from the light of her kitchen and again when the perpetrator took her across a field under a full moon. On at least two occasions, she was face to face with her attacker with an excellent opportunity to observe his identity. The victim initially described her assailant as between sixteen and eighteen years old and between five feet ten inches and six feet tall, as weighing between 180 and 200 pounds, and as having a dark brown complexion. The victim's initial description offered to police clearly matched the defendant in every detail.

Police permitted the victim to observe the defendant as she walked past the suspect in a hallway. Only after the police had Biggers speak did the victim identify him as the man who had raped her. To obtain a voice identification and at the victim's request, the police required Biggers to say, "Shut up or I'll kill you." Upon seeing Biggers and after hearing his voice, her identification of him as the perpetrator proved instantaneous and positive. She testified that it was petitioner's voice that "was the first thing that made me think it was the boy."[19]

During the seven months between the rape and her identification of the defendant, the victim had looked at countless mug shots, viewed suspects in her own home, and observed many in-person lineups and photographic arrays but had never identified any suspect.

The trial court jury convicted Biggers of rape, and he had no success with direct appellate review. A petition for a writ of habeas corpus was granted by a federal district court and affirmed by the Court of Appeals for the Sixth Circuit. The Supreme Court of the United States granted certiorari.

Legal Issue:

Where a rape victim has been permitted to walk past an arrested suspect and made a positive identification based on visual inspection and hearing a voice sample, does such a suggestive identification process, in the absence of a standard lineup or photographic array, violate a defendant's right to due process under the Fourteenth Amendment?

The Court's Ruling:

The justices held that although the identification process might be somewhat suggestive, the procedure used here could meet due process standards where there was little likelihood of an erroneous misidentification, as tested by the five-factors test.

Essence of the Court's Rationale:

* * *

III

We have considered on four occasions the scope of due process protection against the admission of evidence deriving from suggestive identification procedures. In *Stovall v. Denno*, 388 U.S. 293 (1967), the Court held that the defendant could claim that "the confrontation conducted . . . was so unnecessarily suggestive and conducive to irreparable mistaken identification that he was denied due process of law." *Id.*, at 301–302. . . .

Subsequently, in a case where the witnesses made in-court identifications arguably stemming from previous exposure to a suggestive photographic array, the Court restated the governing test:

> "[W]e hold that each case must be considered on its own facts, and that convictions based on eyewitness identification at trial following a pretrial identification by photograph will be set aside on that ground only if the photographic identification procedure was so impermissibly suggestive as to give rise to a very substantial likelihood of irreparable misidentification." *Simmons v. United States*, 390 U.S. 377, 384 (1968).

* * *

Some general guidelines emerge from [our] cases as to the relationship between suggestiveness and misidentification. It is, first of all, apparent that the primary evil to be avoided is "a very substantial likelihood of irreparable misidentification." *Simmons v. United States,* 390 U.S., at 384. While the phrase was coined as a standard for determining whether an in-court identification would be admissible in the wake of a suggestive out-of-court identification, with the deletion of "irreparable" it serves equally well as a standard for the admissibility of testimony concerning the out-of-court identification itself.

* * *

We turn, then, to the central question, whether under the "totality of the circumstances" the identification was reliable even though the confrontation procedure was suggestive. As indicated by our cases, *the factors to be considered in evaluating the likelihood of misidentification include the opportunity of the witness to view the criminal at the time of the crime, the witness' degree of attention, the accuracy of the witness' prior description of the criminal, the level of certainty demonstrated by the witness at the confrontation, and the length of time between the crime and the confrontation.* [Emphasis added.] Applying these factors, we disagree with the District Court's conclusion.

* * *

We find that the District Court's conclusions on the critical facts are unsupported by the record and clearly erroneous. The victim spent a considerable period of time with her assailant, up to half an hour. She was with him under adequate artificial light in her house and under a full moon outdoors, and at least twice, once in the house and later in the woods, faced him directly and intimately. She was no casual observer, but rather the victim of one of the most personally humiliating of all crimes. Her description to the police, which included the assailant's approximate age, height, weight, complexion, skin texture, build, and voice, might not have satisfied Proust but was more than ordinarily thorough. She had "no doubt" that respondent was the person who raped her. In the nature of the crime, there are rarely witnesses to a rape other than the victim, who often has a limited opportunity of observation. The victim here, a practical nurse by profession, had an unusual opportunity to observe and identify her assailant. She testified at the habeas corpus hearing that there was something about his face "I don't think I could ever forget."

There was, to be sure, a lapse of several months between the rape and the confrontation. This would be a seriously negative factor in most cases. Here, however, the testimony is undisputed that the victim made no previous identification at any of the showups, lineups, or photographic showings. Her record for reliability was thus a good one, as she had previously resisted whatever suggestiveness inheres in a showup. Weighing all the factors, we find no substantial likelihood of misidentification. The evidence was properly allowed to go to the jury.

Affirmed in part, reversed in part, and remanded.

Case Importance:

Neil v. Biggers stands for the principle that identifications constitute a crucial part of the criminal justice process, during which due process standards must be properly honored. Where the five-factors test is applied consistently and properly, the chance of an irreparable misidentification becomes remote.

measure whether a particular identification process comported with due process and eliminated any significant chance of irreparable misidentification. When considering a claim involving an alleged improper identification, courts must consider the opportunity of the witness to view the criminal at the time of the crime, the witness's degree of attention, the accuracy of the witness's original description of the criminal, the level of certainty demonstrated by the witness at the time of the confrontation, and the length of time that had passed between the crime scene identification and the confrontation. A proper analysis by a trial court of these factors, called the "totality of the circumstances test," should result in only proper eyewitness identifications being admitted to evidence by trial court judges.

In *Neil v. Biggers,* officers paraded a suspect past the complaining victim in a rape case. Previously, the victim-witness had looked at mug books and photographs and had attended in-person lineups for about six months and had identified no one. When she walked past the suspect in a hallway, she indicated that she was very sure he was the perpetrator. At the crime scene, she had a good opportunity to see his face and body and paid close attention during the crime, and her original description proved quite accurate. The six-month delay was viewed as the weakest part of her identification but did not destroy it because of her level of certainty. The *Neil* Court approved the courtroom use of eyewitness identification of the suspect, even though he was not represented by counsel at the time of his identification. Consistent with *Kirby,* since the suspect had not been formally charged with a crime, he did not possess the right to counsel at the time of his identification by the victim.

The *Neil* five-factors eyewitness identification test may be applied to virtually any type of identification process, from an in-person lineup to a photographic array. An interesting and somewhat suggestive procedure occurred in *Manson v. Brathwaite,*[20] where a trained police officer observed a drug dealer during an undercover narcotics purchase. Subsequently, the officer described the suspected drug dealer to a fellow officer in such detail that the fellow officer believed he knew the identity of the suspect. The second officer obtained a photograph of the suspected drug dealer and placed it on the original officer's desk. When the undercover officer looked at the photograph, he instantly recognized the drug suspect. At the time of the viewing of the photograph, the suspect did not have counsel and was not under arrest.

The Supreme Court upheld the identification of Brathwaite by the undercover officer by using the five-factors test of *Neil v. Biggers* and concluded that, under the circumstances, such a procedure did not violate due process. The officer had been trained in observation of suspects, especially details relating to identification. He had a fairly clear view of the suspect, and little time had transpired between the original view and the identification. The officer was sure of his identification, and the suspect description matched the description originally offered by the officer.

Many states have adopted the *Neil v. Biggers* five-factors test or some slight variation for evaluating eyewitness identification issues. Kansas follows its own test, which incorporates some of the *Neil* case and adds some slightly different considerations. According to a Kansas case, the factors used to determine eyewitness identification are as follows:

(1) The opportunity of the witness to view the actor during the event; (2) the witness's degree of attention to the actor at the time of the event; (3) the witness's capacity to observe the event, including his or her physical and mental acuity; (4) whether the witness's identification was made spontaneously and remained consistent thereafter, or whether it was the product of suggestion; and (5) the nature of the event being observed and the likelihood that the witness would perceive,

remember and relate it correctly. This last area includes such factors as whether the event was an ordinary one in the mind of the observer during the time it was observed, and whether the race of the actor was the same as the observer's. *Kansas v. Long,* 721 P.2d 483 at 493 (1986)

In a recent Kansas case, a trial court used the test for eyewitness identification to determine whether an accused robber had been identified consistent with fundamental fairness. In the robbery, the perpetrator entered the store with a bandanna over his lower face, acted as if he had a firearm up his sleeve, and threatened the clerk. The robber was face-to-face with the clerk, who looked away only long enough to retrieve the money. The robber immediately left the scene and removed the bandanna as he entered his car. Within minutes, the police captured a man who matched the description and had the clerk identify him. Following admission of the eyewitness identification at trial and his conviction, the defendant appealed, alleging a violation of due process involving an alleged misidentification offered at trial by the clerk-victim. The appellate court considered the degree of attention offered by the clerk and noted that the eyewitness was completely focused on the robber, the clerk's ability to perceive the robber was unimpeded, and the two were in close proximity. The appellate court felt that the clerk properly described the appearance of the robber. The victim offered information concerning the robber's sideburns, which he could see under the bandanna, and the victim's description of the robber, especially his height, was quite accurate. The appellate court noted with approval that the trial court properly considered whether the event was ordinary to the witness and whether the race of the perpetrator was the same as that of the witness. An armed robbery, according to the court, was not an ordinary event to the store clerk, so that facts surrounding the event should have been memorable to the victim. When the appellate court considered all the factors, it affirmed the conviction, since it determined that there was little likelihood of misidentification by the convenience store clerk.[21] This type of trial and appellate court analysis serves to prevent misidentification of defendants by meeting due process standards under both state and federal constitutions.

9. CURRENT APPLICATION OF IDENTIFICATION PROCEDURES

Since for several years the Supreme Court of the United States has not heard a major case that altered the due process requirements of eyewitness identification, the general framework involving the right to counsel and to due process remains relatively settled law. Demonstrative of the generally accepted identification process is a case from the Court of Appeals for the Seventh Circuit, *United States v. Traeger,*[22] where the defendant alleged that his identification in a bank robbery case contained constitutional errors.

In *Traeger,* the defendant contended that a bank teller's identification of him as the robber should have been suppressed. At the crime scene, the teller had an excellent view of the robber and made a certain identification three weeks following the crime. According to Traeger, his constitutional right to due process had been violated because the lineup, as composed, was unduly suggestive. The defendant was much taller and much more robust than the other men in the lineup, a fact, he alleged, that made him stand out from the others. The identification process occurred three weeks after the robbery, with all the participants dressed in traditional jail orange jumpsuits. In the beginning stages of the lineup, all the men were seated, which disguised height differentials, but subsequently, the men were asked to stand one by one. Since the defendant was by far the largest of the participants, he contended that the lineup procedure was unduly suggestive. The Court of Appeals noted that it normally engaged in a two-step process in evaluating such a claim:

> First, we ask whether the defendant established that the identification procedure was unnecessarily suggestive. If it was, we ask whether, under the totality of the circumstances, the identification was reliable despite the suggestive procedures. In determining the reliability of an identification, we consider five factors: (1) the witness' opportunity to view the criminal at the time of the crime, (2) the witness' degree of attention, (3) the accuracy of the witness' prior description of the criminal, (4) the level of certainty that the witness demonstrated at the time of the confrontation, and (5) the time elapsed between the crime and the confrontation. *See Cossel v. Miller,* 229 F.3d 649, 655 (7th Cir. 2000) (citing *Neil v. Biggers,* 409 U.S. 188, 199–200, 34 L. Ed. 2d 401, 93 S. Ct. 375 (1972)). *Traeger* at 474

In reviewing the material facts, the *Traeger* Court determined, from viewing photographs of the lineup, that even though the defendant was much larger in stature and more robust than the other participants, the differences were not so great as to create an unduly suggestive lineup. The court also found that the bank teller had ample opportunity to view the robber while she was getting money from her drawer and that her level of attention appeared to have been elevated by the fact that she was the victim of a robbery. She accurately described Traeger as an individual who was in his mid-thirties, "who was 6'3" tall, weighed 300 to 350 pounds, was unshaven, and wore a blond ponytail."[23] The Court rejected the defense argument concerning unfair suggestiveness because Traeger wore an ankle strap restraint during the lineup. The barely visible plastic ankle restraint would not be recognizable as a restraint unless one were intimately acquainted with the criminal justice system, and there was no evidence that the bank teller focused on Traeger's feet at the lineup.[24]

Ultimately, the Court of Appeals rejected defendant Traeger's complaints based on the alleged improper identification procedures because the Court followed the suggestions offered by the Supreme Court in *Neil v. Biggers,* mentioned previously. While most state courts have followed the principles suggested in *Neil* and reconfirmed by the Court in *Manson v. Brathwaite*[25] when deciding identification issues, some states have decided to pursue a more in-depth evaluation and may reject identifications, based on state case law. States are free to offer greater procedural safeguards and follow more stringent concepts of due process concerning identification and to reject procedures that would pass muster under the minimal federal constitutional standards.[26]

10. THE INITIAL APPEARANCE AND THE PRELIMINARY HEARING

Although a preliminary hearing is not a required step under the Constitution of the United States, many states use it as an additional screening device for criminal cases, especially where a grand jury has not returned an indictment or a grand jury is not expected to be used. Some states dispense with a preliminary hearing completely where a grand jury has returned an indictment[27] because the probable cause determination has been made previously by the grand jury. As is the case in many legal proceedings, the statutory right to a preliminary hearing is a waivable right, and an informed defendant may dispense with this legal procedure.[28] Unlike a probable cause only hearing, the preliminary hearing is adversarial and permits the confrontation and cross-examination of prosecution witnesses by the defendant. As a general rule, states follow the rules of evidence at preliminary hearings.[29] Where a state chooses to use the preliminary hearing, it must grant a defendant the Sixth Amendment right to counsel; where a defendant is indigent, there is a right to free counsel.[30]

The Supreme Court first recognized the right to counsel at a preliminary hearing in *Coleman v. Alabama,* 399 U.S. 1 (1970) (see Case 12.2). In *Coleman,* the defendants had been granted a preliminary hearing in an assault with intent to commit murder prosecution, but the indigent defendants were not represented by counsel. In deciding the case, the Court noted that an accused requires the guidance of counsel in every step of a criminal prosecution and that the Sixth Amendment right to counsel extends beyond the actual trial. The *Coleman* Court determined that a preliminary hearing constituted a critical stage of the criminal justice process, at which time the assistance of counsel was required by the federal constitution.

Consistent with the Sixth Amendment right recognized in *Coleman,* the California Penal Code provides that the defendant be allowed to have counsel during a preliminary hearing:

> The magistrate shall immediately deliver to the defendant a copy of the complaint, inform the defendant that he or she has the right to have the assistance of counsel, ask the defendant if he or she desires the assistance of counsel, and allow the defendant reasonable time to send for counsel. Cal. Penal Code § 859 (Mathew Bender 2003)

Most states allow a defendant a reasonable time in which to obtain legal counsel and will proceed with a preliminary hearing when the attorney for the defendant can be present.

As a general rule, at the beginning of a preliminary hearing, the government calls the witnesses who will be able to offer sufficient evidence to demonstrate probable cause to believe that the defendant has committed the alleged crime or crimes. The witnesses are subject to cross-examination by the defense, which may enable the attorney for the accused to cast sufficient doubt to destroy probable cause. In most cases, the defendant's attorney is not successful in having the case dismissed but can gather evidence about the government's theory of the case and how the prosecution will probably proceed if the case goes to trial. An additional benefit to the defendant is that the witnesses who do testify at a preliminary hearing have the effect of "freezing" their testimony, and the subsequent trial testimony must match what was given at the preliminary hearing.

Demonstrative of the general theory that the preliminary hearing shall not become a mini-trial on the merits, many jurisdictions do not allow defendants to call witnesses to rebut the general testimony placed on the record by the prosecutor

CASE 12.2

Leading Case: The Sixth Amendment Right to Counsel at a Preliminary Hearing

Coleman v. Alabama
Supreme Court of the United States
399 U.S. 1 (1970)

Case Facts:

An Alabama court convicted Coleman and some associates of assault with intent to murder a Mr. Reynolds. At the trial, Reynolds testified that he had been engaged in changing an automobile tire when three men approached him. One of the men shot Reynolds, and there was evidence that Coleman put his hands on Mrs. Reynolds. As a car approached, the men ran away after one of them shot Reynolds a second time. The victims positively identified Coleman and the others as the perpetrators.

During the pretrial stage of the prosecution and at the preliminary hearing, the state of Alabama failed to furnish Coleman with legal representation to advise him of legal issues presented. Although Alabama law does not require a preliminary hearing, when one is held, a variety of defendant's rights become involved. Among the issues to be determined at an Alabama preliminary hearing are whether there is probable cause to present the case to the grand jury and whether to allow bail and in what amount for bailable crimes. Upon appeal, Coleman argued that Alabama's failure to provide him with appointed counsel at the preliminary hearing unconstitutionally violated the Sixth Amendment right to counsel, a "critical stage" of the prosecution.

Legal Issue:

Where a preliminary hearing is an optional step in the criminal process and a defendant is not required to advance any defenses, is a preliminary hearing considered a "critical stage" of the criminal justice process for which the right to counsel under the Sixth Amendment exists?

The Court's Ruling:

The Court determined that the Sixth Amendment right to counsel was required at a preliminary hearing because the justices determined that the preliminary hearing constituted a "critical" stage of the criminal process. The justices noted that the assistance of an attorney might expose flaws in the prosecution's case, can "freeze" adverse testimony that may be used at trial, and should assist in discovering the prosecution's theory of the case.

Essence of the Court's Rationale:

II

This Court has held that a person accused of a crime "requires the guiding hand of counsel at every step in the proceedings against him," *Powell v. Alabama,* 287 U.S. 45, 69 (1932), and that that constitutional principle is not limited to the presence of counsel at trial.

It is central to that principle that in addition to counsel's presence at trial, the accused is guaranteed that he need not stand alone against the State at any stage of the prosecution, formal or informal, in court or out, where counsel's absence might derogate from the accused's right to a fair trial. *United States v. Wade, supra,* at 226.

Accordingly, the principle of *Powell v. Alabama* and succeeding cases requires that we scrutinize *any* pretrial confrontation of the accused to determine whether the presence of his counsel is necessary to preserve the defendant's basic right to a fair trial as affected by his right meaningfully to cross-examine the witnesses against him and have effective assistance of counsel at the trial itself. It calls upon us to analyze whether potential substantial prejudice to defendant's rights inheres in the particular confrontation and the ability of counsel to help avoid that prejudice. *Id.* at 227.

Applying this test, the Court has held that "critical stages" include the pretrial type of arraignment where certain rights may be sacrificed or lost, *Hamilton v.*

Alabama, 368 U.S. 52 (1961). [Other citations omitted.]The preliminary hearing is not a required step in an Alabama prosecution. The prosecutor may seek an indictment directly from the grand jury without a preliminary hearing. *Ex parte Campbell,* 278 Ala. 114, 176 So.2d 242 (1965). The opinion of the Alabama Court of Appeals in this case instructs us that under Alabama law the sole purposes of a preliminary hearing are to determine whether there is sufficient evidence against the accused to warrant presenting his case to the grand jury, and if so to fix bail if the offense is bailable. The [Alabama] court continued:

> At the preliminary hearing . . . the accused is not required to advance any defenses, and failure to do so does not preclude him from availing himself of every defense he may have upon the trial of the case. Also *Pointer v. State of Texas* [380 U.S. 400 (1965)] bars the admission of testimony given at a pre-trial proceeding where the accused did not have the benefit of cross-examination by and through counsel. Thus, nothing occurring at the preliminary hearing in the absence of counsel can substantially prejudice the rights of the accused on trial. 44 Ala.App., at 433; 211 So.2d. at 921.

* * *

The determination whether the hearing is a "critical stage" requiring the provision of counsel depends, as noted, upon an analysis "whether potential substantial prejudice to the defendant's rights inheres in the . . . confrontation and the ability of counsel to help avoid that prejudice." *United States v.* *Wade, supra,* at 227. Plainly the guiding hand of counsel at the preliminary hearing is essential to protect the indigent accused against an erroneous or improper prosecution. First, the lawyer's skilled examination and cross-examination of witnesses may expose fatal weaknesses in the State's case, that may lead the magistrate to refuse to bind the accused over. Second, in any event, the skilled interrogation of witnesses by an experienced lawyer can fashion a vital impeachment tool for use in cross-examination of the State's witnesses at the trial, or preserve testimony favorable to the accused of a witness who does not appear at the trial. Third, trained counsel can more effectively discover the case the State has against his client and make possible the preparation of a proper defense to meet that case at the trial. Fourth, counsel can also be influential at the preliminary hearing in making effective arguments for the accused on such matters as the necessity for an early psychiatric examination or bail.

The inability of the indigent accused on his own to realize these advantages of a lawyer's assistance compels the conclusion that the Alabama preliminary hearing is a "critical stage" of the State's criminal process at which the accused is "as much entitled to such aid [of counsel] . . . as at the trial itself." *Powell v. Alabama, supra,* at 57.

Case Importance:

This case demonstrated that the justices on the Supreme Court were committed to due process by extending the right to counsel to any part of the criminal process where the guiding hand of a lawyer could assist a defendant, whether indigent or not.

or to summon witnesses to impeach the prosecutor's witnesses. In the interests of justice, California follows a slightly different process from the traditional preliminary hearing procedure. When the examinations of prosecution witnesses in preliminary hearings in California are complete, any witness the defendant may produce shall be sworn and examined. The limitations on defense witnesses are that

> the magistrate shall require an offer of proof from the defense as to the testimony expected from the witness. The magistrate shall not permit the testimony of any defense witness unless the offer of proof discloses to the satisfaction of the magistrate, in his or her sound discretion, that the testimony of that witness, if believed, would be reasonably likely to establish an affirmative defense, negate an element of a crime charged, or impeach the testimony of a prosecution witness or the statement of a declarant testified to by a prosecution witness. See Cal. Penal Code § 859 (Mathew Bender 2003)

Essentially, the defense witnesses are allowed to testify if such evidence would clearly be devastating to the finding of probable cause to believe that the defendant had committed the crime or crimes.

When the preliminary hearing results in a finding by the judge or magistrate that probable cause exists, the court orders that the defendant continue to be held in custody and that the prosecutor's office take steps to continue the prosecution. In jurisdictions that are permitted to initiate serious criminal prosecutions by the use of information rather than a grand jury, the prosecutor then begins the steps that result in an information being filed by the prosecutor in the court of general jurisdiction where the case is to be tried.

11. BAIL ISSUES PRESENTED AT A PRELIMINARY HEARING

In many jurisdictions, once the judge or magistrate has determined that probable cause exists to hold the felony defendant further, the court moves to address the issue of whether to grant bail or to order pretrial detention. If an offense is subject to bail under state law, the judge must consider the relevant factors in determining what type of bail would be appropriate. Some states allow a variety of assets to be pledged to meet the required monetary amount of bail. A cash bail is sometimes required, but approved property such as stocks and bonds or real estate holdings within the court's jurisdiction are generally considered permissible types of assets. The most important factor for a judge is to set the amount of bail. In making an evaluation of the defendant and the charged crime for bail purposes, the judge may be limited by an excessive bail provision in the state's law or constitution. However, many states hold by legislation, constitution, or case law that some offenses are not bailable, so any concern of excessive bail under these circumstances does not become an issue.[31]

When a defendant is or may be entitled to bail, the defense attorney has a variety of arguments to offer about bail in that particular case, the amount of bail, and the conditions under which bail may be offered. A fairly extensive number of decided cases offer both the defense attorney and the counsel for the government a wide range of issues to litigate concerning bail. The question of bail often arises at an arraignment or at the preliminary hearing.

12. GENERAL BAIL JURISPRUDENCE

Among other rights, the Eighth Amendment to the Constitution of the United States guarantees that "excessive bail shall not be required." A bail that has been set at an amount higher than the minimum reasonably calculated to fulfill the aims and purposes of bail may be deemed "excessive" under the Eighth Amendment. Bail allows a criminal defendant to be released from formal government custody in exchange for the payment money or the pledge of property of a value sufficient to ensure the defendant's return to court at all proper times. The rationale for conditionally releasing a person who has been accused of a crime rests on the primary consideration of the pretrial presumption of innocence.[32] Pretrial release permits the accused to freely consult with counsel, to interview and search for favorable witnesses, to assist in the preparation of an appropriate defense, and to continue gainful employment.

The assets pledged or paid as bail usually must meet state or local statutory requirements concerning type and location of the collateral, as well as the value of the property. Even where sufficient property has been pledged as bail, the conditional freedom always involves the risk that a defendant might flee and fail to return when required. For this reason, if new factors become obvious or if new conditions arise in the time prior to trial, an adjustment of the amount or a reconsideration of the conditions of bail may be held at any time upon the request of either party. Offering bail is, at best, a calculated risk-weighing decision where a judge gambles that a defendant will perform consistent with the pledges and promises made in court.

Bail limitations have existed from the time of the common law, when bail was not available for all types of alleged crimes, especially the more serious offenses. Where the crime charged carries a potential life sentence or the death penalty, a judge or magistrate might refuse to set bail at any amount. Under local law or pursuant to practice, judges may deny bail where the danger to the community appears to be great, particularly in instances involving sexual crimes or drug-related offenses. The resulting situation ensures that the defendant will not flee and does not give rise to a claim of "excessive bail," since a judge denied bail completely.

While states frequently grant pretrial bail, the bail portion of the Eighth Amendment has not yet explicitly been incorporated into the Due Process Clause of the Fourteenth Amendment. Therefore, it cannot be stated with certainty whether this part of the Eighth Amendment applies to state bail practice. In any event, the states generally permit bail to be granted on terms and conditions that mirror or are substantially similar to the federal bail jurisprudence under the Eighth Amendment.[33]

In a leading case that remains good law, *Stack v. Boyle,* 342 U.S. 1 (1951), the Supreme Court determined that the factors used to set bail are subject to individual determination by taking due consideration for the personal circumstances of each person charged in federal prosecutions (see Case 12.3). Felony bail cannot be automatically set based on the charge or the past history of other persons charged with the same offense. Courts should consider the nature and circumstances of the defendant and of the crime, the strength of the evidence, the general character of the accused, and the ability of a defendant to pay for release. Bail that has been set at a greater amount than necessary to assure that the accused individual will not flee is considered "excessive." A federal judicial official must make a unique determination for each defendant.

For state felony cases, a judicial official generally must consider numerous factors in determining the appropriate bail amount, while giving due consideration to the individual circumstances of a particular defendant. Considerations underpinning the bail decision involve an individual analysis of the defendant's past history under pretrial release, the defendant's ties to the local community, the defendant's work history and financial resources, the seriousness of the crime, the strength of the evidence, the potential penalty if convicted, and the likelihood that the defendant will continue criminal conduct or otherwise endanger individual members of the community. Although the primary bail consideration centers around the issue of whether the

CASE 12.3

Leading Case: Federal Bail Determinations Require Individual Consideration

Stack v. Boyle
Supreme Court of the United States
342 U.S. 1 (1951)

Case Facts:

A federal grand jury returned an indictment against twelve defendants for violating the Smith Act, 18 U.S.C. sections 371 and 2385, that involved advocating the overthrow of the government of the United States and conspiracy with other conspirators to do the same. Subsequent to their arrest in New York, a federal district judge set bail at amounts ranging from $2,500 to $10,000 by taking into consideration the various factors affecting each defendant. When the defendants arrived in California, and pursuant to the prosecution's request that the amounts of bail be increased, the district court elevated bail to $50,000 for each defendant.

Defendant Stack filed a motion for a reduction in bail on the basis that the amount as determined violated the excessive bail prohibition of the Eighth Amendment. In support of the motion for bail reduction, the petitioners cited their varying financial situations, family relationships, health, prior criminal records, and other information. The prosecution did not focus on individual characteristics of each defendant during the bail reconsideration hearing. In opposition to the bail amount change, the prosecution argued that since other persons previously convicted of violating the Smith Act had jumped bail, a high bail was absolutely necessary for these defendants.

The federal district court denied the motion to reduce bail and refused to grant a motion for a writ of *habeas corpus*. The two decisions were affirmed by the Court of Appeals for the Ninth Circuit, and the Supreme Court of the United States granted certiorari.

Legal Issue:

In a federal prosecution, is the amount of bail excessive where it is set without reference to individual circumstances in an amount greater than the minimum level necessary to assure the appearance of each defendant for all appropriate times?

The Court's Ruling:

Recognizing that bail considerations involve both the Eighth Amendment and federal statutes, the Court vacated the trial court's determination of bail to require that the judge look at the individual circumstances and situations of each defendant and set bail at the minimum amount necessary to assure attendance at all trial proceedings.

Essence of the Court's Rationale:

* * *

From the passage of the Judiciary Act of 1789, 1 Stat. 73, 91, the present Federal Rules of Criminal Procedure, Rule 46(a)(1), 18 U.S.C.A., federal law has unequivocally provided that a person arrested for a non-capital offense shall be admitted to bail. This traditional right to freedom before conviction permits the unhampered preparation of a defense, and serves to prevent the infliction of punishment prior to conviction. Unless this right to bail before trial is preserved, the presumption of innocence, secured only after centuries of struggle, would lose its meaning.

The right to release before trial is conditioned upon the accused's giving adequate assurance that he will stand trial and submit to sentence if found guilty. *Ex parte Milburn*, (1835) 9 Pet. 704, 710, 9 L.Ed. 280. . . . Bail set at a figure higher than an amount reasonably calculated to fulfill this purpose is "excessive" under the Eighth Amendment.

Since the function of bail is limited, the fixing of bail for any individual defendant must be based upon standards relevant to the purpose of assuring the presence of that defendant. The traditional standards as expressed in Federal Rules of Criminal Procedure are to be applied in each case to each defendant. . . . It is not denied that bail for each petitioner has been fixed in a sum much higher than usually imposed for offenses with like penalties and yet there has been no factual showing to justify such action in this case. The Government asks the courts to depart from the norm by assuming, without the introduction of evidence, that each petitioner is a pawn in a conspiracy and will, in obedience to a superior, flee the jurisdiction. . . .

If bail in an amount greater than that usually fixed for serious charges of crimes is required in the case of any of the petitioners, that is a matter to which evidence should be directed in a hearing so that the constitutional rights of each petitioner may be preserved. In the absence of such a showing, we are of the opinion that the fixing of bail before trial in these cases cannot be squared with the statutory and constitutional standards for admission to bail.

★ ★ ★

The Court concludes that bail has not been fixed by proper methods in this case and that petitioners' remedy is by motion to reduce bail, with right of appeal to the Court of Appeals. Accordingly, the judgment of the Court of Appeals is vacated and the case is remanded to the District Court with directions to vacate its order denying petitioners' applications for writs of habeas corpus and to dismiss the applications without prejudice. Petitioners may move for reduction of bail in the criminal proceeding so that a hearing may be held for the purpose of fixing reasonable bail for each petitioner. *It is so ordered.*

Case Importance:

Felony bail considerations must be made with reference to individualized factors, including the strength of the government's case, defendant's prior record while on bail, and danger to the community, among other considerations. Where bail is to be offered, each defendant must be evaluated based on individual circumstances.

defendant will return for all required court appearances, the federal Bail Reform Act of 1984 interjected additional requirements for some federal prosecutions.[34]

13. FEDERAL BAIL PRACTICE: RECENT CONSIDERATIONS

Congress moved to correct some perceived abuses in federal bail practice, most notably the tendency of drug-trafficking defendants to post large bail amounts and flee the jurisdiction of the United States. In passing the Bail Reform Act of 1984,[35] the Congress continued most of the typical requirements for bail but changed the basic philosophy of federal bail in a few situations. The act directed federal courts specifically to look at the type of crime charged, the weight of the evidence, the defendant's physical and mental condition, any history of drug or alcohol abuse by the defendant, and the potential danger presented by the defendant toward any person and toward the community. The act changed federal bail practice in cases where the defendant was charged with specific drug offenses, a crime of violence, a life imprisonment crime, a crime for which the penalty could be greater than ten years, or where the accused had been convicted of two similar crimes within the past ten years. In these situations, the attorney for the federal government may ask for a pretrial detention order. In addition, where the federal prosecutor presents evidence that the person might flee, could present a danger to any community member, or might obstruct justice by threatening potential witnesses or jurors, bail may be denied altogether.[36]

In *United States v. Salerno*,[37] the Supreme Court upheld the constitutionality of portions of the Bail Reform Act of 1984 affecting federal pretrial detention. The *Salerno* Court rejected arguments that the practice of holding some defendants in custody pending trial constituted pretrial punishment and noted that pretrial detention orders served to prevent dangers to the community, a legitimate regulatory goal. The Court stated that although the Eighth Amendment prohibited excessive bail, the language of the amendment did not address the issue of whether bail should be available in a particular case and under what circumstances bail could be denied completely.

Although the federal Bail Reform Act of 1984 contemplated that federal courts would grant bail to many persons, only two situations were recognized by the statute.[38] When a court is faced with a bail request, it may either grant release on any reasonable condition or conditions or order detention without bail. If a court grants bail, the accused is deemed released, no matter what conditions are ordered by the judge or how severe or limited the conditions of release might be. In *Reno v. Koray,*[39] the court granted the defendant presentence release to a community treatment center, where the order required him to be confined to the physical premises of the center without permission to leave for any reason. The plain English meaning of these conditions suggests that the defendant remained in government custody rather than being free to roam abroad at his own discretion. When the defendant desired credit toward time served at the center, the *Koray* Court held that he had been released and not denied bail so that he could not apply the time toward his sentence. The lesson of the case is that a person may be "released" under conditions of bail that seem almost like being in full custody; thus a person facing a sentence might want to reconsider whether pretrial or presentence release serves an appropriate purpose where the federal prosecutor's case appears strong.

The Bail Reform Act of 1984 mandated that a federal arrestee be granted a detention hearing at his or her first appearance before a judicial official. Such a hearing could be delayed up to five days at an arrestee's request or up to three days on motion by the government. Figure 12.1 shows the federal court form used to permit detention until the mandated bail hearing pursuant to the present federal Bail Reform Act of 1984.

At issue in *United States v. Montalvo-Murillo*[40] was the question of what remedy should be available for the arrestee if a detention hearing had been delayed significantly longer than the federal statute permitted through no fault of the arrestee. To resolve a dispute among federal courts of appeal, the Supreme Court granted certiorari to determine the remedy for failure to grant a detention hearing at the first appearance of an arrestee. The Court held that a federal court does not lose jurisdiction to make a detention determination under the Bail Reform Act even where the act has not been followed to the letter. The Court held that a court may issue a detention order even if the government has not followed the time requirements of the law. According to the *Montalvo-Murillo* Court, "Magistrates and district judges can be presumed to insist upon compliance with the law without the threat that we must embarrass the system by releasing a suspect certain to flee from justice."[41]

In contrast to the practice of felony bail and the litigation that accompanies it, criminal cases involving misdemeanor offenses generally do not require such detailed analysis of individual factors. Typically, alleged misdemeanors and violations of local municipal ordinances are bailable with little reference to any factor other than a local predetermined bail schedule.[42]

Regardless of whether the charged offense constitutes a felony or misdemeanor, once the amount of bail has been judicially determined, the defendant, or a person

✎ AO 470 (Rev. 12/03) Order of Temporary Detention[43]

UNITED STATES DISTRICT COURT

District of _____

_____

UNITED STATES OF AMERICA	**ORDER OF TEMPORARY DETENTION**
	PENDING HEARING PURSUANT TO
V.	**BAIL REFORM ACT**

_____
Defendant

Case Number: _____

Upon motion of the _____ , it is ORDERED that a

detention hearing is set for _____ * at _____
                                              Date   *Time*

before _____
                    Name of Judicial Officer

_____
Location of Judicial Officer

Pending this hearing, the defendant shall be held in custody by (the United States marshal)

(_____) and produced for the hearing.
              Other Custodial Official

Date: _____   _____
                                                                          Judge

_____

*If not held immediately upon defendant's first appearance, the hearing may be continued for up to three days upon motion of the Government, or up to five days upon motion of the defendant. 18 U.S.C. § 3142(f)(2).

A hearing is required whenever the conditions set forth in 18 U.S.C. § 3142(f) are present. Subsection (1) sets forth the grounds that may be asserted only by the attorney for the Government; subsection (2) states that a hearing is mandated upon the motion of the attorney for the Government or upon the judicial officer's own motion if there is a serious risk that the defendant (a) will flee or (b) will obstruct or attempt to obstruct justice, or threaten, injure, or intimidate, or attempt to threaten, injure, or intimidate a prospective witness or juror.

FIGURE 12.1 Temporary Detention Order in Federal District Court Pending Bail Hearing.

acting on behalf of the defendant, may personally pay or pledge the full amount. Not infrequently, the accused does not possess the complete bail amount or own approved values of property and must resort to a commercial bail bondsman. Typical bond practice requires the defendant to pay 10 to 15 percent of the full bail to the bondsman in exchange for the bondsman's executing a pledge for the complete amount to the government. Bail posted through a bondsman is money that will not be returned to the defendant, even if he or she fully complies with all conditions of bail.

To assist in the orderly preparation of a defense, the issue of bail may be of extreme importance to a defendant, but the defendant may desire to assert other constitutional rights prior to trial. In some cases, the trial might occur too rapidly following notification of charges to allow adequate preparation; conversely, delay in getting to trial may create other problems and challenges for a defendant. Federal constitutional protections granted to all accused defendants include the Sixth Amendment right to a speedy trial; defendants also possess similar additional protections under state laws and state constitutions. Regardless of the source of the right, the guarantee of a speedy trial is a right that must be asserted prior to trial, or it may be deemed to have been waived.

14. RIGHT TO A SPEEDY TRIAL: REASONABLE TIME REQUIREMENTS

The Sixth Amendment to the United States Constitution reads as follows:

> In all criminal prosecutions, the accused shall enjoy the right to a *speedy and public trial,* by an impartial jury of the State and district wherein the crime shall have been committed, which district shall have been previously ascertained by law, and to be informed of the nature and cause of the accusation; to be confronted with the witnesses against him; to have compulsory process for obtaining witnesses in his favor, and to have the assistance of counsel for his defence. (Emphasis added.)

The literal language of the Sixth Amendment states that in all prosecutions of a criminal nature, the accused has the right to a speedy trial. As a practical matter, a criminal trial may be delayed for a variety of reasons. The defendant's request for additional time to formulate a defense, the prosecution's need to prepare its case, and the resolution of pretrial motions are appropriate reasons to delay the start of a trial. Prior to 1967, the Sixth Amendment speedy trial right clearly applied only in federal criminal trials, but following the Court's decision in *Klopfer v. North Carolina,*[44] the right to a speedy trial became a constitutional requirement enforceable against the states through the Due Process Clause of the Fourteenth Amendment. In addition to the constitutional provision, Congress passed the Speedy Trial Act of 1974,[45] which helps move federal criminal cases to the top of trial dockets. States also have statutory speedy trial statutes designed to ensure that criminal matters generally receive expeditious resolution. In any case, a defendant has an improved chance of having a case dismissed based on a speedy trial statutory violation than on federal or state constitutional grounds; statutes are more specific in their provisions, making it easier to demonstrate a prosecution deficiency with legal requirements.

From a policy perspective, prompt resolution of criminal matters allows a defendant to plan for the future and allows society to make a proper disposition of the case and move forward. Having criminal cases resolved fairly rapidly prevents a non-bailed defendant from extensive preresolution punishment and disruption or termination of employment. Additionally, a fairly quick trial allows the accused's defense to remain fairly fresh, before the memory of witnesses has had much chance to fade. A trial held within a reasonable time also limits the period of public scrutiny of the defendant's affairs, which is an additional justification for a quick resolution of the defendant's legal difficulties. If there were no imperative to resolve criminal cases, a prosecutor could allow an accused to wallow in uncertainty for months or years, always wary that a prosecution could be initiated at any time.[46] Such an extended delay is not normally practiced by the prosecution, however; the government generally has the burden of proof concerning most trial issues, and delay in proceeding to trial usually works in a defendant's favor as the memory of prosecution witnesses becomes less clear with the passage of time or as witnesses die or disappear.[47]

15. SPEEDY TRIAL STATUTES

Criminal defendants may also file pretrial motions concerning speedy trial rights based on federal law and state statutory and constitutional provisions. Typically, state and federal speedy trial statutes attempt to provide a timetable with which the prosecution must comply, subject to carefully delineated exceptions. Most statutes include provisions to prevent the release of a defendant due to a mere nonconformity with the time requirements.

Because both society and the accused possess an interest in a fairly rapid resolution of criminal cases, the state function of administering justice arguably is best served by freeing the innocent and incarcerating wrongdoers as soon as possible. Without the statutory right to a swift resolution of a criminal case, a defendant would face an uncertain future and would be forced to contend with difficulties in planning for the future, with maintaining employment, in meeting the expenses of litigation, and with diminished availability of witnesses and testimony. Problems concerning availability of defense witnesses become especially acute where crispness and detail of testimony prove crucial. Further prejudice to the defendant's reputation and community standing occurs while criminal charges are pending, a factor that leads to much personal anxiety and stress. Of special concern is the prejudice suffered by a defendant who is unable to make bail and must remain incarcerated pending trial. In such a case, a speedy resolution becomes imperative.

16. SPEEDY TRIAL: WHEN THE TIME BEGINS TO RUN UNDER THE SIXTH AMENDMENT

The time aspect of the constitutional speedy trial right begins to run when a person has been arrested for a particular crime and has been either retained in custody or released on bail. The period also begins to run when a person has been indicted or has had an information filed against him or her. Only by taking one of these steps has the prosecution indicated that a criminal case has been selected for which a speedy resolution becomes meaningful. The constitutional right to a speedy trial also applies to individuals incarcerated in a foreign jurisdiction (another state) who have been indicted or had an information filed in the current state. In order not to violate the Sixth Amendment, the jurisdiction lacking custody must attempt to procure the presence of the defendant or risk a violation of the right to speedy trial. The noncustodial state may not use the excuse that unavailability is the defendant's problem where the convict is the "guest" of a foreign jurisdiction.[48]

17. TO DETERMINE WHETHER A VIOLATION EXISTS: THE FOUR-FACTORS TEST

To determine whether the federal constitutional right to a speedy trial has been violated, courts should look to four factors as described by the Court in *Barker v. Wingo* (see Case 12.4).[49] According to the *Barker* Court, attention should be directed to the length of the delay, the reason for the delay, the defendant's assertion or nonassertion of the right, and prejudice to the defendant. The length of the delay may prove determinative that the right has been violated. Case law seems to indicate that the passage of time *alone* will rarely prove sufficient to constitute an infraction,[50] but time, in concert with other factors, may tip the scales in the direction of a violation.

The Court applied *Barker v. Wingo* and the five-factor test in *Doggett v. United States*. In that case, the defendant had been indicted in 1980 for drug-related offenses but not arrested until late 1988. In intervening time, he had been residing openly in the United States for almost six years.[51] Doggett's location could have been easily discerned except for governmental negligence. On speedy trial grounds, the *Doggett* Court overturned Doggett's conviction for drug offenses based on the length of the delay and the presence of presumed, but unproven, prejudice. Even though Doggett proved unable to present specific instances of prejudice to his case, the Court accepted the presence of prejudice by citing the extremely long wait between indictment and arrest. The *Doggett* decision reaffirmed the principle that the remedy for a violation of the Sixth Amendment right to speedy trial is an absolute dismissal of the charges with prejudice or, where there has been a conviction, a reversal of the decision with no chance to retry the defendant.

The second factor mentioned in *Barker* involved the reason for the delay. Acceptable reasons include time used for psychiatric examination, defense requests for continuances, and absence or illness of necessary prosecution witnesses. Crowded court dockets and postponements purposely used or created to hinder the defense have not proven acceptable as reasons for delay. Where a defendant has requested a continuance, the right to a speedy trial has been effectively waived to the extent of the request.

The *Barker* Court noted that asserting or failing to assert the right to a speedy trial constitutes the third factor courts must consider. While some continuances may enhance the prosecution's case, normally the defense benefits from a delay because the burden of proof rests with the government. Where the defendant remains silent and does not *assert* the right, a waiver will not conclusively be presumed, but the silence of the defendant in failing to assert the constitutional right will not materially enhance a speedy trial contention.

The final factor cited by the *Barker* Court as important to a determination of a speedy trial violation was prejudice to the defendant. Prejudice should be viewed in the

CASE 12.4

Leading Case: The Four-Factor Test Used to Determine Speedy Trial Violations

Barker v. Wingo
Supreme Court of the United States
407 U.S. 514 (1972)

Case Facts:

Following two brutal homicides, Silas Manning and Willie Barker, the petitioner, were indicted for the murders. The trial court appointed attorneys for the pair on September 17 and set a tentative trial date of October 21, 1958. Since the Commonwealth of Kentucky had a stronger case against Manning and the prosecutor felt that Barker could only be convicted if Manning testified against Barker, the trial court granted the first of what eventually became sixteen continuances. Barker's trial finally began on October 9, 1963, some five years following his murder indictment. Barker spent ten months in custody prior to being released on pretrial bail.

The primary reason for the lengthy delay prior to Barker's trial was the difficulty of obtaining a valid conviction of Manning, so that Manning could be forced to testify against Barker. Subsequent delays involved the prosecutor and the health of his witnesses. Following Manning's conviction, the prosecutor requested a continuance of Barker's case for the twelfth time and Barker objected. The court granted the twelfth continuance in February 1962, and two subsequent continuances in June and September of 1962. Barker did not object to the latter two continuances. In February 1963, Barker's trial was set for March 19. On the March trial date, the prosecutor requested another continuance, to which Barker objected and requested a dismissal of the case. The judge set the case for a June trial in 1963. The June trial date came and went due to the continued illness of the former sheriff. The trial court announced that if the case were not tried in the October term of court for 1963, that the case would be dismissed with prejudice.

At the October trial, Manning testified against Barker with the result that Barker was convicted of murdering the elderly couple and sentenced to life in prison. Barker argued that his trial should never have

occurred because his rights under the speedy trial provision of the Sixth Amendment had been violated and the case should have been dismissed. The Supreme Court of the United States granted certiorari to consider whether the Sixth Amendment right to a speedy trial had been violated.

Legal Issue:

Where valid reasons existed for the prosecution to seek trial delays for longer than five years, does the length of the delay, without more, violate the Sixth Amendment right to a speedy trial?

The Court's Ruling:

The Justices decided that the length of time was only one factor to consider in evaluating whether the Sixth Amendment right to speedy trial has been violated. The court noted that the reasons for the delay, the defendant's assertion or nonassertion of the right, and prejudice to the defendant's case were three other factors that must be considered in making the determination.

Essence of the Court's Rationale:

[The Court noted that the right to speedy trial is somewhat different from other constitutional rights that protect an accused. Society has an interest in a rapid resolution of a criminal case but a defendant may wish to delay because a prosecutor's case generally gets weaker with time. The right to speedy trial is a somewhat vague concept that does not allow an easy determination of when the right has been violated. The Court reaffirmed that the remedy for the violation of the right to speedy trial is a dismissal of the case without the chance to bring in a second time.]

(continued)

III

[Tthe defendant suggested that the court follow one of two approaches.] . . . The first suggestion is that we hold that the Constitution requires a criminal defendant to be offered a trial within a specified time period. The result of such a ruling would have the virtue of clarifying when the right is infringed and of simplifying courts' application of it.

* * *

We find no constitutional basis for holding that the speedy trial right can be quantified into a specified number of days or months. The States, of course, are free to prescribe a reasonable period consistent with constitutional standards, but our approach must be less precise.

The second suggested alternative would restrict consideration of the right to those cases in which the accused has demanded a speedy trial. Most States have recognized what is loosely referred to as the "demand rule," although eight States reject it. . . . Under this rigid approach, a prior demand is a necessary condition to the consideration of the speedy trial right. . . .

Such an approach, by presuming waiver of a fundamental right from inaction, is inconsistent with this Court's pronouncements on waiver of constitutional rights. The Court has defined waiver as "an intentional relinquishment or abandonment of a known right or privilege." *Johnson v. Zerbst,* 304 U.S. 458, 464 (1938).

* * *

[The Court rejected a set elapsed time test and a requirement that the defendant has to demand a speedy trial.]

IV

A balancing test necessarily compels courts to approach speedy trial cases on an *ad hoc* basis.

* * *

The length of the delay is to some extent a triggering mechanism. Until there is some delay which is presumptively prejudicial, there is no necessity for inquiry into the other factors that go into the balance. . . . To take but one example, the delay that can be tolerated for an ordinary street crime is considerably less than for a serious, complex conspiracy charge.

Closely related to length of delay is the reason the government assigns to justify the delay. [A deliberate delay for no good reason would run against the prosecutor. Negligence and overcrowded courts would not be as severe considerations. Delay that is the government's fault is a factor in the defendant's favor]. . . . Finally, a valid reason, such as a missing witness, should serve to justify appropriate delay.

We have already discussed the third factor, the defendant's responsibility to assert his right. Whether and how a defendant asserts his right is closely related to the other factors we have mentioned. The strength of his efforts will be affected by the length of the delay, to some extent by the reason for the delay, and most particularly by the personal prejudice, which is not always readily identifiable, that he experiences. The more serious the deprivation, the more likely a defendant is to complain. The defendant's assertion of his speedy trial right, then, is entitled to strong evidentiary weight in determining whether the defendant is being deprived of the right. We emphasize that failure to assert the right will make it difficult for a defendant to prove that he was denied a speedy trial.

A fourth factor is prejudice to the defendant. Prejudice, of course, should be assessed in the light of the interests of defendants which the speedy trial right was designed to protect. This Court has identified three such interests: (i) to prevent oppressive pretrial incarceration; (ii) to minimize anxiety and concern of the accused; and (iii) to limit the possibility that the defense will be impaired. Of these, the most serious is the last, because the inability of a defendant adequately to prepare his case skews the fairness of the entire system. If witnesses die or disappear during a delay, the prejudice is obvious. There is also prejudice if defense witnesses are unable to recall accurately events of the distant past. Loss of memory, however, is not always reflected in the record because what has been forgotten can rarely be shown.

* * *

Case Importance:

The four-factors test provides a benchmark against which alleged violations of the right to speedy trial can be measured. The length of the delay and prejudice to the defendant's case are related and carry the most weight in making this evaluation.

light of the interests of defendants, which the speedy trial right was designed to protect. The *Barker* Court identified three such prejudicial interests: the prevention of oppressive pretrial incarceration, the diminution of anxiety and concern of the accused, and a limitation of the possibility that the defense case might be impaired.[52] Of the three, the most crucial is the third, because the inability of a defendant adequately to prepare his or her case tilts the fairness of the criminal justice system. If witnesses die or disappear during a delay, the prejudice becomes apparent. Prejudice may originate where defense witnesses are unable to accurately recall events of the distant past.

Applying the *Barker* factors to an allegation of a speedy trial violation, a Minnesota appellate court determined that a defendant's right to a speedy trial had been violated. In *State v. Nesgoda,*[53] the prosecution filed a complaint against the defendant in February 2002 that charged him with burglary. In May 2002 the three-week continuance was granted to the prosecution and an additional continuance was granted based on the prosecutor's request. In February 2003, the government and the defendant agreed to an indefinite continuance because a government witness had to resolve a criminal case before he would testify for the prosecution. About a year and a half later, in July 2004, the defendant made his first demand for a speedy trial. At this time, the government witness was confined to a psychiatric ward of the prison hospital and was not able to testify. In October 2004, the prosecution requested a continuance that was denied. At a hearing March of 2005, more than eight months after the demand for a speedy trial, the defendant requested dismissal of the charges, which the trial court granted. The appellate court sustained the trial court decision after considering the four factors cited in *Barker v. Wingo* (see Case 12.4). The court noted that when the length of delay becomes presumptively prejudicial it triggers a preview of the other three factors. The appellate court noted that more than eight months passed between the speedy trial demand and the district court's dismissal of the case. In evaluating the second factor, the reason for the delay, nothing the defendant did caused the delay, and the defendant had earlier agreed to an indefinite postponement of the trial. Even though the prosecution did nothing to cause the witness to be unavailable, it must be diligent in bringing a case to trial. In this case, the defendant clearly asserted his right to a speedy trial. The court then considered prejudice to the defendant's case and his person and evaluated three interests that a speedy trial right protects. The court noted that among these interests were preventing extensive pretrial incarceration, minimizing a defendant's concern and anxiety, and preventing prejudice to the defendant's case. It will be difficult for a defendant to point toward specific prejudice when an excessive delay, according to the appellate court, compromises the reliability of the trial that may not be provable or identifiable. In approving the dismissal of the burglary charges with prejudice, the court concluded "that the eight-month delay after the speedy-trial demand was excessive, especially considering that more than three years had passed since Nesgoda was charged, and that, therefore, the delay presumptively compromised the reliability of a trial."[54] Admittedly, not all courts would dismiss a case on Sixth Amendment speedy trial grounds as quickly as did the trial court in this case, but in this case, the prospects for a trial in the near term were not promising, a factor that may have motivated the court.

To prevail on a federal constitutional claim of a Sixth Amendment right to a speedy trial, prejudice to the merits of a defendant's case appears to be the primary factor in winning a motion to dismiss a criminal prosecution. Sheer length of time, even in the absence of clear prejudice, may permit a trial court to find a violation, although length of time accompanied by prejudice to the merits of the case may stand the best chance of winning the motion for a defendant. Prejudice may include extensive pretrial incarceration, loss of job, stress to the defendant, or loss of witness testimony due to death or fading memory. Where a strong indication of prejudice appears and coexists in the presence of a sufficient level of the three other factors, a court may conclude that the government has violated a defendant's Sixth Amendment right to a speedy trial.

18. REMEDY FOR VIOLATION OF SIXTH AMENDMENT RIGHT TO SPEEDY TRIAL

Where the criminal defendant has prevailed on a Sixth Amendment speedy trial claim, courts have struggled to formulate an appropriate remedy. Some jurisdictions devised a method whereby a sentence would be reduced by the duration of the speedy trial violation, a remedy that ignored any prejudice to the defendant. However, the Court in *Strunk v. United States*[55] determined that the remedy must include a prejudicial dismissal of the case. Where prejudice to the defendant, such as the death of a witness, has occurred, a reduction in length of sentence would do nothing to cure that prejudice and ensure fairness in a trial involving facts from the distant past. Therefore, outright prejudicial dismissal remains the sole remedy for a violation of the Sixth Amendment right to a speedy trial. This drastic remedy creates pressure on trial courts to reject pretrial motions to dismiss and has the effect of sending speedy trial issues to appellate courts for resolution. However, it is crucial that the issue be raised at the pretrial stage, or the defendant runs a strong chance that an appellate court will rule that a waiver has occurred by virtue of failure to raise the issue in a timely manner.

19. DOUBLE JEOPARDY: A REQUIRED PRETRIAL MOTION

Along with other motions that an accused must make prior to trial is the requirement—where a prior trial may have adjudicated the case that the prosecution is attempting to bring a second time, or where the defendant faces a second punishment for a crime for which punishment jeopardy had already attached—to alert the prosecution of a double jeopardy claim. The constitutional prohibition against double jeopardy has been interpreted as a prohibition against a second trial for the same crime arising from one set of operative facts by the same sovereign jurisdiction and a prohibition against double punishment for the same offense. According to the Supreme Court, the double jeopardy provision offers three separate protections:

> It protects against a second prosecution for the same offense after acquittal. It protects against a second prosecution for the same offense after conviction. And it protects against multiple punishments for the same offense. *North Carolina v. Pearce,* 395 U.S. 711, 717 (1969)

Where the prosecution is unaware that it is about to transgress the constitutional prohibition, the defendant has the legal duty to make the prosecution aware of the problem prior to trial. According to the Fifth Amendment of the Constitution of the United States, "No person shall . . . be subject for the same offence to be twice put in jeopardy of life or limb." The Fifth Amendment prohibition against trying a criminal defendant twice for the same crime is based on the theory that the state, with all its resources, should try a defendant once and not exhaust the defendant's assets and will to resist with a series of consecutive trials. A judicial interpretation of the Fifth Amendment double jeopardy provision generally prevents imposing successive punishments for the same crime. For example, in one case, a defendant had been convicted of capital murder, but the jury could not unanimously agree on a penalty, so pursuant to state law, the judge sentenced the defendant to life in prison. When an appeals court overturned the conviction, the state planned to retry the case with death penalty specifications; the defendant contended that the judge's imposition of the life sentence effectively acquitted him of the death penalty, and to place him in jeopardy of losing life would constitute double jeopardy. The Supreme Court of the United States disagreed, saying the double jeopardy clause would not be offended, since the original jury had never acquitted him of the death penalty; it just failed to reach an agreement, constituting a hung jury that never reached a decision on the merits of the penalty. Hung juries do not prevent a retrial of either the case or the penalty phase.[56]

As a general rule, the contention that the prosecution may violate the defendant's rights under the double jeopardy provision of the state or federal constitution must be made prior to a trial on the merits. A defendant with adequate representation who pleads guilty to gain other favorable outcomes generally waives the right to complain on the appellate level or mount a collateral attack about an alleged double jeopardy violation.[57] However, under some circumstances and in the interests of justice, Texas allows a double jeopardy claim to be raised on appeal for the first time where the undisputed facts demonstrate a clear violation of double jeopardy on the face of the case record.[58]

20. REQUIREMENTS TO CLAIM A VIOLATION OF DOUBLE JEOPARDY

To prevail, a defendant must have first been placed in jeopardy prior to the claim that a subsequent prosecution runs afoul of the United States Constitution. Jeopardy has been determined to attach when the judge begins to hear evidence from the first witness in a bench trial[59] and when the jury is empaneled and sworn in a jury trial.[60] As the Court of Appeal for the Second Circuit recently noted:

> it is firmly established that the "attachment of jeopardy" occurs not only with a verdict but more generally at the "point in criminal proceedings at which the constitutional purposes and policies [of the clause] are implicated." *Serfass* [*v. United States*], 420 U.S. at 388. As a result, the Supreme Court has long recognized that jeopardy attaches in a jury trial after the jury has been empaneled and sworn, see *Kepner v. United States*, 195 U.S. 100, 128, 24 S. Ct. 797, 49 L. Ed. 114 (1904), and in a bench trial when the judge begins to hear evidence. *Wade v. Hunter*, 336 U.S. 684, 688, 69 S. Ct. 834, 93 L. Ed. 974 (1949); *McCarthy v. Zerbst*, 85 F.2d 640, 642 (10th Cir.), cert. denied, 299 U.S. 610, 57 S. Ct. 313, 81 L. Ed. 450 (1936).[61]

Pretrial motions and pretrial dismissals have not generally been considered proceedings during which jeopardy attaches.[62] For example, if a defendant successfully obtains dismissal of an indictment on technical grounds, a subsequent indictment and trial are not barred, since the defendant was never placed in jeopardy. Similarly, a prosecutor could take a case to successive grand juries if the first grand jury failed to return an indictment, without encountering any problem concerning initial jeopardy.

Demonstrative of the concept of double jeopardy is the case of *Benton v. Maryland,* 395 U.S. 784 (1969) (Case 12.5), where the defendant had been tried for burglary and larceny. Subsequent to his jury conviction of burglary and his acquittal of the larceny count, his convictions were reversed due to grand and trial jury irregularities. The court offered an option for reindictment and retrial that Benton selected. Upon his reindictment and retrial, the jury convicted Benton of both burglary and larceny, though the first jury had aquitted him of the latter charge. Upon his appeal, the Supreme Court held that the Fifth Amendment provision protection against double jeopardy applied through the Due Process Clause of the Fourteenth Amendment to limit the states. Since Benton had once been at jeopardy for the larceny charge and had been acquitted, to try him again constituted a violation of the double jeopardy provision.

21. ALLEGING DOUBLE JEOPARDY VIOLATION: REQUIREMENT OF SAME OFFENSE

The case of *United States v. Dixon*[63] demonstrates the principle that successive prosecutions must be for the same offense to qualify as a double jeopardy violation. The *Dixon* Court held that the defendant had been subjected to prosecution twice for the same crime where he had been released on pretrial bail and was under a court order to commit no new crimes. While free, he was arrested for drug use, a direct violation of pretrial release. At the end of a lengthy contempt of court hearing, he was found guilty of criminal contempt of court for his bail violation involving use of cocaine. When he came to trial for his drug offense committed while on bail, Dixon claimed a violation of double jeopardy because a trial court had already taken judicial action on his most recent drug offense. The Supreme Court ruled in Dixon's favor on the double jeopardy issue, since the court order to commit no new crimes and the subsequent criminal contempt conviction included the same elements as the drug charge. In effect, Dixon had been tried twice for the same criminal conduct.

22. SEPARATE OFFENSES: THE *BLOCKBURGER* TEST

Proper application of double jeopardy claims and resolution of allegations of violations of double jeopardy require courts to determine whether a course of conduct constitutes two separate crimes or whether the government is prosecuting twice for the same offense. In *Blockburger v. United States,*[64] the defendant had completed the illegal sale of a controlled substance and immediately made a second sale of the same drug to the same person, separated by only a brief interval. The defendant alleged that there was only one offense, not two separate transactions. According to the

CASE 12.5

Leading Case: Selective Incorporation of the Prohibition Against Double Jeopardy

Benton v. Maryland
Supreme Court of the United States
395 U.S. 784 (1969)

Case Facts:

The state of Maryland indicted and tried Benton for both burglary and larceny. The jury convicted him of the burglary charge and found Benton innocent of the larceny count. Prior to the time his appeal would have been heard, the Maryland Court of Appeals decided a case that invalidated a portion of the Maryland constitution that had required jurors to swear their belief in the existence of God.

Benton was given an option for reindictment and retrial since both the grand jury which indicted Benton and the petit jury which convicted him had been selected under the invalid constitutional provision. He selected the option and received a new trial, which resulted in a conviction for *both* burglary and larceny.

During the pretrial stage of the second prosecution, Benton alleged that the Fifth Amendment provision against double jeopardy precluded his being retried on the larceny charge since he had already been acquitted of the charge at the first trial. By making the double jeopardy argument prior to the second trial, the issue was properly preserved to be raised on appeal. The trial court denied Benton's contentions, and the Maryland Court of Special Appeals considered the double jeopardy claim but denied relief. Maryland's highest court refused discretionary review. The Supreme Court granted certiorari.

Legal Issue:

Does the Fifth Amendment prohibition against double jeopardy apply to the states through the Due Process Clause of the Fourteenth Amendment to prevent a second state trial of a charge of which the defendant has previously been acquitted?

The Court's Ruling:

In construing the Fifth Amendment prohibition against double jeopardy, the Court determined that the provision applied against the states so that a judgment of acquittal to a crime operated to prevent a second trial for that crime.

Essence of the Court's Rationale:

III

In 1937, this Court decided the landmark case of *Palko v. Connecticut*, 302 U.S. 319. Palko, although indicted for first-degree murder, had been convicted of murder in the second degree after a jury trial in Connecticut state court. The State appealed and won a new trial. Palko argued that the Fourteenth Amendment incorporated, as against the States, the Fifth Amendment requirement that no person "be subject for the same offense to be twice put in jeopardy of life or limb." The Court disagreed. Federal double jeopardy standards [at that time in history] were not applicable against the States. Only when a kind of jeopardy subjected a defendant to "a hardship so acute and shocking that our polity will not endure it," *id.*, at 328, did the Fourteenth Amendment apply. The order for a new trial was affirmed. In subsequent appeals from state courts, the Court continued to apply this lesser *Palko* standard. *See, e.g., Brock v. North Carolina*, 344 U.S. 424 (1953).

Recently, however, this Court has "increasingly looked to the specific guarantees of the [Bill of Rights] to determine whether a state criminal trial was conducted with due process of law." *Washington v. Texas*, 388 U.S. 14, 18 (1967). . . . [W]e today find that the double jeopardy prohibition of the Fourteenth Amendment represents a fundamental ideal in our constitutional heritage, and that it should apply to the States through the

(continued)

Fourteenth Amendment. Insofar as it is inconsistent with this holding, *Palko v. Connecticut* is overruled.

Palko represented an approach to basic constitutional rights which this Court's recent decisions have rejected. . . . Our recent cases have thoroughly rejected the *Palko* notion that basic constitutional rights can be denied by the States as long as the totality of the circumstances does not disclose a denial of "fundamental fairness." Once it is decided that a particular Bill of Rights guarantee is "fundamental to the American scheme of justice," *Duncan v. Louisiana, supra,* at 149, the same constitutional standards apply against both the State and Federal Governments. *Palko*'s roots had thus been cut away years ago. We today only recognize the inevitable.

The fundamental nature of the guarantee against double jeopardy can hardly be doubted. Its origins can be traced to Greek and Roman times, and it became established in the common law of England long before this Nation's independence. As with many other elements of the common law, it was carried into the jurisprudence of this Country through the medium of Blackstone, who codified the doctrine in his Commentaries. "[T]he plea of *autrefois acquit,* or a former acquittal," he wrote, "is grounded on this universal maxim of the common law of England, that no man is to be brought into jeopardy of his life more than once for the same offence." Today, every State incorporates some form of the prohibition in its constitutional or common law. As this Court put it in *Green v. United States,* 355 U.S. 184 (1957), "[t]he underlying idea, one that is deeply ingrained in at least the Anglo-American system of jurisprudence, is that the State with all its resources and power should not be allowed to make repeated attempts to convict an individual for an alleged offense, thereby subjecting him to embarrassment, expense and ordeal and compelling him to live in a continuing state of anxiety and insecurity, as well as enhancing the possibility that even though innocent he may be found guilty." This underlying notion has from the very beginning been part of our constitutional tradition. Like the right to trial by jury, it is clearly "fundamental to the American scheme of justice." The validity of petitioner's larceny conviction must be judged, not by the watered-down standard enunciated in *Palko,* but under this Court's interpretations of the Fifth Amendment double jeopardy provision.

IV

It is clear that petitioner's larceny conviction cannot stand once federal double jeopardy standards are applied. Petitioner was acquitted of larceny in his first trial. Because he decided to appeal his burglary conviction, he is forced to suffer retrial on the larceny count as well. As this Court held in *Green v. United States, supra,* at 193–194.

[c]onditioning an appeal of one offense on a coerced surrender of a valid plea of former jeopardy on another offense exacts a forfeiture in plain conflict with the constitutional bar against double jeopardy.

* * *

V

Petitioner argued that his burglary conviction should be set aside as well. He contends that some evidence, inadmissible under state law in a trial for burglary alone, was introduced in the joint trial for both burglary and larceny, and that the jury was prejudiced by this evidence. The question was not decided by the Maryland Court of Special Appeals because it found no double jeopardy violation at all. . . . We do not think that this is the kind of determination we should make unaided by prior consideration by the state courts. Accordingly, we think it "just under the circumstances," 28 U.S.C. Section 2196, to vacate the judgment below and remand for consideration of this question. The judgment is vacated and the case is remanded for further proceedings not inconsistent with this opinion.

It so ordered.

Case Importance:

The *Benton v. Maryland* case overruled the case of *Palko v. Connecticut,* 302 U.S. 319 (1937), and had the effect of incorporating the Fifth Amendment prohibition against double jeopardy into the Due Process Clause of the Fourteenth Amendment so that an acquittal in a criminal case could not be retried by the prosecution. Following this case, the double jeopardy provision had the same effect in both state and federal courts.

Blockburger Court concerning separate offenses, the sale of each quantity of drug was separated into a distinct transaction, which created a separate, though virtually identical, new offense that occurred at a different time from the first offense. Therefore, no violation of double jeopardy prohibition could be successfully argued.

Under current double jeopardy interpretation, a prohibited prosecution would follow where the government obtained a conviction or acquittal for robbery and proceeded to try the defendant for *armed* robbery arising from the same facts as the initial prosecution. The test for determining whether a second prosecution is for the "same offense" involves a consideration of whether each of the two criminal offenses under consideration requires proof of an additional fact or element that the other does not.[65] Robbery and armed robbery are examples of crimes that could not be prosecuted successively by the same sovereign if the charges arose from the same criminal act because each offense does not require proof of an element different from the other.

In an effort to generate clarity in the context of double jeopardy, the Court in *United States v. Dixon* suggested:

> In both the multiple punishment and multiple prosecution contexts, this Court has concluded that where the two offenses for which the defendant is punished or tried cannot survive the "same-elements" test, the double jeopardy bar applies. See, e.g., *Brown v. Ohio,* 432 U.S. 161, 168–169 (1977); *Blockburger v. United States,* 284 U.S. 299, 304 (1932) (multiple punishment); *Gavieres v. United States,* 220 U.S. 338, 42 (1911) (successive prosecutions). The same-elements test, sometimes referred to as the "*Blockburger*" test, inquires whether each offense contains an element not contained in the other; if not, they are the "same offence" and double jeopardy bars additional punishment and successive prosecution. 509 U.S. 688, 696–697

Where each of the acts of which a defendant stands accused contains an element different from the other, the acts will be considered separate offenses, and prosecution will not be barred by the double jeopardy clause. In the same manner, where one of the crimes for which an accused is to stand trial contains a unique element that the proof of the other does not require, there is no bar to being tried for each crime, since they are considered separate offenses. However, where a defendant has been charged with two separate theories of committing the same crime, such as intentional murder and felony murder of the same victim, regardless of which crime the jury convicts, the defendant may be punished only one time for the single death without running afoul of the double jeopardy clause.[66]

23. DUAL SOVEREIGNTY DOCTRINE: SUCCESSIVE PROSECUTION FOR SAME ACTS PERMITTED

Successive prosecutions are not prohibited under the Fifth Amendment double jeopardy provision where the same act or conduct violated the laws of two separate sovereign jurisdictions. As a result, citizens can be subject to the criminal laws of both the state and federal government or of two separate sovereign states of the United States for the same act or course of conduct. Therefore, under what is known as the dual sovereignty doctrine, successive prosecutions by two separate and sovereign states for the same act or acts are not prohibited by the double jeopardy provision of the Fifth

Amendment. In *Heath v. Alabama*,[67] the defendant had been accused of hiring two men to kill his pregnant wife by first taking her from Alabama to Georgia, where the men killed her. Heath pled guilty to murder in Georgia. To his surprise, Alabama subsequently extradited him from Georgia and charged him with the murder of his wife. The Alabama trial court convicted Heath of the death of his wife and sentenced him to death. His double jeopardy claim failed in the Supreme Court when it held that Heath had committed two separate offenses by committing murder under Georgia law and murder under Alabama law. As the *Heath* Court noted:

> The dual sovereignty doctrine is founded on the common law conception of crime as an offense against the sovereignty of the government. When a defendant in a single act violates the "peace and dignity" of two sovereigns by breaking the laws of each, he has committed two distinct "offences." 474 U.S. at 88

The crimes were described and made criminal both by the sovereign state of Georgia and by the sovereign state of Alabama. Murder in Georgia was not the same crime as murder in Alabama; the one act violated the peace and dignity of Georgia and also violated the peace and dignity of Alabama. Thus, the dual convictions were appropriate, and the convictions were upheld by the Supreme Court. Proof for each crime was different, since separate statutes were violated, and each homicide offense required proof of an element not found in the other crime.

The dual sovereignty doctrine applies when the separate prosecutions involve the federal government and a state in successive prosecutions. The state of Illinois properly prosecuted an alleged bank robber after he had been acquitted of federal charges stemming from his robbery of a federally insured savings and loan association. In *Bartkus v. Illinois*,[68] the trial court considered a pretrial motion to dismiss the state charges but rejected the defendant's plea of *autrefois acquit,* or prior (former) acquittal. Illinois successfully prosecuted Bartkus on robbery charges involving the same transaction that had been the subject of the failed federal prosecution. The Supreme Court approved of the successive federal and state prosecutions on the theory that each jurisdiction was sovereign and the same act constituted two separate crimes under the dual sovereignty doctrine.[69]

Following similar legal reasoning, the double jeopardy clause did not prevent a Kentucky prosecution for driving under the influence of alcohol in a case where the defendant fled Kentucky and was apprehended by Indiana police. The Kentucky prosecution occurred following the arrest and guilty plea by the defendant to a driving under the influence charge in Indiana. Since two separate sovereigns elected to try the defendant for violation of the respective law of each state, no double jeopardy violation occurred under the circumstances.[70]

Since the protection of the Fifth Amendment's provision against double jeopardy was designed to relieve a defendant of unfair multiple trials, it must be asserted prior to the start of the second trial to be effective in preventing the second trial. Therefore, as a general rule, the assertion of the right not to be tried twice for the same crime requires that the objection be raised during the pretrial phase to give the trial judge a chance to rule on the objection to the second trial. Failure to raise the issue at the appropriate time runs a strong risk that the right has been waived. Since the prohibition against being tried twice would be lost if the defendant could not immediately appeal the trial court's ruling, as a general rule, an adverse ruling on double jeopardy grounds allows an immediate appeal prior to the alleged second trial. As the Supreme Court noted in *Abney v. United States:*

> [A]spects of the guarantee's protections would be lost if the accused were forced to "run the gauntlet" a second time before an appeal could be taken; even if the accused is acquitted, or, if convicted, has his conviction ultimately reversed on double jeopardy grounds, he has still been forced to endure a trial that the Double Jeopardy Clause was designed to prohibit. Consequently, if a criminal defendant is to avoid exposure to double jeopardy, and thereby enjoy the full protection of the Clause, his double jeopardy challenge to the indictment must be reviewable before that subsequent exposure occurs. 431 U.S. 651, 662 (1977)

As a general rule, the sovereign government, whether state or federal, may not wear a defendant down by successive trials over the same events without violating the double jeopardy provision of the Fifth Amendment. However, the provision against double jeopardy does not create an absolute prohibition against successive trials. Some occasions and situations will allow second trials, such as where there has been a successful defendant appeal, a hung jury, or a lawfully declared mistrial, especially if the defendant requests the mistrial declaration.[71]

24. SUMMARY

In the time between the initiation of a criminal case and the actual trial, pretrial motions may help focus the issues at trial by resolving and eliminating problems that would otherwise have to be considered in the middle of a trial. Legal arguments involving venue and jurisdiction should be resolved during the pretrial stage. Some motions that may be mandatory, such as an allegation that the right to a speedy trial has been violated or that the upcoming trial will violate principles against double jeopardy, need to be resolved prior to trial because the resolution of these issues may dispose of the need for a trial.

Legal issues concerning identification both prior to trial and during the trial must meet standards of due process, and it may involve questions of whether there is a right to counsel at some identification procedures. A postindictment, postinformation in-person lineup requires the presence of legal counsel under the Sixth Amendment unless a defendant waives that right. Preindictment, preinformation in-person lineups do not require the presence of legal counsel, and photographic arrays never require the presence of a defendant's counsel. Where there is some questions concerning the accuracy or reliability of an eyewitness identification, the five-factors test under *Neil v. Biggers* should be considered. The opportunity for view, the degree of prior attention given by the witness, the accuracy of the prior description, the length of time since the crime scene view, and the certainty of the witness are important considerations when evaluating eyewitness identification.

Once a defendant has been taken into custody, where a judge has issued an arrest warrant or a grand jury has returned an indictment, there is no immediate need to seek a judicial determination of probable cause. However, where the arrest has been based upon a police officer's decision about probable cause or upon an information filed by a prosecutor's office, the arrestee must have a judicial determination of probable cause within forty-eight hours. Different jurisdictions use varying labels to describe early hearings in the criminal justice process. An initial appearance may involve a mere reading of the charges against a defendant, the appointment of indigent trial counsel, and bail considerations. There is no constitutional right to a preliminary hearing, but where one is granted, generally a defendant has the right to counsel and the right to confront and cross–examine adverse witnesses. However, some jurisdictions do not permit a defendant to call any witnesses. Bail considerations may arise at a preliminary hearing if they have not been considered at a prior time. Bail should be based on the individual defendant's situation and not exclusively on the nature of the criminal charge. Under prior federal law, bail was the presumption, but changes made in the federal Bail Reform Act of 1984 permits the denial of bail in a variety of situations.

Federal defendants have a Sixth Amendment right to a speedy trial in federal prosecutions. State defendants have not only the Sixth Amendment right to a speedy trial but, in most jurisdictions, a state constitutional and a state statutory right to a speedy trial. Under the Sixth Amendment, if the federal constitutional right to speedy trial has been violated, absolute prejudicial dismissal is the only remedy. Under the federal statutory right to a speedy trial and most state statutes, absolute dismissal is the remedy as well. The length of the delay, the reason for the delay, the defendant's assertion or nonassertion of the right, and prejudice to the defendant's case are the four factors used to determine whether the constitutional right to a speedy trial has been violated.

If a defendant believes that he or she has once prior been in jeopardy for the same exact offense, the defendant must file a pretrial motion alleging this error. Jeopardy is said to attach in a jury trial when the jurors take their oaths as jurors in the case and in a bench trial when the judge begins hearing the evidence from the first witness. Unless a defendant wins an appeal on the merits or a judge declared a mistrial for manifest necessity, a defendant cannot be tried again once jeopardy has attached. The theory is that, with all its wealth and resources, a government should not be able to wear down a defendant through a series of repeated trials until the government obtains a conviction.

REVIEW EXERCISES AND QUESTIONS

1. When does the right to have counsel present exist at an in-person lineup? How does the assistance of counsel benefit a suspect who is a participant and a target in a postindictment or postinformation in-person lineup?

2. As a legal and practical matter, why is there no right to counsel at a photographic array (photographic lineup)?

3. The Supreme Court has approved the exhibition of individual suspects to a victim in some situations. Is this practice a violation of due process? Why or why not?

4. In the case of *Neil v. Biggers,* the Supreme Court developed a five-factor test to measure whether eye-witness identifications met the standard of due process. What are the factors in this test? Does this

approach seriously reduce the chance of an irreparable wrong identification? Why or why not?

5. The preliminary hearing has been determined to be a "critical stage" of the criminal justice process. What assistance may an attorney offer a defendant who is subjected to a preliminary hearing?

6. What are some of the factors that courts consider in setting a monetary amount of bail?

7. Under what circumstances and in which situations may a federal court deny bail?

8. When does the Sixth Amendment right to a speedy trial begin to run? What are the factors used to determine whether the constitutional right to speedy trial has been violated?

9. Abdul Cohen engaged in the production of the recreational pharmaceutical known as methamphetamine. His success produced a great deal of cash, and since Cohen did not use methamphetamine, he was able to save money and retire from the business of producing and selling it. He moved to southern California and began a life of leisure. Due to previous investigatory work, Arkansas police presented sufficient evidence of Cohen's illegal activity to a prosecutor, who used the evidence to procure an indictment against Cohen. Despite initial efforts to find Cohen, prosecution efforts failed, and police ended efforts directed toward his arrest. Due to his cache of cash, Cohen had no need to use credit cards or do other things that would produce an evidentiary trail that would have disclosed his location and identity. He lived openly and was ignorant of the indictment back in Arkansas. California life was good! Four years after his indictment, his small fishing boat was hit by a large yacht, and he required medical treatment that involved rescuers and police officers. This experience with law enforcement agents disclosed his true identity, and he was extradited to Arkansas to face trial. Two of the men who presented evidence at the earlier grand jury proceeding had passed away, and one defense witness Cohen wanted to call in his defense could not be located. An Arkansas judge denied bail, and Cohen's trial did not commence until a year after his arrest, which was four years after his indictment. In a pretrial motion, Cohen requested that the charges of manufacturing and selling methamphetamine be dismissed on the grounds that he did not receive a speedy trial. What factors should the court consider? How should it rule?

10. Explain the concept of double jeopardy, and give an example where a court should refuse to allow a second trial to begin.

HOW WOULD YOU DECIDE?

1. In the Court of Criminal Appeals of Tennessee

A trial jury convicted defendant Guy Martin of aggravated robbery and intentionally evading arrest in a motor vehicle. Martin contended that the trial court erred when it denied his motion to suppress the victim's out-of-court identification based on a photographic array that he contended violated his rights to due process. In the photographic array, the defendant was the only person who wore braids, and this factor, the defendant contends, made the photographic array unduly suggestive that he was the guilty party.

The victim had ample time to observe the two men who, at gunpoint, carjacked her vehicle when she was in the process of loading her children into her car. The first male ordered her to give him the car keys and stated that if she screamed, he would shoot her. The woman tried to get her son out of the car, but one of the defendants had already removed the child. Somehow, the woman's daughter exited the car herself. Neither of the two carjackers wore a mask, and the victim was able to get a good look at their faces.

Several days later, the police arranged the photographic array, and the victim, Latasja Vardaman, identified the second defendant, Johnson, as one of the perpetrators. Subsequently, the police summoned the victim to the police station, where she picked out the second defendant, Johnson, from a second photographic array. When police picked up Johnson, he identified Guy Martin as the primary defendant and the ringleader of the pair. Police prepared a photographic array in which defendant Guy Martin was displayed as the only person with braided hair. The trial judge determined that the photographic array was not improperly suggestive, and the court found that the men who were depicted in the array looked sufficiently similar that no person stood out from the remaining photographs.

The defendant appealed his aggravated robbery conviction.

How would you rule on the defendant's contention that the photographic array used to identify the defendant violated due process because it was unduly suggestive?

The Court's Holding:

Out-of-court eyewitness identifications, as well as in-court identifications, may be challenged on constitutional grounds. A defendant's right to due process is violated if, under the totality of the circumstances, "the photographic identification procedure was so impermissibly suggestive as to give rise to a very substantial likelihood of irreparable misidentification." *Simmons v. United States*, 390 U.S. 377, 384, 88 S. Ct. 967, 19 L. Ed. 2d 1247 (1968); *Stovall v. Denno*, 388 U.S. 293, 302, 87 S. Ct. 1967, 18 L. Ed. 2d 1199 (1967); *see also State v. Strickland*, 885 S.W.2d 85, 88 (Tenn. Crim. App. 1993). "Suggestive confrontations are disapproved because they increase the likelihood of misidentification, and unnecessarily suggestive ones are condemned for the further reason that the increased chance of misidentification is gratuitous." *Neil v. Biggers*, 409 U.S. 188, 198, 93 S. Ct. 375, 34 L. Ed. 2d 401 (1972). Examples of impermissibly suggestive identification procedures include:

> That all in the lineup but the suspect were known to the identifying witness, that the other participants in a lineup were grossly dissimilar in appearance to the suspect, that only the suspect was required to wear distinctive clothing which the culprit allegedly wore, that the witness is told by the police that they have caught the culprit after which the defendant is brought before the witness alone or is viewed in jail, that the suspect is pointed out before or during a lineup, and that the participants in the lineup are asked to try on an article of clothing which fits only the suspect. *United States v. Wade*, 388 U.S. 218, 233, 87 S. Ct. 1926, 18 L. Ed. 2d 1149 (1967) (footnotes omitted)

Although an identification procedure might be unnecessarily suggestive, the ensuing identifications may be admissible at trial if the identification was nonetheless reliable. *Neil*, 409 U.S. at 199–201. The factors to be considered in determining the reliability of the identification include:

> [T]he opportunity of the witness to view the criminal at the time of the crime, the witness' degree of attention, the accuracy of the witness' prior description of the criminal, the level of certainty demonstrated by the witness at the confrontation, and the length of time between the crime and the confrontation. *Id.* at 199; *see State v. Edwards*, 868 S.W.2d 682, 695 (Tenn. Crim. App. 1993)

In this case, we agree with the trial court that the photographic lineup was not unduly suggestive. The photographic array depicted six African American males of similar age with similar facial characteristics, hair color and hair length. The hairstyles of the men in the photographic array were similar enough that no one man stood out merely because of a distinctive hairstyle. In addition, the victim testified at trial that she identified Appellant from the lineup based on his eyes in the photograph, not his hairstyle. Moreover, even if the lineup had been suggestive, we find the victim's identification of Appellant to be nonetheless reliable. The victim had plenty of time to view Appellant during the robbery, Appellant's face was unmasked, and the victim had no idea that Mr. Johnson had already implicated Appellant in the crime at the time that she easily identified him from the photographic lineup. Under these circumstances, we find the victim's identification of Appellant reliable. Appellant is not entitled to relief on this issue.

* * *

At the outset, we acknowledge that it is well-settled that the identification of a defendant as the perpetrator of the crime is a question of fact for the jury to determine. *State v. Strickland*, 885 S.W.2d 85, 87 (Tenn. Crim. App. 1993). Viewing the evidence in a light most favorable to the State, the victim made a positive identification of Mr. Johnson from a photographic lineup at the police station. Then, after the police interviewed Mr. Johnson, he admitted his involvement in the robbery and implicated Appellant as the second individual involved in the robbery. At that point, the victim was able to identify Appellant from a photographic lineup. The victim again positively identified Appellant at trial and testified that during the encounter, she had approximately two minutes to observe Appellant and Mr. Johnson and that neither man was wearing a mask. We determine that the proof offered at trial was more than sufficient to support Appellant's conviction for aggravated robbery. Appellant is not entitled to relief on this issue.

[Appellant's convictions were affirmed.] *See State v. Martin*, 2007 Tenn. Crim. App. LEXIS 588 (2007).

HOW WOULD YOU DECIDE?

2. In the United States District Court for the District of Minnesota

In a United States District Court on January 20, 2004, the federal government charged defendant Mohamed Abdullah Warsame with conspiracy to provide material support and resources to a listed foreign terrorist organization and with providing support and resources to a listed foreign terrorist organization, in violation of 18 U.S.C. § 2339B. In a superseding indictment that included the original charge, Warsame was also charged on June 21, 2005, with making false statements in violation of 18 U.S.C. § 1001(a)(2). In September 2006, he filed a motion to dismiss the charges against him based on a violation of his right to a speedy trial under the Sixth Amendment to the United States Constitution. Earlier in the case, in February 2004, the trial court issued one of several orders granting continuances consistent with the federal Speedy Trial Act in which both defense and prosecution joined. Some of the evidence was classified information that was desired by the defense, and to allow the defense to see the data, the prosecution had to meet procedures under the Classified Information Procedures Act. Several more delays in 2005 were caused by problems with the statute, and both sides filed numerous pretrial motions, including motions to suppress evidence.

Defendant Warsame remained in custody in a maximum-security setting for the whole time from his arrest until he petitioned for a dismissal of the charges.

Other requests that caused delays in 2006 came from defendant Warsame and involved data collected by the National Security Administration. Many of the delays were caused by governmental delays beyond the prosecutor's office, and some were caused by the defendant's motions. According to the District Court, the

> defense filed the instant motion to dismiss on September 22, 2006. Since that time, the Court has engaged in proceedings under CIPA [Classified Information Procedures Act] and has continued to oversee the prosecution's compliance with its discovery obligations. Specifically, the Court reviewed potential discovery on November 21, 2006, December 13, 2006, and February 27, 2007, and the prosecution will be providing additional information for the Court's review.

The federal judge prepared to rule on the defendant's federal constitutional speedy trial motion to dismiss the case.

How would you rule on the defendant's contention that the delays caused by federal security and secrecy laws and by other pretrial motions violated his Sixth Amendment right to a speedy trial and that the criminal prosecution should be dismissed with prejudice?

The Court's Holding:

[The trial judge reviewed the Sixth Amendment requirement that the accused must be granted the right to a speedy trial. The judge also gave due consideration to the federal Speedy Trial Act.]

The Supreme Court has identified four relevant inquiries in a claim involving the Sixth Amendment right to a speedy trial: 1) whether delay before trial was uncommonly long; 2) whether the government or the criminal defendant is more to blame for that delay; 3) whether, in due course, the defendant asserted his right to a speedy trial; and 4) whether he suffered prejudice as a result of the delay. *Doggett v. United States,* 505 U.S. 647, 651, 112 S. Ct. 2686, 120 L. Ed. 2d 520 (1992) (citing *Barker v. Wingo,* 407 U.S. 514, 530, 92 S. Ct. 2182, 33 L. Ed. 2d 101 (1972)). Courts refer to these four inquires as the *Barker* factors.

The Sixth Amendment right to a speedy trial attaches at the time of arrest or indictment, whichever comes first. Here, the right to a speedy trial attached on January 20, 2004, and over three years have passed since that date. To trigger speedy trial analysis, the defendant must allege that the interval between accusation and trial has crossed a line "dividing ordinary from 'presumptively prejudicial' delay." *Doggett,* 505 U.S. at 651–52. The Eighth Circuit has held that a 37-month delay is presumptively prejudicial. *United States v. Walker,* 92 F.3d 714, 717 (8th Cir. 1996); *cf. Titlbach,* 339 F.3d at 699 ("A delay approaching a year may meet the threshold for presumptively prejudicial delay . . ."). The delay here is presumptively prejudicial, so the Court must engage in the speedy trial analysis and weigh the *Barker* factors.

The first *Barker* factor is the length of delay, which has been uncommonly long. The second factor is the reason for the delay. As explained above, the delay can be primarily attributed to the need to provide the defendant with discovery derived from classified materials. The blame for this delay is not attributable to defendant, but this fact does not make the delay inexcusable. The Court believes that the prosecution and the Court have acted with reasonable diligence in working through the discovery issues in this case, and there is certainly no indication of bad faith. The delays experienced thus far have been largely inevitable given the unusual and complex nature of cases that implicate national security interests. As for the third *Barker* factor, Warsame has asserted his right to a speedy trial in due course by bringing this motion at this time.

The final factor considers whether defendant has suffered prejudice because of the delay. Prejudice may arise in the form of oppressive pretrial incarceration, anxiety and concern of the accused, and the possibility that dimming memories and loss of exculpatory evidence will impair the defense. Warsame has been held in the Administrative Control Unit of the Minnesota Department of Corrections facility at Oak Park Heights since February 2004. This is a maximum-security setting that allows few privileges and little contact with other people. . . . Warsame has been provided with increased recreational time, reading materials, and canteen privileges. It is nevertheless clear that uncommonly long pretrial detention under maximum-security conditions is a source of some prejudice for defendant. However, the most serious form of prejudice is impairment of the defense. Importantly, there is no indication that the delay here has impaired the defense in any way. The extent of the delay in this case is unfortunate, but the Court notes that the primary cause of the delay has been the efforts to provide discovery materials vital to the defense.

Based on its consideration of the *Barker* factors, the Court concludes that Warsame's constitutional right to a speedy trial has not been violated. See *Uniterd States v. Warsame,* 2007 U.S. Dist. LEXIS 16722 (D.C. D. Minn. 2007).

ENDNOTES

1. Court have territorial jurisdiction where the crime must have occurred within the geographical territory covered by the court. In addition, courts may have special or limited subject matter jurisdiction and must not exceed their respective subject matter. If a court fails to have jurisdiction over the area or topic, a motion to dismiss the case may be proper.
2. See, for example, *People v. Venegas,* 74 Cal. Rptr. 2d 262 (1998), where the Supreme Court of California considered the admissibility of DNA testing under the rules of evidence and prior case law.
3. *Simmons v. United States,* 390 U.S. 377, 384 (1968).
4. See, for example, Donald A. Dripps, "Miscarriages of Justice and the Constitution," 2 *Buff. Crim. L. R.* (1999), and Keith A. Findley, "Learning from Our Mistakes: A Criminal Justice Commission to Study Wrongful Convictions," 38 *Cal. W. L. Rev.* 333 (2002).
5. *United States v. Wade,* 388 U.S. 218 (1967).
6. Ibid. at 221.
7. Ibid. at 218.
8. Justice Brennan, in *United States v. Wade,* 388 U.S. 218, 232 (1967), at n.17.
9. The concept of formal charge does not include an arrest for federal constitutional purposes on the theory that the government has not made a clear decision on prosecution. See *Kirby v. Illinois,* 406 U.S. 682 (1972).
10. One could argue that in a photographic array, the same vices that legal counsel should prevent by being present in a postindictment, postinformation lineup could easily happen with no one present to complain.
11. 406 U.S. 682 (1972).
12. 413 U.S. 300 (1973).
13. Ibid. at 313.
14. Ibid. at 317.
15. See *Moore v. Illinois,* 434 U.S. 220 (1977).
16. 388 U.S. 293 (1967).
17. 394 U.S. 440 (1969).
18. 409 U.S. 188 (1972).
19. *Biggers v. Tennessee,* 390 U.S. 404, 406 (1968).
20. 432 U.S. 98 (1977).
21. *Kansas v. Hunt,* 69 P.3d 571, 577 (2003).
22. 289 F.3d 461 (2002).
23. Ibid.
24. Ibid.

25. 432 U.S. 98 (1977).

26. For some alternative state approaches to identification problems that generally offer additional protections to defendants, see *Commonwealth v. Henderson,* 411 Mass. 309 (1991); *State v. Ramirez,* 817 P.2d 774 (Utah 1991); and *People v. Adams,* 53 N.Y.2d 241 (1981).

27. See Ohio Rules of Criminal Procedure, Crim. R. 5(B)(1).

28. See Cal. Penal Code § 860 ". . . a defendant represented by counsel may when brought before the magistrate as provided in Section 858 or at any time subsequent thereto, waive the right to an examination before such magistrate. . . ."

29. See Ohio Rules of Criminal Procedure, Crim. R. 5(B)(2).

30. See *Coleman v. Alabama,* 399 U.S. 1 (1970).

31. See Constitution of the State of Ohio, Article I, § 9: Bill of Rights. Most jurisdictions provide for a complete denial of bail in some cases. Demonstrative of this concept is the case of Ohio law, which does not allow bail for persons charged with capital offenses where the proof is evident or the presumption strong. Similarly, bail can be denied to a person who is charged with a felony where the proof is evident or the presumption great, and who poses a potential serious physical danger to a victim of the offense, to a witness to the offense, or to any other person or to the community.

32. See *Stack v. Boyle,* 342 U.S. 1 (1951), for the rationale about setting bail amounts.

33. Demonstrative of bail practice is the legal formulation of the state of Ohio. See the Ohio Revised Code, Section 2937.23, and Article I, Section 9, Ohio Constitution, for an example of typical bail practice.

34. 18 U.S.C. § 3141 *et seq.*

35. Ibid.

36. 18 U.S.C. § 3142(e). Where a judge has conducted a hearing under the act and when the judicial official ". . . finds that no condition or combination of conditions will reasonably assure the appearance of the person as required and the safety of any other person and the community, he shall order the detention of the person prior to trial."

37. 481 U.S. 739 (1987).

38. See 18 U.S.C. § 3585(a) and (b).

39. 515 U.S. 50 (1995).

40. 495 U.S. 711 (1990).

41. Ibid. at 721.

42. See Ohio Rules of Criminal Procedure, Crim. R. 46(G). Anderson 2001. "Bond schedule. Each court shall establish a bail bond schedule covering all misdemeanors including traffic offenses, either specifically, by type, by potential penalty, or by some other reasonable method of classification."

43. http://www.uscourts.gov/forms/ao_470.pdf.

44. 386 U.S. 213 (1967).

45. Speedy Trial Act of 1974, 18 U.S.C. § 3161 *et seq.*

46. The outer limit for a criminal prosecution would involve the statute of limitations. However, some states do not have a statute of limitations for all crimes, and the trend has been to lengthen the existing time limitations.

47. "Delay is not an uncommon defense tactic. As the time between the commission of the crime and trial lengthens, witnesses may become unavailable or their memories may fade. If the witnesses support the prosecution, its case will be weakened, sometimes seriously so. And it is the prosecution which carries the burden of proof. Thus, unlike the right to counsel or the right to be free from compelled self-incrimination, deprivation of the right to speedy trial does not per se prejudice the accused's ability to defend himself." *Barker v. Wingo,* 407 U.S. 514, 521 (1972).

48. See *Smith v. Hooey,* 393 U.S. 374 (1969). Where a defendant has been charged in one jurisdiction while serving time in another, upon request, the noncustodial jurisdiction has a duty to attempt to obtain custody for trial or risk violating the speedy trial portion of the Sixth Amendment.

49. 407 U.S. 514, 530–531 (1972).

50. See *Dillingham v. United States,* 423 U.S. 64 (1975), where a twenty-two-month delay between arrest and indictment and an additional twelve-month delay following indictment to trial did not constitute a violation of the Sixth Amendment right to a speedy trial. The delay alone was not sufficient to demonstrate a violation.

51. 505 U.S. 647 (1992).

52. *Doggett v. United States,* 505 U.S. 647, 654 (1992).

53. 2006 Minn. App. Unpub. LEXIS 34 (2006).

54. Ibid.

55. 412 U.S. 434 (1973).

56. See *Sattazahn v. Commonwealth of Pennsylvania,* 537 U.S. 101 (2003).

57. *Mays v. Indiana,* 790 N.E.2d 1019 (2003).

58. *Duval v. Texas,* 59 S.W.3d 773, 776, 777 (2001).

59. See *Downum v. United States,* 372 U.S. 734, 738 (1963).

60. See *Crist v. Bretz,* 437 U.S. 28 (1978).
61. *United States v. Dionisio,* 503 F.3d 78, 83, 2007 U.S. App. LEXIS 22132 (2nd Cir. 2007).
62. See *Serfass v. United States,* 420 U.S. 377 (1975).
63. 509 U.S. 668 (1993).
64. 284 U.S. 299, 304 (1932).
65. Ibid.
66. *Washington v. Johnson,* 113 Wn. App. 482; 54 P.3d 155 (2002).
67. 474 U.S. 82 (1985).
68. 359 U.S. 121 (1959).
69. Bartkus could have been tried and convicted in the Illinois state court even if he had originally been convicted of the federal charges. Double jeopardy would not apply because of the dual sovereignty doctrine.
70. *Commonwealth of Kentucky v. Stephenson,* 82 S.W.3d 876; 2002 Ky. LEXIS 165 (2002).
71. *United States v. Newton,* 327 F.3d 17 (1st Cir. 2003).

CHAPTER 13

Trial Procedure and Legal Rights

Learning Objectives

1. Describe what the right to a trial by jury involves, and articulate when the right to a trial by jury exists under the federal constitution.
2. Be able to explain the process by which a defendant can waive the right to a trial by jury.
3. Distinguish some of the different views on the number of jurors in criminal cases, and explain why states might want to have smaller juries and/or nonunanimous juries.
4. Explain how the Sixth Amendment right to a jury trial was determined to be a fundamental right that had to be enforced against the state criminal justice systems.
5. Understand the requirement that trial jurors must be chosen from a panel of potential jurors that is representative of a fair cross section of the people living within the court's jurisdiction.
6. Evaluate and articulate the differences between federal jury practice and the states' constitutional options to alter the number of jurors and to experiment with nonunanimous verdicts.
7. Demonstrate knowledge of when the right to free legal counsel exists for a person too poor to afford private assistance by explaining when a person can be granted free legal assistance.

Chapter Outline

1. Trial by Jury: A Constitutional Right
2. Application of the Right to a Trial by Jury
3. Selective Incorporation of the Sixth Amendment into the Due Process Clause
4. Determining Whether the Right to a Jury Trial Exists
5. Selecting Jurors from a Fair Cross Section of the Jurisdiction
6. Violation of the Fair Cross Section Requirement: Proof and Remedy
7. Waiver of the Right to a Trial by Jury
8. Jury Size: Difference in State and Federal Requirements
9. State Efforts to Reduce the Size of Juries
10. The Concept of Jury Unanimity: Variety in State Juries
11. Combination of Smaller Juries with Nonunanimous Verdicts
12. Trial by Jury: Issues Involving Racial and Gender Discrimination
13. Removal of Prospective Jurors: Proper and Improper Rationales

Key Terms

Challenge for cause
Fair cross section requirement
Federal jury size
Nonunanimous jury verdicts
Peremptory challenge
Petit jury
Petty offense compared with serious offense

Requirement of unanimity
Right to appointed counsel
Selective incorporation
Six-person jury
Trial by jury
Voir dire of the jury
Waiver of trial by jury

1. TRIAL BY JURY: A CONSTITUTIONAL RIGHT

The concept that a group of individuals selected from the community should sit in judgment as a jury when one of their number is accused of a crime was well known to the American colonists prior to the Revolutionary War. This practice continued in the colonies after the Revolution to the time when the United States Constitution replaced the Articles of Confederation. The Framers of the Constitution guaranteed the right to a trial by jury for defendants accused of federal crimes in Article III, Section 2, where they wrote:

> The trial of all crimes, except in cases of impeachment, shall be by jury; and such trial shall be held in the State where the said crimes shall have been committed; but when not committed within any State, the trial shall be at such place or places as the Congress may by law have directed.

Although this section of Article III indicates that all crimes shall be tried by jury, in reality only persons accused of federal crimes received this guarantee, and the right to a trial by jury in the several states remained a creature of state law or the constitution of an individual state. The federal guarantee was reiterated in Amendment Six as part of the Bill of Rights when the Framers wrote:

> In all criminal prosecutions, the accused shall enjoy the right to a speedy and public trial, by an impartial jury of the State and district wherein the crime shall have been committed, which district shall have been previously ascertained by law, and to be informed of the nature and cause of the accusation; to be confronted with the witnesses against him; to have compulsory process for obtaining witnesses in his favor, and to have the assistance of counsel for his defence.

This restated and reinforced right to a trial by jury required only the federal government to grant a trial by jury; the original intent of the amendment was not to give any guarantee to individual defendants in state criminal cases. The legal theory, often repeated in a variety of ways, was that there was a fear of a strong national government, in relation to which the local states would have little power. For this reason, limitations on power and authority were placed on the national government because the people in the states could control the way their respective state governments dealt with people with respect to criminal law and procedure.

2. APPLICATION OF THE RIGHT TO A TRIAL BY JURY

The Sixth Amendment guarantee that "in all criminal prosecutions" the accused person shall have the right to have the case heard "by an impartial jury of the State and district" where the crime was committed could be interpreted as a guarantee to state criminal defendants. However, the reference to "the State" in the Sixth Amendment referred to the place of the trial, not the violation of state law. As originally conceived, this guarantee required the federal government to grant jury trials in federal criminal cases but left the states free to determine whether, when, and under what circumstances to offer a jury trial. Under the original legal theory, a state could amend its constitution and eliminate the particular state's jury requirement without running afoul of the federal Constitution. In a slightly different vein, a state could determine that the traditional jury of twelve should be reduced in number or could alter the jury system to allow for nonunanimous verdicts. In fact, both changes have been tried by some states without transgressing any jury guarantee in the federal Constitution.

During the 1960s, the Supreme Court of the United States, under Chief Justice Earl Warren, began to decide cases involving the right of due process emanating from the Fourteenth Amendment. As various cases came to the United States Supreme Court, the justices took the position that some of the rights mentioned in the Bill of Rights were so crucial to fundamental fairness that they should be incorporated into the Due Process Clause of the Fourteenth Amendment. This gradual application of the Due Process Clause, based on case-by-case analysis, was known as the selective incorporation doctrine. As part of this doctrine, the Warren Court decided that the right to a trial by jury was so fundamental that it must be considered part of due process and enforced in state courts.

3. SELECTIVE INCORPORATION OF THE SIXTH AMENDMENT INTO THE DUE PROCESS CLAUSE

The Sixth Amendment jury trial provision was selectively incorporated into the Due Process Clause of the Fourteenth Amendment and made applicable to the states in *Duncan v. Louisiana* (see Case 13.1).[1] According to *Duncan,* since a jury trial was considered to be among the fundamental principles of liberty and justice that were part of the foundation of all our civil and political institutions, the federal Constitution through the Due Process Clause of the Fourteenth Amendment required the states to offer jury trials. The Court also considered that the right to a jury trial was "basic in our system of jurisprudence"[2] and "a fundamental right, essential to a fair trial."[3] It is somewhat surprising, perhaps, that the Supreme Court concluded that

CASE 13.1

Leading Case Brief: The Right to a Jury Trial Is a Fundamental Right That Is Incorporated into the Due Process Clause of the Fourteenth Amendment

Duncan v. Louisiana
Supreme Court of the United States
391 U.S. 145 (1968)

Case Facts:

Appellant Duncan observed two of his cousins in a conversation with four white boys. Since racial incidents had occurred in the recent past, he stopped to see if anything was amiss. Duncan urged his cousins to come with him and was about to enter his automobile when a small altercation developed.

According to the white youths, appellant Duncan slapped one of them on the arm while Duncan and his partisans offered a story that indicated Duncan had only lightly touched the elbow of one of the white boys. As a result of the encounter and following a criminal complaint by the white boys, Duncan was charged with simple battery for which the maximum penalty was two years imprisonment and a $300 fine. The trial court rejected Duncan's request for a jury trial, citing Louisiana law, which granted jury trials only where imprisonment at hard labor or the death penalty were potential sentences.

The trial court, sitting without a jury, rendered a conviction for simple battery and imposed a sentence that required Duncan to serve sixty days in the parish prison and pay a $150 fine. Having objected at trial to properly preserve the jury trial issue, Duncan requested that the Supreme Court of Louisiana hear the case. After the state supreme court declined to consider the case, Duncan applied to the Supreme Court of the United States for a grant of certiorari. Subsequently, the Court granted the writ.

Legal Issue:

Consistent with the Sixth Amendment, must a crime be considered a serious criminal offense for which a jury trial must be offered where the maximum punishment for that crime is up to two years' imprisonment and a $300 fine?

The Court's Ruling:

Following its decision that the Sixth Amendment right to a trial by jury constituted a fundamental right and must be incorporated into the Due Process Clause in the Fourteenth amendment, the Court decided that the right to a jury trial existed for serious cases and that an offense for which two years was the maximum punishment was a serious offense that deserved a trial by jury.

Essence of the Court's Rationale:

* * *

I

* * *

The test for determining whether a right extended by the Fifth and Sixth Amendments with respect to federal criminal proceedings is also protected against state action by the Fourteenth Amendment has been phrased in a variety of ways in the opinions of this Court. The question has been asked whether a right is among those "fundamental principles of liberty and justice which lie at the base of all our civil and political institutions," *Powell v. State of Alabama,* 287 U.S. 45, 67 (1932); whether it is "basic in our system of jurisprudence," *In re Oliver,* 333 U.S. 257, 273 (1948); and whether it is "a fundamental right, essential to a fair trial," *Gidedon v. Wainwright,* 372 U.S. 335, 343–344 (1963). The claim before us is that the right to trial by jury guaranteed by the Sixth Amendment meets these tests. . . . The position of Louisiana, on the other hand, is that the Constitution imposes upon the States no duty to give a jury trial in any criminal case, regardless of the seriousness of the crime or the size of the punishment which may be imposed. Because we believe that trial by jury in criminal cases is fundamental to the American scheme of justice, we hold that the Fourteenth Amendment guarantees a right of jury trial in all criminal cases which—were they to be tried in a federal court—would come within the Sixth Amendment's guarantee. Since we consider the appeal before us to be such a case, we hold that the [federal] Constitution was violated when appellant's demand for jury trial was refused.

The history of trial by jury in criminal cases has been frequently told. It is sufficient for present purposes to say that by the time our Constitution was written, jury trial in criminal cases had been in existence in England for several centuries and carried impressive credentials traced by many to the Magna Carta. Its preservation and proper operation as a protection against arbitrary rule were among the major objectives of the revolutionary settlement which was expressed in the Declaration and Bill of Rights of 1689.

* * *

The constitutions adopted by the original States guaranteed jury trials. Also, the constitution of every State entering the Union thereafter in one form or another protected the right to jury trial in criminal cases.

Even such skeletal history is impressive support for considering the right to jury trial in criminal cases to be fundamental to our system of justice, an importance frequently recognized in the opinions of this Court.

* * *

The guarantees of jury trial in the Federal and State Constitutions reflect a profound judgment about the way in which law should be enforced and justice administered. A right to jury trial is granted to criminal defendants in order to prevent oppression by the Government. Those who wrote our constitutions knew from history and experience that it was necessary to protect against unfounded criminal charges brought to eliminate enemies and against judges too responsive to the voice of higher authority. The framers of the constitutions strove to create an independent judiciary but insisted upon further protection against arbitrary action. Providing an accused with the right to be tried by a jury of his peers gave him an inestimable safeguard against the corrupt or overzealous prosecutor and against the complaisant, biased, or eccentric judge. If the defendant preferred the common-sense judgment of a jury to the more tutored but perhaps less sympathetic reaction

of the single judge, he was to have it. Beyond this, the jury trial provisions in the Federal and State Constitutions reflect a fundamental decision about the exercise of official power—a reluctance to entrust plenary powers over the life and liberty of the citizen to one judge or to a group of judges. Fear of unchecked power, so typical of our State and Federal governments in other respects, found expression in the criminal law in this insistence upon community participation in the determination of guilt or innocence. The deep commitment of the Nation to the right of jury trial in serious criminal cases as a defense against arbitrary law enforcement qualifies for protection under the Due Process Clause of the Fourteenth Amendment, and must therefore be respected by the States.

* * *

In determining whether the length of the authorized prison term or the seriousness of other punishment is enough in itself to require a jury trial, we are counseled by *District of Columbia v. Clawans, supra,* to refer to objective criteria, chiefly the existing laws and practices in the Nation. In the federal system, petty offenses are defined as those punishable by no more than six months in prison and a $500 fine. In 49 of the 50 States crimes subject to trial without a jury, which occasionally include simple battery, are punishable by no more than one year in jail. Moreover, in the late 18th century in America crimes triable without a jury were for the most part punishable by no more than a six-month prison term, although there appear to have been exceptions to this rule. We need not, however, settle in this case the exact location of the line between petty offenses and serious crimes. It is sufficient for our purposes to hold that a crime punishable by two years in prison is, based on past and contemporary standards in this country, a serious crime and not a petty offense. Consequently, appellant was entitled to a jury trial and it was error to deny it.

The judgment below is reversed and the case is remanded for proceedings not inconsistent with this opinion.

Case Importance:

The Court determined that the right to a trial by jury in a particular state was a fundamental right protected by the Sixth Amendment to the United States Constitution in a situation where a person was charged with a serious crime. The Court did not determine the point at which a crime must be considered serious.

the right to a trial by jury is fundamental to justice even though so many defendants decide to reject jury trials and instead opt for a trial by a judge. Once *Duncan* made the jury trial mandatory on the states, regardless of what the state constitutions had to say about the matter, the states were required to grant jury trials in much the same manner as did the federal government.

Even though the Sixth Amendment speaks of allowing a jury trial in all criminal cases, the Drafters of the Sixth Amendment did not contemplate that the trial of every minor offense should culminate in a jury trial. Once the right of trial by jury was required of the states, the Supreme Court had to determine exactly what the right meant in state courts and whether it might mean something different than in federal courts. In support of allowing petty offenses to be tried without juries, *Baldwin v. New York*[4] held that a jury trial is constitutionally required in a state case only where the potential sentence is greater than six months' incarceration. Thus, a reading of *Duncan v. Louisiana* and *Baldwin* requires a state to offer jury trials in serious cases punishable by incarceration longer than six months and permits a state to require bench trials for petty offenses for which six months or less is the maximum penalty. However, nothing in the Sixth Amendment prevents a state from offering a jury trial where the maximum penalty of incarceration in less than six months.

4. DETERMINING WHETHER THE RIGHT TO A JURY TRIAL EXISTS

Precisely what crimes should be considered a "petty" offense has been the subject of litigation by individuals who have contended that some crimes, because of the fact of incarceration, significant fine, or collateral consequences, should be considered serious crimes. As a general rule, an offense with a maximum penalty of six months or less is presumed to be a petty offense, unless a state legislature has added additional penalties that are sufficiently severe to indicate that the legislature considered the offense to be serious. There is authority for the proposition that if an offense was recognized by the common law as sufficiently serious to warrant a jury trial, then modern versions of old common-law crimes might merit trial by jury based on the seriousness of the offense rather than the length of time for which incarceration might be imposed.[5] If defendants had been successful in convincing the Supreme Court that other factors besides length of incarceration should classify other offenses as serious for Sixth Amendment purposes, such a decision would have had the effect of extending the right to a jury trial to additional situations.[6] In *Blanton v. City of North Las Vegas*, 489 U.S. 538 (1989), the litigants contended that the offense of driving under the influence of alcohol should be construed as a serious offense for which the Sixth Amendment would mandate a jury trial. While the *Blanton* Court admitted that a crime's seriousness was to be judged by the maximum allowable custodial penalty,[7] and the Court was willing to consider the other penalties attached to the crime, it was not persuaded that the Nevada legislature considered the offense a serious crime. Thus, driving while intoxicated in Nevada did not require a trial by jury, but in some other contexts in other states, an allegation of driving while intoxicated may give rise to the right to a jury trial.[8]

The fact that a particular defendant might receive more than six months of incarceration due to multiple counts being tried at the same time does not require a trial by jury so long as the maximum sentence authorized for each offense is six months or less. In one case[9] where a defendant had been charged with two counts of obstructing the United States mail, he argued that the total potential penalty should be the benchmark for determining whether a jury trial was constitutionally required. The Supreme Court of the United States determined that the Sixth Amendment guarantee of the right to a trial by jury does not extend to petty offenses, even where the total sentences for several petty offenses might result in a sentence longer than six months. Multiple offenses did not change the seriousness of each individual offense.

Although adults possess the right to a jury trial based on the predetermined circumstance of the potential length of sentence, young persons tried in juvenile courts generally do not have that right. According to the constitutional interpretation in *McKeiver v. Pennsylvania,* a person who is to be subjected to a juvenile adjudication in a juvenile court has no Sixth Amendment right to trial by jury.[10] Many practical considerations have impact if a juvenile were to be granted a jury trial: Privacy has generally been a hallmark of juvenile adjudications, and privacy would cease to exist if a jury were empaneled to hear a juvenile case. Nothing prevents a state from offering a jury trial to a juvenile,[11] but it has never been interpreted as a constitutional mandate applicable in state trials. If however, a juvenile is certified as an adult or is otherwise tried as an adult in a nonjuvenile court, the usual standards determine whether a right to a jury trial exists.

5. SELECTING JURORS FROM A FAIR CROSS SECTION OF THE JURISDICTION

To meet constitutional requirements and as a general rule, the actual jury empaneled must have been selected from a fair cross section of the community. This requirement does not come from the text of the Sixth Amendment but is derived from a traditional understanding of how the justice system can assemble a fair jury.[12] Even though the juries must have been selected from a pool of prospective jurors that meets the fair cross section requirement, the Supreme Court has never imposed a requirement that the actual jury selected in a given case mirror the component groups making up the fair cross section.[13] The Sixth Amendment requirement that the pool from which jurors are chosen must be a fair cross-section of the community is a means of assuring not a representative jury but a fair jury. In a dissent, Justice Marshall noted that the fair cross section requirement existed to guard against the exercise of arbitrary power and to ensure that the common sense judgment of the community will act as a hedge against an overzealous or mistaken prosecutor. Marshall added that the fair cross section requirement helped preserve public confidence in the criminal justice system and helped implement our belief that sharing in the administration of justice is a phase of civic responsibility.[14]

One of the rationales for requiring that identifiable groups be included in the fair cross section is that otherwise the exclusion of identifiable groups or segments of the community prevents the excluded groups from sharing the civic responsibility of the administration of justice.[15] Congress has expressed the view that the requirement that a jury should be chosen from a fair cross section of the community is fundamental to the American system of justice.[16] For a defendant to claim a violation of the fair cross section requirement, the defendant must allege and prove that the underrepresented group is distinctive and identifiable, that the particular group has been systematically excluded from potential jury service, and that the group's underrepresentation is unfair and unreasonable.[17]

To generate a pool of potential jurors, the jurisdiction must devise a method whereby all distinctive groups are represented and included as members of the jury pool. For example, to call for jury service all citizens whose names appear on a list of income tax payers would fail to generate a representative pool, since the poorest citizens may not be included within the class of people who pay income taxes. Relying on voter lists of the jurisdiction, supplemented by adult drivers' license data, generally produces a sufficiently fair cross section of the population. A defendant does not possess the right to have an actual jury chosen that reflects the precise demographic composition of identifiable groups within the community, but the actual array of prospective jurors must generally be representative of a fair cross section of the community.

6. VIOLATION OF THE FAIR CROSS SECTION REQUIREMENT: PROOF AND REMEDY

Where a defendant believes that the jury was not chosen appropriately, the defendant usually must meet the burden of proof by presenting evidence that establishes a prima facie violation. As a general rule, a defendant's evidence should demonstrate that the identifiable group alleged to be excluded from potential jury service has distinctive group characteristics in the community, that the representation of this group in the jury pool is not fair and reasonable considering the number of such persons in the community, and that the underrepresentation is due to recurring attempts to exclude the group during the jury selection process.[18] Where a trial jury has been chosen from a pool of citizens in an irregular manner that failed to follow the state statute exactly but still produced a randomly selected jury pool that was not based on race, the fair cross section requirement was properly met, and the jury was not constitutionally defective.[19] Merely demonstrating that African American and Hispanic persons constituted distinctive groups within the community was insufficient to prove a violation of the fair cross section requirement in the absence of proof that the jury pool excluded members of the recognizable groups and that any underrepresentation was the result of a systematic effort at exclusion.[20]

Where a defendant has reason to believe that his or her jury has been selected from a group that did not fairly represent a cross-section of the population in the court's jurisdiction, the initial burden rests with the defendant to raise the issue. A defendant must offer an allegation that the jury was not selected from a fair cross section and is required to offer proof that the alleged underrepresented group has distinctive characteristics and has a group identity, that the distinctive group has been systematically excluded by the legal system from eligibility for jury service, and that the underrepresentation of the group is unfair and unreasonable.[21]

7. WAIVER OF THE RIGHT TO A TRIAL BY JURY

Most constitutional rights, whether state or federal, may be waived by criminal defendants who desire to forgo the protections that the constitutional rights normally provide. Waiver of a right to a jury trial often occurs within the context of a negotiated plea bargain, and so long as the defendant understands the significance and substance of the rights being released, waiver is appropriate.

Some defendants, as trial strategy, may waive the federal or state right to a trial by jury in order to obtain a bench trial. Waiver of a jury trial might be an appropriate legal strategy, especially where some of the evidence is particularly gruesome or other "rough" facts might have a tendency to inflame the passions of a jury. Under the theory that most judges have seen and heard almost anything and everything, rough evidence may have less effect on a "case-hardened" judge. Where a defendant desires to waive the right to a jury trial, most states, through court decision or law, require that the trial judge make a concerted inquiry into this preference. For example, in Alabama, a defendant cannot waive a jury trial unless the waiver gains the consent of both the prosecutor and the trial judge. Additionally, the defendant may waive personally in writing, in open court, or through the trial counsel if the waiver is made in open court and the defendant is present.[22] Similarly, Ohio courts allow a defendant to waive the right to a jury trial, but the waiver must be made in open court after arraignment and after the defendant has consulted with an attorney. The waiver must be contained in writing, signed by the defendant, and filed in the case as part of the record.[23] A failure to follow the strict Ohio requirements will be ineffective to waive a trial by jury and has the effect of removing jurisdiction of the court to hear the case. Michigan uses a form (Figure 13.1) to formally waive the right to a jury trial following proper advisement.

In a Louisiana case,[24] the reviewing court determined that a defendant properly waived the right to trial by jury in a robbery and kidnapping case, even though the defendant did not know that a Louisiana jury could reach a verdict where ten of twelve jurors agreed. The trial judge had personally addressed the defendant in open court to ensure that the defendant's waiver was being done freely, voluntarily and intelligently and with the assistance of counsel. The defendant contended that the discussion with the trial judge was too general for him to have made a knowing and intelligent decision when he did not know that a twelve-person jury could render a verdict on a vote by ten jurors. The reviewing court held that the trial judge was only required to determine whether the defendant made a jury trial waiver on a knowing and intelligent basis and was not required to explain to him the intricacies of jury voting.

In one habeas corpus case that was heard by a federal district court,[25] the defendant contended that his attorney failed to properly represent him in a criminal cause of action by allowing him to waive his right to a trial by jury. As a general rule, the waiver of the Sixth Amendment right to a jury trial must be made in a voluntary, knowing, and intelligent manner. In this particular case, the attorney previously had discussed the matter with the client, made sure that the client had taken his medication properly and examined the client under oath in open court concerning the matter, and both the client and the attorney had signed a waiver form. In rejecting the habeas corpus

Original - Court
1st copy - Defendant/Juvenile
2nd copy - Defendant/Juvenile attorney
3rd copy - Prosecutor

Approved, SCAO[26]

STATE OF MICHIGAN ___ JUDICIAL DISTRICT ___ JUDICIAL CIRCUIT ___ COUNTY PROBATE	WAIVER OF TRIAL BY JURY AND ELECTION TO BE TRIED WITHOUT JURY	CASE NO.

ORI
MI-   Court address   Court telephone no.

THE PEOPLE OF

☐ The State of Michigan

☐ _____

v

Defendant's/Juvenile's name, address, and telephone no.

CTN	SID	DOB

☐ Juvenile   In the matter of _____

I, _____ , defendant/juvenile in the above case, hereby voluntarily
   Name (type or print)

waive and relinquish my right to a trial by jury and elect to be tried by a judge of the court in which the case may be pending. I

fully understand that under the laws of this state I have a constitutional right to a trial by jury.

_____   _____
Date   Signature

_____
Defendant/Juvenile attorney signature   Bar no.

_____
Name (type or print)

Prosecutor's consent:

_____
Signature   Bar no.

_____
Name (type or print)

THE COURT FINDS:

1. Defendant/Juvenile has been arraigned and properly advised of the right to a jury trial.

2. Defendant/Juvenile has had an opportunity to consult with counsel.

3. Waiver occurred in open court as required by law.

Approved:

_____   _____
Date   Judge   Bar no.

MCL 712A.2d(7); MSA 27.3178(598.2d)(7),
MCL 763.3; MSA 28.856,
MCR 6.402(B)

MC 260 (6/97) **WAIVER OF TRIAL BY JURY AND ELECTION TO BE TRIED WITHOUT JURY**

FIGURE 13.1   Example of Waiver of Jury Trial Form.

petition of Langel, the district judge noted the defendant had been informed of his constitutional right to a jury trial and that if he waived the right, a judge would make a determination of guilt or innocence. The judge also noted that it was undisputed that the defendant had signed a jury waiver form and therefore, he could not overcome the presumption of correctness that attached to the trial court determination. Where a defendant properly waives the right under the Sixth Amendment to a trial by jury, so long as it was done intelligently and voluntarily, second-guessing that decision after a guilty verdict will not normally result in a new trial.

8. JURY SIZE: DIFFERENCE IN STATE AND FEDERAL REQUIREMENTS

The trial jury in a criminal case generally consists of twelve persons who possess citizenship, are representative of the local community, and are empaneled to hear or judge a case. Federal criminal trials require twelve-person juries who generally must reach a verdict by a unanimous vote[27] but may, with the consent of both parties, constitutionally render a verdict with fewer than twelve jurors.[28] The rules of criminal procedure for federal courts permit the use of a jury smaller than twelve if the judge and the parties consent in a written stipulation.[29] A federal court judge may allow a jury of eleven persons to return a verdict, even where the parties refuse to stipulate to a smaller jury, if deliberations have begun and the court finds good cause to excuse one of the twelve jurors.[30] State practice varies, since the tradition of a jury of twelve is not a federal constitutional requirement imposed by the United States Constitution upon the states.[31] However, most serious state criminal trials involve twelve-person juries, and where a trial verdict carries the possibility of the death penalty or life in prison, a jury of twelve is used.

Where a defendant possesses a right to a jury trial in a state criminal case, generally he or she may agree to accept a jury of fewer jurors than the state statute dictates. The right of a defendant to consent to a smaller jury stems from the right to completely waive a jury trial, and the same procedural safeguards that are required when formally waiving a jury trial should be followed prior to permitting a defendant to accept a reduction in jury size.[32] Among the reasons a defendant might wish to waive a right to a statutorily required number of jurors might be illness among the sitting jurors, removal of a juror for cause during a trial, or juror misconduct when alternative jurors are not available. The consent might be in the defendant's best interests, since the particular jury might appear to be leaning favorably toward the defendant, and there would be a desire to keep that jury rather than accept a mistrial.

The jury hears the evidence and renders a verdict based on the facts and evidence presented by each party. To produce a decision, juror balloting, in most criminal cases, must be unanimous for either a conviction or an acquittal. The general rule is that a less than unanimous vote requires that the case be retried before a different jury. The costs of a jury trial (or retrial) to a municipality, county, or state can be significant, especially if the trial is lengthy. To be required to retry a case that has been terminated without a verdict because of a hung jury creates additional expense to the jurisdiction and has caused states to experiment with methods of reducing costs without reducing the quality of justice. In one Georgia case, where the jury vote generally had to be unanimous given the type of case for which the defendant was on trial, the foreman of the jury sent a notice that the jury was deadlocked eleven to one and at two jurors were having some problems with that vote. Georgia procedure permits a nonunanimous verdict if the prosecution and defense agree. The defendant must make that decision freely and voluntarily after being told that he has the right to demand a unanimous jury verdict. After agreeing to accept the eleven-person jury vote and after having been convicted, the defendant unsuccessfully appealed, arguing that his counsel had encouraged him to accept the eleven-person verdict and that he did not intelligently waive his right to a unanimous verdict. The reviewing court found no merit in the defendant's allegations and approved the verdict based upon eleven jurors voting to convict.

9. STATE EFFORTS TO REDUCE THE SIZE OF JURIES

With a view to reducing expenditures for jury trials, some states have experimented with different approaches designed to minimize the size of the jury while maximizing the chances that it will come to a verdict.[33] Smaller juries cost less to empanel and pay than a full jury of twelve, and the time that the judge or the attorneys spend on voir dire of the jury is reduced. Presumably, a smaller jury will be able to deliberate and reach a decision in a shorter amount of time. A common criticism of smaller juries revolves around the argument that opportunities for minority participation will be reduced as the jury size shrinks. The government costs required for selecting and managing the jury system of the several states are significant, so measures that make their respective systems less expensive and more decisive have proven attractive. The goal is to balance cost reduction with the maintenance of an appropriate level of justice, consistent with fairness and due process.

In *Williams v. Florida* (Case 13.2),[34] the Court approved unanimous six-person juries in a serious, noncapital case. The Court noted that the selection of the number twelve was probably a historical accident, even though that number appears in the Bible in connection with the twelve tribes and the Twelve Apostles. Since the required number of jurors may have been pure happenstance, and since the original intent of the Framers of the Sixth Amendment concerning jury size remains unknown, the *Williams* Court approved Florida's use of a six-person jury as consistent with the United States Constitution. Following Florida's example, Connecticut allows the use of unanimous six-person juries in serious prosecutions not involving the death penalty or life imprisonment cases. In a sexual assault case,[35] one defendant made the argument that where the sexual assault might have been accomplished by different types of sexual activities, the jury might not have been unanimous in determining which type of sexual activities supported the conviction for sexual assault. The appellate court held that so long as a jury returned a unanimous six-person verdict, there was no real concern that the jury had failed to unanimously determine which specific acts supported the conviction for sexual assault.

In utilizing the theory of *Williams,* Florida and other states that adopted the six-person jury could enjoy the financial benefits of lower costs, as well as the probability of fewer hung juries and thus fewer retrials. Of course, if a six-person jury offered monetary savings and other benefits, an even smaller jury would further enhance

CASE 13.2

Leading Case Brief: Sixth Amendment Does Not Require Twelve-Person Jury in Most State Criminal Trials

Williams v. Florida
Supreme Court of the United States
399 U.S. 78 (1970)

Case Facts:

Prior to his trial for robbery, defendant Williams filed a pretrial motion to request a twelve-person jury for his trial. Under Florida law, Williams was entitled to a six-person jury. In contending that he should have a traditional jury of twelve, Williams noted that a twelve-person jury was the size commonly used at the time of the adoption of the Constitution and the Sixth Amendment. The trial court denied Williams' pretrial motion to have a twelve-person jury empaneled. The smaller jury convicted Williams as charged, resulting in a sentence of life in prison.

The Florida District Court of Appeal affirmed Williams' conviction and rejected, among other claims, Williams' argument that he possessed the Sixth Amendment right to have a twelve-person jury consider his case. In acting on Williams' petition, the Supreme Court granted a writ of certiorari to consider whether the Sixth Amendment requires a twelve-person jury in a serious, noncapital state prosecution.

Legal Issue:

In serious, noncapital state criminal prosecutions, does the Sixth Amendment require a jury of twelve persons?

The Court's Ruling:

Since there was no indication that the Framers of the Sixth Amendment intended to require the common-law usage of twelve jurors, it is not an explicit requirement so long as a modified jury system serves the function of the traditional jury of twelve.

Essence of the Court's Rationale:

* * *

While "the intent of the Framers" is often an elusive quarry, the relevant constitutional history casts considerable doubt on the easy assumption in our past decisions that if a given feature existed in a jury at common law in 1789, then it was necessarily preserved in the Constitution. Provisions for jury trial were first placed in the Constitution in Article III's provision that "[t]he Trial of all Crimes . . . shall be by Jury; and such Trial shall be held in the State where the said Crimes shall have been committed." The "very scanty history [of this provision] in the records of the Constitutional Convention" sheds little light either way on the intended correlation between Article III's "jury" and the features of the jury at common law.

* * *

We do not pretend to be able to divine precisely what the word "jury" imported to the Framers, the First Congress, or the States in 1789. It may well be that the usual expectation was that the jury would consist of 12, and that hence, the most likely conclusion to be drawn is simply that little thought was actually given to the specific question we face today. But there is absolutely no indication in "the intent of the Framers" of an explicit decision to equate the constitutional and common-law characteristics of the jury. Nothing in this history suggests, then, that we do violence to the letter of the Constitution by turning to other than purely historical considerations to determine which features of the jury system, as it existed at common law, were preserved in the Constitution. The relevant inquiry, as we see it, must be the function that the particular feature performs and its relation to the

(continued)

purposes of the jury trial. Measured by this standard, the 12-man requirement cannot be regarded as an indispensable component of the Sixth Amendment.

The purpose of the jury trial, as we noted in *Duncan,* is to prevent oppression by the Government.

> "Providing an accused with the right to be tried by a jury of his peers gave him an inestimable safe-guard against the corrupt or overzealous prosecu-tor and against the compliant, biased, or eccentric judge." *Duncan v. Louisiana, supra,* at 156.

Given this purpose, the essential feature of a jury obvi-ously lies in the interposition between the accused and his accuser of the commonsense judgment of a group of laymen, and in the community participation and shared responsibility that results from that group's determination of guilt or innocence. The performance of this role is not a function of the particular number of the body that makes up the jury. To be sure, the num-ber should probably be large enough to promote group deliberation, free from outside attempts at intim-idation, and to provide a fair possibility for obtaining a representative cross-section of the community. But we find little reason to think that these goals are in any meaningful sense less likely to be achieved when the jury numbers six, than when it numbers 12—particu-larly if the requirement of unanimity is retained. And, certainly the reliability of the jury as a fact finder hardly seems likely to be a function of its size.

* * *

We conclude, in short, as we began: the fact that the jury at common law was composed of precisely 12 is a historical accident, unnecessary to effect the purposes of the jury system and wholly without significance "except to mystics." *Duncan v. Louisiana, supra,* at 182 (Harlan, J., dissenting). To read the Sixth Amendment as forever codifying a feature so incidental

to the real purpose of the Amendment is to ascribe a blind formalism to the Framers which would require considerably more evidence than we have been able to discover in the history and language of the Constitution or in the reasoning of our past decisions. We do not mean to intimate that legislatures can never have good reasons for concluding that the 12-man jury is prefer-able to the smaller jury, or that such conclusions—reflected in the provisions of most States and in our federal system—are in any sense unwise. Legislatures may well have their own views about the relative value of the larger and smaller juries, and may conclude that, wholly apart from the jury's primary function, it is desir-able to spread the collective responsibility for the deter-mination of guilt among the larger group. In capital cases, for example, it appears that no State provides for less than 12 jurors—a fact that suggests implicit recog-nition of the value of the larger body as a means of legitimating society's decision to impose the death penalty. Our holding does no more than leave these considerations to Congress and the States, unrestrained by an interpretation of the Sixth Amendment that would forever dictate the precise number that can con-stitute a jury. Consistent with this holding, we conclude that petitioner's Sixth Amendment rights, as applied to the States through the Fourteenth Amendment, were not violated by Florida's decision to provide a six-man rather than a 12-man jury.

The judgment of the Florida District Court of Appeal is Affirmed.

Case Importance:

The Court's approval of a six-person jury in a serious state criminal case indicates that the Sixth Amend-ment right to a trial by jury in a state case is not an identical right to the federal jury trial right. Under the Sixth Amendment, the states have some freedom to innovate their criminal jury procedure.

these advantages. Moving in the direction of a smaller jury system, Georgia attempted to reduce the six-person jury to a five-person jury for noncapital cases. In *Ballew v. Georgia,*[36] the Court refused to approve the five-person jury trial for serious, non-capital cases[37] on the theory that it would prove too small to allow for effective group deliberation and might produce a greater number of inaccurate verdicts. The *Ballew* Court noted:

> [R]ecent empirical data suggest that progressively smaller juries are less likely to foster effective group deliberation. At some point, this decline leads to inaccurate

factfinding and incorrect application of the common sense of the community to the facts. Generally, a positive correlation exists between group size and the quality of both group performance and group productivity. *Ballew v. Georgia,* 435 U.S. 223, 232–233, n. 11 (1978)

The *Ballew* Court also noted that the smaller the group, the less likely it would be to overcome any biases held by its members and obtain an accurate result. Neither the financial nor the time-savings benefit of smaller juries influenced the Court; the benefit to Georgia would not offset the substantial threat to the constitutional guarantees that the Court believed would occur if it permitted Georgia to reduce the jury from six to five. Six-person juries are permissible, but the verdicts they render must be unanimous. In a Florida case, however, a defendant was permitted to waive his right to a six-person jury and have his case decided by the remaining five members. Since the right to a trial by jury has been deemed a waivable right, and although the federal Constitution has been construed as requiring at least a unanimous six-person jury in a state criminal case, a defendant may waive the right to a six-person jury and choose to accept the verdict from a five-member jury.[38]

In situations where a defendant has the right to a twelve-person jury, as a general rule, where the defendant consents, a decision may be rendered by fewer than twelve.[39] This situation may occur where a juror becomes ill and alternate jurors are not available. In a recent Illinois case,[40] the defendant was entitled by the state constitution to a jury of twelve persons. At the start of the trial, while jury selection was under way, the prosecution and the defense agreed that an alternate juror was not necessary in the prosecution for driving while intoxicated. When one juror became ill at the start of the trial, the judge continued the trial with the remaining eleven jurors, and the defendant made no objection at that time. The eleven-person jury convicted the defendant of her alcohol-related offense. However, the defendant appealed her conviction on the ground that she did not personally sign any waiver or orally agree on a jury of eleven. The Appellate Court of Illinois held that a defense counsel has the power to stipulate on behalf of a defendant that a smaller jury would be acceptable, and no reversal is necessary if the defendant has not been prejudiced. In addition, the defendant was well aware that there were not twelve jurors, and she offered no objection. The general rule that may be distilled from this case is that a jury of twelve is a waivable number and that states may proceed to trial with fewer than twelve jurors where a defendant's counsel agrees to the reduction and where the defendant has made no objection.

10. THE CONCEPT OF JURY UNANIMITY: VARIETY IN STATE JURIES

In another area of jury reform, Louisiana and Oregon eliminated the unanimity requirement for serious, noncapital cases, permitting a 9-to-3 jury vote to be sufficient for either a conviction or an acquittal. Allowing nonunanimous jury verdicts lessened the number of hung juries, consequently lowering the number of retrials required and saving money for the adopting jurisdictions. The Supreme Court approved the procedure despite allegations that a nonunanimous verdict called into question whether proof beyond a reasonable doubt was possible where three persons believed in innocence. In *Johnson v. Louisiana,*[41] the Court upheld the nonunanimous verdict of 9 to 3 and rejected the contention that three dissenters would tend to impeach the vote of the other nine. In a companion case, the Court rejected an argument that the Sixth Amendment requires jury unanimity to give effect to the burden of proof in criminal cases. The Court held that the reasonable doubt standard, while perhaps mandated by due process requirements, had no merit, since, in any event, the Sixth Amendment did not require proof beyond a reasonable doubt.[42]

11. COMBINATION OF SMALLER JURIES WITH NONUNANIMOUS VERDICTS

With costs savings available through the use of less than unanimous verdicts and reduced expenditures with smaller juries, it was not surprising that some state jurisdictions would try to achieve greater savings by combining the two concepts. However, efforts to unite reduction in juror numbers with nonunanimous jury verdicts ran aground in *Burch v. Louisiana,*[43] where the Court ruled that a nonunanimous six-person jury (a 5-to-1 vote) was not constitutionally permissible in serious, noncapital cases. According to the *Burch* Court, even though the state of Louisiana possessed a substantial interest in reducing the time and expense associated with administering its system of criminal justice, the state's interest proved to be an insufficient justification for its use of nonunanimous six-person juries. Where the state had reduced its jury size to the minimum permitted by the Court, any attempt to introduce nonunanimity in the legal equation began to threaten constitutional principles. The line had to be drawn somewhere concerning voting practice. The Court found the line in *Burch* and refused to move further away from the traditional unanimous vote of twelve persons of the community.

12. TRIAL BY JURY: ISSUES INVOLVING RACIAL AND GENDER DISCRIMINATION

The federal Constitution, state constitutions, and case law require that fair and unbiased juries be empaneled as part of a guarantee of a fair trial. Although both the prosecution and the defense desire a fair jury trial, most often each side prefers a jury more "fair" to that side than the other. In the not so distant past, various strategies were employed by states and by various individuals, for a variety of reasons, to keep persons of color and other minorities from serving on juries altogether or from serving on some juries in particular. The use of the poll tax[44] prevented many minorities from registering to vote,[45] which kept them from being selected when prospective jurors were summoned from voting lists. Literacy tests[46] as a prerequisite for voting registration had an effect similar to the poll tax, which indirectly prevented minority members of society from serving as jurors. In the past, some jurisdictions used what has been called a "key man" system, which resulted in members of identifiable minority groups being underrepresented on trial and grand juries. Where courts appointed key men to select potential jurors, the tendency was to pick potential jurors who were known to the key men and not to select other members of society who were members of minority groups.[47] Key man jury selection schemes have been known to keep minorities from jury service when white men were the key men doing the selecting.[48] Where jury service was permitted, other methods and intimidation had been devised to prevent particular individuals from seeing jury duty.

For more than 125 years, the Supreme Court has considered state-sponsored racial discrimination a transgression of the guarantees of the Fourteenth Amendment's Equal Protection Clause. In *Strauder v. West Virginia,* the Court held that a state violated the Fourteenth Amendment guarantee of equal protection of the laws when it put a black defendant before a jury "from which [all] members of his own race have been purposefully excluded."[49] The Court invalidated a state statute that provided only white men could serve as jurors. This case seems to have been the genesis of the Supreme Court design to remove factors involving racial discrimination from the courts in general and from jury selection in particular. The Court has continued its efforts to remove racism when it appears in the state or federal justice system. As an example, with respect to racially motivated efforts to exclude potential jurors, in 2005 the Supreme Court reversed a conviction and death sentence where the prosecution used peremptory challenges to remove ten of eleven black potential jurors. In *Miller-El v. Dretke,*[50] the Court offered the opinion that happenstance was unlikely to have produced the racial disparity demonstrated by the large number of potential black jurors who were removed from jury service when white prospective jurors with similar views and opinions were not removed. Where provable racial discrimination appears in a case before the Supreme Court, the justices seem united in their determination to end such discrimination as a way to foster fair trials and to meet the requirements of the Constitution.

Gender discrimination in the selection of jurors, whether the trial involves a criminal case or a civil case, has been prohibited since the landmark case of *J.E.B. v. Alabama ex rel. T.B.,* 511 U.S. 127 (1994), where the defendant in a paternity case objected to the government using its peremptory challenges to remove all men from the jury that was to determine paternity. The defendant contended that for the government, representing the mother, to purposefully remove all male jurors on the basis of gender violated his rights to equal protection of the laws under the Fourteenth Amendment. The Court, speaking by analogy in racial terms, noted that although a defendant has no right to have a jury composed in whole or part of members of his own race, a defendant has the right to be tried by a jury whose members were selected by following nondiscriminatory standards. To pass muster under equal protection standards, classifications based on gender require an exceedingly high level of justification to meet equal protection standards. The Court refused to permit clear gender discrimination in jury selection and noted that whether discrimination is based on race or gender, it causes harm to the litigants, the community, and to the individual prospective jurors who are improperly excluded from civic participation in the court process. In reversing the Alabama Court of Civil Appeals, the Supreme Court stated, "When state actors exercise peremptory challenges in reliance on gender stereotypes, they ratify and reinforce prejudicial views of the relative abilities of men and women."[51]

In the selection of trial jurors, neither the parties nor the court may base exclusion of any state or federal juror based on the individual's race or gender due to the violation of equal protection[52] that harms the individual defendant, the excluded juror, and the community as a whole.

13. REMOVAL OF PROSPECTIVE JURORS: PROPER AND IMPROPER RATIONALES

During the jury selection process, both the prosecution and the defense are permitted to remove from a prospective jury any juror who can be shown to have a bias, prejudice, or interest involving the case. Since bias, prejudice, or interest may affect the juror's view of the merits of the case and could result in a decision on an improper basis, both parties are permitted unlimited removals of prospective jurors for cause. Alternatively, peremptory challenges to prospective jurors permit the prosecution or defense to remove any particular juror for any reason or for no stated reason. Each party generally has a limited number of peremptory challenges that may be asserted in a given case. A constitutional limitation on the use of peremptory challenges exists where a party uses a constitutionally prohibited, though unstated, reason to remove a potential juror. A defendant may not exercise a challenge to remove a prospective juror *solely* on the basis of the juror's gender, ethnic origin, or race. If a defendant could prove that a prosecutor both had used peremptory challenges to remove prospective black jurors and had historically followed a pattern of doing so, a violation of equal protection would be proven.[53] In *Swain v. Alabama,* the defendant was unable to demonstrate that the prosecutor in his case had practiced discrimination based on race because he could not prove that the prosecutor demonstrated a pattern of discrimination. Under the *Swain* test, a prosecutor who discriminatorily removed jurors in only one case was not likely to have a verdict disturbed on appeal based on equal protection grounds. The virtually insurmountable burden that a defendant had to meet required proof of a pattern of discrimination, data that would be expensive and difficult to obtain from the prosecutor's office and probably not available anywhere else.

14. PROVING IMPROPER RATIONALES FOR USING PEREMPTORY JUROR CHALLENGES

Swain v. Alabama remained good law until the Court faced a similar claim in an updated setting. In *Batson v. Kentucky,*[54] the judge conducted voir dire examination of the jury venire[55] and excused certain jurors for cause (see Case 13.3). Subsequently, the prosecutor used peremptory juror challenges to remove all four blacks from the jury, which left an all-white jury to hear the case of an African American defendant. The defendant could not meet the *Swain* test by showing that the prosecutor, in trial after trial, whatever the crime and whoever the defendant, had systematically removed blacks from serving as jurors. The Court announced that the *Swain* test had been slowly eroded by later decisions and that, henceforth, a defendant could establish a prima facie case of purposeful discrimination solely on evidence concerning the prosecutor's use of peremptory challenges in the very case at bar. According to *Batson,* the defendant would have to show that he or she is a member of a cognizable racial group and that the prosecutor exercised peremptory challenges

CASE 13.3

Leading Case Brief: Racial Discrimination in the Use of Peremptory Challenges Violates Sixth Amendment and Equal Protection Clause

Batson v. Kentucky
Supreme Court of the United States
476 U.S. 79 (1986)

Case Facts:

A Kentucky grand jury indicted petitioner Batson, an African American, on charges of second-degree burglary and receipt of stolen goods. At the start of his trial, the judge conducted voir dire examination of the venire, excused certain jurors for cause, and permitted the parties to exercise peremptory challenges as they wished. Skillfully, the prosecutor used the allotted peremptory challenges to strike all four black persons from the trial jury. The final selections resulted in a jury of only white persons. Defense counsel objected to the way the jury had been selected. Defendant contended that the prosecutor's use of peremptory challenges to exclude members of defendant's race from the jury panel violated the petitioner's rights under the Sixth and Fourteenth Amendments to have a jury selected from a fair cross section of the community and to equal protection. The trial judge observed that the parties were entitled to use their peremptory challenges to "strike anybody they want to." The judge denied the petitioner's motion, reasoning that the cross section requirement applies only to selection of the venire and not to selection of the trial jury itself.

Following his conviction on both charges, Batson appealed to the Supreme Court of Kentucky. He continued his argument that the prosecutor's use of peremptory challenges based on the race of specific jurors deprived him of his right to a proper jury trial under the Sixth Amendment. Petitioner also contended that the facts showed that the prosecutor had engaged in a "pattern" of discriminatory challenges in this case and established an equal protection violation under *Swain v. Alabama*, 380 U.S. 202 (1965). In rejecting Batson's claims, the Kentucky Supreme Court noted that, in another case, it had relied on the rule of *Swain v.*

Alabama and had held that a defendant alleging lack of jury selection from a fair cross section must demonstrate a systematic exclusion of a group of jurors from the venire. Batson had failed to make this demonstration, so the Supreme Court of Kentucky affirmed Batson's convictions. The Supreme Court of the United States granted certiorari to hear the case.

Legal Issue:

Where a state prosecutor used peremptory challenges with an apparent purpose to remove all members of a defendant's race from the trial jury, did such use of peremptory challenges violate a defendant's rights under the Sixth Amendment and under the equal protection clause of the Fourteenth Amendment?

The Court's Ruling:

A defendant's constitutional right to a fair trial has been violated when a prosecutor uses peremptory challenges to systematically eliminate members of the defendant's race from sitting on the jury. Where proven racial discrimination exists in a particular case, any conviction based on that discrimination will be reversed.

Essence of the Court's Rationale:

* * *

This case requires us to reexamine that portion of *Swain v. Alabama*, 380 U.S. 202 (1965), concerning the evidentiary burden placed on a criminal defendant who claims that he has been denied equal protection through the State's use of peremptory challenges to

(continued)

exclude members of his race from [serving on] the petit jury.

I

In *Swain v. Alabama,* this Court recognized that a "State's purposeful or deliberate denial to [African Americans] on account of race of participation as jurors in the administration of justice violates the Equal Protection Clause." *[Swain]* 380 U.S., at 203–204. This principle has been "consistently and repeatedly" reaffirmed, in numerous decisions of this Court both preceding and following *Swain.* We reaffirm the principle today.

A

More than a century ago, the Court decided that the State denies a black defendant equal protection of the laws when it puts him on trial before a jury from which members of his own race have been purposefully excluded. *Strauder v. West Virginia,* 100 U.S. 303 (1880). The decision laid the foundation for the Court's unceasing efforts to eradicate racial discrimination in the procedures used to select the venire [i.e., the group] from which individual jurors are drawn.

* * *

II

A

Swain required the Court to decide, among other issues, whether a black defendant was denied equal protection by the State's exercise of peremptory challenges to exclude members of his race from the petit jury.

* * *

Accordingly, a black defendant could make out a prima facie case of purposeful discrimination on proof that the peremptory challenge system was "being perverted" in that manner. For example, an inference of purposeful discrimination would be raised on evidence that a prosecutor, "in case after case, whatever the circumstances, whatever the crime and whoever the defendant or the victim may be, is responsible for the removal of [African Americans] who have been selected as qualified jurors by the jury commissioners and who have survived challenges for cause, with the result that no [African Americans] ever serve on petit juries." Evidence offered by the defendant in

Swain did not meet that standard. While the defendant showed that prosecutors in the jurisdiction had exercised their strikes to exclude blacks from the jury, he offered no proof of the circumstances under which prosecutors were responsible for striking black jurors beyond the facts of his own case. *[Swain],* at 224–228.

* * *

The [current] standards for assessing a prima facie case in the context of discriminatory selection of the venire have been fully articulated since *Swain.* These principles support our conclusion that a defendant may establish a prima facie case of purposeful discrimination in selection of the petit jury solely on evidence concerning the prosecutor's exercise of peremptory challenges at the defendant's trial. To establish such a case, the defendant first must show that he is a member of a cognizable racial group, and that the prosecutor has exercised peremptory challenges to remove from the venire members of the defendant's race. Second, the defendant is entitled to rely on the fact, as to which there can be no dispute, that peremptory challenges constitute a jury selection practice that permits "those to discriminate who are of a mind to discriminate." *Avery v. Georgia,* 345 U.S., at 562. Finally, the defendant must show that these facts and any other relevant circumstances raise an inference that the prosecutor used that practice to exclude the veniremen from the petit jury on account of their race. This combination of factors in the empanelling of the petit jury, as in the selection of the venire, raises the necessary inference of purposeful discrimination.

In deciding whether the defendant has made the requisite showing, the trial court should consider all relevant circumstances. For example, a "pattern" of strikes against black jurors included in the particular venire might give rise to an inference of discrimination. Similarly, the prosecutor's questions and statements during *voir dire* examination and in exercising his challenges may support or refute an inference of discriminatory purpose. These examples are merely illustrative. We have confidence that trial judges, experienced in supervising *voir dire,* will be able to decide if the circumstances concerning the prosecutor's use of peremptory challenges creates a prima facie case of discrimination against black jurors.

Once the defendant makes a prima facie showing, the burden shifts to the State to come forward with a neutral explanation for challenging black jurors.

* * *

In this case, petitioner made a timely objection to the prosecutor's removal of all black persons on the venire. Because the trial court flatly rejected the objection without requiring the prosecutor to give an explanation for his action, we remand this case for further proceedings. If the trial court decides that the facts establish, prima facie, purposeful discrimination and the prosecutor does not come forward with a neutral explanation for his action, our precedents require that petitioner's conviction be
Reversed.

Case Importance:

Batson reaffirmed the principle that where a case presents provable evidence of racial discrimination, the Court finds such discrimination intolerable and contrary to the Constitution and the Fourth Amendment guarantees of due process and equal protection. Where provable discrimination exists, the Court will reverse, or remand as appropriate, any resulting conviction.

to remove members of the defendant's race from the jury. The defendant must show that the facts raise an inference that the prosecutor excluded the jurors due to race, implicating the Equal Protection Clause of the Fourteenth Amendment. The burden then shifts to the prosecutor to come forward with a race-neutral explanation for challenging African American jurors, and a court must determine whether the defendant has carried its burden of proving intentional discrimination. *Batson* effectively overturned the *Swain* test and substituted a more rational and workable approach that makes the allegation and proof of racial discrimination an easier path to follow. In *Batson,* the Court recognized that when a defendant makes an allegation of intentional racial discrimination on the part of the government in jury selection, such a claim raises issues concerning the basic fairness of the trial at hand, as well as the fairness of other trials within that particular judicial system.

Following an allegation and offer of prima facie proof of discrimination in the use of peremptory challenges, a trial court must sort through the evidence offered by both the defense and the prosecution and render an initial decision on the allegation. One Connecticut court identified numerous factors that should be considered in determining whether a prosecutor has used peremptory challenges in an unacceptable and discriminatory manner. The court noted that the issues include but are not limited to the following:

> (1) [T]he reasons given for the challenge were not related to the trial of the case . . . (2) the [party exercising the peremptory strike] failed to question the challenged juror or only questioned him or her in a perfunctory manner . . . (3) prospective jurors of one race [or gender] were asked a question to elicit a particular response that was not asked of the other jurors . . . (4) persons with the same or similar characteristics but not the same race [or gender] as the challenged juror were not struck . . . (5) the [party exercising the peremptory strike] advanced an explanation based on a group bias where the group trait is not shown to apply to the challenged juror specifically . . . and (6) the [party exercising the peremptory strike] used a disproportionate number of peremptory challenges to exclude members of one race [or gender].[56]

While the ultimate racial composition of the seated jury may not be determinative of the allegation of discrimination, it remains a factor that many courts consider in evaluating the prosecutor's explanation.[57]

Under the dictates of equal protection, defense attorneys may not exercise peremptory challenges in a racially discriminatory manner, and a trial judge does not cure the evil by permitting the prosecution to practice an equal degree of racial discrimination in an effort to level the field. In *Louisiana v. Lewis,*[58] when the defense began to exercise peremptory challenges with a view to removing white citizens from the jury, the prosecution objected, citing the *Batson* case. The ultimate court response involved allowing the prosecution the same latitude in striking prospective black jurors. When the defendant appealed his conviction, he contended that the prosecution practiced jury discrimination outlawed in *Batson*. The defendant proved successful in obtaining a reversal of his conviction because he demonstrated purposeful racial discrimination by the prosecution during the jury selection process, even though, arguably, he had engaged in similar discriminatory jury selection.

Where other factors that are not race related appear, prospective jurors who may be female or black or male or white may be excluded from jury service so long as there are nongender and nonracial reasons for striking them from jury service through peremptory challenges. In *Rice v. Collins,*[59] a black prospective juror had been excluded from jury service because, according to the prosecutor, she had rolled her eyes when fielding a question from the judge. In addition, she was young, and the prosecutor feared that she might be unfairly tolerant of drug crimes, and she was single and lacked strong ties to the local community. The Supreme Court accepted these reasons as not being based on race and such factors could properly be considered by a prosecutor or defense counsel in excluding prospective jurors from serving in state criminal cases.

Although a member of a racial minority can use the *Batson* test for judging discrimination in jury selection, the same theory may be employed by a member of a racial majority. In *Powers v. Ohio,*[60] a white man objected to the prosecutor's use of peremptory challenges that removed seven black prospective jurors from the jury array. In deciding that a member of the majority racial group could use the *Batson* test, the Court focused on the rights of jurors rather than on those of a defendant. As the *Powers* Court noted:

> [T]he Equal Protection Clause prohibits a prosecutor from using the State's peremptory challenges to exclude otherwise qualified and unbiased persons from the petit jury solely by reason of their race, a practice that forecloses a significant opportunity to participate in civic life. An individual juror does not have a right to sit on any particular petit jury, but he or she does possess the right not to be excluded from one on account of race. 499 U.S. 400, 409

In a further decision involving jury selection that involved racial discrimination, a white man had used peremptory challenges in a manner similar to what the prosecutor did in *Powers*. The defendant used his challenges to remove African Americans from the jury, partly because the victim in the case was a person of color. In *Georgia v. McCollum,*[61] the Court held that criminal defendants cannot use peremptory challenges based on race because the practice offends the Equal Protection Clause of the Fourteenth Amendment, and it harms the individual juror by subjecting him or her to open and public racial discrimination. In addition, such a racially discriminatory practice creates harm to the community by undermining public confidence in the jury system.

Just as the prosecutor in *Batson* had been prohibited from using racial criteria, the Court applied similar reasoning to prevent a defendant from doing the same thing.[62]

In selecting a jury, neither the prosecution nor the defense should pursue legal strategies designed to remove representatives of identifiable groups from jury service. Although the use of a racial animus in jury selection clearly transgresses the Constitution, the pursuit of gender goals resulting in discrimination was not always considered illegal. In *J.E.B. v. Alabama ex rel. T.B.*,[63] the government of Alabama used nine of its ten peremptory challenges allowed under state law to remove all males from a trial jury in a paternity case. The rationale of the state of Alabama was based on its perception that men who would otherwise be legally qualified to serve as jurors might be more sympathetic and receptive to the arguments of a man charged in a paternity action. In a sense, the Alabama government was following a stereotype that men would not be fair and impartial in a paternity case. It could attempt to argue that it was not actively pursuing gender discrimination; it was attempting to secure a fair trial. The opposite view held by the defendant, that women equally qualified might be more sympathetic and receptive to the arguments of the child's mother, caused the defense to use peremptory challenges to remove female jurors. According to the Supreme Court, using gender as the factor in exercising peremptory challenges cannot be constitutionally supported since it is based on the very stereotypes the law condemns. The *J.E.B.* Court cited *Strauder v. West Virginia* in noting that the "defendant does have the right to be tried by a jury whose members are selected pursuant to nondiscriminatory criteria."[64] The *J.E.B.* Court went on to conclude that the Equal Protection Clause of the Fourteenth Amendment prohibits gender discrimination where it is based on the belief that jurors will possess stereotypical gender-based prejudices and decide cases based on that bias.

The purpose of selecting a proper jury for a trial is to insulate the defendant from an unfair or overzealous prosecutor or judge. This role cannot be successfully implemented where a jury is too small in number, where it has been selected based on racial characteristics, where an agreement of a significant number of the majority is not required for a decision, or where gender discrimination taints the selection of the jury. The goal of equal justice requires a jury that is selected appropriately and consistently with constitutional dictates.

15. EVOLUTION OF THE SIXTH AMENDMENT RIGHT TO TRIAL COUNSEL

As originally contemplated by the Framers of the Sixth Amendment, the right to a jury trial existed for the most serious federal offenses and for some of the less serious offenses, according to the practice of the common law. However, precisely when the right to a jury trial existed was not clearly drawn, even with reference to the common law. In addition, the Sixth Amendment appeared to permit the assistance of counsel to prepare one's criminal defense but did not advise a defendant how to find legal representation or address how a poor person would be able to afford an attorney. The original intent of this right was that if a defendant could afford to pay for an attorney, he or she could have legal assistance in the preparation and presentation of a defense. The right to have the assistance of counsel would have little value to a person who could not afford to pay a lawyer. If the government, be it state, local, or federal, viewed a criminal matter as sufficiently important that it hired a lawyer to act as a prosecutor, it would seem that a defendant should be able to fairly meet the government by using a lawyer for the presentation of a defense. The inability to afford a proper defense created a legal mismatch for most indigent defendants. This handicapping of impoverished defendants with no defense counsel who faced professionally trained prosecutors existed from the founding of the nation until 1966.

In a now-famous case, Gideon v. Wainwright, 372 U.S. 335 (1963). Florida had charged the defendant with a serious felony but had not offered to furnish him with legal assistance. As a result, an impoverished Gideon proceeded to trial without counsel for having allegedly broken into and entered a poolroom with intent to commit a misdemeanor, a crime that was considered a felony. At his trial, where he was convicted, Gideon requested the assistance of counsel, but the judge followed state law and refused to appoint an attorney. Attorneys on Gideon's behalf initiated the appellate process but had no success in Florida state courts. Gideon successfully applied for a writ of certiorari to the Supreme Court of the United States. With a bit of irony, that Court appointed free attorneys for Gideon to argue his case in the Supreme Court.

16. CONSTITUTIONAL RIGHT TO COUNSEL: FELONIES AND MISDEMEANORS

When Gideon's case reached the nation's top court in *Gideon v. Wainwright,*[65] the Court held that an indigent defendant charged with a serious, noncapital offense has the right to have appointed legal counsel to assist in his defense. The *Gideon* Court concluded that having the assistance of counsel was a fundamental right essential to a fair trial and that to force someone to trial without an attorney created a violation of the Sixth Amendment as applied to the states through the Due Process Clause of the Fourteenth Amendment. As Justice Black noted:

> From the very beginning, our state and national constitutions and laws have laid great emphasis on procedural and substantive safeguards designed to assure fair trials before impartial tribunals in which every defendant stands equal before the law. This noble ideal cannot be realized if the poor man charged with crime has to face his accusers without a lawyer to assist him. *Gideon v. Wainright,* 372 U.S. 335, 344 (1963)

For the very first time, the Court recognized the existence of the right to free legal counsel for any defendant charged in a state felony case when the accused could not afford to hire an attorney. The generally accepted view was that this decision significantly leveled the inherent advantages of the prosecution and helped move the states toward a fair criminal justice system. Yet to come was the extension of the right to counsel to other offenses of a less serious nature.

Following *Gideon,* in a series of cases culminating in *Argersinger v. Hamlin*[66] and *Scott v. Illinois,*[67] the Court extended the right to free assistance of counsel to any crime for which incarceration might be imposed. In *Argersinger,* the defendant was an indigent who was tried for an offense punishable by incarceration for up to six months, a $1,000 fine, or both. He was actually given a ninety-day jail sentence after his court trial, at which he was given no right to court-appointed counsel. The state of Florida refused to grant free counsel on the ground that such a right extended only to trials involving serious offenses punishable by more than six months in prison. The Supreme Court rejected Florida's holding and determined that in the absence of counsel, no jail time may be given upon a conviction of an indigent who cannot afford legal representation and who has not been offered free assistance of counsel. In effect, if a judge determines not to appoint counsel for an indigent, the judge cannot later impose a jail or prison sentence. Incarceration cannot be imposed either at the end of a trial or later for a probation violation. As a further limitation, a conviction may not be used under a multiple offense statute or as a "strike offense" in a three-strikes law context to convert a subsequent misdemeanor into a felony with a prison term.[68]

Where the right to counsel exists under the Sixth Amendment in a criminal case, the right would be somewhat hollow if there were no standards to govern the competency of an appointed attorney. Under *Strickland v. Washington,* 466 U.S. 668 (1984), the Court determined that the Sixth Amendment guarantee of the right to counsel also included the right to effective assistance of counsel. The concept of effective assistance of counsel contemplates that the attorney for a defendant was able to offer guidance, assistance, and performance to ensure a fair trial, but not necessarily one that a defendant always wins. In order for an appellant to win an appeal based on a claim of ineffective assistance of counsel, the appellant must demonstrate that the "counsel's representation fell below an objective standard of reasonableness" and that "the deficient performance prejudiced the defense."[69] In a habeas corpus petition, the appellant would have to bring forth some evidence that his or her attorney had failed to make an investigation of the facts where that approach would have been reasonable, that the attorney failed to exercise due diligence to discover evidence of innocence or other evidence helpful to the accused, that the attorney had failed to properly prepare for trial, or that the representation during the trial fell dramatically below acceptable standards, given the complexity or simplicity of the case. As a general rule, there is a strong presumption that a defense attorney's performance in a given case falls within a wide range of professional conduct. According to the *Strickland* Court,

> Judicial scrutiny of counsel's performance must be highly deferential. It is all too tempting for a defendant to second-guess counsel's assistance after conviction or adverse sentence, and it is all too easy for a court, examining counsel's defense after it has proved unsuccessful, to conclude that a particular act or omission of counsel was unreasonable. A fair assessment of attorney performance requires that every effort be made to eliminate the distorting effects of hindsight, to reconstruct the circumstances of counsel's challenged conduct, and to evaluate the conduct from counsel's perspective at the time.[70]

An additional burden for an appellant who claims ineffective assistance of counsel is the requirement that the defendant must demonstrate his case experienced prejudice. This is another way of saying that the appellant must show that there some reasonable likelihood or probability that, but for the attorney's deficiency, the outcome in the defendant's criminal case would have been different. As a result of the standards announced by the *Strickland* Court, few appellants will succeed in obtaining new trials based on the incompetency of prior legal counsel.

17. SUMMARY

Although the Sixth Amendment holds that in all criminal prosecutions the defendant shall enjoy the right to a speedy and public trial by an impartial jury, not every criminal case merits a trial by jury under the Sixth Amendment. Article III, Section 2, of the Constitution of the United States also mandates that the "trial of all crimes, except in cases of impeachment, shall be by jury," but this provision has not been interpreted to mandate a jury trial for every minor federal criminal transgression. Due to the process of selective incorporation, the Supreme Court incorporated the Sixth Amendment and its guarantee of a trial by jury into the Due Process Clause of the Fourteenth Amendment and made the right to a jury trial applicable to the states in the 1968 case of *Duncan v. Louisiana.* A subsequent case, *Baldwin v. New York,* determined that the right to a jury trial was constitutionally required in state cases only where the potential sentence was greater than six months' incarceration. Juvenile courts are not constitutionally required to grant a trial by jury to juveniles tried in juvenile courts, but juveniles certified as adults who stand trial in adult court must be given the right to trial by jury as if the juvenile were an adult.

The actual selection of a trial jury requires that due process and fundamental fairness be exercised when deciding who shall sit as jurors. The general rule requires that the jury be chosen from a group that represents a fair cross section of the different types of people residing within the jurisdiction. However, the actual jury seated need not be a mirror image of the identifiable groups that compose the fair cross section of the community. A defendant who believes that a jury was not selected from a fair cross section of the community has the burden of proof to establish a violation. The defendant must demonstrate that an identifiable group was precluded from representation or that underrepresentation of an identifiable group was based on an intentional design.

Although a federal criminal jury must have twelve individual jurors, state juries may have fewer than twelve but must have at least six members. Twelve-member juries in state cases are not required by the Sixth Amendment to render a verdict based on unanimity, and a 9-to-3 vote has been determined by the Supreme Court to be consistent with the Constitution. A six-person state jury must reach a verdict by a unanimous vote.

To assure that improper racial or gender issues have not intruded in a way that would influence a jury's deliberations, the use of peremptory challenges to remove prospective jurors based on race or gender is prohibited. Race and/or gender may not be a consideration or basis on which to prevent a prospective juror from serving. Persons being considered for jury duty may be removed when there is evidence that an prospective juror may not be able to render a fair and impartial verdict based on the evidence presented. Except for race or gender, an attorney may remove a person from jury service for any reason or no reason by exercising a peremptory challenge to the seating of that prospective juror. Peremptory challenges are usually limited in number, but challenges for cause do not have a numeric limitation.

The right to a trial by jury might not mean very much unless an individual has the right to counsel to assist in that person's defense. Where there is any chance that a conviction might result in a defendant's incarceration, free legal counsel must be given to a person who qualifies as an indigent. The right to counsel applies whether the charged crime is a felony or is a misdemeanor, so long as there is any potential for incarceration.

REVIEW EXERCISES AND QUESTIONS

1. Explain why the Sixth Amendment right to a trial by jury originally applied only in federal criminal prosecutions.

2. The language in the Sixth Amendment suggests that a jury trial should be available to every federal defendant. When does the right to a jury trial arise under present interpretations of the Sixth Amendment?

3. What purposes are served by having a jury drawn from a representative, fair cross section of the community? Are there any other obvious purposes or benefits from selecting jurors from this pool?

4. In a prosecution for sexual assault, the prosecutor objected to the defendant's attorney's use of a peremptory challenge to remove a prospective female juror from serving on the panel. The prosecutor alleged that the juror was being excused because she was female and noted that the sexual assault involved the defendant's alleged act against a female. The defense countered that its questioning of the prospective female juror indicated that

she had a relative who had been raped and that she thought police officers usually arrested the guilty and not the innocent. Is gender discrimination being practiced by the defense attorney, or is the prosecutor correct that the juror has been excluded for legal reasons? Explain your arguments and any assumptions that you add to this case.

5. Federal juries must have twelve persons in criminal cases, but the states have some freedom to experiment with juror numbers. Why would states want to permit juries with fewer members than the traditional twelve?

6. What are some of the reasons why some states have reduced the numbers of jurors below twelve for many criminal cases?

7. What factor determines whether an indigent defendant must be given legal counsel?

8. Why should criminal defendants who are too poor to afford legal counsel be granted access to free attorneys who assist in presenting their defense?

HOW WOULD YOU DECIDE?

1. In the United States Court of Appeals of Arizona, Division One

The defendant, Erin Crowell, had been cited for violating the Scottsdale, Arizona, city code that regulated nude performances by exotic dancers or adult service providers. The code permitted nude dancing but provided restrictions that the dancing women must honor. The prosecutor alleged that Crowell violated three provisions of the ordinance in that she had exotically danced

without a permit, had danced less than three feet from a patron, and had allowed a patron to place money on her person or costume. The penalties might possibly be consecutive, resulting in more than six months of incarceration. A penalty of a $2,500 fine or no more than six months' imprisonment was the maximum that could be given for each offense. The defendant argued that she should have the right to a jury trial because the ordinance preventing her conduct involving nude dancing was a direct outgrowth of common-law offenses prohibiting indecent exposure. Regulating the right to a jury trial, in addition to federal constitutional case law, is the Arizona state constitution, Article 2, Section 23, which provides that "[t]he right of trial by jury shall remain inviolate." To decide whether a defendant has a right to a jury trial under this provision, the court had to determine whether the defendant's alleged offenses had a "common law antecedent that guaranteed a right to trial by jury at the time of Arizona statehood." *Derendal v Griffith,* 209 Ariz. at 425, P36, 104 P.3d at 156 (2005).

How would you rule on the defendant's contention that she has the right to a jury trial for her alleged exotic dancing infractions?

The Court's Holding:

[The appellate court reaffirmed that the right to a trial by jury shall remain inviolate and that the court must determine whether the offense that has been accused in this case was one that had a common law antecedent that would have guaranteed the right to trial by jury at the time Arizona became a state. According to the court, if the right to a jury trial did not exist in the federal Constitution, the court will evaluate the right to jury trial based on case law interpreting the Sixth Amendment of the United States Constitution. The court also noted that the defendant did not allege that that the ordinances carry additional consequences that might render them so serious as to warrant a jury trial pursuant other parts of the Arizona constitution or federal case law.]

In determining whether there is a common-law, jury-eligible antecedent to a modern offense, we compare the character of the modern offense with that of the common-law offense. *Id.* at 419, P10, 104 P.3d at 150 ("We have further held that when the right to jury trial for an offense existed prior to statehood, it cannot be denied for modern statutory offenses of the same 'character or grade.'" (quoting *Bowden v. Nugent,* 26 Ariz. 485, 488, 226 P. 549, 550 (1924))).

The court in *Derendal* cited several cases as examples of modern crimes with common-law antecedents. *Id.* at 419-20 & n.4, PP11–12, 104 P.3d at 150–51 & n.4. In

Bowden, "a defendant charged with operating a poker game in violation of a city ordinance was entitled to a jury trial because the charge was similar in character to the common law crime of conducting or maintaining a gambling house and the elements of the crimes were substantially similar." *Id.* at P11 (citing *Bowden,* 26 Ariz. at 490, 226 P. at 550). Likewise, in *Urs v. Maricopa County Attorney's Office,* a charge of reckless driving, defined as "driv[ing] a vehicle in reckless disregard for the safety of persons or property," was similarly akin in "character" to the common-law offense of "operating a motor vehicle so as to endanger [any] property [or] individual." *Id.* at 420, P12, 104 P.3d at 151 (alterations in original) (discussing *Urs,* 201 Ariz. 71, 74, P10, 31 P.3d 845, 848 (App. 2001)).

* * *

In determining whether the offenses at issue in this case share the character of a common-law antecedent, we focus on the elements of the offenses. We regard a jury-eligible, common-law offense as an antecedent of a modern statutory offense when the modern offense contains elements comparable to those found in the common-law offense. *Id.* at 419, P10, 104 P.3d at 150; *see id.* at 420, P11, 104 P.3d at 151 (noting that elements of the modern crime in *Bowden* were "substantially similar" to the historical offense).

Crowell argues that, like the Tucson ordinance at issue in *Lee [prohibiting nude dancing and exposure],* the Scottsdale City Code provisions she is accused of violating have as their common-law antecedent the crime of indecent exposure, entitling her to a jury trial. She contends, and Scottsdale does not deny, that one charged with indecent exposure at common law was entitled to a jury trial.

[The court determined that she was not eligible for a trial by jury because the offenses were punishable only by six months or less and that the ordinance did not prohibit nude dancing; it merely regulated it. Therefore, it was different from the prior common law that outlawed indecent exposure and gave a jury trial to those accused of that crime due to the character of the crime. Here exotic nudity was not viewed in the same level of seriousness as purposely being indecent out in public, so no jury trial was available based on the crime.] See *Crowell v. Jejna,* 161 P.3d 577; 2007 Ariz. App. LEXIS 108 (2007).

HOW WOULD YOU DECIDE?

2. In the United States Court of Appeal for the Eleventh Circuit

A Florida highway patrol officer stopped a rental car for speeding in which the defendant, William Downs, was riding. His girlfriend was the driver of the car, which had been rented by another relative. Another officer arrived with a drug-sniffing dog and permitted the dog to conduct a sniff test outside and around the car. The dog's conduct indicated that controlled substances were probably inside the vehicle. Eventually, the officers found that it contained a large amount of hidden crack cocaine. On appeal, Downs contended, among other legal issues, that the jury selection process resulted in a racially imbalanced jury, thereby violating his constitutional rights. Although the defendant objected at trial to the lack of African Americans on the panel and requested that the court reject the jury so that a new jury could be empaneled, he never offered any proof that members of his race had been purposely excluded from jury service. Defendant Downs argued that he had a right to have his actual jury reflect a fair cross section of the community, and he contended that his right to equal protection of the law had been violated since his jury panel was racially imbalanced. He failed to object to any specific peremptory challenge exercised by the government, and he did not offer to show or otherwise prove that African Americans had been systematically excluded from the jury pool. The defendant simply offered no evidence to support his allegations. The trial judge did not act on his unproven accusations of constitutional deficiencies in his case.

How would you rule on the defendant's contention that his right to equal protection of the laws was impaired because of his allegation that the jury pool did not represent a fair cross section of the people in the judicial district and that the actual jury selected did not have a balance of members of his race on the panel?

The Court's Holding:

[The circuit court noted that the Supreme Court of the United States has never required that petit (trial) juries mirror the racial or ethnic makeup of the jurisdiction where the trial is being held. The circuit court agreed with defendant Downs that he has legal standing to object to a race-based exclusion of jurors, whether or not the defendant and the excluded jurors shared the same race. In rejecting Downs' appellate arguments, the circuit court determined that:

Downs did not establish a violation of either his fair cross-section right or his equal protection right. While Downs pointed out to the district court that there were no African-Americans in the jury pool, he failed to show that this exclusion was systematic, and he offered no proof that the underrepresentation was unfair or unreasonable, but rather, simply asked the court to impanel a new jury with African-Americans on it. *Cf. Berryhill* [*v. Zant*], 858 F.2d at 638 [1088] (defendant claiming fair cross-section violation must show that distinctive group is *systematically* excluded from the jury source). Moreover, his equal protection claim fails because although he pointed out that African-Americans were not represented on the venire, he made no allegation, never mind a showing, that the venire was selected under a practice providing an opportunity for discrimination. And he requested only that the court impanel a new jury, a request the district court properly denied because Downs had not made the requisite showing for his requested remedy. *See Cunningham* [*v. Zant*], 928 F.2d at 1013 [1991]. Accordingly, we discern no error on either of the grounds Downs asserts concerning the jury selection process.

* * *

Affirmed [the convictions]. See *United States v. Downs,* 217 Fed. Appx. 841, 2006 U.S. App. LEXIS 27236 (8th Cir. 2006).

ENDNOTES

1. 391 U.S. 145 (1968).
2. *In re Oliver,* 333 U.S. 257, 273 (1948).
3. *Gideon v. Wainwright,* 372 U.S. 335, 343–344 (1963).
4. 399 U.S. 117 (1970).
5. *Crowell v. Jejna,* 161 P.3d 577, 2007 Ariz. App. LEXIS 108 (2007).
6. But see *Sassano v. Brown,* 2006 U.S. Dist. LEXIS 90025 (D. N.J. 2006). A federal district court ruled that driving while intoxicated is a petty offense for which no right to a jury trial exists, even where the defendant was jailed for 180 days, had his license and registration revoked for ten years, and was fined $1,000 dollars, $300 in court costs, and other surcharged penalties. See *Sassano v. Brown,* 2006 U.S. Dist. LEXIS 90025 (D. N.J. 2006).
7. For the offense and under the circumstances, the *Blanton* litigants faced a maximum of six months' incarceration under Nevada law.
8. See *Solem v. Helm,* 463 U.S. 277, 280, n. 4 (1983).
9. *Lewis v. United States,* 518 U.S. 322 (1996).
10. 403 U.S. 528 (1971).
11. See ALM [Annotated Laws of Massachusetts] GL ch. 119, § 55A (2007), where a child who has received a complaint against him or her or has been indicted as a youthful offender in juvenile court has the right to a trial by jury.
12. *Holland v. Illinois,* 493 U.S. 474, 480 (1990).
13. Ibid., 482.
14. Ibid., 495.
15. *Taylor v. Louisiana,* 419 U.S. 522, 530 (1975).
16. Ibid.
17. See *United States v. Downs,* 217 Fed. Appx. 841, 2006 U.S. App. LEXIS 27236 (11th Cir. 2006).
18. See *Duren v. Missouri,* 439 U.S. 357, 364 (1979).
19. See *Boston v. Bowersox,* 202 F.3d 1001; 1999 U.S. LEXIS 30660 (8th Cir. 1999).
20. *United States v. Brown,* 1997 U.S. App. LEXIS 13812 (2nd Cir. 1997).
21. See *United States v. Downs,* 217 Fed. Appx. 841, 2006 U.S. App. LEXIS 27236 (11th Cir. 2006).
22. *Davis v. State,* 2003 Ark. App. LEXIS 112 (2003), citing Rule 31.1 and Rule 31.2 of the Arkansas Rules of Criminal Procedure.
23. *Ohio v. Baer,* 1998 Ohio App. LEXIS 4152 (10th App. Dist. 1998).
24. See *State v. Campbell,* 960 So. 2d 363, 2007 La. App. LEXIS 1302 (2007).
25. *Langel v. Burt,* 2006 U.S. Dist. LEXIS 36476 (N.D Iowa 2006).
26. http://courts.michigan.gov/SCAO/courtforms/ generalcriminal/mc260.pdf.
27. *Hawaii v. Mankichi,* 190 U.S. 197, 245 (1903). Justice Harlan, in dissent, offered his view on federal juries: "Whatever may be the power of the states in respect of grand and petit juries, it is firmly settled that the Constitution absolutely forbids the trial and conviction, in a federal civil tribunal, of anyone charged with crime otherwise than upon the presentment or indictment of a grand jury and the unanimous verdict of a petit jury composed, as at common law, of twelve jurors."
28. *Patton et al. v. United States,* 281 U.S. 276, 312; 50 S. Ct. 253, 263 (1930).
29. *Federal Rules of Criminal Procedure,* Rule 23(b)(2).
30. Ibid., Rule 23(b)(3).
31. *Jordan v. Massachusetts,* 225 U.S. 167 (1912). "In criminal cases, due process of law is not denied by a state law which dispenses with a grand jury indictment and permits prosecution upon information, nor by a law which dispenses with the necessity of a jury of twelve, or unanimity in the verdict." *Jordan* was cited with approval in *Johnson v. Louisiana,* 406 U.S. 356 (1972), a case that held that less than unanimous verdicts in state criminal cases do not offend the Sixth Amendment as applied to the states.
32. See *Kansas v. Roland,* 15 Kan. App.2d 296; 807 P.2d 705; 1991 Kan. App. LEXIS 149 (1991).
33. For example, see Utah Constitution Art. I, § 10. [Trial by jury.] "In capital cases the right of trial by jury shall remain inviolate. In capital cases the jury shall consist of twelve persons, and in all other felony cases, the jury shall consist of no fewer than eight persons. In other cases, the Legislature shall establish the number of jurors by statute, but in no event shall a jury consist of fewer than four persons. In criminal cases the verdict shall be unanimous. In civil cases three-fourths of the jurors may find a verdict. A jury in civil cases shall be waived unless demanded."
34. 399 U.S. 78 (1970).

35. See *State v. Griffin,* 97 Conn. App. 169, 903 A.2d 253, 2006 Conn. App. LEXIS 381 (2006).

36. 435 U.S. 223 (1978).

37. Ballew was initially sentenced to concurrent terms of one year in prison and a $1,000 fine for showing an obscene film, *Behind the Green Door.*

38. See *Blair v. Florida,* 698 So. 2d 1210; 1997 Fla. LEXIS 1338 (1997).

39. *Godfrey v. State,* 2005 Tex. App. LEXIS 4050 (2005).

40. See *People v. Barrier,* 359 Ill. App. 3d 639, 834 N.E.2d 616, 2005 Ill. App. LEXIS 865 (2005).

41. 406 U.S. 356 (1972). Accord, *Apodaca v. Oregon,* 406 U.S. 404 (1972).

42. See *Apodaca v. Oregon,* 406 U.S. 404, 411–412 (1972). Although the Court notes that the Sixth Amendment does not require proof beyond a reasonable doubt, the Due Process Clause of the Fourteenth Amendment was construed in *In re Winship,* 397 U.S. 358 (1970), as requiring proof beyond a reasonable doubt for proof of guilt in criminal cases.

43. 441 U.S. 130 (1979).

44. A poll tax was a levy imposed on those citizens who wished to vote. The Supreme Court held that the tax constituted a violation of the Equal Protection Clause of the Fourteenth Amendment in *Harper v. Virginia,* 383 U.S. 663 (1966). Prior to this decision, if a citizen had not paid the poll tax, he or she could not vote. If a person were not on the voting rolls, there was a virtual certainty that a call to jury service would not be forthcoming, since jury service was often based on being listed as a voter.

45. *South Carolina v. Katzenbach,* 383 U.S. 301 (1966).

46. *Oregon v. Mitchell,* 400 U.S. 112 (1970).

47. One key man system in Tennessee involved three jury commissioners who compiled a list of qualified potential jurors from which the actual grand jurors were selected at random. The Tennessee judge having criminal jurisdiction made all appointments of forepersons for the county grand juries. See *Rose v. Mitchell,* 443 U.S. 545 n.2 (1979). A key man system formerly followed in Texas allowed a state judge to appoint three to five jury commissioners who selected persons for jury duty who were believed to have a sound mind and who were of good moral character. But these key man systems did not always select from a fair cross section of the community. See *Castaneda v. Partida,* 430 U.S. 482, 484 (1977).

48. *Hernandez v. Texas,* 347 U.S. 475, 479 (1954), and *Castaneda v. Partida,* 430 U.S. 482, 484 (1977).

49. 100 U.S. 303 (1880).

50. 545 U.S. 231 (2005).

51. *J.E.B. v. Alabama ex rel. T.B,* 511 U.S. 127, 140 (1994).

52. The equal protection clause of the Fourteenth Amendment does not appear in the Fifth Amendment; the requirement of equal protection is deemed to be included within the Fifth Amendment's Due Process Clause.

53. *Swain v. Alabama,* 380 U.S. 202 (1965).

54. 476 U.S. 79 (1986).

55. Voir dire of the jury occurs when the judge asks questions of the prospective jurors concerning bias, interest, or prejudice in their beliefs. In some jurisdictions, the court asks the questions posed by the attorneys, and some jurisdictions allow the attorneys to do the questioning of the potential jurors. The word *venire* refers to the whole body of citizens summoned by the sheriff under an old writ called *venire facias* that directed the sheriff to summon qualified citizens of the jurisdiction to serve as jurors. The modern term *jury venire* refers similarly to the body composed of citizens qualified to serve as petit (trial) or grand jurors.

56. *Connecticut v. Morales,* 71 Conn. App. 790, 804 A.2d 902, 2002 Conn. App. LEXIS 453, n.17 (2002).

57. In many cases, the defendant may face significant hurdles in proving that the prospective jurors removed actually possessed a particular racial identity or racial-ethnic identity. In *Collado v. Miller,* 157 F. Supp. 2d 227, 233; 2001 U.S. LEXIS 11788 (2001), the court noted that the defendant failed to show that challenged prospective jurors with Hispanic-sounding surnames were, in fact, Hispanic at all, or whether they simply carried Hispanic-sounding surnames with some different ethnic identity.

58. 795 So.2d 468; 2001 La. App. LEXIS 1938 (2001).

59. 546 U.S. 333 (2006).

60. 499 U.S. 400 (1991).

61. 505 U.S. 42 (1992).

62. In the interests of ensuring a fair trial, consistent with due process and equal protection, a white criminal defendant has the right to challenge state discrimination against African Americans in the selection of a grand jury foreman. In *Campbell v. Louisiana,* 523 U.S. 392 (1998), the court concluded that any accused suffers an "injury in fact" when a grand jury's composition has been tainted by racial discrimination. This theory applies equally to trial jury composition.

63. 511 U.S. 127 (1994).
64. 100 U.S. 303, 305 (1880). While *Strauder v. West Virginia* was a criminal case and *J.E.B. v. Alabama ex rel. T.B.* was a civil matter with criminal enforcement overtones, the prohibition against gender discrimination was not limited by the Court to civil cases; the decision was all-encompassing.
65. 372 U.S. 335 (1963).
66. 407 U.S. 25 (1972).
67. 440 U.S. 367 (1979).
68. See *Baldasar v. Illinois,* 446 U.S. 222 (1980).
69. *Strickland v. Washington,* 466 U.S. 668, 687 (1984).
70. Ibid., 689.

Appellate Practice and Other Posttrial Remedies

Learning Objectives

1. Explain that the federal Constitution does not provide any right of appeal in a criminal case.
2. Be able to articulate why, in the interests of fairness and justice, a government should permit appeals of criminal convictions.
3. Develop an understanding of why a state supreme court might choose to hear a particular criminal appeal, and give an example of a case a state supreme court would probably choose to hear.
4. Orally detail how a state criminal case may eventually be heard by the Supreme Court of the United States.

5. State why the Sixth Amendment right to counsel applies only to the first appeal that is given as a matter of legal right and does not apply to subsequent appeals.
6. Explain the requirement that a defendant's trial attorney must properly make objections during the trial in order to preserve the trial record for appeal purposes.
7. Be able to explain and discriminate between the concepts of plain error and harmless error.
8. Describe the options might be available to the prosecution and to the defense following a successful appeal by the adverse party.

Chapter Outline

Key Terms

Collateral attack

Federal issue or federal question

Indigent right to appellate counsel

Indigent right to transcript

Notice of appeal

Plain error rule

Reversible error

Right to appeal

Writ of certiorari

Writ of habeas corpus

1. THE RIGHT TO APPEAL

[T]he right of review in an appellate court is purely a matter of state concern.
McKane v. Durston, 153 U.S. 684, 688 (1894)

To the present time, the Constitution of the United States imposes no duty and fails to require any state to provide appellate review of any criminal conviction. Although the right to appeal from a verdict rendered in a criminal trial would seem to be one of those constitutional rights found deeply embedded in the Due Process Clause of the Fifth or the Fourteenth Amendments, a federal constitutional right to a criminal appeal does not exist.[1] Justice Scalia, concurring in an earlier case,[2] stated, "Since a State could, as far as the federal Constitution is concerned, subject its trial court determinations to no review whatever, it could *a fortiori* subject them to review which consists of a nonadversarial reexamination of convictions by a panel of government experts." The source for Justice Scalia's view on appellate rights comes from the language in an old case, which noted, "[T]he right of review in an appellate court is purely a matter of state concern."[3] From the perspective of the United States Supreme Court, states would not have to give any review to criminal case determinations but have chosen to do so as a matter of state constitution,[4] state law, or state court decision.

Although a state is not required by the federal Constitution to grant any right of appeal from a trial court, all states permit at least one appeal from an initial court judgment. However, states do not and are not required to automatically allow appeals from an intermediate court of appeal to the top state court.[5] Justice Ginsburg recently reaffirmed the Court's position when he noted that states need not appoint counsel to aid an indigent person in discretionary appeals to a state's supreme court or to the Supreme Court of the United States.[6] In allowing at least one appeal, states may not condition this appeal in such a manner that the possibility or opportunity of a meaningful appeal depends upon the wealth of the appellant. As the Supreme Court of the United States once noted, "There is no meaningful distinction between a rule which would deny the poor the right to defend themselves in a trial court and one which effectively denies the poor an adequate appellate review accorded to all who have money enough to pay the costs in advance."[7]

A state's grant of the right to an appeal is not an absolute right and may be forfeited if a convicted defendant fails to appear for sentencing or escapes following a guilty verdict. Where a defendant has skipped bail after conviction or has intentionally not appeared as ordered for sentencing, at least one jurisdiction applies the "escape rule."[8] Under the escape rule theory, the right of appeal on the merits is ended, and trial and appellate courts will not hear any postconviction motions. The escape rule limiting appeal and other relief applies only to errors that occurred prior to and up to the time of escape and do not include errors after the defendant's return to custody. The forfeiture of the right to appeal does not depend on the length of time that the convicted defendant has been absent from justice, whether it is fifteen days or more than ten years.[9]

The primary rationale for allowing appeals following a conviction is the desire to correct errors or unfairness that may have improperly influenced the court verdict. Although both prosecution and defense attorneys are obligated by their oaths taken upon bar admission to support the United States Constitution and laws and to support and defend their respective state constitutions and state laws, it is unlikely that every law and rule has been properly applied and enforced in every criminal trial. Errors in procedure and practice, in admission and exclusion of evidence, in impeachment and cross-examination, in jury selection and exclusion, in the opening and closing statements, and in a variety of other areas create a virtual certainty that no criminal trial will be error-free. Some errors are so inconsequential that their effect on a verdict is minimal, but others may affect the outcome of a trial. Where a defendant can demonstrate a significant error to an appellate court, a reversal of the conviction may be the proper judicial remedy.

The zealous urge to prevail in a criminal case may prompt a defense counsel or a prosecutor to pursue a course of action that is, in the legal sense, erroneous. Some of these problems are of a minor order of magnitude, and when considering the whole body of evidence in a criminal case, the error is not of great concern to either party. Such small errors are not deemed to have created any lasting effect on the trial or any substantial influence on the overall outcome. In contrast, some errors have such a tremendous effect on the direction and outcome of a trial that it becomes impossible to say what the outcome of the case would have been without the error. The prosecutor and the defense counsel probably will have different opinions about which errors have affected the outcome of a criminal case. One way to test the effect of a legal or constitutional mistake on a trial is taking the case to an appellate court and allowing a panel of judges to review it. Upon careful consideration of the appellant's briefs and oral argument by the parties, an appellate court renders an opinion on whether the alleged errors require reversal of the conviction.

2. THE APPEAL PROCESS: GENERALLY

The courts in most states have a process for appeal that takes the case from the trial court to an intermediate court of appeal as a matter of statutory right, with the possibility of having the top court in the state hear the case, at its discretion. The move from the trial court to the court of appeal occurs as a matter of legal right because a court of appeal generally has no discretion concerning whether to hear a case. If the outcome is not favorable to the defendant in the court of appeal, additional litigation is possible within that state court system. Though theoretically it is possible to get a case to a state supreme court, in most instances the top state courts have the right to choose the cases they wish to hear.[10] A state supreme court may exercise its discretion to consider a case that has important public policy or legal ramifications. Where two separate courts of appeal within the same state have decided similar issues that have resulted in divergent and incompatible legal theories, a state supreme court, in the exercise of its discretion, may decide to take such a case to resolve the conflict between the lower courts of appeal. If a case contains a legal theory that has been decided in a way that is inconsistent with an earlier state supreme court decision, the state's high court may take the case and use it as a vehicle to revisit the issue or to adopt the new view offered by the lower court.

3. THE FIRST APPEAL: THE COURT OF APPEALS

The appellate procedure usually requires the aggrieved defendant to file a notice of appeal within a set period of time following the entry of the verdict. A failure to file the notice of appeal may preclude a higher court from considering the case. Subsequent to the notice of appeal, the defense attorney consults the trial transcript and conducts legal research covering the disputed areas of law, which is incorporated within a legal brief presented to the appellate court and served on the prosecutor. In a similar manner, legal research and writing result in a brief in which the prosecutor's office presents its view of the legal merits of the case. In some cases, the attorneys for both sides simply submit the legal briefs and allow the appellate court to render its decision based on the briefs in the absence of oral argument. More typically, each side may determine that the best chance to prevail involves personally addressing the judges and putting the best face possible on the case.

Once the appellate judges have read the briefs and listened to and participated in oral arguments, they take the case under advisement and, in due course, render a decision. Appellate decisions may take several directions. Perhaps the most common resolution in criminal cases is that the trial court decision is upheld and the conviction stands. The conviction also could be reversed, with directions to the trial court to dismiss the case and allow the defendant to walk free. The defendant's conviction could be reversed, and the appellate court could order a retrial of the case. In many jurisdictions, an appellate court has the power to reduce the level of offense and to enter a conviction for a lesser included offense that the court considers appropriate under the circumstances.

4. THE APPELLATE ROLE OF A STATE SUPREME COURT

When the appellate court has rendered its decision, the prosecution and defense are faced with some hard decisions. If the appellate court has rendered a verdict in the defendant's favor and has ordered a retrial or some other disposition, the attorneys for the government may request that the supreme court of the state consider hearing the case. As a general rule, state supreme courts have almost total discretion over which cases they take. While there may be some cases under state law that state supreme courts must hear, criminal appeals do not normally fit into this category. Upon careful analysis of the appellate court decision, a prosecutor's office may conclude that its best efforts should be directed toward a retrial because the legal conclusions may predict a lack of success at the state supreme court level. If the appellate court has upheld the conviction of the defendant, few options realistically remain. The defense attorney may suggest that the case be appealed to the state supreme court, realizing that there is only a small possibility that the top court will take the case. The appeal to a state supreme court may be a necessary prerequisite prior to filing a habeas corpus petition in the state or federal court system. For this reason, even though success in the supreme court may be only a distant hope, the attempt to obtain a hearing in a state supreme court may pave the way for appellate litigation in other courts.

If either party has proven successful in getting a review by the state's supreme court, each side prepares a revised brief that targets the latest legal theories on the issues and prepares for oral arguments in front of the high court. A process similar to that followed in the intermediate court of appeal is repeated at the supreme court level. Each attorney tries to convince the court that his or her position is the most logical, reasonable, and intelligent resolution of the legal issues. While the decision rendered by a state supreme court is probably the final resolution of the criminal case, either party may request a rehearing by the top court. Actually obtaining a rehearing, however, remains a remote possibility.

5. SUPREME COURT OF THE UNITED STATES: ONLY A POTENTIAL FOR REVIEW

A relatively small number of state supreme court decisions are successfully appealed to the Supreme Court of the United States, which, like state supreme courts, generally has control concerning whether to hear a particular case. Consistent with the Supreme Court's discretion in accepting cases, Rule 10 of the Rules of the Supreme Court states, "Review on a writ of certiorari is not a matter of right, but of judicial discretion. A petition for a writ of certiorari will be granted only for compelling reasons."[11] If the United States Supreme Court deems a case sufficiently important, the case involves a federal question, and four justices vote to hear it, the Court grants a writ of certiorari. The Court is more likely to hear a case in which a state supreme court has decided a federal question in a manner that is in conflict with another top state court or a case in which a state court has decided an important federal issue that should be settled by the Supreme Court of the United States.[12] Because the Supreme Court has no power to interpret state law or to reconsider the conclusions of fact based on what was presented at a state trial court, the Court must restrict its selection of cases and its decisions to cases involving federal questions. For that reason, to invoke the jurisdiction of the Court, litigants often contend that some federal right belonging to a defendant has been violated by the state government in bringing the case to trial and pursuing the criminal suit.

6. APPELLATE ASSISTANCE TO THE DEFENDANT: THE RIGHT TO COUNSEL

The Sixth Amendment guarantees that a person accused of a crime has the right to the assistance of counsel. Although this right is often thought to be primarily a right to counsel at trial, it has been extended to a variety of other situations. Assistance of counsel is available to the person undergoing custodial interrogation,[13] to a person in a postindictment or postinformation lineup,[14] and to a defendant involved in a preliminary hearing,[15] among other times. However, it is at the trial when assistance of counsel proves the most meaningful and its absence is so devastating.[16] The value of appeal counsel to a defendant is almost the same as the importance of trial counsel because the pursuit of an appeal requires careful legal maneuvering and contending with arcane procedural paths to obtain meaningful appellate review.

In *Douglas v. California* (Case 14.1),[17] a California trial court convicted the petitioners of thirteen felonies, including robbery and attempted murder. Douglas and his friend, both indigents, had rejected the assistance of counsel at their trial because they believed that the attorney was not properly prepared for trial. However, their preparation and performance in court as their own attorneys also proved to be inadequate, since they were convicted on all charges. At the time, California law allowed appeals by indigents but first required an appellate court to look over the trial record to preliminarily consider the merits of the appeal. If the appellate court determined that it would be an advantage to a defendant to have appellate counsel, it would appoint such counsel but otherwise deny the assistance of counsel for appellate purposes. In Douglas' case, the appellate court conducted the review and concluded that an appointed counsel for the appeal would not benefit the defendant or the court. A person in Douglas' position would be able to pursue an appeal so long as he possessed sufficient financial resources to afford an attorney. Because Douglas possessed no money, and the appellate court screened his case away, he had no avenue to make his one statutory appeal effective.

The Supreme Court considered the *Douglas* case with reference to an earlier one in which the kind of an appeal depended on the amount of money a person had. In *Griffin v. Illinois,* the Court observed that there could be no justice where justice depended on the amount of money a person possessed and held that a state may not grant appellate review in a way that discriminates against convicted defendants on account of their poverty.[18] In Douglas' case, the type of appeal he would have received would have been based on his ability to pay for private legal counsel, in the absence of a court determination on preliminary merits of the case. If he could have afforded legal counsel for appeal, he could have obtained the same appellate scrutiny as any other person. The Supreme Court found in favor of Douglas' argument that he should have a right to free counsel for his first appeal granted as a matter of right. Thus, an indigent defendant must be granted free assistance of counsel for the initial appeal. For Douglas and for future defendants, this decision assured a modicum of equality among the class of individuals who pursue criminal appeals.

The *Douglas* Court was not very clear in stating the constitutional basis of its decision. In *Ross v. Moffitt,* 417 U.S. 600 (1974) (see Case 14.3), Justice Rehnquist attempted to offer an explanation concerning the basis for the *Douglas v. California* decision:

> The precise rationale for the *Griffin* and *Douglas* lines of cases has never been explicitly stated, some support being derived from the Equal Protection Clause of the Fourteenth Amendment, and some from the Due Process Clause of that Amendment. Neither Clause, by itself, provides an entirely satisfactory basis for the result reached, each depending on a different inquiry which emphasizes different

CASE 14.1

Leading Case Brief: An Indigent Must Receive Free Appellate Legal Counsel for the First Appeal

Douglas v. California
Supreme Court of the United States
372 U.S. 353 (1963)

Case Facts:

Following the filing of a thirteen-count information, which included robbery, assault with a deadly weapon, and assault with intent to commit murder against defendants Douglas and Meyes, the defendant-petitioners were tried together and convicted on all counts. Prior to the trial, the single public defender appointed as counsel to represent both defendants requested a continuance so that separate counsel could be appointed. The trial court denied the motion, and petitioners dismissed the defender, claiming he was unprepared, and again renewed motions for separate counsel and for a continuance. Subsequent to the conviction, petitioners requested, and were denied, the assistance of counsel on appeal, even though they were indigents. Under the California procedure at that time, the District Court of Appeal reviewed the record of the trial and came to the conclusion that the appeal was not meritorious and therefore refused to appoint appellate counsel. Although they pursued their appeal in the absence of an attorney, the appeal was heard without assistance of counsel, and their convictions were affirmed. The Supreme Court of California denied a discretionary review and the Supreme Court of the United States granted a writ of certiorari.

Legal Issue:

Where the merits of the one appeal that an indigent legally possesses have been decided without the benefit of legal counsel and the fact of indigency was the only reason for lack of counsel, has there been a violation of the Sixth Amendment right to counsel as applied to the states through the Due Process Clause of the Fourteenth Amendment?

The Court's Ruling:

After hearing the arguments, the Supreme Court decided that where the quality and presentation of an indigent defendant's first appeal depends on the ability to afford appellate legal counsel, an unconstitutional line has been drawn between the poor and the rich person. With considerations of due process, indigent appellants must be granted free legal counsel for the first appeal that is granted to every convicted person.

Essence of the Court's Rationale:

* * *

[T]he type of an appeal a person is afforded in the District Court of Appeal hinges upon whether or not he can pay for the assistance of counsel. If he can, the appellate court passes on the merits of his case only after having the full benefit of written briefs and oral argument by counsel. If he cannot, the appellate court is forced to prejudge the merits before it can even determine whether counsel should be provided. At this stage in the proceedings, only the barren record speaks for the indigent, and, unless the printed pages show that an injustice has been committed, he is forced to go without a champion on appeal. Any real chance he may have had of showing that his appeal has hidden merit is deprived him when the court decides on an ex parte examination of the record that the assistance of counsel is not required.

* * *

[W]here the merits of the one and only appeal an indigent has as of right are decided without benefit of counsel, we think an unconstitutional line has been drawn between rich and poor.

(continued)

When an indigent is forced to run this gauntlet of a preliminary showing of merit, the right to appeal does not comport with fair procedure. In the federal courts, on the other hand, an indigent must be afforded counsel on appeal whenever he challenges a certification that the appeal is not taken in good faith. *Johnson v. United States,* 352 U.S. 565. The federal courts must honor his request for counsel regardless of what they think the merits of the case may be; and "representation in the role of an advocate is required." *Ellis v. United States,* 356 U.S. 674. In California, however, once the court has "gone through" the record and denied counsel, the indigent has no recourse but to prosecute his appeal on his own, as best he can, no matter how meritorious his case may turn out to be. The present case, where counsel was denied petitioners on appeal, shows that the discrimination is not between "possibly good and obviously bad cases," but between cases where the rich man can require the court to listen to argument of counsel before deciding on the merits, but a poor man cannot. There is lacking that equality demanded by the Fourteenth Amendment where the rich man, who appeals as of right, enjoys the benefit of counsel's examination into the record, research of the law, and marshalling of arguments on his behalf, while the indigent, already burdened by a preliminary determination that his case is without merit, is forced to shift for himself. The indigent, where the record is unclear or the errors are hidden, has only the right to a meaningless ritual, while the rich man has a meaningful appeal.

We vacate the judgment of the District Court of Appeal and remand the case to that court for further proceedings not inconsistent with this opinion.

Case Importance:

Due process demands that where a state permits an appeal of a criminal conviction and where a fair and meaningful appeal requires the guiding hand of appellate counsel, a state must provide an attorney for the first level of appeal.

factors. "Due process" emphasizes fairness between the State and the individual dealing with the State, regardless of how other individuals in the same situation may be treated. "Equal protection," on the other hand, emphasizes disparity in treatment by a State between classes of individuals whose situations are arguably indistinguishable. *Moffit* at 608–609

In an effort to meet the requirements of *Douglas v. California,* the California procedure adapted to the revised requirements for granting a meaningful appeal to those of indigent status. In *Anders v. California,* 386 U.S. 738 (1967), the court-appointed appellate counsel had a copy of the trial transcript but refused to write a formal brief or otherwise pursue the appeal. After looking over the transcript, the appellate attorney concluded that there was no merit to the case. The attorney filed a "no merit" notice with the court of appeal. The court examined the record and affirmed the judgment of conviction. On a petition for a writ of habeas corpus, which Anders filed six years later, the court found the appeal lacked any merit. Upon appeal of the rejection of the writ, the California Supreme Court dismissed the habeas corpus application. Anders appealed to the Supreme Court of the United States, which reversed the California court result. The *Anders* Court suggested the following procedure, which, if followed, would meet the requirements of due process:

The constitutional requirement of substantial equality and fair process can only be attained where counsel acts in the role of an active advocate in behalf of his client, as opposed to that of *amicus curiae.* The "no merit" letter and the procedure it triggers do not reach that dignity. Counsel should, and can with honor and without conflict, be of more assistance to his client and to the court. His role as advocate requires that he support his client's appeal to the best of his ability. Of course, if counsel finds his case to be wholly frivolous after a conscientious examination of it, he should so advise the court and request permission to withdraw. That request must, however, be accompanied by a brief referring to anything in the record that might arguably support the appeal. A copy of counsel's brief should be furnished the indigent, and time allowed him to raise any points that he chooses; the court—not counsel—then proceeds, after a full examination of all the proceedings, to decide whether the case is wholly frivolous. If it so finds, it may grant counsel's request to withdraw and dismiss the appeal insofar as federal requirements are concerned, or proceed to a decision on the merits, if state law so requires. On the other hand, if it finds any of the legal points arguable on their merits (and therefore not frivolous), it must, prior to decision, afford the indigent the assistance of counsel to argue the appeal. *Anders* at 744

Despite the precedent of the *Douglas* case *and* the suggestions contained in the *Anders* case, the strength of a defendant's appeal may still have some relationship to the financial well-being of a defendant but still pass constitutional muster. In *Smith v. Robbins,* 528 U.S. 259 (2000), the Supreme Court approved a California process in which the appellate attorney for the defendant evaluates the merits and grounds for an indigent's appeal (Case 14.2). If the attorney finds strong grounds for the appeal, the appellate process continues along the typical path. However, if the facts of the case are less promising from an appellate perspective, California permits a reduced level of appellate advocacy. Where the attorney determines that the appeal possesses no meritorious legal basis, he or she files a brief with the appellate court attesting that no appealable issues exist. In contrast, a person who could afford a privately retained attorney would be able to have the case briefed and heard by the court of appeals on its merits, rather than having an attorney merely look over the record and potentially determine that no real meritorious appealable issues exist. According to the *Robbins* Court, the indigent appellate procedure does not have to be followed exactly as prior cases had proposed it should. The Court noted that proper appellate procedure was a "prophylactic framework" that it had established in *Douglas v. California* and later cases and was not to be viewed as a constitutional straitjacket. The states were permitted wide latitude in administering appellate procedures for indigents, subject to minimum standards of due process under the Fourteenth Amendment.

States may choose to terminate additional assistance of counsel for indigents following the one appeal granted as a matter of right by state laws or constitutions. The federal constitution does not prohibit continued indigent legal assistance following the first appeal, but it does not mandate a state to continue to expend scarce state resources in funding any and all postconviction appeals that a convicted defendant might desire. In *Ross v. Moffitt,* 417 U.S. 600 (1974), an indigent wanted court-appointed appellate counsel to assist him in his discretionary appeals beyond the first level (Case 14.3). In rejecting the argument favoring court-appointed counsel for discretionary appeals, Justice Rehnquist noted that the appellate level is significantly different from the trial level because the defendant has actually been convicted of a crime, stripped of the presumption of innocence, and had one appeal as a matter of right. Under either the Due Process Clause or Equal Protection Clause of the Fourteenth Amendment,

CASE 14.2

Leading Case Brief: States May Develop Screening Procedures to Eliminate Completely Frivolous Indigent First Appeals

Smith v. Robbins
Supreme Court of the United States
528 U.S. 259 (2000)

Case Facts:

A state court jury in California convicted Lee Robbins of second-degree murder. Upon appeal, the court appointed counsel, who, after looking at all the material, concluded that appeal would be frivolous and of no merit. The attorney filed a brief with the state court of appeal, which complied with the appellate procedure developed to meet constitutional dictates emanating from *Anders v. California*, 386 U.S. 738 (1967). The new procedure, established in *People v. Wende*, 25 Cal.3d 436 (1979), allowed an appellate attorney, if the attorney concluded that a case had no merit, to file a brief with the appellate court that summarizes the procedural and factual history of the case, with citations of the record. He also attests that he has reviewed the record, explained his evaluation of the case to his client, provided the client with a copy of the brief, and informed the client of his right to file a pro se supplemental brief. He further requests that the court independently examine the record for arguable issues. Unlike under the *Anders* procedure, counsel following *Wende* neither explicitly states that his review has led him to conclude that an appeal would be frivolous (although that is considered implicit, see *Wende*, 25 Cal.3d at 441–442, 600 P.2d at 1075) nor requests leave to withdraw. Instead, he is silent on the merits of the case and expresses his availability to brief any issues on which the court might desire briefing.

The procedure was followed in Robbins' case, and the court of appeal agreed with the attorney's evaluation of the case that no arguable issues remained in the case. The court of appeal even considered two issues Robbins personally raised in a supplementary filing and denied Robbins' petition.

After Robbins exhausted his direct postconviction remedies, he filed a petition for a writ of habeas corpus in the appropriate federal district court. Robbins alleged that he had been denied the effective assistance of appellate counsel because his lawyer's brief to the court of appeal failed to comply with the suggestions in *Anders v. California* for cases where the attorney found no merit in the appeal. According to the district court, if an issue might arguably have supported an appeal, it should have been included in the brief and since it was not, the district court concluded that a writ of habeas corpus should have been issued because the deviation in delivery of legal services amounted to deficient performance by counsel. The Ninth Circuit Court of Appeal agreed with the district and concluded that the brief filed by the appellate attorney was deficient because it did not, as the *Anders* procedure required, identify any legal issues that arguably could have supported the appeal. The Supreme Court of the United States granted certiorari.

Legal Issue:

Must states, while ensuring due process and adequate appellate equality between indigent litigants and wealthier persons, follow exactly the suggestion of *Anders v. California*, 386 U.S. 738 (1967)?

The Court's Ruling:

A state need not require a court-appointed indigent's attorney to formally file an appellate brief containing legally unsupportable issues. So long as a state provides a method to address appellate issues that have merit, the state's indigent appellate process will meet the requirements of due process under the Fourteenth Amendment.

Essence of the Court's Rationale:

II

A

In *Anders,* we reviewed an earlier California procedure for handling appeals by convicted indigents. Pursuant to that procedure, Anders' appointed appellate counsel had filed a letter stating that he had concluded that there was "no merit to the appeal," *Anders,* 386 U.S. at 739–740. Anders, in response, sought new counsel; the State Court of Appeal denied the request, and Anders filed a *pro se* appellate brief. That court then issued an opinion that reviewed the four claims in his *pro se* brief and affirmed, finding no error (or no prejudicial error). *People v. Anders,* 167 Cal.App.2d 65, 333 P.2d 854 (1959). Anders thereafter sought a writ of *habeas corpus* from the State Court of Appeal, which denied relief, explaining that it had again reviewed the record and had found the appeal to be "'without merit.'" *Anders,* 386 U.S. at 740 (quoting unreported memorandum opinion).

We held that "California's action does not comport with fair procedure and lacks that equality that is required by the Fourteenth Amendment." *Id.* at 741. We placed the case within a line of precedent beginning with *Griffin v. Illinois,* 351 U.S. 12 (1956), and continuing with Douglas, *supra,* that imposed constitutional constraints on States when they choose to create appellate review. In finding the California procedure to have breached these constraints, we compared it to other procedures we had found invalid and to statutory requirements in the federal courts governing appeals by indigents with appointed counsel. We relied in particular on *Ellis v. United States,* 356 U.S. 674 (1958) *(per curiam),* a case involving federal statutory requirements, and quoted the following passage from it:

> "If counsel is convinced, after conscientious investigation, that the appeal is frivolous, of course, he may ask to withdraw on that account. If the court is satisfied that counsel has diligently investigated the possible grounds of appeal, and agrees with counsel's evaluation of the case, then leave to withdraw may be allowed and leave to appeal may be denied." *Anders, supra,* at 741–742 (quoting *Ellis, supra,* at 675).

In *Anders,* neither counsel, the state appellate court on direct appeal, nor the state *habeas* courts had made any finding of frivolity. We concluded that a finding that the appeal had "no merit" was not adequate, because it did not mean that the appeal was so lacking in prospects as to be "frivolous":

> We cannot say that there was a finding of frivolity by either of the California courts or that counsel acted in any greater capacity than merely as amicus curiae which was condemned in *Ellis.* 386 U.S. at 743.

* * *

[A]ny view of the procedure we described in the last section of *Anders* that converted it from a suggestion into a straitjacket would contravene our established practice, rooted in federalism, of allowing the States wide discretion, subject to the minimum requirements of the Fourteenth Amendment, to experiment with solutions to difficult problems of policy. In *Griffin v. Illinois,* 351 U.S. 12 (1956), which we invoked as the foundational case for our holding in *Anders,* see *Anders,* 386 U.S. at 741, we expressly disclaimed any pretensions to rulemaking authority for the States in the area of indigent criminal appeals. We imposed no broad rule or procedure, but merely held unconstitutional Illinois' requirement that indigents pay a fee to receive a trial transcript that was essential for bringing an appeal.

* * *

III

Having determined that California's *Wende* procedure is not unconstitutional merely because it diverges from the *Anders* procedure, we turn to consider the *Wende* procedure on its own merits. We think it clear that California's system does not violate the Fourteenth Amendment, for it provides "a criminal appellant pursuing a first appeal as of right [the] minimum safeguards necessary to make that appeal 'adequate and effective,'" *Evitts v. Lucey,* 469 U.S. 387, 392 (1985) (quoting *Griffin,* 351 U.S. at 20 (plurality opinion)).

* * *

In determining whether a particular state procedure satisfies this standard, it is important to focus on the underlying goals that the procedure should serve—to ensure that those indigents whose appeals are not frivolous receive the counsel and merits brief required by *Douglas,* and also to enable the State to "protect

(continued)

itself so that frivolous appeals are not subsidized and public moneys not needlessly spent," *Griffin, supra,* at 24 (Frankfurter, J., concurring in judgment). For, although, under *Douglas,* indigents generally have a right to counsel on a first appeal as of right, it is equally true that this right does not include the right to bring a frivolous appeal and, concomitantly, does not include the right to counsel for bringing a frivolous appeal.

* * *

Since Robbins' counsel complied with a valid procedure for determining when an indigent's direct appeal is frivolous, we reverse the Ninth Circuit's judgment that the *Wende* procedure fails adequately to serve the constitutional principles we identified in *Anders.* But our reversal does not necessarily mean that Robbins' claim that his appellate counsel rendered constitutionally ineffective assistance fails. For it may be, as Robbins argues, that his appeal was not

frivolous and that he was thus entitled to a merits brief rather than to a *Wende* brief.

* * *

The judgment of the Court of Appeals is reversed, and the case is remanded for further proceedings consistent with this opinion.

* * *

Case Importance:

Indigents will be able to pursue meaningful appeals with the assistance of appointed counsel but will not be permitted to file appeals that have absolutely no merit in law. The Court balanced the need for indigents to have attorneys for appeal purposes against the need for a state to conserve scarce financial resources in a manner that justice should be served.

the fact that a defendant wants to pursue additional litigation at the appellate level does not require a state to provide counsel for every legal maneuver a defendant might wish to pursue.

7. APPELLATE ASSISTANCE TO THE DEFENDANT: THE INDIGENT'S RIGHT TO A TRANSCRIPT

Essential to prosecuting a criminal appeal, besides the assistance of counsel, is the ability to get an appellate court to hear a defendant's case. The process of getting a criminal appeal in front of an appellate court involves more than just giving the notice of appeal. Appellate briefs that clearly state the legal reasons the defendant thinks the case should be reversed need to be prepared and served on the opposing counsel and transmitted to the court of appeals. The cost of an appeal varies with the complexity of the criminal case, the legal issues involved, the length of the original criminal trial, and to some extent, the jurisdiction.

In *Griffin v. Illinois,*[19] state law gave defendants a right to an appeal, but a full, direct appellate review could be obtained only by furnishing the appellate court with a report of the trial proceedings, certified by the trial judge. These documents were considered difficult to prepare without an expensive stenographic transcript of the trial proceedings. Because Griffin had no funds with which to purchase a transcript, he filed a motion in the trial court that a certified copy of the entire record, including a stenographic transcript of the proceedings, be furnished to him without cost. When the State of Illinois refused to furnish the trial transcripts, Griffin initiated a suit to force the state to pay for the transcript. When the case reached the United States Supreme Court, the Court expressed some concern that the only reason full appellate

CASE 14.3

Leading Case Brief: Due Process Does Not Require States to Fund Indigent Appeals Beyond the First Posttrial Appeal

Ross v. Moffitt
Supreme Court of the United States
417 U.S. 600 (1974)

Case Facts:

Pursuant to an indictment that charged Claude Frank Moffitt with two counts of forgery and with uttering, a North Carolina trial court convicted him on the charges. Moffitt had the benefit of legal counsel for his first appeal. In one case, involving a discretionary appeal, Moffitt wanted to appeal to the Supreme Court of North Carolina but was denied the assistance of a free attorney. In the other case, the North Carolina courts appointed counsel to prepare for an appeal to the Supreme Court of North Carolina. When Moffitt desired that counsel be appointed for an appeal to the Supreme Court of the United States, the North Carolina courts refused. In arguing for the right to free counsel as an indigent, Moffitt contended that the due process clause of the Fourteenth Amendment required that the state of North Carolina provide him with legal counsel for his appellate litigation. North Carolina courts rejected his contention, and he perfected his appeal to the Supreme Court of United States. When he pursued litigation in the federal court system, he had some initial success in the district courts, but the Fourth Circuit, 483 F.2d at 654, reversed portions of the federal district decision and remanded the case back to the lower courts. The Supreme Court granted Moffitt's request for certiorari.

Legal Issue:

In a state criminal proceeding, does due process require a state to furnish free legal counsel to indigent criminal appellants to pursue appeals beyond the initial appeal following trial?

The Court's Ruling:

The Justices determined that due process and fundamental fairness do not dictate that free counsel be given to indigent defendants because a state is not obligated to give any convicted defendant any appeal.

Essence of the Court's Rationale:

* * *

II

This Court, in the past 20 years, has given extensive consideration to the rights of indigent persons on appeal. In *Griffin v. Illinois,* 351 U.S. 12 (1956), the first of the pertinent cases, the Court had before it an Illinois rule allowing a convicted criminal defendant to present claims of trial error to the Supreme Court of Illinois only if he procured a transcript of the testimony adduced at his trial. No exception was made for the indigent defendant, and thus one who was unable to pay the cost of obtaining such a transcript was precluded from obtaining appellate review of asserted trial error. Mr. Justice Frankfurter, who cast the deciding vote, said in his concurring opinion:

> . . . Illinois has decreed that only defendants who can afford to pay for the stenographic minutes of a trial may have trial errors reviewed on appeal by the Illinois Supreme Court. *Id.* at 22.

The Court in *Griffin* held that this discrimination violated the Fourteenth Amendment.

Succeeding cases invalidated similar financial barriers to the appellate process, at the same time reaffirming the traditional principle that a State is not obliged to provide any appeal at all for criminal defendants. *McKane v. Durston,* 153 U.S. 684 (1894).

(continued)

***

The decisions discussed above stand for the proposition that a State cannot arbitrarily cut off appeal rights for indigents while leaving open avenues of appeal for more affluent persons. In *Douglas v. California,* 372 U.S. 353 (1963), however, a case decided the same day as *Lane, supra,* and *Draper, supra,* the Court departed somewhat from the limited doctrine of the transcript and fee cases and undertook an examination of whether an indigent's access to the appellate system was adequate. The Court in *Douglas* concluded that a State does not fulfill its responsibility toward indigent defendants merely by waiving its own requirements that a convicted defendant procure a transcript or pay a fee in order to appeal, and held that the State must go further and provide counsel for the indigent on his first appeal as of right. It is this decision we are asked to extend today.

This Court held unconstitutional California's requirement that counsel on appeal would be appointed for an indigent only if the appellate court determined that such appointment would be helpful to the defendant or to the court itself. The Court noted that, under this system, an indigent's case was initially reviewed on the merits, without the benefit of any organization or argument by counsel. By contrast, persons of greater means were not faced with the preliminary "ex parte examination of the record," *id.* at 356, but had their arguments presented to the court in fully briefed form. The Court noted, however, that its decision extended only to initial appeals as of right. . . .

***

We do not believe that the Due Process Clause requires North Carolina to provide respondent with counsel on his discretionary appeal to the State Supreme Court. At the trial stage of a criminal proceeding, the right of an indigent defendant to counsel is fundamental and binding upon the States by virtue of the Sixth and Fourteenth Amendments. *Gideon v. Wainwright,* 372 U.S. 335 (1963). But there are significant differences between the trial and appellate stages of a criminal proceeding.

***

This is not to say, of course, that a skilled lawyer, particularly one trained in the somewhat arcane art of preparing petitions for discretionary review, would not prove helpful to any litigant able to employ him. An indigent defendant seeking review in the Supreme Court of North Carolina is therefore somewhat handicapped in comparison with a wealthy defendant who has counsel assisting him in every conceivable manner at every stage in the proceeding. But both the opportunity to have counsel prepare an initial brief in the Court of Appeals and the nature of discretionary review in the Supreme Court of North Carolina make this relative handicap far less than the handicap borne by the indigent defendant denied counsel on his initial appeal as of right in *Douglas.* And the fact that a particular service might be of benefit to an indigent defendant does not mean that the service is constitutionally required. The duty of the State under our cases is not to duplicate the legal arsenal that may be privately retained by a criminal defendant in a continuing effort to reverse his conviction, but only to assure the indigent defendant an adequate opportunity to present his claims fairly in the context of the State's appellate process. We think respondent was given that opportunity under the existing North Carolina system.

***

The judgment of the Court of Appeals' holding to the contrary is Reversed.

Case Importance:

Prior to *Ross,* settled case law guaranteed free counsel to indigent defendants for all trials where the possibility of incarceration existed. Generally states have chosen to grant free counsel for the first appeal allowed all convicted defendants. Appellants, who desire to litigate beyond the first appeal, and for whom states choose not to provide legal counsel for those subsequent appeals, have not been subjected to a violation of either due process or equal protection. A state does not have to grant free legal counsel to every post-trial remedy that a defendant might desire to pursue.

review was not available to Griffin was because he was too impoverished and that a person in better financial shape would have available a different legal remedy. The *Griffin* Court did not hold that a trial transcript had to be furnished in every case, but it did state that if a transcript was central to pursuing a meaningful appeal, the state was bound to furnish a free transcript.

The philosophy of *Douglas v. California* and of *Griffin v. Illinois* tends to indicate that the first appeal must be provided in a meaningful manner to all defendants, including those who are poor or of modest means, so that the type of justice one receives is not the type of justice that one can afford. These two cases and others involving related but similar issues are not recent decisions, but the Supreme Court of the United States has remained constitutionally sensitive to issues involving wealth that have the effect of denying substantially equal justice.

8. LAYING THE GROUNDWORK FOR AN APPEAL: PRESERVING THE RECORD

During the trial, the defense counsel initiates the groundwork that allows an appeal if one is needed in the event of a conviction. Whenever the opposing side commits an error or the attorney believes that the judge made an erroneous ruling on procedure or on the admission or exclusion of evidence during the trial that is believed to be significant, the defense counsel raises an objection. If the judge does not resolve the objection in favor of the defendant, this objection may become one of the grounds for a subsequent appeal. As potential appealable errors multiply throughout the course of a criminal trial, the trial attorney builds a significant record for appellate purposes. The defense generally is required to raise an objection at the time the alleged error occurs so that the trial judge is made aware of the problem and has a chance to correct it, instead of waiting for an appeal with the hope of a reversal. The court's time and the attorney's time are more beneficially spent correcting errors as they occur, rather than waiting to address the errors during the appellate process and potentially creating the need for a complete new trial.

9. THE PLAIN ERROR RULE: ABILITY TO APPEAL WITHOUT PRESERVING THE RECORD

Even where the defense attorney failed to notice errors committed by the judge, errors by the prosecution, or jury misconduct, some errors may be so egregious and outrageous that an appellate court would consider reversing a case even though they were observed by no one involved in the trial. This theory, known as the plain error rule,[20] is an exception to the general rule that an objection must be made at the trial to preserve the issue for appeal. Under the Federal Rules of Criminal Procedure, a plain error is one that affects substantial rights and may be considered by a reviewing court even where the error was not brought to the attention of the trial court.[21] In explaining how to evaluate plain error, an Alabama court stated that the standard of review under the plain error rule was stricter than in cases when an issue had been properly raised during the trial of the matter and that the plain error argument applied only where the error was particularly outrageous and seriously affected the fairness or integrity of the judicial proceedings.[22]

The best chance for an appellate reversal of a conviction under the plain error rule may exist where breaches of constitutional rights have occurred and where no functionary of the court system took notice during the trial. For example, plain error could be demonstrated where the prosecutor used evidence that clearly had been taken in violation of that defendant's Fourth Amendment rights against illegal searches, and through inadvertence, negligence, or ignorance, the defense counsel made no objection during the trial. Plain error has occurred where a trial court neglected to instruct the jury concerning one of the elements of the crime.[23] The plain error rule could be applied by an appellate court where a prosecutor used a coerced confession, known to the defense trial attorney, without objection. Such a fundamental breach of a constitutional right should trigger an appellate attorney's ability to successfully argue the plain error rule upon appeal. As Justice Brennan, speaking of the plain error rule, stated in dissent in *United States v. Frady:*

> The Rule has been relied upon to correct errors that may have seriously prejudiced a possibly innocent defendant, *see, e.g., United States v. Mann,* 557 F.2d 1211, 1215–1216 (CA5 1977), and errors that severely undermine the integrity of the judicial proceeding, *see, e.g., United States v. Vaughan,* 443 F.2d 92, 94–95 (CA2 1971). The plain error Rule mitigates the harsh impact of the adversarial system, under which the defendant is generally bound by the conduct of his lawyer, by providing relief in exceptional cases despite the lawyer's failure to object at trial. 456 U.S. 152, 180 (1982)

In using the plain error rule to reverse a defendant's conviction of sexual imposition upon his twelve-year-old stepdaughter, an appellate court held that evidence of prior criminal activity involving assault and stalking of adult women was admitted for the limited purpose of showing that defendant had committed other criminal acts and was not properly admissible for any reason.[24] The appellate court noted:

> The testimony relating to accusations of assault and stalking is unrelated in nature to the offense of sexual imposition upon a child. This testimony suggests that Appellant generally engages in violence toward adult females. This is highly inflammatory. The only evidence of Appellant's guilt is the recanted testimony of a child with no attendant physical evidence. Because we cannot say that there is no reasonable possibility that the evidence relating to the 1993 accusations contributed to Appellant's conviction, the trial court's error in its admission is an abuse of discretion and grounds for reversal.

Allowing the evidence to be admitted constituted plain error, even in the absence of any objection. In addition, the trial court committed plain error when it failed to give a limiting instruction that should have directed the jury not to consider the evidence of the prior accusations of adult assault and stalking as constituting any proof of the crime charged, sexual imposition. This type of error was prejudicial, and the admission of evidence denied him his constitutional right to a fair trial and was the basis for reversal under the plain error rule.

By following the principles that support the plain error rule, justice may be done by appellate courts when an attorney for a defendant has allowed an important legal point to pass unnoticed that, but for this theory, could result in substantial injustice.

10. SUBJECT MATTER JURISDICTION: ALWAYS AN APPEALABLE ISSUE

An issue that is always assertable upon appeal concerns the jurisdiction of the original trial court to hear the case. Even when no objection was made at a trial, if later developments indicated that the crime occurred in a different state than the one in which the trial was held, it would become obvious that the trial court had no jurisdiction over the offense or the offender. The issue of jurisdiction over the crime is generally not a waivable defect and can be properly raised upon appeal, even though no one raised the issue at, before, or during the trial.

11. THE APPELLATE PROCESS: MAKING IT WORK

Only final orders and judgments may be appealed by a defendant. Preliminary orders and rulings by a trial judge are not normally appealable, except that the prosecution can appeal orders and rulings in many situations because the prosecution can obtain no retrial if unfair rulings are permitted to stand. As a general rule, a defendant's appeal may be taken only when the criminal conviction has reached a final judgment; prior to that time, an appellate court does not have jurisdiction. For example, in appeals from Ohio trial courts, the appellate court does not have jurisdiction until there has been a plea or verdict, a sentence had been conferred, the judge has signed the judgment entry, and the paperwork exhibits the time stamp of the clerk of court to indicate that the judgment has been entered into the court's journal.[25] Only then does the appellate court have jurisdiction. Similar protocols are required in most jurisdictions to indicate that a final judgment has occurred, from which an appeal may be taken.

Where a criminal appeal from a trial court decision has been briefed and argued before the appellate court, a variety of outcomes are possible when the court arrives at a decision. For the defendant, the best possible resolution is for the appellate court to reverse the trial court decision and remand with instructions to dismiss the case with prejudice.[26]

In most cases, a court of appeals affirms a trial court verdict, a decision that will most likely withstand additional litigation. A court's decision to affirm may be based on a clear view that the prosecution made its case beyond a reasonable doubt and that no substantial error affected the defendant's rights. Even an error that may appear to have a significant influence derogatory to a defendant's case may not cause an appellate court to reverse a conviction where the court deems it to be "harmless error" beyond a reasonable doubt. In *Chapman v. California,* 366 U.S. 18 (1967), where the defendant's Fifth Amendment privilege against self-incrimination had been violated by the prosecution, the Supreme Court reversed the conviction since it could not say beyond a reasonable doubt that the constitutional violation had no effect on the outcome of the case (Case 14.4). However, if there had been little chance that the error affected the outcome of the case, and the result would have been the same even in the absence of the error, the *Chapman* Court would have affirmed the convictions.[27]

CASE 14.4

Leading Case Brief: Constitutional Errors in Criminal Trial May Be Evaluated Using the Harmless Error Standard

Chapman v. California
Supreme Court of the United States
386 U.S. 18 (1967)

Case Facts:

A California trial jury convicted Ruth Chapman of the robbery, kidnapping, and murder of a bartender. In the exercise of her privilege against self-incrimination, Chapman chose not to testify in her defense. The prosecutor offered extensive negative comments on her failure to testify. The constitutional interpretation at the time of the trial permitted the prosecutor to comment upon her failure to testify and allowed the jury to be told that it could draw adverse inferences from her failure to testify. Subsequent to the trial, but before Chapman's case had been considered on appeal by the California Supreme Court, the Supreme Court decided *Griffin v. California*, 380 U.S. 609 (1965), which held as invalid California's constitutional provision and practice of commenting on a defendant's failure to testify, on the ground that it put a penalty on the exercise of a person's right not to be compelled to be a witness against himself, guaranteed by the Fifth Amendment to the United States Constitution and made applicable to the states by the Fourteenth Amendment.

The California Supreme Court agreed that the defendants had been subjected to an unconstitutional violation of rights by the lower court and the prosecutor who tried the case, but the Court refused to reverse Chapman's decision because it invoked the "harmless error rule." The harmless error rule holds that where a constitutional or other error has occurred, the verdict will stand despite the error if the reviewing court can determine that beyond a reasonable doubt, the error was not determinative of the outcome. The Supreme Court of the United States granted certiorari.

Legal Issue:

May a court use harmless error analysis to sustain a conviction where a defendant's federal constitutional rights have been violated?

The Court's Ruling:

The Court determined that not all constitutional errors that occur during a criminal trial are so harmful to a defendant's case that an automatic reversal is constitutionally required. Where the error or errors would not have affected the result in the case, as tested by a beyond a reasonable doubt standard, a reversal of a conviction is not appropriate.

Essence of the Court's Rationale:

* * *

II

We are urged by petitioners to hold that all federal constitutional errors, regardless of the facts and circumstances, must always be deemed harmful. Such a holding, as petitioners correctly point out, would require an automatic reversal of their convictions and make further discussion unnecessary. We decline to adopt any such rule. All 50 States have harmless error statutes or rules, and the United States long ago, through its Congress, established for its courts the rule that judgments shall not be reversed for "errors or defects which do not affect the substantial rights of the parties." 28 U.S.C. § 2111. None of these rules, on its face, distinguishes between federal constitutional errors and errors of state law or federal statutes and rules. All of these rules, state or federal, serve a very useful purpose insofar as they block setting aside convictions for small errors or defects that have little, if any, likelihood of having changed the result of the trial. We conclude that there may be some constitutional errors which, in the setting of a particular case, are so unimportant and insignificant that they may, consistent with the Federal Constitution, be deemed harmless, not requiring the automatic reversal of the conviction.

III

In fashioning a harmless constitutional error rule, we must recognize that harmless error rules can work very unfair and mischievous results when, for example, highly important and persuasive evidence, or argument, though legally forbidden, finds its way into a trial in which the question of guilt or innocence is a close one. What harmless error rules all aim at is a rule that will save the good in harmless error practices while avoiding the bad, so far as possible.

* * *

We prefer the approach of this Court in deciding what was harmless error in our recent case of *Fahy v. Connecticut,* 375 U.S. 85. There we said: "The question is whether there is a reasonable possibility that the evidence complained of might have contributed to the conviction." *Id.* at 86–87. Although our prior cases have indicated that there are some constitutional rights so basic to a fair trial that their infraction can never be treated as harmless error, this statement in *Fahy* itself belies any belief that all trial errors which violate the Constitution automatically call for reversal. At the same time, however, like the federal harmless error statute, it emphasizes an intention not to treat as harmless those constitutional errors that "affect substantial rights" of a party.

* * *

IV

Applying the foregoing standard, we have no doubt that the error in these cases was not harmless to petitioners. To reach this conclusion, one need only glance at the prosecutorial comments compiled from the record by petitioners' counsel. . . . [T]he state prosecutor's argument and the trial judge's instruction to the jury continuously and repeatedly impressed the jury that from the failure of petitioners to testify, to all intents and purposes, the inferences from the facts in evidence had to be drawn in favor of the State—in short, that, by their silence, petitioners had served as irrefutable witnesses against themselves. And though the case in which this occurred presented a reasonably strong "circumstantial web of evidence" against petitioners, 63 Cal.2d at 197, 404 P.2d at 220, it was also a case in which, absent the constitutionally forbidden comments, honest, fair-minded jurors might very well have brought in not-guilty verdicts. Under these circumstances, it is completely impossible for us to say that the State has demonstrated, beyond a reasonable doubt, that the prosecutor's comments and the trial judge's instruction did not contribute to petitioners' convictions. Such a machine-gun repetition of a denial of constitutional rights, designed and calculated to make petitioners' version of the evidence worthless, can no more be considered harmless than the introduction against a defendant of a coerced confession. See, *e.g., Payne v. Arkansas,* 356 United States 560. Petitioners are entitled to a trial free from the pressure of unconstitutional inferences.
Reversed and remanded.

Case Importance:

Even though the errors in this case were not harmless errors and dictated a reversal of the conviction, errors that do not have the effect of changing the outcome of a criminal case may generally be deemed to be harmless errors that do not require a reversal of a case.

The harmless error standard mentioned in the *Chapman* case has been followed in a variety of cases. In the federal court system, according to Rule 52 of the Federal Rules of Criminal Procedure, a harmless error is any error, defect, irregularity, or variance that does not affect the substantial rights of a defendant. The harmless error rule has been used to preserve criminal convictions in various contexts and involving various errors. In *Neder v. United States,* 527 U.S. 1 (1999), the harmless error rule was applied to uphold a conviction where the jury instruction omitted an element of the offense. In *Arizona v. Fulminante,* 499 U.S. 279 (1991), the erroneous admission of evidence of a coerced confession in violation of the Fifth Amendment's guarantee against self-incrimination was deemed to be subject to the harmless error standard. But where other types of constitutional issues have arisen, the harmless error rule may not be applied.

However, the Court refused to follow the harmless error rule in *Vasquez v. Hillery,* 474 U.S. 254 (1986), which involved admitted racial discrimination in the context of a grand jury. The Court rejected the use of the harmless error rule and overturned a murder verdict. Essentially, the Court held that racial discrimination can never be harmless error and must have affected substantial rights of the defendant when practiced by the government. In a Louisiana case decided by the Fifth Circuit Court of Appeals, *Pickney v. Cain,*[28] the defendant had alleged a violation of equal protection due to racial discrimination in the selection of the grand jury foreperson, but the claim had been procedurally defaulted so the court declined to reach the racial discrimination claim. This decision, which did not go to the Supreme Court, calls into question the theory of automatic reversal for any case where racial discrimination may exist, since the *Pickney* court felt that the outcome would not have changed even if the defendant had prevailed in his discrimination claim.

The Court refused to follow the harmless error rule in a case where a defendant had been denied the right to select his own retained attorney under the Sixth Amendment.[29] The Supreme Court agreed with the lower court that a Sixth Amendment violation is not subject to harmless error analysis because the choice of counsel affects the way a trial is conducted and is not merely an error in the trial process. A denial of the use of a retained counsel, according to the Court, is not subject to a demonstration of actual prejudice; prejudice to the defendant is presumed.

In a small number of cases where constitutional or other errors substantially affect a defendant's rights, a court of appeals reverses the case and orders a new trial, based on errors at the trial that substantially affected the original decision. Errors of sufficient magnitude to require a reversal include erroneous admission or exclusion of evidence, constitutional violations prior to or during the trial, prosecutorial misconduct, insufficiency of evidence, and jury misconduct, among other possibilities. If the appellate court orders a retrial, the prosecution must rethink its overall strategy and decide whether to retry the individual as originally charged, offer a reduction in the charge in exchange for a plea bargain, or not try the case again.

Alternatively, either the prosecution or the defense, depending on which side prevailed at the court of appeals, may elect to pursue the appeal to the next level. In most states, that is the highest court of the state, often known as the supreme court. Since a court at this level generally possesses discretion over which cases it hears, the defendant may have a difficult time interesting the court in a single criminal case, but a prosecutor who has lost a case in the court of appeals may have a slightly easier time in getting the court to take the case. Where the top court of a state accepts a case from a state appellate court, the case resolution has much the same possible outcome as when the court of appeals first considered it.

12. ADVERSE APPELLATE RESULTS: THE NEXT STEP

The prosecution has options where the state's highest court remands a case for retrial if the high court's decision was based on the United States Constitution; similarly, the defendant has options if the case involves a federal question.[30] In either situation, when the case concerned an error involving a federal question, the losing appellate party may choose to petition the Supreme Court of the United States to consider the case. Such an option may be effectively removed where a top state court decided a particular case based on adequate and independent state law grounds.[31] In most situations, the Supreme Court declines review and does not issue a writ of certiorari.

Where the court of appeals or the supreme court of the state has returned a case to the lower court for a retrial, the prosecutor must start the prosecution from the beginning. Alternatively, a prosecutor could decide that the evidence in the case does not support a successful retrial at the same level of severity and opt for trial for a lesser offense or opt not to retry the case at all. The prosecutor could conclude that where a person has won a reversal after many years in custody, the jurisdiction's penal needs have been met by the time already served and choose not to pursue the case further. At any appellate level, the prosecutor could ask the reviewing court to reconsider the case a second time or, if the intermediate appellate court has made the decision, the prosecution may request that the top court in the jurisdiction consider the case. Upon retrial, some rules and limitations govern what crime the prosecutor may charge the individual with having committed. On the assumption that a defendant has been tried for first-degree murder, has been convicted, and has had the case reversed, the prosecutor may try the individual a second time for first-degree murder. Alternatively, if a defendant has been charged with first-degree murder but has been convicted only of second-degree murder, which was later reversed on appeal, the prosecution may not prosecute the defendant for first-degree murder. The legal theory in this case focuses on the fact that the original trial court acquitted the defendant of first-degree murder and convicted of second-degree murder. A violation of the Fifth Amendment provision against double jeopardy would occur if the state were permitted to retry the defendant for the top level of murder. This limitation would also apply if the defendant had been originally charged only with second-degree murder, had been convicted of second-degree murder, and became subject to a retrial. The prosecution could not elevate the charge to first-degree murder on the retrial. These principles apply in any situation where the government wishes to levy a higher charge than was the subject crime at the first trial; in general, where there has been a conviction for a lesser offense, the government may not recharge at a higher level.

While double jeopardy provisions prevent a prosecutor from trying a defendant for a second time for a higher offense following a reversal, that type of limitation does not apply when a defendant has successfully procured a new trial and has been charged a second time for the same level of offense.[32] Following a second trial, case precedent allows a judge to give an enhanced sentence upon reconviction, based on events that have come to light concerning the defendant's conduct since the first trial. The information may have come to the judge's attention from evidence presented at the second trial, from a subsequent presentence report, from the conduct record of the defendant while incarcerated on the original charge, and/or from general information available at the time of sentencing that was not presented at the earlier sentencing proceeding. A jury can impose an enhanced sentence following the second trial without offending due process so long as it remains unaware of the prior sentence and the sentence enhancement could not have been given vindictively.[33] Sentence enhancement coexists with and is complementary to an extended sentence, whether imposed under a habitual offender statute or under three-strikes legislation.

13. COLLATERAL ATTACK: THE WRIT OF HABEAS CORPUS

If a defendant has pursued a direct criminal appeal through the state appellate system and has not received satisfaction, the convicted defendant may consider pursuing a collateral attack that can be mounted in a state or federal court. If the defendant complains of an illegal detention that arose from state court action, the defendant cannot take an appeal to a federal circuit court of appeal unless a judge in a circuit or district court issues a certificate of appealability. If a district judge denies a certificate of appealability, the habeas corpus litigant may request a certificate from the appropriate court of appeals.[34]

In mounting a collateral attack on the conviction by filing a petition for a writ of habeas corpus, the defendant may initiate an action in the state criminal court that rendered the conviction or may file the petition in a federal district court. The general rule dictates that the defendant must have raised and fully litigated all potential legal issues at the proper times, whether at trial or upon appeal, so that the relevant courts have had an opportunity to correct any errors. An exception exists where the defendant is able to demonstrate that good cause existed for a failure to object or otherwise raise the issue at the proper time and that prejudice to the defendant's case has resulted. If the defendant succeeds in demonstrating good cause as the basis for the procedural default, as well as "actual prejudice" to the case, there is a slight possibility of federal habeas corpus relief.[35]

In a collateral attack requesting a federal writ of habeas corpus, the defendant must allege that he or she is being held in violation of the United States Constitution, federal law, or treaty. Whether the defendant seeks federal or state habeas corpus, there must be a demonstration that all other possible avenues of relief have been pursued,[36] that relief has not been forthcoming, or that the pursuit would be futile.[37] Federal requirements decree that a litigant is not deemed to have exhausted all state remedies if the defendant has the right, under the law of the state that rendered the conviction, to raise, by any available procedure, any federal question that is the center of the habeas corpus petition.[38] Where a federal district court determines that a defendant has remaining and unresolved state law claims, as a general rule the district court must dismiss the petition. However, the defendant may return to federal court once the requisite exhaustion of remedies has occurred.[39] If a defendant meets the exhaustion test, the federal court entertains the petition for the writ, but the burden of proof is on the applicant, who has the duty to rebut the presumption of state court correctness by clear and convincing evidence.[40]

Where a federal district court has denied a defendant's application for a writ of habeas corpus, an appeal of that denial of the writ may be made to the proper federal circuit court of appeal. The notice of appeal must be filed with the circuit court within the allotted time, or the court cannot hear the case. Since the time limits for filing the notice of appeal are considered to be jurisdictional in nature, when the notice of appeal is not filed in a timely manner or within any extension granted by court rule, the federal court of appeals has no jurisdiction to hear a defendant's habeas corpus case.[41]

When filing for a writ of habeas corpus, the defendant must allege the factual underpinnings of all of the constitutional errors in the case and is not permitted to save any errors to assert during later litigation in a subsequent habeas petition. A failure to bring all the claims at one time generally constitutes a waiver, and those claims are forever barred as a basis for requesting a writ of habeas corpus. Part of the legal necessity of having some finality to a habeas petition surrounds the concept that there is no formal res judicata effect to a habeas corpus petition, whether granted or denied. Without a concept like abuse of the writ, a petitioning defendant could offer requests for relief without limit or merit, and courts would have to entertain them. Under modern court practice, the ready availability of appellate review dictated the need for some modification of the common-law rule that allowed endless habeas corpus petitions. Thus, under the legal theory of abuse of the writ, where a defendant brings a second or successive habeas corpus petition, a court generally dismisses the petition.[42] The government has the burden of pleading "abuse of the writ with particularity."[43] If the prosecution produces evidence that writ abuse has occurred, the burden of going forward with the evidence shifts to the other party. The defendant must demonstrate that there has been no abuse of the writ in seeking successive habeas corpus relief[44] involving an old claim or one that should have been included in the earlier habeas petition.

Where a federal district court grants the writ, the defendant does not normally gain immediate freedom but remains in custody pending further litigation by the prosecution. The attorney for the state might decide to appeal the district court decision to the appropriate federal circuit court of appeal. Alternatively, if the federal district court denies the writ of habeas corpus, the defendant has a right of appeal similar to that of the prosecution. Once a court of appeal renders a judgment, either side is free to request a review (apply for a writ of certiorari) by the Supreme Court of the United States.

A federal defendant who claims the right to be released on the ground that the sentence was imposed in violation of the Constitution or laws of the United States is permitted to file an application for a writ of habeas corpus in the court that rendered the conviction with a request to vacate, set aside, or correct the conviction or sentence.[45] The federal prisoner must make a similar demonstration of exhaustion of remedies to be entitled to consideration for relief. Upon a favorable ruling in favor of the defendant, the federal prosecutor may appeal the decision; if the court fails to grant the writ of habeas corpus, the defendant may choose to appeal to the relevant federal circuit court of appeal and pursue a path that is similar to a state defendant in the federal court system seeking the same remedy.

In the event that the state or federal habeas corpus litigant has reached the end of the process in a federal circuit court of appeal, the defendant may petition the Supreme Court of the United States to hear the case. In cases that come to the Court on the basis of habeas corpus, the Court either takes the case or refuses to consider the merits. There is no recourse other than to request that the Court reconsider its refusal, a path that does not normally result in a different decision.[46]

14. SUMMARY

While there is no federal constitutional right to appeal any criminal conviction, all jurisdictions within the United States permit at least one appeal as a matter of statutory law, state constitutional law, or federal law. The purpose of an appeal is to correct errors that occurred during a trial that have affected substantial rights of the defendant. As a general rule, only where an appellate court can determine that a trial court error affected the outcome of the case, and that the verdict would have been different but for the error, does the court reverse a criminal conviction. Where racial discrimination in a criminal case has been proven, courts generally reverse the case, even though the error may not have been outcome determinative.

To file an appeal, a defendant must generally file a notice of appeal and meet the procedural requirements involving the filing of an appellate brief and appellate reply brief and must follow any other rules of the appellate court system. Since all states provide for at least one appeal, every convicted defendant who desires to appeal a criminal conviction may have the benefit of one appeal. Following the initial appeal, obtaining a review by a state supreme court is a difficult matter because those courts take cases based on judicial discretion. An even more difficult path exists for a state defendant who wants to appeal to the Supreme Court of the United States because this court takes cases based on the discretion of four justices and requires an issue involving a federal law, a federal treaty, or the Constitution of United States.

Every indigent defendant pursuing the first appeal granted as a matter of right is guaranteed the assistance of an attorney to file, brief, argue, and present the appeal. Where a meaningful appeal requires a transcript or other official documents, those items must be provided to the indigent litigant free of charge. A meaningful appeal should not be based upon whether a criminal defendant can afford to pay for appellate legal counsel.

Errors that occurred at a trial must have been noted and brought to the court's attention by the trial counsel through an objection or otherwise to preserve that issue for appeal purposes. If an error occurred and the trial attorney did not object and offer the trial judge a chance to correct the error, as a general rule that error has not been properly preserved for appeal purposes. Where an outrageous error affected a defendant's substantial rights and an error that should have been obvious to all parties at the criminal trial was not noticed, an appeal based on the concept of plain error may allow this error to be argued on appeal, despite the absence of any trial objection. If there is some defect in the court's subject matter jurisdiction, lack of subject matter jurisdiction is an error that may always be brought up at any time on appeal, despite the fact that it was never mentioned during the trial.

Where a defendant has pursued an appeal as a matter of right, taken the case through the state appellate system, and exhausted all state legal remedies, the defendant may ask for writ of habeas corpus within the state judicial system. If this initial request is denied, as a general rule it may be appealed through the state appellate system. Upon exhaustion of state remedies, the state litigant may request, but with little hope of success, the Supreme Court of the United States to consider the habeas corpus petition. The state litigant may later request a writ of habeas corpus from a federal district court contending that he or she is being detained in violation of a federal law, treaty, or the Constitution. Properly pursued, this avenue may allow a habeas litigant to reach the Supreme Court of the United States.

REVIEW EXERCISES AND QUESTIONS

1. Are there effective differences between the types or results of appellate justice that an indigent appellant might expect when compared with a wealthier individual? Are these differences especially significant?

2. Could a particular state decide not to grant any appeal following a conviction in a criminal court? Would the Supreme Court of the United States find such a practice unconstitutional?

3. Assume that an attorney appointed to represent an indigent person who has been convicted of a criminal offense determines that there is absolutely no merit in the legal sense to pursuing a criminal appeal. What type of process could a state arrange that would allow the attorney to meet obligations to the court and to the client under this set of circumstances?

4. In a case involving domestic violence, the defendant did not take the witness stand in his own defense, and the prosecutor noted to the jury during closing arguments that the defendant had the right to take the stand and testify and that the defendant knew what really happened and chose not to tell the jury. For some reason, neither the judge nor the defense attorney was paying close attention at this particular point in the closing moments of the trial. No objection was made by the defendant's trial counsel to the prosecutor's inappropriate argument. Does the newly appointed appellate counsel have a chance to argue that the plain error rule should permit the appellate counsel to argue that the case should be reversed? Explain how the plain error rule operates.

5. Explain the concept of "harmless error" and why appellate courts that find such an error in a criminal case do not always reverse the verdict and remand for a new trial.

6. What are the possible outcomes following a successful appeal for a defendant? What steps may a prosecutor take following a defendant's appellate victory? Explain.

HOW WOULD YOU DECIDE?

1. In the Court of Appeals of Ohio

The defendant's former girlfriend, Ms. Stoddard, called police for help because Timothy Wamsley had beaten her and bloodied her face after he had broken down the door to her apartment. Police arrested the defendant when they observed him leaving her apartment through the broken door area. The prosecution called Stoddard as a witness to assist the prosecutor in proving that Wamsley committed aggravated burglary when he broke her door down prior to beating and kicking her. Her testimony indicated that the defendant was not welcome inside her apartment and that she had retrieved a hidden key she kept outside her apartment so that the defendant could not use it to enter. One of the elements of aggravated burglary that the prosecution must prove that the defendant committed is a trespass to her rights in the apartment, and the trespass must have been done knowingly.

In essence, the trial court judge omitted a jury instruction on one of the elements of the crime, that the jury must find that the defendant knowingly committed a trespass. Although the defendant received a conviction for aggravated burglary, on appeal he argued that the trial court committed reversible error in failing to charge the jury that it must find, among the other elements that constitute aggravated burglary, that the defendant knowingly trespassed by interfering with his former girlfriend's property: "Knowingly enter(s) or remain(s) on the land or premises of another."[47] Appellant Wamsley argued that the error in failing to charge the jury was of such great magnitude that the error should have been obvious and apparent to the trial court, even in the absence of any objection. Defendant-appellant Wamsley appealed his conviction of aggravated burglary and his four-year prison sentence.

How would you rule on the defendant's contention that the trial court's failure to offer a jury instruction on one of the elements of the crime constituted plain error, for which the defendant should have his conviction reversed and be granted a new trial?

The Court's Holding:

[The Court of Appeals noted that a trespass can be committed knowingly, recklessly, or negligently, depending on the facts of the case. It noted that the trial court did instruct the jury on the concept of trespass, and it noted that a person who enters onto the land or premises of another, without privilege, may be guilty of trespass, but the trial court neglected to explain that the jury must find that the trespass was done "knowingly."]

Appellant contends that this omission by the trial court is a due process violation because the jury could not have found him guilty beyond a reasonable doubt of all the elements of the crime if the trial court did not tell the jury exactly what constitutes all the elements of the crime. Appellant also contends that, even though his attorney did not object to this omission in the jury instruction, the error is harmful, prejudicial, and constitutes plain error.

* * *

Appellant correctly argues that the jury must be instructed on all the elements of criminal trespass when the crime charged is aggravated burglary. Since the definition of criminal trespass contains a culpable mental state, that mental state is one of the essential elements of criminal trespass, and by extension, one of the elements of aggravated burglary. *State v. Campbell* (1997), 117 Ohio App.3d 762, 773, 691 N.E.2d 711. This is such an obvious conclusion that it is rarely discussed in the caselaw as anything other than an established principle.

In the instant case though, Appellant's counsel did not object to the jury instructions. Generally speaking, a failure to object to a trial error waives all but plain error

on appeal. *State v. Underwood* (1983), 3 Ohio St.3d 12, 3 Ohio B. 360, 444 N.E.2d 1332, syllabus. "The failure to object to a jury instruction constitutes a waiver of any claim of error relative thereto, unless, but for the error, the outcome of the trial clearly would have been otherwise." *Underwood, supra,* 3 Ohio St.3d 12, 444 N.E.2d 1332, at syllabus.

Appellant contends that the error is of such magnitude that the plain error rule should be invoked. To constitute plain error, the error must be obvious on the record, and the error must be so fundamental that it should have been apparent to the trial court without objection. *State v. Tichon* (1995), 102 Ohio App.3d 758, 658 N.E.2d 16. "Notice of plain error . . . is to be taken with the utmost caution, under exceptional circumstances and only to prevent a manifest miscarriage of justice." *State v. Long* (1978), 53 Ohio St.2d 91, 7 O.O.3d 178, 372 N.E.2d 804, paragraph three of the syllabus. The decision to conduct a plain error review is discretionary with the reviewing court. *State v. Noling,* 98 Ohio St.3d 44, 2002 Ohio 7044, 781 N.E.2d 88, at P62.

* * *

In [this case] the appellant's culpable mental state with respect to the trespass was an issue at trial. One of the defenses Appellant raised at trial was that he could not have committed a trespass because the Dresden Avenue apartment was, in effect, his apartment. Considerable evidence was presented concerning Appellant's prior access to the Dresden Avenue apartment, whether he had a key, whether he paid rent, how often he stayed there, and his prior living arrangements with the victim.

* * *

Based on the fact that the trial court failed to instruct the jury on all the essential elements of the offense of aggravated burglary, Appellant was denied his constitutional right of due process, and this constitutes plain error. Appellant's third assignment of error is sustained. The judgment of conviction and sentence for one count of aggravated burglary rendered by the Columbiana County Court of Common Pleas is vacated and the case is remanded.

See *State v. Wamsley,* 2006 Ohio 5303, 2006 Ohio App. LEXIS 5298 (2006).

HOW WOULD YOU DECIDE?

2. In the Supreme Court of the United States

After having been accused of criminal sexual activity, the defendant, Dwayne Halbert, entered a plea of *nolo contendere* and was convicted of two counts of second-degree criminal sexual assault. Under the circumstances of the plea that Halbert entered, the trial court was unable to appoint legal counsel to assist in his appeal because his *nolo contendere* plea ended his right to free legal counsel under Michigan law. On two subsequent occasions, Halbert requested the appointment of appellate counsel. The Michigan procedure contemplated that the intermediate appellate court would take a preliminary look at the merits of the claims that a convict made in his or her application to determine whether to appoint an attorney. Since filing a petition to the intermediate appellant court was a difficult procedure to successfully accomplish without help, Halbert desired some legal assistance. Halbert wanted an attorney to help him prepare an application for permission to appeal to an intermediate Michigan court, stating that his sentence had been computed incorrectly and that he needed an attorney to preserve his legal issues before undertaking an appeal. When Michigan courts refused to consider his case, where he merely wanted counsel to assist him for one appeal past the trial court, he obtained a writ of certiorari from the Supreme Court of the United States. On this appeal, he relied on *Douglas v. California*, which held that a person would be given free counsel for the first appeal. Michigan contended that since he pled guilty, he had no right to counsel and that Halbert's case was controlled by *Moss v. Moffitt*, which held that any appeal past the first one did not carry with it any right to free legal counsel. The only way that Halbert could obtain free legal counsel after his *nolo contendere* plea was to petition for permission to appeal to the intermediate Michigan appellate court.

How would you rule on the defendant's contention that under the United States Constitution he has a right to an appeal, even after he entered a nolo contendere *plea and a trial court entered a verdict of guilt?*

The Court's Holding:

[The Supreme Court of the United States noted that the Constitution of the United States imposes no obligation on the states to grant any sort of criminal appeal. It noted that where a state decides to allow criminal defendants to appeal convictions, it must do so in a fundamentally fair way, which may include granting free assistance of counsel to indigent appellants. In *Douglas v. California*, 372 U.S. 353 (1963), the Supreme Court held that free counsel must be made available to the first appeal that is granted as a matter of right if a litigant could not afford to pay for a lawyer. The Court reviewed its decision in *Griffin v. Illinois*, 351 U.S. 12 (1956), that required states to furnish the free trial transcript when those were essential to making a first appeal. The Court noted that the first appeal is the one that generally has the opportunity to correct errors that have occurred in the case. Subsequent appeals may not be as important as the first appeal, with respect to the error correction function, and that factor played a role in the decision in *Ross v. Moffitt*, 417 U.S. 600 (1974), where the Court determined that a state need not furnish free counsel for subsequent appeals following the first one.]

* * *

A defendant convicted by plea who seeks review in the Michigan Court of Appeals must now file an application for leave to appeal pursuant to Mich. Ct Rule 7.205 (2005). In response, the Court of Appeals may, among other things, "grant or deny the application; enter a final decision; [or] grant other relief." Rule 7.205(D)(2). If the court grants leave, "the case proceeds as an appeal of right." Rule 7.205(D)(3). The parties agree that the Court of Appeals, in its orders denying properly filed applications for leave, uniformly cites "lack of merit in the grounds presented" as the basis for its decision.

* * *

Persons in Halbert's situation are particularly handicapped as self-representatives. As recounted earlier this Term, "[a]pproximately 70% of indigent defendants represented by appointed counsel plead guilty, and 70% of those convicted are incarcerated." *Kowalski,* 543 U.S., at 140, 160 L. Ed. 2d 519, 125 S. Ct. 564 (Ginsburg, J., dissenting). "[Sixty-eight percent] of the state prison populatio[n] did not complete high school, and many lack the most basic literacy skills." Ibid. (citation omitted). "[S]even out of ten inmates fall in the lowest two out of five levels of literacy—marked by an inability to do such basic tasks as write a brief letter to explain an error on a credit card bill, use a bus schedule, or state in writing an argument made in a lengthy newspaper article." Ibid. Many, Halbert among them, have learning disabilities and mental impairments. See U.S. Dept. of Justice, Bureau of Justice Statistics, A. Beck & L. Maruschak, *Mental Health Treatment in State Prisons*, 2000, pp. 3–4 (July 2001), http://www.ojp.usdoj.gov/bjs/pub/pdf/mhtsp00.pdf (identifying as mentally ill some 16% of state prisoners and noting that 10% receive psychotropic medication).

* * *

[There are issues that anyone may raise after a *nolo contendere* plea, such as double jeopardy, jurisdiction of the court, sufficiency of the evidence at a preliminary hearing, preserved entrapment arguments, and claims of ineffective assistance of counsel, among others.]

Michigan's very procedures for seeking leave to appeal after sentencing on a plea, moreover, may intimidate the uncounseled. See *Kowalski,* 543 U.S., at 141–142, 160 L. Ed. 2d 519, 125 S. Ct. 564 (Ginsburg, J., dissenting). Michigan Ct. Rule 7.205(A) (2005) requires the applicant to file for leave to appeal within 21 days after the trial court's entry of judgment. "The defendant must submit five copies of the application 'stating the date and nature of the judgment or order appealed from; concisely reciting the appellant's allegations of error and the relief sought; [and] setting forth a concise argument . . . in support of the appellant's position on each issue.'" *Kowalski,* 543 U.S., at 141, 160 L. Ed. 2d 519, 125 S. Ct. 564 (Ginsburg, J., dissenting) (quoting Rule 7.205(B)(1)).

* * *

We are unpersuaded by the suggestion that, because a defendant may be able to waive his right to appeal entirely, Michigan can consequently exact from him a waiver of the right to government-funded appellate counsel. See Tr. of Oral Arg. 14. Many legal rights are "presumptively waivable," post, at 637, 162 L. Ed. 2d, at 577 (Thomas, J., dissenting), and if Michigan were to require defendants to waive all forms of appeal as a condition of entering a plea, that condition would operate against moneyed and impoverished defendants alike. A required waiver of the right to appointed counsel's assistance when applying for leave to appeal to the Michigan Court of Appeals, however, would accomplish the very result worked by *Mich. Comp. Laws Ann.* § 770.3a (West 2000): It would leave indigents without access to counsel in that narrow range of circumstances in which, our decisions hold, the State must affirmatively ensure that poor defendants receive the legal assistance necessary to provide meaningful access to the judicial system. See *Douglas,* 372 U.S., at 357–358, 9 L. Ed. 2d 811, 83 S. Ct. 814; *M.L.B. v. S.L.J.,* 519 U.S. 102, 110–113, 136 L. Ed. 2d 473, 117 S. Ct. 555 (1996); cf. *Griffin v. Illinois,* 351 U.S. 12, 23, 100 L. Ed. 891, 76 S. Ct. 585 (1956) (Frankfurter, J., concurring in judgment) (ordinarily, "a State need not equalize economic conditions" between criminal defendants of lesser and greater wealth).

[The Supreme Court vacated the decision against Halbert in the Michigan Court of Appeals and remanded for further proceedings.] See *Halbert v. Michigan,* 545 U.S. 605 (2005).

ENDNOTES

1. *Halbert v. Michigan,* 545 U.S. 605, 610 (2005).
2. *Martinez v. Court of Appeal of California,* 528 U.S. 152, 165 (2000).
3. *McKane v. Durston,* 153 U.S. 684, 688 (1894).
4. See N.M. Const. art. VI, § 2, Supreme court; appellate jurisdiction. "Appeals from a judgment of the district court imposing a sentence of death or life imprisonment shall be taken directly to the supreme court. In all other cases, criminal and civil, the supreme court shall exercise appellate jurisdiction as may be provided by law; provided that an aggrieved party shall have an absolute right to one appeal."
5. See *Ross v. Moffit,* 417 U.S. 600, 610 (1974).
6. *Halbert v. Michigan,* 545 U.S. 605, 610 (2005).
7. *Griffin v. Illinois,* 351 U.S. 12, 18 (1965).
8. See *Loveall v. State,* 215 S.W.3d 753, 2007 Mo. App. LEXIS 402 (2007) and *State v. Vaughn,* 223 S.W.3d 189, 2007 Mo. App. LEXIS 780 (2007).
9. Ibid., 757.

10. Demonstrative of the discretion possessed by state supreme courts is the procedure followed by the Michigan Supreme Court. *Mich. Comp. Laws Ann.* § 770.3(6): Further review of any matter appealed to the court of appeals under this section may be had only upon application for leave to appeal granted by the supreme court.

11. Rules of the Supreme Court of the United States, Rule 10, Considerations Governing Review on Certiorari. Adopted July 26, 1995.

12. Ibid.

13. See *Miranda v. Arizona,* 384 U.S. 436 (1966).

14. See *Gilbert v. California,* 388 U.S. 263 (1967).

15. See *Coleman v. Alabama,* 399 U.S. 1 (1970).

16. See *Gideon v. Wainwright,* 372 U.S. 335 (1963).

17. 372 U.S. 353 (1963).

18. 351 U.S. 12 (1956).

19. Ibid.

20. USCS *Fed Rules Crim Proc R* 52 (Mathew Bender 2007).

21. Ibid.

22. *Marshall v. State,* 2007 Ala. Crim. App. LEXIS 138 (2007).

23. See *Penson v. Ohio,* 488 U.S. 75, 79 n. 1 (1988).

24. *State v. Smith,* 2006 Ohio 45, 2006 Ohio App. LEXIS 44 (2006).

25. See *State v. Williams,* 2007 Ohio 1897, 2007 Ohio App. LEXIS 1750 (2007), referencing *Ohio Crim. R.* 32 (2007).

26. See *Burks v. United States,* 437 U.S. 1 (1978). The *Burks* Court held that the double jeopardy provision of the Fifth Amendment precluded a second trial once the appellate court determined the evidence insufficient to sustain the jury's verdict of guilty, and the only proper remedy available is to enter a verdict of acquittal. A retrial would not be barred if the reversal were based on trial error rather than on a failure of the prosecution to prove its case.

27. The harmless error analysis has been applied, inter alia, where a jury instruction omitted an element of the crime, *Neder v. United States,* 527 U.S. 1 (1999); where an error in jury instructions proved not to be harmless error, *O'Neal v. McAninch,* 513 U.S. 432 (1995); in cases where the prosecution failed to disclose exculpatory evidence to the defense, *Kyles v. Whitley,* 514 U.S. 419 (1995); and where a jury instruction inadequately covered the concept of reasonable doubt, *Sullivan v. Louisiana,* 508 U.S. 275 (1993).

28. 337 F.3d 542, 2003 U.S. App. LEXIS 14566 (5th Cir. La. 2003).

29. See *United States v. Gonzales-Lopez,* 548 U.S. 140, 2006 U.S. LEXIS 5165 (2006).

30. A federal question may be considered part of the case where the federal Constitution, federal law, or a federal treaty has been implicated in the case in some fashion. For example, a federal question exists where a defendant has alleged that her apartment was illegally searched and evidence seized in violation of the Fourth Amendment as applied to the states. If a federal question exists, an appeal to the Supreme Court of the United States is possible.

31. For information concerning the doctrine that federal courts will not reverse state court decisions where they rest upon adequate and independent state grounds where no federal question is involved, see, e.g., *Murdock v. City of Memphis,* 87 U.S. 590 (1875); also see *Michigan v. Long,* 463 U.S. 1032, 1040 (1983), where Justice O'Connor noted, "Respect for the independence of state courts, as well as avoidance of rendering advisory opinions, have been the cornerstones of this Court's refusal to decide cases where there is an adequate and independent state ground." See also Westling, "Advisory Opinions and the 'Constitutionally Required' Adequate and Independent State Grounds Doctrine," 63 *Tulane L.Rev.* 379, 389, and n. 47 (1988).

32. See *North Carolina v. Pearce,* 395 U.S. 711 (1969).

33. See *Chaffin v. Stynchcombe,* 412 U.S. 17 (1973).

34. See Federal Rules of Appellate Procedure, Rule 22(b).

35. See *Engle v. Isaac,* 456 U.S. 107 (1982). See also *Reed v. Ross,* 468 U.S. 1 (1984), where the Supreme Court believed that there was good cause shown for not raising the issue during the trial and appellate stages, and that the issue properly could be first raised in a habeas corpus request.

36. *Ex parte Hawk,* 321 U.S. 114, 116–117 (1944). In a per curiam opinion, the Court stated, "Ordinarily an application for *habeas corpus* by one detained under a state court judgment of conviction for crime will be entertained by a federal court only after all state remedies available, including all appellate remedies in the state courts and in this Court by appeal or writ of certiorari, have been exhausted."

37. 28 U.S.C. § 2254(b)(1) (Mathew Bender 2003).

38. 28 U.S.C. § 2254 (c) (Mathew Bender 2003).

39. See *Rose v. Lundy,* 455 U.S. 509 (1982). The *Rose* Court held that a federal district court must dismiss habeas corpus petitions containing both exhausted and unexhausted claims.

40. 28 U.S.C. § 2254 (e) (Mathew Bender 2003).

41. See *Bowles v. Russell,* ___ U.S. ___, 2007 U.S. LEXIS 7721 (2007).

42. See, generally, *McCleskey v. Zant,* 499 U.S. 467, 477–503 (1991).

43. Ibid., 482.

44. Ibid.

45. 28 U.S.C. § 2255 (Mathew Bender 2003).

46. But see *Boumediene v. Bush,* 127 S.Ct. 1478, 2007 U.S. LEXIS 3783 (2007), where certiorari was denied in a habeas corpus case but where the Court reversed itself and granted certiorari. *Boumediene v. Bush,* 127 S.Ct. 3078, 2007 U.S. LEXIS 8757 (2007).

47. Ohio Revised Code § 2911.21(A)(1).

APPENDIX A

The Constitution of the United States

THE PREAMBLE

We the people of the United States, in order to form a more perfect union, establish justice, insure domestic tranquility, provide for the common defense, promote the general welfare, and secure the blessings of liberty to ourselves and our posterity, do ordain and establish this Constitution for the United States of America.

ARTICLE I

Section 1. All legislative powers herein granted shall be vested in a Congress of the United States, which shall consist of a Senate and House of Representatives.

Section 2. The House of Representatives shall be composed of members chosen every second year by the people of the several states, and the electors in each state shall have the qualifications requisite for electors of the most numerous branch of the state legislature.

No person shall be a Representative who shall not have attained to the age of twenty five years, and been seven years a citizen of the United States, and who shall not, when elected, be an inhabitant of that state in which he shall be chosen.

Representatives and direct taxes shall be apportioned among the several states which may be included within this union, according to their respective numbers, which shall be determined by adding to the whole number of free persons, including those bound to service for a term of years, and excluding Indians not taxed, three fifths of all other Persons. The actual Enumeration shall be made within three years after the first meeting of the Congress of the United States, and within every subsequent term of ten years, in such manner as they shall by law direct. The number of Representatives shall not exceed one for every thirty thousand, but each state shall have at least one Representative; and until such enumeration shall be made, the state of New Hampshire shall be entitled to choose three, Massachusetts eight, Rhode Island and Providence Plantations one, Connecticut five, New York six, New Jersey four, Pennsylvania eight, Delaware one, Maryland six, Virginia ten, North Carolina five, South Carolina five, and Georgia three.

When vacancies happen in the Representation from any state, the executive authority thereof shall issue writs of election to fill such vacancies.

The House of Representatives shall choose their speaker and other officers; and shall have the sole power of impeachment.

Section 3. The Senate of the United States shall be composed of two Senators from each state, chosen by the legislature thereof, for six years; and each Senator shall have one vote.

Immediately after they shall be assembled in consequence of the first election, they shall be divided as equally as may be into three classes. The seats of the Senators of the first class shall be vacated at the expiration of the second year, of the second class at the expiration of the fourth year, and the third class at the expiration of the sixth year, so that one third may be chosen every second year; and if vacancies happen by resignation, or otherwise, during the recess of the legislature of any state, the executive thereof may make temporary appointments until the next meeting of the legislature, which shall then fill such vacancies.

No person shall be a Senator who shall not have attained to the age of thirty years, and been nine years a citizen of the United States and who shall not, when elected, be an inhabitant of that state for which he shall be chosen.

The Vice President of the United States shall be President of the Senate, but shall have no vote, unless they be equally divided.

The Senate shall choose their other officers, and also a President pro tempore, in the absence of the Vice President, or when he shall exercise the office of President of the United States.

The Senate shall have the sole power to try all impeachments. When sitting for that purpose, they shall be on oath or affirmation. When the President of the United States is tried, the Chief Justice shall preside: And no person shall be convicted without the concurrence of two thirds of the members present.

Judgment in cases of impeachment shall not extend further than to removal from office, and disqualification to hold and enjoy any office of honor, trust or profit under the United States: but the party convicted shall nevertheless be liable and subject to indictment, trial, judgment and punishment, according to law.

Section 4. The times, places and manner of holding elections for Senators and Representatives, shall be prescribed in each state by the legislature thereof; but the Congress may at any time by law make or alter such regulations, except as to the places of choosing Senators.

The Congress shall assemble at least once in every year, and such meeting shall be on the first Monday in December, unless they shall by law appoint a different day.

Section 5. Each House shall be the judge of the elections, returns and qualifications of its own members, and a majority of each shall constitute a quorum to do business; but a smaller number may adjourn from day to day, and may be authorized to compel the attendance of absent members, in such manner, and under such penalties as each House may provide.

Each House may determine the rules of its proceedings, punish its members for disorderly behavior, and, with the concurrence of two thirds, expel a member.

Each House shall keep a journal of its proceedings, and from time to time publish the same, excepting such parts as may in their judgment require secrecy; and the yeas and nays of the members of either House on any question shall, at the desire of one fifth of those present, be entered on the journal.

Neither House, during the session of Congress, shall, without the consent of the other, adjourn for more than three days, nor to any other place than that in which the two Houses shall be sitting.

Section 6. The Senators and Representatives shall receive a compensation for their services, to be ascertained by law, and paid out of the treasury of the United States. They shall in all cases, except treason, felony and breach of the peace, be privileged from arrest during their attendance at the session of their respective Houses, and in going to and returning from the same; and for any speech or debate in either House, they shall not be questioned in any other place.

No Senator or Representative shall, during the time for which he was elected, be appointed to any civil office under the authority of the United States, which shall have been created, or the emoluments whereof shall have been increased during such time: and no person holding any office under the United States, shall be a member of either House during his continuance in office.

Section 7. All bills for raising revenue shall originate in the House of Representatives; but the Senate may propose or concur with amendments as on other Bills.

Every bill which shall have passed the House of Representatives and the Senate, shall, before it become a law, be presented to the President of the United States; if he approve he shall sign it, but if not he shall return it, with his objections to that House in which it shall have originated, who shall enter the objections at large on their journal, and proceed to reconsider it. If after such reconsideration two thirds of that House shall agree to pass the bill, it shall be sent, together with the objections, to the other House, by which it shall likewise be reconsidered, and if approved by two thirds of that House, it shall become a law. But in all such cases the votes of both Houses shall be determined by yeas and nays, and the names of the persons voting for and against the bill shall be entered on the journal of each House respectively. If any bill shall not be returned by the President within ten days (Sundays excepted) after it shall have been presented to him, the same shall be a law, in like manner as if he had signed it, unless the Congress by their adjournment prevent its return, in which case it shall not be a law.

Every order, resolution, or vote to which the concurrence of the Senate and House of Representatives may be necessary (except on a question of adjournment) shall be presented to the President of the United States; and before the same shall take effect, shall be approved by him, or being disapproved by him, shall be repassed by two thirds of the Senate and House of Representatives, according to the rules and limitations prescribed in the case of a bill.

Section 8. The Congress shall have power to lay and collect taxes, duties, imposts and excises, to pay the debts and provide for the common defense and general welfare of the United States; but all duties, imposts and excises shall be uniform throughout the United States;

To borrow money on the credit of the United States;

To regulate commerce with foreign nations, and among the several states, and with the Indian tribes;

To establish a uniform rule of naturalization, and uniform laws on the subject of bankruptcies throughout the United States;

To coin money, regulate the value thereof, and of foreign coin, and fix the standard of weights and measures;

To provide for the punishment of counterfeiting the securities and current coin of the United States;

To establish post offices and post roads;

To promote the progress of science and useful arts, by securing for limited times to authors and inventors the exclusive right to their respective writings and discoveries;

To constitute tribunals inferior to the Supreme Court;

To define and punish piracies and felonies committed on the high seas, and offenses against the law of nations;

To declare war, grant letters of marque and reprisal, and make rules concerning captures on land and water;

To raise and support armies, but no appropriation of money to that use shall be for a longer term than two years;

To provide and maintain a navy;

To make rules for the government and regulation of the land and naval forces;

To provide for calling forth the militia to execute the laws of the union, suppress insurrections and repel invasions;

To provide for organizing, arming, and disciplining, the militia, and for governing such part of them as may be employed in the service of the United States, reserving to the states respectively, the appointment of the officers, and the authority of training the militia according to the discipline prescribed by Congress;

To exercise exclusive legislation in all cases whatsoever, over such District (not exceeding ten miles square) as may, by cession of particular states, and the acceptance of Congress, become the seat of the government of the United States, and to exercise like authority over all places purchased by the consent of the legislature of the state in which the same shall be, for the erection of forts, magazines, arsenals, dockyards, and other needful buildings;—And

To make all laws which shall be necessary and proper for carrying into execution the foregoing powers, and all other powers vested by this Constitution in the government of the United States, or in any department or officer thereof.

Section 9. The migration or importation of such persons as any of the states now existing shall think proper to admit, shall not be prohibited by the Congress prior to the year one thousand eight hundred and eight, but a tax or duty may be imposed on such importation, not exceeding ten dollars for each person.

The privilege of the writ of habeas corpus shall not be suspended, unless when in cases of rebellion or invasion the public safety may require it.

No bill of attainder or ex post facto Law shall be passed.

No capitation, or other direct, tax shall be laid, unless in proportion to the census or enumeration herein before directed to be taken.

No tax or duty shall be laid on articles exported from any state.

No preference shall be given by any regulation of commerce or revenue to the ports of one state over those of another: nor shall vessels bound to, or from, one state, be obliged to enter, clear or pay duties in another.

No money shall be drawn from the treasury, but in consequence of appropriations made by law; and a regular statement and account of receipts and expenditures of all public money shall be published from time to time.

No title of nobility shall be granted by the United States: and no person holding any office of profit or trust under them, shall, without the consent of the Congress, accept of any present, emolument, office, or title, of any kind whatever, from any king, prince, or foreign state.

Section 10. No state shall enter into any treaty, alliance, or confederation; grant letters of marque and reprisal; coin money; emit bills of credit; make anything but gold and silver coin a tender in payment of debts; pass any bill of attainder, ex post facto law, or law impairing the obligation of contracts, or grant any title of nobility.

No state shall, without the consent of the Congress, lay any imposts or duties on imports or exports, except what may be absolutely necessary for executing its inspection laws: and the net produce of all duties and imposts, laid by any state on imports or exports, shall be for the use of the treasury of the United States; and all such laws shall be subject to the revision and control of the Congress.

No state shall, without the consent of Congress, lay any duty of tonnage, keep troops, or ships of war in time of peace, enter into any agreement or compact with another state, or with a foreign power, or engage in war, unless actually invaded, or in such imminent danger as will not admit of delay.

ARTICLE II

Section 1. The executive power shall be vested in a President of the United States of America. He shall hold his office during the term of four years, and, together with the Vice President, chosen for the same term, be elected, as follows:

Each state shall appoint, in such manner as the Legislature thereof may direct, a number of electors, equal to the whole number of Senators and Representatives to which the State may be entitled in the Congress: but no Senator or Representative, or person holding an office of trust or profit under the United States, shall be appointed an elector.

The electors shall meet in their respective states, and vote by ballot for two persons, of whom one at least shall not be an inhabitant of the same state with themselves. And they shall make a list of all the persons voted for, and of the number of votes for each; which list they shall sign and certify, and transmit sealed to the seat of the government of the United States, directed to the President of the Senate. The President of the Senate shall, in the presence of the Senate and House of Representatives, open all the certificates, and the votes shall then be counted. The person having the greatest number of votes shall be the President, if such number be a majority of the whole number of electors appointed; and if there be more than one who have such majority, and have an equal number of votes, then the House of Representatives shall immediately choose by ballot one of them for President; and if no person have a majority, then from the five highest on the list the said House shall in like manner choose the President. But in choosing the President, the votes shall be taken by States, the representation from each state having one vote; a quorum for this purpose shall consist of a member or members from two thirds of the states, and a majority of all the states shall be necessary to a choice. In every case, after the choice of the President, the person having the greatest number of votes of the electors shall be the Vice President. But if there should remain two or more who have equal votes, the Senate shall choose from them by ballot the Vice President.

The Congress may determine the time of choosing the electors, and the day on which they shall give their votes; which day shall be the same throughout the United States.

No person except a natural born citizen, or a citizen of the United States, at the time of the adoption of this Constitution, shall be eligible to the office of President; neither shall any person be eligible to that office who shall not have attained to the age of thirty five years, and been fourteen Years a resident within the United States.

In case of the removal of the President from office, or of his death, resignation, or inability to discharge the powers and duties of the said office, the same shall devolve on the Vice President, and the Congress may by law provide for the case of removal, death, resignation or inability, both of the President and Vice President, declaring what officer shall then act as President, and such officer shall act accordingly, until the disability be removed, or a President shall be elected.

The President shall, at stated times, receive for his services, a compensation, which shall neither be increased nor diminished during the period for which he shall have been elected, and he shall not receive within that period any other emolument from the United States, or any of them.

Before he enter on the execution of his office, he shall take the following oath or affirmation:—"I do solemnly swear (or affirm) that I will faithfully execute the office of President of the United States, and will to the best of my ability, preserve, protect and defend the Constitution of the United States."

Section 2. The President shall be commander in chief of the Army and Navy of the United States, and of the militia of the several states, when called into the actual service of the United States; he may require the opinion, in writing, of the principal officer in each of the executive departments, upon any subject relating to the duties of their respective offices, and he shall have power to grant reprieves and pardons for offenses against the United States, except in cases of impeachment.

He shall have power, by and with the advice and consent of the Senate, to make treaties, provided two thirds of the Senators present concur; and he shall nominate, and by and with the advice and consent of the Senate, shall appoint ambassadors, other public ministers and consuls, judges of the Supreme Court, and all other officers of the United States, whose appointments are not herein otherwise provided for, and which shall be established by law: but the Congress may by law vest the appointment of such inferior officers, as they think proper, in the President alone, in the courts of law, or in the heads of departments.

The President shall have power to fill up all vacancies that may happen during the recess of the Senate, by granting commissions which shall expire at the end of their next session.

Section 3. He shall from time to time give to the Congress information of the state of the union, and recommend to their consideration such measures as he shall judge necessary and expedient; he may, on extraordinary occasions, convene both Houses, or either of them, and in case of disagreement between them, with respect to the time of adjournment, he may adjourn them to such time as he shall think proper; he shall receive ambassadors and other public ministers; he shall take care that the laws be faithfully executed, and shall commission all the officers of the United States.

Section 4. The President, Vice President and all civil officers of the United States, shall be removed from office on impeachment for, and conviction of, treason, bribery, or other high crimes and misdemeanors.

ARTICLE III

Section 1. The judicial power of the United States, shall be vested in one Supreme Court, and in such inferior courts as the Congress may from time to time ordain and establish. The judges, both of the supreme and inferior courts, shall hold their offices during good behavior, and shall, at stated times, receive for their services, a compensation, which shall not be diminished during their continuance in office.

Section 2. The judicial power shall extend to all cases, in law and equity, arising under this Constitution, the laws of the United States, and treaties made, or which shall be made, under their authority;—to all cases affecting ambassadors, other public ministers and consuls;—to all cases of admiralty and maritime jurisdiction;—to controversies to which the United States shall be a party;—to controversies between two or more states;—between a state and citizens of another state;—between citizens of different states;—between citizens of the same state claiming lands under grants of different states, and between a state, or the citizens thereof, and foreign states, citizens or subjects.

In all cases affecting ambassadors, other public ministers and consuls, and those in which a state shall be party, the Supreme Court shall have original jurisdiction. In all the other cases before mentioned, the Supreme Court shall have appellate jurisdiction, both as to law and fact, with such exceptions, and under such regulations as the Congress shall make.

The trial of all crimes, except in cases of impeachment, shall be by jury; and such trial shall be held in the state where the said crimes shall have been committed; but when not committed within any state, the trial shall be at such place or places as the Congress may by law have directed.

Section 3. Treason against the United States, shall consist only in levying war against them, or in adhering to their enemies, giving them aid and comfort. No person shall be convicted of treason unless on the testimony of two witnesses to the same overt act, or on confession in open court.

The Congress shall have power to declare the punishment of treason, but no attainder of treason shall work corruption of blood, or forfeiture except during the life of the person attainted.

ARTICLE IV

Section 1. Full faith and credit shall be given in each state to the public acts, records, and judicial proceedings of every other state. And the Congress may by general laws prescribe the manner in which such acts, records, and proceedings shall be proved, and the effect thereof.

Section 2. The citizens of each state shall be entitled to all privileges and immunities of citizens in the several states.

A person charged in any state with treason, felony, or other crime, who shall flee from justice, and be found in another state, shall on demand of the executive authority of the state from which he fled, be delivered up, to be removed to the state having jurisdiction of the crime.

No person held to service or labor in one state, under the laws thereof, escaping into another, shall, in consequence of any law or regulation therein, be discharged from such service or labor, but shall be delivered up on claim of the party to whom such service or labor may be due.

Section 3. New states may be admitted by the Congress into this union; but no new states shall be formed or erected within the jurisdiction of any other state; nor any state be formed by the junction of two or more states, or parts of states, without the consent of the legislatures of the states concerned as well as of the Congress.

The Congress shall have power to dispose of and make all needful rules and regulations respecting the territory or other property belonging to the United States; and nothing in this Constitution shall be so construed as to prejudice any claims of the United States, or of any particular state.

Section 4. The United States shall guarantee to every state in this union a republican form of government, and shall protect each of them against invasion; and on application of the legislature, or of the executive (when the legislature cannot be convened) against domestic violence.

ARTICLE V

The Congress, whenever two thirds of both Houses shall deem it necessary, shall propose Amendments to this Constitution, or, on the application of the legislatures of two thirds of the several states, shall call a convention for proposing amendments, which, in either case, shall be valid to all intents and purposes, as part of this Constitution, when ratified by the legislatures of three fourths of the several states, or by conventions in three fourths thereof, as the one or the other mode of ratification may be proposed by the Congress; provided that no amendment which may be made prior to the year one thousand eight hundred and eight shall in any manner affect the first and fourth clauses in the ninth section of the first article; and that no state, without its consent, shall be deprived of its equal suffrage in the Senate.

ARTICLE VI

All debts contracted and engagements entered into, before the adoption of this Constitution, shall be as valid against the United States under this Constitution, as under the Confederation.

This Constitution, and the laws of the United States which shall be made in pursuance thereof; and all treaties made, or which shall be made, under the authority of the United States, shall be the supreme law of the land; and the judges in every state shall be bound thereby, anything in the Constitution or laws of any State to the contrary notwithstanding.

The Senators and Representatives before mentioned, and the members of the several state legislatures, and all executive and judicial officers, both of the United States and of the several states, shall be bound by oath or affirmation, to support this Constitution; but no religious test shall ever be required as a qualification to any office or public trust under the United States.

ARTICLE VII

The ratification of the conventions of nine states, shall be sufficient for the establishment of this Constitution between the states so ratifying the same.

Done in convention by the unanimous consent of the states present the seventeenth day of September in the year of our Lord one thousand seven hundred and eighty seven and of the independence of the United States of America the twelfth. In witness whereof We have hereunto subscribed our Names,

G. Washington—President and deputy from Virginia

New Hampshire: John Langdon, Nicholas Gilman

Massachusetts: Nathaniel Gorham, Rufus King

Connecticut: Wm. Saml. Johnson, Roger Sherman

New York: Alexander Hamilton

New Jersey: Wil. Livingston, David Brearly, Wm. Paterson, Jona. Dayton

Pennsylvania: B. Franklin, Thomas Mifflin, Robt. Morris, Geo. Clymer, Thos. Fitzsimons, Jared Ingersoll, James Wilson, Gouv Morris

Delaware: Geo. Read, Gunning Bedford Jun., John Dickinson, Richard Bassett, Jaco. Broom

Maryland: James McHenry, Dan of St Thos. Jenifer, Danl Carroll

Virginia: John Blair, James Madison Jr.

North Carolina: Wm. Blount, Richd. Dobbs Spaight, Hu Williamson

South Carolina: J. Rutledge, Charles Cotesworth Pinckney, Charles Pinckney, Pierce Butler

Georgia: William Few, Abr Baldwin

Attest: William Jackson

A P P E N D I X   B

The Bill of Rights and Other Amendments to the Constitution

[The First Ten Amendments to the Constitution are known as the Bill of Rights.]

AMENDMENT I

(1791)

Congress shall make no law respecting an establishment of religion, or prohibiting the free exercise thereof; or abridging the freedom of speech, or of the press; or the right of the people peaceably to assemble, and to petition the Government for a redress of grievances.

AMENDMENT II

(1791)

A well regulated Militia, being necessary to the security of a free State, the right of the people to keep and bear Arms, shall not be infringed.

AMENDMENT III

(1791)

No Soldier shall, in time of peace be quartered in any house, without the consent of the Owner, nor in time of war, but in a manner to be prescribed by law.

AMENDMENT IV

(1791)

The right of the people to be secure in their persons, houses, papers, and effects, against unreasonable searches and seizures, shall not be violated, and no Warrants shall issue, but upon probable cause, supported by Oath or affirmation, and particularly describing the place to be searched, and the persons or things to be seized.

AMENDMENT V

(1791)

No person shall be held to answer for a capital, or otherwise infamous crime, unless on a presentment or indictment of a Grand Jury, except in cases arising in the land or naval forces, or in the Militia, when in actual service in time of war or public danger; nor shall any person be subject for the same offence to be twice put in jeopardy of life or limb; nor shall be compelled in any criminal case to be a witness against himself, nor be deprived of life, liberty, or property, without due process of law; nor shall private property be taken for public use, without just compensation.

AMENDMENT VI

(1791)

In all criminal prosecutions, the accused shall enjoy the right to a speedy and public trial, by an impartial jury of the State and district wherein the crime shall have been committed, which district shall have been previously ascertained by law, and to be informed of the nature and cause of the accusation; to be confronted with the witnesses against him; to have compulsory process for obtaining witnesses in his favor, and to have the Assistance of Counsel for his defence.

AMENDMENT VII

(1791)

In suits at common law, where the value in controversy shall exceed twenty dollars, the right of trial by jury shall be preserved, and no fact tried by a jury, shall be otherwise reexamined in any Court of the United States, than according to the rules of the common law.

AMENDMENT VIII

(1791)

Excessive bail shall not be required, nor excessive fines imposed, nor cruel and unusual punishments inflicted.

AMENDMENT IX

(1791)

The enumeration in the Constitution, of certain rights, shall not be construed to deny or disparage others retained by the people.

AMENDMENT X

(1791)

The powers not delegated to the United States by the Constitution, nor prohibited by it to the States, are reserved to the States respectively, or to the people.

[The Amendments that follow the Bill of Rights.]

AMENDMENT XI

(1798)

The judicial power of the United States shall not be construed to extend to any suit in law or equity, commenced or prosecuted against one of the United States by Citizens of another State, or by Citizens or Subjects of any Foreign State.

AMENDMENT XII

(1804)

The electors shall meet in their respective States, and vote by ballot for President and Vice-President, one of whom, at least, shall not be an inhabitant of the same state with themselves; they shall name in their ballots the person voted for as President, and in distinct ballots the person voted for as Vice-President, and they shall make distinct lists of all persons voted for as President, and of all persons voted for as Vice-President and of the number of votes for each, which lists they shall sign and certify, and transmit sealed to the seat of the Government of the United States, directed to the President of the Senate; The President of the Senate shall, in the presence of the Senate and House of Representatives, open all the certificates and the votes shall then be counted; the person having the greatest number of votes for President, shall be the President, if such number be a majority of the whole number of Electors appointed; and if no person have such majority, then from the persons having the highest numbers not exceeding three on the list of those voted for as President, the House of Representatives shall choose immediately, by ballot, the President. But in choosing the President, the votes shall be taken by states, the representation from each State having one vote; a quorum for this purpose shall consist of a member or members from two-thirds of the States, and a majority of all the States shall be necessary to a choice. And if the House of Representatives shall not choose a President whenever the right of choice shall devolve upon them, before the fourth day of March next following, then the Vice-President shall act as President, as in the case of the death or other constitutional disability of the President. The person having the greatest number of votes as Vice-President, shall be the Vice-President, if such number be a majority of the whole number of Electors appointed, and if no person have a majority, then from the two highest numbers on the list, the Senate shall choose the Vice-President; a quorum for the purpose shall consist of two-thirds of the whole number of Senators, and a majority of the whole number shall be necessary to a choice. But no person constitutionally ineligible to the office of President shall be eligible to that of Vice-President of the United States.

AMENDMENT XIII

(1865)

Section 1. Neither slavery nor involuntary servitude, except as a punishment for crime whereof the party shall have been duly convicted, shall exist within the United States, or any place subject to their jurisdiction.

Section 2. Congress shall have power to enforce this article by appropriate legislation.

AMENDMENT XIV

(1868)

Section 1. All persons born or naturalized in the United States, and subject to the jurisdiction thereof, are citizens of the United States and of the State wherein they reside. No State shall make or enforce any law which shall abridge the privileges or immunities of citizens of the United States; nor shall any State deprive any person of life, liberty, or property, without due process of law; nor deny to any person within its jurisdiction the equal protection of the laws.

Section 2. Representatives shall be apportioned among the several States according to their respective numbers, counting the whole number of persons in each State, excluding Indians not taxed. But when the right to vote at any election for the choice of Electors for President and Vice-President of the United States, Representatives in Congress, the executive and judicial officers of a State, or the members of the Legislature thereof, is denied to any of the male inhabitants of such State, being twenty-one years of age, and citizens of the United States, or in any way abridged, except for participation in rebellion, or other crime, the basis of representation therein shall be reduced in the proportion which the number of such male citizens shall bear to the whole number of male citizens twenty-one years of age in such State.

Section 3. No person shall be a Senator or Representative in Congress, or elector of President and Vice-President, or hold any office, civil or military, under the United States, or under any State, who, having previously taken an oath, as a member of Congress, or as an officer of the United States, or as a member of any State legislature, or as an executive or judicial officer of any State, to support the Constitution of the United States, shall have engaged in insurrection or rebellion against the same, or given aid or comfort to the enemies thereof. But Congress may by a vote of two-thirds of each House, remove such disability.

Section 4. The validity of the public debt of the United States, authorized by law, including debts incurred for payment of pensions and bounties for services in suppressing insurrection or rebellion, shall not be questioned. But neither the United States nor any State shall assume or pay any debt or obligation incurred in aid of insurrection or rebellion against the United States, or any claim for the loss or emancipation of any slave; but all such debts, obligations and claims shall be held illegal and void.

Section 5. The Congress shall have power to enforce, by appropriate legislation, the provisions of this article.

AMENDMENT XV

(1870)

Section 1. The right of citizens of the United States to vote shall not be denied or abridged by the United States or by any State on account of race, color, or previous condition of servitude.

Section 2. The Congress shall have power to enforce this article by appropriate legislation.

AMENDMENT XVI

(1913)

The Congress shall have power to lay and collect taxes on incomes, from whatever source derived, without apportionment among the several States and without regard to any census or enumeration.

AMENDMENT XVII

(1913)

The Senate of the United States shall be composed of two Senators from each State, elected by the people thereof, for six years; and each Senator shall have one vote. The electors in each State shall have the qualifications requisite for electors of the most numerous branch of the State legislatures.

When vacancies happen in the representation of any State in the Senate, the executive authority of such State shall issue writs of election to fill such vacancies: *Provided,* that the legislature of any State may empower the executive thereof to make temporary appointments until the people fill the vacancies by election as the legislature may direct. This amendment shall not be so construed as to affect the election or term of any Senator chosen before it becomes valid as part of the Constitution.

AMENDMENT XVIII

(1919)

Section 1. After one year from the ratification of this article, the manufacture, sale, or transportation of intoxicating liquors within, the importation thereof into, or the exportation thereof from the United States and all territory subject to the jurisdiction thereof for beverage purposes is hereby prohibited.

Section 2. The Congress and the several States shall have concurrent power to enforce this article by appropriate legislation.

Section 3. This article shall be inoperative unless it shall have been ratified as an amendment to the Constitution by the legislatures of the several States, as provided in the Constitution, within seven years from the date of the submission hereof to the States by Congress.

AMENDMENT XIX

(1920)

The right of citizens of the United States to vote shall not be denied or abridged by the United States or by any State on account of sex.

Congress shall have power to enforce this article by appropriate legislation.

AMENDMENT XX

(1933)

Section 1. The terms of the President and Vice-President shall end at noon on the twentieth day of January, and the terms of Senators and Representatives at noon on the third day of January, of the years in which such terms would have ended if this article had not been ratified; and the terms of their successors shall then begin.

Section 2. The Congress shall assemble at least once in every year, and such meeting shall begin at noon on the third day of January, unless they shall by law appoint a different day.

Section 3. If, at the time fixed for the beginning of the term of the President, the President-elect shall have died, the Vice-President-elect shall become President. If a President shall not have been chosen before the time fixed for the beginning of his term, or if the President-elect shall have failed to qualify, then the Vice-President-elect shall act as President until a President shall have qualified; and the Congress may by law provide for the case wherein neither a President-elect nor a Vice-President-elect shall have qualified, declaring who shall then act as President, or the manner in which one who is to act shall be selected, and such person shall act accordingly until a President or Vice-President shall have qualified.

Section 4. The Congress may by law provide for the case of the death of any of the persons from whom the House of Representatives may choose a President whenever the right of choice shall have devolved upon them, and for the case of the death of any of the persons from whom the Senate may choose a Vice-President whenever the right of choice shall have devolved upon them.

Section 5. Sections 1 and 2 shall take effect on the 15th day of October following the ratification of this article.

Section 6. This article shall be inoperative unless it shall have been ratified as an amendment to the Constitution by the legislatures of three-fourths of the several States within seven years from the date of its submission.

AMENDMENT XXI

(1933)

Section 1. The eighteenth article of amendment to the Constitution of the United States is hereby repealed.

Section 2. The transportation or importation into any State, Territory, or possession of the United States for delivery or use therein of intoxicating liquors, in violation of the laws thereof, is hereby prohibited.

Section 3. This article shall be inoperative unless it shall have been ratified as an amendment to the Constitution by conventions in the several States, as provided in the Constitution, within seven years from the date of the submission hereof to the States by the Congress.

AMENDMENT XXII

(1951)

Section 1. No person shall be elected to the office of the President more than twice, and no person who has held the office of President, or acted as President for more than two years of a term to which some other person was elected President shall be elected to the office of the President more than once. But this Article shall not apply to any person holding the office of President when this Article was proposed by the Congress, and shall not prevent any person who may be holding the office of President, or acting as President, during the term within which this Article becomes operative from holding the office of President or acting as President during the remainder of such term.

Section 2. This article shall be inoperative unless it shall have been ratified as an amendment to the Constitution by the legislatures of three-fourths of the several States within seven years from the date of its submission to the States by the Congress.

AMENDMENT XXIII

(1960)

Section 1. The District constituting the seat of government of the United States shall appoint in such manner as the Congress may direct:

A number of electors of President and Vice-President equal to the whole number of Senators and Representatives in Congress to which the District would be entitled if it were a State, but in no event more than the least populous State; they shall be in addition to those appointed by the States, but they shall be considered, for the purposes of the election of President and Vice-President, to be electors appointed by a State; and they shall meet in the District and perform such duties as provided by the twelfth article of amendment.

Section 2. The Congress shall have power to enforce this article by appropriate legislation.

AMENDMENT XXIV

(1964)

Section 1. The right of citizens of the United States to vote in any primary or other election for President or Vice-President, for electors for President or Vice-President, or for Senator or Representative in Congress, shall not be denied or abridged by the United States or any State by reason of failure to pay any poll tax or other tax.

Section 2. The Congress shall have power to enforce this article by appropriate legislation.

AMENDMENT XXV

(1967)

Section 1. In case of the removal of the President from office or of his death or resignation, the Vice-President shall become President.

Section 2. Whenever there is a vacancy in the office of the Vice-President, the President shall nominate a Vice-President who shall take office upon confirmation by a majority vote of both Houses of Congress.

Section 3. Whenever the President transmits to the President pro tempore of the Senate and the Speaker of the House of Representatives his written declaration that he is unable to discharge the powers and duties of his office, and until he transmits to them a written declaration to the contrary, such powers and duties shall be discharged by the Vice-President as Acting President.

Section 4. Whenever the Vice-President and a majority of either the principal officers of the executive departments or of such other body as Congress may by law provide, transmit to the President pro tempore of the Senate and the Speaker of the House of Representatives their written declaration that the President is unable to discharge the powers and duties of his office, the Vice-President shall immediately assume the powers and duties of the office as Acting President.

Thereafter, when the President transmits to the President pro tempore of the Senate and the Speaker of the House of Representatives his written declaration that no inability exists, he shall resume the powers and duties of his office unless the Vice-President and a majority of either the principal officers of the executive department or of such other body as Congress may by law provide, transmit within four days to the President pro tempore of the Senate and the Speaker of the House of Representatives their written declaration that the President is unable to discharge the powers and duties of his office. Thereupon Congress shall decide the issue, assembling within forty-eight hours for that purpose if not in session. If the Congress, within twenty-one days after receipt of the latter written declaration, or, if Congress is not in session, within twenty-one days after Congress is required to assemble, determines by two-thirds vote of both Houses that the President is unable to discharge the powers and duties of his office, the Vice-President shall continue to discharge the same as Acting President; otherwise, the President shall resume the powers and duties of his office.

AMENDMENT XXVI

(1971)

Section 1. The right of citizens of the United States, who are eighteen years of age or older, to vote shall not be denied or abridged by the United States or by any State on account of age.

Section 2. The Congress shall have power to enforce this article Amendment by appropriate legislation.

AMENDMENT XXVII

(1992)

No law, varying the compensation for the services of the Senators and Representatives, shall take effect, until an election of Representatives shall have intervened.

Glossary

Abandonment: The Act that indicates a person has no future use for or claim to property and that no expectation of privacy remains in the property.

Administrative probable cause: The level of suspicion, knowledge, or belief necessary to obtain a warrant for a noncriminal search of a home, business, or other location where the occupier of the premises will not consent to a search; a level of probable cause that requires a much lower level of suspicion or reason to justify a search directed toward enforcing administrative, zoning, or safety regulations.

Administrative search: A governmental search designed to enforce a civil (as opposed to criminal) law or regulation; a search conducted under a lower standard of probable cause than criminal probable cause that may or may not require a warrant, depending on the circumstances. Administrative probable cause may be based on the passage of time, the nature of a building, or the condition of an area of a city, and does not have to be specific to the location being subjected to an administrative search.

Administrative search: business: A search of a commercial establishment to enforce zoning and regulatory and safety programs that can be conducted on a reduced level of probable cause that is lower than that required for criminal probable cause. Absent consent or other theory permitting entry, an administrative search usually requires a warrant.

Administrative search: home: A search of a private dwelling, not directed at a finding of criminal wrongdoing but focused on assuring compliance with zoning, safety, architectural, and other regulatory programs, that does not require traditional probable cause but does require a warrant or some recognized exception to a warrant.

Adverse prosecutorial comment: A violation of the Fifth Amendment privilege against self-incrimination occurs whenever a prosecutor calls attention to the fact that a defendant has not testified in his or her criminal case. A prosecutor's comment may constitute a reversible error, depending on the circumstances.

Affidavit: A written and sworn statement of fact or of belief given under oath and signed in front of a person legally qualified to execute oaths.

Affidavit for a warrant: The written and sworn statement offered by a law enforcement official to a judicial official that describes the facts and circumstances that the official believes constitute probable cause sufficient for the judicial official to issue a search or an arrest warrant.

Airport passenger search: A consent-based search of airline passengers and luggage designed to detect the presence of objects that could be used to hijack the aircraft or to cause harm to the passengers or crew. The search must be reasonable and no more extensive or intrusive than necessary to meet the goal of airline safety.

Alford **plea:** A plea of guilt to the charges, admitting to the truthfulness of the accusation while at the same time alleging that the defendant is not guilty of the charges.

Amicus curiae: An organization or a person not a party to a lawsuit who receives court permission to file a brief supporting the position of one party in an existing lawsuit with a view toward influencing the outcome; literally, "friend of the court."

Appellate process: The legal steps that a convicted defendant must pursue to have a higher count consider whether the defendant had a fundamentally fair trial.

Arraignment: An early postarrest hearing of the criminal justice process in which the charges are read to the arrestee, where counsel is often appointed, where bail may be set, and where the court typically asks the arrestee to enter a plea to the charges.

Arrest: The seizure of the body of a person, under the authority of a government, for whom probable cause exists to warrant a person of reasonable caution to hold the belief that the seized person has committed a crime or crimes.

Arrest in the home: A warrant is required for police to make a lawful seizure of a person who is inside that person's home. Several exceptions to the general rule allow a warrantless arrest under exigent circumstances (an emergency), hot pursuit into the home, or consent to enter the home.

Arrest of third party in home: A warrantless seizure of a person while he or she is a guest at another person's home violates the Fourth Amendment.

Articles of Confederation: The document that organized the American national government following the conclusion of the Revolutionary War. The national charter proved to be a weak form of central government that could not raise armies properly and had no power to regulate trade among the states. The form of government under the Articles of Confederation was replaced by a stronger national government under the Constitution of the United States in 1789.

Attachment of jeopardy: A defendant is deemed to have been once at risk of a criminal conviction when a judge at a bench trial begins hearing evidence from the first witness and when the jury has been empaneled and sworn in a trial to a jury.

Attenuation: See **Doctrine of Attenuation.**

Automatic standing: The principle that anyone "legitimately on the premises" who becomes the subject of a police search has legal grounds to contest the illegality of the search under the Fourth Amendment. This doctrine has no application in federal trials and has been rejected in most state criminal proceedings.

Bail: The method of procuring the release of a person accused of a crime by payment of money; an amount of money or approved property that a judge or magistrate believes will cause an arrested person to comply with all conditions of release and to appear at court at all appropriate times; pretrial release on conditions set by the court.

Bailable offense: Any offense that a legislature has determined would be appropriate for pretrial release on conditions; any offense other than those that a state or the federal legislature has determined do not merit consideration of pretrial release.

Bail provision of Eighth Amendment: The part of the Eighth Amendment that prohibits excessive federal bail and regulates the manner in which federal bail statutes may be structured by Congress; the section of the Eighth Amendment that has never been incorporated into the Due Process Clause of the Fourteenth Amendment and therefore does not apply to the states and does not regulate state bail practice.

Bench trial: Where the defendant elects to have the judge or a three-judge panel hear and decide the case in which the defendant has waived various legal rights, especially the Sixth Amendment right to a trial by jury.

Bill of Rights: The first ten Amendments to the Constitution.

Bivens remedy: The court-created remedy for an egregious violation of the Fourth Amendment by federal law enforcement officials in which the wronged individual may file a federal civil suit for money damages against the agents.

Blockburger test for double jeopardy: Offenses are separate offenses for double jeopardy purposes if each crime requires proof of an element that the other does not. See Blockburger v. United States 284 U.S. 299 (1932).

Blood alcohol tests: Scientific examinations that are conducted to determine the alcoholic content of individuals' blood following arrests for driving while intoxicated; they do not violate the Fifth Amendment privilege against self-incrimination.

Bond: An amount of money or the value of assets placed with a court to obtain pretrial release of an accused; in misdemeanor cases, the amount of money set by a court, police agency, or statute to ensure the subject's appearance in court at all appropriate times.

Breach of plea agreement: Following the execution of a negotiated plea, if either party fails to perform its respective obligations, the plea may be withdrawn and the parties will be left where they were prior to the plea agreement. In some cases, specific performance of a plea agreement may be possible.

Burden of proof: The quantum of evidence required to be produced by the prosecution to win a criminal case; a level of proof required to be demonstrated in affirmative defenses for criminal cases; the prosecution must introduce evidence to prove the case beyond a reasonable doubt.

Case in Chief: The part of a trial when the prosecution and the defense introduce their evidence.

Case in rebuttal: The portion of a criminal trial when the prosecution attempts to offer evidence to counter the proof previously offered by the defense party.

Case in rejoinder: The portion of the criminal trial when the defense attempts to rebut evidence offered by the prosecution during its case in rebuttal.

***Carroll* doctrine:** Judicial principle that permits a warrantless search of a moving or readily movable motor vehicle for which probable cause exists; an exception to the Fourth Amendment warrant requirement that permits searches of readily movable or moving vehicles, boats, and aircraft. See *Carroll v. United States,* 267 U.S. 132 (1925).

Challenge for cause: The concept that a prospective juror can be removed for bias, interest, or prejudice in a criminal case where the attorney for a party can demonstrate lack of impartiality. Challenges for cause are theoretically unlimited in number.

Closely (heavily) regulated industry: A business or industry that has traditionally been subject to intensive or pervasive governmental regulation such that persons engaging in such a business or industry may expect a diminished expectation of privacy and may expect searches of their premises without prior notice, probable cause, or warrant. Firearms and explosives manufacturing, the production of distilled spirits, and automobile dismantling are examples of businesses and industries that have traditionally been closely regulated by different levels of government.

Collateral attack: When a defendant has exhausted all direct state and federal appellate reviews and appeals without success and files court papers requesting that a court issue a writ of habeas corpus if it finds that the defendant is currently being held under a judgment in violation of, respectively, the state or federal constitution or laws.

Collateral estoppel: Where a fact necessary to the prosecution of a second but different case against the defendant has been clearly found in the defendant's favor at the first trial, the defendant cannot be forced to relitigate the same fact a second time at a second trial involving the same sovereign.

Compelled testimony: No witness has the right to refuse to testify in front of a grand jury where the witness has been given use or transactional immunity that is coextensive with the protections of the Fifth Amendment.

Competency: The mental ability of a defendant to comprehend the nature and importance of court proceedings and to have sufficient mental comprehension to properly assist counsel in preparing a defense; the requirement that a witness in a court case take an oath to tell the truth, to have possessed original perception of the events, to have a recollection of what happened, and to have the ability to communicate the facts to the judge or jury.

Composition of grand jury: Members of a grand jury must be selected from a pool of citizens who represent a fair cross section of the jurisdiction.

Concept of standing: The requirement under the Fourth Amendment that an aggrieved party must demonstrate that a personal right of his or hers has been violated in order to be permitted to argue for suppression of evidence illegally seized in violation of the rule of *Mapp v. Ohio,* 367 U.S. 643 (1961), and the Fourth Amendment. See *Rakas v. Illinois,* 439 U.S. 128 (1978).

Confession: The free and voluntary act by an accused of admitting to the material elements of a crime that are generally sufficient to generate proof beyond a reasonable doubt if believed by a trier of fact.

Consent search: A search conducted by a governmental agent following the granting of permission by the individual holding dominion and control over the object or premises; a search justified where the occupier of the premises freely and voluntarily relinquished his or her Fourth Amendment rights and permitted a search. Voluntariness of consent is measured by the "totality of the circumstances" test.

Counsel: Every accused possesses the right to an attorney under the Sixth Amendment, and where the accused has insufficient funds to afford legal representation, the government must furnish reasonably competent legal representation.

Curtilage: The area surrounding a dwelling house that might reasonably fenced and in which the house occupier has an expectation of privacy under the Fourth Amendment.

Custody: For *Miranda* purposes, when a governmental agent deprives an individual of his or her freedom of movement in any significant manner; one of the two triggering factors under *Miranda* that require police officers to offer *Miranda* warnings.

Derivative evidence: Evidence discovered or disclosed by reference to exploiting other evidence already known; evidence that may be excluded if the original evidence was "tainted" or illegally seized under the Fourth Amendment. See *Wong Sun v. United States,* 371 U.S. 471 (1963).

Determination of bail amount: The factors that courts use to evaluate the amount of money or approved property required to assure that a bailed defendant will appear at all appropriate times. Courts consider, among other factors, the strength of the prosecution's case, the alleged offender's prior history while on bail, the severity of the charged offense, the alleged offender's ties to the community, the wealth of the individual, and whether the alleged offender will harm members of the community or witnesses in the case.

Doctrine of attenuation: The theory that an illegally seized item of evidence, normally excluded under the Fourth Amendment's exclusionary rule, may be admissible where that evidence and the act of illegal seizure have significant separation by time and distance sufficiently to break the chain of causation between the evidence and the illegal seizure.

Double jeopardy: A provision of the Fifth Amendment of the United States Constitution that has been construed to prohibit an individual from being tried twice for the same crime prosecuted by the same sovereign jurisdiction unless the defendant waives the constitutional protection by appealing a conviction.

Drug courier profile: A set of characteristics developed from past encounters with drug dealers and traffickers that may be used to identify persons who are not known to be involved in the drug trade but who may be drug carriers based on their possession of the stereotypical characteristics. The profile may include demeanor, age, travel origin or destination, time of arrival at a transportation facility, lack of luggage or use of expensive luggage, and other factors. When properly applied, law enforcement agents may use the profile to briefly stop and inquire about a person's travel plans and ask other routine questions.

Dual sovereignty: The concept that each of the several states is sovereign for the purposes of determining its criminal law and that the federal government is sovereign for the purposes of determining its criminal law. A state's prosecution of a person following a prosecution by a different state for the same act does not constitute a violation of double jeopardy, and both the federal government and one of the states may successively prosecute an individual for one act that consists of two separate crimes.

Dual sovereignty doctrine: A person may be prosecuted successively by one state and then another or by the state and then by the federal government for the same acts, which constitute different crimes under two or more separate jurisdictions. See *Heath v. Alabama,* 474 U.S. 82 (1985).

Due process: A constitutional guarantee found in the Fifth and Fourteenth Amendments to the United States Constitution that mandates the state and central governments to treat individuals with "fundamental fairness" when interacting with them, whether the situation involves lawmaking or law enforcement.

Due Process Clause of the Fourteenth Amendment: The constitutional guarantee that the governments of the states will treat all persons found within their borders with "fundamental fairness" in all interactions between a state government and an individual.

Effect of discrimination: Where racial discrimination has been proven to have tainted a criminal case, the case will be reversed and will not generally be decided using the harmless error doctrine.

Emergency administrative search: A search directed toward discovering items or conditions that pose actual or potential harms to the general public or to a specific group of persons. It does not require a warrant and may not require administrative probable cause. Examples of emergency administrative searches include entry to a farm to destroy tubercular cattle, seizure of botulism-tainted tuna, and confiscation of misbranded prescription drugs.

Emergency exception: The doctrine that permits governmental action under the Fourth Amendment where life or property may be in danger, and when compliance with usual procedural requirements would not be reasonable.

Emergency exception to *Miranda*: An excuse for conducting limited custodial interrogation of an arrestee where an immediate danger exists to the safety of the arresting officer or other persons; permissible custodial interrogation generally characterized by the presence of an unlocated firearm or explosive device. See *New York v. Quarles,* 467 U.S. 649 (1984).

Exceptions to warrant: Arrest warrants will not be required to arrest within the home where exigent circumstances exist, where the arrest follows a hot pursuit, or under circumstances of consent. Search warrants generally will not be required for motor vehicle searches and are not necessary for consent searches, inventory searches, exigent circumstances, and searches incident to lawful arrests.

Excessive bail: For federal bail purposes and under many state interpretations, bail has been deemed excessive when it has been set at an amount higher than the amount minimally necessary to assure a defendant's appearance at all appropriate times.

Exclusionary rule: A court-made rule that prevents the use of evidence illegally seized in violation of the Fourth Amendment during the prosecution's case in chief; a court-made rule designed to ensure respect for the Fourth Amendment by law enforcement officials by removing the incentive to conduct illegal searches and seizures.

Executory plea: A negotiated plea that had received mutual assent by the parties but has not been performed by both sides. Either party may withdraw at any time from an executory plea agreement since no constitutional rights are enforceable in an executory plea bargain due to lack of performance.

Exigent circumstances: An emergency situation characterized by a law enforcement official lawfully entering private premises or property without a warrant; situations where life may hang in the balance, which justifies an extraordinary law enforcement response involving a warrantless search and/or seizure.

Expectation of privacy: A judicially recognized constitutional right based on the Fourth Amendment that limits governmental intrusion on areas of a person's life, property, papers, and effects. An expectation of privacy is not absolute and may be breached by a demonstration of an important and sufficient governmental interest.

Eyewitness identification: A process in which a witness to a crime identifies the proper person, following procedures that must meet due process requirements to prevent misidentification; a process involving a lineup, photographic array, or one-on-one show-up where the law enforcement agents do not attempt to steer or otherwise assist in making an identification and during which the defendant may have a right of counsel.

Factors used in determining bail: In making a bail decision, courts typically consider the strength of the prosecution's case, prior history while on bail, severity of the charged offense, the alleged offender's ties to the community, the wealth of the individual, and whether the alleged offender will harm members of the community or witnesses in the case.

Fair cross section requirement: The concept that the pool of citizens from which a grand jury or a trial jury is to be selected must represent identifiable groups within the judicial community. Where identifiable groups have been intentionally excluded, there is the possibility of reversible error.

Federal jury size: The Sixth Amendment right to a trial by jury has been judicially determined to require a jury of twelve unless a defendant consents to a lower number.

Federal question: Denotes that a particular cause of action may be tried in a federal court as federal cause of action; in the appellate or habeas corpus context, where a legal issue involves a federal law, the federal Constitution, or a federal treaty, it may be litigated in a federal court.

Felony: A serious offense for which the punishment may include a heavy fine and/or significant imprisonment (often longer than one year) up to life imprisonment or the death penalty; an offense of a serious nature that is more than a misdemeanor but less than treason.

Fifteenth Amendment: A post–Civil War change in the constitution that prevented a denial of the right to vote based on previous conditions of servitude.

Fifth Amendment privilege: The constitutional right granted to every person to not serve as a witness against him or herself. A defendant has no duty to assist the prosecution in obtaining a conviction of the defendant.

Fifth Amendment privilege at lineup: A defendant has no constitutional right to refuse to participate in a lineup, even though it may prove to be a link in a chain of evidence that results in a conviction.

First hearing: The initial appearance of an arrestee before a judicial official where probable cause to hold may be judicially evaluated, where a not guilty plea or no plea may be entered, where the charges are read to the arrestee, and where the judge may set a bail amount.

Fourth Amendment: The portion of the Bill of Rights that generally requires warrants for searches and seizures but has been construed to permit warrantless arrests in most situations.

Fourteenth Amendment: A post-Civil War change in the Constitution that decreed all persons born in the United States are citizens and guaranteed all persons due process of law.

Frisk: A limited search of the outer garments of a detainee to discern whether the individual possesses a weapon or weapons that could be used to harm the officer or surrounding persons. See *Terry v. Ohio,* 392 U.S. (1968).

Fruit of the poisonous tree doctrine: A corollary to the exclusionary rule whereby evidence may be excluded from an individual's criminal trial where the individual would have normally possessed no standing to suppress evidence; the theory that excludes evidence from a defendant's trial when the evidence was derivatively obtained in violation of the defendant's Fourth Amendment rights and would not have been discovered but for the violation of the defendant's rights. See *Wongsun v. United States,* 371 U.S. 471 (1963).

Functional equivalent of international border: Any location similar to an airport or seaport where products and people enter or leave a nation, and where customs and immigration services may be required. Searches and seizures conducted at these locations have minimal Fourth Amendment limitations concerning probable cause or scope of search.

Functional equivalent of interrogation: Where police speak in front of a suspect in their custody in a manner that is clearly designed to elicit an incriminating response from a suspect who has decided not to talk following receipt of *Miranda* warnings; any words or actions on the part of the police (other than those normally incident to arrest and taking a person into custody) that the police should know are reasonably likely to elicit an incriminating response from the suspect.

Fundamental fairness: Description often given to explain the essential dictates of the Fifth and/or Fourteenth Amendment requirement of due process; the proposition that the government must offer each accused person sufficient notice and opportunity to be heard and to have a meaningful opportunity to defend against criminal charges.

Good faith exception: A judicially recognized exception to the *Mapp* exclusionary rule that permits prosecution use of evidence illegally obtained where the searching officers were reasonably unaware of the defect in the search warrant; permits use of illegally seized evidence where the judge or magistrate has made an error in issuing a search warrant and the law enforcement officials acted in an "objectively reasonable" manner and were ignorant of the error.

Grand jury: A group of qualified persons, eligible to be voters (often numbering from nine to twenty-four) selected from a fair cross section of the community whose function is to determine whether probable cause exists to believe that a person has committed a specific offense or offenses; a body of persons who make the determination of whether to indict a person.

Grandjury indictment: The process where a person is formally charged with a crime following a majority vote of a grand jury.

Grand jury secrecy: limitations: The secrecy surrounding a grand jury proceeding cannot be violated except to prevent an injustice in a separate case (and therefore the need for disclosure is greater than the need for continued secrecy). However, individual grand jury witnesses may reveal the substance of offered testimony, and grand jurors may speak after the grand jury's term has expired.

Grand jury standard: probable cause: To render an indictment, the grand jury, by a majority vote, must be convinced that a person of reasonable caution, when presented with the facts and circumstances, would conclude that a particular person had committed a particular crime or crimes.

Grand jury target: The individual who the prosecutor believes committed the crime or crimes and who is the subject of the grand jury's particular investigation.

Guilty plea: Admission by a criminal defendant that he or she is guilty of the crime or crimes for which charges have been alleged; a confession of guilt that allows the trial court to impose a sentence; a plea that waives the right to a jury trial, the right to confront and cross-examine adverse witnesses, the Fifth Amendment privilege against self-incrimination, the right to force witnesses to testify on one's behalf, the right to complain of violations of protections against illegal search and seizure, and generally, the right to appeal the conviction.

Guilty plea effect: Upon acceptance of a guilty plea, the defendant has given up the right to a trial by jury, the right to contest most grand jury issues, the right to be represented by counsel at trial, the privilege against self-incrimination, the right to compel witnesses to testify, the right to confront and cross-examine adverse witnesses, the right to contest Fourth Amendment issues, the right to a public trial, the right to a speedy trial, and the right to an appeal.

Habeas corpus: a common-law writ that survives to the present that permits a criminal defendant or convict to request that a court issue the writ where the individual can prove that he or she is being held in violation of the particular state constitution or the national constitution; a writ that will permit the person who is illegally held to be freed from present custody or obtain a new trial where the defendant demonstrates that he or she has been held illegally in absence of due process of law.

Hearsay: A statement offered in court substantially repeating a statement made by someone outside that court and offered for its substantive truth; in-court statements made by a witness who is quoting someone else who was not under oath and made a statement while outside the court.

Hot pursuit: An exception to the usual requirement of a warrant where an arrest is effectuated within the arrestee's home or other place by directly following the suspect inside the structure; the doctrine that permits a warrantless arrest within a suspect's home where probable cause to arrest exists and the officer closely followed the suspect inside after a chase.

Identification of defendant: An eyewitness must make a fairly positive determination that the defendant is the one responsible for the crime and must make this determination in a manner that comports with due process for the accused.

Identification: the *Neil* five-factors test: In order to determine whether an eyewitness had made a proper identification of a suspect, the court must evaluate the opportunity of the witness to view the criminal at the time of the crime, the witness's degree of attention, the accuracy of the witness's original description of the criminal, the level of certainty demonstrated by the witness at the time of the confrontation, and the length of time between the crime scene identification and the confrontation. See *Neil v. Biggers,* 409 U.S. 188 (1972).

Impeachment: The art of placing a courtroom witness in a position where the truthfulness of the witness's testimony is called into question; a showing that the witness may intentionally not be telling the truth or a demonstration that for any of several reasons the witness may have been mistaken concerning what the witness thought he or she observed.

Impeachment use of confession: The principle that a confession taken in violation of the *Miranda* warnings, but not in violation of the Fifth Amendment privilege against self-incrimination, may be used to cast doubt on a defendant's testimony when a defendant takes the witness stand and offers evidence that is contradictory to the *Miranda*-barred statement or confession.

Impeachment use of *Miranda*: Evidence that has been received in violation of the principles of *Miranda* may be used to impeach a defendant where the defendant takes the witness stand and offers a contradictory story from the one given subsequent to a defective *Miranda* warning.

Improper steering: The making of subtle or overt suggestions to witnesses by government law enforcement agents during identification procedures. A violation of due process may render the eyewitness's testimony excluded from admission to evidence.

Independent source rule: An exception to the exclusionary rule that permits the use of evidence that has been discovered through an illegal means where the evidence also has a lawful means of discovery; introduction of evidence discovered during an illegal search and seizure so long as the evidence was later obtained independently by legal law enforcement activity unrelated to the initial illegality.

Indictment: The written product of a grand jury issued when a simple majority of the members conclude that probable cause exists to believe that a particular person has committed a specific crime or crimes; a true bill returned by a grand jury that charges a person with a crime.

Indigent right to appellate counsel: Where a state or the federal government allows one appeal as a matter of statutory right, a person too poor to afford to hire an attorney to pursue the appeal must be furnished with free counsel to prosecute the first appeal.

Indigent right to transcript: Where an appeal requires a trial transcript to obtain meaningful appellate review, a person who is too poor to afford the price of a transcript is entitled under due process to have the proper number of transcripts prepared at governmental expense.

Individual show-up: The identification procedure conducted prior to indictment or the filing of an information where the police exhibit a single suspect to an eyewitness for possible identification.

Infamous crime: Under the Fifth Amendment, the crime required to initiate a federal criminal prosecution must be an offense punishable by hard labor or death or otherwise labeled an infamous crime.

Informants: Individuals, whether paid or unpaid, who deliver information to law enforcement officials in an effort to assist in the apprehension of criminals or to frustrate criminal plans; individuals who must have a sufficient level of believability to help establish probable cause for arrest or for search.

Information: One method of initiating a serious criminal case whereby the prosecutor, in a writing filed with the proper court, accuses, in plain language and with sufficient particularity, a person with having committed a specific crime or crimes; a method of initiating a criminal lawsuit that often requires that the potential defendant waive his or her right to a grand jury indictment and consent to the entering of criminal charges against him or her.

Infrared scan: A process that uses a thermal imaging device, which detects heat escaping from homes or other structures, to produce a picture that assists law enforcement agents in determining whether a building is being used to grow marijuana. The use of this technology to uncover details of the interiors of private homes implicates the Fourth Amendment and generally constitutes an illegal search when conducted without a warrant.

Initial appearance: Often called an arraignment; the first instance where an accused meets a magistrate or judge to hear a reading of the charge(s) against him or her and where the accused may make an initial plea or response.

International border search: Persons crossing a United States international border may be searched for any reason and without a showing of probable cause, since the Fourth Amendment has a diminished effect on international travelers at the point of entry or exit of the nation.

Interrogation: The process of acquiring information from a suspect or eyewitness; under *Miranda,* questioning a suspect by speaking in a declarative voice with a view toward eliciting incriminating statements from the arrestee; the functional equivalent of questioning a suspect while in custody.

Inventory search: An exception to the usual requirement of probable cause to search that permits a warrantless inventory or cataloging of items found on an arrestee or items in the immediate dominion and control of the arrestee.

Inventory search: motor vehicle: A lawful search not requiring probable cause that police may conduct following receipt of a vehicle as evidence or for safekeeping. The purpose is to protect police from false claims of loss of personal items and to protect the owner from theft of personal property while the property remains in police custody. If a police agency has and follows a written policy regulating these searches, criminal evidence produced by the search will be admissible in court.

Inventory search: personal property: Police may without a warrant and without probable cause conduct a search of personal property that comes into police custody or possession following an arrest. The purpose is to protect police from false claims of loss of personal items and to protect the owner from theft of personal property while it is in police custody. If a police agency has and follows a written policy regulating these searches, criminal evidence produced by the search will be admissible in court.

Inventory search policy: Every jurisdiction that wishes to conduct searches based on an inventory search theory must have and routinely follow a departmental policy that regulates inventory searches. In the absence of policy regulation, the parameters of an inventory search will have no limits, and the search will be deemed unreasonable under the Fourth Amendment.

Involuntary confession: Where the mind and will of an accused are overcome by governmental tactics, and he or she offers evidence sufficient to meet the standard of proof beyond a reasonable doubt.

Jeopardy: When a defendant has been placed in danger of losing money, freedom, or life; it attaches to a defendant in a bench trial when the judge begins hearing the first witness and attaches in a jury trial when the jury has been empaneled and sworn.

Judgment: The decision rendered by a judge or jury following a trial, or the entry made by a judge following the acceptance of a negotiated plea.

Jury instructions: Guidelines of the law that the trial judge rends to the jury before it retires to consider the case; the law to be applied to the case.

Knock and announce: Fourth Amendment requirement that law enforcement officials notify occupants of real property that police are outside and have the legal authority of a warrant to enter. The necessity of notice is not absolute, and notice need not be given where the announcement would clearly expose police officers to unreasonable levels of risk or where officers reasonably believe that evidence might be destroyed.

Lesser included offense: An offense below the initially charged offense that lacks one or more elements necessary to prove the more serious offense. For example, second-degree murder would be a lesser included offense of first-degree murder, since second-degree murder would not require proof of premeditation.

Limitations on scope: Refers to the extent that a police officer may lawfully search for a specifically defined object.

An officer may only search where an object or material might reasonably be found and may not search in places where the object could not be hidden. For example, in an automobile an officer could lawfully search for drugs almost anywhere, but if a stolen desktop computer were the object of the search, the officer could not lawfully look for it in the automobile console.

Lineup: An identification process whereby a witness observes several individuals, one of whom may be the police suspect, and is requested to indicate whether the person the witness observed at the crime scene is a member of the array; an identification procedure that requires the presence of counsel for the defendant if the process occurs following an indictment or the filing of an information.

Material witness: An observer of the essential elements of the crime whose presence in court may be essential to the prosecution or the defense; an essential witness who may be placed under bail or kept in official custody to ensure his or her presence at a criminal trial.

Miranda warnings: Legal advisement that must be made by a governmental official to an arrestee concerning constitutional rights that must be explained prior to any interrogation; a warning to a person who is in custody that the individual has the right to remain silent and to consult with counsel prior to speaking, that anything that is said may be used against the individual in a court of law, and that a free lawyer is available for the arrestee. See _Miranda v. Arizona,_ 384 U.S. 436 (1966).

Misdemeanor: A criminal violation that is less severe than a felony; an offense often punished by custody of less than a year (time varies by jurisdiction) and/or a fine; a criminal violation that is punishable by local incarceration rather than custody in a state prison.

Misdemeanor bail: An amount of bail or bond that normally does not involve individual consideration of a defendant and is set by a fee schedule based on the type of crime that has been charged.

Motion to suppress: A request, normally filed with the court prior to trial, that seeks to have evidence excluded from consideration by the judge or jury; a pretrial request that the judge order evidence illegally seized in violation of the Fourth or Fifth Amendment excluded from trial consideration.

Necessary conditions for warning: To be required to offer the *Miranda* warnings, custody of a subject must exist, and police must desire to conduct interrogation of the subject.

Neutral and detached judicial official: A person who serves in a judicial capacity who has authority to issue arrest and search warrants, has no preconceived reason to either grant or refuse to grant a warrant, and makes his or her decision based only on the merits of the evidence.

Nolo contendere: The Latin phrase denoting that a defendant has decided not to put on a defense and to allow the judge to determine guilt or innocence, most frequently resulting in a guilty adjudication.

Nontestimonial evidence: Evidence that does not come from the mouth of a witness and may include conduct; physical evidence that may have the operative effect of proving guilt but has not been deemed to have the same effect as speech.

Nonunanimous jury verdicts: In state cases, the right to a jury trial does not dictate that a jury of twelve must be used to comply with the Sixth Amendment requirement of unanimity, which is required in federal criminal prosecutions.

Notice of appeal: The procedural requirement that alerts the trial court that a convicted defendant plans to appeal the conviction. As a general rule, if the defendant fails to notify the trial court within thirty days, the right of appeal extinguishes by operation of law.

Open field doctrine: The principle that an uncovered field, which the occupier has not taken steps to prevent individuals from observing, is not a house or an effect and does not merit Fourth Amendment protection. Erection of a farm or cattle fence has been held to be insufficient to create an expectation of privacy in an open field. See *United States v. Dunn,* 480 U.S. 294 (1987).

Parole: Discharge from traditional confinement prior to the time originally scheduled for release; early discharge from custody under conditions that may include staying away from specific individuals, not consuming alcohol, not gambling, not committing additional crimes, maintaining employment, and/or other conditions believed relevant to rehabilitation.

Particularity of description: A requirement under the Fourth Amendment that items that are the subject of a search must be clearly and carefully described, so that any law enforcement official may know what items can be seized and what items are not subject to seizure. In the context of a search warrant, the items must be carefully described in language placed on an affidavit for a search warrant, and this description is carried over to the language used in a subsequent search warrant.

Peremptory challenge: The practice of removing a prospective petit juror from trial service for any reason or no particular reason by requesting that the prospective juror be excused from further jury consideration; a method of eliminating a trial juror without offering a reason for so doing, limited by the fact that removal cannot be based on the race or gender of the prospective juror.

Personal property: Property that is not attached to land or a building that is generally movable.

Petit jury: The jury of citizens that determines the guilt or innocence of the accused.

Petty offense compared with serious offense: A trial by jury must be accorded to any defendant who faces more than six months in custody.

Photographic array: The functional equivalent of an identification lineup conducted by law enforcement officials by the use of still photographs of persons who are similar in appearance to the suspect; a method of identifying suspects that does not require the presence of an attorney for the accused, regardless of whether an indictment been issued or information has been filed.

Plain error rule: The principle that, in the interests of justice, an appellate court may reverse a criminal conviction based on an extreme error that was not preserved for appeal by an objection at trial and would not normally be considered by an appellate court.

Plain feel doctrine: A corollary of the plain view doctrine that permits instantaneous seizure of the object whose criminal nature becomes immediately apparent to a law enforcement officer who senses the seizable material during a lawful pat-down or frisk of a person.

Plain feel search: See **Plain feel doctrine.**

Plain view doctrine: An exception to the usual requirement that an officer possess probable cause prior to conducting a search; permits the warrantless seizure and introduction of evidence taken by an officer who was lawfully in a position to observe the seizable property.

Plea: The response a defendant offers to a judge during an arraignment, preliminary hearing, or other early judicial hearing that takes the form of a plea of guilty, a plea of not guilty, or a plea of nolo contendere.

Plea bargain: Where a defendant agrees to plead guilty to a specific charge or charges in exchange for the government's agreement to dismiss other charges and/or for an agreed sentence or recommendation of sentence; an agreement by the government to lower the level of the criminal charge in exchange for the defendant's agreement to admit guilt to the lesser crime.

Preliminary hearing: An early hearing in the criminal justice process where a court determines probable cause to detain, where the bail amount may be set, where early psychiatric examinations may be requested, and where the prosecution may be required to put on a prima facie case.

Pretrial detention: When a judge or magistrate denies bail to an arrestee and the accused must remain in full custody awaiting trial; under the federal Bail Reform Act of 1984, a person deemed to be dangerous to others or who has been accused of particular federal crimes may be denied bail completely and kept in custody until and during trial.

Prima facie case: The level of evidence sufficient to convict if no adverse evidence were introduced; the level of evidence necessary to survive a motion to dismiss for lack of proof beyond a reasonable doubt.

Private employer search: Where workers employed by private corporations are subject to Fourth Amendment searches of personal property and searches of the person under the order of a government where the search may be based on less than probable cause. For example, federal railroad regulations specify testing employees for drugs or alcohol upon the occurrence of specified events like train wrecks or the personal injury of a worker.

Privilege against self-incrimination: The right of an accused under the Fifth Amendment to refuse to testify or otherwise give evidence against himself or herself. See *Malloy v. Hogan,* 378 U.S. 1 (1964), and *Schmerber v. California,* 384 U.S. 757 (1966); one of the constitutional rights that law enforcement officers must explain to a person who is in official custody prior to initiating interrogation.

Probable cause: Where the facts and circumstances known to a person of reasonable caution would permit him or her to conclude that seizable property would be found in a particular place or that a particular person has committed a particular crime.

Probable cause arrest: A seizure of a person when the police officer has sufficient reason to believe a person has committed an offense.

Probable cause only hearing: A judicial procedure that must be held within forty-eight hours after arrest when a person has been arrested without a warrant and without an indictment; the hearing determines only probable cause to hold the individual.

Probable cause to arrest: The level of proof that a police officer must have to take a subject into custody lawfully; the level of proof that would permit a person of reasonable caution to form the belief that a particular person had committed or was committing an offense for which an arrest was permitted.

Probation: Release of a convicted person by the judicial system without that person serving the sentence of incarceration; release prior to execution of sentence on condition that the convict obey the law, maintain employment, not drink alcohol, not consume recreational pharmaceuticals, or not gamble, among other possible conditions.

Protective sweep: A cursory inspection of premises beyond the area permitted under a search warrant (or arrest warrant) for the purposes of discerning whether other persons might be present who might harm the officers or frustrate the search or arrest; a quick and limited search of the premises, incident to an arrest, conducted to protect the safety of police officers and others, which is narrowly confined to a cursory visual inspection of places in which a person might be hiding.

Public safety exception to *Miranda*: Where an arrestee presents or appears to present an immediate danger to the safety of the arresting officer or other persons, the officer is permitted to interrogate the subject concerning the danger prior to offering the warnings required by *Miranda;* permissible custodial interrogation generally permitted when unresolved dangers to the public exist. See *New York v. Quarles,* 467 U.S. 649 (1984).

Rationale for bail: The purposes for granting bail: It assists the defendant in planning a defense with his or her attorney, it allows the defendant to freely search for and interview witnesses, it prevents preconviction punishment, and it preserves the presumption of innocence while assuring the defendant's appearance before a court as appropriate.

Rationale for double jeopardy: The purposes for forbidding double jeopardy: This prevents the prosecution, with all the resources of the state, from continuing to retry a defendant until, through successive prosecutions, it wears down the defendant's will to oppose the government; a government should have one and only one chance to make its case or refrain from additional efforts toward one defendant.

Real property: Land, generally known as real estate and property that cannot be considered personal property.

Reasonable basis to suspect: The standard of proof necessary for a police officer to initiate a brief stop of a person where there exists some question as to whether the individual is involved in criminal activity. If the suspicion extends to a fear that the subject may be armed and dangerous, a pat-down of the subject's outer garments is permissible. This standard will allow a brief motor vehicle stop where there is articulable reason to suspect that criminality may be present.

Reasonable suspicion: Virtually the same as probable cause in some contexts; may be used in the context of a *Terry v. Ohio* type of search in which the terminology may be phrased as "reasonable basis to suspect criminal activity," which would permit a police officer to initiate a brief detention, discussion, and perhaps a pat-down of a suspect.

Reduced expectation of privacy: juveniles: Children do not have the same Fourth Amendment rights as adults and can be searched by school officials on a showing of less than probable cause. Public school children, with parental consent, can be forced to submit to drug screens as a condition of engaging in after-school activities like football or the Latin club.

Requirement of unanimity: Federal criminal cases must be decided by unanimous jury verdicts.

Requirement to claim double jeopardy: Defendant must allege and prove that the same sovereign is attempting to try him or her a second time for a crime that has already been adjudicated to a conclusion; defendant must show that the crime or crimes the prosecution wants to try for a second time do not have a separate element different from the first crime charged.

Reservation of right to appeal: Where a defendant enters a plea of guilty but specifically does not give up all rights of appeal, such that he or she reserves the right to appeal one or more narrow legal issues as part of a plea bargain.

Right assertable against government: Constitutional rights possessed by defendants that they may use to prevent evidence seized against their rights from being used by a government to prove guilt. Examples include alleged *Miranda* and self-incrimination violations, as well as the right to demand a jury trial.

Right to a grand jury indictment: Absent waiver, all serious federal criminal prosecutions must be initiated by the use of a grand jury, but states are free to develop individual alternatives because the right to a grand jury indictment has never been applied to the states through the Due Process Clause of the Fourteenth Amendment.

Right to counsel: A benefit given to all accused persons under the Sixth Amendment to the federal Constitution, as well as a right granted by state constitutions. The right includes the furnishing by the government of free legal counsel to those accused individuals who cannot afford to hire attorneys.

Right to counsel: postarrest limitations: No general right to counsel exists following an arrest unless other procedures, like interrogation, a postindictment lineup, or a postinformation lineup, occur.

Right to counsel: postindictment: A defendant has the right to counsel at all critical stages of the criminal justice process.

Right to counsel: postinformation: A defendant has the right to counsel following the filing of an information against the defendant, since proceedings following the filing of an information are considered critical stages of the criminal process.

Right to remain silent: A constitutional right guaranteed under the Fifth Amendment that permits a person to refuse to assist the government in prosecuting a criminal case against that individual; a right guaranteed by the Fifth Amendment and reinforced by the case of *Miranda v. Arizona,* 384 U.S. 436 (1966), allowing a person in custody to refuse to speak with police about any substantive matter.

Rule of inevitable discovery: The exception to the exclusionary rule that allows the admission of evidence that has been illegally discovered where the evidence clearly would have been discovered by lawful means at a later time. See *Nix v. Williams,* 467 U.S. 431 (1984).

Scope of frisk: The area on the person or in a place that may be searched under the rationale of *Terry v. Ohio* and its progeny. A frisk following a lawful stop allows an officer to pat down the outer garments of a subject with whom the officer is dealing in an effort to ascertain whether the subject is armed and may extend to any area of outer clothing under which weapons may reasonably be hidden.

Scope of search: The places where law enforcement officials may lawfully look where an object of the search could reasonably be hidden. Example: cocaine could be hidden almost anywhere, but a stolen television could not be found in a medicine chest above a bathroom sink.

Scope of search of a home: The type and extent of a search of a home that can be considered reasonable based on the size and type of property that is the object of a home search. Searching officers may search for an object in any home location where the object of the search could reasonably be hidden.

Scope of search of a motor vehicle: The type and extent of a search that may be conducted of a motor vehicle when due consideration has been given to the object of the search. Officers may search anywhere inside a motor vehicle, including any containers, that could reasonably be the location of seizable property.

Search: A governmental inspection, survey, or examination of the premises of a person's home, automobile, papers, person, or other area where private material may be stored.

Search incident to arrest: A specialized type of search that requires only a lawful arrest of a person as its justification; a search that permits inquiry into areas under the immediate "dominion and control" of the arrestee, such as a purse or backpack and personal effects, but does not generally include a search of an entire house or automobile.

Secrecy of grand jury: purpose: A grand jury is not open for public scrutiny because there is no such constitutional requirement, and secrecy prevents targeted individuals from escaping or influencing witnesses or jurors, while it protects those individuals who are never indicted.

Seizure: The act by law enforcement officials of acquiring dominion and control over a person, property, or contraband.

Selective incorporation: The process whereby the Supreme Court of the United States, on a case-by-case basis, determined that various rights in the Bill of Rights should be incorporated into the Due Process Clause of the Fourteenth Amendment.

Separate offense interrogation: Where an arrestee has requested counsel following receipt of *Miranda* warnings, the law prohibits any additional police interrogation on any separate offense unrelated to the offense for which the person is in custody.

Serious criminal case: For purposes of the Sixth Amendment, any offense that carries a maximum penalty of more than six months in prison creates the right to a jury trial for a defendant.

Silver platter doctrine: Legal theory, no longer used, whereby a federal officer who had illegally seized evidence in violation of the Fourth Amendment could offer the evidence for use by a state official in a state prosecution.

Six-person jury: The smallest trial jury that has been approved by the Supreme Court of the United States for state cases as not violating the Sixth Amendment right to a trial by jury so long as unanimity is maintained.

Sixth Amendment right to a speedy trial: While not specifying any particular time frame, the Sixth Amendment, as interpreted, requires that an accused be tried within a reasonable time following arrest, indictment, or the filing of an information.

Specific performance: In cases of plea bargains breached by the prosecution, the trial court has discretion to allow the defendant to completely withdraw the original plea and start the prosecution anew, or to order that the prosecution exactly perform the duties under the plea bargain to which it had originally agreed.

Speedy trial: The requirement under the Sixth Amendment, federal law, state law, and/or state constitution that a person accused of a crime be brought to trial within a specific time or within a reasonable time following the filing of an information, apprehension, or indictment. The remedy for a violation of the Sixth Amendment speedy trial right is prejudicial dismissal against the prosecution. See *Barker v. Wingo,* 407 U.S. 514 (1972).

Speedy trial: factors to consider: The four-factors test evaluates the length of time, the reason for the delay, the defendant's assertion or nonassertion of the right, and prejudice to the defendant and the case.

Stale probable cause: The rationale sufficient to search for an object may exist only for a short time, since some illegal activity depends upon movement of the object. When the probable cause becomes stale, the search for the object becomes unreasonable under the Fourth Amendment. Example: Drug dealers must move their product and sell it as part of the normal course of business, so that probable cause for a search at a particular time for a particular place may not exist several days later. Probable cause for arrest does not typically become stale, since the information pointing to a particular perpetrator does not often change with the passage of time.

Standing: The legal position that an accused must hold to be able to successfully litigate a motion to suppress evidence under the exclusionary rule of *Mapp v. Ohio* and the Fourth Amendment; the position of possessing a reasonable expectation of privacy under the Fourth Amendment.

Statutory right to a speedy trial: Many states and the federal government have laws that help enforce both the Sixth Amendment and state constitutional rights to speedy trials by specifying the time requirements necessary to

meet the goal of having swift trials. These laws have the effect of moving criminal cases in danger of not meeting time requirements to the top of the docket.

Stop and frisk: The reasonable limited restriction on freedom of movement and the potential limited search of the outer garments permitted under the doctrine announced in *Terry v. Ohio,* 392 U.S. 1 (1968); limited detention or search permitted whenever an officer observes unusual conduct that leads the officer to suspect criminal activity, and the officer reasonably believes that the person with whom he or she is dealing may be armed and dangerous.

Stop and identify: A rejected theory, related to the stop and frisk doctrine, that would allow police officers to stop anyone who seemed out of place or who seemed remotely suspicious, and that would allow a police officer to force a subject to give a positive identification. No person who is merely abroad in the night or day can be required to carry identification.

Straight plea: When a defendant pleads guilty to exactly the charges that the prosecutor has levied, without any promises or consideration made by the prosecution.

Subpoena: A lawful order issued by a court of competent jurisdiction commanding an individual to appear in court or another place under penalty of law for failure to comply; an order requiring a person to personally appear and bring particularly described items to court at a specified time is called a *subpoena duces tecum.*

Suggestiveness at lineup: Where improper steering or undue influencing of eyewitnesses occurs during an in-person lineup, an in-person show-up, or a photographic lineup (array), a violation of due process has occurred that generally will require exclusion of the evidence.

Suspicionless public school search: Schools may require that children, with parental consent, submit to drug screens and testing as a condition of playing sports or engaging in extracurricular activities.

Suspicionless workplace search: A privately or publicly employed worker, holding a position where the safety of the public could be injured, may be required to submit to a warrantless drug test or screen as a condition of continued employment. Probable cause or reasonable suspicion is not required to make this search reasonable for some occupations.

Testimonial evidence: Oral evidence offered from the witness stand or by deposition by a witness who has taken an oath to tell the truth and who is generally subject to cross-examination.

Thermal imaging: The picture produced when police subject a building to a scan with an infrared detector to measure the differences in the heat signature offered by particular parts of the building. The imaging machine converts infrared radiation into an image based on the relative warmth or coolness of the surface of the building. For example, on the screen of an infrared scanner, white indicates a relatively hot surface, gray colors demonstrate cooler temperatures, and black indicates a relatively cold surface. See *Kyllo v. United States,* 533 U.S. 27 (2001).

Thirteenth Amendment: A post-Civil War constitutional change to the Constitution that abolished slavery in the United States.

Time limitations on detention: A person cannot be held in custody in the absence of a judicial or grand jury determination of probable cause for longer than forty-eight hours, but the remedy for a person who has been held longer without judicial intervention is not automatic release. See *Riverside v. McLaughlin,* 500 U.S. 44 (1991), Also, under the stop and frisk rationale, a subject may be detained only for a brief time without the detention maturing into an illegal arrest.

Totality of the circumstances test: A test used to determine whether an informant has met the requirements necessary for a judge or police officer to be able to find probable cause for an arrest or search. See *Illinois v. Gates,* 462 U.S. 213 (1983). Also, a test used to determine whether a person has given a valid consent to search the person or an area controlled by the person, involving an analysis of the person's age and education, coerciveness of the circumstances, knowledge of the right to refuse consent, and other factors.

Transactional immunity: The type of immunity given to a witness and potential defendant in which the government gives up its right to pursue criminal sanctions against the individual in exchange for testimony against other defendants; a type of immunity under which the defendant or target can never be prosecuted for crimes for which the immunity extends.

Trial by jury: A federal and state constitutional right where members of the community are called to sit in judgment of the defendant to determine guilt or lack of guilt; a process of determining whether the prosecution has proven its case by having a body of community members numbering usually twelve evaluate the evidence to determine whether guilt beyond a reasonable doubt exists.

Trial by the court: Where the defendant elects to have the judge or a three-judge panel hear and decide the case in which the defendant has waived various legal rights, especially the Sixth Amendment right to a trial by jury.

Two-pronged test: The test to determine whether an informant has sufficient standing to permit the facts offered by the informant to equal probable cause for a search or arrest; under *Aguilar v. Texas,* 378 U.S. 108 (1964), the informant's story must contain sufficient facts that would equal probable cause, and there had to be sufficient reason to believe that the informant was telling the truth. The requirements of the two-pronged test were overruled by the Supreme Court in *Illinois v. Gates,* 462 U.S. 213 (1983).

Unexplained flight: Where an individual takes immediate steps to place distance between the individual and a police officer upon observing the officer's presence and some additional factor is present. Nervous, evasive behavior in a high-crime area, coupled with flight upon sight of a police officer, may be sufficient to meet the reasonable-basis-to-suspect standard for a stop and frisk under *Terry v. Ohio.*

Unlawful arrest: An arrest for which probable cause does not exist; a warrantless arrest conducted within the home of the arrestee in the absence of exigent circumstances.

Unlawfully seized evidence: admissible: A grand jury may consider illegally seized evidence because the Fourth Amendment and the exclusionary rule possess very little application at a grand jury proceeding.

Use immunity: A guarantee offered by the prosecution to a prospective witness, typically at a grand jury proceeding, that the prosecution will not affirmatively use the information offered by the witness against that same witness; a type of immunity that is coextensive with the protections of the Fifth Amendment privilege against self-incrimination that still permits the government to use independently sourced evidence to prosecute the immunized person.

Vehicle forfeiture search: A warrantless search having no limitations on its scope that does not require probable cause and that is conducted by law enforcement agents following the acquiring of custody of a vehicle that is subject to forfeiture under the laws of the jurisdiction. No person possesses an expectation of privacy under the Fourth Amendment in a motor vehicle that is owned by a government or that is subject to forfeiture.

Vicarious standing: A generally unsuccessful legal theory whereby an individual who has not personally been the victim of a Fourth Amendment violation attempts to suppress evidence where the evidence is sought to be offered against that person or a third party.

Voir dire of jury: An inquiry under the direction of the trial judge or the trial attorneys in which jurors are questioned concerning possible bias or interest in the case in which they are about to be seated; an interrogation of a prospective witness concerning the witness's qualifications.

Voluntary abandonment: Behavior that indicates a person has no further desire to retain ownership or possession of property.

Voluntary confession: Evidence offered without governmental duress or compulsion by a suspect or defendant that includes admissions containing all the elements necessary to prove guilt of the crime in question.

Waivable rights: Legal entitlements belonging to a defendant that an accused may knowingly and intelligently determine to relinquish as part of a plea bargain or a straight plea of guilt.

Waiver: The decision by an accused to forgo some statutory or constitutional protections, which requires that the decision be based on knowledge and understanding of the right being relinquished. A decision not to obtain the benefits of the *Miranda* warnings and subsequent submission to interrogation constitutes a waiver of the right against self-incrimination. A waiver is the intentional abandonment of a known right or privilege.

Waiver of privilege: The decision of an accused not to assert a Fifth Amendment privilege against self-incrimination and to offer a free and voluntary confession to the crime alleged.

Waiver of right to indictment: A federal defendant may decline to force the government to procure an indictment and, usually as part of a plea bargain, allow the government to file an information against the defendant.

Waiver of trial by jury: Under the Sixth Amendment, the process under which a defendant may choose to have a criminal case decided by a judge rather than by a jury; the waiver must be done knowingly, intelligently, and with understanding of the rights being relinquished.

Warrant: A legal order of a court directed to a law enforcement official to seize a particular person or property and return the individual or property to the court.

Warrant exception for vehicles: Where probable cause to search a motor vehicle exists, the general rule allows an immediate warrantless search of the vehicle whose scope is regulated by the nature of the objects of the search.

Warrant requirement for house: Police may neither warrantlessly search a place of residence nor warrantlessly arrest a resident inside a home. The home possesses the highest expectation of privacy under the Fourth Amendment and generally requires a warrant or some exception for law enforcement officials to breach its privacy.

Warrant to arrest: A court order based on probable cause issued by a neutral and detached judicial official directed to law enforcement agents ordering them to obtain official custody of a particularly described individual.

Weapons frisk of automobile: A cursory and limited search of the interior of a motor vehicle, permitted when a person is stopped under a stop and frisk standard, that permits the officer to ascertain whether weapons are in close proximity that could be used to frustrate the purpose of the brief stop. The officer must possess a reasonable belief based on specific and articulable facts that warrant an officer in believing that the subject may be dangerous and that the subject could gain immediate control of weapons.

Writ of assistance: Blanket warrant used by British officials that permitted searches of homes and effects of colonists in the absence of any individual suspicion; a blank search warrant that allowed British Crown officials to search private houses for personal items, personal documents and effects, and other evidence that could be used in court to convict the possessor.

Writ of certiorari: The court order that indicates the Supreme Court of the United States will hear a case from a state appellate or state supreme court; the court order granted when four justices of the Supreme Court of the United States vote to hear a case.

Writ of habeas corpus: A common-law writ that survives to the present that allows a criminal defendant or convict to petition a court when the individual believes that he or she is being held in violation of the particular state constitution or the national Constitution; a writ that will permit the person who is illegally held to be freed from custody or obtain a new trial, if the applicant for the writ demonstrates that he or she has been held illegally in absence of due process of law.

Table of Cases

Index

THE CRIMINAL

POLICE

COURTS

ENTRY INTO THE SYSTEM

PROSECUTION & PRETRIAL SERVICES

ADJUDICATIO

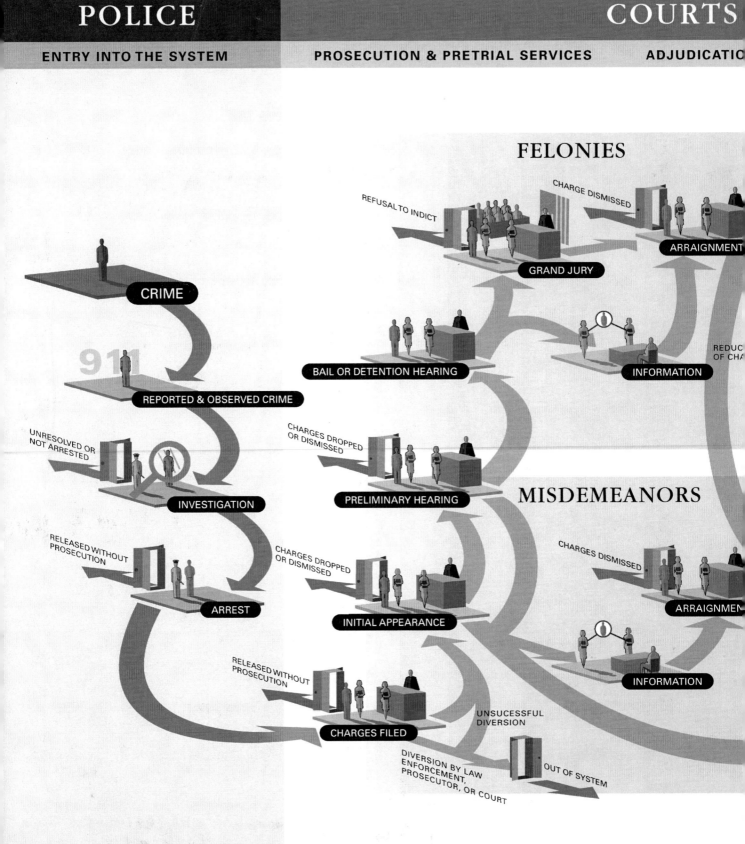

FELONIES

MISDEMEANORS

CRIME

REPORTED & OBSERVED CRIME

UNRESOLVED OR NOT ARRESTED

INVESTIGATION

RELEASED WITHOUT PROSECUTION

ARREST

RELEASED WITHOUT PROSECUTION

CHARGES FILED

REFUSAL TO INDICT

GRAND JURY

CHARGE DISMISSED

ARRAIGNMENT

BAIL OR DETENTION HEARING

INFORMATION

REDUC OF CHA

CHARGES DROPPED OR DISMISSED

PRELIMINARY HEARING

CHARGES DROPPED OR DISMISSED

INITIAL APPEARANCE

CHARGES DISMISSED

ARRAIGNMEN

INFORMATION

UNSUCESSFUL DIVERSION

DIVERSION BY LAW ENFORCEMENT, PROSECUTOR, OR COURT

OUT OF SYSTEM